LINGUISTICS

D0209966

LINGUISTICS
An Introduction

Donna Jo Napoli

New York   Oxford
OXFORD UNIVERSITY PRESS
1996

Oxford University Press

Oxford   New York
Athens   Auckland   Bangkok
Calcutta   Cape Town   Dar es Salaam   Delhi
Florence   Hong Kong   Istanbul   Karachi
Kuala Lumpur   Madras   Madrid   Melbourne
Mexico City   Nairobi   Paris   Singapore
Taipei   Tokyo   Toronto

and associated companies in
Berlin   Ibadan

Published by Oxford University Press, Inc.
198 Madison Avenue, New York, New York 10016

Oxford is a registered trademark of Oxford University Press, Inc.

Library of Congress Cataloging-in-Publication Data

Napoli, Donna Jo, 1948–
Linguistics : an introduction / Donna Jo Napoli.
p.   cm.   Includes bibliographical references and indexes.
ISBN 0-19-509175-2 (alk. paper)
1. Linguistics.   I. Title.
P121.N36   1996
410—dc20   95-20587

1 3 5 7 9 8 6 4 2

Printed in the United States of America
on acid-free paper

Preface

Language weaves together the fabric of our society. Yet even the educated have rarely studied it as a phenomenon—a problem in and of itself—rather than as a tool for access to something else. The same educated people who have not studied language analytically may well have theories as to how language works and may often not hesitate to expound these theories, blissfully unaware of their glaring inadequacies. None of this would be alarming if personal theories of language structure did not affect our daily interactions with people. But they do. Some of our most damaging racial, ethnic, and socioeconomic prejudices are based on our linguistic ignorance and our utterly stupid ideas about language.

So you need this book. You may be picking it up because you are required to for a class, or because you have to for your own research. I'm telling you now, be glad. A basic knowledge of linguistics is as fundamental to intelligent daily living as a basic knowledge of mathematics. No, it's even more fundamental, because language plays a part in our experiences virtually every day of our lives.

This is an introductory text to linguistic theory. It contains no more discussion of why someone might want to study linguistics than the comments in this preface and remarks early in Chapter 4, and it contains only rare mentions of the applications of linguistics to other fields. Discussion of the applications of linguistic theory cannot be handled adequately without a firm foundation in the core of linguistics, which you will get with this book. In other words, first things first.

Thus this book explores in a comprehensive way the core areas of the analysis of language: the sound systems, the word and phrase systems, and the meaning systems. It accordingly contains five chapters: Phonetics, Phonology, Morphology, Syntax, and Semantics. Each chapter is divided into sections, but the sections are often merely ways to organize the discussion and, so, rarely deal with a topic in its entirety. The text is followed by problem sets. The languages from which the data in the discussion and problem sets are drawn vary, but you will find problem sets that deal with American Sign Language, English, Italian, and Japanese in every chapter. New terminology appears in small capitals the first time it is brought up. An index lists these terms and tracks them through the book. Another index gives genetic and geographic information on languages mentioned. Neither the text nor the problem sets are interrupted by bibliographical references. Instead, a list of references for both can be found at the end of the book.

This book can be used in a course in a college or university, for nonmajors or majors, at the undergraduate or graduate level. The discussion is meant to be user-friendly and to invite you, with step-by-step help, into the technical aspects of language and the formalism that linguists use. Let me tell you right off: Linguistics is a technical field. Each chapter starts with a deceptive simplicity but gets hard fast. You need to pay close attention from the very beginning, because each new discussion relies on the knowledge and skills built up cumulatively from what precedes. But don't worry—you get breaks from the technical material now and then. A large part of Chapter 3 should make you happy in this regard.

Since the intended audience for this book varies so widely, individual instructors may well select only certain portions of chapters for close coverage. The problem sets vary enormously in the level of sophistication they require, and, again, instructors should choose the problem sets accordingly. I have starred particularly difficult problem sets and I have indicated when a particular question within a problem set is more difficult than the rest of the problem set. There is more material in this book than most introductory linguistics courses cover, even at the graduate-student level, even in a full year course. And the problem sets vary from work that first-year college students should be able to do to work that one might expect only graduate students to be able to do.

Nevertheless, I urge you—be you student or teacher—to read each chapter in its entirety. (Although there is no need to actually do all the problem sets, do read them.) There are three reasons for this. First, fundamental concepts are scattered throughout each chapter and in the problem sets, as well, so selective reading may result in serious gaps. In fact, I do not hesitate to make reference to material learned in the problem sets of an earlier chapter.

Second, I have found that introductory courses in linguistics often cover only what are considered "the basics." But what people label the basics frequently is limited to material that is out of date. For example, an introductory course in linguistics may teach phonology as though linear phonology is the entire story. When I was in graduate school, linear phonology was, in fact, the whole of phonology. That's why I thought phonology was boring. But today we know much more about the sound systems of the world's languages, and phonology today is spectacularly beautiful. It would be a pity not to let the introductory student get a glimpse of this beauty, just as it would be a pity not to let the introductory student know that there is life after traditional 1970s-style transformational syntax, just as it would be a pity not to let the introductory student know that morphology is now a seething cauldron of ideas that over the next few decades can only lead to drastic revisions in how we view language. So, teachers—please urge your students to at least skim the whole of each chapter.

But the third reason is the most important. Face the facts: Most people who study linguistics take only a single course in it—the introductory course. The introduction-to-linguistics course at an institution should, therefore, be the one the most effort goes into, not the least. It should supply as comprehensive a vision of the core of linguistics as possible. This is a teacher's one shot at most people—a linguist's one chance to get them to understand how language works. Please, let's take careful aim.

But this book need not be used only in a classroom setting. It can be used as a manual for teaching yourself linguistics in the privacy of your home. If you do this, however, you will need to find some way to get feedback on the problem sets, for reading linguistics without doing problem sets is tantamount to self-deception. **You simply cannot learn what linguistics is really about unless you do problem solving.** You may tell yourself that you don't really want to learn what linguistics is about—you just want to get some appreciation for the human faculty of language or for the world's languages. But I don't believe even that goal can be attained without taking an active role in investigating language—the type of active role that comes from facing data on your own and learning to recognize its complexities. So please do at least some of the problem sets. You will need to find a partner or two to read and do problem sets with. If you go at it systematically in this way, with a lot of determination and hard work, I believe the book can be useful even outside a classroom.

My fondest hope is that psychologists, anthropologists, sociologists, computer scientists, philosophers, literary critics, and anyone else who finds that a rudimentary knowledge of linguistics is important to their own field will pick up this book and study it. I have found that people in related fields have shockingly different ideas of what linguistics is from the ideas that linguists have. What defines the field of linguistics is not just the material that linguists study, but the way they look at data, the manner in which they argue, and the range of conclusions they find sensible in light of the data. Linguists, regardless of their theoretical bias, regardless of the component of the grammar that they specialize in, have an unmistakable mindset, and this book tries to give you insight into a linguist's way of looking. I hope this book can help to bridge the gap that I have too often noticed in discussions between linguists and scholars of other disciplines.

And now I must correct what I said in the previous paragraph. My fondest hope of all is that all sorts of people, not just academics, will pick up this book. No, I don't expect to ever see the plumber and the baker have conversations about relative-clause strategies in Hebrew vs. Romanian, for example. Yet I would love to see them smile at a language use that is unusual to them, and appreciate the system of the person who produced the interesting utterance. Yes, that's truly my fondest hope.

Linguistics is a rich, formal, exciting field. And once you have read this book, you will see the world differently. I mean this seriously. Unlike in other fields, you, the native speaker of your language, are in total command of all the relevant data for writing a complete grammar of that language before you ever begin studying linguistics. That means that you can challenge theories immediately—the instant you understand a theory, you can go looking for data whose analysis presents problems for or confirms various theories. Right from the start you are not reliant on the teacher as some sort of exalted authority. Linguistics empowers you. This power lets you feel confident in what you learn, and it helps you to unlearn wrong things and start over. For example, if anyone tells you the word for "mother" is the same in all languages, you can think of the more than one hundred languages you've looked at in this book, and then think of the fact that there are well over five thousand languages spoken today and you can laugh. If anyone tells you the sounds of one language are beautiful while the sounds of another are ugly, you can agree or disagree, but in either case you'll be able to explain to that person the features of the sounds that that person is judging positively or negatively. And, most important of all, if you are someone who has been careful to speak "properly" or "grammatically," you may continue to speak as you always did, but you will be disabused of the misconception that any one form of speech is more proper than another. And this realization will lead you to recognize the forces that have made us, as a society, label any particular convention, whether it be a language convention or any other type of convention, "proper." You will see conventions exposed in a new light. And enlightenment is what education is all about. That's the world that linguistics opens to you.

Welcome to your new world.

Swarthmore D.J.N.
September 1995

Acknowledgments

So many people helped me on this book in so many ways that it is a futile act to try to remember all of them. But I engage in many futile acts. So here goes.

For help throughout, start to finish, I thank Wendy Cholbi, Claire Lecomte du Nouy, Sandy Lin, David McKay, Naomi Nagy, John Voss, and an anonymous reviewer.

For help on Chapter 1, I thank Stuart Davis, Carr Everbach, Uri Ko, Kathleen Lawton, Cris Moddeé, Marina Nespor, and Bill Reynolds. For help on Chapter 2, I thank Shannon Allen, Gene Buckley, Uri Ko, Cris Moddeé, Bill Reynolds, and Hadass Sheffer. For help on Chapter 3, I thank Emmon Bach, Gene Buckley, Jack Hoeksema, Mika Hoffman, Uri Ko, Cris Moddeé, Sharon Peperkamp, and Bill Reynolds. Chapter 3 is also infused with the results of conversations years ago with Dwight Bolinger and Richard Janda. For help on Chapter 4, I thank Michael Hegarty, Rod Johnson, Cris Moddeé, Emmie Quotah, and Natsuko Tsujimura. For help on Chapter 5, I thank Ted Fernald, Uri Ko, Kathleen Lawton, and Emmie Quotah. Chapter 5 also bears the marks of conversations a decade ago with Rod Johnson.

For trouble-shooting various problems sets regarding sign languages, I thank Carol Neidle, Carol Padden, Ronnie Wilbur, and Sandra K. Wood. For help in drawing some of the figures on American Sign Language (ASL) in Chapter 3, I thank Wendy Cholbi.

For help on certain details of Italian and Greek, I thank Marina Nespor and Rosaria Munson. For help on certain details of Japanese and on the problem sets involving Japanese, I thank Mutsuko Endo Hudson, Kaori Kitao, and Natsuko Tsujimura. For help on certain details of French, I thank Stephen J. Hannahs. For help on certain details of Turkish, I thank Beryl Hoffman. For help on certain details of Latin, I thank Gil Rose. For help on certain details of Bulgarian, I thank Roumyana Izvorski. For help on certain details of Greek, I thank Stephen Epstein and Don Ringe. For help on computer jargon, I thank Michael Gelman.

Finally, I thank Swarthmore College and the National Science Foundation. Swarthmore helped me by granting me a Eugene M. Lang Faculty Fellowship for the academic year 1994–1995, by allowing me to have a student research assistant through the Joel Dean Summer Grant program in the summer of 1994, and by contributing half the funds for setting up the Swarthmore Phonetics Laboratory in 1989. The other half of the funds for the laboratory were contributed by the National Science Foundation through Instrument and Laboratory Improvement grant no. USE-8950990 to Swarthmore College.

Thank you all.

Contents

LINGUISTICS

1

Phonetics

Chapter Organization–for the Instructor

This chapter covers a lot, probably more than you've ever tried to handle in an introductory course, where phonetics is often the area of linguistics that gets short shrift. But I urge you to try to cover as much of it as you can. A solid knowledge in phonetics is an invaluable foundation for phonology. With it, the current approaches to phonology seem insightful and delightful. Without it, they can seem arbitrary.

We begin with articulatory phonetics, going through the consonants of English, from the front of the mouth back toward the throat, introducing distinctive features as they become necessary for distinguishing among the consonants. We then look at consonants from other languages with the goal of being representative rather than exhaustive. Then we move to an inventory of the vowels of American English, adding in new distinctive features and recognizing the variety of types of syllable nucleus. We augment this with vowels from other languages. Finally we move into acoustic phonetics, covering pitch and intensity. We study formants and learn to read several kinds of information from spectrograms. An appendix displays the International Phonetic Alphabet (IPA) and distinctive features of commonly found consonants.

Okay, let's go

Here's the situation. You live in America and you speak American English (the English spoken by native speakers in the United States of America). You have a pen pal in New Guinea. Your pen pal writes and reads English but has never heard the language spoken. Your pen pal asks you in a letter how to pronounce English. What do you do?

You make a tape recording and mail it to New Guinea. But guess what? Your pen pal has no tape recorder—and no source of electricity anyway.

At this point you have to get clever. You decide to describe the sound of English. You might begin word by word, say with the word *dear* (since that's how you start your monthly letters to this pen pal). If you know your pen pal's language (which is Ku Waru, since your pen pal is a Papua New Guinea Highlander of the Nebilyer Valley in the Western Highlands Province), you might try comparing the sounds of *dear* with the sounds of some word or words in Ku Waru. Nice try, but I won't let you get away with it. I declare you are a less well-traveled American and, in fact, you had never even heard of Ku Waru before you began writing to your pen pal.

At this point you might try to find out what languages, if any, you both have a speaking knowledge of. Let's say you discover one and it's Italian (an Indo-European language in the Romance family). So now you decide to compare the sounds of the word *dear* (as you say it) to sounds in Italian words. If you are a good speaker of Italian, you have a little problem right off with "d." That's because the Italian "d" of *dirò* 'I will say,' for example, isn't quite the same as the American one. You might not be sure what the differences are, but your ear detects them. If you are a poor speaker of Italian, you might not even know the two "d"s are not the same, and you might go blithely on to the next sound in *dear*.

Let's say somehow or other you get to this next sound.

And now the real trouble starts, for unless your ear is like a stone, you have to notice that the VOWEL sound in the English word lasts longer and changes somehow in quality, while the vowel sound in the Italian word, which starts out the same (or close to the same) as the sound in the English word, maintains a steady quality. What are you going to do? What is the change in vowel QUALITY in the middle of this English word that isn't happening in the Italian word?

Let's say somehow or other you get past this problem and hit the "r."

Yikes. How can both the English "r" of *dear* and the Italian "r" of *dirò* go under a single title or rubric? They don't sound very much alike at all.

If you don't know what the Italian word sounds like, this discussion may have left you cold. But think of Spanish, French, Chinese, Vietnamese, Swahili, Amharic, whatever language you have ever heard even in passing in a shopping mall or in a line at the movies. Whether you ever found out its name or not, you must have heard another language at some point in your life. So you know very well that the sounds of the world's languages are not all the same. That's the point. That's exactly the point.

So what do you do?

Articulatory Phonetics

You talk about what we all have in common: physiology. And that's precisely what linguists do. They describe language sounds based on how the body produces them. This is called ARTICULATORY PHONETICS. Let's see how it works.

To begin, list twelve MONOSYLLABIC words of English (that is, words consisting of precisely one syllable). Any twelve. Here's a typical list:

car	dog	house	law	my	knee
rip	I	walk	few	ma	sleep

Look at them. Look at all those letters. Say each word. Is there any word there that is written with a vowel that you can't hear? Sure: *house*—just look at that final "e." But look a little closer. See the MEDIAL vowel combinations (in the middle of the word) in *sleep* and *house*? Are there really two equally prominent vowels in the middle of each of these words? We will find out that the answer is no.

Is there any word there that is written with a CONSONANT that you can't hear? Sure: *knee* (the "k") and, for most of us, *walk* (the "l"). Again, though, a closer look should make you stop at *law*. Say it. Compare it to *few*. Unless you are from one of a few areas in the American South, you probably don't pronounce a final "w" in *law*.

So ORTHOGRAPHY (spelling) can include symbols (here, Roman alphabet letters) that don't correspond to any sound in the word.

Now look again at these words. Do you hear any sounds (whether consonant or vowel sounds) that aren't represented by a written letter? Sure: in *my*. Where's the letter corresponding to the vowel sound(s) we hear? Perhaps you had a high school English teacher who told you "y" could be a sort of honorary vowel, so you feel sure that "y" does, indeed, represent the vowel sound(s) that follows "m" in *my*. You may be confident that the letter "y" in *my* does not represent the same sound as the letter "y" in the word *you* at the start of this sentence. One is the honorary vowel (so to speak) and the other is a consonant. In fact, you're right. And you can demonstrate this difference yourself.

To see this we need to consider one more word: *high*. Say *my* and *high*. They rhyme, right? So they end with the same sound. Now put two fingers in your mouth sideways, so that one pushes up and the other presses down. Try to say *high*. It doesn't sound too bad. Keep your fingers there and try to say *you*. It sounds awful. Do it again. The final sound of *high* can be said with your two fingers in your mouth like that, but the initial sound of *you* can't be. That means that these sounds are not identical. So the final sound of *my* (which is the same as the final sound in *high*) and the initial sound of *you* are not identical. In other words, "y" does not always represent the same sound, and your high school English teacher was not a fool.

Before going on with our discussion of the sounds in *my*, stop for a moment and explain why, in the experiment we just did, we used *high* and *you* instead of contrasting *my* and *you* directly. What irrelevant interference does *my* present? Sure, you got it. The "m" can't be said with the fingers in the mouth like that, because to say "m" we have to close our lips. So we had to switch to a new word that didn't have sounds like "m."

Returning to *my*, though, we find that even if we allow "y" to represent something vowellike, that still can't be the whole story for most speakers of English. Unless you speak a southern variety of English, you have three sounds in the word *my*. To see this, compare *my* to *ma*. Both words start with the same consonant and then go into the same vowel sound. But the sounds of *my* keep going after the sounds of *ma* have stopped. There are three sounds in *my*, but only two sounds in *ma*. Can you hear that? Say them quickly, then slowly, then quickly. Do you see? When you say both words quickly, it can be very difficult to hear that *my* involves two vowel sounds. But the slow pronunciation should help you. When you say *ma* very very slowly, you simply hold onto a single vowel sound for a long time. But when you say *my* very very slowly, you can hear the change from one vowel sound to another and you can feel the tongue change position from low in the mouth to high. If you are still having trouble, look into a mirror as you pronounce each word slowly. You will see the jaw stay quite open at the end of *ma*; but the jaw will move from very open to more nearly closed at the end of *my*. That's because *ma* consists of a consonant and one vowel, but *my* consists of a consonant and two vowels. So no matter how clever we might be about categorizing "y" (as sometimes vowellike and other times a consonant), we still have to face the fact that *my* has only two letters, but three sounds. Somehow a sound is not represented by a letter (or else a single letter is representing more than one sound).

If you are a southerner, you may feel left out in the cold right now. You pronounce *my* with only two sounds: a consonant and a vowel. The remarks below, however, should make the point for your speech as well (the point being that the orthography of a word can have fewer letters than the sounds of that word), so please bear with me.

What's going on with *few*, another word on our list of monosyllabic words of English? Compare it to the child's exclamative *phoo*. The initial sound in both is [f] (so orthography fails us once more) and they share a vowel. But *few* is longer than *phoo*—it has more sounds. Listen to what comes between the initial consonant and the vowel that is common to both words. *Few* has another sound after the initial consonant that is missing from *phoo*. But *few* has no letter between the "f" and the written letter "e" to represent that sound.

So the orthography of a word can fail to represent sounds that actually occur in a word.

And you already noticed that the [f] sound can be represented by the letter "f" or the letters "ph" (in our discussion of *few* vs. *phoo*).

And now, to complete the picture, think about the initial sounds of *cat* and *celery*. No identity there. So a given letter can represent more than one sound.

We have seen four shortcomings of orthography in English. First, letters can appear that correspond to no sound. Second, sounds can occur that correspond to no letter. Third, different letters can correspond to a single sound. Fourth, a single letter can correspond to different sounds. In other words, there is no beautifully clean correspondence between sounds and letters in English.

This is no accident. It has to do with the history of our language and the fact that our spelling reflects pronunciations used when the spelling conventions were adopted. Language changes over time but orthography is fixed at a certain time and reflects only the pronunciation of a certain group of people at that certain time. (You'll get a chance to discuss some issues related to this fact in Problem Set 1.1.)

What matters to us now is that our Roman alphabet will not allow us to have a one-to-one correspondence between the sounds of English and written symbols. For this reason, we are not going to use that alphabet, but, instead, a new system called the INTERNATIONAL PHONETIC ALPHABET (or IPA), in which there is a one-to-one correspondence between sounds and symbols. When we write words in the IPA, we say we are TRANSCRIBING those words into IPA. Fortunately for us, many of the symbols in the IPA are based on the Roman alphabet, so we will have many fewer new symbols to learn than a linguistics student who uses a different alphabet or a nonalphabetic writing system. In the appendix at the end of this chapter, the IPA is explained. The meaning of the DIACRITICS (that is, the marks added to these symbols to indicate various modifications in sounds) introduced in this chapter are also given. Feel free to consult the appendix whenever you need to.

From here on out, every time we talk about a sound, we will use the IPA symbol for that sound. Furthermore, when we speak of consonants and vowels, we will be speaking of sounds, not of letters.

Minimal Pairs and Consonants

Okay, let's return to our list of twelve monosyllabic words. Let's try to come up with all the consonants of English. We can start on this task by considering the word *my* again. I claim that *my* is a separate word of English from *by*. You agree with me, right? They mean two different things—that's what makes them different words. However, they also sound different—and the difference is minimal: They contrast on only one sound. (Be careful here: Sometimes two different words can sound the same, as in *red* and *read*. These are

HOMONYMS. What we are concerned with in the text is words that differ in both their meaning and their sound.) For this reason pairs like *my* and *by* are called MINIMAL PAIRS. **The fact that *my* and *by* are different words means that the difference between them–which amounts to the difference between [m] and [b]—is DISTINCTIVE in English:** this difference matters to us in identifying and distinguishing between words. **Single sounds that are distinctively different from other sounds in whatever language we are considering are called PHONEMES.**

What other consonant phonemes does English make use of? Take the word *my* and form as many minimal pairs with it as you can. You should come up with several. Write them all down. Then organize them according to the physiology used to speak them. I'll help you. Right now please put your hand over the paragraph immediately below, so that you can't see it. Now, answer: what parts of the body do you use in making sounds that are parts of words? List them. Once you've done that, read the next paragraph.

You should have come up with at least these: lips, teeth, tongue, roof of mouth.

Don't limit yourself just to considering the mouth, however. What else? Your nose, definitely. To see this, say the words:

cat   can

Now pinch your nose shut and say them again. *Cat* sounds the same; but *can* doesn't. Focus on the vowel and what follows it. Say these two words again. With your nose pinched, *cat* has three sounds made in the ORAL CAVITY (the mouth), but *can* is different. With your nose pinched, the initial consonant of *can* sounds the same, but the vowel and the final consonant sound different. That's because while you are still making the vowel, you prepare to make the [n] by opening up the NASAL CAVITY (in a way you will learn later—you do this whether you have pinched your nose shut or not). The vowel is therefore NASALIZED. Feel how that nasalized vowel resonates inside your nasal cavity? But what makes this nasalized vowel different from the vowel if your nose was not pinched shut is that the air that passes into the nasal cavity cannot escape through the nose. The final consonant is also different for the same reason—the air in the nasal cavity cannot pass out through the nose, as it normally does in making [n]. Now take the little hum that we can make to signal a positive response, as in "mmmhmmm." Say it. Now pinch your nose shut and try to say it. See the difference? So the nasal cavity is involved in making [m], as well.

What else is involved in making language sounds?

Warning: By this time you have learned that when I ask a question, I quickly answer it. That can lead you to simply stop bothering to try answering for yourself. Please don't get lazy. This book will be much more valuable to you if you read along with one hand ready to cover the material that follows a question mark. Okay? Be a sport—try it my way.

I'll repeat the question: What else is involved in making language sounds? Your lungs, of course. And the part of your throat that leads into your windpipe. In fact, different languages can use sounds made by activity in different areas of the throat all the way down to and including your voice box (the LARYNX, the front protuding part of which you might call the Adam's apple). The air passages above your larynx are known as the VOCAL TRACT.

Other factors are involved in making and distinguishing language sounds. But for now I want you to concentrate just on the oral cavity. Starting at the very front of the mouth and moving inward toward the throat, organize the minimal pairs you have come up with according to whether they do something significant at some given point, which we will call the PLACE or POINT OF ARTICULATION. You should come up with a list that includes:

(1)	**m** my	**p**	pie	**b**	by
(2)		**f**	fie	**v**	vie
(3)		**θ**	thigh	**ð**	Thy
(4)	**n** nigh	**t**	tie	**d**	die
		s	sigh		
				l	lie
(5)		**ʃ**	shy		
(6)				**ɹ**	rye
(7)				**g**	guy
				w	why
(8)		**h**	high		

The letters and symbols are from the IPA. The words following them begin with the sounds these symbols stand for. You should have all these consonant phonemes that I've listed here (unless you find *nigh* so totally archaic that you skipped it), in the same numbered lists I've put them in, although you may well have ordered them differently within those lists. However, you might have been unsure whether to put [w] in the list in 1, since it uses the lips, or in the list in 7 (where I put it), since it uses the back of the tongue. In fact, [w] has two places of articulation, a PRIMARY one inside the mouth (your tongue bunches and the thick back of it rises toward the top of the back of the mouth—can you feel it?) and a SECONDARY one at the lips. We'll return to the idea of secondary articulations later.

Some of you might have put words like *cry*, *fly*, and *sly* on your lists. Actually, while spelling is often not terribly helpful in English in figuring out how many sounds we have in a word, in examples like these the spelling can be instructive, for each of these words begins with a consonant CLUSTER (a series of more than one consonant). Still, you were being sensitive to the fact that there is something unusual about the second consonant in each of these words, unusual with respect to place of articulation. When we discuss "r"-like and "l"-like sounds later, you can return to these three words and then you can explain for yourself why you might not have recognized at first that they begin with two consonants.

Each of the sounds in 1–8 is made at the same place of articulation as the other sounds in that same example. We say that each example in 1–8 contains HOMORGANIC sounds (sounds made at the same place of articulation). So [m], [p], and [b], for example, are homorganic.

We now have seventeen consonant phonemes of English. But there are more. To show there are more, we'll have to change the standard word that we've been using for forming our minimal pairs. Let's take the word *moo* and try forming minimal pairs with it by varying the initial consonant. Write them down. Let's repeat the lists above and fill in the new consonants where they fit (and for those of you who were unhappy with *nigh*, you can now use *new* to fill in the consonant [n]:

(1)	m my	p	pie	b	by
(2)		f	fie	v	vie
(3)		θ	thigh	ð	thy

(4)	n	nigh/new	t	tie	d	die
			s	sigh	z	zoo
					l	lie
(5)			ʃ	shy		
			ʧ	chew	ʤ	Jew
(6)					ɹ	rye
					j	you
(7)			k	coo	g	guy
					w	why
(8)					h	*h*igh

We have added in five more consonants: [z], [ʧ], [ʤ], [j], and [k]. And this is as far as we can go with minimal pairs that contrast by the initial consonant. (You might notice that two of these symbols, [ʧ] and [ʤ], are complex in the sense that they look like a combination of two symbols. In fact, the sounds these symbols signify are, arguably, equally complex. We will go into this when we talk about affricates.)

However, there are still two more consonant phonemes of English. One of them occurs only in a syllable-final position in words in English, which is why we couldn't find it using minimal pairs that contrasted on their first sound. So now let's form minimal pairs by varying the final consonant rather than the initial one. Take the word *sip*. Vary the final consonant and you'll come up with many words that are only minimally different from it, including:

sib (short for *sibling*), sin, sit, Sid (a proper name),
sis, sill, sing, sick, cig (short for *cig*arett*e*)

The new consonant is the final sound in *sing*, and it's made in the same place [k] and [g] are made. Its IPA symbol is [ŋ], which is called "eng" or "engma," so enter it in the list in 7 like so:

(7)	ŋ	sing	k	coo	g	guy
					w	why

The last consonant phoneme for us to find occurs word-initially only in words that are borrowed from French (another Romance language like Italian, spoken in France) and maintain a strong French flavor. You know it as the first sound in the name *Zsa Zsa Gabor* (at least as Americans say it) and in the word *genre*. However, it can occur medially or in word-final position in many words that we do not today associate with French, such as *vision* and *garage*. Minimal pairs for this sound are hard to find, but consider the medial sounds in:

confusion   Confucian
allusion   Aleutian

This sound is written as [ʒ], and you can now fill it into the list in 5:

(5)			ʃ	shy	ʒ	genre
			ʧ	chew	ʤ	Jew

Our final list of the consonants of English contains these twenty-four:

(1)	m	my	p	pie	b	by
(2)			f	fie	v	vie
(3)			θ	thigh	ð	thy
(4)	n	nigh/new	t	tie	d	die
			s	sigh	z	zoo
					l	lie
(5)			ʃ	shy	ʒ	genre
			ʧ	chew	ʤ	Jew
(6)					ɹ	rye
					j	you
(7)	ŋ	sing	k	coo	g	guy
					w	why
(8)			h	*h*igh		

When we refer later to the examples in 1–8, please use this final list.

Places of Articulation and Articulators

Each of the lists in 1–8 groups homorganic sounds. Move around the various parts of your mouth. What can move? Your lips, your tongue, your bottom jaw. But your top jaw stays fixed. For this reason, we talk about an ARTICULATOR, which moves, and a point or place of articulation which that articulator moves toward. The articulators are along the bottom of the mouth. The places of articulation are along the roof of the mouth.

What are the various places of articulation on the roof of the mouth? You have a top lip and top teeth, of course. Now stick your tongue behind your teeth and run the TIP of it along the roof of your mouth as far back as you can go. The bony ridge behind your upper teeth is called the ALVEOLAR RIDGE. The hard part of the roof of the mouth that rises up behind the ridge is called your HARD PALATE. The tip of your tongue can easily reach to the point where the palate starts to get more fleshy, although it can't travel very far onto that fleshiness. That part is called the SOFT PALATE or the VELUM. And when your tongue is curled back like this, the tongue is said to be RETROFLEXED.

Go to a mirror now and look in your mouth. You can see a little fleshy part hanging down back there. That's called the UVULA, and sounds made at the uvula or directly behind it are called UVULAR sounds. The area inside the throat deeper than the uvular area is called the PHARYNX and sounds made there are called PHARYNGEAL. The area below the pharynx is called the larynx, and it produces LARYNGEAL sounds.

Now consider the parts of the bottom of your mouth. Again you have a lip and teeth. But you also have a tongue, which can be used in many different ways. We will talk about the tip of the tongue, the BLADE (the wider part behind the tip), the BACK or DORSUM, and the ROOT. If you close your mouth and rest your tongue flat inside it, the tip will be right behind the bottom teeth, the blade will line up with the hard palate, and the back will line up with the velum.

In Figure 1.1 you can see all these areas labeled.

The drawing shown in Figure 1.1 is called a MIDSAGITTAL SECTION, because it shows what we would see if we could take a picture of the inside of the middle of the head.

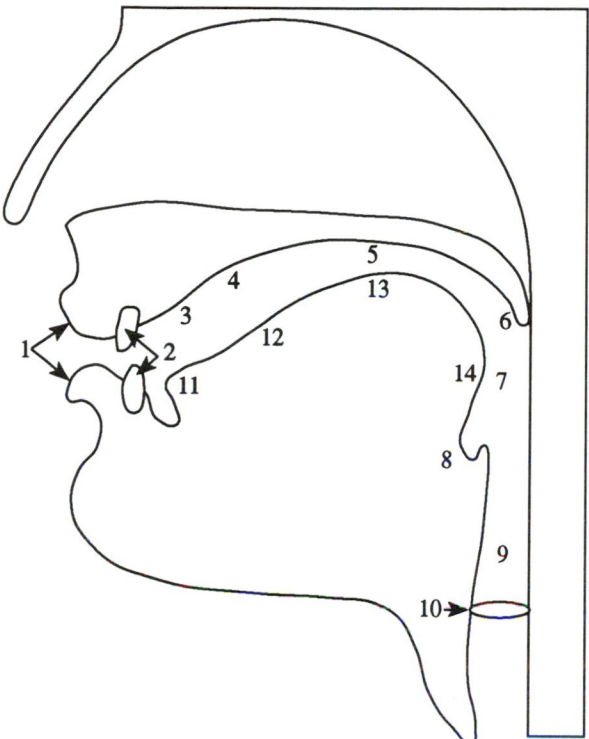

Figure 1.1. The numbers in this figure correspond to the following points of articulation and articulators: (1) lips; (2) teeth; (3) alveolar ridge; (4) hard palate; (5) velum; (6) uvula; (7) pharyngeal area; (8) epiglottis; (9) laryngeal area; (10) larynx with vocal cords; (11) tip of tongue; (12) blade of tongue; (13) back of tongue; and (14) root of tongue.

Okay, now look at the sounds listed in 1, which I have augmented with [w]:

[m]   [p]   [b]
            [w]

What is their place of articulation? (top lip) What is their articulator? (bottom lip) These are called the BILABIAL SOUNDS. We say that any sound which makes use of either or both of the lips has the FEATURE of [+LABIAL].

As our discussion progresses, we will introduce more and more features, which we will use as classification devices for sounds. **All of the features we talk about will be BINARY (so [+ labial] contrasts with [− labial], for example, and every relevant sound has the value of + or − for each feature). And a given sound will have several features, which we group together into what we call a FEATURE BUNDLE.** The usefulness of this notion will become apparent later.

All four of the sounds discussed above, [m], [p], [b], and [w], are made with the same articulator and same place of articulation. So what makes them different sounds? What other features are we using to distinguish between them?

We have already noted that [w] is doubly articulated. (It has two places of articulation and two articulators.) So we can hold off on further discussion of [w] for the moment.

But what distinguishes [m], [p], and [b]?

We noted above that in making [m] the air flows through the nasal cavity. In fact, for [p] and [b] the whole velum is raised so that it touches the back wall of the vocal tract and it closes off the flow of air into the nasal cavity, forcing all of it to escape through the oral cavity. (This might surprise you. You might have thought the velum was stationary. It's not.) But for [m] the velum is lowered, and both the oral and nasal cavities fill with air from the lungs. This contrast is shown in Figure 1.2*a* (with [m]) and 1.2*b* (with [b]). Compare the position of the velum in Figure 1.2*a* and *b*. In Figure 1.2*b* the velum is raised in preparation for making the oral sound [b].

We call sounds with a lowered velum NASALS (which is the name of the feature that distinguishes sounds made with airflow through the nasal cavity). So we can distinguish [m] from [p] and [b] by the fact that [m] is nasal but the other two are oral. We say that [m] has the feature of [+NASAL], while [p] and [b] have the feature of [−nasal].

Now we need to distinguish [p] from [b]. Take a piece of paper and hold it up flat in front of your mouth less than an inch from your lips. Say *pad*. Now say *bad*. The paper should get pushed away from your mouth more at the start of *pad* than at the start of *bad*. Now put your hand, palm facing you, right in front of your mouth. Repeat the experiment. You can feel a puff of air at the beginning of *pad* that you don't feel at the beginning of *bad*. (Some speakers can feel a puff of air at the beginning of both, but it is stronger and more explosive at the beginning of *pad* than at the beginning of *bad*.) That strong puff or explosion is called ASPIRATION. We say that the [p] of *pad* is aspirated, but the [b] of *bad* is not. The feature we use to indicate aspiration is [+SPREAD GLOTTIS], because the spreading of the VOCAL CORDS at the release of a complete closure causes the aspiration. (The vocal cords, the space between them, and the area around them together are called the GLOTTIS.) We write an aspirated [p] in this way: [pʰ]. In fact, in my speech every occurrence of [p] above should have been written as [pʰ].

Phonemes and Allophones

We now have a nice difference between those two sounds. Unfortunately, if you are an Italian speaker or a French speaker or a German speaker or a Japanese speaker or a speaker of many other languages and you try that same experiment (with the paper and then with the hand), you will not be able to reveal a difference between [p] and [b]. That's because these languages don't aspirate either sound.

And, in fact, there are times when the speaker of English doesn't aspirate this sound. Repeat our experiments, saying the minimal pair *lap* and *lab*. The paper doesn't move for either sound. You don't feel a puff on your palm for either sound. Neither [p] nor [b] is aspirated in these words. That's not to say that you can't aspirate the [p]. If you want to, you can add aspiration, perhaps to give an emphatic focus. But normally you don't. And this contrasts with the situation in *pad* vs. *bad*, where the aspiration is obligatory on the first consonant in the first word.

Make a list of several minimal pairs that contrast [p] and [b] in initial position and then several that contrast [p] and [b] in final position. What do you notice? Now don't do the experiment—just consider the minimal pairs *pill* and *Bill* and *tap* and *tab*. In which word do you expect [pʰ]? You should expect it in *pill*.

Now make a list of several POLYSYLLABIC words that have [p] and [b] somewhere other than in word-initial or word-final position—words such as *repeat, imbecile, compound*,

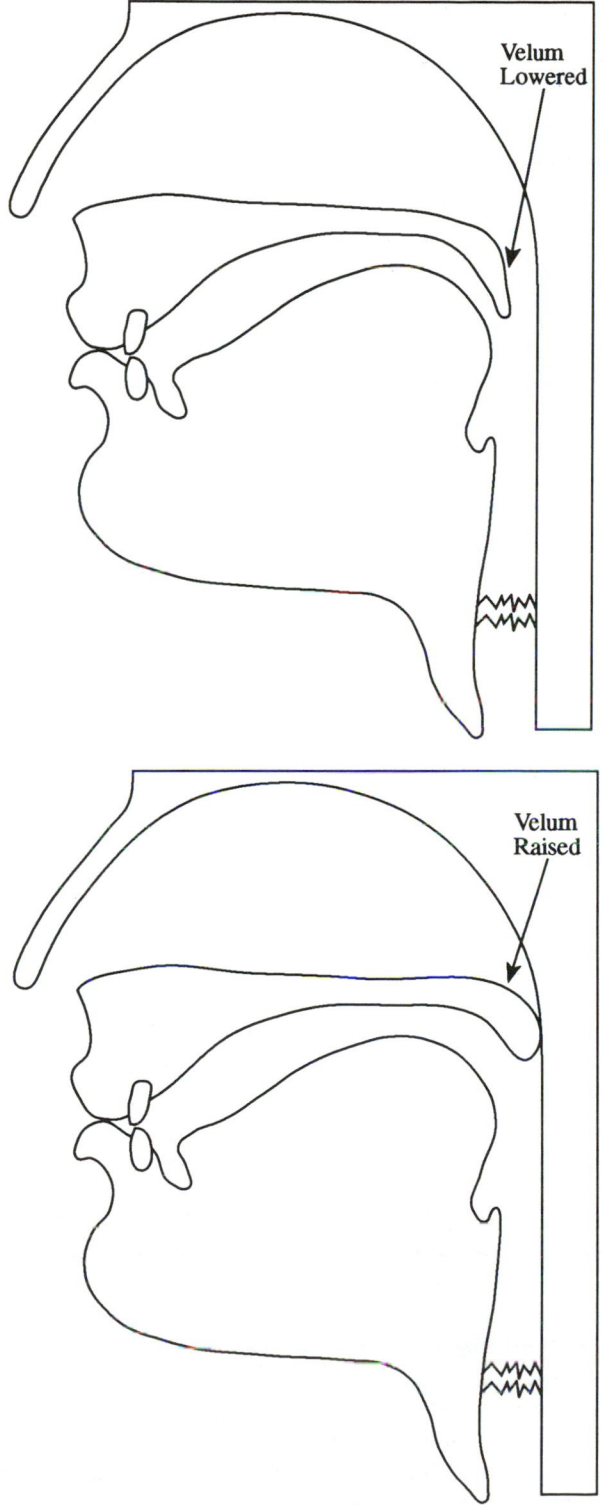

Figure 1.2. (*a*) The lips meet. The velum is lowered. The vocal cords vibrate (as indicated by wavy lines in the larynx). (*b*) The lips meet. The velum is raised (so air does not pass through the nasal cavity). The vocal cords vibrate.

rebuke, etc. Is [b] ever aspirated? (no) Is [p] in these words? Okay, so in general, is it word-initial position or syllable-initial position that we find [pʰ] in? (syllable-initial)

Now consider another question: When [p] occurs in syllable-initial position, is it always aspirated? To answer this one, consider words such as:

potato	punctual	potentate	preponderance
coupon	rampage	capacious	apiary
campus	tapping	reparations	copulate

You should feel quite sure that in word-initial position we find [pʰ]. And I hope you feel rather sure that in the second row of words we also find [pʰ]. But in the third row you probably do not aspirate the [p]. Can you hear that? In all of these words, the [p] or [pʰ] is syllable-initial (you will learn about how to syllabify words later and in the section "Syllable Types" in Chapter 2), yet not all of them require aspiration. We find that when [p] is initial to (that is, begins) a truly unstressed syllable, the [p] is typically not aspirated.

In other words, it is predictable that in the initial position of a stressed syllable we will find [pʰ] and not [p] in English (although we'll find [p] in Italian). And it is predictable that [b] will never be aspirated in English. For this reason we say that the feature of [+spread glottis] in some instances of [p] is **not distinctive in English—it is RE-DUNDANT. It is a difference that occurs automatically in a certain PHONOLOGICAL ENVIRONMENT or CONTEXT or CONDITION.** (Here initial position of a syllable is the phonological environment for aspiration.) We say, therefore, that [p] and its aspirated counterpart [pʰ] are not separate phonemes, but, instead, ALLOPHONES of a single phoneme. That is, our basic phoneme is /p/, which we write between slanted lines (a point I'll return to). But when /p/ finds itself in the initial position of a stressed syllable, it gets aspirated and it comes out as [pʰ]. (A symbol between brackets represents the sound as we say it.)

The simplest way to recognize whether two sounds are separate phonemes or allophones of a single phoneme is to look for minimal pairs. If you are lucky enough to find a minimal pair, the two sounds in question are separate phonemes. If you don't find a minimal pair, you need to check further, since not every sound will participate in a minimal pair with every other sound. (You already knew that. Remember how we started forming minimal pairs using *my* for a standard, but then we had to switch to using *moo* because not all of our English consonants participated in a minimal pair with *my*?)

What you'll be looking for is predictability. If you can see that one sound occurs only in a given environment or in a restricted set of environments, and another very similar sound occurs in all other environments, then you are probably dealing with allophones, where the sound that occurs in "all other environments" is the BASIC or UNDERLYING form, and the sound that occurs only in a given environment or in a restricted set of environments is the DERIVED form. When we write our sounds using the IPA, we make a distinction between what we know must be the underlying form and what we actually say. What we know must be the underlying form we write between slanted lines, and we call it our PHONEMIC or UNDERLYING REPRESENTATION (UR). What we actually say we write between square brackets, and we call it our PHONETIC REPRESEN-TATION (PR).

The importance of the distinction between UR and PR will become clear when we turn to Chapter 2 (and see particularly the section called "Why Have UR and PR?"). But even now it's worth it for you to be aware of this distinction.

To see how we use this terminology, let's contrast *sip* with *pass*. The last sound of *sip* can be pronounced as [p] or [pʰ] (or, actually, a couple of other pronunciations, as well— but let's consider only these two here). If we say it as [p], then it has an identical UR and PR: /p/ and [p]. The first sound of *pass*, on the other hand, must have a different UR and PR: /p/ and [pʰ].

An important fact about phonemes and allophones is that two sounds which may be allophones of a given phoneme in one language might well be separate phonemes in another language. For example, there are languages in which the feature of [+spread glottis] on any consonant is distinctive, and thus /p/ and /pʰ/ are separate phonemes. We will be talking more and more about allophones in this chapter and throughout Chapter 2, so don't worry if you're not yet comfortable with this idea. You will be.

Voicing

Let us return now to our discussion of the distinctive difference between /p/ and /b/. We have learned that we cannot point to aspiration as that difference. There must be another difference that is a distinctive difference, for even though [p] is not aspirated in syllable-final position in English, we still can distinguish it from [b] in that position. And even though Italians and Japanese do not aspirate [p] in any position, they still can distinguish it from [b]. So there has to be some other difference between the two—a difference that is not predictable from context.

Let's start again with *tap* and *tab*. Put your hand on your throat so your palm covers your larynx. Say the words. Can you feel more vibrations in your hand at the end of *tab*? You should be able to. Try putting both hands over your ears, forming a suction with your palms. Now say them. See how *tab* seems to reverberate more inside your head?

Actually, because the [p] and the [b] follow vowels in these examples, it may be hard for you to feel the difference with either of those tests. So if you are having difficulty, you could try getting ready to say *pan*, but don't actually say it. Just close your lips and do whatever it is you do before you say the initial consonant. Now do the same for *ban*. With each, put your hand over your larynx, and then put your palms over your ears. Do you feel the difference? If you are still having difficulty, just believe me for now that the [b] reverberates more in your head than the [p] does, and when we get to the discussion of [f] vs. [v], you can try these two tests again, simply holding the [f] sound for several seconds and then holding the [v] sound for several seconds, first with your hand over your larynx and then with your palms over your ears. I guarantee you will feel the difference then.

The difference here is in your vocal cords. They are vibrating quickly with [b], but they are not vibrating or only barely vibrating with [p]. This distinction is called VOICING. We say that [p] (and [pʰ], as well) is VOICELESS and [b] is VOICED; [p] has the feature [−voiced] and [b] has the feature [+voiced]. Try whispering the words *pad* and *bad*. Can you tell the difference? Aspiration allows us to distinguish between the two words. But now whisper the words *tap* and *tab* with no aspiration on the final consonants. When we whisper, the vocal cords don't vibrate, so the voicing distinction in the final consonants is lost. Can you hear how the difference between word-final [p] and [b] is removed with whispering?

Many people can still distinguish between *tap* and *tab* when whispered, but that is because they are paying attention to another difference between the words. Say *tap* and *tab* again, this time without whispering. Pay close attention to the vowel sound. Can you see a difference? The vowel in *tab* is slightly longer than the vowel in *tap*. It appears to be a language universal that vowels have greater DURATION or QUANTITY before voiced consonants than before voiceless consonants. When people whisper, they maintain a lengthened vowel before a consonant that would be voiced if they weren't whispering. It is the vowel LENGTH difference that allows you to distinguish *tap* from *tab* when they are whispered, since the rest of these words are identical when whispered.

For English speakers the distinction between voiced and voiceless consonants is relatively light. For speakers of Italian it is a strong distinction. That's one reason why when an Italian says something like, "Bello" ('pretty'), people often think the remark is exclamatory. But even said as a cool judgment, the Italian word *bello* simply starts with a fully voiced [b]—in contrast to the lightly voiced [b] of English.

The whole idea of having a feature to a certain degree (such as light voicing vs. full voicing) is disturbing. Most discussions of phonetics treat the features as being binary in value—a sound either has a feature or it doesn't. And in the rest of this book we will follow that convention. However, if you ever do your own research in phonetics and phonology, you might well have to pay attention to varying degrees of a feature.

We have now seen three of the major ways sounds can be distinguished. One is by their articulator and place of articulation. (So far we've discussed only bilabial sounds, with a passing remark on affricates.) Another is by whether the air flow goes into the nasal cavity (that is, whether or not the sound has the feature [+nasal]). And a third is by whether the vocal cords are vibrating (that is, whether or not the sound has the feature [+voiced]). So we have the following feature bundles for these three consonants:

[p]:   [+labial, −nasal, −voiced]
[b]:   [+labial, −nasal, +voiced]
[m]:   [+labial, +nasal, +voiced]

(These feature bundles are incomplete. As we learn more features, you can fill in their value—plus or minus—for these three consonants.)

Actually, we have seen a fourth way that sounds can be distinguished—by the feature of [±spread glottis]. In English this feature is not distinctive (as we argued above when discussing /p/), but in other languages it often is.

All right, we're ready to move on to additional features. Look back at our examples in 1–8. Is there any other group of phonemes which, like /m/, /p/, and /b/, have the same place of articulation and same articulator, but differ by nasality and/or voicing? Sure. Look at 7 again:

[ŋ]   [k]   [g]
      [w]

This situation is entirely parallel to the bilabials. Here we a nasal, a voiceless oral sound, a voiced oral sound, and the doubly articulated [w]. These sounds are called VELAR. The back of the tongue is the articulator, and, in fact, the only part of the tongue that we ever move toward the velum is the back of the tongue. Which of the velar sounds is the nasal?

([ŋ]) Which of the other two is [−voiced]? ([k]) Is either of them [+spread glottis]? ([k] is when in syllable-initial position—so in that position we write it as [kʰ].)

If we want to distinguish the sounds in 1 (the bilabials) from the sounds in 7 (the velars) in terms of features, we can say that the former are [+labial], while the latter are [−labial]. This doesn't work beautifully, however: the problem is [w], for [w] is a LABIALIZED velar, so it is [+labial]. Therefore we need to add another feature, and we have already discussed it: the back of the tongue pulls toward the velum in making all the sounds in 7, so we say that the velars are [+BACK]. Thus the velars in the top row of 7 are distinguished from the bilabials by at least two features: they are [−labial] and they are [+back].

Before going on, let's linger a moment over [w]. Give a feature bundle for [w] with respect to the features we know so far:

[w]:   [+labial, −nasal, +voiced, +back]

Is [w] ever aspirated? No. So it is also [−spread glottis]—but in English we would not list this feature, since it is not distinctive. As you continue meeting new features in this chapter, you should return to the consonants we have already discussed and enrich their feature bundles accordingly.

Okay, let's go on. When I asked you to find a group of sounds that seemed to contrast internally in the same way the sounds in 1 did, you might well have also wanted to list the examples in 4:

[n]   [t]   [d]
      [s]   [z]
            [l]

The problem here is that we have more than three sounds made with the same articulator and at the same place of articulation. The articulator is the tip of the tongue (or, for many speakers of English, the blade of the tongue). The place is, for English, back toward the bony alveolar ridge, and for the Romance languages and many of the languages of Europe, immediately behind and touching the teeth. These sounds are often called the DENTAL sounds, even though in English they are made on or just in front of the alveolar ridge. (Sounds made on the alveolar ridge are called ALVEOLAR sounds.) As with the velar sounds, the parts of the tongue that can be involved are automatically limited since the tip and blade of the tongue are the only parts we can bring to the area behind the teeth or to the alveolar ridge. (If you have been playing around with these sounds, you may realize that the remarks in this paragraph do not pertain as much to [l] as they do to the other five sounds. Please have patience. We will get to a discussion of [l].)

For each of the sounds in 4 now, give a feature bundle with respect to the features we have discussed above—that is, give a list with the values for the features labial, nasal, spread glottis, voiced, back. All of them are [−labial, −back]. Which is [+nasal]? ([n]) Which are [−voiced]? ([t] and [s]) Which is [+spread glottis] in syllable-initial position? ([t]—which is then written as [tʰ]) But that is as far as we can go. We have no way yet to distinguish between the voiceless sounds [t] (in positions in which it is [−spread glottis]) and [s], and between the voiced sounds [d], [z], and [l], yet we know our language cares about the distinctions between these sounds. So the dental sounds in 4 force us to find more features that distinguish between sounds.

Manner

Let's start by examining [t] and [s]. Compare *toe* to *sew*. Certainly we have the aspirated [tʰ] here, while [s] is not aspirated. But there's more to it than that—and you know it, since *mat* and *mass* are distinctly different, yet both end in a consonant that is [−spread glottis]. Try to hold onto the initial consonant of *toe* and then of *sew*. That is, try to increase its duration or length. Can you? For *toe*, lengthening the [tʰ] means having a longer silence before the sound is RELEASED (that is, before the closure formed by the tongue against the alveolar ridge is opened). For *sew*, lengthening the [s] means hissing for a longer period. The air flow is completely stopped in the oral cavity in making both [t] and [tʰ], but the air flow is continuous in the oral cavity in making [s]. For this reason, we say that the MANNER of air flow differs between these sounds. We call /t/ (in both its allophones [t] and [tʰ]) a STOP (or PLOSIVE) and we say that it has the feature [−CONTIN-UANT], while [s] has the feature [+continuant].

Let me warn you about terminology here. We say that sounds are [−continuant] if the air flow in the oral cavity is completely cut off at some point in making the sound. Thus even though the air may flow continuously through the nose on some sounds (as it does with [n]), a nasal sound will be [−continuant] if the air flow in the oral cavity stops. Not all linguists call nasals stops, however. So the terms *stop* and *noncontinuant* are not interchangeable. I will often refer to oral stops to distinguish them from nasals.

Look again at our bilabial sounds in 1 for a moment now:

[m]   [p]   [b]

Are they [+continuant] or [−continuant]? All three are [−continuant] because the air flow in the oral cavity is completely stopped. (Did this throw you off? Remember: while the air flow is never blocked in the nasal cavity for [m], the important question for the determination of this feature is what happens in the oral cavity.) What about our velar sounds in 7?

[ŋ]   [k]   [g]
          [w]

Again, all these are [−continuant], except [w]. Since the lip closure is not complete for [w], the air flow in the oral cavity is never totally stopped.

Which of the sounds in 4 are [−continuant]?

[n]   [t]   [d]
      [s]   [z]
           [l]

Yes, the top row. That's why I organized these sounds into rows.

Make a full list of the stops of English now and of the nasals:

stops: p, b; t, d; k, g
nasals: m, n, ŋ

Look again at 4, repeated above. Both the second and third row of 4 contain sounds that are all [+continuant]. We have already noticed that we can distinguish between [s] and [z] by the feature of voicing. But we are lacking a way to distinguish [z] from [l].

What differs between these two sounds? (If you do not make the [l] of *lie* with the tip or blade of the tongue touching the alveolar ridge, again, I ask for your patience. Many people do. So we are now on a hunt for a difference between [z] and [l] for those speakers. Bear with me and we will get to a more detailed discussion of [l], I promise.) We are going to get subjective here as we find another difference in manner of air flow, so loosen your shoulder muscles and let it happen. Hum a tune you like with the sound [z]. Now hum that same tune with the sound [l]. Which one sounds more melodic? Which one, in contrast, sounds more buzzy? Why is [z] buzzy? Make a [z] and hold it. What's happening to the air flow to make it so turbulent? It's being forced against the inside of the teeth and the oral cavity is being reduced because of the shape and placement of the tongue. Can you feel that? In contrast the air flow in making [l] is smooth and unobstructed. Yet the tip of the tongue is touching the roof of the mouth as you say the initial consonant of *lie*, just as it is in saying the dental stops. How is that air flow escaping? The air passes freely around the sides of the tongue. See?

We call [+continuant] sounds which involve air turbulence FRICATIVES or SPIRANTS. Look across your twenty four consonants of English:

[m]	[p]	[b]
	[f]	[v]
	[θ]	[ð]
[n]	[t]	[d]
	[s]	[z]
		[l]
	[ʃ]	[ʒ]
	[ʧ]	[ʤ]
		[ɹ]
		[j]
[ŋ]	[k]	[g]
		[w]
	[h]	

Which of them are fricatives? You should be asking which of them you can hold (that is, which are [+continuant]) and have a hiss or buzz to them. Why are some hissy while others are buzzy? That difference is voicing. List now the fricatives in pairs that differ only by voicing. You should come up with four pairs:

fricative pairs: f, v; θ, ð; s, z; ʃ, ʒ

(If you listed [ʧ] and [ʤ], you were correctly noticing their hissy or buzzy quality. But neither of these sounds begins as a [+continuant]. We'll discuss them in detail later.) The last two pairs of fricatives in the list here are called the SIBILANTS. The sibilants are our most turbulent sounds. Compare the pair of [f] and [v] to [θ] and [ð]. Can you hear a difference in turbulence between these pairs? You may well not be able to. I can't. Yet rules that affect sounds (PHONOLOGICAL RULES, which you will learn about in Chapter 2) often group [f] and [v] with the sibilants, treating them as though they are highly turbulent or STRIDENT. We make note of the difference here with the feature of STRIDENCY. We say that [f] and [v] and all the sibilants are [+STRIDENT], while the fricatives [θ] and [ð] are [−strident].

There is one more fricative of English that does not come in a pair: [h]. If you came up with it yourself, great. If you didn't, that's not surprising—it is a difficult sound to describe. I'm going to hold off on discussing it until after we've looked at the other consonants of English.

Laterals

Go back to [l] now. Earlier I treated [l] in the word *lie* as though it had the same place of articulation as [t], [d], [n], [s], and [z] in the appropriately minimally contrasting words. But for many speakers, this is not true. In saying the word *lie* there are many speakers whose tongue does not make contact with the top of the mouth. And for all speakers, we could easily find words containing /l/ that didn't involve this place of articulation. Describing the sounds associated with /l/ is more complicated than describing any other phoneme we have yet faced, because /l/ has allophones that can be remarkably different from one another. Say the word *little*. There are two instances of the phoneme /l/ in this word, each having a different PR (phonetic representation)—that is, each being a different allophone. The initial instance is like the initial consonant sound of *lie*, which is the allophone we have already considered. But the second instance is new. We call the first LIGHT or CLEAR or HIGH *L* (because the tip of the tongue is high), written as [lˆ], and the second DARK or VELARIZED or LOW *L* (because the back of the tongue is bunched a little toward the velum and the tip of the tongue is low), written as [lˇ]. What is the shape of your tongue as you make the two sounds? Certainly the blade of the tongue is fairly wide and flattened out in both, though not much else of the shape may be similar. But the crucial common feature is that the air flows freely around the sides of the tongue—this is the defining feature of "l"-like sounds, and we call it LATERAL. We say that both allophones are [+lateral]. Thus you should not feel terribly bad about admitting them as allophones of the single phoneme /l/ in English. Go through the list of English consonants. Are any of the others [+lateral]? No.

Dark and light *l* are not the only allophones of /l/ in English. Say the word *million*. Now try to isolate the INTERVOCALIC sound (the sound between the vowel sounds). Say it over and over. What is its place of articulation? Yes, the palate. Consider the shape of the tongue as you make this sound. It isn't terribly similar to the shape of the tongue as you made either of the other allophones of /l/, because now the blade of the tongue is high. But still the blade is wide and flattened. And can you tell that the air flow is still lateral? This palatal allophone of /l/ is written as [ʎ]. While we will be sure in our transcriptions of English to distinguish between [l] and [ʎ], we will lump light and dark /l/ together and transcribe them simply as [l]. There are two reasons why we will not be conscientious about distinguishing between light and dark allophones of /l/. First, it will ease transcription. But the second reason is the more important one: no language I know of makes a phonemic distinction between light and dark laterals, although many make a phonemic distinction between other laterals, such as the dental and the palatal. So it is important that you note the distinction between dental and palatal laterals, but less important for you to note the distinction between light and dark laterals.

All of our various "l"-like sounds are lateral; that's what unifies them. Nevertheless, [l] cannot be said to have a distinctive place of articulation, as we have just seen. We will say that [l] is UNDERSPECIFIED for place of articulation. Instead, its place of articulation varies according to the sounds we find preceding or following it. In fact, the phoneme we call "l" is likely to have allophones in any language that has this sound. This is going to become an important point when we talk about underspecification in the sections "Dissimilation" and "Underspecification Theory in Lexical Phonology" in Chapter 2.

When we first met the idea of allophones above, I told you that sounds which were allophones in one language can be separate phonemes in another. Let me demonstrate that point here. Italian has three lateral consonant sounds. One is a dental; one is a long dental (a dental of double duration, indicated with a colon after the consonant symbol); and one is a palatal. Now consider the following words of Italian, where I have written before each one the IPA symbol for the intervocalic lateral sound and I have written after each translation the IPA transcription for the whole word (with a vowel you will meet later):

[l]	pala	'shovel'	[pala]
[l:]	palla	'ball'	[pal:a]
[ʎ]	paglia	'straw'	[paʎ:a]

These words are a MINIMAL TRIPLET (like a minimal pair), differing only in the lateral consonant. What does this say about these three lateral sounds in Italian? Are they separate phonemes or are they allophones of a single phoneme? If you don't know the answer right off, reread the earlier paragraphs concerning allophones. Do you know now? The fact that the words above differ in sound by only the one SEGMENT and also differ in meaning (that is, they form a minimal triplet) is the key. I expect you to say that these three lateral sounds are three separate phonemes in Italian: /l/, /l:/, and /ʎ/. Actually, that isn't exactly how linguists say it. Notice that the quality of /l/ and /l:/ is identical—they have all and only the same features. What differs is duration. So we say that Italian, unlike English, has distinctive length on its consonants (although not on its vowels).

The point of the above discussion of Italian is that the palatal lateral [ʎ] is an allophone of /l/ in English, but it is a separate phoneme from /l/ in Italian.

But another point has fallen out of that discussion, a fact about language that we could not have learned simply from looking at English alone: duration can make a sound distinctively different from another sound. We saw above that Italian has distinctive length on consonants. A colon after an IPA symbol means a lengthened segment of sound. Lengthened segments are called GEMINATES. Thus the consonant [l] differs distinctively from the lengthened or geminate consonant [l:] in Italian. Many languages, in fact, use duration to distinguish between sounds, particularly between vowel sounds. The Slavic language Czech has distinctive length on vowels, for example, and the Uralic-Yukaghir language Finnish of Finland uses duration distinctively for both consonants and vowels.

Inventory of Features Thus Far

At this point we can benefit from making an inventory of the new terminology we have been developing. First, we talked about articulators and places of articulation. We've looked at three places of articulation thus far and discussed the sounds found there: bilabials, dentals or (in English) alveolars, and velars. In this discussion two features were relevant to the place of articulation and articulators:

labial,   back

Second, we talked about whether the vocal cords were vibrating and whether they were spread to make aspiration. The relevant features were:

voiced,   spread glottis

Third, we talked about the manner of the air flow, noting that we have oral stops, nasals, fricatives, and laterals. There were four relevant features here:

continuant,   nasal,   strident,   lateral

Are you comfortable with that? If not, I suspect your worry is about calling nasality a manner of air flow. The other three features all deal with how the air moves in the oral cavity, but nasality deals only with the fact that air moves through the nasal cavity, not with how it moves in that cavity.

But think about that fact a moment. Certainly there is nothing analogous to the tongue inside the nasal cavity. And the tongue is one thing that allows us to stop the air flow to create sounds that are [−continuant] and to direct the air flow around it to create sounds that are [+lateral]. There is also nothing analogous to the teeth or lips. So we cannot direct the air flow against an obstruction to create sounds that are [+strident]. Therefore, saying a sound is [+nasal] says all that is relevant about its manner of air flow in the nasal cavity.

However, saying a sound is [+nasal] may not be all that is necessary to describe the manner of the air flow in its entirety. If the air flow were continuous in both the oral and nasal cavities at once for a given sound, we would need to say more about the manner of air flow for that sound. Does any such sound actually occur? In other words, do we ever get a nasal that does not correspond to an oral stop? Certainly not among the nasals we have discussed thus far. ([m] corresponds to the oral stop [b]; [n] corresponds to the oral stop [d]; and [ŋ] corresponds to the oral stop [g].) And in most languages of the world that have nasals, most of those nasals in most of their uses are [−continuant]. This is not, however, a necessity. We have already noted that vowels can be nasalized. (Look back at our discussion of *cat* vs. *can*.) And you will learn in Problem Set 1.3 that at least one of our English nasals has an allophone that does not correspond to an oral stop. Nevertheless it is an unusual or MARKED occurrence for a nasal consonant to be [+continuant]; the UNMARKED nasal consonants are all [−continuant]. In other words, generally, nasal consonants correspond to oral stops. And you may come across the term "nasal stops" in your readings.

Also, as you will see in Problem Set 1.3, a sound can be both [+nasal] and [+strident].

What about the features of nasal and lateral? Are they mutually incompatible? If we were to have a sound that was [+nasal, +lateral], that would mean that the velum was lowered and that the air that passed through the oral cavity went around the sides of the tongue. If laterals are [+continuant], then such a sound would also be [+continuant], so it would be marked (given that nasals are typically [−continuant]). But the question I want you to consider is whether such a consonant is possible at all. Try to nasalize the initial sound of *lie*. See? You can do it. But it's certainly odd. I don't know if any languages of the world make use of nasalized laterals.

Since it came up, I will indulge in a brief aside here. In the previous paragraph, there is a sentence that begins, "If laterals are [+continuant] . . ." According to our definition of continuancy, laterals are continuant because the airflow is continuous around the sides of the tongue. However, in some languages laterals pattern with stops on phonological rules. That is, laterals and stops will behave the same way, when other sounds will behave differently. For this reason, some linguists have defined the notion of continuancy in such a way as to give laterals the value of [−continuant]. We have not done that, and we will not, in fact, look at any languages in which laterals pattern with stops. But you should be aware that this controversy exists, simply because it can help you to understand a very basic point: **while our physiological apparatus is the basis for our description of the sounds of language, the choice of which differences between sounds we will elevate to the status of distinctive features is based not solely on physiology, but on phonological behavior, too.** Without a doubt, as linguists study the sound systems of more and more languages, the features that we choose to list as distinctive features will change somewhat to accommodate the new findings and to accommodate the resulting new ways in which we look at already-familiar data.

Now go back to the set of 1–8. Again beinning at the front of the mouth, let's consider sounds whose articulator and place of articulation we haven't yet discussed. We come to 2:

[f]   [v]

What is the place of articulation for these sounds? (top teeth) The articulator? (bottom lip). These are called the LABIODENTALS. Give a feature bundle for these fricatives. You should come up with [+labial, −back, −nasal, +continuant, +strident, −lateral, −spread glottis]. As for voicing, [f] is [−voiced] and [v] is [+voiced]. Since no other sounds we have discussed thus far have the same feature bundles, there is no need for us to distinguish them further at this point.

Now we arrive at the sounds in 3:

[θ]   [ð]

Describe the place of articulation and the articulator. Not surprisingly, these are called the INTERDENTALS. Give a feature bundle for these fricatives. You should come up with: [−labial, −back, −nasal, +continuant, −strident, −lateral, −spread glottis]. Which of them is voiced? ([ð]). Again, these feature bundles are different from those for every other sound we've described thus far, so we can pass on without further details here.

We have already covered the sounds in 4 ([t], [d], [n], [s], [z], and [l]), so let us move on to 5. Consider the sounds in the first row of 5:

[ʃ]   [ʒ]

([ʃ] is sometimes written as [š]) and [ʒ] is sometimes written as [ž].) Which of them is voiced? ([ʒ]) What is the articulator for these sounds? (the tip or blade of the tongue) What is the place of articulation? (Right behind the alveolar ridge.) These fricatives are [−labial, −back, −nasal, +continuant, +strident, −lateral, −spread glottis]. But this feature bundle is the same as that of another pair we have already discussed. Which other pair? That's right—the other sibilants, [s] and [z]. So we need a feature to distinguish between the two pairs. And we already know that they differ by place of articulation. So we now introduce the new feature of [+ANTERIOR]: those sounds that are made with the primary place of articulation being at or in front of the alveolar ridge are [+anterior]; those behind are [−anterior].

Now consider the sounds in the next row of 5:

[tʃ]   [dʒ]

([tʃ] is sometimes written as [č]) and [dʒ] is sometimes written as [ǰ].) Which of them is voiced? ([dʒ]) Are these really made at the same place of articulation as the postalveolar fricatives [ʃ] and [ʒ] in the first row of 5? Many linguistics books say these sounds are made on the hard palate—that is, further back than the postalveolar fricatives. But that isn't the full story. These sounds are complex in nature. Say them as slowly as you can. Can you see? They start out with a complete closure and then slowly release. The complete closure is on the alveolar ridge and along the sides of the palate. The DELAYED RELEASE (a term that we will now include in our features and abbreviate as DEL REL) means that the air is forced through a gradually enlarging passageway, so these sounds are definitely [+strident]. **Complex sounds that begin as a stop and end as a fricative are called AFFRICATES.** In English each of these two affricates behaves as though it is a single consonant phoneme with respect to phonological rules, and their complex nature is reflected in their IPA symbols ([tʃ] and [dʒ]). In other languages, however, they may better be analyzed as a sequence of two consonants, a stop and a fricative. We would then transcribe them as [t] followed by [ʃ] and [d] followed by [ʒ]. Their feature bundle as single consonants, not considering voicing, is: [−labial, −back, −nasal, −continuant, +strident, −lateral, −spread glottis, +del rel, −anterior]. Notice that even without introducing the feature of delayed release we could have distinguished these sounds by their feature bundles, since the fact that they are [−continuant] makes them different from the postalveolar fricatives. It's worth it to learn the feature of delayed release, however, since this one feature can pick out all affricates as a class.

"r"-sounds

We now come to the sounds in 6:

[ɹ]   [j]

Let us first consider [ɹ]. No book on phonetics that I know of groups [ɹ] with the palatal sounds. Instead, they typically list [ɹ] with the alveolar sounds. Is the [ɹ] of *rye* an alveolar sound the way you say it? Not if you use the actual point at which the tongue touches the top of the mouth for your criterion. The sides of the tongue are raised against the inside of the top teeth on the sides of the hard palate. Perhaps the tip of your tongue is pointing upward, and if it is, it is pointing toward the alveolar ridge (and, hence, the classification as alveolar in many texts). Probably your lips are protruding. We know that /ɹ/ is a phoneme of English. Is every PR of /ɹ/ identical? Of course not. (You may have already realized that the PR of any phoneme can vary somewhat from its UR.) Compare the initial sound of *rye* to the final sound of *car*. Notice that your lips are not protruding on *car*. Yet I know of no symbol to distinguish between these two allophones of /ɹ/. What that suggests is that linguists have not found it necessary to have an additional symbol here. Why? Probably because there is no language in which the two sounds differ distinctively. Can you understand the logic here? If not, reread this paragraph.

My description of the tongue, teeth, and lips when making [ɹ] may not have matched the description you would have given. Please do not get overly concerned about the differences. This sound, like the laterals, and much more so than the other sounds we have yet discussed, varies in its place of articulation based on the sounds around it, so much so that it can even be said not to really have its own distinct place of articulation. So again we are dealing with a phoneme whose place of articulation is underspecified. But one thing we should be able to agree upon is that the blade of the tongue is raised when we make [ɹ]. We can now meet another feature, CORONAL. We say a sound is [+coronal] if we move the tongue blade toward the teeth, alveolar ridge, or hard palate to make it.

List our [+coronal] consonants thus far. This feature is needed because certain phonological rules make use of it. When this feature was first proposed, the interdentals were considered [−coronal]. Today, however, many linguists call the interdentals [+coronal]. By this point you are familiar with this sort of controversy, and you can guess that linguists found the interdentals behaving like coronal sounds in the phonological rules of some languages and they therefore changed their judgment of the value of this feature for these sounds.

But there is another point I'd like to make here: **Not all linguistics texts and articles use the features we discuss in this chapter to mean precisely the same thing.** So be sure to try to figure out exactly how an author is using the term as you follow that author's discussion. Let us return now to our consideration of "r"-like sounds.

Do you know any other language that has an "r"-sound that sounds like English [ɹ]? Be careful here. Don't be led astray by spelling. Many sounds that we identify as "r"-like occur in other languages, but they may well not be identical to [ɹ]. In Spanish, for example, we get a repeated TAP, called a TRILL, on the dental area. The symbol for this sound is [r], and it is truly a dental sound. Say the English word *pudding*. The intervocalic sound here is a single tap or FLAP, very similar to the repeated tap of the trill, although it can be made on the alveolar area; its symbol is [ɾ]. Can you tell that it is a little farther forward than both [d] and [t] in English? In French, on the other hand, the "r"-like sound we get is a voiced uvular fricative. The symbol for this sound is [ʁ].

Many different types of sounds go under the rubric of *r*, then, including trills, taps, a fricative, and the English [ɹ], which is often called an APPROXIMANT. (The term "approximant" covers continuant sounds that produce no audible friction. Many works in linguistics mark the laterals as approximants.) And these so-called "r"-sounds do have some things in common (although the French [ʁ] is an exception). They are [+voiced, +continuant, −strident]. They are also highly melodic. In this way they are like the nasals and the laterals, and unlike the oral stops, affricates, and fricatives.

We can see a major division among consonants here: The first set is the SONORANTS (nasals, laterals, approximants). The second set is the OBSTRUENTS (stops, affricates, fricatives). These features—sonorant and obstruent—are two sides of the same coin. The sonorants are our most vowellike consonants and we will discuss them further after we have discussed the vowels. For now, just add sonorant to your list of distinctive features. (We could as easily have chosen obstruent for the feature. We chose sonorant because sonority will become an important concept in our discussions.)

The oral sonorant consonants, that is, the "r"-like sounds and the lateral sounds, are called the LIQUIDS, although the term *liquid* is not typically used as a feature name. The liquids form a natural class in that they participate in phonological rules in a similar or identical way in many languages. (Remember that we'll meet phonological rules in Chapter 2.) In English you can feel relatively secure in grouping them together even from a purely phonetic perspective because they do not have a distinctive place of articulation, as already mentioned. Instead, [ɹ] and [l] vary in place of articulation quite a lot—much more than the stops, for example—according to context.

The second sound in 6 is [j]. Compare [ɹ] and [j]. Go back and forth between them. Their major difference is the shape of the tongue. For [j] the middle of the tongue is high, coming very very close to closure with the palate, yet not closing fully. We say that sounds that raise the blade or back of the tongue high up toward the roof of the mouth are [+HIGH] (which is the name of another feature).

Which other sounds that we've discussed thus far are [+high]? Actually, we are once more in a controversial area. Surely the affricates [tʃ] and [dʒ], and the postalveolar fricatives [ʃ] and [ʒ] are candidates worth considering. But the alveolar fricatives [s] and [z] are not, since even if you say them with the blade of the tongue, the tongue body is distinctly lower than when you say the postalveolar fricatives. You will find some linguists marking these affricates and the postalveolar fricatives as [+high], although others will mark them as [−high]. But everyone marks the alveolar fricatives as [−high].

The controversy over the highness of these affricates and postalveolar fricatives has two parts. First, it is clear that these sounds are made with the tongue blade (so they are [+coronal]), but does the tongue body rise in the process? And if it does, is this raising phonologically important? That is, do languages make use of this information when putting sounds together into larger units? For these affricates and postalveolar fricatives some languages seem to treat them as [+high], whereas other languages don't seem to offer such evidence. In Chapter 2 you will see many instances in which sounds change their features when preceded or followed (or both) by certain other sounds. When you get there, you can ask yourself whether or not the changes you consider offer evidence that a particular affricate or fricative is [+high]. (See in particular Problem Set 2.4.) In languages that lack relevant evidence about highness for these sounds, it is possible that such sounds are underspecified for this feature.

What about the velars with respect to highness? They are clearly [+high].

To return to [j], is [j] sonorant or obstruent? (sonorant) It is neither nasal nor liquid, however. Instead, [j] is an approximant (like the English [ɹ]). It is also often called a GLIDE. (This term is usually applied only to [j], [w], and [h], and we will make only minimal use of it.)

We are now at 7, the velars:

[ŋ]   [k]   [g]
        [w]

You should have no trouble, using all the features we have discussed thus far, giving a feature bundle for these sounds.

So we turn to [h]. Give a feature bundle for it. Is this sound back? No, because the back of the tongue is not bunched up toward the velum. If this sound has to fit into one of our groups of oral stops, nasals, fricatives, affricates, liquids, or approximants, which one does it seem most like? Certainly it is a continuant and oral, so the only real choices should be fricative, liquid, or approximant. But notice that the other liquids and approximants which we have discussed are voiced, while [h] is as close to silence as any of the sounds we've discussed thus far gets. In fact, [h] is produced merely by spreading the glottis and letting the air flow out from the lungs (so it is [+spread glottis]), without any point of articulation or articulator in the oral cavity. So [h] is a fricative (though it's [−strident]).

Many books list [h] as [+sonorant]. Given how we've developed this chapter thus far, you probably think of fricatives as being [−sonorant]. There are at least two reasons for considering [h] a sonorant. First, acoustically, [h] appears to be equivalent to the voiceless counterpart of the vowel [ə]—a vowel we will discuss later. (If you have a phonetics laboratory available to you, you can demonstrate that for yourself.) Second, sonority is fundamentally a feature of sounds that have freedom of airflow in the vocal tract. Now the fricative sound of [h] is made in the larynx. If the larynx is an articulator of the vocal tract, then [h] should be considered [−sonorant]. But if the larynx is not an articulator of the vocal tract, then [h] should be considered [+sonorant]. It appears that languages vary as to whether their phonological rules treat the larynx as an articulator of the vocal tract or not. So [h] sometimes participates in phonological rules as though it is a sonorant consonant, and we therefore often find [h] listed as a glide. The most sensible guide then is how [h] behaves in the language that you are analyzing. You may mark it as [+sonorant] in one language and [−sonorant] in another.

In our discussion we have come up with **thirteen distinctive features for English: voiced, spread glottis, labial, back, nasal, anterior, continuant, strident, lateral, delayed release, sonorant (which is the opposite of obstruent), coronal, and high**. Of these, eleven were needed in order to distinguish one sound from another. But two of them, sonorant and coronal, were introduced for other reasons. There are no two sounds of English that are identical except for their value on the feature of sonority or for their value on the feature of coronality. There are other languages (as I will mention later for sonority), however, in which these features may be distinctive. And we will see that these two features turn out to be very useful when we write phonological rules.

These are all the consonant features we are going to discuss. Certainly there are more ways that we could classify consonant sounds if we wanted to. But the question for us is not how detailed we can get in describing sounds, but what the minimal amount of detail is that we need in order to handle whatever linguistic phenomena we want to look at.

Think about that point a moment. If we discussed, say, two dozen features of sounds, when only perhaps three were relevant to a given phenomenon, the twenty-one superfluous features would be in the way. They might tend to mask the real nature of the phenomenon. For that reason, linguists opt for the minimal set of features (or any other mechanism) necessary to handle a problem. The features we have discussed above turn out to be adequate for our purposes in discussing phonological rules, so we will not introduce new ones. But if you approached other sorts of problems in the study of language sounds, you might well want to consider additional features.

Beyond English

At this point we have discussed all the consonants of English. (See the Appendix at the end of this chapter, which lists all these consonants with their place and manner as well as with their distinctive feature values.) But we haven't discussed the full range of consonants found in the languages of the world. Among the things we've left out are many fricatives and some oral stops and nasals, particularly in the rear parts of the vocal tract. Fricatives can be made at every possible place of articulation, so let's start at the front of the mouth and fill in those that are missing.

Put your lips together lightly. Now force air through them. If you let a pocket of air form behind the top lip, you will wind up making a trill. This bilabial trill, [ʙ], is a sound you might make if you were fed up or disgusted with something. But it is also a consonant in a very few languages, such as Kele (also spelled "Gele") and Titan, Indo-Oceanic languages spoken in the Admiralty Islands of Papua New Guinea.

If, instead of forming an air pocket behind the top lip, you keep your lips taut as you force the air between the lips, you will make a bilabial fricative, and you can choose to voice it or not. [ɸ] is voiceless; [β] is voiced. Bilabial fricatives are commonly found: Japanese (a language isolate in the Altaic phylum, spoken in Japan) makes use of the voiceless one; Spanish (another Romance language, spoken in Spain), of the voiced one.

Now make an alveolar [l]. Then try forcing the air very hard around that lateral. You'll come up with a lateral fricative, which you can voice ([ɬ]) or not. (To indicate lack of voicing on a normally voiced sound, you can put a diacritic—a small circle—under the sound.) Welsh (a Celtic language of the Indo-European family spoken in Wales) and Zulu (a Bantu language spoken in South Africa) both use lateral fricatives, as do many languages. The approximant alveolar lateral is [+sonorant], while the fricative lateral is [−sonorant]. This is the first instance we've seen in which the feature of sonority can be the distinguishing feature in a minimal pair.

Now put the tip of your tongue at the front of your hard palate (but well behind the alveolar ridge). You will have to curl it backward to do this. Make an oral stop. If it's voiceless, it will sound like a strangely muffled [t]. (In fact, this sound is sometimes considered a speech impediment for speakers of English.) Recall that sounds made with the tongue curled back like this are called retroflexed. ([ʈ] is the voiceless retroflexed stop; [ɖ] is the voiced one). Make a retroflexed nasal now. ([ɳ]) Retroflexed stops and nasals occur in many of the major languages of India, including Hindi-Urdu (an Indo-Iranian language spoken also in Pakistan) and Malayalam (a Dravidian language). You can also make retroflexed fricatives by lowering the tongue so the closure is incomplete. Do it. The symbols for them are [ʂ] and [ʐ]—and Vietnamese (an Austro-Asiatic language spoken in Vietnam) and Malayalam make use of them, as do many other languages. You can make both retroflexed liquids there. Try it. (The "r"-like one, [ɽ], will be a tap or flap, not a trill, right?) The symbol for the lateral is [ɭ].

Now put the blade (not tip) of your tongue to your palate. Make an oral stop. You can voice it ([ɟ]), or not ([c]). This is, of course, where the palatal lateral ([ʎ]), and the approximant ([j]) we have already discussed, are made. A palatal nasal ([ɲ]) is also made here, and you will learn about it in Problem Set 1.3. Italian makes use of the palatal nasal and liquid; Hungarian (a Uralic-Yukaghir language spoken in Hungary) makes use of both palatal stops. Now make a fricative, simply by lowering the tongue the slightest bit and forcing the air through the reduced passageway. If you're having trouble, try saying the word *huge*. Most speakers start this word with a palatal voiceless fricative. Practice voicing ([ʝ]) and devoicing ([ç]) the fricative. German (an Indo-European language of the Germanic family) uses the voiceless palatal fricative. Greek (an Indo-Hittite language spoken in Greece) uses both voiced and voiceless palatal fricatives.

Now make a [k]. Then don't complete the closure and you'll be making a voiceless velar fricative, like at the end of the word *Bach* under the German pronunciation. The symbol for this fricative is [x]. Say it and then voice it ([ɣ]). Vietnamese and Greek use both velar fricatives. You can also make a lateral there ([ʟ]). Try it. Some languages spoken in Papua New Guinea use velar laterals, but they are rare. And you can make an approximant similar to the lateral and similar to [j], written with the symbol [ɰ].

You can make fricatives behind the velum in the uvular area, but in order to do it, it helps to know how to make non-nasal stops back there. Make a [k] between [ɑ] sounds. ([ɑ] represents the vowels in *mamma*.) So say [ɑkɑ]. Now try to swallow it a bit, so the closure is in the uvular area. That's the voiceless uvular stop [q] (which the western Semitic language Arabic makes use of). (If you have trouble making this, then wait until I've discussed ejectives and come back to it then.) Now make the voiced uvular stop [ɢ]. Once you can make those stops, make the uvular nasal [ɴ]. All three of these consonants occur in Inuit (an Eskimo-Aleut language spoken in Alaska and Canada), Quechua (an Amerind language spoken in the Andes), and some other languages native to the Americas, which are in the Amerind family. Okay, now raise the velum (so it's no longer a nasal sound) and try easing up on the closure so that you get the voiced ([ʁ]) and voiceless ([x]) uvular fricatives. (Recall that the voiced one is the French "r"-sound.) And now sort of gargle a bit while you voice and you will be making the uvular trill [ʀ]. Amazing, huh?

Now go even deeper in your throat. You won't be able to make stops in the pharyngeal area, but you can make fricatives there. Make a sound like you're clearing your throat. Now voice it. You've just made the pharyngeal fricatives [ħ] ([−voiced]) and [ʕ]. Fricatives are the only types of sounds that are made in the pharynx, and both Classical and modern varieties of Arabic use these fricatives, as do Hebrew (a Semitic language spoken in Israel) and some of the languages of the Caucasus Mountains.

You already know how to make a glottal fricative—that's what [h] is. Now make an [h], but add voicing, to get [ɦ]. You should sound like a dying person or a monster. You can also make a stop here. Make an extended [ɑ] and stop the air in the middle of it at the glottis. The glottal stop [ʔ] is always voiceless and you can hear it in the medial position of American English and British English (English spoken by native speakers in Great Britain) pronunciations of words like *button* and the exclamation *uh-oh*. You can also hear it when teachers read words off a list in a spelling test; they will often put a glottal stop before a word that begins with a vowel, such as *apple*, so that the word seems to get a jumpstart. The feature [+CONSTRICTED GLOTTIS] is used for any sound that involves complete closure of the vocal cords, such as [ʔ] (and we will meet more such sounds later).

Some languages use other sounds made deep in the vocal tract, called EPIGLOTTAL sounds. Without a tape recording and/or a teacher to help you, I doubt you can make these sounds on your own. The symbol for the voiceless fricative is [ʜ]; for the voiced fricative is [ʢ]; and for the voiced stop is [ʡ]. The Semitic languages (a family in the Afro-Asiatic phylum) are the main users of these sounds.

Furthermore, some languages make a double articulation of [ʃ] and [x] written as [ɧ]. This one I think you can produce on your own; try it. You are already familiar with double articulations from having looked at affricates and at the labialized velar [w] (which, by the way, is another approximant, like [ɹ], [j], and [ɰ]). You will meet more doubly articulated sounds later in this chapter.

Where I have failed to give an example of a language that uses a particular sound, this gap is due to my lack of knowledge. But the IPA introduces all these symbols, so I assume that there must be languages that make use of all these sounds.

Ejectives, Implosives, and Clicks

Languages also have other stop consonants which are made in the same areas as the ones we've discussed, but for which other aspects of the air flow vary. One such type of sound is called an EJECTIVE. The stops we've looked at thus far all depend on PULMONIC air pressure—that is, air pressure from the lungs. To make an ejective, the glottis closes so that the air pressure builds up behind. Then you make a momentary closure somewhere else in the vocal tract and release it along with the glottis, thus getting GLOTTALIC pressure. The sound sort of pops from your mouth. All ejective sounds are, by definition, [+constricted glottis].

Let's try to make some ejectives. Perhaps the easiest one to start with is an ejective velar, written as [k']. (An ejective air pressure is indicated by an apostrophe after the regular IPA symbol.) Put it between [ɑ]s again and go back and forth between the pulmonic and the glottalic stop, like so: [ɑkɑ] [ɑk'ɑ]. Now try it for the palatal, retro-flexed, alveolar, and bilabial stops. All of them are voiceless. You can also make a uvular ejective. It sounds very much like the "glug" sound from an emptying bottle. (And if you had trouble making uvular stops earlier, now make this ejective and then try opening the glottis and doing a regular pulmonic uvular stop.) Ejectives are very common. They are found in many Amerind languages (such as Lakhota) and Athapascan languages (such as Navajo), in several African languages (such as Hausa, a Chadic language of Nigeria, and Swahili, a central Bantu language), and in some languages of the Caucasus region (such as Georgian).

You can also close the glottis, and when you release it, suck air into the lungs instead of letting it go out the vocal tract. That is, the AIRSTREAM is INGRESSIVE rather than EGRES-SIVE. Sounds made in this way are inverse ejectives and are typically called IMPLOSIVES. Like the ejectives, they are typically [+constricted glottis] (although they do not have to be, as mentioned in the next paragraph). Unlike the ejectives, both voiced and voiceless implosives are found in language, although voiceless implosives are rare. Again, it may take some practice to learn how to make these sounds, and, strangely enough, you might have an easier time doing it if you start in the uvular area. Make a uvular ejective (the bottle "glug"). Then make a uvular implosive and go back and forth between them as quickly as you can, ejecting and sucking, in alternation. Once you get the hang of it, you can make implosives at all the other stop points, although retroflexed implosives do not have symbols in the IPA, so I assume they do not occur in language. An implosive air pressure is indicated by a rightward curved hook on the upper left or right portion of the regular IPA symbol, so the voiced bilabial implosive, for example, has the symbol [ɓ] and the voiced uvular implosive has the symbol [ʛ]. Zulu makes use of both ejective and implosive bilabials, as do many other languages of Africa and some languages of the Americas and of India, such as Sindhi (an Indo-Iranian language).

By the way, it is perfectly possible to have ingressive pulmonic air pressure, but it is rare. The Penutian language Maidu (of northern California) is the only language I have found listed as making use of it.

Finally, there is one more thing we can do with air that doesn't involve the lungs or the glottis. We can form a complete closure somewhere in the oral cavity and then move the articulator to produce a suction. The release of this suction is called a CLICK. Sounds made with this sort of suction are called VELARIC pressure sounds (as opposed to pulmonic or glottalic pressure sounds). You already know how to make a bilabial click: it's identical to the kiss sound and it's written as [ʘ]. You are also familiar with the affricate click that touches both the alveolar and palatal areas and sounds like a scolding noise or a noise that means, "What a shame!" It is written as [!]. You can move that click forward to behind the dental area and make [|], also written as [ǀ]. And you are familiar with the alveolar lateral that sounds like encouragement to a horse to speed along, written as [‖]. (This is made by opening only one side of the mouth and clicking that same side of the tongue.) You can also easily make an alveopalatal click that sounds very much like a cork popping from a bottle, [≠]. Make all of them now. You can find clicks in many languages used as interjectional noises. But they are common as phonemes primarily in some languages of southern Africa: Zulu, Xhosa, Nama, Bushman, and Hottentot use a variety of clicks.

The clicks you've just made (with the exception of the bilabial and lateral ones) involve pulling the tongue down and back to rarefy the air behind the closure. But you could also push the tongue upward and compress the imprisoned air to make an inverse click. Try going back and forth with the alveolar affricate click, regular then inverse then regular and so on.

Breathy Voice, Whispery Voice, and Creaky Voice

At this point you have been introduced to all the consonants listed in the IPA. However, there are other things you can do to these consonants. Compare the pair *bloom* and *plume*. Focus on the lateral sound. Say the words quickly, then slowly. What's the difference between the two laterals? Certainly that in *plume* has a more airy quality to it. Can you hear it? Try it again. It is very difficult for an English speaker who is not trained in phonetics to detect this difference. Try getting ready to say *bloom*, but then say it without the [b]. Then do the same for *plume*, without the [p]. If you really have yourself all prepared to make the [b] first, and then all prepared to make the [p] first, you should be able to notice that the lateral starts differently in each. That's because the lateral in *bloom* is voiced, while that in *plume* is voiceless. The IPA marks voiceless sounds that are typically voiced with a small circle under the regular IPA symbol, such as [l̥]. (Another way to mark them is to use the corresponding capital letters, for example: [L].) For those of you who are still having difficulty hearing the difference, don't despair—you're not alone. A more noticeable [l̥] is after an [s] in an unstressed syllable, as in *whistling* [wɪsl̥ɪŋ]. Can you hear it now? Once you learn to hear that one, then you should be able to hear the [l̥] of *plume*, too.

Can you guess why this lateral is voiceless in *plume* but voiced in *bloom*? If you don't know how to begin guessing, then say many words with a lateral and put them in two lists according to whether they are voiced or not. You might come up with something like:

Voiced	*Voiceless*
lose	slow
alter	claim
pail	please
glue	flavor
pearl	schlep (from Yiddish)

(Yiddish is a High Germanic language spoken by Jews of eastern Europe.) Now can you see? The voiced [l] occurs in many phonological environments, but the voiceless one in English occurs only as part of a consonant cluster where the first consonant is voiceless. What does this tell us about the status of the voiceless one? Is it a phoneme of English or is it an allophone of /l/? It's an allophone (and now we have met yet one more allophone of /l/). But in another language it might be a separate phoneme.

Now that you know how to make and look for voiceless laterals, find instances in English of voiceless "r"-like sounds and voiceless nasals.

The difference between voiceless and voiced sounds is a difference in PHONATION. For voiceless sounds our vocal cords are generally separated and the air passes between them without causing vibration. For voiced sounds our vocal cords are generally close together and the airflow causes them to vibrate.

We can also separate the glottis and use a substantial enough airflow to make the vocal cords vibrate a bit, despite their separation. Say [h] again. Now keep saying it, but increase the airflow as much as you can. You have now made a BREATHY or MURMURED [h]. And you can add this breathy quality on top of your ordinary speech—that is, to all consonants and vowels. Some linguists call this Marilyn Monroe talk, and it is indicated by two horizontally arranged dots under the regular IPA symbol. Breathiness on a vowel is in a sense analogous to aspiration on a voiceless oral stop. The language Kuy, a minority language of the Mon-Khmer family spoken in eastern Thailand and some areas of Cambodia and southern Laos, uses breathy vowels, which contrast distinctively with nonbreathy vowels.

We can also add a WHISPERY quality by removing all voicing. This is something you are probably quite used to doing. Many languages have voiceless vowels (such as French, Japanese, and Comanche, an Uto-Aztecan language in the Amerind phylum of the western United States), but typically they are allophones of voiced vowels, rather than phonemes.

And we can speak in a CREAKY voice, as if we were making the low sound of a rusty hinge on a door in telling a horror story. (This is indicated by the diacritic tilda, ~, under the regular IPA symbol.) Here all sounds involve vibration of the glottis, but only one end of the vocal cords can vibrate. When we discuss formants, we will talk more about exactly what's happening in the larynx as we make a creaky voice. For now, it is enough that you can make a creaky voice and detect one when you hear it.

Try taking a word with all voiced sounds in it and imposing breath on it. Now try giving a whispery quality to the word. Be careful not to totally whisper, because then all the sounds will be voiceless. There's a difference. And now say it in a creaky voice.

Another common way consonants in various languages can be different from those we've already discussed is in the addition of a secondary articulation. You are already familiar with the idea of secondary articulation from our discussion of [w]. We called the labialization here secondary. Take [k] and [g] and give them a secondary labialization. You come out with the initial sound of words like *queen* and *guana*. Labialization is indicated with a raised *w*: [k^w], [g^w]. Try labializing other consonants. Do you find any that seem to occur in English? Certainly labialized alveolar stops occur in English. Find examples. (the initial consonants in *twin*, *Dwight*, and the like) Typically it is stops that are labialized, but other sounds may be, as well.

Consonants can also have a secondary articulation in the palatal area (Russian makes use of palatalized stops), in the velar area, and in the pharyngeal area. Again, this typically happens with oral stops. And the release of such a stop can be accompanied by a quick lowering of the velum (to give a nasal release) or by a widening and flattening of the tongue (to give a lateral release). (Here you may need an instructor's demonstration to help you make the sounds.)

This is not the whole story. Other fine distinctions can be made. The point is not for you to memorize what goes on in language, but for you to be sensitized to the sorts of things that can happen, so that you can listen for them.

Minimal Pairs and Vowels

Just as orthographic consonants in English do not have a one-to-one relationship with consonant sounds, the same is true for vowels. So please fight off tendencies to revert to any short list of vowels your grade school teacher may have given you.

With that caveat in mind, let's begin by trying to understand what a vowel is and how a vowel differs from a consonant. We have already introduced the vowel [ɑ] (as in *mamma*). Say this [ɑ] and compare it to the consonant sounds. What do you notice about it? Which consonant sounds does it seem to have the most in common with? Certainly [ɑ] is a continuant and it's voiced—and we will find that all our vowels are (by definition) continuants, and voiced in the unmarked situation. Yet the vowels do differ from the consonants. With respect to articulatory phonetics, the vowels are made with no obstruction in the vocal tract whereas the consonants have varying degrees of obstruction, from very little (with the approximants and liquids) to complete (with the stops). Still, you may have trouble swallowing the claim that the first vowel in the word *ear*, for example, involves any greater or smaller obstruction than the obstruction made by the liquid at the end of that same word.

Fortunately, we don't have to rely solely on articulatory phonetics to see the differences between vowels and consonants. Vowels differ quite remarkably from consonants in ways we can see both from acoustic phonetics (which we will talk about later) and from phonological rules. That is, the vowels play different sorts of roles from the consonants when we put sounds together to make words. That's what we'll focus on first.

To see this, compare [ɑ] to [z], for example, which is also [+continuant, +voiced]. (Notice that in this discussion the sounds are consistently between square brackets. That is because all we care about is how they sound as we say them, not what they might have been in underlying representation.) Say monosyllabic words that contain [ɑ] and monosyllabic words that contain [z]. What do you notice about them? Say a monosyllabic word that contains both [ɑ] and [z], such as *Oz* [ɑz] (as in the wizard's land) or *shah's* [ʃɑz] (as in having to do with the shah of Iran). Maybe you're starting to get an inkling of the difference. Try comparing [ɑ] to another voiced continuant, such as [v]. Look at the word *von* [vɑn] as in the last name *von Beethoven*. Now make up monosyllabic nonsense words that contain three sound segments, choosing only from the list of [z], [v], and [ɑ]. You have undoubtedly made up [zɑz], [zɑv], [vɑz], [vɑv], and [ɑvz]. That is, you can have two consonants, but only one [ɑ]. What happens if you put two instances of [ɑ] into your nonsense word? English does not form minimal pairs in which one word has a short vowel (a single vowel) and the other has a long vowel (a sequence of two identical vowels.) (But some languages, do, as we'll discuss later.) So if we're going to make a nonsense English word with two instances of [ɑ], those instances will be in separate syllables. The result in English is a polysyllabic word such as [ɑzɑ] or [zɑvɑ].

Syllables

Give me any two-syllable word of English. You might have given *father*, or thousands of others. Give me any three-syllable word of English. You might have given *unlikely*, or thousands of others. Give me any four-syllable word of English. You might have given *American*, or thousands of others. How are you choosing which words have three syllables and which have four? What are you counting? In musical terms, you might say you are counting beats. Each syllable consists of a single beat.

And now you have found one of the major differences between consonants and vowels: in the unmarked case vowels are crucial to the beat of a syllable. We say they form the NUCLEUS of the syllable and that they are [+SYLLABIC]—they carry the beat. And in the unmarked case consonants are [−syllabic] and they appear either preceding the nucleus of the syllable, in the ONSET, or following the nucleus, in the CODA. Thus in a syllable like [vɑn], the onset consists of [v], the nucleus consists of [ɑ], and the coda consists of [n]. Is it possible for a syllable to have no coda in English? Certainly. Think of the word *pa* [pʰɑ]. Is it possible for a syllable to have no onset in English? Again, of course. Think of the word *Oz* [ɑz]. But every syllable must have a nucleus, by definition, since every syllable has a beat.

Syllabic Consonants

Now while consonants typically are not SYLLABIC (that is, they typically don't carry the beat of a syllable) and vowels typically are syllabic, we find that there are some syllabic uses of certain consonants in English as well as some nonsyllabic uses of certain vowels. The vowel [ɑ] is always syllabic, so we'll hold off on a discussion of nonsyllabic vowels for a moment. But we can now discuss syllabic uses of consonants. Do you remember which consonants we claimed above were the most vowellike? The sonorant consonants. Consider first the liquids. Can you think of a word that contains a syllable that has no vowel, but instead has a syllabic liquid? Let me give you one for [l]: *bottle* [ˈbɑ.r̩l]. (The diacritic of a small vertical line under a consonant shows that this consonant is [+syllabic]. So [l] is nonsyllabic and [l̩] is syllabic. A period indicates a syllable boundary. And an acute accent, ´, over a vowel, or, in some books, a raised ´ before a syllable, indicates that that vowel (or syllable) receives PRIMARY WORD STRESS. By convention when transcribing monosyllabic words, we leave out the stress mark, even though the word may be fully stressed.) Now you can easily find others. What about a syllabic use of [ɹ]? Consider the word *work* [wɹ̩k]. Again, you can now easily find others.

Turn now to the nasals. Can you find a syllabic use of any of them? Examples with the bilabial and alveolar nasals are easy to come by (such as the minimal pair *prism* [pʰɹɪ́.zm̩], *prison* [pʰɹɪ́.zn̩], both of which use a vowel in the first syllable that we haven't yet discussed). But for some speakers the velar nasal can also be syllabic, as in the first syllable of the word *ingot* [ŋ̩.gət] (which uses a vowel in its second syllable that we haven't yet discussed).

The only other sonorant consonants are the glides, [h], [w], and [j], the last two of which are often called the SEMIVOWELS. No glides can be syllabic in English, however, a point we return to later.

The liquids and nasals—that is, the sonorants minus the glides—are the only consonants that can be syllabic in English. However, other languages may make use of no syllabic consonants or of a range of other syllabic consonants. The Imdlawn Tashlbiyt dialect of Berber, an Afro-Asiatic language family spoken in various parts of northern Africa west of Egypt, particularly in Morocco, demonstrates one extreme case, for in this language any consonant (as well as any vowel) can be syllabic, whether it is sonorant or obstruent. This is a highly marked language for syllabicity, of course.

Sonority

Let us take a moment now, before we go on with our discussion of the vowels, to look a little more closely at the feature of sonority and its role in the shape of the syllable. Consider monosyllabic words in English that contain clusters of two consonants in either onset or coda, or both. List them. Start with the bilabial consonants and ask what clusters they can initiate. Then go to the labiodentals, and so on, into the mouth. Your list should begin with such examples as:

onset clusters

[pʰl], [pʰɹ]	please, proud
[bl], [bɹ]	bloom, bread
[fl], [fɹ]	fly, fry
[θɹ]	thread

Considering only the contrast of obstruent vs. sonorant, what can you say about the ordering of these two types of sounds within an onset cluster? Obstruents precede sonorants. Now consider coda clusters. Make another list. It should contain examples like:

coda clusters

[lp], [ɹp]	help, burp
[lb], [ɹb]	bulb, suburb
[lf], [ɹf]	elf, smurf
[lθ], [ɹθ]	health, earth

Once more you can see a contrast between obstruents and sonorants, but this time the sonorant comes first. Can you put these two statements of the distribution of sonorants vs. obstruents together into one generalization? Sonorants occur closer to the nucleus of the syllable; obstruents occur at the periphery of the syllable.

In fact, there is much more that we could say. Sometimes languages allow clusters containing more than one sonorant and/or more than one obstruent, or a sonorant plus an obstruent. English does this. And there are rules regulating the order of different consonants within a cluster. It has been proposed that there is a SONORITY HIERARCHY among sound segments:

vowels, glides, liquids, nasals, fricatives, affricates, and oral stops

In fact, within the fricatives and affricate/stop groups, the voiced segments are more sonorous than the voiceless segments. When languages form syllables, they usually arrange sounds within a syllable so that those closer to the nucleus are more sonorant. English presents exceptions to this generalization that you will explore a bit in Problem Set 1.4. English is not alone in being exceptional. Thus this generalization should be considered a kind of metric for evaluating the naturalness of a syllable, rather than as a principle for creating syllables. In fact, we will see in the section "Syllable Types" in Chapter 2 that the sonority hierarchy can be helpful in understanding how languages syllabify words.

Okay, at this point I hope you feel comfortable with our treating the vowels as different sorts of animals from consonants. And if you don't, then perhaps after we have discussed acoustics a bit later, you will. But for now let's turn to an articulatory phonetic description of the vowels of English.

Vowels and Diphthongs

Think about the features we've learned for the consonants. Are any of them relevant to [ɑ]? Certainly. [ɑ] is voiced; it doesn't use the lips in any way; the tongue is not bunched in the back of the mouth; it is not nasal; it is continuant; it is not strident; it is not lateral; it has no aspiration so it is not spread glottis; it can't have a delayed release because it has no closure to start with; the tongue body is not high in the mouth; it is a sonorant sound; and the tip or blade of the tongue is not raised in any way so it's not coronal. In other words, all of the features we have talked about for consonants could easily be used in describing vowels. Nevertheless, only some of the features used to talk about consonants are used to talk about vowels, and other features particular to vowels will need to be introduced. That's because there is little point in saying a vowel is [+continuant] or [+sonorant], for example, if all vowels have those features. (But if we had cause to gather together all the vowels and all the continuant consonants with a single feature, for example, we could use [+continuant].) Furthermore, what distinguishes vowels from one another more than anything else is the shape and size of the RESONATING CHAMBER—that is, the oral cavity. Vowels are resonant sounds made with much less closure in the oral cavity than most consonants, and this is what we will focus on now.

Say the baby-talk words *meemee*, *mama*, and *moomoo* (as in a child calling attention to self, calling to the mother, and mimicking the noise of a cow). Try to make the vowel sound in each syllable as short and clipped as you can. (In musical terms, give it a staccato quality.) With a short vowel in each one, we transcribe these three words into IPA like so:

[mí.mi]   [mɑ́.mɑ]   [mú.mu]

The three vowels we are hearing are [i], [ɑ], and [u].

Probably you did not make a short vowel for two of these three words until I asked you to. Go back to your original pronunciation of *meemee* and *moomoo*. Say them several times. Then take off the initial nasal consonant and say the vowels in isolation. Contrast these longer vowels to the short staccato vowels I asked you to produce. What are the differences? One difference, of course, is duration. The short vowel takes up one TIMING SLOT (or unit of time), while the longer one takes up two timing slots. But there is another difference. Can you hear that the quality of the longer vowels changes? I asked you to pronounce them with staccato style so that you could isolate a single vowel sound here, without the vowel change at the end.

Say the words *beat* and *bit*. Now say them with staccato vowels. You have now met a fourth vowel, the vowel in *bit*: [ɪ] (often written as a script "i," and called iota). We transcribe *bit* as [bɪt]. When you say *beat* staccato style, with only one timing slot for the vowel, we have [bit]. When many of you say *beat* in the normal style, with two timing slots for the vowels, we have [biɪt]. (If you are having trouble saying and hearing [bit] in contrast to [biɪt] and my directions to use staccato style don't help, try starting the word and holding the initial vowel without ending the word. Can you hear and produce the difference now?)

For many speakers of American English the normal pronunciation of *beat* involves a DIPHTHONG, a combination of a syllabic vowel and a nonsyllabic vowel. Which part of the diphthong in [biɪt] is the [+syllabic] part? The first vowel. We will indicate that the second vowel is nonsyllabic with the diacritic ˎ below the vowel, like so: [biɪ̯t]. That is, just as syllabic consonants are marked with a special diacritic, so nonsyllabic vowels are marked with a different special diacritic—because both situations are the less-typical case. The [−syllabic] part of a diphthong is often called a glide. In fact, you will find linguistics articles that transcribe the second part of this diphthong with the glide [j]. However, you know that this part of a diphthong is different from [j]. (If you don't remember, go back to our discussion early in this chapter of the final sound in *my* in contrast to the initial sound in *yes*.) The final sound in *my* is a [−syllabic] instance of the vowel [ɪ]; but the initial sound in *yes* is the consonant [j]. Transcribe *my*. You can do it. ([maɪ̯]) (We will return to thorny issues of glides and diphthongs in Chapter 2, particularly in Problem Set 2.2. So if you are full of questions now, please hold onto them.)

A similar situation holds for the vowels in *moomoo*. Say the words *cooed* (as in what a pigeon does) and *could*. If you say them normally, the first one has two timing slots for the vowel sounds, but the second one has only one timing slot. Say the first one staccato. You come up with [kʰud]. This contrasts with the second one: [kʰʊd]. Now say *cooed* in your normal style (not staccato). Can you hear the diphthong? Many American English speakers have a diphthong here, which would give us the transcription [kʰuʊ̯d].

Not all American English speakers, however, have a diphthong in *beat* or *cooed*, and even for those who do, the diphthongization is slight and hard to hear, because the two vowels in each of these diphthongs are so similar to each other. ([i] is only slightly higher than [ɪ], and [u] is only slightly higher than [ʊ]—which is also often written as closed omega [ɷ].) Some speakers instead have a long vowel in each of these words. (And there are some words that perhaps all speakers have only a long vowel in, such as *cease* [si:s].) If you are among the speakers who say [bi:t] rather than [biɪ̯t] and [kʰu:d] rather than [kʰuʊ̯d], then go to a movie or turn on the radio and listen closely. You will almost assuredly be able to hear the diphthongs in words like this within a few moments if you are looking for them, because this diphthongization, while delicate, is prevalent in many varieties of English.

One way to think of diphthongs is to consider them vowels in motion. You start out with one vowel and move into another vowel. In the two examples with diphthongs that we have discussed thus far, the nonsyllabic part is second. This is called an OFF diphthong or glide (or, depending on your terminology, a FALLING diphthong or glide). You can also have the nonsyllabic part come first in an ON diphthong (or a RISING diphthong), as in the word *piano* ([pʰɪ̯æno]). And you can have TRIPHTHONGS in which nonsyllabic vowels surround the syllabic vowel. English has some triphthongs, as in *cute*. Can you hear the rising and falling glide on either side of the [u]? Transcribe *cute*. ([kʰɪ̯uʊ̯t])

English is a difficult language to get started talking about vowels in because English makes such frequent use of diphthongs. But now that you know what a diphthong is, you can be sensitive to them and you can revert to staccato speech to avoid them. So we're ready to face vowels head on now.

Front, Back, High, Low

Let's contrast [i] to [u] to [ɑ].

For [i], describe the shape and position of the tongue. Is it high in the mouth (that is, close to the roof) or not? Yes, it's as high as vowels get in that part of the mouth. What do I mean by "that part of the mouth"? The palate. So [i] is often called a palatal vowel. Now consider the bunched up part of the tongue (the part that comes up toward the palate) and contrast that position to the position of the tongue in [u] and [ɑ]. Would you say the bunching for [i] is in the front of the mouth or the back in contrast to [u]? Certainly the bunching is not very far forward at all, but [i] is definitely in the front when compared with [u], right? [i] is called our FRONT, high vowel. And we have now met two features that are relevant to vowels: front and high. Front is not to be confused with anterior for consonants. Anterior is a feature of sounds made at or in front of the alveolar ridge. But the vowels need a resonating chamber—so they can't be made too far forward in the mouth. The hard palate is as far forward as the vowels get. Likewise, high for vowels is not as simple as the feature high for consonants. With consonants, we mark them as + or − for highness and that is the only feature we have for tongue height. That's because consonants call for some sort of partial or total obstruction of the airflow somewhere in the mouth, so if the tongue is crucially involved in making a given sound, it won't be terribly low in the mouth. But for vowels, the important part is the shape and size of the resonating chamber. So a very low tongue position will be relevant to the quality of the sound. Therefore, with vowels we will speak not only of highness, but of lowness. [i] is a high vowel. Is any vowel we've discussed yet low? Certainly: [ɑ]. These two vowels are at the extreme ends of the scale from high to low. But many other vowels come in along that scale. And some of these vowels are nearer to the middle of the scale than to either end. They are called the MID vowels and we say they are [−high, −low].

What about [u] with respect to the features of high and front? [u] also is a [+high] vowel. But now the tongue is bunched up in the velar area. Is [u] as high as [i]? Look back at our midsagittal section in Figure 1.1. The roof of the mouth slopes downward from the hard palate to the velum. So, because of our physiology, [u] is lower than [i]. But the important point is that [u] is as high as it can be for the velar area, so it is [+high]. Now about frontness, [u] is [−front]. But just as we made a three-way distinction with consonants between [+anterior], [+back], and [−anterior, −back] sounds, we will have reason to do the same for vowels (when we meet the central vowels). So [u] is a [+back] vowel.

Go back and forth between [i] and [u] several times. They contrast on frontness and they are similar on height. But that isn't the full story. Can you notice anything else different between them? Listen to them. What about PITCH? If you can't hear a difference, whisper the two sounds. Can you hear it now? [i] has the higher pitch of the two. Oh, certainly you can change the pitch on a vowel. Sing [i] from a low to high pitch. Do the same for [u]. But if we are just talking normally and not making any attempt to control our pitch, [i] has a naturally higher pitch than [u]. Why is that? Do an experiment now. Take two bottles of the same shape and size. Fill one with water half way. Fill the other with water one-fourth of the way. Now blow across the tops of the bottles so the air resonates in the space in the bottles not filled with water. Which has a higher pitch? The one that has more water in it. Why? Smaller resonating chambers give higher pitch. We will discuss why this is so when we turn to acoustics. But for now, draw your own version of Figure 1.1 and draw in the tongue as it would be for making [i] (bunched up at the palatal area). Now draw in the tongue as it would be for [u] (bunched up at the velar area). Where is the resonating chamber for each sound? It is the space in front of the bunched up portion of the tongue. So now you can see why [i] is naturally higher in pitch: the resonating chamber in front of it is smaller than the resonating chamber in front of [u].

Vowels definitely differ on their natural pitch. We will not, however, discuss this matter further here, because in this section we are talking about what we can notice in producing sounds (articulatory phonetics), not what we can notice in receiving sounds (acoustic phonetics). So please just lay this sort of difference in vowels aside and consider only the features of front, back, high, and low.

Tense and Lax

Put your tongue in the position to say [i]. Surround that sound with [b] and [t]—say [bit]. (We're back to staccato vowels here to avoid diphthongs.) Now say *bait*. Does it have a diphthong or not? Probably you say it with a falling diphthong. (And this is true even if you say *beat* with a long vowel rather than a diphthong.) If so, say it staccato. You can transcribe the staccato pronunciation with the new vowel [e]: [bet]. (Some books call this CLOSED "e".) How would you transcribe the normal pronunciation? ([beɪt]). Is the bunched-up part of the tongue high in the mouth or not? It's not very high, but it's also not flat like with [a]. So [e] is our first front mid vowel; its features are [+front, −high, −low]. Now say [i] and [e] in succession. Then try to slide between the two. Stop midway on that slide. Surround the vowel here with [b] and [t]. Do you recognize the word you're producing? It's *bit* again: [bɪt]. We say that this front vowel is also [+high]. So how can we distinguish [i] from [ɪ] with a feature bundle?

Unfortunately, we cannot see the articulatory difference here, but perhaps you can feel it. Say [i] and [ɪ] staccato style. Does one seem to involve more tension in the tongue? In fact, to make [i], inside the pharynx we project the tongue root forward, creating a larger pharyngeal opening. We say the [i] has the feature of [+ADVANCED TONGUE ROOT], or just [+ATR] for short. We also say that [i] is a TENSE vowel, whereas [ɪ] is LAX.

Okay, now pronounce in staccato style the words we've talked about so far: *beat*, *bit*, *bait*—[bit], [bɪt], [bet]. Say just the vowel sounds in succession: [i], [ɪ], [e]. Now let the tongue lower just a little. What word do you get? *Bet*—[bɛt]. We call [ɛ] EPSILON or OPEN "e." Here we have another [−high, −low] vowel that is [+front], just like [e]. Which of the two is [+ATR]? ([e])

If you find yourself unable to feel the tension difference between the [+ATR] vowels ([i] and [e]) and the [−ATR] ones ([ɪ] and [ɛ]), you're not alone. There is another way you can help yourself remember them. Say all the words we've been working on to find these vowels. What can you say about vowels with respect to diphthongs? When we are dealing with monosyllabic words, the tensed vowels typically occur only in diphthongs with a lax vowel, but the lax ones can occur in a syllable that does not have a diphthong. When we have a diphthong in English, which vowel is the syllabic one: the tense or lax vowel? The tense one.

Okay, lower the tongue even more. Put the new vowel that you are making between [b] and [t]. What word do you have? *Bat*, written as [bæt]. This vowel is [+low, +front]. Can you tell if it is tense or lax? If you can't feel whether the tongue root is advanced, listen for a diphthong. If it has a diphthong, it must be tense. If it doesn't have a diphthong, it could be tense or lax. It has no diphthong, right? And, in fact, this vowel is [−ATR]. We name [æ] ASH, or DIGRAPH.

So we have discussed five front vowels. We have also discussed the high back vowels [u] and [ʊ], as in the words *cooed* and *could*. (The first has a diphthong.) Which of these vowels is [+ATR]? ([u]) Now lower the tongue to midway and keep the same consonants surrounding the vowel. What word do you get? *Code*. When you say this word in ordinary style, does it have a diphthong or not? Yes—[kʰoʊ̯d]. (And, again, even if you say *cooed* with a long vowel rather than a diphthong, you probably have a diphthong in your pronunciation of *code*.) Get rid of the glide and just say the vowel in isolation: [o], sometimes called "closed o." Now lower the tongue a bit and what new word do you get with this new vowel? *Cawed* (as in what a crow did): [kʰɔd], where [ɔ] is called OPEN "o" or BACKWARDS "c."

At this point we come to a major split in American English speech. While NATIVE SPEAKERS along the east coast, including the South, as well as speakers in Los Angeles and San Francisco, pronounce the word *cawed* with [ɔ], most of the rest of the speakers in America pronounce this word with [ɑ]. **(A native speaker of a particular language is one who learned the language before the onset of puberty. A grammar of a language is always based on the linguistic behavior of native speakers only, since language learned after the onset of puberty is rarely of the same competence as native competence.)** In fact, the vowel [ɔ] does not occur in the speech of these American English speakers at all. So if you are a speaker who does not have [ɔ] in your variety of English, you will have to treat this vowel like you would any other sound from a foreign language and simply learn how to produce it and how to recognize it. If you let your tongue slide between [ɑ] and [o], you should be able to pick out a middle point that is close to [ɔ]. Do that now until you feel comfortable producing this vowel.

Now compare [o] with [ɔ]. Both are [+back, −high, −low]. So which one is [+ATR]? ([o]) (Here your diphthong test should have been a big help, right?)

Okay. We now have four back vowels. At this point we have one more front vowel than back vowel. Many books in linguistics list [ɑ] as the missing low back vowel. Other books call it a CENTRAL vowel. We will call it a back vowel because in many languages phonological rules group [ɑ] with the back vowels. However, there is one feature that the other back vowels have that [ɑ] does not have. To see this, hold a mirror in front of you and say the front vowels, and then the back vowels, leaving out [ɑ]. What do you notice about the lips? The back vowels in English are [+ROUND]—they call for rounding of the lips. But [ɑ] is [−round].

There are, however, more vowels than just these front and back ones. Say the word *but*. This vowel is [ʌ], called CARET or UPSIDE-DOWN "v." Can you feel where the tongue slightly bunches? Is it front, central, or back? I hope that you didn't say it was front. Many books classify it as central, others as back. We'll return to this later.

Now say the word *roses*. In the second syllable of this word we meet yet another vowel, called SCHWA [ə]. Is this vowel higher or lower than [ʌ]? It's a bit higher, but it may be hard for you to convince yourself of that because we have no minimal pairs for these two vowels. In fact, for most speakers of English, [ə] occurs only in unstressed syllables and [ʌ] occurs only in stressed syllables. You might want to adopt that convention for yourself as you transcribe English words. We say that [ʌ] is a low vowel (though not as low as [ɑ]), while [ə] is a mid vowel. Is [ə] front, central, or back? This is one vowel that linguists agree should be classified as central. Some people pronounce the second syllable of *roses* with a higher central vowel, written as [ɨ]. One way to see if you do is to say "Rosa's roses" (with an American English pronunciation of *Rosa*: [ɹoʊ̯zə]). If the words differ, you probably use [ə] in the final syllable of *Rosa's* and [ɨ] in the final syllable of *roses*.

Beyond (Standard) English

These vowels pretty much cover the vowels we find in what you might call standard American English. However, there are other vowels that occur in natural language, some of which occur in various regional varieties of American English. You probably are very aware of that fact already if you have been contrasting my pronunciation of the words I've discussed thus far with your own—for the quality of vowels is the most noticeable difference between varieties of English. For example, in Boston some people might pronounce the word *Harvard* without either "r"- sound and with both vowels pulled back and slightly rounded, written as [ɒ]: [hɒ́.vɒd]. Contrast that to the more central vowel of a midwesterner saying [hɑ́ɹ.vɹ̩d], or another type of Bostonian using a front vowel, as in [hǽ.vɹ̩d], or an even lower front to central vowel, written with [a], as in [há.vɹ̩d]. And notice that here the Bostonian is using the same vowel that southerners use in words such as *my* [ma].

Another way we can find more vowels is to play with the feature of roundness. In American English, front and central vowels are [−round]. But they don't have to be that way. So make [i]. Now round your lips and say the new front round vowel: [y] (which is often written as [ü]). Do you know a language that makes use of the high front round vowel? French does (as in the word *tu* 'you' [ty]); so does German (as in the word *Tür* 'door' [tyr]). German also makes use of the lax high front round vowel [ʏ] (which you make by rounding [ɪ]). Now take your mid vowel [e] and round it. You get the new vowel [Ø] (often written as [ö], and found in the French word *peu* 'a little' and the German word *Söhne* 'sons'). Now take your lax mid front vowel [ɛ] and round it. You get the new vowel [œ] (often written as [ɔ̈], and found in the French word *peur* 'fear').

You can also take your back vowels and unround them. Try it for the tense vowels first. You get the high vowel [ɯ] and the mid vowel [ɣ] (which is also written as [ë]), both found in Korean. You can also unround your lax mid back vowel. What you get may well be identical to [ʌ], and some books list this vowel not as a central vowel but as a back unrounded vowel, as I said above.

As with consonants, this isn't the whole story, but it's enough to get you sensitized to the sorts of distinctions you should listen for. The appendix at the end of this chapter gives details of these vowels and their features.

Acoustic Phonetics

Distinctions in the physical properties of the sounds that your ear receives are our next focus.

There are at least three different audible characteristics of language sounds: pitch, loudness (or INTENSITY), and quality. So far when discussing how we make sounds, we have concentrated on the quality of those sounds. Let us turn now to the other two characteristics, both of which are called SUPRASEGMENTALS. In a language like English, only quality is essential to recognition of the phoneme: we can hold the quality of a sound steady and change its pitch and intensity without changing its identity as a phoneme. Nevertheless, the pitch and intensity of a sound are important, and when we put sounds together to make words, we pay particular attention to these suprasegmentals, as you will learn in our discussion of Metrical Phonology in Chapter 2. For now let's just try to understand what these two suprasegmentals are.

Consider a pendulum. If you set it moving, it will swing upward to one side, then back toward its resting point, pass through that point, and continue on in an upward arc to the other side. At a certain point it will reverse direction again and go back to the resting point. At this point we say the pendulum has completed one CYCLE of movement. Now it passes through the resting point and heads upward on the first side again, beginning the second cycle of movement. Repetitive movement like this is called PERIODIC.

Now pluck a guitar string. Your pluck has set the string in motion, and the motion is periodic. Do you see that? Give me other examples of periodic movement.

Not all motion is repetitive or periodic. Swing your arm once through the air. That's an APERIODIC movement. Drop a book on the floor. That's an aperiodic movement.

Okay, now pluck the guitar string again (or any other string that is tightly attached at both ends). You can see its periodicity. But what you don't see is that your pluck has also set the air in motion. That string moved to one side, displacing the air on one side of it— thus compressing it. Then it moved to the second side, rarefying the air on the first side and compressing it on the second side. (Of course, much more air is compressed if the guitar string causes a larger surface, called a soundboard, to move, also. But let's just assume our guitar string isn't even attached to a guitar, but only to a peg at each end so that all we have to discuss is the movement of the string and its affect on the air.) Each time the guitar string makes a cycle of movement, the air likewise makes a cycle of movement. But the molecules in the air touch other molecules, which are likewise compressed and rarefied in a pattern. We say the guitar string has set up a periodic SOUND WAVE, which is a regularly increasing and decreasing sequence of air pressure that is transmitted out in every direction from the string.

Let's take a moment here to consider that fact. All sound must travel through a MEDIUM. The air is our typical medium for speech sounds. Can you guess what happens if we hang a bell inside a closed jar and then suck out all the air in the jar and ring the bell? There is no sound. That's because there is no medium to carry the sound wave. What do you think happens if we hit a spoon on a metal table? Try it. Hit the bowl of a spoon very hard on the edge of a metal table, then hit it very hard on the edge of a wooden table. What do you hear besides the smack of the spoon? The metal table probably set up a buzzing sound. The wooden table probably did not. That's because metal is a more efficient medium for carrying sound waves than wood is; metal absorbs less of the sound internally than wood does. When you hit the spoon on these two tables, you set up other vibrations, called sympathetic vibrations, that travel through the metal or wood and are prolonged by the metal or wood.

Pitch

Okay, now let's return to our discussion of the vibrations of the guitar string. We say that the amount of time it takes for a vibration to complete a cycle of compression and rarefaction is its period. (And for the sake of a simpler exposition, we will hereafter use the term "cycle" to mean one compression and rarefaction.) The number of periods that a sound wave has in a given amount of time is its FREQUENCY. For speech sounds we use one second as our measure of time. So the frequency of a sound would be how many cycles a sound wave executes in one second (or how many periods it has in one second). The unit of measure here is the HERTZ, abbreviated as Hz. For example, if a cycle of a sound wave takes 0.01 second to complete, that means that in a full second it will repeat 100 times. We say that sound has a frequency of 100 Hertz. In case you haven't used much mathematics in your life recently, let's go over this. You can take what we just did above and restate it as: One second divided by 0.01 second = 100 Hz. (An [l], for example, is a sound that has a frequency in the range of about 100 to 125 Hz.) If a cycle of a sound wave repeats every 0.1 second, what would its frequency be? (10 Hz. One second divided by 0.1 second = 10 Hz.)

Let's put this into a formula. Let 1 stand for one second. Let p stand for period (the amount of time it takes for a single cycle). Let f stand for frequency (Hz). So we have just realized that in general:

$$\frac{1}{p} = f$$

Now let me ask you a new question that draws on the same information: If a sound had a frequency of 1,000 Hz, how long would it take a cycle of that sound wave to repeat? In other words, what would the p of that sound be? (0.001 second) You can answer this by plugging in values to the formula above. And you can manipulate the formula so that you isolate p on one side:

$$\frac{1}{f} = p$$

Let's talk a bit more about the experiment you did above when we were discussing the relative pitches of [i] and [u]. You filled one bottle with water halfway and another with water one-quarter of the way. Now think about what you did to the air inside the bottle when you blew across the top. You set the air in motion. When the moving air molecules hit an obstruction, they bounced off and traveled in another direction, until they hit another obstruction and then bounced off again. If you keep blowing, the air motion inside will keep repeating. If you have two cavities of different sizes (like two bottles filled to varying degrees with water, or two bottles of different sizes), the frequency of the air motion will be faster in the smaller one. That's due to a fact of physics that I feel ill-equipped to explain to you. Essentially, smaller bottles make higher frequencies because the stiffness of the air inside the bottle is inversely proportional to the volume.

Consider the specific case of our bottles that are partially filled with water. The space in the bottle that is not occupied by water is the resonance cavity for the air. Now do you remember which cavity produced a higher pitch? (the smaller one) Okay, now can you state the relationship between frequency and pitch? The higher the frequency (that is, the shorter the periods of a sound are), the higher the pitch. Thus Hertz can be thought of as a measure of pitch.

However, the relationship between pitch and Hertz isn't really perfect. That's because even sounds for which Hertz cannot really be measured—that is, even sounds that have no frequency—have pitch. We will return to this point. But first, let's talk about these other types of sounds.

Intensity

Not all sounds have a frequency. What sorts of sounds would set up a sound wave that was not repeating? Aperiodic sounds, of course. A slap of your hand on a table, for example, sets a sound wave in motion, but it is not a repeating sound wave, because the slap is nothing like a vibrating string. In Figure 1.3 we can see the sound wave set up by a tuning fork (1.3A) and the sound wave set up by a clap of hands (1.3B). The boxed area in 1.3A and 1.3B is enlarged at the bottom of each figure. The wave for the tuning fork is periodic; that for the hands clapping isn't.

The horizontal axis measures time, starting from zero, which marks the moment when the sound begins. The vertical axis measures air pressure, where zero is the pressure before the sound begins. The movement of this wave above the horizontal axis going through the center of each graph shows compression of air. The movement of this wave below the horizontal axis shows rarefaction of air. We call the height of the wave its AMPLITUDE. Tell me—if you want to make a louder sound with your guitar string, what can you do? You pluck it harder, right? That means you displace the string more. There-fore, the air around the string is displaced more. Therefore, the compression and the rarefaction are both greater. What does that mean about the amplitude of the sound wave? How will it be affected? It will increase. Do you see that? So the vertical axis on Figure 1.3 is measuring the intensity of the sound. We measure intensity in DECIBELS, abbreviated as dB. We say a given sound is so-many decibels. If we increase the intensity of a sound by 5 dB, we are doubling the intensity of the sound. Typically increases of less than 1 dB are not noticed by our ears.

Say these continuous sounds for five seconds each: [m], [z], [e], [l]. Can you hear a difference in intensity among them? As with pitch, we can easily vary the intensity of a sound: say [z] softly and then say [z] loudly. But without any instructions about varying intensity, you might have noticed that these sounds have different natural intensities, just like the vowels and consonants have different natural pitches. We have an INTENSITY CLINE that goes from most intense to least intense:

vowels, glides, liquids, nasals, voiced fricatives,
voiced oral stops, voiceless vowels, voiceless
fricatives, and voiceless oral stops

If you couldn't hear the intensity difference among the four sounds I asked you to say, that's okay. Many people have trouble hearing it. (I'm in that group.) What can you notice about the intensity cline? Does it remind you of anything else we've discussed? Certainly. **It starts out very much like the sonority hierarchy, although it differs once we get past the middle of the cline. This tells us that intensity is a correlate or factor of sonority in many instances.**

Back to Pitch

Let us return now to our discussion of pitch. Look back at Figure 1.3. You can count cycles by counting the highest peaks. What is the frequency of the sound wave of this tuning fork? To figure this out, take a close look at the enlargement of the boxed part of 1.3A. Start at any fixed point and estimate how many seconds it takes for a cycle to repeat. For example, if we start at time 0.033, we find a completed cycle by 0.0353. So it takes approximately 0.0023 second for a repetition. Actually, if your eye is good enough, you can see that it takes closer to 0.00228 second for a cycle. So how many cycles would we have in one full second? To find this, you divide one second by 0.00228. The answer is 439. That's pretty close; this tuning fork gives the note A, and its frequency is 440 Hz.

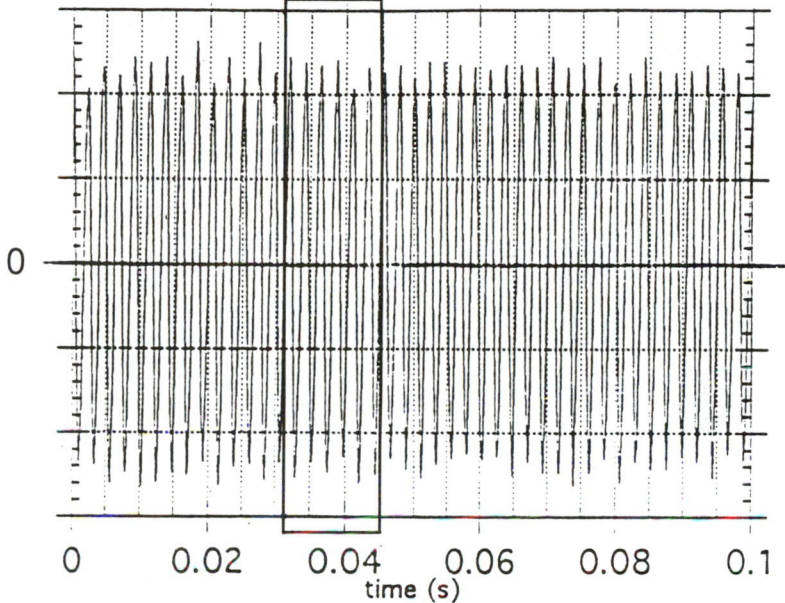

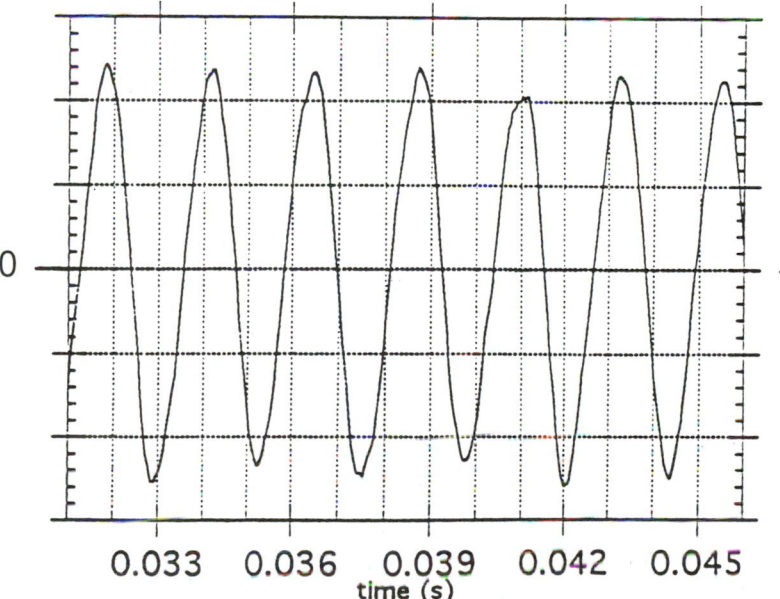

Figure 1.3A. The sound wave of a tuning fork. (The note is A.) The lower figure is an enlargement of the boxed in area of the upper figure. The horizontal axis measures time from the moment the sound begins in seconds. The vertical axis measures air pressure, where 0 is the pressure before the sound begins.

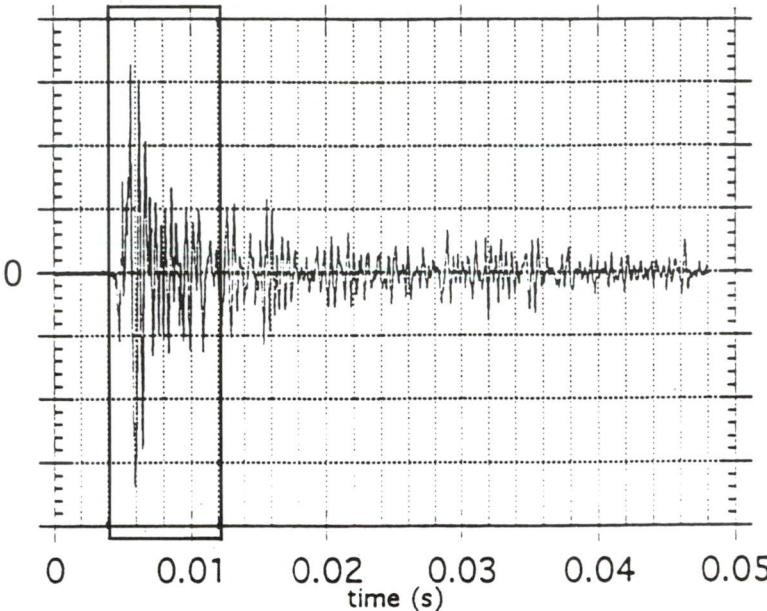

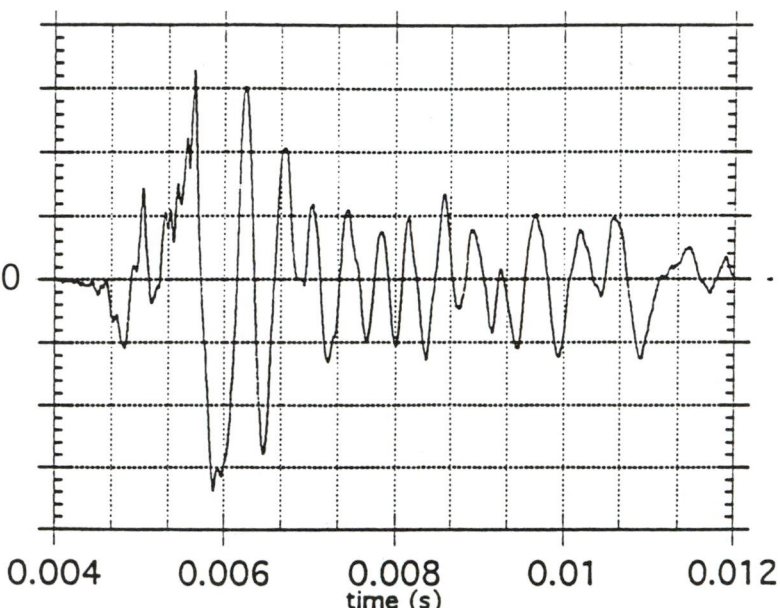

Figure 1.3B. The sound wave of clapping hands. The lower figure is an enlargement of the boxed in area of the upper figure. The horizontal axis measures time in seconds. The vertical axis measures air pressure.

We say the tuning fork has a pure sound (at least when the sound travels through air, not through other media) because what we are hearing is its FUNDAMENTAL FREQUENCY, uncluttered by any sympathetic resonances.

But even aperiodic sounds can be said to have pitch, although they have no defined frequency. You know this; your ear tells you this. Say [s] and then say [ɑ]. [s] is a voiceless sound, so the vocal cords aren't vibrating. (You'll learn the relevance of this fact immediately below.) Furthermore, the cavity in the mouth is highly occluded, so we have an irregular, random pattern of noise. But you can hear a pitch difference between [s] and [ɑ] all the same. Which is higher? [s], very clearly, no? So [s] has a pitch, even though no COMPONENT of its sound wave is periodic. And that's why Hertz do not really equal pitch.

So how do we measure the pitch of an aperiodic sound? We do it by using a mathematical formula. We take a fixed interval of time and we look at the sound wave during that interval. In effect, we declare that that interval is the period of the sound. We choose how long an interval of time to look at based on certain properties of the particular sound we are analyzing (and I will not go into those properties here). We do this not because the sound actually has a period, but because in this way we can then speak of the Hertz of the sound. (Tell me, what would be the Hertz of a sound that had a period of 0.0005 second? 2,000 Hz, right? What would be the Hertz of a sound that had a period of 0.00025 second? 4,000 Hz. Many consonant sounds of English fall in the 2,000- to 4,000-Hz range.

Now, let's go back to periodic sounds. Your vocal cords are a lot like a guitar string. And your vocal tract contains the body of air through which the sound wave set up by your vocal cords passes. When you make a [+voiced] sound, the vocal cords vibrate in a periodic way. The sound wave moves through the oral and, sometimes, the nasal cavity. But inside those cavities, the air bangs against the various obstacles and sets up other vibrations with their own frequencies—SYMPATHETIC RESONANCES. These additional sound waves form a complex sound wave with the one set up by the vocal cords. And what that wave looks like depends directly on the shape of the vocal tract, which you control by movements of your tongue and teeth and velum and lips. In other words, the sympathetic resonances are major contributors to what makes voiced sounds distinct from one another. Consider a sound wave for [l], given in Figure 1.4.

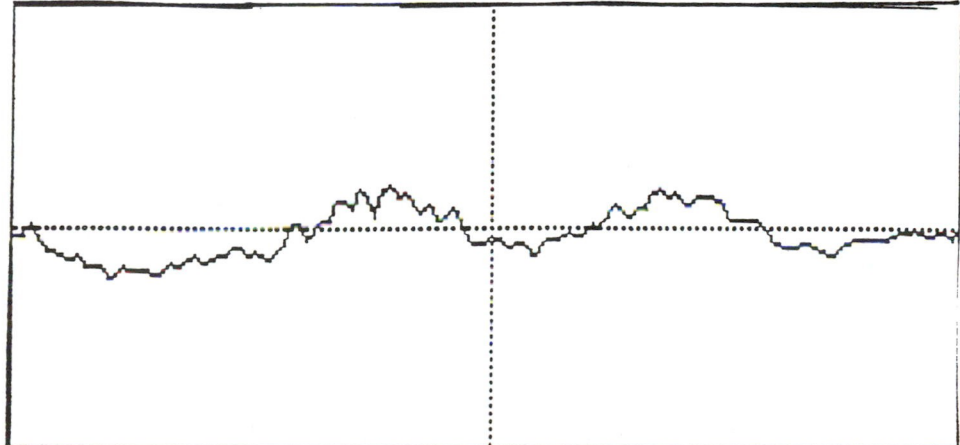

Figure 1.4. Sound wave of [l].

Compare this sound wave to those for the tuning fork in Figure 1.3A and the hands clapping in Figure 1.3B. You can certainly see that the sound in Figure 1.4 is periodic. But you can also see that the sound wave for [l] is complex: The minor peaks between these highest peaks show the sympathetic resonances due to the shape of the vocal tract.

Think now about the shape of the vocal tract. For which kinds of sounds do we have the least occlusion and hence the greatest opportunity for sympathetic resonances? The vowels, of course. But also the nasals, the liquids, and the approximants.

Formants

Consider first the vowels. Acoustically they are complex because they have a fundamental frequency (like the tuning fork has), plus they have sympathetic vibrations at whole-number multiples of their fundamental frequency. For example, if the fundamental frequency is 100 Hz, there will be sympathetic vibrations, called HARMONICS, at 200, 300, 400, etc., Hz. The vocal cords produce the fundamental frequency, and this frequency determines the perceived pitch of the sound. The vocal cords also produce all the harmonics. Most of the harmonics are not significant; however, all vowels have at least four harmonics that are more prominent, called OVERTONES or FORMANTS. The formants for a particular vowel correspond to the resonances of the vocal-tract shape as you say that vowel. We can say that the harmonics are shaped by the resonances of the vocal cavities. The formant with the lowest frequency is called the FIRST FORMANT.

When we ended our discussion of consonants, we talked briefly about different kinds of phonation. One was called the creaky voice. Make a noise like the creaking of a door in a horror story. Now say this whole sentence with that creaky voice. You cannot see what you are doing, but can you guess where the significant changes are taking place? In the larynx, and that's why speaking in a creaky voice is also called LARYNGEALIZATION. Inside your voice box at one end you have the arytenoid cartilages. To make a creaky voice, you pull the arytenoid cartilages tightly together so that the vocal cords at that end of the voice box are also pulled together so tightly that they cannot vibrate. But the vocal cords do vibrate on the opposite end. The result is a very low pitched sound. Sing [ɑ] from as high up as you can go to as far down as you can go comfortably. Now go even lower. Probably you are now laryngealizing the [ɑ].

Creaky voice is of interest to us now because it can help us hear the overtone known as the first formant. Say the back vowels with a creaky voice, sliding from [ɑ] to [u]. Can you hear a pitch change? It is gradual and somewhat delicate, but if you do this a few times, maybe you can hear it. **We are finding a falling pitch as the back vowels rise.** Now say the front vowels with a creaky voice, sliding from [æ] to [i]. Can you hear the pitch change? Again, **the pitch falls as the vowels rise.** In other words, **the first formant has an inverse relationship to vowel height. This is very nice, for it tells us that our vowel height distinction, which we made on articulatory grounds, has an acoustic correlate.** (Indeed, fine distinctions in vowel height are a bit suspicious on purely articulatory grounds, so this finding is welcome.)

The SECOND FORMANT of vowels can also be heard by using a special phonation, that of whispering, whereby the vocal cords don't vibrate (so there is no fundamental frequency). Start at the high front vowel [i], go down the front of the mouth gradually to [æ], then move on to [ɑ] and go up the back of the mouth to [u], whispering the whole way. What do you notice about the pitch? It falls continuously.

I know of no way to hear the THIRD or FOURTH FORMANTS of the vowels, but this is not a terrible problem since these two formants are quite high and they vary little from vowel to vowel (although you will discover something about them if you do Problem Set 1.7). Furthermore, the fourth formant can vary considerably according to the quality of individual voices. (In fact, the fourth formant is useful for speech recognition and identification systems.) So the important formants for recognizing the quality of vowels are the first and second (although if you do Problem Set 1.7, you will discover that the third formant can tell us about the feature of rounding).

Spectrograms

Speech scientists have found a way to give us a visual representation of the component frequencies of sounds: the spectrogram. In Figure 1.5 you see a spectrogram for the vowels [i], [ɑ], and [u], as Bill Reynolds (an American phonologist) says them.

The horizontal axis measures time, just as the horizontal axis for our sound waves in Figures 1.3 and 1.4 did. The vertical axis, however, measures hertz, and we have markers every thousand hertz. Intensity is now shown by increased darkness. The resonant frequencies of a sound are the loudest parts, so they show up as the dark horizontal bars. Now you can easily see the four formants we've just been talking about; I have labeled them for each vowel. You can see that the first formant of [ɑ] is higher than the first formant of both [i] and [u] (as you discovered by saying the vowels in a creaky voice), and the second formant of [ɑ] is midway between the second formant of [i] (which is higher than it) and the second formant of [u] (which is lower than it, as you discovered above by whispering the vowels).

There is another important piece of information we can glean about these sounds from this figure. Look at the vertical STRIATIONS (the vertical marks). These show momentary increases in acoustic energy due to a single cycle of movement. If the cycle is very short, the striations will be closer together than if the cycle is long. So higher-pitched sounds (for which the cycles are short) will have the striations more densely packed together than lower-pitched sounds. That means that the formants on the front vowels will typically be

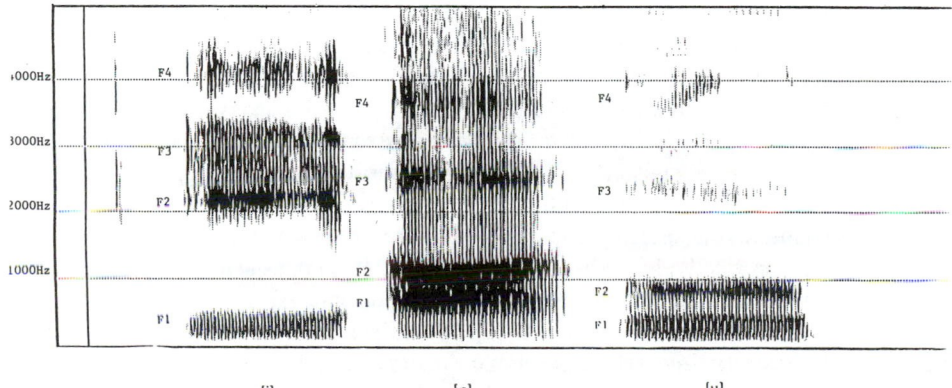

Figure 1.5. Spectrograms of the vowels [i], [ɑ], and [u], with the four most prominent formants labeled.

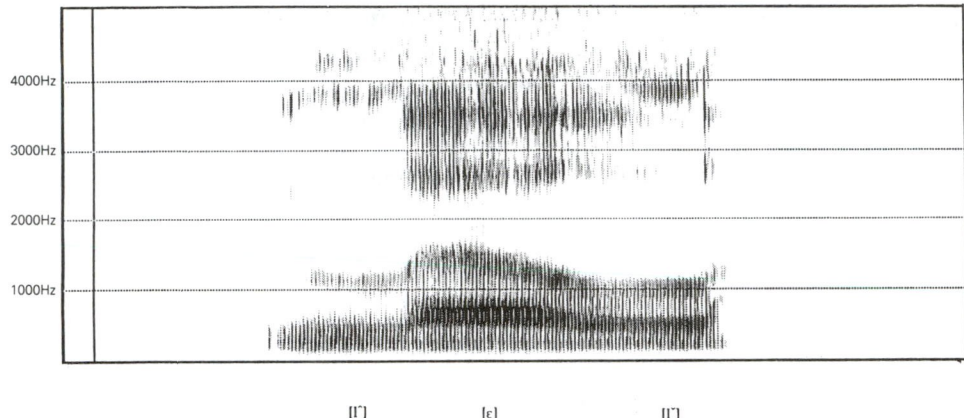

Figure 1.6. Spectrogram for the sounds [1ˆ ε 1ˇ].

denser (and thus appear darker) than the formants on the back vowels. This contrast between [i] and [u] is particularly striking in Figure 1.5.

Now consider the spectrogram in Figure 1.6. Here the speaker is going from a light lateral to a dark lateral with the open mid front vowel between—that is, [lˆ ε lˇ]. The vowel in the middle is easy to see. Contrast the laterals on either side of it to the vowel in the middle. How many formants do you see for these laterals? (Please ignore the striations at the very bottom for now. We will account for them when we discuss Figure 1.7.) Only three of significant intensity, right? As compared to the vowels, which formant seems to be missing? The third—can you see that? For most speakers in most contexts the third formant is of such weak intensity that it does not appear clearly on a spectrogram. What about the comparative intensity of the liquids' formants as compared to the vowels' formants—do you see a difference? The intensity is less on the liquids.

You are going to explore formants for nasals in Problem Set 1.6, so we won't consider them here. But what do you guess happens on a spectrogram when we nasalize a vowel? Both vowels and nasals have their own formants. When we nasalize a vowel, the vowel's formants have the nasal's formants superimposed. That means nasalized vowels will show up as very dark wherever the two sets of formants overlap. It also means that you may see more than four formants for the vowel, if one of the nasal's formants does not overlap with any of the vowel's formants. We call the extra formants PSEUDOFORMANTS. While English does not nasalize vowels in a distinctive way (in contrast to French, for example), certain regional varieties of American English are characterized by partially nasalized vowels, particularly before a nasal consonant, and many speakers of English may partially nasalize their vowels just as an individual (rather than regional) characteristic.

What do you think the spectrograms of [s] and [z] will look like? Will the striations on the spectrogram be relatively high or relatively low? Think back to the pitch of [s] as compared to [ɑ]. So you expect striations at the upper end. All fricatives, in fact, have quite high pitch. Say [s] and compare it to [f]. Which is higher? [s] is. So even though all fricatives will have striations relatively high on the spectrogram, you will be able to see a difference between [s] and [f] in that [s] will be higher and its striations will be denser (hence looking darker). In fact, [s] and [z] have quite dark striations on spectrograms. Do you expect to see formants for [s] and [z]? No, these sounds don't resonate in the oral

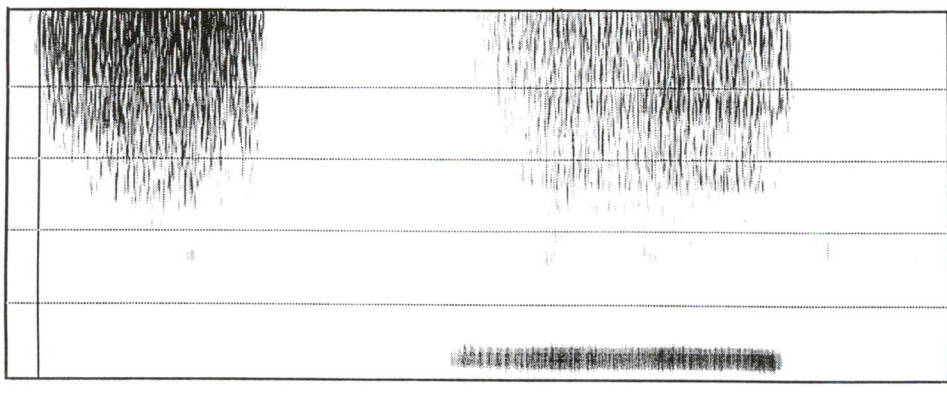

[s]   [z]

Figure 1.7. Spectrograms for [s] and [z].

cavity. They are hissy and buzzy, not melodic. We can see their spectrograms in Figure 1.7.

Can you guess what the dark stuff at the very bottom of the spectrogram for [z] represents? It runs along the time bar and extends up to around 250 Hz. Notice that this is a major difference between [s] and [z]—so that fact should help you to guess what this dark mark is. This is called the VOICE BAR and it shows the frequency of the vocal cords. All voiced sounds will have a voice bar on their spectrogram, while voiceless ones will not. (I didn't point out the voice bar in Figs. 1.5 and 1.6 both because it is difficult to see on those figures and because all of our sounds in those figures were voiced, so no contrast could be made.)

What do you think the spectrograms of [k] and [g] will look like? Try to make a [k] in isolation of any other sound. If you're having trouble, say the word *tack* and then say it again, without pronouncing anything but the final consonant. There's complete silence, and then a voiceless release. How about with [g]? Say the word *tag*, and then say it again, pronouncing only the final consonant. You are voicing those vocal cords before you release. So there will be nothing on the spectrogram for [k], followed by relatively high striations. But there will be a voice bar for [g], followed by similar high striations. What if you pronounce *cool* and *ghoul*, and isolate the initial consonants? The aspiration on the initial voiceless consonant will come out as a moment of silence, before the onset of voicing (of the following vowel). In Figure 1.8 you can see the spectrograms of these four words. Just based on how the words begin and end, can you label which spectrogram represents which word? (The words are in the order *tack, tag, cool, ghoul*.)

Stop for a moment and look back at the spectrograms of the vowels in Figure 1.5. Compare the spectrogram of [u] there to the spectrogram of the [u] in the middle of *cool* and *ghoul*. Notice that the formants for this vowel are not identical in the two utterances. When [u] is pronounced in isolation, the formants stay relatively steady (and when I recorded the vowels in Fig. 1.5, I asked the person I was recording—Bill Reynolds—to be careful to avoid diphthongization). But when [u] is pronounced as part of a word, the formants begin in a certain way and end in another certain way, with only their middle part reliably close to the formants we see of the vowel in isolation. Why is that? Certainly, there may be a slight falling diphthong for the words in Figure 1.8 for many speakers, and

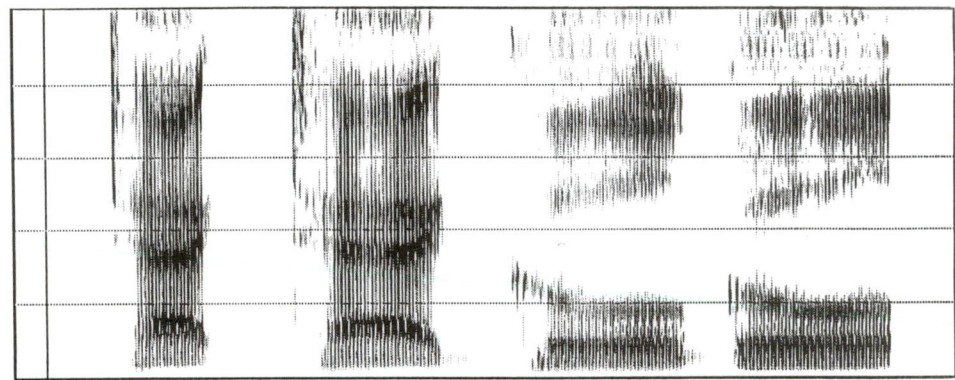

Figure 1.8. Spectrograms for four words, with attention to velars.

I believe there is for the speaker I recorded here. But there is more difference than just that: The sounds preceding and following any given sound can affect that sound's beginning and ending, respectively. That is, the initial [tʰ] vs. [kʰ] and the final choice of [k], [g], or [l] affect the sounds in the middle of the words. **Given that utterances are generally made up of syllables, and that syllables generally have vowels as their nucleus, we can think of consonants as different ways to begin or end vowels.** (You will find this way of looking at things useful as you do Problem Set 1.8.)

Figure 1.9 shows a spectrogram of the sentence *I like Staymen apples*. Can you see the diphthong in the first syllable? Cover the figure a moment and ask yourself what you expect to see happen to the first formant of the vowel [ɑ] (in the word *I*) as it moves into the [−syllabic] vowel [ɪ]. Remember, the first formant varies inversely to height. So you expect the first formant to fall. Now what do you expect the second formant to do as we move from the [+syllabic] to the [−syllabic] vowel? Remember that the second formant falls continuously from the high front vowel down to the bottom of the mouth and then keeps falling as we go up the back of the mouth. So we expect the second formant to rise in this diphthong. Now look at the figure. Do these formants behave as you expected? Aren't you happy?

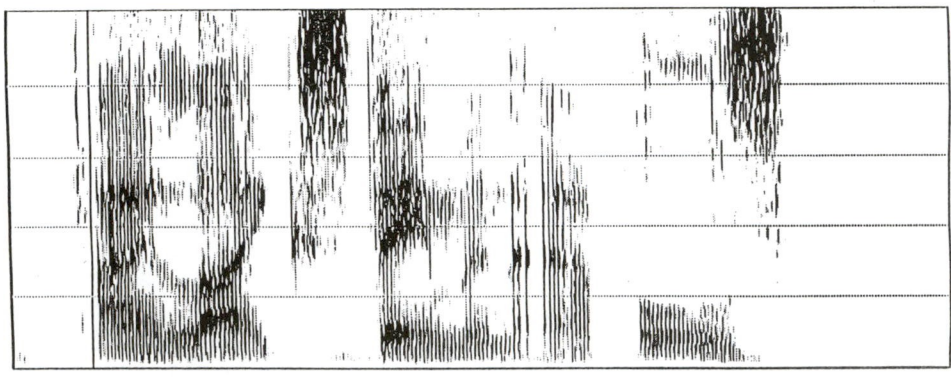

   [aɪ]   [l]   [aɪ]   [k] [s] [t] [eɪ]   [m]   [n] [æ] [p]   [l]   [s]

Figure 1.9. Spectrogram for the sentence *I like Staymen apples.*

Cover the IPA transcriptions below the spectrogram and examine this spectrogram, trying to locate every sound segment in the utterance on the spectrogram. I think you can do it. Let's talk about the obstruents first. Do you see the silence at the [k] of *like*, the [t] of *Staymen*, and the [pʰ] of *apples*? Can you see the high-pitched striations that mark the fricative [s] of *Staymen* and the final fricative [s] of *apples*? (In Problem Set 2.9 you will learn that many speakers would have a [z] as the final sound of *apples*, but this speaker had [s].)

Now let's turn to the sonorants. Can you see the same diphthong in *I* and *like*? Do you see the [l] that comes between them? (The [l] should have only three formants of significant intensity. Unfortunately, the second formant shows up more darkly than expected. There's a lesson here: speakers vary so spectrograms vary.) Do you see the diphthong in the first syllable of *Staymen* and the [m] that immediately follows it? Notice that the [m] has formants, like the vowels, but fewer. (You'll deal with this issue in Problem Set 1.6.) Can you see any difference between the nucleus of the first and the second syllables of *apples*? The first one is more intense, right? The same is true for the nuclei of the first and second syllables of *Staymen*. **So we can now see that intensity is a correlate of stress.** How does the spectrogram show you that the [l] in the second syllable of *apples* is the syllabic segment and that there is no vowel here? Can you see that there are only three relatively intense formants, whereas all vowels have four? Compare the [−syllabic] [l] of *like* to the [+syllabic] [l] of *apples*. Do you see any difference there? The syllabic one is more intense. (This is very difficult to see on this particular spectrogram, but if you compare the first formants for the two laterals, you might be able to see the intensity difference.)

That's all we're going to say about acoustics, even though, as you by now know (given the way I tend to end each major discussion in this chapter), there's much more to say. It's time for us to pass on to the job of looking at the principles that govern what happens when we put sounds together into larger units. That's called PHONOLOGY, and that's the matter of Chapter 2.

Appendix

International Phonetic Alphabet: Consonants

In Appendix Table 1 the consonants discussed in this chapter are shown (including one that comes up in the problem sets). Across the top are labels for place.

Affricates and other doubly articulated sounds are not included since the reader can put together all the relevant information on them by considering their component sounds. The following abbreviations are used: bilab = bilabial; lab-den = labio-dental; inter-den = interdental; alveo = alveolar; post-alveo = postalveolar; retro = retroflex; palat = palatal; uvu = uvular; phar = pharyngeal; glot = glottal; oral = oral stop; tap/f = tap or flap; fric = fricative; lat = lateral; appr = approximant; ejec = ejective; impl = implosive. The symbols I have used for the clicks are not the ones approved by the IPA; however, they are very commonly used, and I prefer them.

Additionally, we have the sounds:

lateral fricative: ɬ
epiglottal fricative: Hʕ
epiglottal voiced stop: ʡ

Appendix Table 1. IPA: Consonants

	Bilab	Lab-den	Inter-den	Dental	Alveo	Post-alveo	Retro	Palat	Velar	Uvu	Phar	Glot
Oral	p b			t	d		ʈ ɖ	c ɟ	k g	q ɢ		?
Nasal	m	ɱ			n		ɳ	ɲ	ŋ	N		
Trill	B			r						R		
Tap/f					ɾ		ɽ					
Fric	ɸ β	f v	θ ð	s	z	ʃ ʒ	ʂ ʐ	ç ʝ	x ɣ	χ ʁ	ħ ʕ	h ɦ
Lat					l		ɭ	ʎ	L			
Appr								j ɹ	ɰ			
Ejec	p'			t'			ʈ'	c'	k'	q'		
Impl	ƥ ɓ			ƭ	ɗ			ƈ ʄ	ƙ ɠ	ʠ ʛ		
Click	ʘ			ǀ		! ‖		ǂ				

NOTE: When two symbols occupy the same cell, the first is voiceless and the second is voiced, except in the click row, where all sounds are voiceless.

And, finally, we have these special symbols for some common doubly articulated sounds:

     rounded velar approximant: w
     alveopalatal affricates: ʤ ʧ
     double articulation of ʃ and x: ɧ

Diacritics

A small circle under an IPA consonant indicates lack of voicing on a normally voiced sound, for example: [ɪ̥].

A tilda, ~, under an IPA symbol indicates creaky voice, for example: [a̰].

A small vertical line under an IPA consonant indicates that this consonant is syllabic, for example: [n̩].

Labialization is indicated with a raised *w*—for example: [kʷ], [gʷ].

Retroflexing is indicated by a rightward-curving hook at the bottom right of a symbol, for example: [n̢].

Ejective sounds are indicated by an apostrophe following the symbol, for example [p'].

Implosive sounds are indicated by a rightward-curving hook at the top right or left of a symbol, for example: [ɗ] and [ɓ].

Length is indicated by a colon following the symbol, for example, [l:].

Breathiness is indicated by two horizontally arranged dots under the symbol, for example [a̤].

A period between symbols indicates a syllable boundary, for example: [la.ka].

Breathy sounds are indicated by two horizontally arranged dots under the symbol.

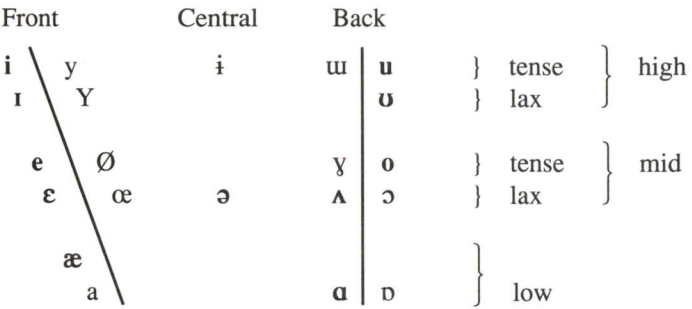

Appendix Figure 1. Vowel chart giving front (unrounded and rounded), central, and back (unrounded and rounded) vowels.

International Phonetic Alphabet: Vowels

In Appendix Figure 1, where symbols come in pairs, the one on the left is unrounded and the one on the right is rounded.

I have listed [a] as a front vowel, but some texts list it as central. I have listed both [ɑ] and [ʌ] as unrounded back vowels, but some texts put one or both as central or even back vowels.

The vowels found in most varieties of American English are typeset boldface.

Diacritics

The symbol ˎ below a vowel indicates that it is nonsyllabic, for example: [aɪ̯].
A rightward hook under a vowel indicates nasalization, for example: [ą].
Alternatively, a tilde can indicate nasalization, for example: [ã].
Tone marks above vowels are ´ for high tone and ` for low tone, for example: [à], [á].
The diacritic ˘ over a vowel indicates very short duration, for example: [ă].
A macron (ˆ) over a vowel indicates long duration, for example: [ā].
Alternatively, a colon after a vowel indicates long duration, for example: [a:].
An acute accent (´) over a vowel can indicate primary stress, for example: [à].

Consonants

Appendix Table 2 shows the values for twelve consonant features discussed in Chapter 1. The features of [spread glottis], [constricted glottis], and [ATR] are not included. Consonants heard in most varieties of American English are boldface. (del-rel = delayed release) A list of words illustrating twenty-seven of these consonants with English words is also shown.

English Words that Use These Consonants

[**p**]: so*p*	[**b**]: so*b*	[**m**]: psal*m*
[**f**]: *f*at	[**v**]: *v*at	
[**θ**]: *th*igh	[**ð**]: *th*y	
[**t**]: ca*t*	[**d**]: ca*d*	[**n**]: ca*n*

Appendix Table 2. Distinctive Features of Most Commonly Found Consonants

	p	b	m	ɸ	β	f	v	θ	ð	t	d	n	s	z	l	r
Anterior	+	+	+	+	+	+	+	+	+	+	+	+	+	+	+	+
Back	−	−	−	−	−	−	−	−	−	−	−	−	−	−	−	−
Continuant	−	−	−	+	+	+	+	+	+	−	−	−	+	+	+	+
Coronal	−	−	−	−	−	−	−	+	+	+	+	+	+	+	+	+
Del-rel	−	−	−	−	−	−	−	−	−	−	−	−	−	−	−	−
High	−	−	−	−	−	−	−	−	−	−	−	−	−	−	−	−
Labial	+	+	+	+	+	+	+	−	−	−	−	−	−	−	−	−
Lateral	−	−	−	−	−	−	−	−	−	−	−	−	−	−	+	−
Nasal	−	−	+	−	−	−	−	−	−	−	−	+	−	−	−	−
Sonorant	−	−	+	−	−	−	−	−	−	−	−	+	−	−	+	+
Strident	−	−	−	−	−	+	+	−	−	−	−	−	+	+	−	−
Voiced	−	+	+	−	+	−	+	−	+	−	+	+	−	+	+	+

	r	ʃ	ʒ	tʃ	dʒ	j	c	ɟ	ç	ʝ	ɲ	ʎ	ɹ	k	g	x
Anterior	+	−	−	−	−	−	−	−	−	−	−	−	−	−	−	−
Back	−	−	−	−	−	−	−	−	−	−	−	−	−	+	+	+
Continuant	−	+	+	−	−	+	−	−	+	+	−	+	+	−	−	+
Coronal	+	+	+	+	+	−	−	−	−	−	−	−	−	−	−	−
Del-rel	−	−	−	+	+	−	−	−	−	−	−	−	−	−	−	−
High	−	+	+	+	+	+	+	+	+	+	+	+	+	+	+	+
Labial	−	−	−	−	−	−	−	−	−	−	−	−	−	−	−	−
Lateral	−	−	−	−	−	−	−	−	−	−	−	+	−	−	−	−
Nasal	−	−	−	−	−	−	−	−	−	−	+	−	−	−	−	−
Sonorant	−	−	−	−	−	+	−	−	−	−	+	+	+	−	−	−
Strident	−	+	+	+	+	−	−	−	−	−	−	−	−	−	−	−
Voiced	+	−	+	−	+	+	−	+	−	+	+	+	+	−	+	−

	ɣ	ŋ	w	ʟ	ɥ	q	ɢ	ɴ	ʀ	χ	ʁ	ħ	ʕ	ʔ	h	ɦ
Anterior	−	−	−	−	−	−	−	−	−	−	−	−	−	−	−	−
Back	+	+	+	+	+	+	+	+	+	+	+	+	+	−	−	−
Continuant	+	−	+	+	+	−	−	−	+	+	+	+	+	−	+	+
Coronal	−	−	−	−	−	−	−	−	−	−	−	−	−	−	−	−
Del-rel	−	−	−	−	−	−	−	−	−	−	−	−	−	−	−	−
High	+	+	+	+	+	−	−	−	−	−	−	−	−	−	−	−
Labial	−	−	+	−	−	−	−	−	−	−	−	−	−	−	−	−
Lateral	−	−	−	+	−	−	−	−	−	−	−	−	−	−	−	−
Nasal	−	+	−	−	−	−	−	+	−	−	−	−	−	−	−	−
Sonorant	−	+	+	+	+	−	−	+	+	−	−	−	−	−	−	−
Strident	−	−	−	−	−	−	−	−	−	+	+	−	−	−	−	−
Voiced	+	+	+	+	+	−	+	+	+	−	+	−	+	−	−	+

[s]: *s*ip   [z]: *z*ip
           [l]: *l*ip
           [ɾ]: la*t*er
[ʃ]: *sh*ade   [ʒ]: illu*s*ion
[ʧ]: *ch*ew   [ʤ]: *J*ew
           [j]: *y*ellow
           [ɲ]: o*n*ion
           [ʎ]: mi*ll*ion
           [ɹ]: *r*ye
[k]: Ric*k*   [g]: ri*g*   [ŋ]: ri*ng*
           [w]: *w*hy
           [h]: *h*igh

Problem Set 1.1: Problems of Orthography and Aspiration in English

1. We noted in the text that there is one consonant phoneme of English that can occur only in syllable-final position ([ŋ]). But there is also one consonant phoneme of English that can occur only in syllable-initial position. Which one?

2. Take the sounds we have written phonetically as:

   [p]   [ʧ]   [ʒ]   [f]

and find as many ways as you can to represent these sounds in writing (orthographically) in English. Give a word to exemplify each way. For some of these sounds there may be several ways. For all there are at least a few. Don't go nuts. Just do the best you can.

3. (a) What are the two consonant sounds of English (sounds that you can find displayed in the appendix) that we always spell identically? Make sure that the sounds you choose cannot be written in English orthography with any other letters. (Hint: Be careful to check for sounds that can be written as a single or a double letter.)

(b) How are they spelled?

(c) Given that these two sounds are always spelled identically, how do we know which sound to make when we read a new word with the letter(s) corresponding to these two sounds? Take a stab at the answer to (c). You won't be graded on this one.

4. Transcribe the intervocalic sound(s) (the sound(s) between the vowels) in *pizza* by using IPA symbols. (Listen carefully as you pronounce the word—you may find some surprises.) Does this sound occur in word-initial position in English? Is it an oral stop, fricative, affricate, liquid, or nasal?

5. We noted in the text that voiceless stops always get aspirated in English in initial position of stressed syllables, but typically not in syllable-final position. What happens in syllable-medial position (that is, when the voiceless stop is neither the first nor the last sound of the syllable)? Make a list of six words you used to answer this question. (You need six. You have three voiceless stops to test, and you need to test each in syllable-onset and syllable-coda clusters. Remember that the onset is the part of the syllable that precedes the nucleus and the coda is the part that follows the nucleus. I'll start you off with both types of examples for /p/: *space*, *apes*.)

6. Find a native speaker of English who pronounces the words *witch* and *which* differently. For most speakers of English, neither of these words involves an *h*, but for some one of them does. Is orthography a help or a hindrance here? Why?

There is something unusual about the [w] in the word which involves an [h]. What is it?

7. Say the words *cool* and *key*. There is a difference between the initial consonants. Describe that difference in terms of the place of articulation and the articulator. Is it a redundant difference or a distinctive difference? If you say it's redundant, give the contexts for each of the two sounds.

8. We have learned that there is a discrepancy between orthography and pronunciation in English, and in the text we attributed this discrepancy to the fact that languages change over time and our orthography reflects the pronunciation of an earlier time.

I now have a question that I hope you will discuss in class: Should we adopt new orthography conventions that reflect today's pronunciations? In discussing this, make a list of the advantages and disadvantages of such spelling reform.

Rising illiteracy in the United States is a problem (as of 1995, when I'm writing this). How would learning to read be affected by spelling reform? Think about what would happen when you read books in which characters from Atlanta, Georgia, are speaking, as opposed to what would happen when you read books in which characters from Brooklyn, New York, are speaking. Will your reading experience be enriched or not?

But also be sure to think of what would happen to you if you learned to read in the IPA and then went to the library to read a book published before the spelling reform. And listen to the variation in pronunciations of all the people around you. Whose pronunciation will you pick as the standard to put in your dictionary? What will happen to the new orthography as spoken language continues to change over time?

Problem Set 1.2: Problems of Orthography in Italian and Japanese

1. Look at the following Italian words in their orthography and their IPA transcription.

cera [tʃera]	culla[kul:a]	già[dʒa]
cosa [kɔza]	amiche [amike]	pace [patʃe]
chiesa [ki̯eza]	Giorgio [dʒordʒo]	Giulio [dʒuli̯o]
ago [ago]	gelo[dʒelo]	chi [ki]
righe [rige]	ghiro [giro]	faccia [fatʃ:a]
amici [amitʃi]	cane [kane]	gufo [gufo]
bacio [batʃo]	ciuccio [tʃutʃ:o]	che [ke]
gatto [gat:o]	Parigi [paridʒi]	laghi [lagi]

(Recall that the colon indicates a geminate. That is, a sound followed by a colon takes up two timing slots. Also, I have used the vowel [a] here and throughout this book. Many Italians, however, use [ɑ] instead.)

Describe the orthographic use of the letter "h" in these examples.

Now consider the orthographic "i" that does not correspond to any vowel in the IPA transcription. Describe the orthographic use of this "i."

2. This question is just for fun. There are no spelling bees in Italy. After about second grade almost no one makes a spelling error. Make a guess why not.

If you know Spanish, do you think there are spelling bees in Spain or Cuba or Argentina?

If you know French, do you think there are spelling bees in France?

3. Now consider the following data on the orthography of Italian vowels (where I have not indicated redundant vowel length):

sella [sél.la]	sera [sé.ra]	slegatura [zle.ga.tú.ra]
dente [dén.te]	bene [bé.ne]	ragazze [ra.gát.se]
esame [e.zá.me]	ieri [i̯é.ri]	gheppio [gép.pi̯o]
umore [u.mó.re]	che [ké]	Ercole [ér.kole]

(These transcriptions are from Zingarelli 1970. They represent a particular variety of Italian—presumably that spoken by Nicola Zingarelli. Italian, like English, shows variation in vowel quality as you move from one variety of Italian to another. If you speak Italian and your speech is not represented by these transcriptions, please treat the data above as though they were from a language unknown to you and use these transcriptions just for the sake of doing this problem set.)

In this list geminate consonants are repeated so that you can see syllable boundaries, indicated by periods. In *ragazze* the written double "z" corresponds to a long voiceless affricate, which I have indicated with a [t] closing one syllable and an [s] opening the next syllable.

Can you predict when a written "e" will correspond to an [e] and when it will correspond to an [ɛ]? Please assume that these data are representative. Ask yourself whether the sounds around the "e" allow you to predict its pronunciation. Ask yourself whether the shape of the syllable allows you to predict its pronunciation. Ask yourself whether the assignment of stress allows you to predict its pronunciation.

Based on your answer, do you believe that [e] and [ɛ] are allophones of a single sound or that they are different phonemes?

Many speakers of Italian claim that they have no minimal pairs in their speech that contrast these two vowels. Does this fact surprise you? If so, why? If not, why not? Many other speakers claim they do have at least one minimal pair. A common example given is:

venti 'twenty' [vén.ti]   venti 'winds' [vén.ti]

(The facts presented here may make you unhappy, because they don't go as neatly with the discussion in the text as one would hope. Language is like that. The distribution of [e] and [ɛ] is affected by historical facts which the ordinary modern speaker may no longer have access to. Thus a distribution which may be predictable at one point in time can become unpredictable at a later period of time. This does not mean Italian is capricious. It means languages change.)

4. Consider the following words written in symbols from the Japanese Katakana. In this writing system, each symbol stands for an entire syllable. Under each symbol I have written a Romanization of that syllable that is very close to IPA. (The differences between this Romanization and IPA are irrelevant to this problem.)

トラィ   ド ラィ   ロ － ス   ロ － ズ
to ra i   do ra i   ro o su   ro o zu

コ － ス ト   ゴ － ス ト
ko o su to   go o su to

(Actually, the words *torai* and *dorai* consist of two syllables, but three moras. You will learn what a mora is in the section "Syllable Types" in Chapter 2. Here each symbol is showing us a mora, rather than a syllable and this writing system, which has traditionally been called a SYLLABARY, is actually a "MORARY"—a term I put in quotes because I just made it up. That detail should not interfere with your ability to answer the questions.)

(a) There is a diacritic that indicates voicing. What is it?

(b) One voiced consonant here does not have that diacritic. Suggest a reason why.

(c) Do you think voicing is a distinctive feature in Japanese? Why? (I have not given you the meaning of any of these words, so your answer has to be based on what you think a reasonable relationship would be between a writing system and the phonemes of that language.)

Now consider the following Japanese words. I have given you the word in katakana, a Romanization, and its translation into English.

ミ ス タ ー   テ リ ー   ホ － ル   ス ク － ル
misutaa   terii   hooru   sukuuru
'Mr.   Terry   Hall'   'school'

テ リ ー   リ ー   ス ク － ル   'Terry Lee School'
terii   rii   sukuuru

メ リ ー   ホ － ル   ス ク － ル   'Mary Hall School'
merii   hooru   sukuuru

These examples are all of English words or names that have been borrowed into Japanese.

(d) Japanese conflates two phonemes of English into one. Which two in English get conflated into which one in Japanese? How is this a natural conflation?

(e) What does the symbol - indicate in Japanese katakana?

(f) Do you think vowel length is distinctive in Japanese? Why or why not?

*Problem Set 1.3: Articulatory Phonetics

1. Give the (a) place of articulation
            (b) articulator
    and (c) manner of articulation
for the sounds corresponding to the italics in these words:

   *f*at   lo*ng*   gara*ge*   *t*unnel   *th*anks

2. For the sounds of the italicized parts of the words in 1 give the voiceless or voiced counterpart if such a counterpart exists. Say whether it is voiced or voiceless.

3. In order for a person to be able to carry a tune in a single, particular sound, what features must that sound have?

4. Give the (a) place of articulation
        (b) articulator
        (c) manner of articulation
    and (d) voicing
of the sounds corresponding to the italics in the words that follow.

    *w*indow   *y*oung   *h*ouse

Now give other words in which at least one of (a)–(d) is different for each of these three sounds. That is, you are trying to find allophones which vary from the three you have described by place of articulation, or by articulator, or by manner, or by voicing. (Notice that here you will be using orthography as your guide. That is, you will consider other words with the written letters "w," "y,", and "h." At this point you probably don't trust orthography very much, but while orthography for English has an extremely poor relationship to phonetic transcription, or PR, it certainly has a much better relationship to the underlying phonemic representation—that is, UR.)

Which one out of (a)–(d) did you most quickly and easily find variations on for each of these three sounds? Which one out of (a)–(d) did you find the most variations on for each of these three sounds? (Of course, for voicing we have only a two-way split: a sound is voiced or voiceless. But for place and articulator and manner, there are several possibilities.) In this way, what other group of sounds are these three glides most like—the nasals, the liquids, the fricatives, or the oral stops?

5. Say the English word *onion*. Consider the intervocalic nasal. How is this nasal different from the nasal in *nose*? Compare their place of articulation. The symbol for this sound is [ɲ]. Is [ɲ] an allophone of /n/ or a separate phoneme? Why?

Now consider the following data on Italian nasals. Before each word I have given the sound of the initial consonant:

    [n]   nomi 'names'
    [ɲ]   gnomi 'gnomes'

Just based on these data, is it possible to tell whether [n] and [ɲ] are separate phonemes or allophones in Italian? Why or why not? If you say it is possible, what are they: separate phonemes or allophones?

6. A typical pattern for languages is to have nasal consonants only at places of articulation where oral stops also occur. That is, nasals are generally homorganic to oral stops. Give a reason for this fact using what you know about the articulatory apparatus.

7. Say *information* slowly and then quickly. Speed should affect your pronunciation. (Hint: Pay particular attention to the sounds in the first two syllables of the word.)

Give two transcriptions of *information* (and you will need to consult the appendix to do this, since you'll need a symbol that wasn't introduced in the text):
    (a) one for fast speech,
and (b) one for slow speech.
    (c) Consider the difference in the two transcriptions in (a) and (b) with respect to the

first nasal sound in *information*. Why do you think this difference occurs? (Notice that nothing like this happens to the second nasal sound in *information*.) As you answer this, be sure to think about the places of articulation and the articulators of the two nasals and of the sound(s) around them. How does this confound your answer to 6 above?

8. Many varieties of Spanish do not have [ʃ] but they do have [ʧ]. What does this suggest about this affricate in those varieties of Spanish? Is it a single phoneme or two?

9. English uses an egressive pulmonic airstream for most sounds in speech. However, there are situations in which we use other types of airstreams. Give an example of a situation in which one might use the following types of sound:
   (a) an ingressive pulmonic voiceless labiodental fricative
   (b) a velaric alveolar lateral
State as precisely as you can what is happening to the airstream as you make these sounds.

10. I want you to think about the application of your knowledge of articulatory phonetics to education of the Deaf. Here's the situation. You are a kindergarten teacher and you have a Deaf child in your classroom. You are supposed to try to help this child learn how to speak English. Assume that the child has no hearing whatsoever (although many people who are Deaf have partial hearing). Assume also that others have worked with this child on speaking before, so the idea of speaking is not new to the child. Explain what you would do and why if you encountered the events described here. (Assume you have the ordinary equipment of a kindergarten. So you have a blackboard, but you have no phonetics lab, for example.)
   (a) You are teaching the alphabet. The child says [bi] as the name of the letter *p*.
   (b) You put up a picture of a doe. The child calls it "no."
   (c) The child says, "Ep," when she clearly means *Help*.
   (d) The child says [wɑɹ] when she means *water*.
NOTE: Please do not take this problem as an endorsement for oral programs for the Deaf. I include this problem simply because oral programs exist and because a basic knowledge of phonetics can give minimal aid to a teacher in such situations.

11. There are two major types of ventriloquism. One is known as "near" ventriloquism. That's when you try to give the impression that the voice coming from you is really coming from some nearby object, such as a dummy. The main object is to move your lips as little as possible and simultaneously move the mouth of the dummy so that the illusion is created. To do this, try retracting your tongue root and talking with your lips slack and slightly apart.

The second type of ventriloquism is called "distant" ventriloquism: You try to give the impression that the voice coming from you is really coming from some distant object, perhaps across the room. To do this, you need to do all you did in near ventriloquism plus add on a change of pitch and phonation. Try closing the posterior section of your vocal cords and, thus, talking with a creaky voice, while still keeping the tongue retracted and the lips slack and slightly apart. If that sounds too awful, try raising the larynx and constricting the muscles of the throat, while keeping the tongue root retracted. This should result in a much higher pitched, muffled voice.

If you get good at it, figure out what you're really doing (since I'm only guessing here, from what I've been able to pick up in encyclopedias), and write a description of it. And throw a party at which you perform. Why not?

Problem Set 1.4: Articulatory Phonetics, Syllable Structure, and Vowels

(NOTE: Question 7 on this problem set is more difficult than the others.)

1. Make a list of monosyllabic words of English that begin with three consonants. What is the first consonant? Characterize the possible second consonants in terms of a feature bundle. Characterize the possible third consonants in terms of a feature bundle. In light of the sonority hierarchy, which aspects of these consonant clusters are surprising and which are expected?

2. Compare these Italian and Spanish cognates:

Italian	Spanish	
Spagna [spa.ɲa]	España [ɛs.pa.ɲa]	'Spain'
stato [sta.to]	estado [ɛs.ta.do]	'state'
scuola [sku̯ɔ.la]	escuela [ɛs.ku̯e.la]	'school'
signore [si.ɲo.re]	señor [se.ɲor]	'mister'
schiavo [skɪa.vo]	esclavo [ɛs.kla.vo]	'slave'
blasfema [blas.fe.ma]	blasfemia [blas.fe.mɪa]	'blasphemy'
tragico [tra.dʒi.ko]	tragico [tra.hi.ko]	'tragic'

Assume the above data are representative. Pay attention to consonant clusters. Does Italian organize its syllable structure according to the sonority hierarchy? Does Spanish? How does Spanish manage to do this, in contrast to Italian?

3. Transcribe the following words:

> fate   fit   fat   feet   fought   foot   fun   phone
> food   fete (it rhymes with *met*)

Whether or not your variety of English uses [ɔ], you should have a different vowel in each of these words (and a diphthong in some of them).

4. Out of the twelve vowels of English discussed in this chapter, which two are missing from the words in 3? (Of course, if you do not have [ɔ] in your speech, then you have only eleven vowels—and only one of the eleven vowels you use is missing from 3. Which one?)

Which of the following words contain the vowel(s) you find missing in 3? Transcribe only those words.

> book   rate   pot   fainted   pawn

5. Transcribe *fight*. Is there a diphthong here? If so, does it contain a rising or falling glide?

6. Write the following in regular English spelling.

(a) [spɪtʃ sáɪntɪsts hæv dəvéləpt məʃínz fɔɹ ɑnǽlɨsɪs]
(b) [íɪvn̩ nom tʃámski hæz ə bɪ̯́θdeɪ]
(c) [pʰliɪz ɹiɪd wətévɹ̩ tʰóʊni mɔ́ɹɪsən ɹɑɪts]

7. These words are not words of English:

[bræft]   [ltos]   [vléɪ.vr̩]   [zo.íʃ]
[dʒí.mʌh]   [kuʊl]

Which of them do you think could become English words (that is, which could be added to our LEXICON—our mental list of all the words of our language) and which could not? Which of them do you think could not be words of any language? State your reasons for both answers. (Be careful. Words without a period inside them are monosyllabic.)

Problem Set 1.5: Features

1. Make a list of all the features discussed in Chapter 1.

(a) Which ones of them deal directly or indirectly with place of articulation?

(b) Which features entail which other features? For example, if a sound is [+sonorant], is there any other feature it has in the unmarked case? Go through all the features, asking yourself which ones entail which others. (This is a tedious exercise, but what you learn will be helpful to you throughout Chapter 2, particularly when you meet Geometric Phonology.)

(c) Which features are incompatible? For each feature, tell which other features (if any) it is incompatible with.

(d) Give the feature bundle for a palatal voiceless oral stop.

(e) List all the distinctive sounds of English that are [+strident].

(f) What feature(s) do these sounds have in common?

[i]   [j]   [tʃ]   [dʒ]

(g) What sound or sounds have these features: [+back, +round]?

(h) Give a feature bundle that will pick out all stops other than the nasals.

2. In Figure 1.10 you see nine signs of American Sign Language, the manual-visual language used by Deaf communities in the United States of America. Only one hand moves in these signs—the dominant hand (right hand for right-handed people; left hand for left-handed people).

These signs show three separate characteristics of signs that distinguish one sign from another. We can think of these as distinctive features of signs. Organize these nine signs into three groups, where each group forms a minimal triplet. That is, for Group 1, hold Feature 1 steady across the three signs and vary Features 2 and 3. For Group 2, hold Feature 2 steady and vary Features 1 and 3. And for Group 3, hold Feature 3 steady and vary Features 1 and 2. Label your groups 1 through 3.

(a) What is Feature 1? Feature 2? Feature 3?

(Clearly you have to come up with your own terms for these features, since they are not any of the distinctive features that we discussed for oral languages. But simply define your terms and then use them.)

Now please try to answer these additional questions. On some of these questions you will be asked to make conjectures. The object, however, is to make intelligent, educated guesses. Please don't forget to consider the suprasegmentals of language.

(b) One way to make a sign emphatic in ASL is to make the movement rapid and

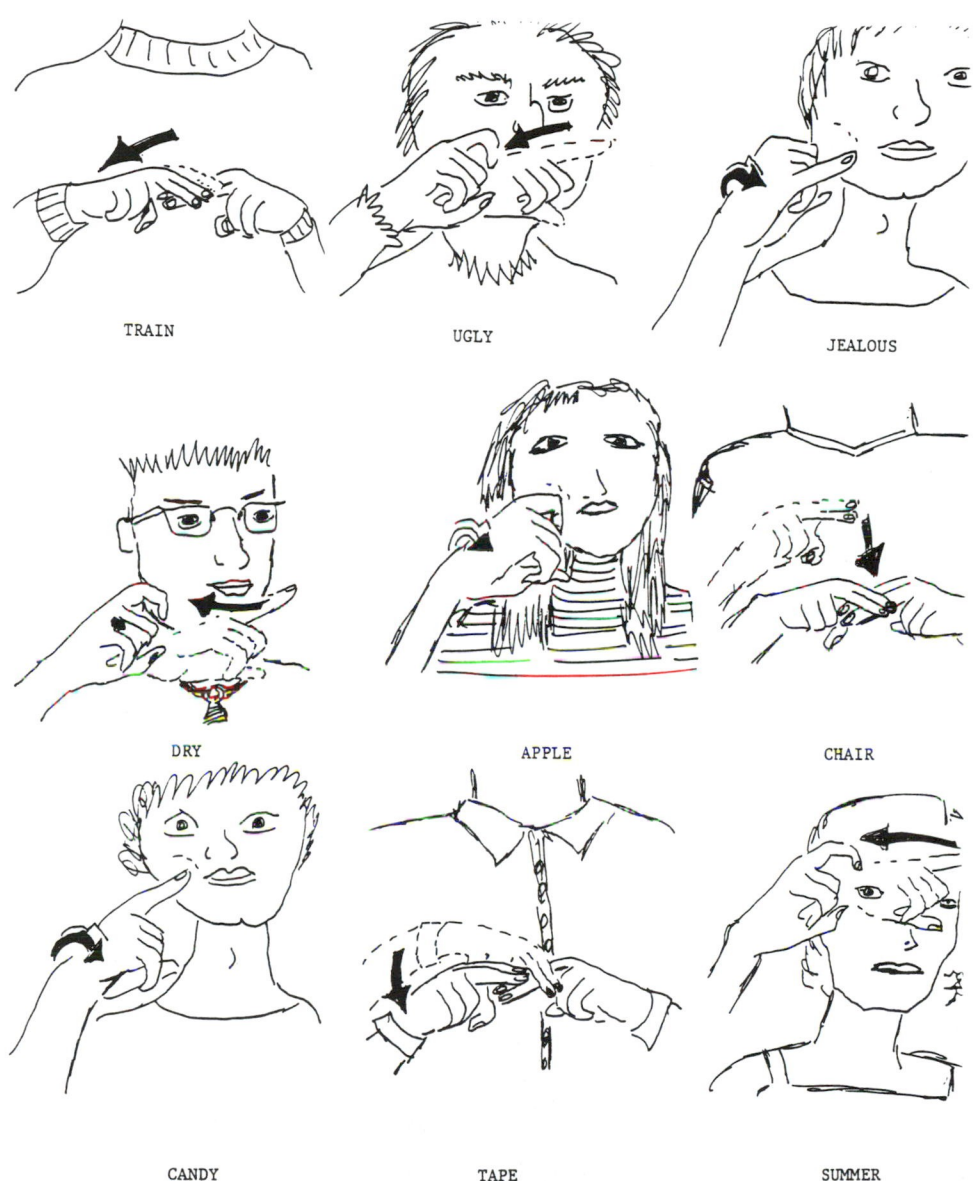

Figure 1.10. Nine signs of ASL, demonstrating three distinctive features.

tense. What would be a phonetic analogue in spoken English? (And, by the way, what would be a graphemic analogue in written English?)

(c) Your hands can make many shapes. Yet only some are actually used in sign languages. In Figure 1.11 you can see four hand shapes. One of these four handshapes does not occur in ASL. Guess which one and explain why you chose it. What would be an analogous fact about spoken English? (I'm asking you here to speculate about why possible handshapes and sounds are not likely to be used as part of a linguistic system. To see the analogy, think of sounds the vocal tract can make, but that aren't used in natural language, and discuss why they aren't used.)

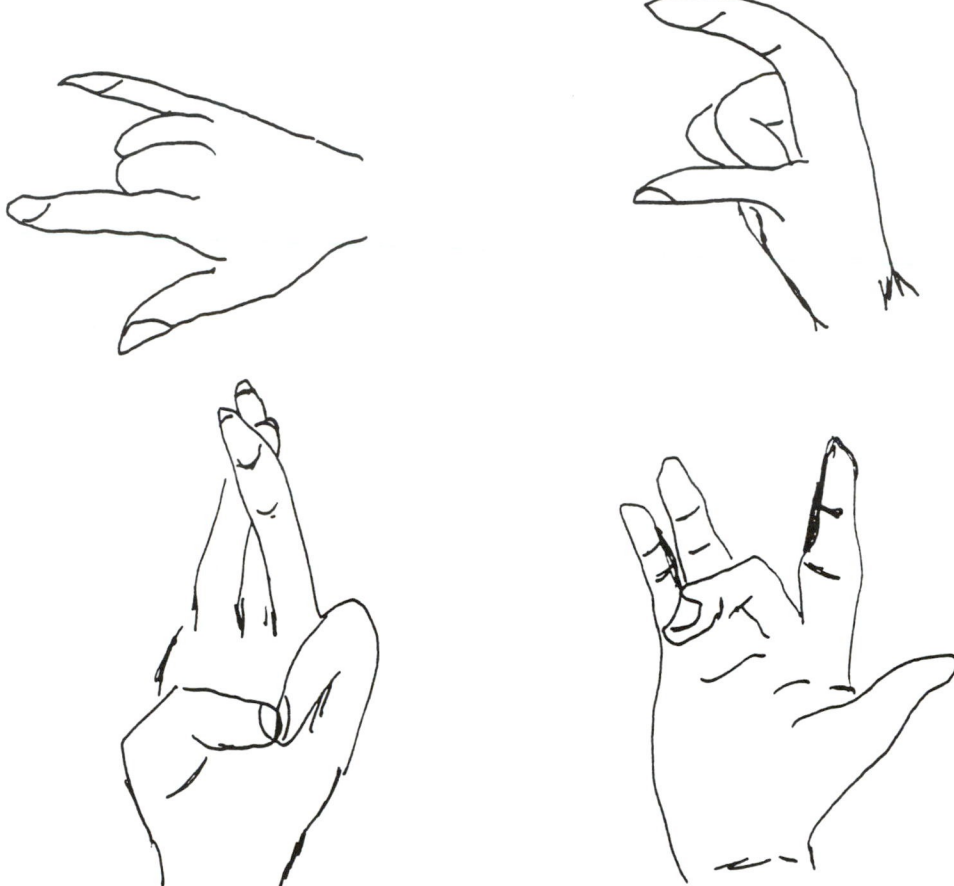

Figure 1.11. Four handshapes, of which one does not occur in ASL.

(d) ASL signs are made in a highly restricted signing space in front of the body, which runs from the top of the head down to the waist, and out to each side as far as the reach of the arms with the elbows bent. What that means is that signs will be made in this signing space and not, for example, in front of the knees or behind the head. Why is this a natural signing space? What is a phonetic analogue in spoken language?

Problem Set 1.6: Acoustic Phonetics without a Laboratory

(NOTE: Question 5 on this problem set is difficult.)

1. Which of the following makes a periodic sound and which makes an aperiodic sound? Explain your answer.

a waterfall   a drum

(If you know the difference between pitched drums, like timpani drums, and unpitched drums, like snare drums, you might want to elaborate on your answer. If not, please just give me the answer you know I'm asking for.)

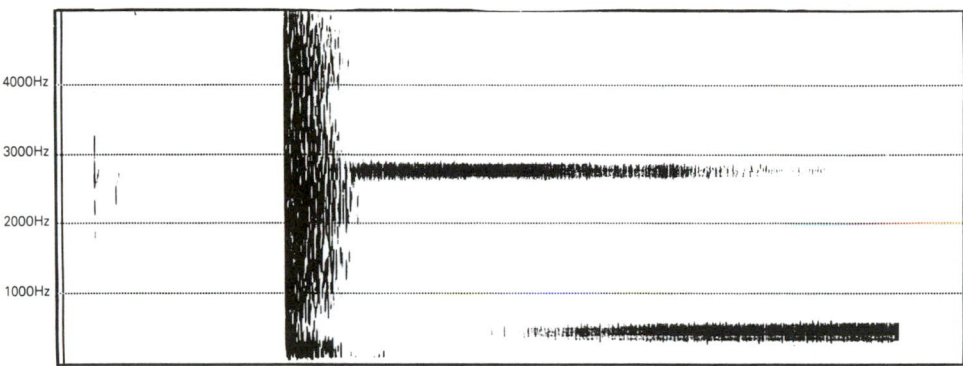

Figure 1.12. Spectrogram for the sounds of a tuning fork hitting a metal table.

2. It is common knowledge that children generally have higher-pitched voices than adult women, who have higher-pitched voices than adult men. In fact, prepubescent voices have a range from 200 to 500 Hz; adult female, from 150 to 300 or even 400 Hz; and adult male, from 80 to 200 Hz. Explain these facts.

3. In Figure 1.12 you have a spectrogram of the sounds that occurred when a tuning fork hit a metal table. We have here the smack of the fork on the table; the pitch of the fork (which is the same fork used in Figure 1.3, so the note here is A); and the pitch of the resonances set up in the table. Label each one and explain how you knew which was which. (The horizontal lines are spaced 1,000 Hz apart. If you are having trouble telling the resonance of the table from the tuning fork, look back at Figure 1.3 and figure out what the Hz of the tuning fork is.)

4. In Figure 1.13 we have a spectrogram of an alveolar nasal followed by a dental nasal. How many (significantly intense) formants do nasals have (assuming [n] is representative of all nasals)? In comparison with vowels, which formant is missing? (If you're having trouble seeing this, compare Fig. 1.13 to Fig. 1.5.) Describe any acoustic differences you see between the alveolar and dental nasals—although these differences are decidedly slight. Would you expect there might be a language which distinctively contrasts dental to alveolar nasals? Why or why not?

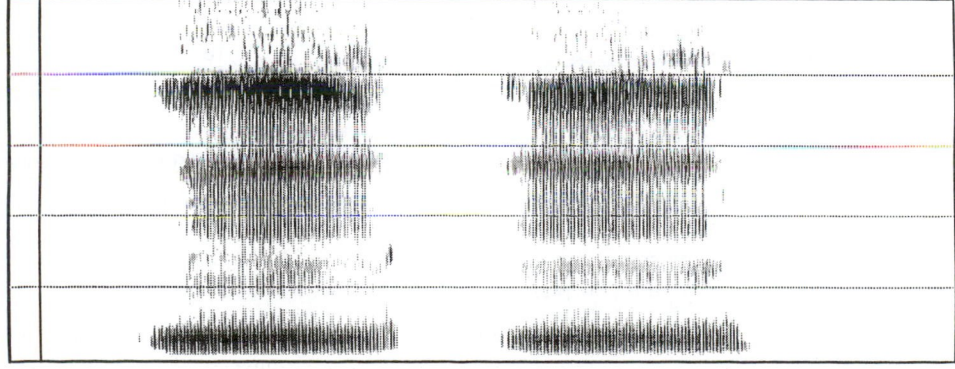

Figure 1.13. Spectrogram for an alveolar nasal followed by spectrogram for a dental nasal.

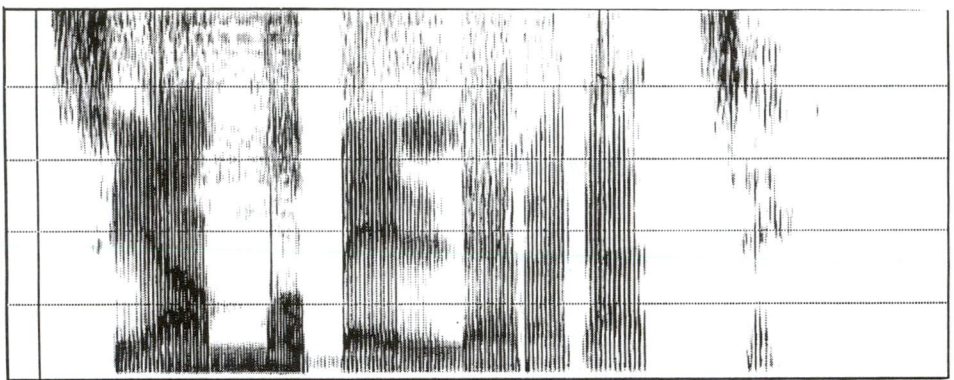

Figure 1.14. Spectrogram of an Italian sentence.

5. In Figure 1.14 you have a spectrogram of a sentence of Italian. Consider the following questions. Tell me which of these questions is theoretically answerable (if you have the experience) from looking at a spectrogram?

  (a) How many vowels are in this utterance?
  (b) Which are the stressed syllables?
  (c) Are there any geminates?
  (d) Are there any syllabic consonants?
  (e) Are there any oral stops?
  (f) Are there any diphthongs?
  (g) Are there any nasals?
  (h) Are there any affricates (stops released as fricatives)?
  (i) Are there any fricatives that are clearly not the release part of a stop—i.e., that are not part of affricates?

  For each question that you say is answerable, answer that question and explain what you looked for in the spectrogram to arrive at your answer. Now label the segments on the spectrogram appropriately wherever possible in light of your answers to these questions.

Problem Set 1.7: Acoustic Phonetics with a Laboratory

1. Do a wide band spectrogram of eight minimal pairs. Does the feature of [+strident] correspond to an acoustic reality? It is your job to find an appropriate set of eight words.

2. Reading spectrograms is confounded by the fact that individual speakers bring their own speech peculiarities to utterances. Record a speaker with a very similar linguistic background to your own—in terms of where the speaker grew up, how old that speaker is, the socioeconomic and educational class that speaker belongs to, the ethnic or racial group that speaker belongs to, gender, and anything else you might guess is pertinent. Now record yourself saying the same sentence(s) that speaker said. Do a wide-band spectrogram and point out any individual peculiarities you or the other person has.

3. If consonants are merely ways to begin or end vowels, tell what the effect of a velar consonant is on ending a vowel. You can do this by looking at appropriate spectrograms.

Make sure that you show it is velars only (and not any other kind of consonant) that cause this effect. And make sure that you show velars cause it on every vowel (not just certain kinds of vowels). You can reduce your job by assuming that voiceless and voiced counterparts of a consonant have the same effect—so test only one of them. You can also reduce your job by assuming that front vowels will be affected as a group, as will back vowels. So test only one representative from the front vowels and only one representative from the back vowels.

4. Lip rounding has an effect on formants. What is that effect? Support your answer by presenting and discussing the spectrograms of at least the vowels [i] vs. [y] and [u] vs. [ɯ].

Now look at the spectrograms for [u] and [o]. Which has more lip rounding? How do you know?

2

Phonology

Chapter Organization—for the Instructor

Current approaches to phonology and morphology simply cannot really be separated. Thus you will find many topics in this chapter that you might have expected to find in a chapter on morphology. I raise those topics here in the hopes of making the transition from phonology to morphology natural—and I point out this mixing to the students later in the chapter when it should make sense to them.

We begin with linear phonology, looking at seven different kinds of sound change and introducing concepts of syllable structure, morphology, and underspecification as they become relevant. We then turn to geometric phonology, illustrating some of the advantages of this theory over linear phonology with regard to the types of sound change studied thus far. We introduce metrical phonology as a complement to geometric phonology, giving formal statements of stress patterns in terms of five parameters. The study of metrical trees is followed by the study of metrical grids. Many languages are discussed, and an examination of English stress leads us to the introduction of lexical phonology, again as a complement theory to geometric and metrical phonology—so that the three can be viewed as subtheories of a single theory. Finally, we look at Optimality Theory as an alternative to all other theories. All along the way we focus on phenomena that make clear how crucial the understanding of phonology is to morphology, preparing us for the next chapter.

Okay, let's go

One of the things we noticed in Chapter 1 is that sound segments vary based on their environment. Thus a lateral in English, which is usually realized as the voiced segment [l], can be realized as voiceless, as in the word *please*. The voiceless segment, [l̥], is an allophone of [l]. Likewise, a nasal can be articulated on the palate, such as the [ɲ] in the word *onion*. So [ɲ] and [n] are allophones. **All the different surface realizations of an underlying phoneme are its allophones**.

Is the distribution of [l̥] vs. [l] random or predictable? You already know the answer. In Chapter 1 (in the section "Breathy Voice, Whispery Voice, and Creaky Voice") you discovered that [l̥] occurs predictably in a syllable onset after a voiceless consonant and [l] does not occur there. In *please*, then, it is the initial [pʰ] that conditions the appearance of the [l̥].

Let's consider again the claim that initial voiceless consonants condition the appearance of the [l̥]. If you were hesitant about this conclusion in Chapter 1, you could try an experiment now. Make up nonsense words that begin with consonant clusters (that is, CC) in which the first consonant is voiced and the second is a lateral. Then make up nonsense words that begin with CC in which the first consonant is voiceless and the second is a lateral. Ask some friends to pronounce the NONCE (that is, made-up) words. You will find that [l̥] occurs predictably after the voiceless consonant and [l] occurs after the voiced one. This kind of exercise is very helpful in phonology; if a sound segment's distribution is predictable from phonological context, then it should show the same distribution in nonce words as in real words of the lexicon.

Now let's look at the nasals. Is the distribution of [n] versus [ɲ] predictable? If you did Problem Set 1.3, you may have already thought about this question. Make a list of as many words as you can in which we hear [ɲ]. You might have listed:

| pinion | minion | canyon | Daniel | spaniel | onion | bunyon |

Let's try to figure out if the context is responsible for the appearance of [ɲ]. First, does there seem to be anything in common about the sound that precedes this [ɲ] in all these words? We find [ɪ], [æ], [ʌ]—all lax [−round] vowels which in these words get stress. Still, the vowels range from high to low, from front to mid (or, depending on how you classify [ʌ], from front to back). Thus the environment preceding the nasal does not seem to be terribly restricted.

What about the environment following this nasal? First, do we ever hear [ɲ] in syllable-final position? No. This fact leads us to suspect that following context is important to the appearance of this nasal. What in fact do we find following this nasal? The high lax front vowel [ɪ] at the start of a diphthong (that is, [ɪ̯]). Thus the distribution of [ɲ] is certainly predictable: It occurs before a nonsyllabic [ɪ], and [n] does not occur there.

Linear Phonology

Now let's go back to our lateral example. We will say that /l/ becomes [l̥] after a voiceless consonant. That is, we are GENERATING [l̥] from /l/. One way to express this particular RULE is with a linear formulation, such as:

$$l \rightarrow \underset{\circ}{l} / \quad \begin{matrix} C \\ [-\text{voiced}] \end{matrix} \quad \underline{\hspace{2cm}}$$

(We have not expressed in this rule the fact that it applies only when both the lateral and the preceding voiceless consonant are within a syllable onset. After you've finished this chapter, come back and rewrite the rule to include that restriction—it will be easy for you to do.) The convention on writing rules in LINEAR GENERATIVE PHONOLOGY is to have the change (a → b), followed by a slash, and then the environment for the change, where a line (the _____) shows the slot in which the changing segment must find itself in order to undergo the rule. If nothing is specified before the slot, that means that the preceding context is not important for the rule. If nothing is specified after the slot, that means that the following context is not important for the rule. The rule devoicing /l/ tells us that the preceding context is important; we must have a voiceless consonant there—but the following context is not important to the change from /l/ to [l̥]. The change from /l/ to [l̥] is called the STRUCTURAL CHANGE of the rule.

Let's stop for a moment and reconsider what we just did. If we know that [l] and [l̥] occur in COMPLEMENTARY DISTRIBUTION (that is, they occur in different phonological environments), we know they are allophones. (Actually, as you know from the discussion of examples like *million* in the section "Laterals" in Chapter 1, there is at least one other lateral allophone: [ʎ]. We will ignore that fact here for the sake of expository clarity.) But how do we know which one is the underlying representation (the UR, a term you know from Chapter 1)? Why should we pick [l] as the UR?

You should have several reasons. First, you learned in Chapter 1 that sonorants are typically voiced. So a voiceless sonorant is special. You might therefore expect that if a voiced and voiceless sonorant are allophones, the voiced one would be the underlying form. Second, you hear [l] much more frequently in English than [l̥]. Just on the basis of frequency, you might expect that the voiced lateral would be the underlying representation. The third reason is the most important of all, and to see it I want you to try to rewrite the rule above turning [l̥] into [l], instead of vice versa. The issue for you is determining the environment—the part of the rule that follows the slash. Do you see how hard it is? You can easily state the distribution of [l̥] (it occurs after a voiceless consonant), so you can easily state the environment in which /l/ becomes [l̥]. But it is much more difficult to state the distribution of [l], and for that reason, it is much more difficult to state the environment in which /l/ becomes [l]. In fact, you could only state this environment in negative terms. That is, you'd have to say that /l/ became [l] everywhere except after a voiceless consonant. Such a statement of the environment certainly sheds no light on what's going on in the rule, and we will in general not allow negative statements of environments. For all these reasons, then, we can conclude that we were right to choose /l/ as our phoneme and derive [l̥] from it.

Why Have UR and PR?

But now let's ask an even more basic question: Why do we want to relate different sound segments via rules anyway? Why do we need to recognize allophones? What is the value of having both a UR and a PR (phonetic representation, a term you learned in Chapter 1)? All of these questions are just different ways of asking the same thing.

A driving force of modern linguistics is the search for explanation. Describing a phenomenon is only the first step. **A true explanation of a phenomenon shows how the phenomenon works with enough insight so as to both account for the patterns observed in the data and to make correct predictions about previously unexamined data.** A rule captures a generalization. As such, it makes predictions about as-yet-untested data.

For example, we came up with our lateral devoicing rule by looking at two lists of only five words each in Chapter 1:

Voiced	Voiceless
lose	slow
alter	claim
pail	please
glue	flavor
pearl	schlep (from Yiddish)

We could have simply said that in the five words in the first list we find [l], and in the five words of the second list we find [l̥]. That would have been a description of the facts. But it would not have been an explanation: It would have failed to recognize a pattern and it would have given us no expectations as to the voicing feature on laterals we might find in other words of the language.

By taking the additional step of noticing that the preceding context is relevant to the voicing feature of the lateral in these particular examples, we are recognizing a pattern. Then, by taking the final step of positing that any time we find a lateral preceded by a voiceless consonant, both within a syllable onset, that lateral will be voiceless, we correctly predict the voicelessness of the laterals in new words we might come across like *plink* and *clean*, but not in new words we might come across like *blink* and *glean*.

Throughout this book we will be striving for accurate and insightful accounts of the data. The quest for explanation will motivate our discussion. And we will find reasons to discuss different levels of representation (parallel to UR and PR in phonology) in the other components of the grammar studied in the following chapters in this book, as well.

Back to the Rules

Returning to the discussion we started earlier about nasals, we can now approach the question of whether [n] or [ɲ] is basic. Which do you think? I hope you said the underlying phoneme was /n/. Can you see how hard it would be to write the environment for a rule that turned [ɲ] into [n], but how easy it is to write the environment for the rule that turns [n] into [ɲ]? The rule in simple words is: /n/ becomes [ɲ] before nonsyllabic [ɪ]. Try to write this rule in the formalism you have just met.

$$\text{n} \rightarrow \text{ɲ} / \underline{\hspace{2cm}} \quad \begin{matrix} \text{ɪ} \\ [-\text{syllabic}] \end{matrix}$$

Easy, right? There are other reasons why you should have said /n/ was the phoneme. [n] occurs more frequently, of course. But also, [ɲ] is a marked sound for English. Why? If you did Problem Set 1.3, you know that typically languages have nasals only in places where they have oral stops. But English has no palatal oral stops (although it certainly does have palatal affricates, which are [−continuant]: [tʃ] and [dʒ]). Thus a palatal nasal is marked in English and we would therefore hope that it is produced by a rule, rather than being part of our phonemic inventory. (In fact, a sound like [ɲ] can be considered marked for all languages, in that sounds made with that point behind the blade of the tongue are marked relative to coronal sounds.)

Both of these types of changes in a sound segment are very common. Our job now is to figure out why.

Assimilation

What feature has changed in the first rule (the one involving the lateral)? Voicing, of course. Do you have any idea why this might happen? Look carefully at the context. Can you see that the voicelessness of the preceding consonant is influencing the voicing feature of the lateral? That is, the lateral is becoming more like the consonant that precedes it for the feature of voicing—it is assimilating for the feature of voicing. How could we rewrite the rule to make this insight into the effect of the rule more obvious? We want to somehow highlight the fact that voicing is what's changing, but no other feature of the lateral is changing. A typical way to do this is:

$$1 \rightarrow [-\text{voiced}] / \quad \underset{[-\text{voiced}]}{C} \quad \underline{\hspace{2cm}}$$

This revised statement of the rule, then, suggests that the feature of voicing is changing to match the feature of voicing on the preceding consonant. The ASSIMILATION rule stated above is to be read as saying that only the indicated feature changes, and no other feature changes unless it is forced to change as a byproduct of the indicated change.

What does that last sentence above mean? Read it again. If you did Problem Set 1.5, you know that some features entail other features. For example, if a sound segment has the feature [+strident], it must also have the feature [−sonorant]. That means that if a rule were to change the feature of a sound segment from being [−strident] to being [+strident], then the sound segment would also have to be [−sonorant] after the application of the rule. So if the input sound segment is [+sonorant], then the rule will necessarily change not only the feature of stridency, but also the feature of sonority. We will not generally write in changes that happen of necessity like this. Can you tell me why? If we wrote in all the concomitant changes, we would clutter up our statement of the rule and perhaps obfuscate the true nature of the rule.

Sometimes the side effects of a rule are more complicated to see. Let's say that our input sound segment is [+sonorant, −nasal]. Then what must its value be for the feature of continuancy? Plus, of course. So if a rule changes the feature of continuancy, then the feature of sonority for our segment will of necessity change, also. But this time it is only because the original sound segment also had the feature of [−nasal] that the concomitant change occurs.

If several changes occur at once, how can you be sure which changes you can perspicuously write as part of the rule formalism and which you should leave out, as side effects? The best way is to stand back from your rule and try to make sense out of it. A statement of a rule that makes the rule seem capricious and arbitrary should be suspect. You want a statement of the rule that gives us a sense of what the rule is all about. Part of making this judgment is having experience dealing with phonological rules—experience that you are only just beginning to gain. But part of it is in being logical and looking for connections.

Consider, for example, the sounds [t] and [ʧ] in Brazilian Portuguese (a Romance language spoken in Brazil). We find that [t] occurs in many phonological environments, but [ʧ] occurs only before [i], where [t] never occurs. For example, we get:

[téɲu] 'I have' [tal] 'such' [kṵátru] 'four'

and:

[ʧívi] 'I had' [párʧi] 'party'

(NOTE: Throughout this chapter and the rest of this book, we will make no distinction between the low vowels [a], [ɑ], and [ɒ], representing them all as [a], unless the difference is of particular interest to us. This is because the sources from which I have taken language examples have almost invariably used simply the symbol [a],

regardless of which of these three vowels actually occur.) Which one do you want to posit as the UR? [t], of course. So our rule will turn [t] into [tʃ]. Give a complete feature bundle for [t] and for [tʃ]. Now list the features they differ on. Delayed release, strident, high, anterior, right? But do we write the rule as changing all these features or just some, where the others will change of necessity? Notice that if [t] becomes [+del rel], it must become [+strident]. So there's no need to mention stridency in the change. This is the only feature we can eliminate purely on our knowledge of how features interrelate.

However, there is other information we need to consider now—information particular to Brazilian Portuguese (BP). In BP there are no oral stops on the palate. Thus if /t/ becomes [−anterior] or [+high] but still stays [−back, −continuant] (as it would in going to [tʃ]), it cannot stay a simple stop. The closest sound to a simple stop made on the palate (closest in terms of differing by the fewest number of features) is an affricate. Thus once we change to either [−anterior] or [+high], we automatically will change to [+del rel]. So we need not mention the change to [+del rel].

The final question, then, is whether we need to mention both [−anterior] and [+high] in the rule change (since either one of them will automatically make our sound also become [+del rel, +strident]). Notice that if a sound segment is [+high], it is automatically [−anterior]. (Both these features correspond to primary articulations. Thus a double articulation—as with a labialized velar or a palatalized dental, etc.—would not affect this statement.) But if a segment is [−anterior], it is not necessarily [+high] (consider all the uvular and pharyngeal sounds). Still, since we are maintaining the feature of [−back], a [−anterior] sound will, in fact, also be [+high]. For this reason, we certainly don't want to mention both features in the rule change. In order to see which one we should choose to mention, let's consider the rule:

$$t \rightarrow tʃ / \text{_____} \ i$$

If we formulate the rule to say the stop is becoming [−anterior], does any motive for the rule jump out at you? Certainly there's nothing about preceding any particular vowel that should favor [−anterior]: All vowels are made behind the alveolar ridge—so in a sense all are [−anterior], and we never talk about the feature of anteriority with regard to vowels. This formulation of the rule, then, gives us no insight into why the change occurs.

If, instead, we formulate the rule to say the stop is becoming [+high], does any motive for the rule jump out at you? Sure. [i] is a high vowel and not all vowels are high. The fact that this change occurs before a high vowel suggests that the relevant feature that is changing is highness—this is another assimilation rule. In fact, in many languages a palatal vowel ([i], [ɪ], or [e]) triggers movement of an adjacent consonant onto the palate. For that reason we will write the rule like so:

$$t \rightarrow [+\text{high}] / \text{_____} \begin{bmatrix} V \\ +\text{high} \\ +\text{front} \end{bmatrix}$$

(By limiting the movement onto the palate to happening before high front vowels only, we have eliminated the possibility of it happening before [e]. And notice that BP has no [ɪ] in its underlying or surface representation, so we do not have to mention the feature [+tense] in order to limit the environment to just [i].) Do you see how simple we have made things just by not mentioning the changes that are automatic?

Now look back at the nasal rule. You should be able to write it now in terms of changing features. When /n/ becomes [ɲ], only one sort of feature is changing. What sort? Features involving point or place of articulation. Do you see that? The nasal has moved from the alveolar to the palatal area. So it goes from being [+anterior] to being [−anterior] and from being [−high] to [+high]. Now do we need to state both features in our change or only one? This is similar to the BP problem above, but now you can do it all by yourself because you know English—you know the inventory of consonants in English. So you can answer this question. If a nasal becomes [−anterior] does it automatically become [+high]? Yes. We do not have any retroflexed nasals in English. So all of our [−anterior] nasals are made on the palate or the velum with the blade or back of the tongue, which means they are all [+high]. On the other hand, if a nasal becomes [+high], does it automatically become [−anterior]? Of course. You can't make [+high] sounds at or in front of the alveolar area. Okay, so we want to state only one of these features in our rule change (because the other one will happen automatically). Which one? Look at the rule again:

$$n \rightarrow ɲ / \underline{\hspace{2cm}} \quad \begin{matrix} I \\ [-\text{syllabic}] \end{matrix}$$

Which feature, anteriority or highness, seems to be most relevant to this change? Again, this is similar to the BP problem above. Consider the environment for the change. I hope you thought immediately about assimilation and said highness. So we will write the rule like so:

$$n \rightarrow [+\text{high}] / \underline{\hspace{2cm}} \quad \begin{matrix} V \\ \left[\begin{matrix} +\text{high} \\ -\text{syllabic} \\ -\text{back} \end{matrix} \right] \end{matrix}$$

You tell me: Why won't this rule turn [n] into [ŋ]? What other feature do [n] and [ŋ] differ on? Backness, of course.

Now tell me: does the formulation of the rule really have to mention that the vowel is not only [+high] but [−back]? This formulation ensures that the change will occur only before nonsyllabic [ɪ], not before nonsyllabic [ʊ]. If there are no words of English that have /n/ before nonsyllabic [ʊ], then we need not mention the feature [−back] in this rule. After you have done Problem Set 2.2, come back to this rule and decide whether to keep the feature [−back]. For now, we'll leave the rule as is.

Let's consider one more common type of rule before taking stock of what we've learned so far. In Spanish we find that the voiced stop [b] occurs in complementary distribution with the bilabial voiced fricative [β]:

| [bráθo] 'arm' | [diβíno] 'divine' | [lóβo] 'wolf' | |
| [xoβ] 'Job' | [ámbos] 'both' | [búr:o] 'burro' | [álβa] 'dawn' |

In general [b] occurs in word-initial position and after a nasal, but [β] occurs between vowels and in word-final position. Exactly the same distributional facts are found for [d] vs. [ð], and for [g] vs. [ɣ], as in:

| [dar] 'to give' | [eláðo] 'ice cream' |
| [gáto] 'cat' | [testíɣo] 'witness' |

In each case only one feature is changing. What is that feature? Continuancy. Can you see that? For the bilabial and the velar I expect you to have no trouble seeing that. But for the dental, you might at first be upset. The [d] is made behind the teeth, whereas the [ð] is interdental. (Actually, the Spanish speaker probably makes this [ð] much closer to behind the teeth than an American English speaker does, but still probably not entirely homorganically to the [d].) Yet if we compare the feature matrices for these two sounds, we can see that continuancy is the only one they differ on. Certainly there are [+continuant] sounds made at the same place of articulation as [d] (several, in fact), but all of them differ from [d] by other features, as well. For example, [z] is [+strident]; [l] and [r] are [+sonorant]; etc. So we have the proper feature change for our rule above right off.

At this point we don't know whether we are going from [b] to [β], or vice versa. Just for the sake of ease of exposition, let's assume for the moment that we are going from [b] to [β].

Now should we just list [b], [d], and [g] as undergoing this feature-changing rule, or is there some more insightful way of going about this? In order to answer this, you need to know that Spanish has no palatal oral stops; however, it does have voiceless stops in all the same places it has voiced oral stops. So the rule is changing voiced oral stops (as a group, regardless of place of articulation) into continuants. What feature bundle will capture all and only the voiced non-nasal stops? [+voiced, −continuant, −nasal].

Finally, we need to look at the environment for the rule. At this point we'll be able to figure out whether we were right to assume that we are going from [b] to [β] or whether we should have posited the opposite direction of change. If [b] becomes [β], what can we see as the environment for this change? It doesn't happen in initial position; it doesn't happen after a nasal. But it does happen between vowels and it does happen after a lateral. You'd need to know more about syllable structure in Spanish to answer this question properly. So let me tell you that it turns out that these stops/fricatives never follow any consonants other than nasals, the liquids, and /s/. Keep in mind that the feature that is changing is continuancy. So we can see that the fricative follows a [+continuant] segment and the stop occurs everywhere else. (Actually, the facts are more complex than this if we look closely at words in which the stops/fricatives follow /s/. If you are interested, this could be a topic for a research paper.)

If we, instead, had said that [β] becomes [b], we would have had to say this change occurs in word-initial position and after a nasal. But there is no way to collapse those two environments. Thus our initial assumption, that we were going from a stop to a fricative, was correct.

We can now write the rule:

$$\begin{bmatrix} +\text{voice} \\ -\text{continuant} \\ -\text{nasal} \end{bmatrix} \rightarrow [+\text{continuant}] \ / \ [+\text{continuant}] \ \underline{\hspace{2cm}}$$

In fact, we can write the rule even more simply by leaving out the feature [−continuant]. Do you see that? If the rule were to apply to a [+continuant] sound, no change would take place.

The change from a stop to a fricative is often called a WEAKENING or LENITION rule. The idea here is that consonants differ from vowels to varying degrees. A voiceless stop, for example, has very little in common with a vowel; a liquid, on the other hand, has much in common with a vowel. Just think of it from the point of view of the sonority hierarchy you read about in the section "Sonority" in Chapter 1. Any rule that makes a consonant more like a vowel when it is happening in the environment of a vowel or a vowellike consonant can be considered a lenition rule, and such a rule would be a particular type of assimilation rule. However, while lenition rules are usually assimilation rules, not all are: Any rule that makes any segment more sonorous can be considered a lenition rule. A lenition rule that turns a stop into a fricative, like the rule in Spanish that we've been talking about, is called a SPIRANTIZATION rule.

The opposite of a lenition rule also occurs and is called a STRENGTHENING or FORTITION rule. Any rule that makes a segment less sonorous is a fortition rule. The typical environment for a fortition rule is postconsonantal, generally after an obstruent, or word-initial, and a typical fortition rule is one that turns a fricative into a stop. Given the typical environment for fortition rules, are fortition rules usually assimilation rules or not? Yes, they are.

This lenition rule for Spanish is the first rule we've written entirely in features. Writing a rule in features suggests that it is more general than a rule that applies to only one sound segment. Can you see why? If a rule applied to only one sound segment, then writing the full set of features to pick out only that sound segment would be no more insightful than just listing the sound segment per se. But if a rule applies to more than one sound segment, we want to zoom in on whatever those segments have in common and write the rule with reference to those features. Thus, whenever it is sensible, write as much of the rule in feature bundles as you can.

Our English lateral rule, so far as we have discussed, applies only to an underlying /l/. But if we were to find out that it applied to other sound segments, then we'd want to write the rule in a more general way. (You will consider this issue further in Problem Set 2.4.) The same is true for our Brazilian Portuguese rule affecting /t/ and our English rule affecting /n/.

Look now at the four rules we have written:

$$l \rightarrow [-\text{voiced}] / \quad \underset{[-\text{voiced}]}{C} \quad \underline{\qquad}$$

$$t \rightarrow [+\text{high}] / \underline{\qquad} \quad \underset{\begin{bmatrix} +\text{high} \\ +\text{front} \end{bmatrix}}{V}$$

$$n \rightarrow [+\text{high}] / \underline{\qquad} \quad \underset{\begin{bmatrix} +\text{high} \\ -\text{syllabic} \\ -\text{back} \end{bmatrix}}{V}$$

$$\begin{bmatrix} +\text{voice} \\ -\text{nasal} \end{bmatrix} \rightarrow [+\text{continuant}] / [+\text{continuant}] \underline{\qquad}$$

In the lateral one, we are changing voicing. In the /t/ and nasal ones, we are changing highness. And in the Spanish voiced stops ones, we are changing continuancy. But all three types of rules have in common the motivation for the change: assimilation. In every case the sound segment changes to become like an adjacent segment for a certain feature, whether that feature be voicing or highness or continuancy. You have seen here that sounds can undergo assimilation for phonation features (here, voicing), place features (here, highness, although we'll have more to say about this later), or manner features (here, continuuancy). Assimilation rules are among the most common phonological rules in the world's languages.

Palatalization

In fact, two of the rules above, the rule of BP involving /t/ and the English nasal rule, are not just assimilation rules; they are also called PALATALIZATION rules. That's because pulling a sound onto the palate is a very common type of sound change. If every instance of pulling a sound onto the palate took place in the environment of another palatal sound (such as the [ɪ] in our nasal rule), palatalization would just be a very common type of assimilation. But, in fact, sometimes palatalization happens in environments where it can't be classified as an assimilation rule. I do not know of any examples of SYNCHRONIC palatalization rules that are not also assimilation rules (a synchronic rule is an alternation that takes place at a particular time in the development of a language, such as today or the twelfth century, etc.), but I can show you one such instance of a DIACHRONIC palatalization rule (a diachronic rule is a change that takes place over time in the development of a language, so that you can point to a period of time when the language had one sound segment in a certain context and then to another period of time when the language had a different sound segment in that same context).

French is a Romance language—which means that it developed from Common Latin (sometimes called PROTOROMANCE). In Latin we find words such as:

[káu̯za] 'thing, cause'   [káza] 'house'   [kavál:u] 'horse'

(In these examples I have given the Accusative form minus the −*m* ending. You will learn about Accusative Case in the section "Back to Latin GF's" in Chapter 4.) In French we find the DESCENDANTS:

[ʃoz] 'thing'   [ʃe] '{at/to} the house of'   [ʃəvál] 'horse'

If we compare the words in the two languages (or you might think of it as in the two different time stages of a single language), we can see that [k] has been palatalized to [ʃ] before a back vowel, not before the expected front vowel if this were an assimilation rule. For this reason we will keep palatalization rules distinct from assimilation rules in our discussion. However, I am on shaky ground here. Many linguists take for granted that palatalization rules are always assimilation rules. So be aware of the fact that I'm not with the majority here.

Not all sound changes can have the effects of assimilating or palatalizing, right? How do you know? If they did, all languages would eventually wind up with words that had lots of sequences of sound segments that shared features except for the possible interference of palatals here and there. So while these two types of change are common, they are not the only types of phonological change.

Loss

What other types of phonological changes might you guess occur? To help you, let me point out something in your own speech. We all have many words we can pronounce in varying ways. Take the word *interesting*, for example. I bet you can pronounce it at least two ways, and you probably have at least heard a third pronunciation. Transcribe them now and describe when you might use each. You should have come up with something like:

[ɪn.tʰəɹ.ɛs.tɪŋ]   [ɪn.tʰɹɛs.tɪŋ]   [ɪ.nɹ.ɛs.tɪŋ]

You might well have transcribed the final consonant as [n] rather than the velar in one or more of these examples. That difference will in no way affect our discussion. You might also have transcribed the fourth segment of the second pronunciation as [ʃ] rather than as the liquid, or you might have transcribed the third and fourth segment of the second pronunciation as the affricate [ʧ] rather than the aspirated stop with the liquid, like so: [ɪn.ʧɹɛs.tɪŋ]. In either of these instances, this just means that you have made a fricative of your liquid, and in the second instance you have interpreted that fricative as combining with the preceding stop to make an affricate. I will not discuss this further here, because the choice between a stop followed by a fricative on the one hand, or an affricate on the other, is based on the phonological behavior of the segment(s), not on their phonetic reality. For now, I will treat all of these transcriptions as equally valid. And, finally, you might have transcribed the first pronunciation with a syllabic liquid and without the schwa. I will return to a discussion of that particular transcription later.

With all those caveats put aside, let's now discuss these three pronunciations. I have indicated syllable boundaries to help you. Which one of these pronunciations seems the fanciest to you, the one you'd be most likely to use in an occasion where you are paying particular attention to speech, such as when a non-native speaker of English asks you to repeat a word because it is a new vocabulary item? The first, of course. (And if you were a teacher saying this word as part of a spelling test, you'd probably use this pronunciation if you were trying to help the students get the orthography right.) The other two belong to casual, fast speech and you might well use only one of them in your daily speech, although I hope you've heard both. What do you notice about both of the casual pronunciations in contrast with the fancy pronunciation? Both of them are shorter. The second pronunciation has one fewer vowel (and therefore one fewer syllable). The third pronunciation has one fewer consonant (the [tʰ] is missing).

Simple LOSS rules will account for both of these pronunciations. And loss rules (or rules that delete sound segments) are common in language.

Now you might not have transcribed the first pronunciation as I did, but rather as:

[ɪn.tʰɹɛs.tɪŋ]

with a syllabic liquid. Actually, I agree with you: in my pronunciation there is a syllabic liquid. A schwa before an [ɹ] often gets lost, and the liquid often becomes syllabic—with the result that we maintain the same number of syllables. You will probably always be a bit perplexed about whether to transcribe a word with this original sequence of sounds as having a schwa plus a liquid or as having just a syllabic liquid. My advice to you, and the advice I follow in this chapter, is that you transcribe the words as you hear them. But then reconsider and use the transcription that most obviously sheds light on the phenomenon you are looking at. I chose to transcribe above with the sequence [əɹ], for example, just so you could see that vowel deletion was a possibility in languages.

As long as we are talking about the difficulties of dealing with this particular sequence of sounds, we might as well go all the way. There is yet another way that you might find the first pronunciation transcribed by linguists:

[ɪn.tʰɚ.ɛs.tɪŋ]

The new symbol here stands for a schwa that ends as an "r"-sound; it is sometimes called SCHWAR. (We say the vowel is RHOTACIZED or "r"-COLORED.) To get from our first pronunciation to this one, we delete the liquid and "r"-color the schwa. Which transcription is correct? Can your ear hear a difference? I don't know if I can or even should be able to. But I hold to my original advice: In the end, use the transcription that will give you insight into the phonological phenomenon you are looking at.

Syllable Types

There is at least one more thing we should say about these particular examples before going on. Consider once again the third pronunciation, in which the [tʰ] is lost. Notice that before the loss, we have a sequence of two consonants: [ntʰ]. Thus this loss has the effect of eliminating a consonant cluster. Languages often simplify clusters to single consonants. In fact, **the most unmarked syllable in any language consists of a single vowel with an optional single consonant. With a few possible exceptions, every language prefers that that single consonant be in the onset of the syllable. Thus (C)V is the most common syllable type.** And we can easily see that if all syllables were of this form, the words of the language would never contain consonant clusters.

The simplification of the cluster to produce [ɪ.nɹ.ɛs.tɪŋ] results not just in avoidance of CC, but also in resyllabification of the nasal. Do you see that? The nasal is now part of the onset of the second syllable. Again, we can see motivation for this change: The resulting syllabification allows us to take a syllable that used to have a coda (the first syllable) and reanalyze it as no longer having a coda. Since syllables with codas are marked, this loss rule takes us from a marked syllable structure to an unmarked one.

At this point let's get a little terminology about syllables under our belts. You know that a syllable can consist of an onset, a nucleus, and a coda. The nucleus and the coda are together called the RHYME (and you will discover why in Problem Set 2.1). If the rhyme contains only one segment (that is, only a nucleus consisting of a single syllabic segment—since we must have a nucleus in every rhyme), we say the syllable consists of one MORA. **If the rhyme contains two or more elements, we say the syllable consists of two moras.** A syllable can have two moras either because the nucleus contains more than one segment (that is, we have a diphthong or a triphthong) or because there is a coda. We have no special name for syllables that have or don't have onsets (and we will see why when we get to a discussion of stress). But we distinguish a few types of syllables based on their rhymes.

We will find reason to talk about SYLLABLE WEIGHT; different languages may define the notion of weight differently. For many languages (such as the Indo-European ancient languages Latin and Classical Greek), a syllable whose rhyme consists of a single short segment in the nucleus is called a LIGHT syllable. Such a syllable has only one mora. A syllable whose rhyme contains more than one element is called a HEAVY syllable. Heavy syllables have two moras. Heavy syllables would include those that have a long vowel or a diphthong and/or at least one consonant in the coda. (Recall that a diphthong is a syllabic vowel preceded or followed by a nonsyllabic vowel.) For other languages (such as the Eskimo-Aleut language Yup'ik of Alaska and Siberia, the Inuit language of St. Lawrence Island, and the Pama-Nyungan language Warrgamay of Australia), syllable weight is defined with respect to nucleus length only: syllables with long vowels or diphthongs are heavy; syllables with short vowels are light. Unless I specifically indicate otherwise, in the rest of this chapter I'd like you to use the first definition of syllable weight: a heavy syllable has two moras.

We also speak of OPEN syllables as being ones that end in a vowel. (Whether the vowel is long or part of a diphthong doesn't matter; an open syllable can be one or two moras—although I'll return to this issue.) CLOSED syllables, of course, would be ones that end in a consonant.

Give me the form of a syllable that is heavy but open. (C_0VV—where the zero subscript to C means any number of consonants including zero.)

If a syllable is light, what must it also be? (Open.) If a syllable is closed, what must it also be? (Heavy—at least with our definition of "heavy" as "consisting of two moras.")

If you are full of questions about diphthongs regarding these classifications of syllable types, good. You should be. Actually, all the heavy syllables we discuss in the text of this chapter that contain diphthongs have falling diphthongs (that is, diphthongs in which the nonsyllabic vowel follows the syllabic vowel—we met these in Chapter 1). Many interesting questions arise regarding the analysis of diphthongs, and of rising diphthongs (in which the nonsyllabic vowel precedes the syllabic vowel) in particular. You will face some of these questions in Problem Set 2.2.

Besides all the proper parts of a syllable, we find that some languages allow an element at the very beginning of the first syllable of a word or at the very end of the last syllable of a word. For example, if you did Problem Set 1.4, you learned that Italian allows an onset cluster consisting of [s] followed by a range of consonants, including voiceless stops. This order, of course, is not in accordance with the sonority hierarchy. We find that such syllables never occur except in word-initial position. That is, an [s] that is medial (word-internal) and that precedes other consonants syllabifies as part of the coda of the preceding syllable, not as part of the onset of the following syllable. In fact, sometimes Italian employs other phonological rules whose effects insure that a medial [s] in a cluster will syllabify as part of a coda. For example, consider the Italian COGNATE of the English word *institute*, which is *istituto*. (Words in different languages which descend from the same source in yet another language are cognates of each other. *Institute*, which came to English via French, and *istituto* are cognates because both of these words descend from a single source in Latin.) The [n] we expected in the first syllable is lost, and the result is that the [s] syllabifies as the coda of the first syllable rather than as part of the onset of the second syllable.

Actually, even when such an [s] occurs in a word-initial syllable, if it can syllabify with the final syllable of the preceding word, it will. For example, in Italian, there are two ALLOMORPHS (phonetic realizations—a parallel concept to "allophones") for the definite article (that is, the word that means 'the') for MASCULINE nouns in the singular that begin with a consonant. One is *il*, and it occurs before nouns that begin with a single consonant (other than certain affricates) and before nouns that begin with a consonant cluster that is in accord with the sonority hierachy (and a few other places—the complexities do not concern us here). Examples include:

il ragazzo 'the boy'   il ceco [il tʃeko] 'the chick pea'
il sogno 'the dream'   il prete 'the priest'

The other is *lo*, and it occurs before a range of other sounds, including an [s] that initiates a cluster. Examples include:

lo stato 'the state'   lo sposo 'the betrothed'
lo schiave [lo ski̯ave] 'the slave'

The [s] syllabifies with the article in these instances.

There is a sense in which the [s] of these words, then, is not really part of the initial syllable. We call it EXTRASYLLABIC.

Okay, now let's take our knowledge of syllable structure and put it to use as we try to understand phonological rules.

We already said above that the consonant loss in English that we discussed above may have been motivated by the need to simplify syllable structure. Loss of both vowels and consonants is common in language and often, though not always, we can see some kind of phonological motivation for the loss.

Let's look now at a vowel loss rule. In Hungarian the plural suffix on nouns takes the form of *ok* or *ek*, as in:

Singular	*Plural*	*Singular*	*Plural*
astal	astalok	ember	emberek
doboz	dobozok	semüveg	semüvegek

(The orthographic *ü* is to be read as the high front rounded vowel [y].) Don't worry about the choice between *ok* and *ek* for now (and after you read about Turkish much later, you can return to this). Please just accept the idea that the underlying representation of the plural suffix contains a vowel. Now consider the following singulars and plurals:

Singular	*Plural*	*Singular*	*Plural*
ayto:	ayto:k	söllö:	söllö:k
fa	fa:k	sürke	sürke:k

What has happened to the plural suffix? The vowel of the plural suffix has deleted. Under what conditions? When the noun ROOT (here the part without any suffix) ends in a vowel, the vowel of the plural suffix is lost. We could write this as:

$$V \rightarrow \text{ø} / V + \underline{\hspace{2cm}} k$$
$$[\mu \text{ plural}]$$

The + indicates the boundary between the root and the suffix. The indication of [μ plural] under the suffix identifies that suffix as the plural suffix. Of course, if there are no other suffixes in Hungarian that begin with a V followed by "k," then there is no need to limit the rule to apply only to the plural suffix vowel. In fact, if there are no vowel sequences in Hungarian, then we could simply say that vowels get lost after vowels. I have not found any examples of Hungarian words that have vowel sequences, but many words have long vowels (including [o:]). Thus, without the relevant knowledge of the phonological rules of Hungarian, I hesitate to simplify the statement of the rule above so drastically. Furthermore, this particular statement of the rule is useful for pedagogical purposes. So I will proceed with it.

Can you guess at a motivation for this vowel loss? Look at the syllable structures of the relevant words if vowel loss had not occurred as opposed to the structures with vowel loss. Without this vowel loss, we would have one syllable ending with a vowel (the final syllable of the root) followed by another syllable beginning with a vowel (the suffix syllable). But Hungarian does not allow an open syllable to be followed by a syllable that has no onset. Rather, syllables that lack an onset occur only in word-initial position. The motivation for this vowel loss rule, then, is the PHONOTACTIC constraint that disallows a sequence of two vowels belonging to different syllables.

But there is more to this vowel loss. Look at the words whose roots end in a vowel. What can you notice about the final vowel of the root after the plural suffix is added? It is always long, whether or not it was long before the plural suffix was added. Thus while the suffix vowel is lost, the time allotted to that suffix vowel, so to speak, its timing slot (a term we learned in the section "Vowels and Diphthongs" in Chapter 1), is not lost, and the final vowel of the root lengthens to fill that slot. (You can consider exactly how the rule that accomplishes this should be written after you have read the rest of this chapter.) You might object that if that is so, we would expect a long final root vowel to become somehow extra-long before the plural suffix. You're right. But Hungarian doesn't allow extra-long vowels. So, again, a phonotactic restriction is at play here.

Actually, this vowel loss rule is not purely phonological. A purely phonological rule concerns only information carried by sounds. But this rule cares not just about sound segments but also about whether those sound segments are part of an AFFIX (here the plural suffix) or part of the root. When we are talking about roots vs. affixes, we are talking about different types of MORPHEMES. Morphemes are often defined as the smallest meaningful units of language, and although that definition will not turn out to be adequate (as we will learn in Chapter 3, see particularly the discussion in the section "Productivity"), that definition can help you here. The symbol we will use for morpheme is "μ" (which is why the plural suffix has [μ plural] under it in our rule). **Many of the rules you will look at in this chapter are really MORPHOPHONOLOGICAL rules rather than phonological rules, per se. That is, they concern information carried by sounds and also information relating to morphemes** (such as the identification of particular morphemes or the recognition of morpheme boundaries). And, unfortunately, in order to talk about the range of phonological theories we need to talk about, we will be constantly making reference to morphemes.

I ask you to try to contain your frustration and use the definition of *morpheme* given here and pretty much fly by the seat of your pants on any issue regarding morphemes until we reach Chapter 3. And I apologize. **This book is organized into chapters that deal with the various COMPONENTS of the GRAMMAR—phonetics, phonology, morphology, SYNTAX (the study of putting words together into phrases and sentences), SEMANTICS (the study of how we interpret language)—where a grammar is a description of all of these components. Most introductory texts that I know of organize chapters in a similar way (although they may take up the components in a different order). However, this organization should not give you the impression that the components of the grammar are cleanly distinct, one from the other. They are not.** So in this chapter we get messy together as we discuss primarily, but not exclusively, phonology.

Epenthesis

What other types of sound changes might you expect to find in language? Again, play around with words in your casual speech and see if you can come up with any other types of differences when contrasting your casual speech to your formal speech. Let me get you started. Say these words in a casual way:

something   sherbet   burglar

Some (many?) people will pronounce them as:

[sʌmpθɪŋ]   [ʃʌɹbəɹt]   [bʌɹgɪ̯ələɹ]

What do you hear with these pronunciations that you might not hear with a fancy pronunciation? In the first word we have the EPENTHESIZED (or added) stop: [p]. In the second word, we have the epenthesized liquid in the second syllable: [ɹ]. In the third word, we have the epenthesized diphthong: [ɪ̯ə]. (If you don't recognize this pronunciation of *burglar* as one you've heard before, perhaps you'd like to substitute an analogous pronunciation of *nuclear*—[nuy̯kʰɪ̯ələɹ]—for it in the discussion below, with appropriate changes.)

You are going to look at the epenthesis of the stop in Problem Set 2.1. So let's now look closely at only the other two. Why do you think the extra liquid (the second [ɹ])appears in *sherbet*? Probably you think the liquid in the first syllable is influencing it. And I bet you're right. While I transcribed this word with a vowel plus a liquid, in my speech I really say it as [ʃɹ̩bɹ̩t]. I transcribed it as I did above only so that you could see the addition of the liquid without worrying immediately about the loss of any vowels. But now you can see that the vowel of each syllable gets lost. (In fact, I'm not sure anyone pronounces these vowels in this word. So you can consider my original transcription, [ʃʌɹbəɹt], as a notational variant of the real transcription, [ʃɹ̩bɹ̩t].) Furthermore, the loss of the vowel allows the liquid to slide into the nucleus as a syllabic consonant. Then both syllables have identical nuclei. And, importantly, the first syllable is open (the preferred syllable type), whereas, before vowel deletion and liquid syllabification, both syllables were closed.

What about the *burglar* example? Transcribe this word before epenthesis: [bʌɹgləɹ]. What type of syllable are both of these? Closed. When we add the diphthong, we create an open syllable in the middle of the word, but we still have a closed syllable on either side: [bəɹgɪ̯ələɹ]. Thus this epenthesis probably has a different motivation. Look again at the transcriptions before and after epenthesis. Before epenthesis the second syllable of the word has a cluster in its onset. After epenthesis, no syllable contains a cluster. Often epenthesis of vowels has precisely this effect: breaking up clusters. (Think about this pronunciation of the word *athlete*: [æθəlit].)

In fact, there is even more to say about this particular example. Consider the pronunciation with epenthesis. I transcribed it with vowels in all syllables for ease of exposition. But now let's transcribe it as it actually sounds, marking off every syllable: [bɹ̩.gɪ̯ə.lɹ̩]. What syllable type do all three syllables belong to? Open. In fact, even without epenthesis, we favor deletion of the vowels: [bɹ̩.glɹ̩]. Again, both syllables are open. Repeatedly we see sound changes (whether they be epenthesis or loss) that bring about the unmarked syllable type—that is, (C)V, an open syllable with no clusters.

Examples of epenthesis often involve vowels. In Yawelmani (a dialect of the Amerind language Yokuts, spoken in California) some verbs have roots that have two forms. One form has the structure CVCC and the other has the form CVCiC. We find the first form before suffixes that begin with a vowel and the second before suffixes that begin with a consonant, as in:

[ʔilk-al] 'might sing'   [ʔilik-hin] 'sings'
[logw-ol] 'might pulverize' [logiw-hin] 'pulverizes'
[lihm-al] 'might run'   [lihim-hin] 'runs'

(Here the - indicates the end of the verb root.) Write the vowel epenthesis rule with our formalism:

$$\varnothing \rightarrow i \;/\; C \underline{\hspace{1cm}} C + C$$

where + indicates the boundary between the root and the suffix. Actually, since we never find sequences of CCC in Yawelmani, the boundary symbol is not needed; this rule is purely phonological. We can rewrite it, then, as:

$$\varnothing \rightarrow i \;/\; C \underline{\hspace{1cm}} C \, C$$

What is the effect of this rule? What might motivate it? Think in terms of consonant clusters. If we didn't have this rule, when consonant-initial suffixes attached to roots of the form CVCC, a sequence of three consonants would be produced. This rule, then, prevents such sequences; it breaks up illicit consonant clusters.

Compensatory Lengthening

Sometimes a lengthening rule (which is, of course, a special type of addition rule) accompanies a loss rule. In Seri, a Hokan language of northwestern Mexico, the PREFIX *si-* goes on verb STEMS. (A stem is a root which might or might not have affixes already attached to it.) There is a class of verb stems for which something special happens with this prefix. If a verb stem in this class begins with a vowel, then when the prefix is attached, we get not *siV* at the start of the new word, but *ssV*. That is, the vowel of the prefix is deleted and the consonant of the prefix is lengthened. We could write this in two steps, where the + indicates the break between the prefix and the stem:

$$i \rightarrow \varnothing \;/\; s \underline{\hspace{1cm}} + V$$
$$\varnothing \rightarrow s \;/\; s \underline{\hspace{1cm}} + V$$

This kind of change, where something is lost and something else consequently lengthens, is called COMPENSATORY LENGTHENING. (Actually, it is possible to analyze this example as not involving compensatory lengthening, if the loss and the lengthening can be argued to be independent from one another. Then the two changes would be two rules, not two steps in a single rule. But we will not go into that, since our interest is just to demonstrate possible types of sound change, not to argue for a particular analysis of Seri verbs. If you want, you can look back at our discussion of the Hungarian plural suffix and consider the compensatory lengthening involved when the root ends in a vowel.)

This is all I'm going to say about compensatory lengthening right now, although we will discuss this type of rule later when we turn to metrical phonology. However, I'd like to leave you with a question to mull over: Why is it that sometimes deletion is accompanied by addition (that is, sometimes compensatory lengthening takes place) and other times deletion can happen without any compensatory addition? We have been searching hard for motivation for our phonological rules. One would hope to find motivation for the compensatory lengthening in Seri. One possibility is that Seri requires that prefixes be of a certain length—so that when deletion occurs in the example case above, addition must also occur to maintain that fixed prefix length. I have no idea whether this possible account is on the right track or not. But it is certainly a testable hypothesis, and it is an example of the kind of hypothesis I hope you will test when you go looking for motivation for whatever phonological rules you discover in your own research.

Metathesis

Another type of sound change can be found by looking at variations in our daily speech or at language mistakes or at children's language. Consider the child who says [pʰsgɛɾi] for *spaghetti*. Or the person who says [æks] for *ask*. What's going on in such examples? We have a reordering, or permutation, of the sound segments. This is called METATHESIS.

An interesting instance of metathesis arises in Hebrew. Typically when a verb is used reflexively (that is, when its Subject and an Object are coreferential, as in the English sentence *Susie likes herself*—you will learn about reflexives in the section "Reflexives" in Chapter 4), the prefix [hit] occurs on the verb stem:

Verb stem	With reflexive	Gloss
[konen]	[hitkonen]	'prepare'
[raʃam]	[hitraʃem]	'mark'
[mina]	[hitmana]	'appoint'

(There are some vowel changes that take place, as well, but we will ignore them here.) However, when the verb stem begins with [s], [ʃ], or [ʦ] (a dental voiceless affricate), we get metathesis of the final [t] of the prefix and the initial consonant of the stem:

[silek]	[histalek]	'remove'
[ʃina]	[hiʃtana]	'change'
[ʦarax]	[hitstarex]	'consume'

Assume that this metathesis is limited to the reflexive morpheme only. Assume further that it occurs only when the initial consonant of the stem is a sibilant. Now try to write the rule. The change here is not a feature change; just write it as the reversal of two segments. You might have written something like:

$$t \quad C \rightarrow C\,t\,/\,hi\underline{\quad\quad} + \underline{\quad\quad}$$
$$\begin{bmatrix} +\text{coronal} \\ +\text{strident} \end{bmatrix} \qquad\qquad [\mu\ \text{reflexive}]$$

The environment here tells us that a [t] in final position of the *hit* reflexive morpheme and a sibilant consonant in initial position of the next morpheme will undergo the rule. The morpheme *hit* does not occur as an independent reflexive marker; it prefixes only onto verb stems. Therefore, there is no need to mark the second morpheme in the environment as a verb stem.

Is there any simpler way to write this rule? Yes. It turns out that there are no other morphemes *hit* in Hebrew, so we needn't mention that this is the reflexive morpheme. Indeed, it appears that Hebrew avoids the sequence of /t/ followed by /s/ in general, so we might well be able to get away with writing this rule as a purely phonological rule—without any reference to morphemes or even morpheme boundaries at all. However, I have chosen to put in the morpheme information so that you can learn how to do that.

Dissimilation

There is yet another type of rule change, but it is relatively less common, and that is DISSIMILATION. Sounds can change in order to be unlike the sounds near them. So far we have looked at changes of segments. Now let's look at change of a different sort.

In the Balto-Slavic language Slovak adjectives agree with the nouns they modify for GENDER (and you will learn about agreement processes in several places in Chapters 3 and 4). There are three genders: masculine, FEMININE, and NEUTER. The root for the adjective meaning 'cruel,' for example, is [krut]. When this adjective modifies a masculine noun, it will be pronounced [kruti:]; when it modifies a feminine noun, it will be pronounced [kruta:]; when it modifies a neuter noun, it will be pronounced [krute:].

However, the root for the adjective meaning 'genuine' is [ri:ʒ]; and its masculine form is [ri:ʒi], the feminine [ri:ʒa], the neuter [ri:ʒe].

The issue for you is what determines whether the masculine, feminine, and neuter endings will be long vowels or short vowels. Consider these data, which are few but representative:

Masculine	Feminine	Neuter	Gloss
[druhi:]	[druha:]	[druhe:]	'other'
[tata:rski]	[tata:rska]	[tata:rske]	'Tartar'
[bi̯eli]	[bi̯ela]	[bi̯ele]	'white'
[tisi:tˢi]	[tisi:tˢa]	[tisi:tˢe]	'thousandth'
[zatʲati:]	[zatʲata:]	[zatʲate:]	'stubborn'

([tʲ] is a dental stop with a secondary articulation on the palate.) Can you see the pattern? Look at the vowels in the roots of these adjectives. When the last syllable of the root has a simple short vowel, the gender suffix is a long vowel. When the last syllable of the root has a long vowel or a diphthong, the gender suffix is a short vowel. Dissimilation here, then, is for duration (not for any segmental feature). (And notice that its effect is a rhythmic alternation. We will be talking about metrical alternations later.)

Let's try writing this rule with our formalism. Can you do it? We are stuck at the start for at least three reasons. First, we need a way to indicate that if the nucleus of the final syllable of the root is long, the suffix V is short and vice versa. We can borrow a symbol from mathematics, using $\pm$ as a value on one nucleus and $\mp$ as a value on the other nucleus (and it doesn't matter which nucleus gets which symbol), which means that if one nucleus has the value + for whatever feature we are interested in, the other has the value − and vice versa. Second, we need a way to indicate variable nucleus length. We have no such feature, and, indeed, phonological theory does not provide us with such a feature. Instead, we will learn a way to handle duration that is more perspicuous later. For the moment, however, we will make up—but only temporarily and only for this one example—a feature that we will call [±duration]. Third, we need a way to indicate a syllable nucleus so that we can then talk about its duration. Let's, just for this single example, use the symbol N for syllable nucleus. Okay, now I think we should be able to write the rule:

$$N[\overline{+}\text{duration}] / \quad N \quad (C_0) + \underline{\qquad}$$
$$[\pm\text{duration}] \quad [\mu \text{ gender}]$$

Did you come up with something like this? Recall that a subscript of zero after the symbol C indicates any number of consonants from zero up. Syllable structure constraints in the particular language will limit the upper number.

Now, even though we can write this rule with our linear formalism, we had to make crucial and disturbing adjustments to do so. We introduced a feature of duration, but unlike our other features, this one concerns not quality but quantity. And unlike the other features we've discussed, duration made reference not to a single segment (here a V), but to the nucleus of a syllable, which can consist of more than one segment. This is a less-than-perspicuous way of going about this problem, and, indeed, phenomena that involve changes in duration like this one provide strong evidence that a linear approach to phonological rules is inadequate.

Let me point out that what Slovak is doing here is in no way unnatural or unusual for a phonological process. When we talked about heavy syllables above, we noted that languages treat syllables with long vowels or diphthongs the same way (regardless of the language's particular definition of syllable weight). Here, again, we see sensitivity to long vowels and diphthongs as a group. So phonological theory needs to face the issue of how to properly treat quantity.

If we write both a long vowel and a diphthong as two vowel slots, then we can say for Slovak that if the root's last syllable has two vowel slots, the suffix consists of one vowel slot. And if the root's last syllable has one vowel slot, the suffix consists of two vowel slots. This way of thinking will allow us to see the phenomenon as operating on the timing of the word rather than on the quality of the sounds.

Is there any sense in which we can say that the suffix has an underlying vowel length? That is, is there any reason you can see to propose that the suffix is underlyingly long or underlyingly short? No. Instead, the length of the vowel in this gender suffix is under-specified (a term we learned in Chapter 1), and it gets determined totally by the root it attaches to. We showed that in the way we wrote our (very unfortunate) linear rule above. And we must remember to hold onto that insight as we consider alternative ways to approach such phenomena.

Before we go on with this line of discussion, let me interrupt to say that **we have discussed seven different types of sound change—assimilation, palatalization, loss, epenthesis, compensatory lengthening, metathesis, and dissimilation—and we will not discuss any other types.** But these are not the only types of sound change. They are merely representative, not exhaustive. Now let us return to our discussion.

The notion of underspecification is not new to you. We recognized in Chapter 1 that the liquids and the glides do not have a well-defined place of articulation out of context. Rather, they take on a place based on the sounds around them. We can say that they are underspecified for place of articulation. In general, if a certain feature of a sound segment or of a morpheme is predictable from context, we say that that segment or morpheme is underspecified for that feature in UR. In fact, we speak of UNDERSPECIFICATION THEORY and we say that one of the principles of this theory is that at UR we have no redundant (or predictable) features present.

Let's think about what we mean when we talk about underspecification regarding place of articulation. Nowhere yet have we said that place of articulation was a single feature. Instead, if you did Problem Set 1.5, you realized that several features directly or indirectly pertain to place of articulation. They are: anterior, labial, back, and coronal. You might be surprised at the inclusion of coronality here, since this feature is relevant to what part of the tongue is used in making a sound—and we have called the tongue an articulator, not a place of articulation. But notice that the blade of the tongue cannot be involved in sounds made far back on the palate. So if a sound is [+coronal], we know that it is made at or in front of the palate. (You might think that similar remarks hold of the feature highness, however, we will replace the feature [high] with a new feature when we talk about sounds made with the dorsum of the tongue. So, for now, we won't consider highness.)

If sounds are going to be underspecified for place of articulation, then we might well find it useful to have a way to group the features relevant to place, and this interest can serve to bring us now to a discussion of another theory of phonology: GEOMETRIC PHONOLOGY.

Geometric Phonology

Look back at the rules we've written so far in this chapter. We wrote them as rules that change features or that add, delete, or permute sound segments. Consider for a moment just the rules we wrote as feature-changing rules. They were typically rules of assimilation. Dissimilation, while it happens, is much less common in language. Now ask yourself: Is there another way we could look at assimilation besides as a feature-changing rule? Think about the elegance that underspecifying segments gives to our rules. If we underspecify for a predictable feature, then assimilation isn't really changing the feature, after all. Instead, assimilation is assigning a feature. And the feature it is assigning is the same feature that some nearby segment has. (That's what assimilation is all about.) We can think of assimilation then as a SPREADING rule, if you will, where the features ASSOCIATED with a given segment spread so that they become associated with another nearby segment, as well.

Given the assimilation rules we've discussed in this chapter so far (in the section "Assimilation"), we can see that voicing, continuancy, and place, at a minimum, must be able to spread. And shortly below you will learn that laterality and nasality also must be able to spread (and you'll learn more about nasality spreading in Problem Set 2.6). It is quite possible that you may come across languages in which other features spread.

What does this mean? So far we have considered features as inherent to individual segments. The idea that the feature on one segment could spread so that it associates with another segment as well means that we have to look at features in a new way. We have to entertain the possibility that features are somehow independent of segments. Theories of phonology that consider features as independent in this way are called AUTOSEGMENTAL theories, with the idea that any feature is potentially an autosegment, an independent (that is, autonomous) creature that has a phonological reality independent of the segment it associates with.

This idea should not be entirely foreign to you. In Chapter 1 we discussed some characteristics of speech that pertain to a larger domain than just individual sound segments. One of them was pitch. We can talk about pitch rising or falling or staying steady over a single segment or over a series of segments (perhaps a syllable) or over a whole word or even a whole phrase. Say the sentence *Janie left town* as a declarative statement. Now say it as a question. Now say it as an exclamation of dismay or disbelief. Your pitch contour varies and it isn't helpful to talk about the pitch on each individual sound segment of the utterance when comparing declaratives to questions or exclamations. Instead, we talk about the PITCH CONTOUR or the INTONATION CONTOUR of the whole utterance. For this reason pitch has been called a suprasegmental feature (as you learned in the section "Acoustic Phonetics" of Chapter 1).

Voicing, continuancy, nasality, laterality, and other such features are unlike the suprasegmentals in that they tend to have more restrictive domains. They never spread across whole utterances, for example. Yet, like the suprasegmentals, these autosegments can have a wider domain than just a single segment.

Let's start over again. When we hear a word like *ran*, for example, what are the most fundamental things, what we might think of as the skeletal things, we know about the segments that make up this word? Since voicing can spread, we know voicing is an autosegment, so let's not include voicing. Likewise, we won't include continuancy or nasality or any features relating to place of articulation. So what remains?

Well, we might mention the feature of sonority. After all, sonority is one of the most important features we have seen in that it is a crucial factor in syllable structure. But even sonority has been argued to be an autosegment (though this is a controversial question). In Finnish, for example, we find that an oral stop assimilates to a preceding nasal, as in the following examples, where we have a verb stem plus an INFLECTIONAL suffix (and we'll talk about inflection in the section "Cycles and the Strict Cycle Condition" later, but you'll have to wait until the section "Inflectional vs. Derivational" in Chapter 3 to learn about it in detail), yielding a new form:

[huonompa + n] → [huonomman] 'bad'
[isäntä + n] → [isännän] 'host'

But an oral stop also assimilates to a preceding liquid:

[virta + n] → [virran] 'to chirp'
[haltu + n] → [hallun] 'possession'

If we want to see this as a single process (and you should be able to give a few reasons why it would be uninsightful not to see this as a single process), then we need to recognize that the sonorant consonants are the ones that trigger the rule: Sonority is spreading. More than sonority spreads, however, because sometimes we see a [t] becoming an [n] and sometimes we see a [t] becoming an [l] or [r]. In other words, [t] can become any sonorant that is homorganic to it. What determines which sonorant it will become? The preceding sonorant, of course. So the features nasal and lateral are also spreading. (Stop now and explain why if nasal and lateral do not spread, but only sonority spreads, [t] will become

[r]. Do you see? [r] is the only dental sonorant that is neither lateral nor nasal. So if the dental [t] becomes sonorant, but not lateral or nasal, it will become [r]. And that's why we do not have to mention any fourth feature in this spreading rule.)

One could, alternatively, say that sonority is not an autosegment and, instead, we have total assimilation in these Finnish examples, triggered by the sonority of the first consonant. We will return to this alternative after we have considered Figure 2.1.

So what can we say the word *ran* consists of if we want to talk about only the skeleton without the autosegments? Surely by now, given that the manner feature of lateral can spread, you suspect that other manner features such as continuancy can also spread. And you're right. Recall our lenition rule in Spanish—that was a spreading rule for the feature of continuancy. So, we're back to that question: What remains? What is truly skeletal?

You might now want to say that the fundamental distinction in sound segments is whether they are consonants or vowels. That seems undeniable at first: let's say that the skeleton of the word *ran* is CVC. This seems clear enough.

But other words are not so easily analyzed in this way. Consider the word *boot*. Transcribe it. [buʊt]. Is the skeleton of this word CVVC? Do you feel entirely comfortable with that analysis? The problem here is the status of the nonsyllabic vowel. We in fact have not yet spoken of two features that can be quite useful: CONSONANTAL and VOCALIC. (Theories of phonology vary on whether both of these features are necessary or simply one. We will use both here without entering the debate.) The nonsyllabic segment that is part of a diphthong or triphthong is often said to be [−consonantal, −vocalic]. So should it be represented as a V just like the syllabic V preceding it in *boot*, or should it be represented as a C just like the C that ends the word *boot*, or is neither completely satisfactory? (After you've done Problem Set 2.2, you can return to this question.)

And what about the word *work*? Transcribe it. [wɹ̩k]. Should this word be represented as having the skeleton CCC? Is the syllabic liquid there to be represented in the same way as the preceding and following nonsyllabic consonants?

Because of questions such as these, we need to augment the features of consonantal and vocalic with the feature of syllabic if we are to put into our skeletal representation the real information we are after. (Please note: The decision to adopt a feature for syllabicity goes against the mainstream. I have justified this decision. But you should realize that most of the literature on phonology will not talk about syllabicity as an autosegment.) We can say that the third segment of *boot* is [+vocalic, −syllabic] and the second segment of *work* is [+consonantal, +syllabic]. So just writing CVVC or CCC alone isn't enough. We need to add the feature of syllabic.

But is the feature of syllabic truly inherent to an individual segment? Look back at our discussion of *burglar*. We said that a common pronunciation is [bɹ̩glɹ̩]. In both syllables a vowel has deleted. But when the vowel deleted, the following liquid became the nucleus of the syllable. It took on the feature of [+syllabic]. But where did that feature come from? I hope you can see it: When the vowel deleted, the feature of syllabicity was not deleted along with it. This feature remained behind and later got associated with the liquid. We can see, therefore, that the feature of syllabicity was stable; it had the property we call STABILITY. **All autosegments have stability in this way; they remain, even if the segment they were associated with deletes.** Only if they never get reassociated with any other segment will they then delete themselves.

So even syllabicity is not inherent to a segment. And without syllabicity it is difficult for us to give satisfactory skeletons in terms of Cs and Vs for all words. Yet we do know that there are three segments in *ran* and *work* and four in *boot*. These segments take up time. So let's represent them simply as Xs, where an X stands for a timing unit. And let's define the representation of this information as being the SKELETAL or TIMING TIER.

timing tiers for: *ran*   *work*   *boot*
XXX   XXX   XXXX

This is the tack we will take for a while in our discussion. However, in many words the issues outlined about the differences between consonants and vowels do not arise. Therefore in many linguistics books and articles you will find the skeletal tier made up of a sequence of C's and V's. And we will present that view later, as well. But for now let's be very careful and use only X's to represent timing slots.

A sequence of X's makes up our timing tier. All the other information that tells us about the sounds of these words will be located on other tiers. We will have a tier for nasality and a tier for continuancy. We will draw ASSOCIATION LINES from these tiers to our timing tier. Let's do that for the word *ran*, and for simplicity's sake let's draw these association lines now only when a feature has the value +:

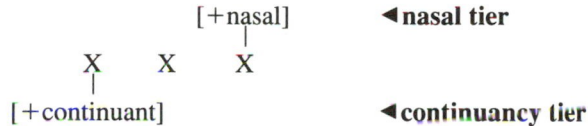

Recall that all vowels are continuous in the oral cavity, so we do not typically talk about the feature of continuancy for vowels. For that reason, I have not associated the feature of [+continuant] with the middle timing slot here. However, if I were going to use that feature of the vowel in a rule, then I would certainly make that association line in my representation. Look back at our discussion of the lenition rule that turned stops into fricatives in Spanish. This happened after continuants, whether those continuants were consonants or vowels. In writing the rule for lenition, we would certainly associate the feature of [+continuant] with the timing slot that the vowel occupied. So unless you want to draw in every single feature on every single tier (and I promise you, you don't), you need to use common sense in your representation, which typically means that you'll draw in only those features you are about to use somehow.

What other tiers will we have? We have already seen that we need a lateral tier. And we have seen that we need tiers for the various places of articulation.

Let's explore place-of-articulation tiers, starting from the front of the mouth and going inward. First, we'll need a tier for labial, which will pull together our bilabial and labiodental sounds, as well as [w] and the [+round] vowels. Second, we'll need a tier for coronal, which will pull together the interdentals, the dentals, and the alveolars (which are all [+anterior]), as well as the postalveolars. Third, we'll need a tier for sounds made with the dorsum of the tongue, a feature we'll label [DORSAL], which will pull together the palatal and velar consonants as well as the vowels. And, finally, we'll need a tier labeled [PHARYNGEAL] for sounds made in the pharyngeal area or that involve advanced tongue root.

You might wonder why we've introduced the feature [+dorsal] rather than making use of the feature [+high] that we already know. The two features are not interchangeable. High consonants are made with a raised blade or back of the tongue. The crucial factor is the height of the tongue—not, really, the point of articulation. But in geometric phonology we are looking not at the height of the tongue, but rather at what part of the tongue is used in making a sound and the place on the roof of the mouth where the tongue makes (or almost makes) contact. So while the two features are quite similar, they are actually different in concept—and only the feature [±dorsal] is applied to consonants in geometric phonology.

You might well wonder how linguists came to precisely these four place tiers: labial, coronal, dorsal, pharyngeal. Certainly if you were asked to name the place tiers, you might have come up with more and different ones. You might, for example, have suggested an anterior tier, to pull together all sounds made at or in front of the alveolar ridge. The matter is an empirical one, and as phonologists have examined phonological rules of more types in more languages, the proposals of which tiers we really need have changed. The four listed here are widely believed to be needed as of the writing of this book.

But the matter of place is even more complex. We find that sometimes all the relevant place features can spread together. Thus we posit another type of tier, what might be called a CLASS tier or a NODE, which lacks content in itself but on which the four tiers of labial, coronal, dorsal, and pharyngeal are DEPENDENT. That way, if, for example, a rule spreads both the labial feature of [+round] and the dorsal feature of [+high], we can say that the whole place node, with all the dependent tiers associated to it, spreads.

The place node isn't the only node. Phonologists have posited a laryngeal node, attached to which are the three tiers of spread glottis (for [h] and all aspirated sounds), constricted glottis (for [ʔ] and all glottalized sounds), and voicing. (You'll explore data that make use of the existence of the laryngeal tier in Problem Set 2.6.) And some phonologists have posited a SUPRALARYNGEAL node to DOMINATE the place node, but we will not make use of such a node in this book.

You might ask whether or not there is a manner node to which the features having to do with manner of airflow attach, such as laterality, stridency, nasality, continuancy. Thus far there is no clear evidence that the manner features group together to act as a unit in phonological rules such as spreading. Accordingly, we will not assume a manner node. In fact, some manner features are relatively uninteresting from the perspective of geometric phonology. The feature of stridency, for example, does not seem to spread, so often linguists will leave it out entirely when drawing a representation of the phonological nodes and tiers.

We should try now to draw such a representation. But let me warn you that it gets quite tricky trying to draw a representation of the interaction of these nodes (these class tiers) and their dependent tiers. You need a little skill at drawing planes and lines. Thus autosegmental theory has, suitably, also been called geometric phonology, and linguists talk of FEATURE GEOMETRY. Rather than my attempting to draw a three-dimensional sketch of this theory, I will give a no-frills model in Figure 2.1 and let the description I've given here fill in the three-dimensionality of it. The only new matters in this figure are the root node, to which the laryngeal and place nodes attach, and the various tiers for manner features and all other features that do not seem to group together (that is, that do not seem to be dependent on a class tier). This shows that the back tier, for example, is associated to the root node only via the dorsal tier and the place node. It also shows that the feature of anteriority, for example, is only interesting if we are discussing a coronal sound. (This is sensible, since if we have a labial sound, it is automatically [+anterior], and if we have a dorsal or pharyngeal sound, it is automatically [−anterior].)

I have placed the features of sonority and consonantality on either side of the root node to indicate that these two features are considered to belong to the skeletal tier. And, while

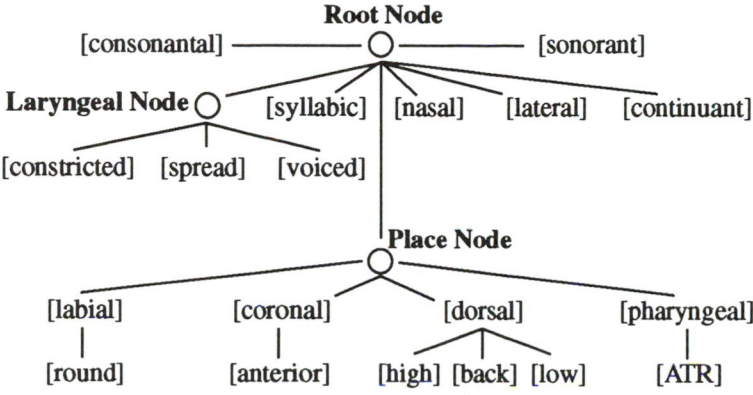

Figure 2.1. No-frills model of the tiers of geometric phonology.

we have discussed the need for both the features of consonantality and syllabicity, most diagrams of the features in autosegmental phonology leave out the feature of syllabicity entirely, equating the feature value of [−consonantal] with [+syllabic]. (I have not done that precisely so that you can see syllabic consonants as being [+consonantal, +syllabic].)

Let me emphasize that how many nodes and tiers there are and how they interrelate is a matter for debate and the specific feature geometry will undoubtedly change as we learn more about phonology. However, the hope is that all languages will arrange the tiers and nodes identically. And it is the existence of the arrangement, not the particular arrangement itself, that gives the theory its value. The beauty of geometric phonology lies in the organization it imposes on features, which determines what groups of features may spread simultaneously, for example.

What kinds of predictions does the theory make, given the geometry in Figure 2.1? First, let's be very specific. Look back at our discussion of the Finnish examples in which an oral stop assimilated to a preceding nasal or liquid. Does our theory predict that such a rule should be possible? And, if so, what node or tier(s) spreads? The features involved (sonority, nasality, laterality) are directly dependent on the root node in Figure 2.1. So all we need to say is that the root node spreads when an oral stop follows a nasal or liquid in the right environment (that is, when we have a verbal stem and an inflectional suffix). If the root node spreads, we get total assimilation.

Now let's consider some general predictions of the theory. We've already seen one, from the principle of stability. If a segment is deleted, the features associated with it might wind up reassociating with a different segment. We saw that happen for the feature of syllabicity. Stability is usually illustrated, however, with examples from TONE LAN-GUAGES.

In a tone language differences of pitch are distinctive in the same way differences of features such as voicing or place are distinctive in English. (Recall that pitch—which is the basis for tone—has to do with the frequency of a sound, and you are familiar with pitch from intonation contours and from singing. Stress, on the other hand, has to do with intensity—that is, loudness—and perhaps, also, with pitch.) For example, in Yoruba, a member of the Niger-Congo family and spoken primarily in the southwestern part of Nigeria, we find the minimal pair:

[kó]   'build'   [kò]   'refuse'

(These words are usually written with a dot below the mid back round vowel, indicating that it is [−ATR]. We won't make use of this detail, so I have omitted it here. In fact, it is not clear that there really is an articulatory distinction between vowels with and without the dot. Instead, the dot may simply be an orthographic convention.)

The ACUTE accent over the vowel in the first word indicates a HIGH TONE ([+hi tone]). The GRAVE accent over the vowel in the second word indicates a LOW TONE ([+lo tone]). (And if we were to draw a feature geometry for Yoruba or any other language that made use of tones, we would include a tone node.) Use your common sense and answer this question: In tone languages will the tone be absolute or relative? That is, will a person have to hit a certain note, for example, in order to say a word such as [kó], or will a person merely have to produce a higher tone on that word than the tone used in saying [kò]? Certainly, people who can't produce fixed musical notes on command are common. So any language that required people to do that would be dooming some speakers to relative incomprehensibility. We wouldn't expect language to do that. Indeed, all tone languages use relative distinctions in pitch, never absolute distinctions. (So if you can't carry a tune, don't worry, you can still learn to speak Yoruba.)

Now tell me, which sound of these words do you think carries the tone, the [k] or the vowel? While you may well have answered, "The vowel," and you would have been right, this answer is much less obvious than the answer to the previous question. If you'll remember from Chapter 1, languages vary enormously in their uses of the consonants, in particular. In some languages, only vowels can be syllable nuclei. In English, vowels and the sonorant consonants other than glides can be nuclei. And in some languages, any consonant whatsoever can be a syllable nucleus. So you might wonder if consonants could carry tone. In fact, both vowels and syllabic consonants can carry tone. And when we hear a tone language, we typically "hear" the tones as belonging to or characterizing whole syllables.

Now if a language were to have only two tones, high and low, we would need to speak about only one feature (we might call low tones [−hi tone]), and in our orthography we would probably indicate only the high tone. But some tone languages have three tones, and the intermediate one is called MID and is either not orthographically marked or is indicated with a MACRON. Yoruba is a three-tone language, and we have, in fact, a third word that minimally contrasts with the pair above for tone:

[kō]   'sing'

Other languages may have four or even five tone levels, and linguists often represent these distinctions by using numbers.

Besides having a single tone, syllabic segments may also have COMPLEX or CONTOUR tones in many languages. In Tangsic, a Wu dialect of Chinese, we find RISING TONES (a combination of L(ow) followed by H(igh)) and FALLING TONES (a combination of H followed by L) as well as LEVEL TONES:

rising: L   H   **falling:** H   L
               _/   _/
        [dhu] 'large'   [ka] 'artificial'

(Actually, the two tones on the first word here are less far apart in pitch than the two tones on the second word, but that is extraneous to our point.)

One of the major breakthroughs in phonological theory that allowed linguists to recognize that features were autosegmental was the discovery that tones display stability. So if a tone-bearing unit is deleted, the tone may well reassociate with a neighboring syllable, and the result can be a contour tone. Can you explain why? If a syllable has L tone, for example, and the nucleus of the preceding syllable, which is H let us say, deletes, then the FLOATING H tone may well DOCK onto the following syllable. But then that syllable will have HL associated with it—so it will be a falling tone.

Tones can also spread. Thus there are tone languages in which some syllables or even whole words are unmarked for tone underlyingly, and the tone of the syllable preceding these syllables or words will spread onto them. It is easy to see why the study of tone languages led to the theory of geometric phonology.

Whether we are talking about tones or any other autosegmental feature, there are certain conventions that linguists have found to prevail. One is that **association lines don't cross.** We assign features on a given tier, say Tier 1, to positions on another tier (usually on the timing tier), say Tier 2, **mapping left to right (or, in the marked case, right to left).**

$$
\begin{array}{llllll}
\text{Tier 1} & x & x & x & x & x \\
& | & | & | & | & | \\
\text{Tier 2} & y & y & y & y & y
\end{array}
$$

(Here I have used "x" to indicate the feature of Tier 1 and "y" to indicate positions on Tier 2.) If some position on Tier 2 does not get the particular feature from Tier 1 assigned to it, then it will either surface without that feature or that feature will spread onto it from the closest spot on Tier 1:

$$
\begin{array}{llllll}
\text{Tier 1} & x & x & x & & x \\
& | & | & |\!\!\searrow & & | \\
\text{Tier 2} & y & y & y & y & y
\end{array}
$$

Here the feature x associated with the third position on Tier 2 has spread onto the fourth position on Tier 2.

Okay, let's go back to our devoicing rule for [l] in English and reconsider it:

$$
l \rightarrow [-\text{voiced}] \, / \quad \underset{[-\text{voiced}]}{C} \quad \underline{\hspace{2cm}}
$$

Describe what this rule does in our new terminology. The feature of voicelessness spreads from a consonant onto a following [l]. Let's write this rule now using feature geometry. To simplify it, we can simply put [l] on our timing tier. Furthermore, since it is only voicing that spreads, let's ignore all the other tiers entirely. **We draw horizontal double bars through an association line to show that it is being dissociated by our rule. We draw broken lines to show association that comes about by our rule.** Try writing the rule now. You should have come up with something like:

$$
\begin{array}{cc}
X & \qquad l \\
| & \nearrow\!\!\!\diagup \\
| \diagup & \ddagger \\
[-\text{voiced}] & [+\text{voiced}]
\end{array}
$$

What does the X in this geometric formulation correspond to in the linear formulation above? The X corresponds to the C that is [−voiced]. Since English does not generally have voiceless vowels, no problem arises by using merely X (a timing slot) for the context of this rule. What indicates the structural change (that is, what indicates the change from [+voiced] to [−voiced] on [l]) in the geometric rule? The broken association line from the feature [−voiced] to [l] shows that [l] becomes voiceless, and the double horizontal bars on the association line from the feature [+voiced] to [l] show that the feature of voicing is dissociated from [l]. These association lines do the job that the arrow did in the linear formulation. (Once you have done Problem Set 2.4, you'll be able to come back and rewrite this rule without having to put in [l]—and you'll do this in Problem Set 2.5.)

We can now also write the rule that turns [bʌɹgləɹ] into [bɹ̩glɹ̩]. For the sake of allowing us to focus on the changes only, let's fill the timing tier with the actual IPA symbols for each consonant and vowel. And since syllabicity is the only feature we are concerned with, let's ignore all other tiers:

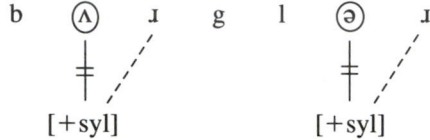

The circles around the vowels indicate that these segments are deleted. Can you see that the feature of syllabicity is being dissociated from the vowels (which delete) and associated with the following [ɹ]?

Does this rule apply just to the word *burglar*? Of course not. In general, certain lax vowels before an [ɹ] delete and the liquid becomes syllabic. So let's rewrite the rule to mention only the relevant segments. But what are the relevant segments? If the rule deletes only certain lax vowels and spreads syllabicity only to [ɹ], we can simply write the rule as below, where I am encoding the feature of [−consonantal] into the symbol V:

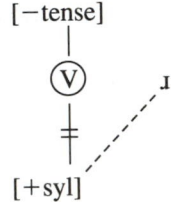

(For the sake of simplicity, I am ignoring the fact that not all lax vowels undergo the rule. I am also not considering the issue of whether the feature of [−tense] associates rightward here, since [ɹ] is [−tense] anyway.)

But is the rule so restrictive? Consider other words that have syllabic consonants in English, words like *label*, *little*, *riddle*. I am not sure if this is the same rule, but if it is, the rule also takes place with [l]. How could we lump together these liquids with features? One way would just be to say there is a feature called [+liquid] or [+approximant] (but [+approximant] would also include the glides, of course). Most linguists do not do this, however. Instead, the liquids would be identified as having the features [+sonorant, +consonantal, −nasal]. We can therefore rewrite the rule more generally. For the sake of expediency again, let's use the symbol C on the timing tier for a segment with the feature [+consonantal], just as we use V to encode [−consonantal].

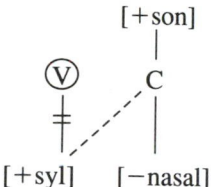

Notice that this does not mean that the features of [+syl] and [−nasal] are on the same tier. Rather, I have put nasality below the timing tier and sonority above it simply to show that these two features are on separate tiers.

Comparing Linear with Geometric Phonology

Of the seven types of rules we have talked about (loss, epenthesis, assimilation, dissimilation, palatalization, metathesis, and compensatory lengthening), which types will be perspicaciously handled by geometric phonology and which seem to you to be equally well handled by linear phonology? Certainly assimilation processes are clearly handled better with geometric phonology, and we already saw that the case of assimilation of oral stops in certain Finnish verb inflections was simply and efficiently handled by spreading the root node. Likewise those instances of palatalization that are assimilation processes are also handled better by geometric phonology. But what about the others?

Since dissimilation involves checking features and changing feature association in such a way that a given segment contrasts with a nearby segment with respect to a particular feature, we could say that geometric phonology, with its feature geometry, should make the nature of the change more apparent.

In fact, dissimilation brings up an interesting theoretical point. In the analysis of tonal languages, it has been proposed that there is an OBLIGATORY CONTOUR PRINCIPLE which bans adjacent identical tones on the tonal tier of a lexical item at UR. So if a word consists of three syllables which have the tones HHL, for example, we would analyze it as underlyingly having only the tonal melody HL, where the first high spreads to cover both of the first two syllables. That is, we would not allow the underlying level to contain two H-tone autosegments in a row.

Dissimilation is an interesting process to consider in similar terms. Some phonologists have claimed that the Obligatory Contour Principle operates on tiers other than the tonal tier. I think dissimilation is responding to something very much like that principle, although, clearly, much more weakly, since dissimilation is not a common process in language. I leave this line of inquiry to the student of phonology. (I return to it briefly in Problem Set 2.6.)

What about loss? Certainly, the loss of a segment off the timing tier is equally handled by either theory. But consider again our analysis of *burglar*. With geometric phonology, we can see the change from coda position to nuclear position of the liquid in each syllable as part of the same process that deletes the vowel—because the floating feature of [+syllabic] docks onto that liquid. With linear phonology, we would have had to write this whole process as two separate rules, where the deletion had to precede the syllabification rule and where the connection between the two was in no way transparent from the formalism. So even loss rules can sometimes be much better handled in geometric phonology.

As for epenthesis, you can consider the value of writing certain epenthesis rules in one theory vs. the other after you have done Problem Sets 2.1 and 2.6. I urge you to come back to this question at that time.

Let's now consider compensatory lengthening, whereby when one segment deletes, a neighboring segment lengthens. Think about this. Where is the deletion taking place? In these instances, is anything being lost off the timing tier? Clearly not. That's the whole point. The timing tier keeps the same number of slots. But one slot (the locus of deletion, you might say) gets dissociated from all features that it was originally associated to. Then the features of a neighboring slot on the timing tier spread onto that slot. So geometric phonology once more allows us to conflate two rules of linear phonology into one process. Without the notion of the timing tier, it would be difficult to make sense out of a process like compensatory lengthening, but with this notion we might even have predicted such processes would take place.

What about metathesis? If you are stumped in trying to find some way that metathesis is better handled by one theory or the other, that's okay because I am, too. You might keep this question in mind if you go on with phonology.

In general linguists today agree about the advantages of geometric phonology over linear phonology. Nevertheless, you need to feel comfortable using both theories because you need access to literature written in both theories. Also, you will find that sometimes even more recent phonology articles will write a rule in linear formalism because the geometric formalism for that particular rule would shed no extra light on the actual workings of the rule and would, in fact, be rather unwieldy to draw. So linear formalism can be used for the sake of clear exposition or expediency.

Metrical Phonology

We're going to backtrack a bit now in order to take off in a different direction. In looking at feature geometry, we broke down sounds into small units that we call autosegments. It's time now to look at larger units. We already noticed early in our discussion that matters larger than just segments and autosegments affect rules of phonology. In particular, we noticed that syllable structure can be the motive behind a given phonological rule. This is particularly true, of course, of rules of loss or epenthesis. We have, therefore, talked about four different levels of structure so far: segments (including autosegments), moras (recall that a light syllable consists of one mora and a heavy syllable consists of two moras), syllables, and words.

Within each of these levels, we can compare items for relative PROMINENCE. For example, let's compare segments on the timing tier. Those that are associated with the feature [+syllabic] are more prominent than the others. As a shorthand way of saying this, we will say syllabic segments are more prominent than nonsyllabic ones (rather than saying timing slots that have the feature [+syllabic] associated with them are more prominent than timing slots without it). And notice that a syllabic segment will always constitute a mora.

With moras, those that consist of or contain (in the case of diphthongs) the syllabic segment will be more prominent than those that consist of the material in the syllable coda.

Now consider syllables. First, you tell me: In the word *friendly*, which syllable seems to you to be prominent? The first. Why? Because it's stressed. So highly stressed syllables are more prominent than weakly stressed or unstressed ones.

We should at this point stop a moment and take up an issue we haven't really faced explicitly: exactly what is stress? If you look back at Figure 1.9 you may notice several physical correlates of stress. In English, stressed vowels often get higher pitch and greater intensity than unstressed vowels in the same word. But this is not a necessity across languages. In Italian, stressed vowels in non-final open syllables are typically longer than unstressed ones (and if you did Problem Set 1.6, you can see this in Figure 1.14). But that's not true (at least not to the same degree) in languages which have distinctive vowel length, such as Finnish. In fact, some linguists have argued that there are no fixed physical correlates of stress across languages. Instead, they say, stress is an integral part of rhythmic structure, and since languages organize their rhythmic structure differently (as you will learn later), stress will be manifested differently across languages.

Okay, so let's return to our discussion of English. We were talking about monosyllabic and disyllabic words. But not all words consist of just one or two syllables. Consider the word *Mississippi*. We have four syllables here. Which is the most prominent? The third. That syllable carries the primary stress. If you can't hear that, try humming the word. Can you hear it now? But there is a SECONDARY STRESS on this word, as well. On which syllable? The first. We analyze this word into two FEET of two syllables each, in which the first syllable of each foot is the prominent one. A foot is the next-larger rhythmic unit after the syllable (and much of the discussion that follows will help you to understand feet). A foot cannot contain more than one stressed (primary or secondary) syllable by definition, although we will find occasion to talk of feet that have no stressed syllables.

So now we have one more level to consider: the foot. And when we compare the two feet of the word *Mississippi*, we can easily see that the last foot, which consists of the final two syllables and which contains the primary stress, is prominent, right?

We can certainly also compare the relative prominence of words within a phrase, but right now let's stop and limit ourselves to a discussion of the prominence relations only up to the level of the word. What we have been talking about is matters of rhythm or meter, the study of which is called PROSODY. We say that the mora (symbolized with μ—the same symbol for morpheme, unfortunately), the syllable (symbolized with σ), the foot (symbolized with F), and the PROSODIC WORD (symbolized with Pw) are the levels from smallest to largest (or lowest to highest) in the PROSODIC HIERARCHY:

Pw   prosodic word
F   foot
σ syllable
μ mora

Given what we know so far, you can identify the unit Pw with the unit of the lexical word. But when we turn to lexical phonology, you will find that there can be a difference between prosodic words and lexical words. (In particular, the prosodic word is the domain of rules that affect stress. But a lexical word may contain some material in addition to the Pw—that is, it may contain affixes that are not seen by the rules that affect stress.)

Let's analyze a given word into these prosodic units. The various levels for *Mississippi*, [mɪsəsɪpi], are:

Pw		[mɪsəsɪpi]			
F	(two feet)	mɪsə		sɪpi	
σ	(four syllables)	mɪ	sə	sɪ	pi
μ	(four moras)	mɪ	sə	sɪ	pi

The levels in the prosodic hierarchy form the DOMAINS relevant to stress or rhythm in a language. And the theory of METRICAL PHONOLOGY accounts for patterns of stress and rhythm.

While the theory of geometric phonology supplanted the theory of linear phonology, the theory of metrical phonology exists side by side with the theory of geometric phonology. The two theories complement each other and handle different sorts of phenomena. Geometric phonology, for example, handles rules of spreading or loss, and metrical phonology handles rules that apply strictly to prosodic domains, being sensitive to and/or affecting the relative prominence of them.

Actually, while it is clear that the prosodic domains of μ, σ, F, and Pw, exist, not all languages make use of all of them in assigning stress. In fact, some languages have phonemic stress—that is, each lexical item comes with a stress that is not predictable. So there are no rules that assign stress in these languages. Spanish is a language whose primary stress is (most probably) phonemic: While it is true that primary stress in Spanish must occur only on one of the last three syllables of a word, we cannot predict which of those syllables it will occur on from looking at the phonological shape of the word. Secondary stress in Spanish, however, is predictable. So a language may lack stress assignment rules entirely or only for primary stress (or, quite commonly, only for secondary stress). In other languages, some morphemes have phonemic stress and others are assigned stress by rule, as in Vedic, a variety of Sanskrit (the ancient Indo-European language of India), and in the Baltic language Lithuanian of Lithuania.

But even among languages that have predictable primary stress throughout the lexicon, the rules that assign stress vary from one language to another, particularly as to which prosodic domains they are sensitive to. One important distinction is at the lowest level: Most languages pay attention to the number of moras in a syllable when assigning stress, but there are some that don't. Since a syllable that contains two moras is a heavy syllable, we say that languages which pay attention to the number of moras in a syllable are QUANTITY SENSITIVE. In a quantity-sensitive language, we find that in a word that contains one or more heavy syllables, stress will typically fall on a heavy syllable, and in a word that contains no heavy syllables, stress will fall on a linearly identifiable syllable (such as the first, last, second, or next to last—we'll return to this). However, the situation can be more complex than that, because the language may superimpose a requirement about where stress can be located. For example, a language may require that the primary stress fall on one of the last two syllables of the word—that is, all words will have final or PENULTIMATE (next to final) stress. In such a language, if the only heavy syllable in the word was the third from the end (the ANTEPENULTIMATE), stress would fall on a light syllable (the final or penultimate) even though the language was quantity sensitive. It's time to stop talking in abstract terms and face some data, so you can feel comfortable about all this jargon.

Bounded Feet

Consider these few words from the nearly extinct language Maranungku, of north-central Australia, in which an acute accent (´) indicates primary stress and a grave accent (`) indicates secondary stress:

tíralk 'saliva'	mérepèt 'beard'	yángarmàta 'the Pleiades'
lángkaràtetì 'prawn'	wélepènemànta 'kind of duck'	

Number each syllable in each word. Circle the primary stressed syllable. Underline the secondary stressed syllable(s). Now state in simple words the stress pattern for this language. We get primary stress on the first syllable and secondary stress on every other syllable thereafter. This language has an ALTERNATING stress pattern, which is quite common in languages around the world. Without even checking to see whether the stressed syllables are heavy or light, tell me whether you think this language is quantity sensitive or not. It gives no indication of being quantity sensitive. All that matters is a syllable's location in the word. Now look back at the words and see if your conclusion is correct. Yes, it is. We can see initial syllables that are light (as in *tíralk*) and initial syllables that are heavy (as in *yángarmàta*), and both types get primary stress. We can see odd-numbered syllables other than the first that are light (as in *lángkaràtetì*) and odd-numbered syllables that are heavy (as in *wélepènemànta*), and both types get secondary stress. And we can see even-numbered syllables that are light (as in *mérepèt*) and even-number syllables that are heavy (as in *yángarmàta*), and both get no stress. So syllable weight plays no role in the assignment of stress in this language, and we need not concern ourselves about the mora level in describing the stress pattern.

If you were to group the syllables of each word together into feet, how many syllables would each foot have? At most two, since a foot cannot contain more than one stressed syllable. (Notice that a final syllable in a word with an odd number of syllables will form a one-syllable foot, a DEGENERATE foot. For now please ignore such feet and you can consider them further when we briefly touch on the issue of degenerate feet.)

Now since this language assigns primary stress to the first syllable and secondary stress to all other odd-numbered syllables, we know we start forming our feet at the left end of the word—that is, we work from left to right as we form feet. Let us assume the convention that **we form the largest feet possible** while still observing whatever other rules the language **imposes.** That means that Syllables 1 and 2 form a foot, Syllables 3 and 4 form a foot, and so on. Since the stressed syllable of the foot is the left syllable, we say these feet are LEFT-HEADED (as opposed to RIGHT-HEADED). And since every foot has no more than two syllables, we say these feet are BOUNDED (as opposed to UNBOUNDED). The final thing we need to say about this language is that when we gather the feet together to form a word, the first foot is the most prominent. (That's what the primary stress indicates.) So at the word level, we also find a left-headed structure. Let us now draw a representation of this metrical analysis for the word *wélepènemànta*:

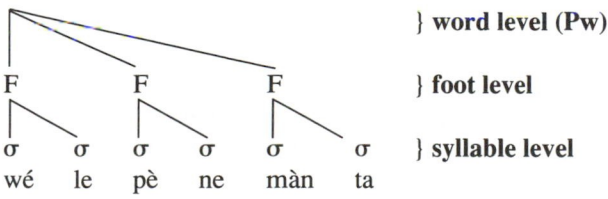

	} **word level (Pw)**
F F F	} **foot level**
σ σ σ σ σ σ	} **syllable level**
wé le pè ne màn ta	

What we have drawn here is known as a METRICAL TREE. A vertical line is drawn over the head of a unit and a slanting line is drawn over nonhead parts. That means that a vertical line is drawn over the more prominent syllable of each foot. So in:

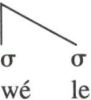

σ   σ
wé   le

wé is the head and *le* is the nonhead. And it means that a vertical line is drawn over the most prominent foot of each prosodic word. In the tree for *wélepènemànta* the first F is the head and the other two are nonheads.

Another way of doing trees is to have all lines slant and to indicate the head with the symbol S (for strong) and the nonhead with the symbol W (for weak). This is easy to do at the foot level for our word above. But at the word level we come across three feet. The contrast of S vs. W, according to many theories of phonology, implies that trees are structurally BINARY. (That is, at most two BRANCHES come together at any given NODE of the tree.) So how do we handle a level that has three parts, such as the word level for *wélepènemànta*, which consists of three feet?

In order to use a consistently binary branching tree for this word, we can follow the convention that whenever two branches come together, one must be labeled S and one must be labeled W, and those labels must correspond to an ultimate difference in stress of the TERMINAL (lowest in the tree) items under the labels. The terminal items are the actual syllables that we hear. In this way, the primary stress would be dominated only by S nodes and the secondary stresses would be IMMEDIATELY DOMINATED by an S node, but the next dominating node up would be W. So the tree would be:

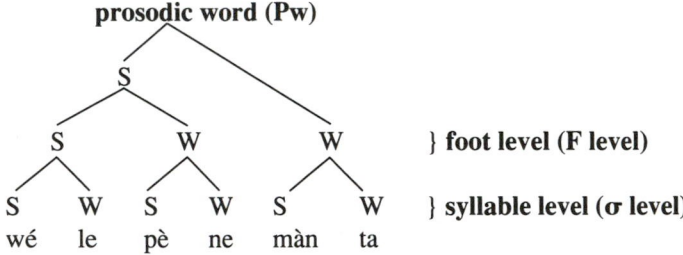

The Pw node here dominates an S on the left and a W on the right, since the word level puts prominence on the left. Each of the three feet nodes also dominates an S on the left and a W on the right, since the foot level puts prominence on the left, as well.

We will draw trees the first way: with a straight line over the head of a unit. That's because the first way allows us to use a single type of tree for languages with unbounded feet and languages with bound feet. But you need to be familiar with both kinds of trees, since the linguistic literature uses both.

Five Parameters

One way to give a formal statement of the stress pattern of Maranungku is to talk about five PARAMETERS, all of which are now familiar to you. They are:

1. Boundedness: This language has bounded feet (here, binary feet).
2. Quantity sensitivity: This language is not quantity sensitive.
3. Headedness at the foot level: This language has left-headed feet.
4. Headedness at the word level: This language is left-headed at the word level (the leftmost foot gets primary stress).
5. Direction: We form feet from left to right.

This particular stress pattern is very common among the languages of the world.

Much more can be said about all of these parameters, but I'll focus here on only a few main points. First, many phonologists would argue that all bounded feet are binary. Others would admit TERNARY feet—that is, feet consisting of three positions (rather than the two positions of a binary foot). (I speak of positions here, rather than syllables, because in some languages feet fill their positions with syllables but in most languages feet fill their positions with moras, as we'll discuss.) You will meet some of the data that have been used to argue for the existence of ternary feet in Problem Set 2.7, although those who would limit the theory to admitting only binary bounded feet have ways to handle such data.

The issue is complex and some have argued that the analysis of poetry is pertinent here. Metrical feet play a role not just in the rhythmic patterns of ordinary speech, but in poetry. And it is clear that some poetic traditions make use of ternary feet (as in the dactylic hexameter line of Homer and Hesiod in Ancient Greek verse and the three different ternary feet of pre-Islamic Arabic verse). In general, the metrical mechanisms of poetry are subject to the rules and principles of phonology of the language. Accordingly, if the poetry (appears to) admit ternary feet, the metrical phonology of the language should (appear to) admit ternary feet. On the other hand, poetry can impose rules (such as an obligatory CAESURA, or syntactic break, in fixed positions) that have no counterpart in the grammar of the language. So perhaps a language could have ternary feet in the poetry but not in the ordinary speech.

Second, while I have listed the parameters as though they are independent of one another, certain of these parameters are correlated with each other in interesting ways. **Bounded feet, for example, can be sensitive to syllable weight or not (a point I'll return to). But unbounded feet typically are quantity sensitive. That is, stress cares either about syllable weight or syllable position or both, but not generally about any other factor.** So if syllable position is not a factor, syllable weight usually is.

Third, **most types of feet are, in fact, quantity sensitive.** The only truly prevalent type of foot that merely counts syllables without regard to the internal structure of the syllable is the **SYLLABIC TROCHEE (consisting of two syllables, left-headed),** which is the foot that Maranungku employs, as we just learned above. Notice that it is called the "syllabic trochee" to make clear the fact that it is a syllable-based foot, not a quantity-sensitive (that is, mora-based) foot.

There are two other prevalent types of bounded feet, and both are quantity sensitive. One is **the MORAIC TROCHEE, in which a foot consists of precisely two moras—that is, two light syllables (˘ ˘) or one heavy syllable (¯).** Cairene Arabic has been argued to employ the moraic trochee, as have many other languages, including English. Here is an example word from Cairene Arabic, where I have marked every light syllable with the symbol ˘ and every heavy syllable with the symbol ¯, and where I have put an x above the head of a foot and parentheses around each foot. The feet are formed from L to R; the final syllable of this word forms a degenerate foot that plays no role in stress assignment (so it is not part of a foot); and at the word level we have right-headedness:

```
(   x   )        word level
(x̱)(x̱ ˳) ˳      foot level
ʔinkása ra
```

This word has four syllables, all light but the first. The first syllable is therefore a foot by itself, as the parentheses at the foot level indicate. The second and third syllables, both of which are light, gather together to make the second foot. And the final syllable, since it is light, cannot constitute a regular foot (since a moraic trochee requires two moras, not just one)—that's what makes it degenerate and that's why we ignore it at the foot and word level.

The other last common type of foot is **the IAMB, which consists of either a light syllable followed by any type of syllable (̆σ), or of a single heavy syllable (̄). Canonically (that is, in the archetypical case), however, the iamb has a heavy syllable in second position.** Many Amerind languages have been argued to employ the iamb, including the Muskogean language Creek, some Inuit languages, some Iroquoian languages (in the Amerind family), and some Algonquian languages (also in the Amerind family). Here is an example word from Creek, with feet indicated. As in the Cairene example above, we form feet from L to R; the final foot in this example is degenerate and plays no part in stress assignment (so, again, it is not part of a foot); and we have right-headedness at the word level.

```
(          x   )       word level
( ˳ x̱)( ˳ x̱) ˳        foot level
tokoɬhokí ta
```

This word has five syllables, all light except the second. Starting from the left, I have gathered them together into feet. Please take our definition of an iamb and justify to yourself now the gathering of the first two syllables into the first foot and the gathering of the third and fourth syllables into the second foot. Let me help you: The first syllable is light, so the second syllable (regardless of its weight) joins it to make up the first foot. The third syllable is also light, so the fourth syllable (regardless of its weight) joins it to make up the second foot.

The salient difference between quantity-sensitive feet and non-quantity-sensitive feet, then, is that the former are defined in terms of moras and the latter are defined in terms of syllables (regardless of how many moras each syllable might consist of). However, even though trochaic feet can be syllabic (as in Maranungku) or moraic (as in Cairene Arabic), there is still something important that allows both to be gathered together under the rubric of "trochee" as opposed to "iamb." Look at the characterizations of both types of trochaic feet above and of the one type of iambic foot we've discussed above. If you'll notice, this inventory of feet would say that **trochaic feet consist of units of the same duration in a sense (either two syllables or two moras), whereas when iambic feet consist of two units, the first must be short and the second may (and canonically does) contrast in length.** This means that trochaic feet and iambic feet are fundamentally different (a finding that scholars of poetics have known for hundreds of years). That fundamental difference has been incorporated into the **IAMBIC/TROCHAIC LAW, which states in part that when a language is quantity sensitive, if we have binary feet, we will put the syllable of greater weight on the right and stress it.**

One final point: **Languages choose a single foot type for their metrical system.**

With just these five parameters and the few remarks above, we can discuss the metrics of any language. So let's play around with them now, using the syllabic trochee of Maranungku as our point of comparison.

You tell me: If you have a language that puts primary stress on the penultimate syllable and secondary stress on alternating syllables before that, what parameters have we changed? Once again, we have syllabic trochees (so we are left-headed at the foot level). But we are right-headed at the word level and now the direction for forming feet is from right to left. Do you see that? Let's go through it step by step.

First, how do we know headedness at the word level? When we describe a language as having primary stress on the last or penultimate syllable, as opposed to on the first or second syllable, we are noticing that the rightmost foot is prominent. That means we are right-headed at the word level.

Okay, now how do we recognize what kind of foot we have? Think about the fact that stress is on the penultimate syllable and on alternating stresses before that. Alternation like that tells us we have binary feet. Now if stress were on the last syllable of the word and alternating before that, we'd gather the last two syllables into a foot and we'd have iambic feet, right? When we have stress on the penultimate syllable, we gather the last two syllables together into a foot and we have a trochaic foot. (We'll come up with a complication for that later, when we discuss extrametricality—but for now, this works.) And since the alternation pattern is entirely regular, mentioning only syllables, we know that the weight of the syllables isn't pertinent. So this language has syllabic trochees.

The last question is: How do we know which edge we start forming our feet from? The direction of forming feet is determined by looking at lots of words and deciding which is the most perspicuous way of describing the facts. If a language has syllabic trochees, then words with an even number of syllables won't tell us about the direction of forming feet. But words with an odd number of syllables will. That's because there will be a **left-over syllable, a syllable that doesn't fit into a foot—a syllable that constitutes a degenerate foot and is probably overlooked by the rules of prosody.** So if you see that extra foot at the right edge of words, then you started forming your feet left to right and your left-over syllable was at the right edge. But if you see that extra foot at the left edge of words, then you started forming your feet right to left and your left-over syllable was at the left edge.

How do we know which edge of the word a left-over syllable will occur on in the language I described above? The very fact that I said that penultimate syllables get stress tells you that there is regularity of stress at the right edge. So we know that irregularity is at the left edge. That means we started forming our feet at the right edge—that's why the right edge displays such regularity. So we form feet right to left.

This is the system found in Warao, an indigenous language of Venezuela, Surinam, and Guyana. (And you will study Warao in Problem Set 2.7.)

What parameter is different if we have a language with stress on the first syllable and alternating syllables thereafter, and the primary stress is on the final foot? Here we have a syllabic trochee again, going from left to right, but at the word level we are right-headed.

Do you see why we're going from left to right? Stress is entirely regular at the left edge of the word, so we formed our feet left to right. Can you justify why we analyze these feet as syllabic trochees? The alternation of stress is regular, regardless of syllable weight, and the first syllable of each foot is the stressed one. Can you explain why we say the word level is right-headed? It is because the final foot gets the primary stress.

I have not found any language with precisely this stress pattern discussed in the literature. However, in Piro, an Arawakan language of Eastern Peru, this system is used with an addition: Before you begin forming trochees from the left, you first form a syllabic trochee at the right edge of the word. In this way, primary stress always falls on the penultimate syllable. Here is an example word:

```
(           x    )       word level
(x   .)    (x   .)       foot level
sàlwayehkáhna
```

What about if we have a language which has primary stress on the second syllable and secondary stress on alternating syllables after that? Such a language forms feet left to right and is left-headed at the word level. (Did you get those two facts right off? You should have. If you're having trouble, go back through the last two examples again, more slowly.) But the big issue is what the foot structure is. This certainly looks like a syllabic iamb (σσ), not the uneven type of iamb we discussed. That is, it looks like the foot consists of two syllables, and the second is prominent. Without any information to the contrary, that is how we should analyze it. But **syllabic iambs are rare in language.** As you have learned, the iamb favors two units of different length (a light and then a heavy syllable). So the iamb is typically a quantity-sensitive foot, not a syllable-based foot. Nevertheless, syllabic iambs do occur and Mapudungan (also known as Mapudungu and Araucanian, the language of the Mapuche people of Chile) makes use of them. Here is an example word:

```
(  x      )       word level
(.  x) (.  x)      foot level
 elú mujù
```

Now what are the parameters if we have alternating stress, starting with primary stress on the first syllable, but with the added fact that any heavy syllable must be stressed, regardless of whether it falls in an odd-numbered position or not? Certainly, such a language would be quantity sensitive, while still maintaining binary left-headed feet. So we have moraic trochees here, formed from left to right, and left-headed at the word level. This is pretty much the system used to stress word roots in the Uto-Aztecan language Cahuilla of southern California. Here is an example word, in which the final consonant does not count for stress assignment (so I have marked the final syllable as light):

```
(x        )       word level
(x̱ )(x̠  ̬)         foot level
qá:nkìʧem
```

You may have many questions about stress in hypothetical situations you can imagine now. For example, what happens in such a language if we have this sequence of syllables: heavy, heavy, light, heavy, heavy? Both of the heavy syllables that flank the light one form feet by themselves. So the light syllable in the middle forms a degenerate foot. Yikes! What's a degenerate foot doing in the middle of a word? Furthermore, this forlorn syllable is in an odd-numbered position, and normally odd-numbered positions in this language get stress. (That's what the alternating stress pattern following the initial primary stressed syllable means.) Do we stress it or not? There are two opposing forces here: one that tells us that degenerate feet shouldn't get stress (something we'll talk about) and one that tells us that a foot in an odd position should get stress (in this particular language). The situation is problematical. This degenerate foot is trapped, in a sense, and this situation has been termed MEDIAL TRAPPING. Languages do many things to avoid medial trapping and we will not go into this issue (although we'll mention it when we discuss degenerate feet more fully). If you want to read about this, there are sources in the bibliography. For now, please don't let your myriad of questions throw you off from the main point of the discussion, which is merely to give you a sense of the richness of metrical systems.

How about if we have primary stress on a final syllable if it's heavy, otherwise on the penultimate, and secondary stress on alternating syllables preceding the primary stress with the additional requirement that every heavy syllable gets stressed? Here we have moraic trochees formed from right to left with a right-headed structure at the word level.

Let's go through that step by step, starting with the easiest things to determine. First, word-level stress is right-headed since the final foot is prominent. That's easy, right? Next, certainly, the foot is quantity sensitive, since heaviness matters. So we have either a moraic trochee or an iamb. If the word ends in a heavy syllable, that syllable gets stressed. If the word ends in two light syllables, the penultimate gets stressed. These two facts alone tell us we have a moraic trochee. (Remember, moraic trochees consist of a single heavy syllable or two light syllables.) And now that we've realized we can identify the foot by looking at the right edge of the word, we know we form feet starting at that edge—so the direction of forming feet is right to left.

Let me point out one complication, however. Notice that if the word ends in a heavy syllable followed by a light syllable, the penultimate gets stressed. Now the penultimate syllable, being heavy, forms a foot by itself. In that situation, the final syllable is a degenerate foot. So even though we started forming feet at the right edge of our word, we can have degenerate feet at our right edge. And, of course, we can still find degenerate feet at our left edge. In quantity-sensitive systems, we can easily find degenerate feet at either end of a word. So determining the parameter of direction for forming feet can be tricky in quantity-sensitive systems and is often a point of debate.

This is the system used by Hawaiian, and here is an example word:

```
(              x  )      word level
  ˘(x̆ ˘)(x̆)(x̆ ˘)       foot level
ke òne  ò:  í o
```

What are the parameters if we have stress on the first syllable if it's heavy, otherwise on the second, and on alternating syllables thereafter with primary stress on the rightmost foot and with the additional requirement that every heavy syllable gets stressed? Take a second to digest those facts.

Okay. Heaviness matters, so we have either moraic trochees or iambs. Now, if both the first and second syllables are light, which one gets stressed? The second. So what kind of foot do we have? An iamb. Which foot gets primary stress? The rightmost, so we are right-headed at the word level. And, finally, we figured out what kind of feet we have by looking at the first two syllables—so that's where the regularity is—and we know we form feet left to right.

In sum, we have iambs (quantity-sensitive iambs), formed from left to right and right-headed at the word level.

This system is very similar to that of Unami, a dialect of Delaware—an Eastern Algonquian language. Unami adds a complication, however: The final foot does not receive stress. Instead, the penultimate foot gets the primary stress. Simply stated, the final foot does not count for metrical purposes. We say that it is EXTRAMETRICAL and we will indicate that by putting angled brackets around the foot. (And you have, in fact, already met instances of extrametricality. The final consonant in the example from Cahuilla is extrametrical. That is, the language simply sets aside final consonants and does not consider them when assigning stress. Also, the final degenerate foot in the examples from Cairene Arabic and from Creek are extrametrical because both of these languages choose to completely overlook degenerate feet in stress assignment. What is different in Unami is that the final foot is not degenerate, but it is still extrametrical.) For example, consider this word:

```
(        x        )        word level
(x̱) (˘   x̱) < (˘ x̱) >    foot level
[en ta máx    ka i:t]
```

This word (which means 'when he found me') has five syllables; the first, third, and last are heavy. So if we start forming iambs from the left, the first syllable is a complete foot. The second and third syllables form a foot (the canonical iamb). And the fourth and fifth syllables form a foot (again, the canonical iamb). But the primary stress falls on the penultimate foot, so the final foot is extrametrical.

Extrametricality is a powerful mechanism. It allows us to mark material at the very edge of a word as outside the metrical domain. A single segment, a mora, a syllable, or a whole foot can be marked as extrametrical. Typically extrametrical units are found at the right edge of a word, but they have been known to occur at the left edge, as well. You will explore the use of extrametricality in Problem Set 2.7.

As long as we are facing more complex issues of this sort, we should go into more detail on a question we raised earlier. Consider a language that has syllabic trochees. How do we analyze words with an odd number of syllables? Depending on the direction parameter (that is, whether the language forms feet going L-R or R-L), the extra syllable will be in final (in a L-R language) or initial (in a R-L language) position. The analogous question comes up for all languages with binary feet—what do we do with a left-over syllable? (Of course, if the feet are moraic trochees or iambs, the issue will not be entirely dependent upon whether the word has an odd or even number of syllables. Do you see why?)

The left-over syllable is a degenerate foot in that it has only one METRICAL POSITION (a syllable of any type in syllabic trochaic meter, and a light syllable in moraic trochaic and iambic meter). Different languages handle degenerate feet in different ways. Many totally ignore degenerate feet with respect to stress assignment. We say those languages have an ABSOLUTE BAN ON DEGENERATE FEET (which is the same as saying that all degenerate feet are extrametrical). **When a language bans degenerate feet, it will have a MINIMAL WORD CONSTRAINT to the effect that no words of the language will be smaller than a single well-formed foot.** Mohawk, a member of the Amerind family spoken in New York and Quebec, and Iroquoi, is such a syllabic trochee language; the Indo-Aryan language Maithili of India and Nepal is such a moraic trochee language; and Cambodian is such an iambic language.

In other languages degenerate feet do fall within the metrical domain, but only under certain conditions. Auca, spoken in Ecuador, is such a syllabic trochee language; Hindi is such a moraic trochee language; and Unami is such an iambic language. And, finally, in a few languages, degenerate feet can even bear primary stress. The Central Algonquian language Ojibwa, spoken in northern Michigan and Canada, is claimed to be such a language. Furthermore, there are times when degenerate feet can occur internal to a word—as we mentioned above, instances of medial trapping. For example, some languages have complex foot formation rules that use both directional parameters. In the Austronesian language Lenakel we form a moraic trochee at the right edge of the word. Then we form moraic trochees across the word going from right to left in nouns but from left to right in verbs and adjectives. Thus a light syllable can get stranded internal to the word in a verb or adjective. Again, how languages treat internal degenerate feet varies. You will get a chance to play a little bit with degenerate feet in Problem Set 2.7.

You might want to take a moment now to look back at the data given above on Maranungku and figure out how this language treats degenerate feet. Are they banned or are they tolerated? In answering this you need to know that Maranungku does not have a minimal word constraint. In particular, monosyllabic words are allowed.

Foot or No Foot

There is one final point we should make before we leave our discussion of stress in languages that have bounded feet. Some languages have stress on the first syllable (such as Czech, the Baltic language Latvian of Latvia, Hungarian), or the last syllable (such as French and the Iranian language Farsi), or the penultimate syllable (as in the Amerind language Aztec and the Balto-Slavic language Polish), with no secondary stress. Do you think such languages have bounded feet? A pattern of alternating stresses has been our major clue thus far in recognizing bounded feet, so these languages do not give the initial impression of having bounded feet. In fact, if the stress is on the very first or very last syllable, we could claim that there was only one foot per word and that that foot was left-headed (for initial stress) or right-headed (for final stress). In other words, a foot and a word are identical. This would be equivalent, really, to saying the language skipped the intermediary level of foot altogether and simply formed a left- or right-headed word directly from the syllables.

Would a similar solution be available for languages with stress on the penultimate syllable? See if you can make use of the notion of extrametricality here. Yes—if the last syllable is extrametrical, then in a penultimate stress language we can skip the foot level and have a right-headed structure at the word level.

So far as I know, there is no language with primary stress on the second syllable and no secondary stresses. If there were, however, a simple analysis could be used: We could analyze the first syllable as extrametrical and then view the rest of the word as being a left-headed structure at the word level, with no foot level. So why don't such languages occur? One possibility is that extrametricality is a mechanism that can be applied onto to the right edge of a word, but not to the left edge. In fact, for a variety of reasons, some phonologists have proposed that extrametricality is limited to the right edge, and certainly this is the unmarked edge for extrametricality.

If a language with primary stress on the second syllable had secondary stresses on alternating syllables, as well, it would look like it had syllabic iambs, which are very rare. Alternatively, again, we could analyze the first syllable as extrametrical and treat such a language as having syllabic trochees. However, given that syllabic trochees are common, if such an analysis were readily available to us, we would expect to find languages with this stress pattern, but, so far as I know, we don't. So the absence of such languages supports our contention above that extrametricality at the left edge is highly marked, if not banned entirely—and thus this analysis is not readily available to us.

Okay, now let's return to the three stress patterns that do occur: initial stress, final stress, and penultimate stress, with no secondary stresses. We find that some languages with these three stress patterns do give other types of evidence of having a foot structure, evidence we will not go into here. In such cases, linguists have proposed binary feet (left-headed moraic or syllabic trochees for initial-stress languages; iambs for final stress languages; syllabic trochees for penultimate-stress languages) and suggested that these languages have a mechanism which suppresses all nonprimary stress, and thus we do not get alternating stress. So while the presence of alternating stress tells us we have binary feet, the absence of it does not conclusively rule against binary feet.

Unbounded Feet

Now let's play with the only parameter we haven't yet: boundedness of feet. As we already pointed out, if a language has unbounded feet, it will be quantity sensitive. And remember, usually when linguists talk of heavy vs. light syllables, they are referring to the distinction between syllables with more than one mora in the rhyme and syllables with only one mora in the rhyme. But specific languages can be sensitive to other distinctions. In Yup'ik heavy syllables are those with long vowels. But syllables with short vowels that end in a coda pattern with light syllables for stress purposes. So if you do any fieldwork of your own in a new language, when you see a pattern that is clearly not alternating and you suspect an unbounded foot structure, be open in looking for what might constitute "weight" in the language. In this chapter, however, we will look at examples of quantity-sensitive languages, in which our original definition of weight holds.

For example, in Classical Arabic we find the following words (the primary stressed syllable is italicized):

[*kub*ba] 'meatloaf'	[ka*ri:m*] 'noble'	[*sa*lima] 'he was safe'
[ta ʕa*lla*ma] 'he learned'		
[ʔumma*hun*na] 'their mother'	[*da*rabaka] 'you'	

Assume that Arabic is a quantity-sensitive language. Go through all these words and circle the heavy syllables. When there is no heavy syllable in a word, which syllable gets stressed? Only two words here contain no heavy syllables, and in both the first syllable is stressed. When there are one or more heavy syllables in a word, which syllable gets stressed? The last heavy syllable.

This stress system is straightforward and relatively common, but it introduces two possibilities that are new to you. Let's talk about the words that do have at least one heavy syllable first. What heads every foot? A heavy syllable. (If you are full of questions at this point about the analysis of *taʕallama*, please be patient. We will turn to it later.) Okay, now we know we have unbounded feet with the head on the heavy syllable. Consider the word *ʔummahunna*. There are two heavy syllables here. Let's put a vertical line over each to show they are heads of feet. Now how can we gather the other syllables into those two feet?

Assume with me for a moment that the final syllable does not form a degenerate foot. So our only real choice to consider at this point is what happens to the second syllable: *ma*. Does it go into the first foot or the second foot?

We will adopt the convention that **all feet must have a head at one end or the other,** never in medial position. This is not arbitrary. Metrical systems clearly put emphasis on the margins of words. Languages generally put primary stress on first or last feet, whether those feet be bounded or not, whether those feet be left-headed or right-headed. We had not faced the possibility of a foot with a medial head before this because the feet we considered were all binary. But now we know we can set aside this possibility even in languages with unbounded feet.

So the proper analysis is the left one, and we can now see that Arabic is left-headed at the foot level. And we know it is right-headed at the word level since the last heavy syllable gets stress, so the last foot is getting stress.

But the conclusion that feet are left-headed was based on the assumption that the final syllable of *?ummahunna* was not degenerate. Without that assumption, the second syllable could have been part of the stressed foot and we would have had right-headed feet.

So we must face the question of what happens to the final syllable: Is the final syllable part of the foot headed by *hun* or is it a degenerate foot? We can answer this only by looking at the words that have no heavy syllables. Such words get initial syllable stress. Since stress can go only on the head of a foot, that means the initial syllable is the head of a foot. But since there are no heavy syllables in the word, we analyze the entire word as a single foot—a single left-headed foot. And since there is only one foot, the head of that foot gets primary stress at the word level. The structure of *salima* is, then:

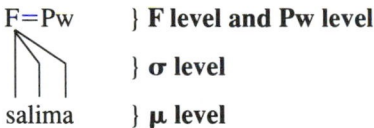

(The F and Pw levels are identical here, since this word consists of a single foot.) So we were, in fact, right in analyzing Arabic as having left-headed feet.

What happens, then, when we get to a word like *ta ʕallama*, which has only one heavy syllable, but that syllable is not the first syllable of the word? All the light syllables preceding the first heavy syllable will be gathered into a single foot that in some sense is degenerate. In this case there is only one such syllable, so it constitutes a headed foot (since we know from having studied the stress of words with no heavy syllables like *salima* that degenerate feet do have a head in Arabic). What happens at the word level? Arabic is right-headed at the word level. So the analysis of this word is then:

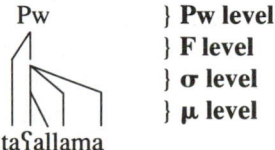

Are you having any difficulties reading off these trees? At the mora level we have five branches, because we have five moras in this word. At the syllable level we have four branches because we have four syllables in this word. At the foot level we have two branches, because we have two feet in this word.

Actually, there are other complications in the stress pattern of Arabic, one of which is explored in Problem Set 2.7. For now, though, we will move on.

So the parameters for Arabic are: (1) unbounded feet, (2) quantity sensitive, (3) left-headed foot, and (4) right-headed at word level. But what is the direction? Do we form our feet going L-R across the word or R-L? Go back to the Arabic words above and form feet L-R, then R-L. Does it make a difference? Will it ever matter? No. **In a quantity-sensitive language with unbounded feet, the parameter of direction is meaningless, because the heads of feet will be determined strictly by the structure of syllables and not by their position in the word.** (So again we have seen a way in which the parameters are correlated one to another.)

Let's take the parameters of Arabic and play with them a little. What would be the parameters of a language which stressed the first heavy syllable, or, if there was none, then the last syllable of the word. Again, we have a quantity-sensitive, unbounded-foot language. At the foot level we must be right-headed (because words with no heavy syllables will form a single foot, and it must have the final syllable as its head). At the word level we must be left-headed (so that the first foot will be stressed).

English Stress

Rather than go further into details of the metrical system of languages that may be exotic to you, let's spend some time on the English stress system, which is actually among the most complex systems studied to date.

Take just five minutes to list as many English nouns containing three or more syllables as you can. You may have come up with words like these:

A	B	C	D
tomato	personality	neighborhood	milk bottle
Seminole	employee	worthlessness	chatterbox
venison	unmusical	beautiful	underwear
Massachusetts	illegible	government	pantyhose
asparagus	appendix	heavenward	dining room

I have arranged them into four lists. Can you figure out the criteria I used to set up these lists? Ask yourself about the morphological breakdown of these words. Think in terms of root morphemes and affixes. Are there any words here that seem to consist of only a single root morpheme, with no affixes of any kind attached? List A gives the monomorphemes. Is there any list that consists of words that have more than one root morpheme, whether or not any affixes are present? Yes, it's List D, which consists of COMPOUNDS. Both Lists B and C consist of words that have a single root morpheme plus one or more affixes. But the affixes in B are of two types: prefixes, or suffixes that begin with a vowel. The affixes in C, on the other hand, are all suffixes that begin with a consonant. While you don't yet know the significance of these facts, let it be your guide to arranging your own words into lists. And if your group of words contains some that have more than one suffix, where one suffix begins with a vowel and the other suffix begins with a consonant, please just set those words aside for now and after you have finished this chapter, you can return to consider them.

For the moment I'd like you to examine only words of the type found in Lists A and B. Concentrate on the words *Seminole*, *Massachusetts*, and *personality*. Hum them. What do you notice about the arrangement of primary and secondary stresses? What is the general pattern here? Do you see that **English favors an alternating stress pattern?** English likes to have its stressed syllables separated by unstressed syllables. So what do you know about the foot structure of English? Don't get too caught up in accounting for every detail at once. I'm asking you for the general tendency. Can you see that **we have binary feet?**

Do we ever have two stressed syllables in a row in the Lists A and B? No. Do we ever have two unstressed syllables in a row? Yes. Where do they fall? They are always the final two syllables of a word. (*personality*, *unmusical*, *illegible*)

Now consider the word *employee*. Some people say this word with primary stress on the penultimate syllable (*emplóyee*); others say it with primary stress on the suffix and secondary stress on the first syllable (*èmployée*) or even on the second syllable (*emplòyée*). If we consider the first pronunciation of this word only, what can we say about the final syllable of all the nouns in Lists A and B? The final syllable is never stressed. Given that we seem to have binary feet and that we sometimes find two unstressed syllables in a row in final position, what do you suspect about the final syllable of English nouns? It is extrametrical. Do you see that? The final syllable does not seem to play a role in stress assignment, whether that final syllable is light (as in *illegible*—where we end in a syllabic [l]) or heavy (as in *appendix*).

On the other hand, if we consider the second pronunciation of *employee* (*èmployée*) or the third pronunciation (*emplòyée*), then we need to allow that this affix is exceptional in that it carries stress (in fact, primary stress). But we can note that once primary stress is established, the tendency for alternating stress kicks in with the second pronunciation (*èmployée*). I will say more about the second and third pronunciations of this particular word below, but for the moment in our discussion please assume the first pronunciation (*emplóyee*).

Okay, now underline all the primary and secondary stressed syllables in Lists A and B. Is English quantity sensitive? Don't let orthography throw you off. Be careful of tense vowels that have a falling diphthong. We find primary stress on both light syllables (as in *aspáragus*) and heavy syllables (*tomáto*). We find secondary stress on both light syllables (*pèrsonálity*—the first syllable has a syllabic liquid) and heavy syllables (*aspáragùs*). But we can discern a certain relationship between syllable weight and stress and if we systematically tease it apart.

First, discount the final syllable of these nouns (since we said it's extrametrical). Now, what can you say about every stressed penultimate syllable? It's heavy, right? Are there any heavy penultimate syllables that don't get stressed? No. So we know that English stresses the penultimate if it's heavy.

What happens if the penultimate isn't heavy? Look at *Seminole*, *venison*, and *asparagus*, for example. The antepenultimate gets stress. This is precisely the pattern we expect if the final syllable is extrametrical and the final foot is a moraic trochee.

What direction do we go in forming the rest of our feet? We can see from a comparison of *Massachusetts* with *personality* that we form our feet from the right to left. Our feet are binary and left-headed. You know they are binary because secondary stresses fall in an alternating pattern to the left of the primary stress. You know they are left-headed, because the stress falls on the left member of each foot. You know the final foot is a moraic trochee and you know the other feet are also trochees, but can you find evidence as to whether the other feet are moraic trochees or syllabic trochees? It is very hard to find, but, in fact, you don't need to. You already know that languages generally make use of only one kind of foot. So if English uses a moraic trochee at all, then it always uses moraic trochees.

Furthermore, primary stress is always on the penultimate syllable or the antepenultimate syllable, so the rightmost foot is prominent and we are right-headed at the word level.

The above discussion is very brief and, in fact, overly simplified. Many nouns of English present questions for this analysis. For example, why does *hurricane* have final secondary stress, if final syllables are extrametrical in nouns? Notice that here we have a diphthong in the final syllable. None of our other examples had a diphthong in the final syllable except *employee* on the pronunciations *èmployée* and *emplòyée*, which are precisely the pronunciations with stress (here primary stress) on the final syllable. Try to find other words that end in long vowels or diphthongs. Is the final syllable of such words generally extrametrical or not? This is a complex matter and I don't mean for you to simply spout an answer, but instead to consider the question, perhaps for future research.

There are other complications in the description of English stress, and you will discover in Problem Set 2.7 that verbs do not follow exactly the same pattern as nouns. But that is all we will do with English stress here.

Metrical Grids

While we have used metrical trees to exhibit the structure of moras, syllables, feet, and words, there is another way to represent metrical structure, with what is called the METRICAL GRID. In fact, we already hinted at this approach when we dealt with the issue of extrametricality in Unami.

A grid representation takes the form of a matrix in which each mora (if the language is quantity sensitive) or syllable defines a column. The rows or levels take the form of x's that mark prosodic prominence. The lowest row is called the first row. Thus the metrical grid corresponding to the metrical tree for the Arabic word *ʔummahunna* is as shown here:

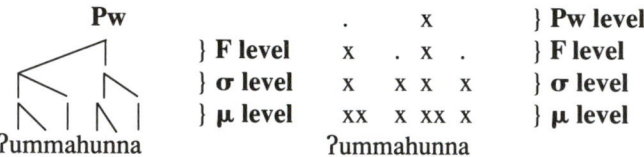

(I have placed a dot in a column if row $n + 1$ does not have an x, but row n does have an x, and row $n + 1$ is the F or Pw level. These dots have no metrical significance. They are expository devices which we will make use of.)

From these grids and trees you may get the impression that in a word with a bimoraic stressed syllable (such as the third syllable of *ʔummahunna*), both moras carry the stress. Actually, there is debate over this issue. It is possible that if one mora is more sonorous than the other, the more sonorous mora carries the stress. It is also possible that if a language has trochaic feet, a heavy syllable that forms a foot will have stress on the left mora, whereas if a language has iambic feet, a heavy syllable that forms a foot will have stress on the right mora. I do not mean to take a stand on this issue—and we will not discuss it further in this text. So please don't read more into these diagrams than I intend.

While you can see that the different rows of a grid correspond quite directly to the same prosodic levels that we see in the tree, the grid need not mark prosodic CONSTITUENCY or unity, while the tree does. Thus, for example, what I have labeled the foot level in the grid need not, in fact, claim any particular grouping of the syllables. Grids can, however, give constituency information, just as trees do, if we allow the convention of parentheses. We will place parentheses in the F level and the Pw level.

Pw		(. x)	} **Pw level**
	} **F level**	(x .) (x .)	} **F level**
	} **σ level**	x x x x	} **σ level**
	} **μ level**	xx x xx x	} **μ level**
ʔummahunna		ʔum ma hun na	

While most information about metrical structure can be conveyed by either trees or grids, we find that grids can be more perspicacious in handling certain kinds of metrical phenomena and in showing us certain principles of metrical phonology.

To see this, let's consider the following question. A binary-foot language favors alternating stress. Now what happens in such a language if it is quantity sensitive and we have two heavy syllables in sequence? Will we get two stresses in a row? Wouldn't two stresses in a row be problematic? In fact, a sequence of two stresses should be considered a STRESS CLASH. And even languages that do not favor an alternating stress pattern (that is, languages with unbounded feet) may be sensitive to stress clashes.

Different languages handle stress clashes in different ways. Some languages tolerate them. But some will try hard to avoid them. Let's consider English, for a moment. Take the word *Tennessee*, which in isolation is pronounced with final primary stress. Let's give a metrical grid for this word, assuming it is to be analyzed as consisting of moraic trochees, going R to L (and here the final syllable is not extrametrical):

$$
\begin{array}{ll}
(\qquad x\ )\ \} & \textbf{Pw level} \\
(\ x\ .)\ (x\ )\ \} & \textbf{F level} \\
x\ x\ x\ \ \} & \textbf{σ level} \\
x\ x\ xx\ \} & \textbf{μ level} \\
\text{Tennessee}
\end{array}
$$

Now think about what happens when we put words together into phrases in English. Consider, for example, the phrase *ugly fingers*. In isolation the two words both have equally strong (initial) word stress. But when we put them together in American English, a phrasal stress rule gives the noun *fingers* a stronger stress than the adjective *ugly*. (This is not true of British English, and all my remarks on English stress in this chapter should be taken as holding for American English only, unless I make an explicit note to the contrary.)

We are ready now to take *Tennessee* and put it together with an initial-stress word, like *walker*, to yield the phrase *Tennessee walker*. Say the words in isolation, then say them in the phrase. Can you hear the change in the stress pattern of the first word? Stress has RETRACTED onto the first syllable: *Ténnessee*. We can represent this change like so:

```
(    .      x  )              (           x  )    } phrase level
(.    x )  (x  )             (x  ← . )   (x  )    } Pw level
(x  .)(x  )  (x  .)          (x  .)(x )  (x  .)   } F level
  x   x   x      x  x   ⇒      x   x   x    x  x  } σ level
  x   x  xx      x  x          x   x  xx    x  x  } μ level
  Tennessee    walker         Tennessee   walker
```

(The fifth, and top, layer here marks the phrasal stress.) This stress retraction was motivated by the need to avoid a stress clash. A stress clash can be defined as a series of two adjacent x's on the same level with no dot between them. Stress clashes are not defined on the mora or syllable level, since stress is assigned only at the foot level and above. The clash here is between the third COLUMN of *Tennessee* and the first column of *Walker*: On the fourth level, the Pw level, we find adjacent x's. English won't tolerate this clash, so it resolves it by stress retraction. (Notice that after stress retraction, we still have a stress clash, between Columns 3 and 4 at the foot level. We cannot resolve this clash, however, for reasons you will learn about immediately below.)

There are other logically possible ways that this clash could have been resolved. The x in the fourth level of *Walker* might have been moved rightward, for example:

```
(    .      x  )              (              x   )
(.    x )  (x  )             (.      x )    (. →x )
(x  .)(x  )  (x  .)   ⇒      (x  .)(x )    (x  . )
  x   x   x      x  x          x   x   x      x  x
  x   x  xx      x  x          x   x  xx      x  x
  Tennessee    walker         Tennessee    walker
```

This stress pattern, *Tennessée walkér*, does not occur, however, so we need to account for why it does not. It has been proposed that the problem with this solution is that we have created discontinuous columns (both columns of *Walker*). We adopt then the CONTINUOUS COLUMN CONSTRAINT, **which says that if a grid column contains an x on level** $n + 1$, **it must contain an x on level** n.

Well, then, how about moving the third-, fourth-, and fifth-level grid marks of the first column of *Walker* together?

```
(    .      x  )              (              .  →x)
(.    x )  (x  )             (.      x )    (. →x)
(x  .)(x  )  (x  .)   ⇒      (x  .)(x )    (. →x)
  x   x   x      x  x          x   x   x      x  x
  x   x  xx      x  x          x   x  xx      x  x
  Tennessee    walker         Tennessee    walker
```

This solution does not violate the Continuous Column Constraint, so something else must be wrong with it; otherwise we'd get this as an allowable stress pattern. The claimed explanation is that the rule that moves grid marks (MOVE X) **can move only one grid mark at a time. In fact, movement must take place only along the level at which the clash occurs,** so the x of the fifth level couldn't move no matter what.

There is yet one more interesting fact about stress clash resolution in English that I'd like to bring up. The stress retraction in *Tennessee walker* was at the Pw level and the movement of the x took place within a Pw (within *Tennessee*). But sometimes stress can retract from one Pw onto a preceding Pw. Let's consider the phrase *a thousand sixteen troops*. In isolation the third word has the stress pattern *sixtéen*, but in this phrase it has the stress pattern *síxteen*. Let's see how that happens.

```
(              .   x)        (.                    x )
(.             x)  (x)       (x            ←.)     (x )
(x  .)  (.     x)  (x)   ⇒   (x  .)    (.   x)     (x )
 x  x   x   x   x             x  x     x   x        x
a thousand sixteen troops   a thousand  sixteen   troops


    (.                x)
    (x         .    )  (x)
⇒   (x  .)   (x  ←.)  (x)
     x  x    x   x   x
    a thousand sixteen troops
```

(I left out the mora and syllable levels for simplicity's sake. Notice that the second syllable of *thousand* appears to be extrametrical, since at the word level we get initial stress. Both of the two top levels here are phrasal.) In our first grid, we find a clash in Columns 4 and 5, at the third level. The left x retracts, but it has to retract all the way back to Column 1. Do you see why? (If it landed on either Column 2 or 3, we'd have a violation of the Continuous Column Constraint.) So stress retraction can move a stress from one word to a preceding word. (Notice that even after this stress retraction, we still have a stress clash in Columns 4 and 5, so we get a second stress retraction, moving an x from Column 4 to Column 3.)

Now consider the phrase *overpaid boss doldrums*. In isolation the first word gets final stress, the second word is a fully stressed monosyllable, and the third word has initial stress. So all three words will clash. Let's see how English resolves this:

```
(            .   x   )        (             .   x   )
(       .    x)  (x   )       (.            x)  (x   )
(.  x)  (x)  (x   )       ⇒   (x  ←.)    (x)  (x   )      ⇒
(x .) (x)  (x)  (x   .)       (x .) (x )  (x)  (x   .)
 x x x   x    x    x           x x x    x    x    x
overpaid  boss doldrums      overpaid   boss doldrums


(.                    x   )
(x             ←.)    (x   )
(x     .  )    (x)    (x   )
(x .) (x)      (x)    (x   .)
 x x x     x      x   x
overpaid      boss      doldrums
```

(I have omitted the mora level again. The top two levels are phrasal levels.) At this point we have resolved two clashes, but others remain. Let's look at the clash in Level 3 between Columns 4 and 5. We might expect that the stress on *boss* could retract. Certainly this would not create a discontinuous column. Nevertheless, we do not do this: *óverpàid boss dóldrums*.

```
        (.              ·              x   )
        (x                     )   (x   )
  ⇒     (x     x)    ←    (.)   (x   )
        (x .) (x)              (x)   (x   .)
        x  x   x              x     x   x
        overpaid            boss  doldrums
```

(The asterisk preceding the phrase *óverpàid boss* indicates ungrammaticality. We'll be using it a lot in Chapter 4.) Look at all the permissible instances of retraction we have discussed and contrast them to this impermissible case. What do you notice? **Retraction takes place only within parentheses—that is, only within prosodic constituents at the relevant level.** This is one more restriction on movement, then, and we will call it the LOCALITY CONSTRAINT.

We have seen three ways that movement is restricted: indirectly by the Continuous Column Constraint, and directly by the Locality Constraint and the restriction that only one x can move at a time and only within the level at which the clash is defined. We will find in Chapter 4 that syntactic movement also obeys certain principles about what can move and where it can move to. (See particularly the sections "Movement as a test for constituency" and "Strict Cyclicity.")

Retraction is not the only way to resolve stress clashes. We could simply delete the stress from one of the two sequential stressed syllables (and English sometimes uses this method when retraction is not possible). I will not go into that here, though, because we have already spent more time on metrical phonology than a book of this sort can reasonably do. So we will now go on to another theory, even though much more could have been said.

Lexical Phonology

Our discussion of metrical phonology leads us naturally into a discussion of our next phonological theory: LEXICAL PHONOLOGY. Consider again the lists of English nouns that we came up with in our discussion of English stress.

A	*B*	*C*	*D*
tomato	personality	neighborhood	milk bottle
Seminole	employee	worthlessness	chatterbox
venison	unmusical	beautiful	underwear
Massachusetts	illegible	government	pantyhose
asparagus	appendix	heavenward	dining room

When we gave our sketch of an analysis (for that's all that we did), we ignored nouns in Lists C and D. For the moment, we will continue to ignore the nouns in List D, and you will consider them yourself in Problem Set 2.9. But we will now compare the nouns in Lists B and C. So we will focus on nouns that consist of a single root plus affixes of varying types.

In the discussion that follows we are going to be talking a great deal about morphology. So the discussion here is a bridge of sorts to the next chapter.

Okay, so let's look now at the list of words in B and C (augmented by your own Lists B and C). Focus your attention on words that contain only one affix, a suffix. (We will take up the issue of prefixes in Problem Set 2.8.) Take those suffixes and make new lists of as many words as you can that use that suffix. For example, from List B, you'll take the suffixes *-ity*, *-ee*, *-al*, *-ible*, and *-ix*. From List C, you'll take the suffixes *-hood*, *-less*, *-ness*, *-ful*, *-ment*, *-ward*. Now you'll form lists of words like these for the suffixes from List B:

-ity: sanity, frugality, acidity, parity, serenity
-al: renal, pastoral, fatal, universal
-ible: edible, fungible, corruptible

and these for the suffixes from List C:

-hood: motherhood, brotherhood, parenthood
-less: careless, clueless, parentless
-ness: blindness, bitterness

All of these affixes are DERIVATIONAL in that their addition to a stem (that is, to a root, or to a root with affixes) derives a new word. *Motherhood* is a different word from *mother* in its sense. *Parentless* is a different word from *parent* in both its sense and the fact that one is an adjective while the other is a noun.

Consider all the words you've come up with in light of what you know about metrical phonology. What can you notice about the stress of the words in your first set of lists (the words which use the suffixes from List B) as opposed to the stress of the words in your second set of lists (the words which use the suffixes from List C)? If you don't see any generalization about stress right off, then take your words and pronounce them first without the suffix, then with it. Compare for example these two pairs (I have italicized the stressed syllable or relevant examples throughout this dicussion in order to bring your attention to the form of that syllable):

*fru*gal fru*ga*lity *mo*ther *mo*therhood

In general when you add a suffix from List B to a word, it may (although it need not) affect the stress of the resulting new word; but when you add a suffix from List C to a word, it cannot affect the stress of the resulting new word.

Let's see why. First let's compare two pairs that both use the same suffix from List B: in one pair the addition of the suffix did not affect the stress and in the other pair it did:

*mu*sic *mu*sical *u*niverse uni*ver*sal

Assume that adjectives follow the same stress rule that nouns follow in English. Now answer these questions.

Why do we get penultimate stress in *music*? Since the last syllable is extrametrical, there's no choice, right?

Why do we get antepenultimate stress in *musical*? The penultimate syllable is light, so stress goes onto the antepenult.

Now why do we get antepenultimate stress in *universe*? The last syllable is extrametrical and the penultimate is light, so the antepenult gets stress.

And why do we get penultimate stress in *universal*? Again, the last syllable is extra-metrical, but the penultimate syllable is heavy, so stress goes onto the penult.

In sum, **the suffixes from List B form a prosodic word with the stem they attach to, so the stress rule applies after the suffix is added.** If you don't see that, go through the above discussion once more. The point is that the stress assignment rule applies to words with the suffix *-al*, like *musical* and *universal*, as a whole, not to some subpart of it.

Now let's look at any word with a suffix from List C and compare it to the word without the suffix. For example, take:

> *pa*rent   *pa*renthood

Why do we get penultimate stress in *parent*? There's no choice, since the last syllable is extrametrical.

But why do we get antepenultimate stress in *parenthood*? Look carefully. The penulti-mate syllable is heavy because it is closed, yet this syllable does not get stress. Instead, the syllable that would have gotten stress if the suffix had not been added is the one that gets stress.

In other words, the suffixes from List C are not part of the prosodic word. They are added on after stress has already been assigned. The stress assignment rule applies only to the subpart *parent* (which is the prosodic word) in the word *parent-hood* (which is the lexical word).

There's at least one other difference between the suffixes in Lists B and C that I think you'll be able to see now. But first consider the words *inept* and *irrelevant*. Do you want to analyze these words as having a negativizing prefix? Most probably. But if so, what does that prefix attach to? With *irrelevant* the answer is obvious: the word *relevant*. But with *inept* we must posit the root *ept*. This root differs from a word in that is must be BOUND; it can never occur FREE as a word of English.

Now what can you say about the suffixes in List B as opposed to the suffixes in List C with respect to the types of roots they can attach to? Do you see that the suffixes in List B can attach to bound roots, as in *parity*, *renal*, *edible*, but the suffixes in List C attach only to free roots? (Actually, you will find that there are exceptions to this statement when you do Problem Set 2.8. But for now, please assume this statement.)

Both of these observations can be accounted for by positing that we have different levels or STRATA in our phonology. In the first level, Level I, we have a set of rules of phonology and of morphology that apply within prosodic words. In the following level, Level II, we have a different set of rules of phonology and of morphology that apply within lexical words. Notice that in *musical*, the prosodic word and the lexical word are identical. But in *parenthood* the prosodic word is just *parent*, while the lexical word is the entire *parenthood*.

If the suffixes in List B are attached during Level I phonology and if the suffixes in List C are attached during Level II phonology, in what order should each type of suffix appear in a word that has both? The Level I suffix should be closer to the root than the Level II suffix, because it will be attached first, since Level I precedes Level II. Do you see that?

Is that, in fact, the case? That is, does our theory (which posits a Level I and a Level II) make correct predictions? Unless you just happen to come across one of a very few problematic instances, you should have no trouble answering yes.

Let's go through the derivation of such a word. Consider *harmoniousness*.

Level I	*har*mony	assign stress
	*har*mony + ous	add suffix *-ous*
	har*mo*nious	assign stress
	———————	
Level II	har*mo*nious + ness	add suffix *-ness*

Lexical Phonology, then, gives us an account of how rules are ordered with respect to one another by offering us an organization of the phonology and morphology that includes levels. We have not previously considered words in which two rules took place, but now you can see that regardless of what theory you adopt for writing your phonological rules, as long as you have a theory that includes a set of rules, questions of rule ordering present themselves. So the theory of Lexical Phonology complements both the theory of geometric phonology and the theory of metrical phonology. It superimposes a set of principles about rule ordering onto these other theories.

Cycles and the Strict Cycle Condition

According to the theory of Lexical Phonology we take our root and during Level I we add whatever Level I affixes we want and we apply all Level I phonological rules, interspersing the phonological rules and the affixations. We may apply several rules during Level I, and a given rule may apply more than once if something happens in between the two applications to supply the environment for the rule. We already saw this above in the derivation of *harmoniousness*, since stress assignment took place twice during Level I. But stress assignment can take place even more times than that. For example, consider the derivation of the word *musicality*. We know that both *-al* and *-ity* are Level I suffixes. And we know that prosodic word stress can apply after the addition of each of those morphemes, as well as to the root word *music*. So the derivation would be:

Level I:	*mu*sic	assign stress
	*mu*sic + al	add suffix *-al*
	*mu*sical	assign stress
	*mu*sical + ity	add suffix *-ity*
	musi*ca*lity	assign stress

Rules that can reapply (as the stress assignment rule above can) are called CYCLIC rules. All the phonological rules of our lexical levels are cyclic rules. However, the rules that add morphemes cannot reapply; that is, we typically do not allow the same morpheme to occur twice in a single word. Yet the rules that add morphemes can be both preceded and followed by cyclic rules. Thus we usually call all the lexical rules cyclic and we presume that the restriction against the same morpheme occurring twice in a single word has some independent explanation (which we won't seek here).

Now take a look at what happened between the various reapplications of the stress assignment rule. We added a morpheme. In general, this is the case. Typically a phonological rule will not apply twice within a given level unless a morpheme has been added between the two applications. As a result, after the first application the rule will apply to segmental material that includes more than one morpheme (it is said to apply "across morpheme boundaries") rather than to material that is all contained strictly within a single morpheme. In fact, in each subsequent application the rule will apply to segmental material that contains more morphemic boundaries than present on the previous application. This result has been codified and is considered to be part of what is known as the STRICT CYCLE CONDITION. **The major idea of the strict cycle condition is that each rule that applies must apply to an equal or larger domain than the previous rule.**

Once we have done all we'll do in Level I, we move on to Level II, adding whatever Level II affixes we want and interspersing the application of whatever Level II phonological rules we want, again allowing reapplication.

Then we move on to Level III, which again will have its own set of affixes and rules, and which again will allow reapplication.

Level III? Yes, some linguists have posited that there are three levels within the LEXICAL COMPONENT of the phonology. Affixes of the third type would be those that have to be added after all affixes of Types I and II. Can you think of any affixes that always come at the very very end of a word, regardless of what other affixes the word has? Consider words like:

swimmingly   differences   salivate   finalized   children's
grammaticalization   analyzes   alphabetical

Take the final affix of each of these words and try to find any word in which this affix can be followed by another. For example, the *-ly* of *swimmingly* is not final in *friendliness* (the difference in orthography between *-ly* and *-li-* should not have thrown you off—you know better at this point, right?); the *-ate* of *salivate* is not final in *salivated*. While many complications come up, I hope you realized that at least four of these affixes must be final: the plural affix in *differences*, the past tense affix in *finalized*, the present-tense agreement affix in *analyzes*, and the genitive affix in *children's* (although you will learn in Problem Set 4.4 of Chapter 4 that there's more to the story about the genitive affix). These affixes have been called inflectional (and we talked about inflectional suffixes in the section "Geometric Phonology" earlier in this chapter). You will study different types of affixes at length in Chapter 3. (Notice that while derivational affixes like *-ize* can change CATEGORY, such as turn an adjective into a verb—as in *neutral* → *neutralize*—inflectional affixes never change the category of a word.) Regular inflections (as opposed to irregular ones, as in the plural *teeth*) are called SECONDARY INFLECTIONS. The only point I want to make here is that this type of inflectional affix is a major motivation for positing a Level III in the lexical component of the phonology.

Postlexical Rules

And by talking about the lexical component of the phonology we have immediately raised a question that we haven't discussed yet: Do all phonological rules take place in the lexicon? Because Lexical Phonology deals with morphological rules, as well as phonological rules, and because, as we have seen, morphological rules can be interspersed with phonological rules, this question automatically raises the sister question: Do all morphological rules take place in the lexicon?

These questions probably did not occur to you before I brought them up. That's because so far in this book all we have considered is the sound system of language and, just briefly, the system for building words—morphology. But there is much more to language. We know that we must put words together into larger units, because we speak in utterances that range from single words to many words. The component of the grammar that handles putting words together is the syntax. And we know that we must interpret our utterances. The interpretive component of the grammar is the semantics.

Surely some words have to serve as input to our syntax. So we know we must have a lexicon that is available for the syntax to pull words from. But are all words fully formed in the lexicon? And do all words take on their final phonological shape in the lexicon? Lexical Phonology aims to answer these questions, and we'll now look at some of the principles it proposes in answering them.

Consider the following data from Italian. We have here the pronunciation of three words when they are spoken in isolation (and we could have picked any of thousands of other words, but for the sake of simplicity we will discuss examples with only these three):

Roma [rɔ́ma]   bimbi [bímbi]   marino [maríno]
'Rome'   'babies'   'marine, pertaining to the sea'

In sentences, however, we find two different pronunciations for them. In the sentences here the pronunciation matches the pronunciation in isolation:

Vuole visitare Roma. '(S)he wants to visit Rome.'
[vu̯ɔ́.le.vi.zi.tá.re.rɔ́.ma]
Sento piangere i bimbi. 'I hear the babies crying.'
[sén.to.pɪ̯án.dʒe.re.i.bím.bi]
Il vento marino sa di sale. 'The sea wind tastes of salt.'
[il.vén.to.ma.rí.no.sá.di.sá.le]

(I have marked every primary stressed syllable in the examples above and below, and I have marked every syllable boundary. No space or other marking has been made at orthographic word boundaries however. In this transcription and others below, I transcribe affricates with a simple symbol if they belong to a single syllable, but as two symbols—a stop followed by a fricative—when they close one syllable and open the next.) But in the sentences here, the pronunciation differs from that in isolation:

Vado a Roma. 'I'm going to Rome.'
[vá.do.ár.**r**ɔ́.ma]
Sento piangere trè bimbi. 'I hear three babies crying.'
[sén.to.pɪ̯án.dʒe.re.tré**b.b**ím.bi]
Mi piace il blù marino. 'I like marine blue.'
[mi.pɪ̯át.ʃe.il.blú**m.m**ar.í.no]

Look carefully. Can you see the difference? In these sentences the first consonant of *Roma*, *bimbi*, and *marino* is double in duration, so it closes the preceding syllable as well as serves as the onset to the first syllable of these words. I have boldfaced the relevant segments.

Now, you certainly cannot be expected to even guess at what particular factors are relevant to whether the first consonant gets doubled or not. But you can tell me something about what type of factors are relevant. So let's follow up on that.

Can phonological factors be relevant? Yes. If you compare the first set of sentences to the second set of sentences, you will see that the three words in question find themselves in different phonological environments in each of the two sentences. So phonological factors could easily enter here.

Let's get a little more specific. Among phonological factors, could metrical factors be relevant? Look very carefully at the data. Do you see any metrical regularity? In fact, every time the initial consonant of our three words gets doubled, the syllable preceding that consonant (the final syllable of the preceding word) is stressed. In many varieties of Italian, stress on the preceding syllable is necessary for the doubling rule to take place.

Okay, now could syntactic factors be relevant? Remember that syntax is that component of the grammar that deals with how we put words together to make larger utterances. Yes, indeed, syntactic factors might very well be relevant, for the doubling happens only when our three words appear with other words, never in isolation. But it is also possible that syntactic factors are not relevant, since we have already noticed that at least one phonological factor (stress on the preceding syllable) is relevant. So perhaps just this phonological factor is enough, and no particular syntactic relationships between the words other than simple linear juxtaposition matter.

You have not yet studied any syntactic relationships, so we are really jumping ahead here. Nevertheless, I think you can go a bit farther with this before we have to drop it. How could we test whether it is just the linear sequence of words that matters or whether some other relationship also matters? While you don't know much about syntax unless you've taken a class in it, you do know some things. For one, you know words can be organized into sentences. So you know that sentences are a syntactic domain or unit (just as moras, syllables, feet, prosodic words, and lexical words are phonological domains). Now how can you use that one bit of knowledge to answer the question of whether syntax is relevant to this doubling? Surely if one sentence ended in a stressed syllable and the next sentence began with one of our three words, if doubling occurred we would think the doubling rule had to be sensitive to purely phonological factors. (Linear juxtaposition of the two words is a phonological factor, as well, in this instance.) But if in that context doubling was impossible, we'd suspect that the stressed syllable had to be part of the same syntactic unit (here, sentence) that our three words were part of. So let's do that test. Consider these sentences, uttered without any kind of sentential pause between them:

Ne ho trovato trè. Roma è la migliore, però.
[ne.o.tro.vá.to.tré.rɔ́.ma.é.la.miʎ.ʎi̯ɔ́.re.pɛ.rɔ́]
'I found three of them. Rome is the best, however.'

Mi sento blù. Bimbi, bimbi dappertutto!
[mi.sén.to.blú.bím.bi.bím.bi.dap.per.tút.to]
'I feel blue. Babies, babies, everywhere!'

Hanno un colore prediletto, però. Marino.
[án.no.un.ko.lɔ́.re.pre.di.lét.to.pɛ.rɔ́.ma.rí.no]
'They have a favorite color, however. Marine.'

(Two of the utterances above are not complete sentences. Please give me that latitude, because I had a terrible time finding examples that made sense. And, of course, you should feel secure that the same syntactic point is being made, since, without a doubt, the utterances that start with *Roma*, *bimbi*, and *marino* are not part of the preceding sentence.) Assume these examples are representative, so we can see that doubling never occurs across a sentence boundary.

Our conclusion, then, is that phonological factors involving only the features internal to words and only linear juxtaposition of words are not the whole story. But still it is not necessarily so that other syntactic factors are involved, for there is yet one more component to consider: semantics. Could the meaning of the word that precedes our three words matter? Look back at the words that didn't trigger doubling:

for **Roma:**   visitare 'visit', trè 'three'
for **bimbi:**   i 'the', blù 'blue'
for **marino:**   vento 'wind', però 'however'

Compare them to the words that did trigger doubling:

for **Roma:**   a 'to'
for **bimbi:**   trè 'three'
for **marino:**   blù 'blue'

You can see that two of the words that did trigger doubling in one syntactic context did not trigger doubling in another syntactic context. That means that either semantics isn't involved, or, if semantics is involved, it goes beyond the simple meaning of individual words. Instead, it must look at the meaning of larger units —and suddenly we are again talking about syntactic units.

But at this point, yet another objection can be made: It is clear that we must have prosodic levels above the level of words, since we know that suprasegmentals such as intonation can extend over larger groups than just words. In fact, you saw in our examples of stress retraction that we need to admit a variety of prosodic phrase levels (look back at the analysis of *overpaid boss doldrums*). Now certainly sentences are prosodic units in this sense. So the data here, even if they show that the unit of sentence is relevant, again need not show that any syntacticosemantic unit is relevant, since the unit of sentence can be identified as a prosodic unit (as well as a syntacticosemantic one).

Nevertheless, we will not have a prosodic unit of sentence until we have put together our words into a sentence. So our rules of syntax must apply before our doubling rule can apply. This is true regardless of whether the factors on the domain of doubling are syntactic, semantic, or prosodic. This rule, in fact, is called "raddoppiamento sintattico" ('syntactic doubling').

We have now met our first rule with a phonological effect that occurs only in an environment that the syntax helps to create, but there are many. And you are familiar with many, of varying sorts. Consider the contraction of:

Peter is nice.

to

Peter's nice.

in comparison to the impossibility of contraction in:

Peter, as I told you, is nice.
*Peter as I told you's nice.

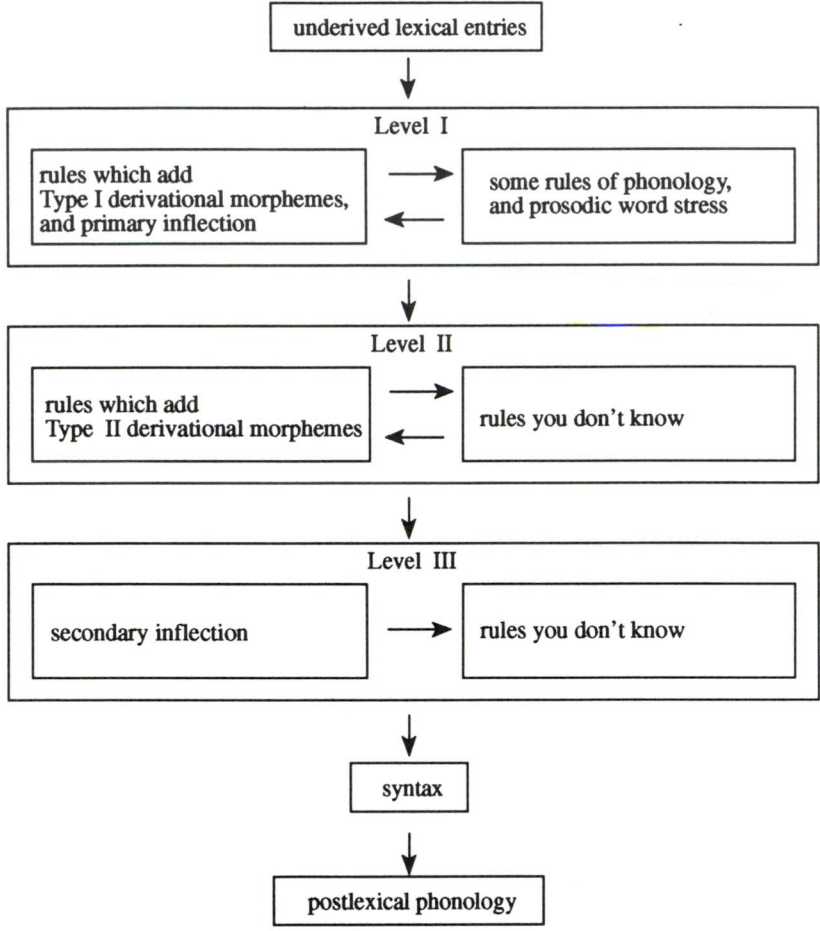

Figure 2.2. Schema for lexical phonology.

This is just one very common example. (The asterisk preceding the second sentence indicates ungrammaticality.)

Rules that have a phonological effect but operate only across word boundaries in a certain context that is at least partially created by the rules of syntax are SANDHI rules. The very existence of sandhi rules tells us that not all of our phonological processes can take place in the lexicon. Instead, we must allow some of them to occur after the syntax, because it is only after the syntax has operated that we have words in sequence in an utterance. So our phonology must have a POSTLEXICAL component in it, which is, in fact, postsyntactic, as well.

Let's take our discussion above and draw a schema for the grammar according to the theory of Lexical Phonology. We will need a set of lexical entities that have not yet been combined into words—the underived lexical entries. This will include all the roots and affixes of our language. We will also need three levels (strata) in which rules of differing types operate on our lexical entries to produce new lexical entries (rules of derivation do this) and to produce new forms of old lexical entries. (Rules of inflection do this.) We have discussed only a small number of these rules. We will then take our newly formed words and allow the syntax to put them together to make phrases and sentences (which is the matter of Chapter 4). Then we will have a level of postlexical phonology that operates on the words in these syntactic phrases and sentences. (Sandhi rules do this, among other types of rules.) So the schema will look like this:

There are several holes in this schema. First, we have completely left out compounding, which you will learn about in Problem Set 2.9 and which we will return to in the section "Compounding" in Chapter 3. Second, you haven't yet heard of PRIMARY INFLECTION. It is the irregular inflection found in plural forms like *teeth* and past-tense forms like *saw*. You will deal with both types of inflection in Problem Set 2.9. Third, we won't be filling in any phonological rules in Levels II and III, unfortunately, except for a brief mention of a stress rule and a nasal assimilation rule in Problem Set 2.9. But I hope that I've given you enough of an idea of this theory so that you can understand its general outline.

One claim of Lexical Phonology is that lexical phonological rules and postlexical phonological rules differ in a number of ways, not just in their ordering with respect to the syntax. For example, **the Strict Cycle Condition is taken to be a principle of lexical rules, not of postlexical rules. Also, (in some versions of Lexical Phonology), if a word formation process, such as the attachment of an affix, creates a prosodic word (that is, a domain for stress), then that word formation process is the result of a lexical rule, never a postlexical rule.**

Underspecification Theory in Lexical Phonology

There are several other important principles and ideas in Lexical Phonology, but we will briefly handle only two more here (and you will meet one other in Problem Set 2.8). Let's look for a moment at vowels. In the data below we see Turkish nouns. (Turkish is an Altaic language spoken in Turkey.) The first column gives the singular form. The second column gives the plural form.

Singular	Plural	
[baʃ]	[baʃlar]	'head'
[dost]	[dostlar]	'friend'
[kul]	[kullar]	'slave'
[kɯz]	[kɯzlar]	'daughter'
[jɨl]	[jɨllar]	'year'
[ders]	[dersler]	'lesson'
[gøl]	[gøller]	'sea'
[diʃ]	[diʃler]	'tooth'
[jyz]	[jyzler]	'face'

(While I have put the above transcriptions between square brackets, I am not sure that I have, in fact, represented a phonetic transcription of the consonants. I am working from other sources which do not always transcribe the examples. The vowels, however, are our focus here and the vowels are accurately transcribed so far as I know.) What are the two allomorphs for plurality? (*-lar* and *-ler*) What determines which plural allomorph a noun will take? Look carefully at the stem vowels. Consult your vowel chart. Is rounding a factor? (No, both allomorphs can follow a stem that has a round vowel or an unrounded vowel.) Is vowel height a factor? (No, both allomorphs can follow a stem that has a low,

mid, or high vowel.) So what distinctive features of vowels are left? Can you see that -*ler*
occurs only after front vowels and -*lar* occurs only after back vowels? (Typically the
central vowels are analyzed as unrounded back vowels in Turkish, as they are in most
languages.) Why is that natural? Because [e] is a front vowel and [ɑ] is not. What kind of a
phonological rule is at play here, in terms of our seven types that we discussed in the first
part of this chapter (listed for you in the section "Dissimilation")? This is an assimilation
or spreading rule. It's different from the other types of assimilation you've seen in two
ways. First, it operates on segments that are not immediately adjacent. And second, it
operates on vowels. This particular type of assimilation rule is known as VOWEL HARMO-
NY, and many languages have it, from languages that are quite different from English (like
Hungarian—and you can now return to our earlier discussion of the Hungarian plural
suffix and consider the harmony there) to languages that are closely related to English
(like Middle High German).

Let's write this rule as a spreading rule. We can indicate that the rule takes place only
with the plural morpheme by the shortcut shown below, in which "μ" now stands for a
morpheme (which you saw before, as in our Hebrew metathesis rule). (Actually, this
spreading rule is a general phonological rule, so it is not necessary to restrict it to applying
to the plural morpheme only. But I'm going to restrict it in the formulation below just to
demonstrate how one might do it.)

There are many questions we must answer. First, do we want to say the plural morpheme is underlyingly -*lar* and that only when the feature of [+front] spreads will the
vowel surface as [e]? Or do we want to say that the plural morpheme has a vowel which is
underspecified for the features of front and back and that it gets these features from the
stem vowel, so that both the features of frontness and backness are spreading? I don't
know which is correct for Turkish, although I have found several books that write the
spreading rule as spreading both front and back. However, if we assume that the underlying morpheme is -*lar*, then we don't have to worry about the features of roundness or
height, since both [e] and [ɑ] are [−round] and since both are the lowest vowels possible
in Turkish with their given value of frontness. For those reasons, please write the rule
assuming that -*lar* is our underlying plural morpheme. You should come out with something like:

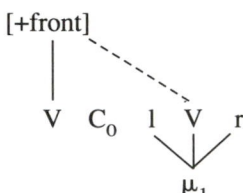

I put a C_0 between the stem vowel and the initial [l] of the plural morpheme. That allows
for zero or more consonants to intervene here. In our examples we had one or two
consonants. So you might well have written "C(C)", where the parentheses around the
second C indicates that it is optional.

Now consider a rule (for which I will give no data) in some unknown language in
which an oral stop between vowels becomes continuant (a spirantization rule, much like
the Spanish spirantization rule we discussed in the section "Assimilation"). Write the rule
in geometric formalism.

$$[+\text{continuant}] \qquad [+\text{continuant}]$$

```
[+continuant]      [+continuant]
   |          \        |
   V          C        V
              |
          [-nasal]
```

Explain why I didn't have to note that the C was [-continuant] in the rule. (If continuancy spreads onto an already-continuant slot, no change will take place, right?)

In this rule formulation I decreed the spreading be from the first vowel rightward. If you made it be from the second vowel leftward, that's fine, too. Without further information, we don't know which is correct in this unknown language.

I want you to compare these two rules now, the one for Turkish plurals and the one for spirantization. In the Turkish rule, is the feature that spreads a predictable feature or not? To answer this, first ask yourself whether vowels in underlying representation will be specified for frontness or not. Assume that the nine vowels given in the column of sample words are all distinctively different from one another. Your answer should be unequivocal: The frontness of a vowel in a noun is not a predictable feature, so it must be specified.

Now look at the spirantization rule. Is the feature that spreads predictable or not? Here we are spreading continuancy from a vowel. If there is any one feature of vowels that absolutely is predictable no matter what language you look at, it's continuancy. (Actually, in English there are several features of vowels that are predictable. List them.) So will continuancy be marked on vowels in UR? No. Vowels will be underspecified for continuancy, given the guideline we adopted much earlier of marking in underlying structure only unpredictable features.

A claim of Lexical Phonology is that **lexical rules will apply to and have access to unpredictable features only, while postlexical rules will fill in and can apply to and have access to predictable as well as unpredictable features.** While this is not a claim that follows as a necessity from the schema of the grammar given above, it is certainly compatible with it. The idea is that earlier forms in a derivation will not have predictable features associated with them. Since the lexical component precedes the postlexical component, it is then compatible with the theory that the lexical component should not deal in any way with redundant features, while the postlexical component should. The upshot of all this is that the rule for Turkish plurals could be a lexical rule or a postlexical rule, while the spirantization rule in the unknown language would have to be a postlexical rule.

Structure Preservation

Consider this question: If lexical rules can see only the unpredictable phonological information, then can a lexical rule ever produce a segment that is not present in UR? That is, could a lexical rule ever produce allophones that are not phonetically identical to phonemes? If you don't know how to begin answering this, let's look back at the Brazilian Portuguese example we talked about in the section "Assimilation." We noted that [t] and [tʃ] occur in complementary distribution, where [tʃ] occurs before [i] and [t] occurs elsewhere. We concluded that the phoneme was /t/ and that the allophone [tʃ] was the result of spreading the feature of [+high] from the vowel onto the consonant. We wrote the rule this way:

$$t \rightarrow [+high] / \underline{\hspace{2cm}} \quad \begin{bmatrix} V \\ +high \\ +front \end{bmatrix}$$

(You can easily rewrite it in autosegmental formalism. Do that now. You can simply put /t/ on the skeletal tier for ease of writing the rule—since the alternative is to give the list of unpredictable distinctive features for /t/ in BP, which you can't be completely sure of without knowing BP.) Does this rule have access to only unpredictable features? Yes, for /t/ is a phoneme, so whatever features we need to indicate /t/ on the skeletal tier are present in UR, and the height and frontness of vowels will also be present in UR. So this rule could easily be a lexical rule so far as we know. But if BP does not have a phoneme /tʃ/, which it does not, then the rule has created a form, the segment [tʃ], that is not present in UR. So the answer to our question is no: The fact that lexical rules apply only to unpredictable information does not entail that lexical rules will produce only segments that are found in the phonemic inventory of the language.

However, the theory of Lexical Phonology has taken on another principle, called STRUCTURE PRESERVATION, which claims that **lexical rules cannot produce segments that are not found in the phonemic inventory of the language. Postlexical rules, however, do not have to be structure preserving in this way.** This principle, as we have just seen, is independent of the other principles we have discussed. And it is this principle which would tell us that the BP palatalization rule must be postlexical, not lexical. It also tells us that the English rule that devoices [l] must be postlexical.

We could certainly go on, looking at more principles of this theory and looking at refinements of the principles we have already discussed. But we will not (although in the section "Theories of Morphology" in Chapter 3 we will deal with certain consequences of Lexical Phonology for morphology), since there is still another theory I'd like to touch on before ending this chapter. But let me just give you a few guidelines for working within the theory of Lexical Phonology.

Here are some questions you should ask yourself as you try to decide whether a rule is lexical or postlexical. (1) Can it apply across word boundaries? Only postlexical rules can do this. (2) Does the rule violate the Strict Cycle Condition? Only postlexical rules can. (3) Must the rule have access to unpredictable features? Only postlexical rules can. (4) Is the rule structure preserving? All lexical rules must be. (5) If the rule attaches an affix, is a prosodic word formed? Only lexical rules can create prosodic words.

Futhermore, there are a few criteria we haven't discussed, two of which I will simply list for you now as questions. None of these other criteria are absolute, however. Instead, they deal with tendencies and frequencies. (6) What kind of process is it? The most common postlexical rules involve feature changing or deletion of segments. (7) Can the output be GRADIENT rather than binary? That is, can the rule change fewer or more features depending on the context? For example, if we have a rule that turns [t] into nothing, [ʔ], or [ɾ] depending on the environment, we have what looks like a gradient rule. Lexical rules are generally binary, but postlexical ones can be gradient in this sense. You will have a chance to consider a third tendency in Problem Set 2.8.

I hope the above paragraph whets your appetite, rather than frustrates you, for we cannot linger here. It's time for our next and final theory of the chapter.

Optimality Theory

With the exception of geometric phonology, which supplanted linear phonology, the theories of phonology that we have examined in this chapter are all complementary and could be viewed as subtheories that make up the whole. Thus a given linguist might use geometric phonology to write a spreading rule, turn around and talk about the five parameters of stress in metrical phonology, and then order all the rules according to principles of Lexical Phonology. But the final theory we are going to look at in this chapter, while it incorporates autosegmentalism and metrical structure, is entirely different: It aims to supplant all other theories with respect to rules.

OPTIMALITY THEORY does not derive PR from UR via a set of rules. Instead, for any particular word many phonological forms are generated at the outset, and the job of the theory is to select from the many forms only that form that indeed occurs in the language. The form that does occur is the most HARMONIC one or the optimal one. Thus there are no phonological rules, and hence there can be no questions or principles about rule ordering.

I will now give you a very brief overview of the theory, and in doing that, I'll introduce a lot of terminology quickly. Try not to be overwhelmed. The concepts are not particularly complex, but the words are new to you. You might want to read with a pencil in your hand and write down the terms and their definitions as I give them.

The theory consists of a GENERATOR, labeled GEN, which generates all the outputs, and a HARMONIC EVALUATOR, labeled H-EVAL, which selects the optimal form.

H-EVAL includes a set of evaluative CONSTRAINTS, which are universal. That is, all languages observe these constraints. But languages differ in how they RANK the importance of the constraints. For example, one language might rank a given constraint, call it C-i, as one of the most important constraints, and never violate it in practice (although **in principle, every constraint may be violated**). Therefore any words generated by GEN that violated C-i would never be chosen as optimal and would not occur in the language. Another language might rank C-i below a different constraint, call it C-j, and never use words that violated C-j, although it might use words that violated C-i. Some languages might never violate several universal constraints. It is even theoretically possible that other languages might violate all universal constraints, although this does not look likely given the studies in Optimality Theory thus far.

All the above may be flying over your head as gobbledygook, because you have no idea what these constraints might look like, and they are, obviously, the heart of the theory. But rather than my giving you a list of constraints, let's try looking at a particular example and then seeing what constraints seem to fall out.

We'll start with Tagalog, a Malayo-Polynesian language of the Philippines. In Tagalog the affix *um* is added to the left edge of a verb stem, sometimes in the initial spot and sometimes after an initial consonant or two. (The sense of the *um* is agentive—similar to the English *-er* added to verbs to derive nouns, as in *walker*, *swimmer*, and so on.) The determining factor for placement of *um* turns out to be the resulting syllable structure of the newly formed word: Tagalog does its best to avoid closed syllables in the resulting word. Let's see how Optimality Theory would handle such a phenomenon.

Consider first the verb stem *abot* 'pass (something), reach for (something).' Let's add *um* to it, starting from the left and moving rightward across the word, so that we generate the forms:

*um*abot   a*um*bot   ab*um*ot   abo*um*t   abot*um*

Now let's evaluate these forms to see which is optimal, given that we want to be sensitive to two constraints.

One constraint is what we mentioned above, that of avoiding codas: *CODA. The asterisk (*) is part of the name of the constraint; it indicates that a coda is to be avoided. You know that English can violate this constraint with relative abandon. (We have codas on many syllables.) But Tagalog ranks this constraint very highly.

*CODA is a member of a FAMILY of constraints that deal with syllable structure. Can you think of other constraints in this family that would make sense? Be very basic here: Think about what seems necessary and what seems most natural or least natural in syllables given the information you've learned in this chapter. Syllable-structure constraints that have been proposed include:

NUC—Syllables have nuclei. (No study that is widely accepted has revealed a violation of NUC in any language.)

ONS—Syllables have onsets. (This follows from the observation that the most common syllable form across languages is CV.)

H-NUC—The nucleus of a syllable will be the most harmonic or sonorant element. (This is simply a codification of the sonority hierarchy.)

And, of course, *CODA.

The second constraint that is most relevant to this phenomenon in Tagalog concerns the fact that *um* prefers the left edge of the word as an attachment site. You are very familiar with the idea that affixes prefer different attachment sites, at least insofar as you have played with both prefixes and suffixes in this chapter. (You will meet more sites for affixes in the section "Beyond English, or The World of Affixes" in Chapter 3.) We can say that there is a constraint which tells us that *um* wants to be at the left edge: EDGEMOST(*um*, L).

EDGEMOST(*um*, L) is a member of the edgemost family of constraints, and you can see that any prefix y- will be sensitive to the constraint EDGEMOST(y, L). All edgemost constraints deal with how far a given linguistic entity (such as the affix *um*) is from a particular edge (L or R). Unlike the syllable-structure constraints, edgemost constraints are not just violated or not, they are violated or not incrementally: the farther *um* is from the left edge of the word, the greater the violation of EDGEMOST(*um*, L).

Again, try to think of other possible members of the edgemost family. Certainly there will be many constraints for suffixes, which all have the form EDGEMOST(x, R), where -x = the suffix. But we could also have edgemost constraints for the placement of stress.

All right, now let's look at our five forms generated by GEN, and see whether or not they violate *CODA and to what extent they violate EDGEMOST(*um*, L). We set up a TABLEAU, which is a matrix with our CANDIDATE forms in the left column and our constraints in the top row. In each CELL of the tableau we put an evaluation of that form with respect to the constraint that heads that column. If the constraint is of the toggle-switch type (that is, it is either violated or not, like the syllable structure family), we put an asterisk in the cell for each violation. An empty cell indicates that the constraint is met. If the constraint is of the incremental type (like the edgemost family of constraints), we put the extent to which the constraint is violated in the cell. For example, with EDGEMOST, we can simply list all the segments between our prefix, in this instance, and the left edge. So let's now set up our tableau and fill in the cells. The affix *um* is capitalized to help you see it. All syllable boundaries are marked, so that you can easily judge whether there is a coda present. (Actually, in marking the syllables, I used the constraint ONS, syllabifying so that a syllable got an onset whenever possible. We are not going to here consider candidates with different syllabification, because ONS is a very high ranking constraint, so those other candidates would have been eliminated as far from optimal right off. However, I was judicious with regard to ONS, excluding from consideration syllabifications that would give an onset cluster that violated the sonority hierarchy. Thus, for example, I did not consider *mb*, in the candidate *aUMbot*, a possible onset.) The left word boundary is marked with # to help you see violations of the edgemost constraint.

Candidates	*CODA	EDGEMOST(um, L)
U.Ma.bot	*	#ø
a.UM.bot	**	#a
a.bU.Mot	*	#ab
a.bo.UMt	*	#abo
a.bo.tUM	*	#abot

Every candidate violates *CODA at least once, and one candidate violates it twice. Only the first candidate does not violate EDGEMOST (*um*, L); all others violate it to greater degrees as we go down the column.

Which form would you predict, based on this tableau, to be the optimal—the one that actually occurs in the language? And you'd be right: It is *umabot*.

Can you tell from this tableau whether *CODA or EDGEMOST (*um*, L) is the higher ranked? No. If EDGEMOST (*um*, L) were the higher ranked, we'd choose *umabot*, since *CODA in this instance would be irrelevant, given that only one form does not violate EDGEMOST (*um*, L). And if *CODA were the higher ranked, we'd still choose *umabot*, because we'd rank four of the forms equally according to *CODA and then use the evaluation of EDGEMOST (*um*, L) to choose between them—and the first candidate would again surface.

Now let's consider the verb stem *gradwet* 'graduate.' How many candidates will you have this time in terms of where *um* can be placed? Eight, right?

UMgradwet	gUMradwet	grUMadwet	graUMdwet
gradUMwet	gradwUMet	gradweUMt	gradwetUM

But given the variety of possibilities for syllabification, we will actually find many more. For example, we could syllabify the form *umgradwet* in these ways:

U.Mgra.dwet	U.Mgrad.wet	U.Mgradw.et
UM.gra.dwet	UM.grad.wet	UM.gradw.et
UMg.ra.dwet	UMg.rad.wet	UMg.radw.et
UMgr.a.dwet	UMgr.ad.wet	UMgr.adw.et

But we won't consider all these possible syllabifications. Again, we will assume the supremacy of ONS as we form the syllables. And again we will not consider syllabifications that would give an onset cluster that violated the sonority hierarchy, such as *mgr*. For the form *UMgradwet*, that leaves us with the first syllable being only *UM*. The second syllable, however, could be *gra* or *grad*. While ONS would favor *gra*, the source I took this example from lists only *grad* in the tableau. I have decided here to include in the tableau only the forms that were included in my source. So please now make your tableau and compare it to mine.

Candidates	*CODA	EDGEMOST(um, L)
UM.grad.wet	***	#ø
gUM.rad.wet	***	#g
grU.Mad.wet	**	#gr
gra.UM.dwet	**	#gra
gra.dUM.wet	**	#grad
grad.wU.Met	**	#gradw
grad.we.UMt	**	#gradwe
grad.we.tUM	**	#gradwet

You might well have have included other forms that differ by syllabification. Please for now consider only the eight I've given here and I will return to a discussion of other possible candidates after we have gone through these eight.

This time it isn't so clear which candidate should emerge as the winner. The first candidate does not violate EDGEMOST (*um*, L) at all, but it has three violations of *CODA. On the other hand, the first two candidates have three violations of *CODA, and all the other candidates have only two, but the candidates with only two violations of *CODA place *um* further and further away from the left edge.

If EDGEMOST (*um*, L) were ranked higher, the first candidate would win, because all other candidates would be eliminated immediately, since they have violations of EDGE-MOST and the first candidate does not.

If *CODA were ranked higher, the candidates with three violations would be eliminated immediately, but all the candidates with two violations would remain. That is, **any candidate with more violations in a given column loses.** We would then look at the edgemost constraint and pick from the remaining viable candidates that with the least severe violation of EDGEMOST (*um*, L), which would be the third candidate.

In fact, the form that surfaces in Tagalog is *grumadwet*, the third candidate. So *CODA is ranked higher. By convention, once we know the ranking of constraints we order them left to right across the tableau with the higher ranked to the left. Also, once a constraint eliminates a candidate, we will put the symbol "!" in the appropriate cell and we will *shade* all rightward cells in that row to show that they no longer can affect the outcome. And, finally, we will mark our optimal candidate with "☞" in the left margin. So now let's go back and fill in the two tableaus above using these conventions.

	Candidates	*CODA	EDGEMOST(um, L)
⇨	U.Ma.bot	**!	#ø
	a.UM.bot	**!	#a
	a.bU.Mot	*	#ab!
	a.bo.UMt	*	#ab!o
	a.bo.tUM	*	#ab!ot

Candidates	*CODA	EDGEMOST(um, L)
UM.grad.wet	***!	#ø
gUM.rad.wet	***!	#g
⇨ grU.Mad.wet	**	#gr
gra.UM.dwet	**	#gra!
gra.dUM.wet	**	#gra!d
grad.wU.Met	**	#gra!dw
grad.we.UMt	**	#gra!dwe
grad.we.tUM	**	#gra!dwet

Okay, now let's return to the issue of syllabification. You might well have come up with an additional eight candidates that differ from those above in having an alternative syllabification:

for candidate 1:   UM.gra.dwet
for candidate 2:   gU.mra.dwet   gU.mrad.wet
for candidate 3:   grU.Ma.dwet
for candidate 4:   none
for candidate 5:   gra.dU.Mwet
for candidate 6:   gra.dwU.Met
for candidate 7:   gra.dwe.UMt
for candidate 8:   gra.dwe.tUM

(I did not consider *mdw* a possible onset or *dw* a possible coda because they violate the sonority hierarchy.) If you add these to your tableau, you will find that six of them violate *CODA only once. And of those six, the form *gU.Mra.dwet* violates EDGEMOST (*um*, L) to the least degree. Yet this form doesn't win. You might be baffled by that fact, and if you are, be consoled; I am also.

The source I took this example from is clearly assuming something about syllabification that would rule out this form. Since *dw* is allowed as a possible onset by my source (as in the analysis of the fourth candidate in the tableau), I will assume that the onset *mr* is illicit (although it is consistent with the sonority hierarchy). Given that, the form that then wins is *grU.Ma.dwet*, which violates *CODA only once and differs from the third candidate in our tableau only by syllabification. Indeed, I don't understand why my source didn't list this candidate and judge it the winner. But do note that this candidate would sound exactly the same to the ear—the only difference is in analysis. Enough said.

Now let's look at a very different type of phenomenon and see how Optimality Theory would handle it—a phenomenon you are very familiar with: the assignment of stress to words that contain derivational suffixes in English. Consider the stem *plácid* and the two words *placídity* and *plácidness*. You have seen how Lexical Phonology accounts for the difference in stress in these two words. Give a Lexical Phonology account right now, please. (If you can't, go back and do a quick review. You'll get it.)

Optimality Theory has no rules, so in a strict sense it can have no rule ordering. However, the theory does allow for the output of one optimization (so to speak) to be the input to the next. In that way we could get the effect of levels and level-ordering. Here, however, let's recognize that the theory offers us a fresh approach and let's simply generate several candidates and choose between them. In this way we can see the insights that the theory has to offer over alternative theories.

Let's start with the analysis of *placídity*. First we generate many forms with *ity* attached to *placid* in varying spots. But English ranks EDGEMOST(*ity*, R) highest, so we don't have to go through all those candidates; we can merely begin with the candidate *placidity*. Did you understand that? In English, suffixes always attach at the right edge of the stem, nowhere else. So this constraint is unviolated in English and therefore it has to be ranked at the top.

The most important question for us, then, is the determination of the prosodic word (the domain to which stress discussions are relevant) vs. the lexical word. We know that in Lexical Phonology we analyzed a word like *placidity* as being both the prosodic word and the lexical word (because *-ity* is a Level I affix, so stress assignment applies after affixation). But in Optimality Theory we need to account for why the analysis of *placidity* as being both the prosodic word and the lexical word is the best analysis.

We now have to meet a new family of constraints: the ALIGN family. This family deals with how we align the various units of a word. For example, do we treat affixes as part of the prosodic word, so that we align the edges of lexical words and prosodic words? The specific member of this ALIGN family that would do this would be written as: ALIGN (Grammatical Unit, Edge, Prosodic Unit, Edge). For short we will write it as Lx ≈ Pw (Lx = lexical word and Pw = prosodic word).

Alternatively, we might treat affixes as outside the prosodic word, so that we align the left edge of a suffix, for example, with the right edge of a prosodic word: ALIGN (Suffix-L, Pw-R). For short we will write this constraint as ALIGN-SFX. One of our jobs will be to figure out the relative rankings for English of Lx ≈ Pw and ALIGN-SFX.

There are many other members in the align family, and some of them are also relevant to the issue before us. One is that we should align the right edge of a prosodic word with the right edge of a syllable: ALIGN(Pw-R, σ-R). For short, we will write it as ALIGN Pw-σ. And since we are going to make use of that constraint, let's also consider ONS, which will be crucial in determining proper syllabification.

Okay, now take the word *placidity* and give me the candidates that would vary on (1) whether the prosodic word aligns with the lexical word or whether the right edge of the prosodic word aligns with the left edge of the suffix, and (2) whether the [d] syllabifies as an onset or a coda. Now make a tableau. We will use the symbol "]" to mark the right edge of a prosodic word. We will use the symbol "|" to mark the left edge of a suffix. We will use periods, as usual, to mark syllable boundaries, and for the sake of simplicity of exposition, we will mark only the syllable boundary that concerns the analysis of the [d]. Please order your constraints across the top of the tableau as I have.

	Candidates	ONS	ALIGN Pw-σ	ALIGN-SFX	Lx ≈ Pw
⇨	placi.d | ity]			*	
	placi.d] | ity		*!		*
	placid. | ity]	*!		*	
	placid.] | ity	*!			*

We know that the best analysis is the first candidate because this is the analysis that wins. (Stress takes the entire lexical word to be identical to the prosodic word.) So now I'd like you to explain why the constraints are ranked as they are in this tableau.

First, why can't ALIGN-SFX be ranked first? Because then the first candidate would be eliminated immediately (as would the third). Okay, now why can't ALIGN-SFX be ranked second? Because then we'd need a first constraint to knock out all of Candidates 2 through 4, but no single constraint does that. So ALIGN-SFX must be ranked third or lower.

That means at least two of the other constraints must be ranked higher and must do the job of together eliminating Candidates 2 through 4. ONS plus ALIGN Pw-σ would do the job, and ONS plus Lx ≈ Pw would do the job. So you know ONS must be one of the two highest constraints no matter what. But no data here can tell you whether ALIGN Pw-σ or Lx ≈ Pw is the other higher constraint. So just bear with me on that until we have looked at more material.

Now, considering the same constraints, give the candidates for *placidness*. This time, however, you do not have the option of considering two syllabifications for the [d], since the suffix begins with the consonant [n], and English does not allow the onset [dn]. (That is, another constraint will wind up eliminating candidates with such syllabification for us.) So you need only consider two candidates, considering the question of whether the prosodic word aligns with the lexical word, or the right edge of the prosodic word aligns with the left edge of the suffix. Make your tableau, using the same constraints in the same ranking.

	Candidates	ONS	ALIGN Pw-σ	ALIGN-SFX	Lx ≈ Pw
	placid. | ness]			*!	
⇨	placid.] | ness				*

Here there were no violations of ONS or ALIGN Pw-σ. That the second candidate wins, even though it violates Lx ≈ Pw, tells us that ALIGN-SFX is ranked higher than Lx ≈ Pw.

So we have now accounted for the rankings, except nothing here has told us that ONS must be ranked higher than ALIGN Pw-σ. Perhaps if you did some additional examples, you'd be able to justify that ranking for yourself.

Notice that as we did the analyses above, we used our knowledge about which candidate the language actually selects to figure out how the constraints are ranked. But once we know the ranking of the constraints in a language, we can then turn to new forms and predict which candidate the language should select. You will do that in Problem Set 2.10.

In sum, Optimality Theory can account for the candidate that surfaces simply by ranking constraints. And one superb insight of Optimality Theory with regard to the particular problem of derivational suffixes and stress in English is that Optimality Theory can account for why derivational suffixes which begin with a vowel are generally part of the prosodic word and derivational suffixes which begin with a consonant are generally outside the prosodic word. Syllabicity is the key, since a suffix that begins with a vowel will attract a final consonant of a stem into the first syllable of the suffix, thereby making it such that if the prosodic word ended before the suffix, the right edge of the prosodic word would not align with the right edge of a syllable. On the other hand, if a suffix begins with a consonant, then this consonant will be in the onset of the first syllable of the suffix, and whether the prosodic word ends before the suffix or after the suffix, the right edge of the prosodic word will always align itself with the right edge of a syllable. (Notice that I brought only derivational suffixes into this discussion, not inflectional suffixes. You might ask yourself whether inflectional suffixes that begin with a vowel, such as *-ing* or comparative *-er*, also are generally part of the prosodic word.)

There are still other types of constraints in Optimality Theory. One family is called the FAITHFULNESS family, and it includes two constraints. PARSE says all segments of a word must be parsed (that is, dominated) by an appropriate node in the prosodic tree. So every segment must be dominated by μ (mora), or σ, or F, or Pw. PARSE, in other words, prohibits what we've called deletion—or the skipping of a segment. But, of course, it can be violated (as can all of the constraints, in theory).

FILL is the other faithfulness constraint. It says that skeletal slots will be filled by segmental material. In other words, it prohibits epenthesis (the insertion of C or V).

Optimality Theory is a new theory and day by day people are coming up with new (families of) constraints. Many questions remain to be answered. We would hope that principles for how languages rank the various constraints would emerge, so that Optimality Theory could play an interesting role in the study of language typology. We would hope that the wild overgeneration of ill-formed candidates would somehow be limited, or that the theory would provide us with a shortcut path through these candidates, so that every evaluation process need not consider huge numbers of candidates.

This ends our discussion of phonology per se, although we will be using the information in this chapter and adding to it in Chapter 3. There are several other theories of phonology that I have chosen not to discuss here in the interest of length. But with a good understanding of the material here, you can approach those other theories on your own and you should find the literature relatively comprehensible.

Let me end by asking you one final question. Given the theories in this chapter, is there a clean division between morphology and phonology? That is, is there a clean division between rules that refer to larger units such as stems and affixes and rules that refer only to distinctive features of sounds? I actually told you at the outset that such a division was impossible, but now I hope you can rally support on your own to convince yourself that the answer to that question must be negative. This chapter, in fact, has already raised many important characteristics of and questions for morphological theory. And that is where we turn in our next chapter.

Problem Set 2.1: Informal Examination of Phonological Rules

1. Make three lists of words that rhyme in English. One list should consist of monosyllabic words. One list should consist of polysyllabic words in which the stress is on the penultimate syllable. And the last list should consist of polysyllabic words with the stress on the antepenult.

(a) What does it mean to say two words rhyme in English? (That is, what must be identical about the words?)

(b) Is the "rhyme" of a syllable (the nucleus and coda together) a misnomer or not?

2. Say the words *dreamt, rinse, youngster*. All of them may be pronounced with an epenthetic consonant.

(a) Give the transcriptions for the pronunciations with the epenthetic consonant.

(b) The epenthetic consonant in each one belongs to a certain class of sounds. What class?

(c) The preceding environment for the epenthetic consonant in each one has something in common. What?

(d) The following environment for the epenthetic consonant in each one has something in common. What?

(e) Account for the epenthetic consonant in articulatory phonetics terms. (That is, what happens in the articulatory apparatus to produce that extra consonant?)

3. In Kihungan, a Bantu language, there is a prefix that goes on verbs which has the form *luN-*, where the N stands for a nasal which varies among [m], [n], and [ŋ]. In fact, some of the time, no nasal shows up at all. Here are some data:

	Stem	*Inflected form*
N + t → tʰ	-tiinis	lutʰiinis 'chase'
N + k → kʰ	-kay	lukʰay 'cut hair'
N + b → mb	-beet	lumbeet 'hit'
N + d → nd	-diik	lundiik 'feed'
N + s → tˢ	-sey	lutˢey 'mock'
N + f → pᶠ	-fut	lupᶠut 'pay'
N + v → mbᵛ	-vaatis	lumbᵛaatis 'dress'
N + h → pʰ	-heek	lupʰeek 'give'
N + l → nd	-lut	lundut 'pass'
N + w → ŋgw	-wiir	luŋgwiir 'obey'
N + j → ŋgj	-jaman	luŋgjaman 'release'

Now answer the following questions. As you do this, assume that a nasal deletes before a voiceless segment. Please understand a symbol with a stop and a superscripted fricative, like [tˢ], to indicate an affricate that fills a single timing slot.

(a) When this prefix is added to a stem that begins with a voiced oral stop, what is the result? Account for which nasal we get.

(b) When this prefix is added to a stem that begins with a voiceless oral stop, what is the result? State a rule (in ordinary words) that will give this result. Must this rule precede or follow the rule that deletes nasals before voiceless segments? Why?

(c) When this prefix is added to a stem that begins with a continuant, we must posit an epenthesis rule (and a following affrication rule, but don't worry about that here). What gets epenthesized? Without considering the example in which the stem begins with [h], but just considering all the other examples with stems that begin with continuants, what determines which consonant gets inserted? (NOTE: This language has no palatal nasals.)

(d) Make a guess as to why we get the result we do with stems that begin with [h].

4. The following is a Japanese haiku:

Fu ru i ke ja	ka wa zu to bi ko mu	mi zu no o to
Ah, old pond	a frog jumps in	the sound of water

All haikus have a fixed number of "groups." I have arranged the Japanese words of this haiku into seventeen groups. Each group consists of a single syllable. But each group consists also of a single mora. I want you to figure out whether the Japanese haiku is a form calling for seventeen syllables (as you may have read in books about poetry) or, alternatively, seventeen moras. You can decide by considering another haiku, one written by the poet Issa, in which the number of syllables is not identical to the number of moras:

Yase	gaeru	makeru	na	Issa	koko	ni	ari
skinny	frog	lose	not(IMP)	Issa	here	LOC	be

'Skinny frog, Don't lose (the fight), Issa is here (cheering).'

(IMP = imperative form; LOC = locative particle.) Japanese has no diphthongs, so each vowel forms the nucleus of a distinct syllable.

First give a syllabic breakdown of the haiku. Then give a mora breakdown. Then decide whether the haiku must be seventeen syllables or seventeen moras.

5. Many languages have language games. Pig Latin in English is one example you might be familiar with. Japanese has a language game called "babibu language." Some examples are:

gakusei → gabakubusebeibi
sora → soboraba
uma → ubumaba
karasu → kabarabasubu
uti → ubutibi

(a) State how the rule works.
(b) Now give the babibu forms for the following words.

kamisori   gakkoo   kanzasi   azisai   kuukoo

(c) How did you handle the geminate vowels in *gakkoo* and *kuukoo* in (b)? If you did Problem Set 1.2, you have a reason to handle them a particular way. Explain why you handled them the way you did.

(d) How did you handle the geminate consonant in *gakkoo* in (b)? Here you had no previous information to help you. Explain what your choices were and why you made the choice you did.

(e) How did you handle the nongeminate consonant cluster in *kanzasi* in (b)? Again you had no previous information to help you. Explain what your choices were and why you made the choice you did.

(f) Look back at what you just learned about the form of the Japanese haiku in Question 4 of this problem set. Given the prosodic unit that the haiku uses, you know something about which units the phonology of Japanese is sensitive to. How do you now think the geminate consonants would be treated in babibu? And how do you now think the nongeminate consonant clusters would be treated in babibu?

(When Japanese borrows foreign words, if the foreign word has a consonant cluster that is not allowed in Japanese, the vowel [u] (or, less often, some other vowel) will often be epenthesized between the two consonants. So in your answers to (d) and (e), if you need to epenthesize vowels, you might assume that the vowel to be inserted is [u].)

*Problem Set 2.2: Diphthongs

1. Some sound segments are open to analysis as being approximants (and thus a type of consonant) or as being nonsyllabic vowels, and in this problem set we are going to call those segments "glides."

Whenever we have a sequence of glide and vowel (in either order), two possible analyses present themselves: Either we have a diphthong, or we have a consonant (which is [−consonantal]) with a vowel.

The choice between these two analyses is basically a question of syllable structure.

That is, is the controversial segment in the nucleus (in which case it is a [−syllabic] vowel) or not (in which case it is a [−consonantal] consonant)?

We can find at least three ways to distinguish between these analyses. The first is based on the Sonority Hierarchy. Some linguists argue that segment types can be broken down into even smaller groups than we did in Chapter 1, giving a number value to the sonority of each group. These are the groups, with voiced obstruents being more sonorous than voiceless ones within each group (which is why some groups have two numbers beneath them).

stop, affricate, fricative, nasal, liquid, glide, hiV, midV, loV
  1 2   3 4   5 6   7   8   9   10   11   12

("Stop" = nonnasal stop; "hiV" = high vowel; "midV"= mid vowel; "loV" = low vowel.) The sonority distance between [n] (which has a value of 7) and [j] (which has a value of 9), for example, would be 2, while the sonority distance between [s] (with value 5) and [t] (with value 1) would be 4.

It has been proposed that within consonant clusters in an onset or a coda, there may be co-occurrence constraints based on sonority distance. A typical constraint would require that two consonants be at least a certain distance apart on the sonority hierarchy. But such constraints don't apply between an element in a nucleus and an element in an onset or coda.

For example, in English we do not permit two sonorant consonants in the onset of a syllable (although we allow them in codas, by the way). That is, there are no sequences of [ml] or [lm] in onsets, for example (although there are in codas, as in [pɑlm] and [fɪlm]).

This means that we can use sonority distance as a way to test whether glides preceding a vowel are part of the onset (consonants) or part of a rising diphthong (nonsyllabic vowels). If such a segment is part of the onset, we might not allow a sonorant consonant to precede it, but if it is part of the nucleus, we might easily find a sonorant consonant preceding it.

Second, we have noted that syllable weight depends on the structure of the rhyme of the syllable. For most languages, a heavy syllable is one whose rhyme contains more than one element or one whose nucleus branches. With either definition, a syllable with a long nucleus (a diphthong or a long vowel) is heavy. So if an open syllable has a glide before a vowel, if that syllable behaves as though it is heavy, then the glide is part of a rising diphthong (and the glide is a nonsyllabic vowel). But if the syllable behaves as though it is light, then the glide is part of the onset (and the glide is a consonant).

In a language that allows closed syllables and that distinguishes only between light and heavy syllables with respect to weight (but does not distinguish between heavy and superheavy syllables—you'll learn about superheavy syllables in Problem Set 2.7), the matter of weight will typically not help us to determine whether a glide that follows a vowel is part of the coda or part of the nucleus. Why not? (Answer this question as part of your problem set, please.)

Third, many languages impose phonotactic restrictions against the co-occurrence of homorganic segments side by side, regardless of whether they both belong to any particular subpart of a syllable. For example, many languages disallow a labial consonant followed by a round vowel, even though the labial is in the onset and the vowel is in the nucleus. However, some languages do the opposite within a nucleus: They require that a glide and a following vowel (or, alternatively, a vowel and a following glide) be homorganic in some way. Thus in such a language, a diphthong might consist of [у̥o] (both elements in the nucleus are [+round]) or [ɪ̥u] (both elements in the nucleus are [+high]), but never [у̥e] or [ɪ̥ɔ], for example. (The elements in the nucleus have no place feature in common.)

Thus, if a glide cannot follow or precede a certain kind of consonant, we know nothing about whether or not the glide is part of the nucleus. But if a glide must follow or precede only a certain kind of vowel, we can suspect that it is part of the nucleus.

Okay, I'd like you now to consider on-glides in English (that is, glides that precede a V). Tell me which is the correct analysis of these two words:

quit: [kwɪt] or [kу̥ɪt]
beauty: [bjuɾi] or [bɪ̥uɾi]

You will get to your final answer step by step by answering all the following little questions. Please be sure to stick to words that are clearly English (and do not seem foreign to you—so don't consider words like French *moi*).

(a) Make a list of words that have a [w]/[у̥] on-glide following an initial consonant. You should come up with words like:

twin   dwarf   thwart   schwa   quote   Gwendolyn

Now make a list of the types of consonants that can precede the [w]/[у̥]. In my speech, two types of consonants are conspicuously absent from the list; labials and sonorants. How could you account for these two facts? (Talk about each fact separately, please.)

(b) Now assume that the following words obey the stress assignment rule we developed in the text, whereby a noun gets stress on the penultimate syllable if it is heavy—otherwise on the antepenult.

équity   réquisite

(I have marked the primary stress for you.) Stress is on the antepenult in these words. Does that mean that the round on-glide counts toward syllable weight or not? How could you account for that fact?

(c) Now consider these data:

queen   swish   sway   dwell   quagmire   swoop   quota   thwart

What can you say about the quality of the vowel that follows our [w]/[у̥]? Is this fact consistent with or problematic for your accounts in (a) and (b) of the value of [w]/[у̥]?

(d) Based on (a)–(c), do you think the round on-glide when it follows an onset consonant is part of the onset or part of the nucleus in English? Give the proper transcription for *quit* now.

(e) Now make a list of words that begin with the [w]/[у̥] on-glide (and no onset consonant preceding the glide). Is this glide in the onset or the nucleus when it begins a word and is not preceded by a consonant? Give at least one argument for your answer or, if you cannot make a determination, explain why you cannot.

(f) Now make a list of words that have a [j]/[ɪ] on-glide following an initial consonant. You should come up with words like:

puny   view   cute   huge   music

Missing from this list in my own speech (although perhaps not in yours) is any combination of a coronal consonant followed by our [j]/[ɪ]. Thus, I don't find [t], [d], [n], [l], [s], [z], [ʃ], [ʒ], [tʃ], [dʒ], or [ɹ] before [j]/[ɪ]. Does the absence of a coronal consonant preceding [j]/[ɪ] tell us anything about syllable structure in general in my speech? Why or why not? If your own speech differs significantly from mine here, please give the relevant data and discuss what they tell us about syllable structure.

(g) Using the same data list you came up with for (f) (yours might differ from mine— in which case, please answer this for each data set), does the range of consonants that can precede [j]/[ɪ] tell us anything about syllable structure in these data? If you say yes, what does it tell us?

(h) Again, using the same data list you came up with for (f), with the same remarks as in (g) about data sets, does the range of vowels that can follow [j]/[ɪ] tell us anything about syllable structure in these data? If you say yes, what does it tell us?

(i) Just based on your answers to (f)–(h), does English treat the palatal on-glide [j]/[ɪ] as part of the onset or part of the nucleus when it follows an onset consonant? Give the correct transcription for *beauty* now.

(j) Now consider these words:

cálculus   cópula   ámulet   Drácula

Did you expect the antepenultimate stress here? How is the stress of these words problematic for your answer to (i)? (One way linguists have handled this is to claim that a rising diphthong can be monomoraic. That is, the nucleus can be a single mora.)

(k) Now make a list of words that begin with the [j]/[ɪ] on-glide (with no onset consonant preceding the glide). Is this glide in the onset or the nucleus when it begins a word and is not preceded by a consonant? Give at least one argument to support your answer or, if you cannot make a determination, explain why you cannot.

2. Now we will consider these same on-glides in Italian. Assume as you do this that Italian, like English, does not allow two sonorants in an onset. Assume also that the data are representative.

(a) Here are Italian words that have [w]/[ɥ] in on-glide position. I will simply put G for glide in the transcription.

buono [bGɔno]   fuoco [fGɔko]   scuola [skGɔla]
nuovo [nGɔvo]   muovere [mGɔvɛre]   luogo [lGɔgo]
suola [sGɔla]   ruota [rGɔta]   vuole [vGɔle]

Given the range of consonants that can precede [w]/[ɥ], do you think this segment is part of the onset or part of the nucleus and why?

(b) Assume that the data in (a) are representative. Given the range of vowels that can follow [w]/[ɥ], do you think this segment is part of the onset or part of the nucleus and why?

(c) Now consider words with the palatal on-glide [j]/[ɪ̯], where, again, I will simply put G for glide:

ieri [Gɛri]	bianco [bGaŋko]	dietro [dGetro]
fiore [fGɔre]	liuto [lGuto]	miagolare [mGagolare]
niente [nGɛnte]	siamese [sGamese]	più [pGu]
rione [rGɔne]	quieto [kwGeto]	chiave [kGave]
ghiera [gGɛra]	tiorba [tGorba]	viola [vGɔla]

Does the range of consonants that can precede [j]/[ɪ̯] tell us anything about whether this glide is part of the onset or the nucleus? If it does, what does it tell us?

(d) Consider again the data in (c). Does the range of vowels that can follow [j]/[ɪ̯] tell us anything about whether this glide is part of the onset or the nucleus? Why or why not?

(The obvious next issue is how these glides affect or don't affect stress in Italian. However, I will not go into it here since stress in Italian is complicated by matters of vowel length.)

Problem Set 2.3: Segmentation

1. A phonetic sequence of two consonants often raises the question of whether in the phonology these behave as a consonant cluster or as a single consonant with double articulation. You are well aware of two such sequences: (1) A stop followed by a homorganic fricative is open to analysis as a single affricate with the feature of [+del rel]; (2) a voiceless stop followed by a glottal stop is open to analysis as a single ejective consonant (that is, a glottalized stop in which phonetically the glottalized stop involves simultaneous release at both the glottis and the oral point of closure, so in a strict sense the two analyses do not really involve phonetic identity). In fact, both pre- and postglottalization can be added to a variety of obstruents (not just voiceless stops) in different languages.

But other types of sequences are equally open to two analyses. For example, (3) a stop followed by a homorganic lateral is open to analysis as a single consonant that begins as a stop and releases laterally. (4) A nasal adjacent to a homorganic oral stop is open to analysis as simply changing the position of the velum (raising or lowering) during one consonant (pre- or postnazalization). (5) Labialization can precede or follow an obstruent, typically a stop.

Furthermore, we can even get multiple articulation. For example, labialize [k] to get [kʷ]. Now add glottalization, to get [kʷ']. Now prenasalize the whole thing, to get [ŋkʷ']. So if you hear such a sequence, you need to consider an analysis with anywhere from one to four consonants (as in [ŋkʔw] or [ŋkwʔ]).

Below are data from Otomí, a Central Amerind language spoken in Mexico. I have written every sound as though it is a full segment. (I am not completely sure of the phonetic value of all the symbols here, since my source was unclear on that point. So please do the problem as though these symbols indicate the sounds we have learned to associate them with in this book.)

(a) bə̀tsí 'child'	(j) tsàpí 'try it'
(b) já 'now'	(k) kwento 'story'
(c) tsʔó 'bad'	(l) ʃų̏di 'morning'
(d) də̌ŋgí 'big'	(m) ʔɲi̧θi̧ 'medicine'

(e) tŏ 'mother-in-law'	(n) tĭni 'he finds it'
(f) ʔjó 'dog'	(o) wade 'chicken'
(g) tʔɯ 'son'	(p) dĕhé 'water'
(h) pá 'day'	(q) gɔʔθo 'all'
(i) pĕtsí 'he has'	(r) hètsʔé 'he sneezes'

Remember that the hook under a vowel indicates nasalization. The diacritics above the vowels indicate high tone (´), low tone (`), or rising tone (˘).

(1) List all the sequences that are potentially open to analysis as a single, multiarticulated consonant.

(2) If you look only at the words that do not contain the sequences you identified in (1), what are the permissible syllable types of Otomí?

(3) If you analyze the sequences you identified in (1) as two or more consonants, what other syllable types must you allow in Otomí?

(4) Just on the basis of your answers to (2) and (3), would you be inclined to analyze these sequences as one consonant or more and why?

(5) If you did Problem Set 2.2, you learned that many languages have phonotactic constraints on the co-occurrence of segment types. English, for example, disallows a coronal consonant to precede the palatal glide. This is an example of a more general phonotactic constraint against sequences of homorganic segments. Given the existence of such constraints in other languages, would you be inclined to analyze homorganic sequences in Otomí as single consonants or consonant clusters? Why?

2. In Figure 2.3 we find seven signs of American Sign Language (ASL): The names of all ASL signs are written in capitals here and throughout this book, following the convention in the ASL literature.

Signs can consist of five different segments:

(a) A movement. We see this in Figure 2.3A. The hand is flat with the fingers spread and the middle and third finger bent together. We will represent this handshape with the symbol [Y̌]. It does not matter for this sign where the hand is located when the movement begins or where the hand is located when the movement ends. All that matters is that [Y̌] moves in a straight line.

(b) A position followed by a movement. We see this in Figure 2.3B. In this sign [Y̌] starts out in the position of sitting on the palm of the other, upturned, hand. Then the [Y̌] moves. Where the [Y̌] is located at the end of the movement does not matter.

(c) A movement followed by a position. We see this in Figure 2.3C. The hands here are flat with spread fingers and the middle finger bent. We will represent this handshape with the symbol [ɣ]. The movement of [ɣ] can start from any position at all, but it must end at the location of the middle finger pointing toward and close to the forehead for the upper hand, and toward and close to the stomach for the lower hand.

(d) A position, a movement, and another position. We see this in Figure 2.3D. The hand in this sign is flat with the fingers together and the thumb separated. We will represent this handshape with the symbol [ḅ]. For this sign [ḅ] is located at the wrist of the other hand, then moves up the arm and stops before the elbow. The positions both before and after movement matter.

(e) A position. We see this in Figure 2.3E. The hand in this sign is flat with all fingers, including the thumb, together. We will represent this handshape with the symbol [B].

That means the structure of these signs is M, PM, MP, PMP, and P, where M =

(A) FLY   (B) TAKE OFF   (C) SICK

(D) IMPROVE   (E) SLEEP

(F) GO UP IN FLAMES   (G) STUDY

Figure 2.3. Seven signs of ASL, with attention to syllable structure.

movement and P = position. (In the linguistic literature on sign languages, you may also find the symbol H for "hold" or the symbol L for "location," instead of the P used here.)

Assume that each of the five signs in Figure 2.3A–E is monosyllabic. Just on the basis of these five signs, if M's and P's are analogous to segments in oral languages, what type of segments are they analogous to? That is, of M and P, which one is a consonant and which one is a vowel? In answering this, first consider just Figure 2.3A–D. Once you've got an initial answer, then look at Figure 2.3E and explain how E can be analyzed consistently with your initial answer.

Now consider the signs in Figure 2.3F and G. F consists of only a movement, since the position the movement starts in and the position the movement ends in can be variable. G consists of only a position. But both of these signs have a SECONDARY MOVEMENT: the fingers of both hands wiggle as the hands move in Figure 2.3F; the fingers of the upper hand wiggle as the hands hold their position in Figure 2.3G.

It has been proposed that secondary movement can occur only on the nucleus of a syllable. We see secondary movement on the M in the sign in Figure 2.3F and on the P in the sign in Figure 2.3G. We often find signs with secondary movement on M, but it has been claimed that the only time secondary movement occurs on P in ASL is when the entire sign consists only of P. Explain these facts in a way consistent with your answer to which is consonantal and which is vocalic between M and P.

Warning: This problem asks you to take M and P as basic segmental types and to assume that only two segmental types are necessary to describe the syllable in ASL. It furthermore assumes that syllables are to be defined with respect to the sign (which is analogous to the word in oral language) rather than with respect to the morpheme. All of these assumptions are found in the literature, but all are controversial. Indeed, a segmental approach to syllable structure in ASL has been shown to be problematic. A more complex approach to the syllable is called for to adequately describe ASL, as argued in some of the references in the bibliography. I have chosen to use this simple model in this problem set because it allows you to build on the knowledge you have of phonology in general at this point.

Problem Set 2.4: Generative Linear Phonology

1. When does /ɹ/ lose voicing in English? Write the rule in linear terms. Can this rule be conflated with our rule for devoicing /l/? If so, write a rule that will cover both changes. If not, explain why not.

2. When does /l/ move onto the palate in English (as in *million*)? Write the rule in linear terms. Can this rule be conflated with our rule for palatalizing nasals? If so, write a rule that will cover both changes. If not, explain why not.

3. Consider the distribution of [s] and [z] in these Italian words:

[sala] 'room'	[kaza] 'house'
[uzo] 'I use'	[askɔlti] 'you listen'
[mostra] 'he/she shows'	[dizerto] 'desert'
[sɔʎːo] 'throne'	[sfera] 'sphere'
[tesːɛre] 'to weave'	[spalːa] 'shoulder'

Even if you know Italian, please consider these data to be entirely representative for the moment.

(a) Are [s] and [z] distinct phonemes or allophones?

If you say they are allophones, which is the UR? Explain your answer. Then write the linear rule which will convert one into the other. If you say they are distinct phonemes, explain your answer.

Now consider these additional data:

[znɛl:o] 'thin'	[zdeɲo] 'distain'
[plazma] 'plasma'	[izlanda] 'Iceland'

(b) If you wrote a rule above in (a), will your rule account for these new data? If so, show how. If not, explain why not. Can you write a revised rule that will account for all the data thus far? If so, do it. If not, explain why not and then write the additional rule needed to handle these data. Classify your rule(s) as one of the seven major types we discussed in the text (loss, addition, assimilation, dissimilation, palatalization, metathesis, compensatory lengthening).

4. Consider the distribution of [t], [tʃ], and [tˢ] in these Japanese words:

[ita] 'board'	[kutʃi] 'mouth'	[tˢuri] 'fishing'
[tokoro] 'place'	[tʃi] 'blood'	[santˢu:] 'three (letters)'
[katta] 'bought'	[hatʃi] 'eight'	[kutˢu] 'shoe'
[te] 'hand'	[motʃi] 'holding'	[motˢu] 'hold'

(a) Are [t], [tʃ], and [tˢ] distinct phonemes or allophones?

If you say they are allophones, which is the UR? Explain your answer. Then write the linear rules which will convert one into the other two. If you say they are distinct phonemes, explain your answer.

(b) If you wrote linear rules for (a), classify those rules according to our seven common types. One of the rules you might have written will classify nicely. The other one resists classification. Why?

(c) In the section titled "'r'-sounds" in Chapter 1 we talked about the fact that there is controversy over the highness of affricates like [tʃ]. In Japanese do you think this affricate is [+high] or [−high]? Why?

Problem Set 2.5: Geometric Phonology

(NOTE: Questions 4 and 5 are more difficult than the others in this problem set.)

1. Rewrite the assimilation rule you wrote in Problem Set 2.4, #1 as a spreading rule in geometric phonology.

2. Rewrite the assimilation rule you wrote in Problem Set 2.4, #2 as a spreading rule in geometric phonology.

3. Consider these data from French:

[fɛ̃] 'end'	[final] 'final'
[bɔ̃] 'good'	[bɔnas] 'tranquility'
[ã] 'year'	[anɥɛl] 'yearly'
[bʁɛ̃] 'brown'	[bʁynɛt] 'brunette'
[vɛ̃] 'wine'	[viɲɔbl] 'vineyard'

(Please ignore the variation in vowel quality across the columns. Also, I have transcribed three of the words in the first column as ending in [ɛ̃], since this is the pronunciation of many younger speakers today. For more conservative speakers the word for 'brown' may end in a rounded front vowel. And, finally, the symbol [ɥ] stands for a high front rounded nonsyllabic vowel; thus I have omitted the diacritic I typically add under vowels to show they are nonsyllabic.)

Assume that the roots for the words in each row are identical across the columns in UR. Assume further that these roots end in a nasal consonant. Based on these data alone, is the distribution of nasal vowels in French predictable? If so, write the rule for nasalization in geometric formalism.

Now consider these data:

[kãtite] 'quantity'
[ɔ̃bʁ] 'shade'
[æ̃bigy] 'ambiguous'

In order to be consistent with your nasalization rule, must these words have underlying nasal consonants or not?

If your original formulation of the rule will not account for the nasal vowels in these last three words, rewrite your rule now to account for them, as well.

This rule is an example of one of the basic principles of geometric phonology. Which principle? Explain your answer.

4. Consider the American English pronunciation

[wʌʧəduṳ̃ŋ̍]

for "What are you doing?" Focus your attention on the affricate. Discuss the generation of this affricate. How does this affricate offer evidence that the feature of continuancy is an autosegment in English? (If you don't see the point here, reread the discussion of contour tones in the text.)

5. In Figure 2.4 you find nine signs of ASL:
These signs are arranged so that the first two of each line go together to make the compound sign that is the third sign of each line. Let me discuss them one by one. (Again, remember that all ASL signs are written in capital letters.)

EAT in Figure 2.4A is an MP sign. The hand has the tips of all fingers, including the thumb, coming together. We will represent this handshape as [Ô]. The [Ô] can start anywhere, but it moves to the mouth.

SLEEP in Figure 2.4B is a P sign. You are familiar with this handshape from Problem Set 2.3. Handshape [B] touches the cheek in this sign.

HOME in Figure 2.4C is a compound, made by putting together the signs for EAT and SLEEP, with modifications that I discuss below. The [Ô] handshape moves to the mouth and then to the cheek.

SLEEP in Figure 2.4D is another sign for "sleep." It is a PMP sign. The hand is flat with the fingers spread in the handshape [5], but the thumb is slightly in front of the hand, instead of sticking out to the side. You can think of this as a relaxed [5] and we will not give it any new symbol. It is located in front of the face, blocking at least one eye and the nose. It closes into the [Ô] handshape as it moves to the chin.

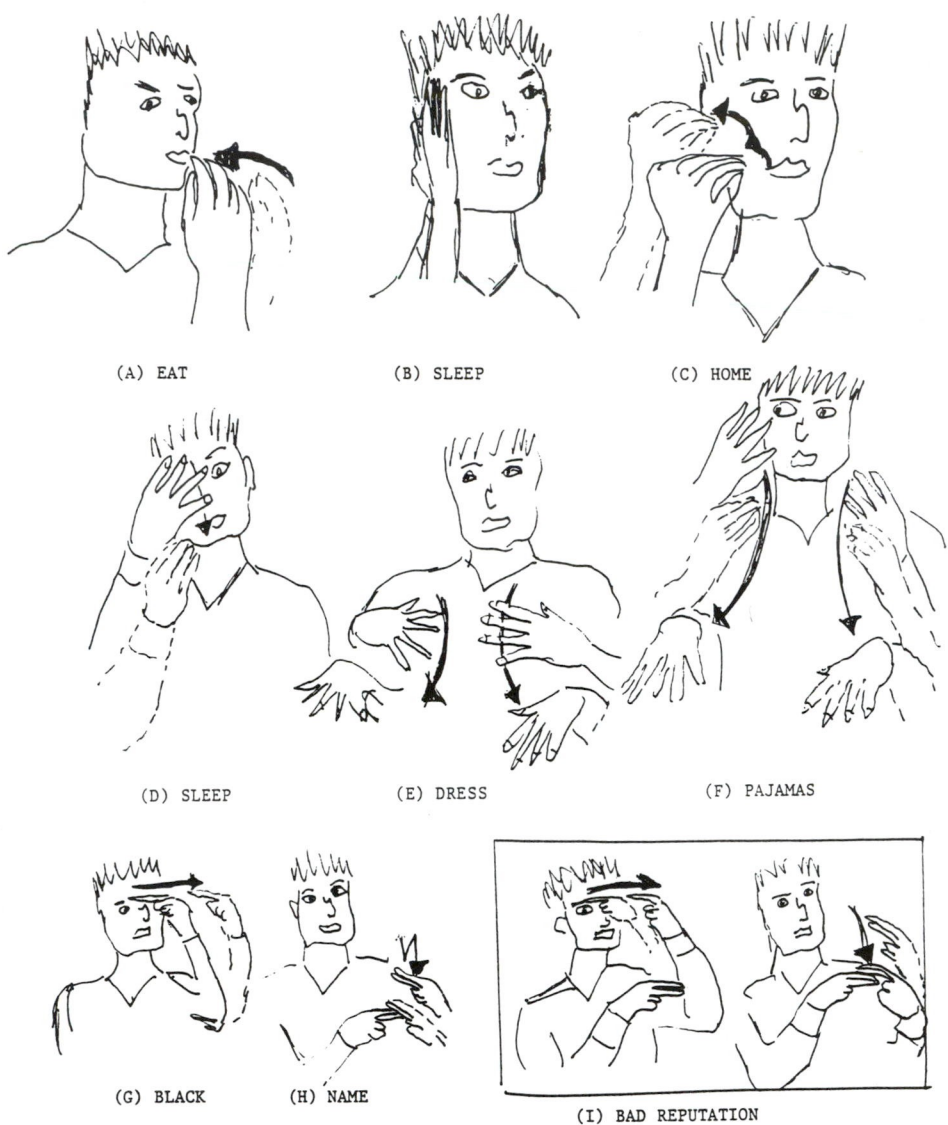

Figure 2.4. Nine signs of ASL, with attention to compound formation.

DRESS in Figure 2.4E is an M sign. The hands can begin in the general area in front of the torso, but they don't touch the body and there is quite a bit of latitude over exactly where they begin. The handshape is [5]. The [5] moves downward and outward. There is no fixed end location.

PAJAMAS in Figure 2.4F is a compound made from putting together the signs for SLEEP and DRESS, again with modifications of the composite signs as I will discuss below. The dominant hand (right hand for a right-handed person, left hand for a left-handed person) begins in front of one side of the face, not blocking either eye or the nose. The [5] moves downward, changing into an [Ô] as it passes the neck and then into a [5] again as it moves down and away from the torso. At the same time the other hand does the same motion with the same handshapes, the only difference being that it begins at a lower place (to one side of the neck rather than to one side of the face).

BLACK in Figure 2.4G is a PM sign. The hand is closed in a fist with the index finger sticking out straight in a [G] handshape. It begins on one side of the forehead, then moves across and out to the side of the head.

NAME in Figure 2.4H is a MPMP sign. Both hands are closed in a fist with the first two fingers sticking out straight in an [H] handshape. The dominant hand can begin movement from any place. It comes down and the bottom finger of the dominant hand hits the top finger of the other hand. Then the movement and position are repeated.

BAD REPUTATION in Figure 2.4I is a compound made from putting together the signs for BLACK and NAME, as always with modifications of the composite signs. The dominant hand begins as a [G] on one side of the forehead. It changes into an [H] as it moves across the face and downward to hit once on the other hand. The other hand stays in an [H] through the entire sign.

(a) If the syllable structures you came up with in Problem Set 2.3, where you studied Figure 4.2, are all the possible syllable structures in ASL, then what is the minimum number of syllables that NAME must have? Give the analysis of the syllables of NAME in terms of P's and M's.

(b) How many syllables do these three compounds (HOME, PAJAMAS, BAD REPU-TATION have and what is their shape? Please answer separately for each compound. (You may find that more than one analysis makes sense to you. That's fine. Just discuss all analyses that are consistent with the data presented and with the information and your answers earlier in this problem set.)

All of these compounds give evidence of phonological rules having applied. That is, none of them is a simple concatenation of two signs. Instead, one or both of the signs that make up the compound has been altered somewhat.

(c) Two of these three compounds lend themselves to an analysis in which assimilation or spreading occurs. Which two? Something different is spreading in each compound. What? What is the direction of spreading (to the left or right) in each of these signs?

(d) One of these compounds undergoes a simplification rule. Which one? Can you suggest any motivation for this simplification?

Warning: This problem set assumes the same approach to ASL syllable analysis as that given in Problem Set 2.3. This approach is controversial and, probably, too simple to be empirically adequate. I refer you to the warning there and to the bibliography for that problem set. I do not believe that a more complex syllable model, however, would affect the theoretical import of the present problem set.

*Problem Set 2.6: Geometric Phonology

1. Consider the following data from Sudanese (A Sudanic language spoken in Sudan):

[mãke] 'to use'	[raris] 'in demand'	[panãs] 'warm'
[combrek] 'cold'	[ŋũliat] 'to stretch'	[tumpuk] 'small heap'
[mãnĩs] 'lovely'	[tarimãq] 'to receive'	[kitaq] 'I'

([c] is a voiceless palatal stop. [q] is a voiceless uvular stop.)

Is the distribution of nasal vowels predictable? If so, write a geometric rule that accounts for nasality on vowels.

Now consider these additional data:

[māhãl] 'to be expensive'   [dahar] 'to eat'   [nãũr] 'to say'
[nĩʔĩs] 'to cool oneself'   [nãĩãn] 'to wet'   [bɤŋhãr] 'to be rich'
[mĩʔãsih] 'to love'   [nĩʔĩr] 'to pierce'

You have learned two new facts about the rule you just wrote. State those facts.

Assume that the data above are totally representative and, furthermore, that the only consonants made in the laryngeal area are [h] and [ʔ]. These data offer evidence that we need a laryngeal node. What distinctive features would link into the laryngeal node? (That is, which features reflect matters of the larynx—vibrations of the vocal cords, opening and closing of the larynx? Of course, these features are linked to separate tiers that then link to the laryngeal node.) Have any of these features been involved in any other spreading rules that you've studied?

Rewrite the rule that nasalizes vowels to account for all the data here.

2. Transcribe the following words. (For polysyllabic words please mark the stressed syllable.)

napped   luffed   rented   clawed   cried   showed   nabbed
loved   rended

(a) What are the three phonetic forms for the regular past-tense morpheme? Write them in IPA. (We call different forms of a single morpheme ALLOMORPHS.

(b) What are the environments for each of these three allomorphs? Answer this in terms of which segments they follow. In your head (not on this homework) go through other regular verbs in the past tense. (Ignore all irregular past-tense morphemes.) Now give me the environments in terms of distinctive features, not just lists of segments.

(c) Which of the three allomorphs would you propose as the underlying form for the past-tense morpheme? Why?

(d) Write the rule responsible for the voicing feature in geometric formalism.

(e) Write the rule responsible for epenthesis or, alternatively, vowel loss in geometric formalism.

(f) Can the two rules in (d) and (e) be conflated in geometric formalism? If so, do it. If not, explain why not.

(g) Discuss the rule in (e) in light of my comments in the text about the Obligatory Contour Principle.

Problem Set 2.7: Metrical Phonology

(NOTE: Questions 2 and 5–7 are more difficult than the others here.)

1. Consider these words from Warao, an Amerind language of Venezuela, Surinam, and Guyana:

yiwàranáę̀   mèḫokóhi   mǫáụ   mǫ̀aụ́pu
yàpurùkitànęḫáse   ìnạwáḫạ   enàḫoròahàkutái

The "y" here is to be taken as the palatal consonant [j]. (My source used a different phonetic alphabet from the IPA and I hesitate to transcribe the examples into IPA since I'm not sure of the phonetic value of all the symbols in that other system.) Please assume that all vowels are syllabic. The diacritic of a little rightward hook under a symbol indicates nasalization. (I have used this rather than the IPA tilde because it is hard to see both a tilde and a stress mark over a vowel.)

(a) State the stress rules for Warao in simple words.

(b) Now give the values for the five parameters for stress in this language. Let me take you through these. First, is the foot bounded or unbounded? Second, is there any evidence of quantity sensitivity? Third, is the foot right- or left-headed? Fourth, is the word right- or left-headed (that is, does the rightmost or leftmost foot receive the primary stress)? And fifth, do we form feet from left to right or right to left?

(c) Does Warao have one of the three most commonly found types of feet (the syllabic trochee, the moraic trochee, the iamb)? (Be careful here: by "iamb" I mean a foot consisting of a light syllable and any second syllable, or a foot consisting of a single heavy syllable.) If so, which one?

(d) Now draw a metrical tree and then a metrical grid for *enròahàkutái*.

2. Consider these words from Warrgamay, a Pama-Nyungan language of Australia:

báda   gagára   gíɟawùlu   ɟuɽágayj-mìri

(Recall that [ɟ] is a voiced palatal stop, and [ɽ] is a retroflex flap. The fourth word has five syllables, of which the third has a glide and a consonant following the vowel.) Assume each of these words is representative of the stress pattern for all words of the same length.

The stress pattern here may be more difficult to discern than that for Warao above. So please follow me step by step.

(a) Are the feet here bounded or unbounded?

(b) Is the direction of forming feet R to L or L to R? (Be careful. Think about the fact that in two- and four-syllable words, the first syllable gets primary stress, but in three- and five-syllable words, the second syllable gets primary stress. Which direction will account for this difference?)

(c) Are these feet left-headed or right-headed?

(d) Is the word level left- or right-headed?

Now consider these additional facts. First, in Warrgamay syllables with a long vowel are heavy; all other syllables are light. Second, long vowels may occur only in initial syllables. Third, whenever the first syllable of a word has a long vowel, that syllable gets primary stress, even in words with an odd number of syllables. An example is:

gí:baɽa

(e) Is this language quantity sensitive?

(f) What kind of foot (syllabic trochee, moraic trochee, or iamb) does this language use?

(g) Two of the words in this problem have degenerate feet. Which two? Which is the degenerate foot and why is it degenerate? How are degenerate feet handled with respect to stress assignment in Warrgamay?

3. What are the values for the five metrical parameters for a language that has primary stress on the second syllable? (Please assume that no syllables are extrametrical.) Where do you expect to find secondary stresses? What do you think will happen to monosyllabic words? An example of such a language is Kungen, an Australian isolate.

óg 'water'   álbmb 'possum'   algálgal 'very straight'
alwán 'sleep'   edjér 'rain'   elbmbélbmbel 'red'
uwál 'gave'   igígun 'keeps going'

In what way is this language unusual with respect to metrical theory? (Think about what kind of foot we have here. Notice that the language allows closed syllables, and ask yourself whether syllable weight plays a role in stress assignment.)

4. What are the values for the five metrical parameters for a language which has primary stress on the first heavy syllable, or, if there are no heavy syllables, then on the last syllable of the word? (Such a language is Komi Jazva, a Permic language of the Finno-Ugric family.)

5. In the text we saw that Classical Arabic places stress on the last heavy syllable of a word, or, in the absence of a heavy syllable, on the first syllable of the word. Actually, the facts are a bit more complicated. Consider these words:

[kitá:bun]   [mámlakatun]   [qá:ʔɪm]

(a) What is surprising here? Which syllable did you expect to get stress in all of these words?

(b) How could we use the notion of extrametricality to account for the stress on these words?

Other facts are even more interesting. Consider these additional words:

[ʔalqʊrʔá:n]   [qa:nú:n]   [karí:m]   [taəkí:r]

(The diacritic ˘ over the schwa indicates a very short vowel.)

(c) Why is the second set of data surprising in light of the first set of data?

(d) In the text we defined a heavy syllable for Arabic as one with a branching rhyme (or two moras). Now let us define a SUPERHEAVY SYLLABLE as one with a branching nucleus plus a coda. State the distinction between the first set of data and the second set of data using the notion of superheavy syllable.

(e) Now use the notion of extrametricality to give a statement of the Arabic stress rule that will cover all the data in the text as well as the data in both sets here. (The ideal situation would be to maintain the rule we came to in the text, by properly noting exactly what is extrametrical in an Arabic word.)

6. In the text we looked briefly at stress on nouns in English. Now let's look at verbs. Consider these:

A	B	C
várnish	revóke	adópt
intérpret	delíght	remínd
cáncel	èntertáin	dìsregárd
embárrass	sùpercéde	insíst
remémber	caróuse	románce

Please limit yourself to considering just these words as you answer (a)–(c).

(a) What is the stress pattern in List A, List B, and List C?

(b) Describe the form of the final syllable in each of these lists. Classify that syllable as light, heavy, or superheavy. (Be careful here. If you did Problem Set 2.2, you know that a palatal on-glide does not contribute to the weight of a syllable in English. Also, consider carefully the nucleus of the final syllables in List B.)

(c) State the stress rule for these English verbs making use of the notion of extrametricality.

(d) What is the foot structure? Do we form feet left to right or right to left? Is English left- or right-headed at the word level? (You probably need to transcribe each word into IPA first, so that you can easily note syllabic consonants and other details that may affect syllable weight.)

Unfortunately, as with our discussion of noun stress in the text, our picture of verb stress is not anywhere near complete. Consider the following two verbs and discuss how they present problems for the rule you stated in (c). Each verb presents a different problem, so be sure to discuss each separately. (Warning: Again, be sure to distinguish between orthography and phonetic realization.)

    mótorìze   caréss

How might lexical phonology account for the stress pattern on *motorize*? (Think here of level ordering.) Could a similar account be offered for *caress*? If not, why not?

7. State how you can predict whether main stress will be on the first syllable or on the second syllable in Alyawarra (which is an Arandic language of central Australia).

ingwá 'night'	Alyáwarra 'Alyawarra'	iylpá 'ear'
kwátja 'water'	túwntjila 'loud'	kwíja 'girl'
píynta 'spring'	walíymparra 'pelican'	yukÚntja 'ashes'

These words are not in phonetic transcription. Please assume that every vowel is syllabic. Also assume that "y" stands for the glide [j]. (I don't know what "j" stands for, but that won't concern you as you do this problem.)

The language here is sensitive to something about syllable structure that we have not discussed with respect to metrics. This language is extremely unusual in this regard and even if you become·a phonologist, you may never run across metrical sensitivity to this factor again.

Can you use the notion of extrametricality to help here? Consider the on-glides [w/u̯] and [j/i̯]. If you use extrametricality to account for the stress in Alyawarra, is your rule more naturally stated if these on-glides are part of the onset or part of the nucleus of a syllable?

8. In Cayuvava, a language of Bolivia, we find primary stress on the antepenultimate syllable and secondary stress on every third syllable before the primary stress, like so: σ σ̀ σ σ σ́ σ σ. Here are two words:

    medàručečèirohíiɲe   'fifteen each'
    čaadàiroròbirohíiɲe   'ninety-nine'

(The symbol "č" stands for [tʃ].)

Discuss all the five parameters for this language. How is this language problematic for metrical theory?

Problem Set 2.8: Lexical Phonology and Prefixes in English

1. How are the two following words problematic for Lexical Phonology? Please discuss them separately, since they raise different problems.

    feckless   developmental

2. In the text we discussed the claims of Lexical Phonology that (1) lexical rules apply only within word boundaries, whereas postlexical rules can apply across word boundaries; (2) lexical rules must obey the Strict Cycle Condition, whereas postlexical ones need not; (3)lexical rules involve only unpredictable feature information, whereas postlexical rules can fill in, specify, or refer to redundant features (this was part of Underspecification Theory); (4) lexical rules never create segments that aren't identical to phonemes in the language, whereas postlexical rules can (this was known as Structure Preservation); and that (5) lexical rules can create a prosodic word, whereas postlexical rules cannot.

There is another claim of Lexical Phonology: **one type of rule applies without exception, whereas the other type of rule can have lexical exceptions.**

(a) Your job now is to figure out whether lexical rules are the ones that have many lexical exceptions or whether postlexical rules are the ones that have many lexical exceptions. In doing this you might consider examples such as the following (an asterisk indicates that the word doesn't exist and ?? indicates that I'm unconvinced the word exists):

    arrive   arrival   *arrivation
    derive   *derival   derivation

You should be able to use one of the five criteria above to determine whether the addition of the affixes *-al* and *-ation* is by lexical or postlexical rules, and, given that determination, you can argue whether lexical or postlexical rules can have lexical exceptions.

(b) Now find one other phonological or morphological rule (not the addition of *-al*, or *-ation*, but something that you come up with) to make another argument for your answer. Please give the relevant data.

(c) Given your answer to (a), determine whether the addition of *-ling* and the addition of *-hood* are by lexical or postlexical rules. In doing this, you might consider examples such as:

    duck   duckling   ??duckhood
    woman   *womanling   womanhood

3. In the text section "Geometric Phonology" you were given data on a Finnish rule involving a verb stem plus an inflectional suffix. In this rule an oral stop assimilates to a preceding nasal or liquid. Look back at those data now. Is this rule lexical or postlexical? Give at least one argument for your answer.

4. In our discussion of Lexical Phonology, we pretty much ignored the behavior of prefixes. There was a reason for this. Think about English stress. What is the direction parameter? In English we start at the right edge of the word and move leftward, correct?

(a) Now what does that suggest about the addition of prefixes? If the base has three or more syllables to start with, should the addition of a prefix be able to affect primary word stress even if the prefix is part of the prosodic word? No. As the first part of answering this question, I want you to explain that "no."

English inflection never takes the form of a prefix. (You'll just have to believe me on that until we do more with inflection in Chapter 3). That means we don't have to ask whether there are any Level III prefixes. So to ask whether prefixes divide into groups like suffixes, what we are asking is whether some belong to Level I and some belong to Level II. I want you to answer that, using the data here and your arguments. (Please limit yourself to these data, because others you may come up with on your own could present complications.)

(b) Consider the negative prefix *un-* and its behavior with respect to stress assignment. Does it behave like a Level I or Level II affix?

| háppy | unháppy | wíse | unwíse | just | unjúst |
| éven | unéven | fáir | unfáir | awáre | unawáre |

(NOTE: You may not be able to account for the stress in these adjectives before the affixation of *un-*). Don't worry about that. All you need to do is consider the interaction of this stress assignment rule (however the rule may work) with the affixation of *un-* in order to answer the question.)

(c) Now consider the negative prefix *in-* with respect to stress assignment. Does it behave like a Level I or Level II affix?

finite ínfinite fámous ínfamous

(NOTE: Again, don't worry about how the stress assignment rule here works. Just compare the stress without *in-* to the stress with *in-*—that's enough to answer the question, regardless of the specifics of the particular stress assignment rule operating here. Also, you may object to my example *infamous* on the grounds that the prefix here does not negate the adjective. I put it in to stir up trouble—because morphology is trouble, as you'll see in Chapter 3.)

Since there are so few examples here, you might also consider:

válid ínvalid (the noun)

and:

píous ímpious

where the nasal has assimilated to the place of the following oral stop.

(d) How is the existence of the following words relevant? Did you expect to find such words?

inept inane indelible indefatigable insipid

(e) The following pairs may be problematic for your answer to (c) depending on something. On what?

| sáne | insáne | fírm | infírm |
| secúre | insecúre | corréct | incorréct |

English has an assimilation rule that can spread certain features onto a nasal from a following consonant. Do not worry about the details of this rule (that is, about which features spread or what kinds of consonants participate in the spread); just assume the existence of the rule, and call it Spread-to-nasal.

(f) Assume that Spread-to-nasal has applied in these words and that in UR they contain the negative prefix *in*-:

illegal   impure   irregular   immoral

Notice that Spread-to-nasal cannot apply to the negative prefix *un*-:

unlawful	*ullawful	unpopular	*umpopular
unreal	*urreal	unmindful	*ummindful

Account for these facts in a Lexical Phonology framework, consistently with your answers to 2 and 3. Be sure to say what level Spread-to-nasal must belong to.

5. In 4 you contrasted the prefixes *in*- and *un*-. Now find any two other prefixes of English and argue that one belongs to Level I and the other belongs to Level II. Give at least one argument for each claim.

Problem Set 2.9: Lexical Phonology, Compounds in English, and French Liaison

1. In the text we did not discuss words of the type in List D, that is, compounds (words with more than one root). Consider these English compounds now:

roller skates	arms merchant	neighborhood bar
math teacher	toothbrushes	whitewashed
pregnancy alert	salinity chart	catlike

Make a long list of compounds, and keep adding to it over the days until this problem set is due. (This is hard to do and the problem set would be much easier if I just gave you a big list. But part of my goal here is to let you learn how to recognize relevant data and organize them. If possible, do this as a group project, so that data gathering is not so time-consuming.) Let your compounds consist of two words only (although in English compounding is ITERATIVE, or RECURSIVE—a term we'll use in the section "Compounding" in Chapter 3, so we can have indefinitely long compounds, such as *undergraduate linguistics language requirement*.) We will speak of them as consisting of word 1 and word 2.

What I'd like you to do is try to figure out where compounding should be ordered in Lexical Phonology. Please assume that it should be a lexical rule. So the issue is, is it in Level I, Level II, or Level III?

In order to do this, please consider the following questions.

(a) Can you come up with a compound in which word 1 contains a Level I derivational affix? If you say yes, give the compound and be sure to show me that this affix truly does belong to Level I. (Show that it is part of the prosodic word for stress assignment and/or that it can attach to a bound root.)

(b) Now do the same for word 2.

(c) Can you come up with a compound in which word 1 contains a Level II derivational affix? Again, if you say yes, give the compound and show me that this affix truly does belong to Level II.

(d) Now do the same for word 2.

(e) Given your answers to (a)–(d), could compounding possibly take place during Level I? Why or why not? Could compounding possibly take place during Level II? Why or why not?

In Lexical Phonology Level I includes the affixation of several derivational affixes, stress assignment, certain other phonological rules, and what has been called primary inflection (a term you met briefly in the text). Primary inflection is responsible for inflection that is achieved via change in vowel quality, as in these plurals:

foot feet   mouse mice   goose geese
[fʊt] [fiɪt]   [maʊs] [maɪs]   [guʊs] [giɪs]

and in these past tenses (one involves both an internal vowel-quality change and a suffix):

sing sang   take   took   sleep slept
[sɪŋ] [seɪŋ]   [tʰeɪk] [tʰʊk]   [sliɪp] [slɛpt]

(Your dialect may have for *sang* [seŋ], without a diphthong. The same point holds: This is primary inflection.)

Level III includes other phonological rules and secondary inflection, such as the regular plurals and regular past-tense affixes here:

cat cats   dog dogs   walk walked   cry cried

(f) Can you come up with a compound in which word 1 contains a Level I primary inflection? If you say yes, give the compound and be sure to show me that this truly is an instance of primary inflection.

(g) Do the same for word 2. Be very careful here. You want to make sure that the plural or past-tense inflection in your example pertains to or has SCOPE OVER only the sense of word 2, not the sense of the whole compound. For example, in *scarecrows* (which uses secondary inflection) the plural sense is of more than one *scarecrow*, not of something that scares more than one crow, so the plural has scope over the whole compound, not over just word 2. If you aren't sure of the scope of your example, give it and discuss why you aren't sure.

(h) Can you come up with a compound in which word 1 contains a Level III secondary inflection affix? If you can, give the compound.

(i) Do the same for word 2, and heed the warning in (g).

(j) Given your answers to (f)–(i), could compounding possibly take place during Level I? Why or why not? Could compounding possibly take place during Level II? Why or why not? Could compounding possibly take place during Level III? Why or why not?

Now consider the following contrasts between compounds on the one hand and phrases of an adjective plus a noun it modifies on the other. (You won't really deal with the concept of phrases until Chapter 4, but just do the best you can here, please.)

You write on a *blackboard* with chalk.
Sue painted the *black board*.
That tree is known as a *redbud* despite its pink blooms.
One stem of that rose bush has a *red bud* at the end.
I'm going to *whitewash* the bench.
I'll do my *white wash* first.

All of these compounds involve component words that are monosyllabic.

(k) For short compounds like this, does word 1 or word 2 get the higher stress? How does that compare to their relative stresses when word 1 modifies word 2 in a phrase (in contrast to a compound)? (NOTE: British English speakers will answer this differently from American English speakers.)

(l) Now look back at all the compound words you've considered during this problem set. Many of them involve polysyllabic component words. Does word 1 or word 2 get higher stress in these longer compounds? Give an example to support your answer.

(m) In Problem Set 2.6 you learned about the regular past-tense affix, which has the allomorphs [t] (after most voiceless consonants), [d] (after most voiced segments), and [əd] (after coronal nonnasal stops, regardless of voicing). Now the addition of [əd] will add a syllable to a verb. Likewise, if you'll give it just a moment's thought you will realize that there are three allomorphs for the regular plural on nouns: [s] as in [kʰæts], [z] as in [dɔgz], and [əz] as in [glæsəz]. Can you give the environments for each? Compare this to the past-tense morpheme. (Isn't English beautiful?)

Warning: Much of the Lexical Phonology literature puts compounding in Level II. You have been led to a different answer here. So don't be surprised if you open another phonology book or article and find compounding located in Level II.

2. French exhibits a rule known as LIAISON, whereby words in larger utterances are sometimes pronounced differently from how they are pronounced in isolation. Here are some examples. In the first of each triplet we see the pronunciation of the word in isolation; in the second, the pronunciation of the word in one kind of context; and in the third, the pronunciation of the word in a different kind of context.

    A. [de] des 'some' (indefinite article, plural)
       [dez] des ennuis 'some troubles'
       [de] des problèmes 'some problems'
    B. [dɑ̃] dans 'in'
       [dɑ̃z] dans une salle 'in a room'
       [dɑ̃] dans la salle 'in the room'
    C. [nu] nous 'us'
       [nuz] Paul nous appelle. 'Paul calls us.'
       [nu] Paul nous repousse. 'Paul rejects us.'

The data are very few, but I think you should still be able to draw some conclusions from them.

(a) Is liaison a lexical or postlexical rule? Give reasons for your answer.
(b) What is the phonological effect or change of the rule of liaison?
(c) Under what phonological condition(s) does liaison take place?
(d) Can you determine whether liaison is a sandhi rule? Why or why not?

Problem Set 2.10: Optimality Theory

1. Give an account in Optimality Theory that explains why we say *creativeness* and not *creatnessive*.

Let's review the relevant constraints:

ONS says a syllable should have an onset.

ALIGN Pw-σ says the right edge of the prosodic word should line up with the right edge of a syllable.

ALIGN SFX says the left edge of a suffix should meet the right edge of the prosodic word.

Lx ≈ Pw says the edges of the lexical word should line up with the edges of the prosodic word.

You learned in the text that these constraints are ranked in English in the order I've listed them, from high to low. So please just assume that as you make your tableau.

Okay, now take the words *creativeness* and *creatnessive* and give me the candidates that would vary on (1) whether the [t] of *create* syllabifies as an onset or a coda, and (2) whether the prosodic word aligns with the lexical word or whether the right edge of the prosodic word aligns with the left edge of a suffix.

For 1, you will have two possibilities for *creativeness*, but only one for *creatnessive*.

For 2, you should consider three possible Pw boundaries (after *creat*, after the first suffix, and after the second suffix) for each of the possible words. For each of *creativeness* and *creatnessive*, you have to consider the possibilities for syllabification of the [t], taking all three of these possibilities for Pw boundary into account.

That means you will have six candidate analyses to consider for *creativeness* and three candidate analyses to consider for *creatnessive*.

Now make a tableau. Please use the symbol "]" to mark the right edge of a prosodic word, and use the symbol "|" to mark the left edge of a suffix. And, as always, use the symbol "." to mark syllable boundaries (but the only syllable boundary you have to worry about is the one that crucially involves the syllabification of the [t]).

In each cell of the tableau you will indicate whether the candidate conforms to the constraint (resulting in an empty cell) or violates the constraint (resulting in an * in the cell). For each column, once a candidate has violated that constraint, you put an ! after the * if there are still other candidates that have not violated that constraint or any higher constraint. Once a candidate has an ! in any cell, that candidate need not be evaluated further.

If a candidate violates a constraint more than once, put an * for each violation in the appropriate cell. This will happen in these candidates. Notice that you have two suffixes, so the constraint of ALIGN-SFX can be violated twice by some of your candidates.

The candidate that has no violations or the lowest-ranked violation is the winner.

Once you have made your tableau, answer these questions:

(a) Which is the analysis that actually occurs in English? (Be sure to give the analysis here. Don't just say *creativeness*; give this word with the proper syllabification and the proper Pw boundary.)

(b) Does Optimality Theory correctly select the analysis you gave in (a)?

2. Assume we have these metrical constraints in English:

STRESS: Each lexical word must get primary stress.

$<\sigma>]_{NP}\#$: Mark the final syllable of NP as extrametrical.

$*[\mu]^F$: Mark a monomoraic foot as degenerate.

Assume that the foot in English is a moraic trochee and that we form feet R-L. Thus two light syllables or one heavy syllable forms a foot, but a stranded light syllable would be degenerate. Assume English bans degenerate feet (that is, they do not get stress).

(a) Any noun in English that consists of two syllables where the first is light presents a serious problem with respect to stress. Why? (Hint: Think about the metrical status of the final syllable in nouns in English. Then remember that a light syllable alone will form a degenerate foot.)

(b) The following word presents these two stress patterns in different varieties of English:

    políce   pólice

One of these words violates $*[\mu]^F$ and the other violates $<\sigma>]_{NP}\#$. Which violates which?

(c) There are four candidates for the analysis of this word into feet, where angled brackets indicate that the material inside them is extrametrical and not available for stress and parentheses indicate that the foot inside them is degenerate and not available for stress:

    po.lice—two feet, both available for stress
    (po).lice—two feet, the first degenerate and not available for stress
    po.<lice>—two feet, the second extrametrical and not available for stress
    (po).<lice>—two feet, the first degenerate and the second extrametrical, neither available for stress

Using these four candidates, set up a tableau with our three metrical constraints across the top. Now for the varieties of English that say:

    políce

figure out whether the proper analysis is

    po.lice   or   (po).lice

by filling in the cells of the tableau you have just set up. (How do you know right off that *po.<lice>* and *(po).<lice>* cannot be the winner? Neither of these has final stress. That's why I'm asking you to focus on the other two candidates.) What is the ranking of these three constraints in these varieties of English?

(d) Now for the varieties of English that say:

    pólice

figure out whether the proper analysis is

    po.lice   or   po.<lice>

by making another tableau with the four candidates and filling in the cells. What is the ranking of these three constraints in these varieties of English?

(e) You have now seen that a simple difference in the order of the ranking of constraints can be responsible for a difference in stress patterns between varieties of English. However, there is one constraint that is ranked highest in all varieties. Which one? Do you expect this constraint to be ranked very high across all varieties of English and perhaps across all languages that use stress? If so, why? If not, why not? (I'm asking for some conjecture here. But informed guesses can be instructive.)

NOTE: The constraints proposed in this problem are not generally used in Optimality Theory. I made them up in order to bring together this theory with what you know about metrical phonology. If you are interested in seeing the constraints proposed in the literature, please consult the references for this problem set.

3

Morphology

Chapter Organization—for the Instructor

This chapter starts by talking about the relationship between sense and form. We contrast lexical morphemes to grammatical ones, analyzing five English words. The analyses lead to theoretical issues, including the notion of head of a word, the Unitary Base Hypothesis, the issue of homophony vs. polysemy, productivity, and evaluative affixes. In the process, a set of criteria emerge for distinguishing derivational from inflectional affixes. A discussion of affix typology leads to a language typology according to morphological characteristics. We consider verbal morphology at length, and the ways new words are added to language. The intent is to give a good descriptive background so we can turn to more theoretical matters.

Prosodic morphology and process morphology follow. We study the interaction of compounding with other word-formation processes as well as with the syntax and semantics. We then move on to bracketing paradoxes in larger and larger domains, encountering word-formation processes that are sensitive to syntactic structure, including Case systems and clitic systems, and we end the chapter ready to move on to syntax.

Okay, let's go

Morphology is the study of word-formation processes and that's what we're going to look at in this chapter.

Give me a monosyllabic word of English. Any monosyllabic word. You might have given any number of words, but let me give you *dog*. What does that word mean? What is the SENSE of it? This is by no means an easily answered question. Grapple with it a while. Maybe you've come up with the idea that the meaning of *dog* is, in fact, an animal. But then, what would the meaning of *unicorn* be? Since we know (or believe) no such animal exists, is this word meaningless? Surely not. If we want to have an idea of the sense of words that will carry from word to word, maybe we need to get more abstract.

Try again. Perhaps you've come up with the idea that the meaning of *dog* is some idea or ideal of a dog—some concept of a dog. Then the meaning of *unicorn* is likewise a concept. But, then, we have a new question: What is a concept? At this point you might start talking about mental images.

Mental Images as Concepts

Once I took a semantics course in which the professor did an experiment with us, and I'm going to do that experiment with you right now. I don't know the source of this experiment and I hereby apologize to the person who devised the experiment if I have distorted it. Take a sheet of paper and a pencil. Relax—no one is going to grade you on this. Put a second sheet of paper over this page right now so that only the line you are reading at this moment shows. Move that sheet of paper down slowly, so that nothing below the line you are actually reading shows. Now give yourself five seconds each to draw the following items (and please draw them now, as you read, and before you uncover the lines below): (1) a person, (2) an animal, (3) a building, (4) a boat, (5) a flower. Okay, now beside each of those five items, I'd like you to draw the following items: (6) a man, (7) a dog or a cat, (8) a house with a chimney and maybe smoke coming out of it, (9) a sailboat, (10) a daisy or a tulip.

For how many of 1–5 were 6–10 identical? In classrooms that I have done this experiment with, most people had at least three identical pairs. Certainly, with awareness of sexism in language (as elsewhere), you might well not have made 1 and 6 identical. And if you grow roses as a hobby, you might not have made 5 and 10 identical. Your philosophical and political attitudes, the particular circumstances of your life, maybe even your mood today could have affected your answers.

But let me ask you, what does this experiment show about the sense of these words? You might object that it shows nothing except the fact that you lack self confidence as an artist, so you draw what's easiest. But isn't drawing a boa constrictor easier than drawing a dog? Isn't drawing a canoe easier than drawing a sailboat?

You might object that in America dogs are the archetypal animals and sailboats are the archetypal boats, so all this experiment shows is the archetypal item of Type X in your culture. You might point out that in Ancient Egypt cats were the archetypal animal and in traditional Inuit culture umiaks are the archetypal boats. And I suspect that your objection has a lot of merit to it.

But let me persist a moment longer. Even admitting the possibility that a house with a chimney might be the archetypal item matching the word *building* in our culture, do you think the person who drew a skyscraper has a different idea of what *building* means from the person who drew a house with a chimney? Do you think the person who drew a pregnant woman has a different idea of what *person* means from the person who drew a man? Are we all constantly using the same words to mean different things? Is there no hope of our understanding one another?

If I've depressed you, lighten up. I don't believe we all go around misunderstanding each other all the time. At least not at the level of the sense of words like *building* and *person*. All I hope to have demonstrated is that some sort of mental image may well not be a totally adequate way of defining concepts. And think of the many many words for which there is no hope that we would ever find any semblance of stability across our various mental images when we hear the word—words like *love, maturity, wisdom*.

The point of the discussion above is twofold. **First, most words do have a sense and it is this sense that allows us to use them to convey information.** Second, defining the notion of sense is not a simple matter. We are not going to pursue the definition further here because this endeavor belongs more properly in a discussion of semantics (and we will return to conceptual issues in meaning in the section "Mental Representations and Conceptual Semantics" in Chapter 5). For now, we will simply use the fact that most words have a sense. The word we started with, *dog*, has a sense.

Arbitrariness

New question: Why does *dog* have the sense that it has? What is there about the word that tells us what it means? Why don't we call dogs *zather* or *boop*? Let's be a little more specific. Is there any subpart in the word *dog* that you can point to and say—that part tells me it is a mammal, or—that part tells me it walks on all fours? Does the sound of the word, the very sound itself, tell us anything about its meaning? Let's say that you have decided to learn a new language, Southwestern Otomí. Do you have expectations about what the word meaning 'dog' will be in Otomí? The word is *ʔyó*. (The accent indicates a high tone; in this transcription the *y* indicates the glide [j], since my source does not use strictly the IPA.)

I hope your answer was a resounding no. You have now discovered one of the most fundamental ideas of linguistics: **the relationship between the phonological shape of a word and its meaning is arbitrary**. And, indeed, the reason we spent so much time talking about the sense of a word was so that you could have a strong-enough idea of what meaning is in order for this generalization to have content for you.

For oral languages, this generalization is equivalent to saying the relationship between sound and meaning is arbitrary. For manual/visual languages, this is equivalent to saying the relationship between sign and meaning is arbitrary. This idea forms the foundation upon which Historical and Comparative Linguistics rests. Historical and Comparative Linguistics is the study of the relationship between the different languages of the world and of how languages change over time. We cannot go into this study in this book because of limitations of time and space. But let's make a quick aside to give you a sense of why the above insight is important to this study.

Tell me: If the relationship between sound and meaning is arbitrary, and if we find two languages in which words with the same or similar meaning have very similar sounds, what can we conclude about the two languages? For example, in German we find *Hund*, *Buch*, and *Katze*, which have similar or identical senses to *hound*, *book*, and *cat* in English. What can we conclude about German and English? Either the similarities are an accident—a pure coincidence—or the languages BORROWED words from one another, or the languages are GENETICALLY RELATED (that is, they descended from a common mother language). It turns out that English and German are genetically related; they share a close common ancestor called PROTO-GERMANIC. We cannot go further with this here, but I encourage you to pick up a book on historical linguistics.

Returning to our claim of arbitrariness between sound and sense, does that mean that there is never a relationship between the sound of a word and its meaning? Of course not. Give me some words of English where you feel quite sure that from the sound of it, you might have predicted a meaning close to what it actually does mean. You might have come up with words like:

quack   meow   cock-a-doodle-doo

The Italian equivalents are:

qua qua   miao   chicchirichi

The similarities are noticeable. If you know anything about the history of English, you might realize that Italian and English are also genetically related languages: They share a more distant common ancestor called Indo-European. For this reason you might not be terribly impressed that the Italian equivalents are so close to the English ones. After all, they could derive from the same sources in Indo-European. So consider the Japanese equivalents:

gaagaa   ɲaaɲaa   kokekokoo

Japanese is not genetically related to English and Italian, so the similarities to the English and Italian words challenge the claim of an arbitrary relationship between sound and meaning. The phenomenon at play here is ONOMATOPOEIA. We say that words whose sound mimics their meaning are onomatopoeic, and animal sounds are among the likely candidates for onomatopoeia in language after language.

While onomatopoeia is evident in language, it is relevant to only a handful of the thousands and thousands of words in English or Italian or Japanese or any other language. Thus onomatopoetic words are a clear, but limited and even expected exception to our claim of arbitrariness.

But are there other types of examples in which just from the sound of a word we have some idea of what it might mean? Consider the made-up word *stode*. Let's say that this is a verb. Do you think that stoding is a quick action or a slow one? Do you think you'd be likely to be joyous or solemn as you do it? If you said you thought it might be a slow action that goes with a solemn attitude, then you might well be making some connection in your head to other words, such as:

stay	stub	stand	stagnate	stupid	stop	stink
stumble	stall	sticky	stain	stoop	stable	stone
stance	stagger	stooge				

Many of our words that begin with *st* have a slow or negative sense to them. This is because in our ancestor language, Indo-European, there was a root **st* that meant 'be/stay.'

Not all our words starting with *st* have this slow or negative sense, however. List some that don't, such as:

style	steep	startle	starling	start	stamp	star

Thus if you didn't feel any slowness or negativity in the nonce verb *stode*, don't worry, you weren't making any sort of mistake. In other words, while *st* at the start of a word may favor a certain vague sense of slowness or negativity, it does not have to. And the reason that it does this has to do with the history of our language and not with the sounds themselves. Thus if we look at genetically unrelated languages, we do not find words beginning with *st* that have a slow or negative sense. In fact, very few languages allow *st* in word-initial position since very few languages allow *st* in the onset of a syllable (and you know why, given the discussion of the sonority hierarchy in Chapters 1—the section "Sonority" and Problem Set 1.4—and 2—the section "Syllable Types").

So what do we do about *st*? Let's see what would happen if we were to identify *st* as a unit of meaning. **We call minimal meaning-bearing units morphemes, a term that we've been using all along in this book (and a term whose definition will be refined repeatedly as we proceed through this chapter).** So our question becomes, what happens if we call *st* a morpheme? When discussing the component parts of a word such as *stub*, we'd identify the *st* morpheme. At that point we'd have two choices. First, we could say *ub* was also a morpheme. But what would *ub* mean? What parts of the sense of *stub* would be contributed by *st* and what parts would be contributed by *ub*? To answer that, we could look for other instances in the language where this same *ub* morpheme occurs without a preceding *st*. But there don't seem to be any. Words like *rub* and *pub* don't have any obvious connection to *stub*. So we haven't gained any explanatory value by calling *ub* a morpheme. Alternatively, we could say both *st* and *stub* are morphemes and that we allow overlapping morphemes in English. It is unclear to me whether or not morphological theory should allow overlapping morphemes. But even if the theory allows this kind of analysis, we must ask ourselves again what semantic contributions to the word *stub* each of the two morphemes would make. The question seems patently unanswerable.

For these reasons, I see only problems resulting from identifying an *st* morpheme in English. Instead, I think we should admit that the fact that *st* used to be a morpheme in an ancestral language manifests itself today in a vague expectation of what the sense of a word that begins with *st* might be. Some linguists employ the term PHONESTHEME to describe such sound sequences, and the term may be useful to you. But I do not know of any systematic theory of how phonesthemes behave; thus, all we can do here is identify them. We will now go on to discuss other, less elusive, matters.

Morphemes: Phonetic Realization

I hope that at this point you feel relatively comfortable about going forward with our claim that there is an arbitrary relationship between the sound of a morpheme and its meaning. So now let's compare the words *dog* and *dogs*. What does the addition of the orthographic "s" add to the sense of *dog*? Plurality, of course. The word *dog* is monomorphemic: It consists of only a LEXICAL morpheme. But the word *dogs* has two morphemes: It consists of the lexical morpheme *dog* plus a GRAMMATICAL morpheme. The grammatical morpheme here is the inflectional plural suffix. And, having read Chapter 2, you are aware of another type of grammatical morpheme, exemplified in a word such as *doggish*. The *-ish* is a derivational morpheme, here deriving an adjective from a noun. (In Chapter 2 and here, I use terms like "noun" and "adjective" without definition. We will discuss such morphosyntactic categories more formally later. For now just start with whatever definition you have from your grammar-school days and add to it the growing amount of information you amass from reading this book.)

In English and many other languages of the world, lexical morphemes are to be identified with roots, another term we have used in earlier chapters. They are what you might think of as the heart of a word, the part without which you couldn't have a word and the part to which all the grammatical morphemes attach. They contribute the meatiest or most salient part of the sense of whatever word they are part of. Most lexical morphemes in English can occur as independent words with nothing else attached to them. That is, most lexical morphemes are free, although you will meet bound lexical morphemes later (lexical morphemes which must have something else attached to them in order to form a word—you met these terms in Chapter 2). The grammatical morphemes, including derivational and inflectional affixes (again, terms we're familiar with from Chapter 2), are generally bound.

You have seen, then, that a morpheme can be smaller than a syllable (like the plural morpheme) or a single syllable (like *dog* or *-ish*). Can a morpheme be two syllables? Try to find a two-syllable word that seems to consist of only one meaning unit.

Be careful here: This is not to say that all morphemes must be meaningful units. Rather, every meaningful unit that is noncompositional (that is, whose meaning is not a composite of the meanings of its subparts) is a morpheme, by definition. But it is arguable that some morphemes are purely functional and not meaningful. We'll return to this point. For right now, let's just look for two-syllable words that consist of a single meaningful morpheme. They are easy to find in English:

fellow   cactus   liver   rabbit   seldom   carrot

You could go on and on. Notice that some of the words in this list have subparts that are homophonous with other words of English. (Homophonous words sound the same, but have different meanings. We met them in Chapter 1 and we will discuss them later in this chapter.) For example, compare the noun *liver*, meaning an internal organ, to the verb *live*. But we do not analyze this word *liver* into two morphemes, with one being *live*, since the sense of *liver* does not by any stretch of the imagination include the sense of *live*. Likewise *fellow* does not include the morpheme *fell*. Instead, each of the words in this list is semantically unanalyzable. So each word is a minimal meaning-bearing unit (that is, a morpheme).

Can you think of a three-syllable word that seems to consist of only one morpheme? This is a little harder, but not impossible:

tomato   marabou   paradise   kangaroo
lecithin   banana

(If you feel *lecithin* is debatable as to whether it includes a suffix, that's fine. So do I. I put it there to goad you.) Can you think of a four-syllable word that seems to consist of only one morpheme? This is quite hard. You may have come up with examples like:

karaoke   salmonella   jacaranda   Massachusetts

(If you feel *karaoke* is debatable, probably you know something about the history of this word in Japanese. For those of us who don't, it belongs on this list.) How about five syllables? It's a tough search.

Sagittarius   jaboticaba   cock-a-doodle-doo

What can you say about the limit on the number of syllables in a single morpheme in English? Generally it's three, right? In fact, most examples have only one or two. That is, the three-, four-, and five-syllable words you've listed probably are borrowings from other languages, where that probability gets greater as the number of syllables gets larger (in my list of four-syllable words, *karaoke* is from Japanese, *jacaranda* from New Latin, and *Massachusetts* from Massachusett—an Algonquian language of the northeast United States), and they may well be polymorphemic in those source languages, or have some other unusual history. *Salmonella*, for example, was coined from the name of the American veterinarian (Daniel Salmon) who discovered the bacteria. Other examples include words that involve a repetition of phonetic parts, including *helter-skelter* and *razzmatazz*. (You will read more about such processes later in the section "Reduplication.")

We'll talk more about borrowing as a source of new words in language briefly later. But we won't follow up on sources similar to that for *salmonella* because this type of coining of new words is relatively rare and definitely sporadic. You might try now to think of others. Surely examples like *pasteurize* (from the scientist's last name, *Pasteur*) are easy to recognize. But recognizing others may require information that most people don't have. For example, *hoodlum*, according to some sources, is derived from the backwards spelling of *Muldoon* (with the final *n* becoming an initial *h*), the name of a gangster in San Francisco in the 1870s.

Let's return now to our discussion of the phonetic realization of morphemes. The important point we were heading toward is that the relationship between morphemes and prosodic units is not fixed in English. In practice it does seem to have an upper limit, although in theory it does not.

Does it have a lower limit? For a word like *sheep*, the addition of the appropriate plural morpheme results in no sound difference whatsoever, yet we know that sometimes *sheep* is singular and sometimes it is plural, since when it is the Subject of a sentence, sometimes it calls for singular verb agreement and sometimes it calls for plural verb agreement:

> One sheep stands in the road.
> Sixteen sheep stand in the road.

(In Chapter 4 we will look at the notions of Subject, Direct Object, and other grammatical functions. For now please use whatever working definitions you have from grade school.) The plural morpheme on the plural word *sheep*, then, is a ZERO morpheme, in that it has a zero realization (that is, zero phonetic material). In fact, some morphemes always have a zero realization (such as many agreement morphemes on verbs in English, as you will learn in Problem Set 3.5). So in English morphemes need not correspond to any prosodic unit whatsoever.

Nevertheless, there is still more we can say about the prosodic size of different kinds of morphemes in English. What kinds of morphemes can be zero: lexical morphemes, grammatical morphemes, or both? Only grammatical, for the absence of a lexical morpheme in a prosodic word would rob the word of the major part of its sense (but you will see a challenge to this in Problem Set 3.3). And what kinds of morphemes are, in fact, larger than two syllables in English, lexical or grammatical? Only lexical. If you look at our grammatical morphemes, they are generally small prosodic units, consisting of zero:

> **derivational**: V → N   cover   cover
> **inflectional**: first-person plural: walk

a single segment:

> **inflectional**: plural: cat*s*

a syllable:

> **derivational**: N → A   music   music*al*
> **inflectional**: progressive aspect: walk*ing*

or two syllables:

> **derivational**: A → N   sane   san*ity*

(I have not included an example of a single-segment derivational morpheme in English, because the only ones I can think of get realized as a syllable—such as the *-y* of *fishy*. I have not included an example of a two-syllable inflectional morpheme in English, because I know of none. Also, in these examples you meet names for notions we have not discussed, such as "person" and "aspect." We will return to these later in the sections "Person, Number, Gender, and Verbal Inflections" and "Verbal Inflections and Affixes.") So, while the relationship between phonetic realization and a morpheme is variable, in general grammatical morphemes are very short in English and lexical morphemes are one syllable or longer.

This is not a universal. In some languages there are clear and fixed correspondences between morphemes and prosodic units. In the Chinese languages of Yuè and Mín, for example, morphemes are (almost always) single syllables.

Lexical and Derivational Morphemes

Above I said *dog* was a lexical morpheme, the plural *-s* an inflectional morpheme, and *-ish* a derivational morpheme. I gave you a definition of "lexical morpheme," but all I've done for the grammatical morphemes is give you examples. Using whatever informal definition you have in your head now about these three types of morphemes, consider the list below and analyze each word into its component morphemes, labeling each morpheme as lexical, inflectional, or derivational.

unfriendliness   wisdom   entertain   mushrooms   pamphlet

(In the discussion that follows, we will spend most of our time looking at the behavior of derivational morphemes. But don't worry, inflections will come up eventually. And you'll get a chance in the section "Inflectional vs. Derivational" to compare derivational and inflectional morphemes point by point.)

Unfriendliness: What are the lexical morphemes in this word? *Friend* is the only one. It is the root morpheme, to which all the others are attached. This particular root morpheme is free. (It can stand alone to form a word.) All the others are affixes. Do you see that the sense of the overall word is the sense of the root morpheme *friend* as acted on by the various affixes?

In what order did we add these affixes? Start with *friend*. The affixes contiguous to this root morpheme are *un-* and *-li*. Does either one get added first? Try it each way, and you'll produce *unfriend* and *friendly* (allowing for the difference in orthography of the morpheme *-li/-ly*). *Unfriend* is not a word of English. Why not? What is wrong with adding *un-* to *friend*? What property of *un-* are we ignoring? Look at other words that consist of two morphemes, where one is the *un-* that means 'not,' such as:

unreal   unwise   uncool   unwell   unsound   unquiet   unsure

What kind of word does this *un-* attach to? Here they are all adjectives. And what kind of word is the result? Another adjective. Do you see that? We say that negative *un-* selects adjectives to attach to.

Is this a necessity? Does *un-* attach only to adjectives, and is the result only adjectives? To find out, let's try attaching *un-* to other morphological categories besides adjectives. If we find *un-* attached to a verb, as in *unzip*, the sense is one of reversal of an action, not negation. In other words, there is a second *un-* in English, the reversal *un-*. So our negation *un-* does not attach to verbs. If we find *un-* attached to a word which could be used as either a noun or a verb, only the verbal sense will appear, as in *unhook* (consider the sentence *Unhook the coat, please*). And, again, the sense is of reversal, not negation. So reversal *un-* can attach only to the verb *hook*, not to the noun *hook*. And our negation *un-* cannot attach to either.

Does either *un-* ever attach to a preposition (P)? The only example I can think of is *untoward*. Here the sense is negation (not reversal) and the result is an adjective, so this is clearly our *un-*. What's interesting is that in my variety of English, at least, there is no adjective *toward*, only a P. I can't say: **That's toward behavior*. However, at an earlier stage of English *toward* used to be an adjective. Thus if *un-* attached to the adjective *toward* at this earlier stage of English, we need not modify our description of what *un-* can attach to.

Nevertheless, there are other examples in which negative *un-* attaches to something other than an adjective, such as *un-* with a noun forming another noun *(uncola)* and *un-* with a FUNCTION WORD forming another function word *(unless*, and we will discuss function words later). And there are examples in which negative *un-* attaches to an adjective but the result is something other than an adjective, such as a noun *(undead* for "vampire"). But so long as such examples are isolated, there is not much to be gained by doing anything other than listing them as exceptions. They should not be taken as an indication that the generalization is in need of revision. The rule, then, is that negation *un-* attaches to adjectives and results in adjectives.

So *unfriend* is ill-formed because negation *un-* cannot (productively) attach to nouns. Therefore, we will first attach *-li/-ly* to the noun *friend* to produce the adjective *friendly*. At this point we have a choice of attaching *un-* or *-ness*. Either result, *unfriendly* or *friendliness*, is good, since both *un-* and *-ness* can attach to adjectives (and *friendly* is an adjective). But, in fact, we must attach one before the other for a different reason. Can you see which order works and which doesn't? Try each of them. If you attach *ness* first, you produce the noun *friendliness*, but we already know that negation *un-* cannot productively attach to nouns, so we cannot now attach *un-*. But if we first attach *un-*, we produce another adjective *(unfriendly)*, and *-ness* can then attach, to produce *unfriendliness*.

In this argument, I assumed that *un-* could not look inside the noun *friendliness* and see the adjective *friendly* and thus attach. Instead, *un-* is limited to seeing only the output of the last morphological rule (the noun *friendliness*, not the internal adjective *friendly*). This restriction has been codified in the ADJACENCY CONDITION (which goes hand-in-hand with the Strict Cycle Condition we discussed in the section "Cycles and the Strict Cycle Condition" of Chapter 2). **The Adjacency Condition states that affixation may be sensitive only to the most recently attached morpheme**—the adjacent morpheme, if we think in terms of cycles (whether the morpheme is linearly adjacent or not).

Our derivation of *unfriendliness*, then, is as follows:

    friend + li
    un + friendli
    unfriendli + ness

We can represent this derivation with a tree:

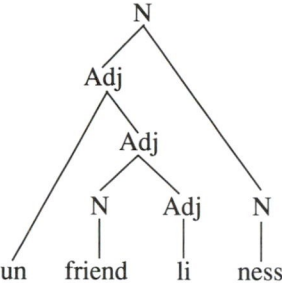

or with labeled square brackets, like so:

```
[ [ un [ [ friend ] li ] ] ness ]
N A   A N       N   A A     N
```

(Often only the right bracket will be labeled, for legibility.)

The labels below the brackets show the category of the word within the brackets, and they point out an important fact. Look carefully. What determines the category of a word? What determines whether *friendly*, for example, will be a noun, a verb, an adjective, or a preposition? The *-ly*. Can you see that? And what determines the category of *unfriendliness*? The *-ness*. The root morpheme provides important parts of the sense, but the affixal morphemes provide other senses, such as negation, and give us the category of the overall word. In other words, **derivational affixes typically HEAD (that is, determine the category of) the word that they derive**.

Notice that the term "head" is used differently here from how we used it in metrical phonology in the section "Bounded Feet" of Chapter 2; the affix that heads a word is not the most prominent part of the word with respect to prosody. It may not even get stress. Furthermore, we will use the term "head" differently again when we turn to syntax (see the section "Phrases" of the next chapter). In morphology the head of a word (or a stem) is the part that determines the category of that word (or stem).

We capture this fact by saying that the **MORPHOSYNTACTIC category (below represented as the subscript $[\alpha]$) of the head of a word (the affix) PERCOLATES up to the word level**, like so:

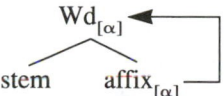

Categories like N, V, and so on, are morphosyntactic because each has a set of morphological properties, but each also has a set of syntactic properties, as we will learn in Chapter 4 (particularly in the section "Homophony and Polysemy").

Because derivational affixes typically determine the category of the stem or word they derive, I put a category label over the affixes *-li-* and *-ness* in our tree for *unfriendliness*. I did not put a category label over *un-*. Should I have? Does *un-* head the word *unfriendly*? It is hard to answer this question, since here *un-* attaches to an Adj and results in another Adj. I really don't know, then, if *un-* is a head. (In fact, the exceptional *uncola* is a noun, and the exceptional *unless* is a function word. So you may feel doubtful that *un-* is a head, just as I do.)

Please be careful to check, as we have just done. We find that most (perhaps all) suffixes in English are heads, but only a handful of prefixes are. Can you give me an example of a prefix that doesn't determine category? *Pre* seems to be one:

V→V   precancel
A→A   prenuptual
N→N   precognition

So, typically, in English words are right-headed (because suffixes are more likely to be heads than prefixes are), but this is not an absolute (and you will look into it further in Problem Set 3.5, where you will consider some prefix heads).

If affixes (particularly suffixes) are generally heads and determine the category of the word, what then determines the category of words that consist of nothing but lexical morphemes? Words like *dog* and *tomato*? Consider the made-up word *prew*. Can you tell from its form whether it's a noun, verb, adjective, or preposition? Compare it to words that rhyme with it in each of those categories, such as *glue, rue, new, to*. In English the category of such words is not predictable. We simply memorize their category, like we memorize their meaning.

But let me ask you a different question. If I were to make up the new word *snew*, do you have any expectations whatsoever about its category? Think about it. Consider the four categories of noun, verb, adjective, and preposition. Is there any that you expect *snew* could not belong to? We do not generally make up new prepositions. Why not? What kind of words are prepositions? How do they function? What kinds of things do they tell us? Consider the prepositions, all of which are italicized, in these sentences:

Jessie left *without* Sam.
I'll buy you a drink *after* the show.
Who's hiding *under* that bridge?
Look *up*!

Prepositions typically give information about relationships, often relationships of space and time, or directions in space or time, and many of the senses English conveys via P's are conveyed via Case endings in other languages (such as Finnish, as you'll see in the section "English Case" of Chapter 4). Nouns, verbs, and adjectives, on the other hand, have a wider range of meanings. We are quite likely to meet up with some new object or action or description as our experiences grow and technology advances, so we may coin new nouns, verbs, and adjectives. But we are much less likely to meet up with new relationships between objects, so we are much less likely to coin new prepositions. For this reason there are few prepositions in any given language (certainly fewer than one hundred in English, even with a very encompassing definition of what a preposition is, and in many languages, only a handful), while there are thousands of nouns, verbs, and adjectives. **We call prepositions a CLOSED CLASS of words, and nouns, adjectives, and verbs OPEN CLASSES.** So when we meet a new word, we may not have positive information about its category, but we are probably safe in assuming it is not a P.

Unitary Base Hypothesis

Before returning to our discussion of *unfriendliness*, I'd like to investigate one other point that came out of our analysis thus far: Affixes select the stem to which they will attach. (Let me remind you of terminology we met in Chapter 2. A stem is a root which might or might not have affixes attached to it, in contrast to a root, which has no affixes attached.) Thus far, we have seen selection based on morphosyntactic category (that is, selection based on whether a stem is a verb, noun, or adjective). However, selection can also be based on a semantic factor (as you will learn in Problem Set 3.3).

It has been claimed that **all word-formation processes select the domain over which they operate and that that domain must be definable as a single morphosyntactic or semantic type. This claim is known as the UNITARY BASE HYPOTHESIS (UBH).**

It follows from the UBH that every affix we look at should restrict the set of stems to which it can attach in a way that should be statable with a single morphosyntactic or semantic statement. It is, in fact, quite common to find affixes that can attach only to adjectives, or only to verbs, or only to nouns. We've come across instances of all three in our analysis of *unfriendliness*. For example, negation *un-* selects adjectives, but not verbs or nouns (although we did note the exceptions *untoward, uncola, unless*). Reversal *un-* selects verbs, but not nouns or adjectives.

The third type of affix, one that can attach only to nouns, we haven't yet discussed, although we came across it. It is seen in the *-ly* of *friendly*. We find it also in several other nouns:

womanly	heavenly	scholarly	ghostly
priestly	kingly	timely	painterly

although it can also attach to a handful of adjectives to produce another adjective:

sickly

As a result, some words ending in *-ly* are AMBIGUOUS as to whether they are adjectives or adverbs, such as:

kindly

Does the fact that this *-ly* can attach to nouns and a handful of adjectives constitute a violation of the UBH? It would only if it were impossible to gather nouns and adjectives together under a single morphosyntactic rubric. But, in fact, while nouns and verbs seem to be polar opposites in morphosyntactic terms, adjectives have properties in common with both, as do prepositions. You will learn about some of these properties in Chapter 4. You can look at it in terms of morphosyntactic features, if you will (similar to phonetically based and phonologically based features). Assume that there are two such features: [±noun] and [±verb]. We can say that the four LEXICAL MORPHOSYNTACTIC CATEGORIES (often called the MAJOR categories) have these feature values:

noun [+noun, −verb]
verb [−noun, +verb]

adjective [+noun, +verb]
preposition [−noun, −verb]

Thus we could say that the *-ly* of *friendly* selects the morphosyntactic categories that have the feature [+noun]. In this way, we have included both noun and adjective.

Can you think of a pairing of categories that shouldn't be possible given the feature analyses above? If an affix selected nouns and verbs only, but never adjectives or prepositions, there would be no way to state that set of categories with a single morphosyntactic restriction. That's because nouns and verbs have no feature in common. Likewise, if an affix selected adjectives and prepositions only, but never nouns or verbs, we would have the same problem. (You will explore this further in Problem Set 3.3.)

Let me ask you one final question before leaving this discussion. Can you find an affix in English that selects only prepositional stems? Go searching. You won't find any. (If you came up with *-ward*, you'll find that it can take stems other than P when you do Problem Set 3.3.) Did that surprise you? We learned above that prepositions are a small, closed set. Now we are finding that prepositions don't seem to be selected as unique stems for affixation.

Make a list of as many words with affixes as you can that have a preposition as the root. You might have come up with words like:

upper (outer, inner)   upward (outward, inward . . .)

Did you make your list quickly? Is your list long? Probably it took you some time and thought, and definitely your list is short. Prepositions in English are relatively inert morphologically speaking. For this reason (and others, including the fact that prepositions form a closed set and that their sense is typically relational) some linguists do not list prepositions among the lexical categories; instead they list noun, verb, and adjective. (Adverbs are considered a related form to adjectives, for reasons you will discover in the section "Modification" of Chapter 4).

Back to *Unfriendliness*

All right, now let's try to answer the question we were faced with at the start: What are the morphemes in *unfriendliness* and what types of morphemes are they? We've seen that the root morpheme *friend* is lexical. We've seen that the affix morphemes are all derivational.

But think about that a moment longer. Perhaps all that *-li* does when we add it to *friend* is derive an adjective from a noun. And maybe all that *-ness* does when we add it to *unfriendli* is derive a noun from an adjective. Or, alternatively, you may feel (as I do) that there's a meaning difference between derivationally related nouns and adjectives that is a product of the very derivation itself—so that *friend* and *friendly*, for example, differ in not just category, but sense. Still, the sense difference is very slight, right?

But what about *un-*? It takes an adjective and derives another adjective, but the two adjectives are not identical, and what differs about them is their meaning—and their meaning differs not slightly, but robustly. So, while linguists typically classify *un-* as a derivational morpheme, it adds the sense of negation and therefore does more than just derive a new word. In other words, the three categories lexical, derivational, and inflectional are not as discrete as you might have expected (or hoped) they would be when you first met those terms.

Homophony

Before we leave our discussion of *unfriendliness*, there is at least one more issue we should discuss. We realized in our examination of *un-* that there are at least two morphemes *un-* in English—one that negates and one that reverses. But there's another morpheme in this word that has a homophonous partner: *-ly*. Consider the *-ly* of a word like *sadly*. This *-ly* sounds the same as the *-li/-ly* we saw above in *unfriendliness*. Is it identical? Certainly not, for this *-ly* heads an adverb. In fact, *-ly* is probably the affix that we are most likely to rely on in identifying adverbs in English. We see it in words such as the following, where it has attached to adjectives:

> madly   unfortunately   obviously   slowly   slightly

The *-ly* in *unfriendliness*, in contrast, attaches typically to nouns to produce adjectives (as we discussed above). We will admit, then, two affixes *-ly*, just as we admitted two affixes *un-*.

Coming to the conclusion that there are two affixes *-ly* was relatively easy to do because the two affixes have different behavior. But in other instances, we may find that conclusions about homophony are hard to come by. For example, is there one morpheme *ear* or two in:

> the ear on your head
> an ear of corn

I feel quite certain these are two morphemes (and historically, these come from different sources), so we have an instance of homophony again. But you may disagree, perhaps noting that the ears of corn stick out like ears on a head. So you may make a lexical connection that I don't make.

Let's take another instance. What about *run*? Are there many morphemes *run*, all homophonous, or do we have an instance in which a single morpheme is semantically flexible so that it can be used in a range of situations?

> We ran two miles.
> Joshua ran the grocery store.
> A woman runs a terrible risk.
> The boss ran us ragged.
> This car just doesn't run right.
> Her stockings ran when she pulled them on.
> The chocolate sauce ran all over my shirt.
> Run these letters over to the mailbox, would you?

If you think there is just one morpheme *run* (as I do), then we have an instance of POLYSEMY (pronounced [pʰəlíˈsəmì])—that is, an instance of one word with multiple related meanings. These are debatable cases, so if you don't agree with me, that's fine. The point is to recognize the debate and why it arises. (By the way, the Dutch cognate for *run*, which is *rennen*, does not have most of the uses exemplified here for English, such as a car running, or running a store or a risk. You can debate with your classmates whether the behavior of cognates sheds any light on the polysemy/homophony debate. The issue baffles me.)

Homophony occurs when two morphemes (or other units, such as words, phrases, or sentences) are identical in sound but not in sense, as we've seen. Let's take a moment to go through the other logical possibilities for the relationships between two morphological forms. Can we have two forms that are identical in sense but not in sound? In English this happens quite a bit:

tooth	dent- (as in *dentist*)
sight	opto- (as in *optometrist*)
nose	rhino- (as in *rhinoplasty*)

Do you know why? Can you see the difference between the free morpheme and the bound one? The free one is of Germanic origin; the bound one was borrowed into English at a much later date from a Latinate (in this instance, French) or Greek source.

Can we have two morphological forms that differ for both sound and sense? Of course. Most pairs of morphemes do.

Can we have two morphological forms that are identical in both sound and sense? Here, probably most morphologists would answer no: If two forms are identical in both sound and sense, they are a single morpheme.

The answer may not really be quite so forthcoming, though. Consider, for example, the verb *break*. We can use it transitively (with an Object, that is):

The children break toys.

or intransitively (without an Object):

Toys break.

Sound is identical here. Is sense identical? The transitive use of *break* includes a CAUSA-TIVE sense that the intransitive lacks. This causative sense could be the product of syntactic mechanisms—and if it were, would that mean we have a single morpheme *break* to start with? And would that single morpheme be allowed to occur in two different structural contexts? Syntacticians (those who study the structure of phrases and sentences) debate the proper way to analyze such sentences. But some of them would say *break* is a single verb and that syntactic and lexical mechanisms account for the ability of *break* to occur in both intransitive and transitive sentences. The causative sense, then, would be the product of the interaction of these syntactic and lexical mechanisms. We won't reach a conclusion here—the point is simply to make you aware that the issues are not always as straightforward as they may appear at first.

What about the adjective *drunk* and the noun *drunk*, as in:

The drunk man came in.
The drunk came in.

Again, sound is identical and sense is certainly very similar (though we'll return to this). But there are significant differences from the morphologist's point of view. The words share a single root, and we would want to derive the noun from the adjective by the addition of a zero morpheme, changing A to N. Thus the two words are not identical in analysis: *Drunk* the noun is polymorphemic and *drunk* the adjective is not. Or maybe it is. We may want to derive *drunk* the adjective from the PERFECT PARTICIPLE of the verb *drink*, in which case *drunk* the adjective consists of three morphemes (a root, a perfect participle morpheme, and a morpheme deriving A from V) while *drunk* the noun consists of those three morphemes plus a fourth morpheme (that derives N from A).

What a mess. We have two forms that have the same sound and sense, yet one may be monomorphemic while the other is polymorphemic. One way out is to look more closely at the sense of these two words. Are they really (close to) identical in sense or not? If categoryhood is a part of sense (as I believe it is), then these forms are not identical in sense, and we can conclude that their analysis does not threaten the claim that if two forms are identical in sound and sense, they are identical morphologically. But even if category-hood is not a part of sense, these forms are not really identical in sense. Look at these sentences:

John is drunk.
John is the worst drunk I know.

In the first sentence, we know John is drunk now, but he might not be charactistically drunk. The drunkenness is PREDICATED of him (that is, assigned to him as a property) at a particular stage in his day (or life), and it is therefore called a STAGE-LEVEL PREDICATE. But in the second sentence, drunkenness is a property of the individual John without regard to time. Even if he's sober right now, we predicate drunkenness of him as charac-teristic. So this is called an INDIVIDUAL-LEVEL PREDICATE. So there really is a semantic difference between the noun and adjective *drunk*, after all. And morphologists can breathe a sigh of relief.

I will not go further with this question here. After you have studied both syntax (in Chapter 4) and semantics (in Chapter 5), you may well want to return to how examples like these bear on morphological issues. For now, I think we can agree that **in the vast majority of instances, when two forms are identical in both sound and sense, they are morphologically identical.** And, given this, we will use identity of sound and sense to identify morphemes, even though we know that such a diagnostic may be problematic in certain instances.

With regard to spoken languages, we have now covered all the logical possibilities for the relationship between sound and sense, on the one hand, and identification of morphemes on the other. But if we look at written language, the factor of orthography makes new possiblities arise. Can we have two morphological forms that are ortho-graphically identical but differ on sound and sense? Surely. consider this noun and verb:

lead (as in *The captains lead their squads*)
lead (as in *There's lead in the paint*)

These morphemes are HOMOGRAPHIC. (They are homograms.)

Can we have two morphological forms that differ in orthography but are identical for sound and sense? This is the same as asking if English has any morphemes that can be spelled two different ways. Several that come to mind are pairs in which one spelling is British and the other is American (as in *colour* vs. *color*), which isn't really the case we're after. But other true examples include the *-y/-ie* seen in *lefty* vs. *leftie*, the two spellings of the interjection *oh* and *o*, the two spellings of the condiment *ketchup* and *catsup*, revisionist spellings side by side with traditional ones like *thru* and *through*, recent politically correct spellings side by side with traditional ones like *wymyn* vs. *women*, and others.

You can ask yourself about the other four logically possible cases that come up from combinations of the three factors of orthography, sound, and sense:

1. two orthographically identical forms that are identical for sound but differ on sense (homonyms, like English *left*);
2. two orthographically identical forms that are identical for sense but differ on sound (like English *either*);
3. two orthographically different forms that are identical for sound but differ on sense (here the Chinese third-person pronoun *ta* might be a candidate, since it has one sound but different orthographic forms according to gender);
4. two orthographically different forms that are identical for sense but differ on sound (synonyms—and we'll talk about issues related to synonymy in the section "Semantic Uses of Lexical Decomposition in Comparing Words" of Chapter 5).

Let's go back now to the two *-ly* morphemes that we identified above. An interesting question now arises. If there are two affixes *-ly*, and one produces adjectives and the other attaches to adjectives (to produce adverbs), we might expect to be able to find words with both of these affixes. Can we? No. English does not allow words like:

    *friendlily   *timelily   *ghostlily

In fact, in language after language, we find that when we expect to find a sequence of homophonous affixes, the expected form does not exist. Indeed, sometimes even if the two affixes are not contiguous, the expected form does not exist. Instead, either we will have a gap in our morphology (which we do for the three nonexistent words above, using paraphrases like "in a friendly way") or we will have a different form from the one we expected, a SUPPLETIVE form.

I don't have any examples to give you of suppletion in English in this particular kind of situation. However, suppletion is common in morphology, particularly in the paradigms of frequently used words. For example, the verb paradigm for *walk* in the present tense is:

    I walk   we walk
    you walk   you walk
    (s)he/it walks they walk

But the corresponding paradigm for *be* (our most used verb) is entirely suppletive:

    I am   we are
    you are   you are
    (s)he/it is   they are

Had *be* had a nonsuppletive paradigm in the present tense, the only two forms would have been *be* and *bes*, like so:

I be	we be
you be	you be
(s)he/it bes	they be

Returning from our tangent on suppletion, we can see that sequences of homophonous affixes don't occur. There is an exception to this statement. In somewhat playful language we can find recursion of nonhead prefixes. That is, a prefix can attach to a form that already has that prefix:

re-rearrange   pre-premedical

But the very fact that the context is playful tells us that these are linguistically self-conscious forms, and, as such, they really aren't reliable indicators of what the grammar naturally produces.

Recognizing Morphemes

Okay, let's move on to *wisdom*. The component morphemes are, I hope, obvious. We have *wis* plus *-dom*. What type of morpheme is each? *Wis* is lexical; *-dom* is derivational. Nevertheless, there are complications with both classifications.

Notice that the adjective corresponding to the first morpheme here is *wise* [wɑɪz]. The nucleus of this syllable contrasts with that of *wis* [wɪz]. Often a morpheme will undergo phonological changes when it is incorporated into a larger word. Sometimes the changes are so great that speakers do not always recognize the two forms as allomorphs (a term we met in Chapter 2). For example, I have asked classes to analyze the word *folly*. Many speakers in my classes have claimed the word is monomorphemic. They have not identified the first syllable with the morpheme *fool*. Are they right? Notice that if we identify the first syllable with the morpheme *fool*, we will have to admit a morpheme *-(l)y*, which turns N into N. This *-(l)y* cannot be identified with the *-ly* that turns N into A *(time, timely)*, nor with the *-ly* that turns an adjective into an adverb *(quick, quickly)*, nor with the diminutive *-y* that turns N into N *(dog, doggy*—we'll talk about diminutives later). So it would be an entirely new morpheme, and we'd hope to find it used in other words than just *folly*.

The question of how many morphemes a word has is interesting from a theoretical perspective. If we ask how many syllables a word has, we will find near uniformity in answers (at least for speakers of the same DIALECT—where a dialect is a variety of speech that is defined by many factors including geographical area and socioeconomic class). But the same question asked about numbers of morphemes can elicit a variety of answers.

Sometimes the rules of the language will help us figure out the correct answer, for these rules can treat a word as monomorphemic or polymorphemic. For example, in Italian an /s/ between vowels becomes voiced (as you learned in Problem Set 2.4). This rule operates within a morpheme. However, in some instances (but not all, by any means) it can cross a morpheme boundary between a root and an affix, as in:

risolvere /ri+sólvere/ → [ri+zólvere] 'resolve'

(I will use + to indicate a morpheme boundary.) But it never operates across a boundary between two root morphemes, as in the compound:

stasera [sta+séra] 'tonight' (literally: 'this night')

Words with more than one lexical morpheme are called compounds, as you know from Chapter 2. So the failure of this rule to apply to *stasera* helps us to recognize that this word is a compound. (It consists of two lexical morphemes.)

Likewise, even though the singular and plural of *sheep* might sound the same in your speech, we know that in some instances we have a monomorphemic singular form *sheep* and in other instances we have a polymorphemic plural form *sheep*, since the rule of Subject-Verb Agreement is sensitive to the morpheme of plurality (as we saw earlier).

But much of the time the rules of the language will not be so helpful. We have to rely, then, on native speaker intuitions. In other words, when we ask a speaker how many morphemes *folly* has, we are implicitly asking whether the speaker associates parts of this word with (parts of) other words (such as *fool*). Some speakers make more associations between the items in their lexicon than others. And the more languages you have studied, the more likely you may be to make the less-obvious associations. Someone who has studied Latin, for example, is quite likely to identify more roots in English than someone who hasn't.

When we use the term "lexical item," we mean not just individual words, but also morphemes and strings of words that have a single sense, like *take care of*. So our comments in the above paragraph mean that even two people who know precisely the same words may have different lexicons, in that one person might recognize the existence of a morpheme that the other person doesn't recognize.

Productivity

Beyond the issue of identifying morphemes and allomorphs is another question. Consider the second morpheme of *wisdom*. What other words do you find it in?

kingdom   fiefdom   stardom   officialdom   freedom

Maybe you've come up with a few others. But, clearly, the number is very small. This morpheme, unlike the adverb-deriving *-ly* discussed above, is relatively UNPRODUCTIVE in that it has been used to produce so few lexical items. Nevertheless, it does have a certain productivity in that it can be used to make up new words if the occasion warrants (though they may be laughable):

rascaldom   serfdom   princedom   dumbdom

Derivational morphemes range widely in productivity, both in the sense of how many lexical items we are generally familiar with that they have been used to produce and in the sense of whether or not and how freely they can be used to produce novel forms. Also, we can predict which categories derivational morphemes will attach to, but we can not predict which particular lexical morphemes they will attach to. For example, consider the morphemes *-ation* and *-al*, both of which can attach to verbs to derive nouns. Some verbs can take both suffixes; some can take only one; and some can take neither:

recite	recitation	recital
reserve	reservation	*reserval
revive	*revivation	revival
deserve	*deservation	*deserval

The variable productivity of derivational morphemes is one property that can help us identify them. (We'll return to this point.)

Furthermore, there is unpredictability (although certainly not total) in the semantic contribution of some derivational morphemes to the overall word. In the sentence:

Her only recitation was brief.

recitation denotes an EVENT of reciting. I cannot think of a sentence in which it means anything else. Contrast that to the sentence:

Do you have reservations this evening, Madam?

If a waiter says it as the woman enters a restaurant, we get quite a different sense from if a (rather formal) lover says it as the woman holds back from entering a bedroom. Only in the first reading does *reservations* denote an act of reserving. In the second reading, I would argue that *reservations* denotes reasons for holding back, not acts of holding back.

If you don't agree with my distinction, we can make the point with other, more obvious examples. Look back at the list of words you have that include the morpheme -*dom*. Do you see a single sense that -*dom* always contributes? Compare *kingdom* to *stardom*, for example. There is a general sense that -*dom* contributes—a sense of state, perhaps. But whether that state is mental (as with *wisdom*) or physical (as with *kingdom*), and what the relationship of that state is to the lexical morpheme that -*dom* attaches to, can vary.

Pressing the point harder, we can return to a question we asked earlier: Can derivational morphemes lack semantic contribution? When we raised this issue before, I posited a meaning difference between derivationally related nouns and adjectives, for example (as in *friend* and *friendly*), that is a product of the derivation itself. But if you didn't agree with me (and many morphologists don't), you might object to my calling adverbial -*ly* a morpheme at all, since I started out by saying morphemes are minimal meaning-bearing units. If all -*ly* does is derive adverbs from adjectives, how does it qualify as a meaning-bearing unit? So, **many would say that we must allow morphemes that simply carry out processes, such as derivation**.

An important point emerges from this discussion: The range of meaning that a derivational affix can contribute and the (limited) unpredictability of this meaning are factors that can help us identify derivational morphemes.

Let's go on now to the next word on our list: *entertain*. How many morphemes does it consist of? Some of you may say this is a single morpheme. Others may want to say that the -*tain* here is the same -*tain* we see in *maintain*, *contain*, *retain*, *pertain*, *obtain*, and so on. The list is surely not long, but it is also not negligible. Indeed, if we allow bound morphemes like -*tain* that have form but whose meaning is arguably (close to) null, we can recognize many networks in our lexicon. (Think of *incur*, *recur*, *concur*, etc.; *converse*, *diverse*, *inverse*, etc.; *discourse*, *intercourse*, *recourse*, etc.; and so on.) And once we allow -*tain* to be a morpheme, then we can identify the *enter* of *entertain* with the *enter* of *enterprise*. In fact, some might claim this is the same *enter* we find in the free verb *enter*.

Once again we are face to face with the idea that morphemes can have form but little or no sense, as we said of certain derivational morphemes and as we're suggesting of -*tain* now. Indeed, *enter* presents a similar situation. The sense of the component morpheme *enter* is not simply somewhat variable from one of these words to another (as in the case of *stardom* vs. *fiefdom*) but indeed quite far apart. (Compare the sense of *enter* in the free verb to that in *entertain*.)

But now we have a new issue before us, for neither *enter* nor *-tain* seems to be a derivational morpheme (unlike *-ly*). What kind of morphemes are *enter* and *-tain*? Are they both lexical? If so, is this word a compound? In Chapter 2 we learned that, in English, compounds receive primary stress on the first member of the compound, not the second (and you might want to look over Problem Set 2.9 again). Yet here we find primary stress on *-tain*. The stress facts militate against a compound analysis of *entertain*.

Alternatively, *-tain* looks like a lexical morpheme of the category V. But then we are forced to claim that *enter-* is a prefix. All in all, the matter is messy (as you have perhaps come to expect morphology to be).

In contrast, recognizing that the word *quickly* has two morphemes allows us to make associations with many other words (all adverbs consisting of an adjective followed by *-ly*) in which the sense or function of each lexical morpheme and of the derivational morpheme *-ly* is consistent from one word to the next. (Compare *quick*, *quicker*, *quickest*, and *slowly*, *sweetly*, *casually*, for example.)

Given these considerations, perhaps you can't get very strongly motivated to argue for anything but a monomorphemic analysis of *entertain*, and that's fine. But if you can, that's also fine (in my opinion, finer) and many (perhaps most) morphologists would agree with you. Nothing we do in this chapter will depend crucially on such distinctions.

Borrowings

Okay, let's pass on to the next word and see what we can learn about word-formation processes from its analysis.

Mushrooms: What are the component morphemes here? For the moment ignore the affix *-s*, since I'm sure we all agree that it is a morpheme, and we'll discuss it thoroughly later. So our first question is how to analyze *mushroom*.

Certainly we have a word *room* in English, but is the second syllable of *mushroom* the same morpheme as in the word *room*? I hope you said no. There is no sense of room in the sense of *mushroom*. Well, what about the fact that we have a word *mush*? In fact, we have both a noun and a verb *mush*. Is either a part of the word *mushroom*? Again, I hope you said no; mushiness is not part of the sense of *mushroom*. (Indeed, we tend to throw out mushy mushrooms when we are cooking.) In fact, this word came into English via French and is an Anglicized pronunciation of the French word meaning 'small thing growing in the moss.' So in English it is a single morpheme, just as *Massachusetts* is (having come to us via an Amerind language). And this single morpheme is lexical.

Since we've raised the issue of ETYMOLOGY (the history of a word), let's look at another word that came to us via French. *Crayfish* was borrowed; the French word for 'crayfish' is *écrevisse* [ekʁəvís]. What steps do you think the French word went through to come out as [kʰɹéɪ̯fɪʃ]? (It may help for you to pronounce the English word *crayfish* with an exaggerated French accent.) Do you see how the final syllable of the French word got REANALYZED in English as *fish*? This type of reanalysis is common. Do you also see how the French syllables were changed so that they matched rules of English syllable structure? For example, the syllable-initial velar stop in French became aspirated in English; the tense high stressed vowel in French became a lax vowel in the English unstressed syllable.

Inflectional vs. Derivational

Now it's time for us to face the -s of *mushrooms*. Since it is an affix, you know it's not lexical. Is it derivational or inflectional? This morpheme is inflectional. And now we need to find some criteria to distinguish derivational from inflectional morphemes. But, in fact, you've already got two.

First, we already learned that derivational morphemes range in productivity. What about this -s? What does it attach to? Nouns. Okay, now make a list of nouns it can attach to.

hat   kitchen   tomato   epiphany   house   region

Keep going. And going. And going. Let me turn the task around: make a list of nouns it cannot attach to. There are several:

*foots   *oxes   *sheeps   *phenomenons   *alumnuses

(You will discuss the correct plurals for these words in Problem Set 3.2.) And you could extend this list, as well, but it will be extremely short in comparison to the list of nouns to which -s can attach.

The point, I hope, is clear: This -s morpheme is productive in a different way from the productivity of derivational morphemes. **In general, inflectional morphemes are productive across an entire category**, not just across a range of members of that category.

Of course, not all inflectional morphemes are productive across an entire category (which is why I couched the above generalization with the introduction "in general"). We just made a list of nouns to which plural -s cannot attach, and the reason plural -s cannot attach to them is that other, irregular plural morphemes attach to them, and the irregularity is precisely that these morphemes are not productive across an entire category (such as the -en of *oxen*). English exhibits irregular inflectional morphemes on both nouns and verbs. So perhaps for English we should say that inflectional morphemes can be productive across an entire category rather than that they are productive across an entire category. Still, I leave the generalization unrevised since my impression is that generally in language (not just in English) inflectional morphemes are productive across entire categories, whereas derivational ones are not.

A second way to distinguish inflectional morphemes from derivational ones is to look at their meaning or function. Derivational morphemes can range from adding very little meaning to quite a bit of meaning, and the meaning they contribute is at least somewhat unstable. Now consider the meaning that our -s contributes. (Be careful: there are other -s morphemes in English. Consider only the one we've been looking at.) It adds plurality, of course. And it does this entirely consistently. **Quite often inflectional morphemes add either a minimal or delicate sense distinction or a very specific sense that is (close to) invariable**. So we can predict the sense of a word with a given inflection from the sense of the stem before the inflection plus our knowledge of the particular inflection—all with a greater degree of reliability than we can for words with derivational affixes.

We have seen a specific sense that an inflectional morpheme can add: plurality. But we have not yet seen an instance in which an inflectional morpheme adds no sense. Consider these Spanish nouns plus modifying adjectives:

   propuesta apropiada   'appropriate proposal'
   comentario apropiado   'appropriate account'

The adjective in these examples consists of the lexical morpheme *apropiad* plus a vowel, where the vowel varies. Can you guess why the vowel varies? Look at the nouns. What do you notice about them? Do you see that the final vowel of the adjective matches the final vowel of the noun? Nouns in Spanish have a fixed gender, either masculine or feminine. (We will discuss gender much further in the section "Person, Number, Gender, and Verbal Inflection.") But adjectives do not have a fixed gender (although some of them have an invariable form). Instead, adjectives take on a gender from the noun that they modify in an AGREEMENT process. The gender affix on the adjective, then, contributes nothing to the meaning of that adjective. Affixes that attach as part of an agreement process often contribute nothing or very little in the way of meaning.

Notice that in the agreement process, the morphology will look at a bundle of features, such as [+s, +f] (for singular, feminine) and SPELL OUT these features in the form of morphemes. (It is unfortunate that this process is called spelling out, when orthography is not involved, but that's how it is. You should learn this terminology because it is useful and common.)

Returning to our major discussion, a third way to distinguish inflectional from derivational morphemes is suggested by the very name "derivational." Derivational morphemes derive new words. *Kindness*, for example, is a different word from *kind* in both its sense and its category. *Sadly* is a different word from *sad* in at least its category (and I think in its sense). *Neighborhood* is a different word from *neighbor* not in category but certainly in sense.

Inflectional morphemes, on the other hand, yield what have sometimes been claimed to be different forms of a single word. This claim is slippery and runs the risk of being circular (that is, we define inflections as those affixes that create a different form of a given word, and we call those affixes that create a different form of a given word inflections). Yet there are at least three ways in which this claim seems sensible.

For one, **inflectional morphemes do not change the morphosyntactic category of the word they attach to**. Derivational morphemes, on the other hand, might (as with -*ness*, compare *happy* to *happiness*) or might not (as with -*hood*, compare *mother* to *motherhood*).

Second, as we already noted, inflectional morphemes contribute either slight or relatively strongly prescribed sense to a word. So *cats* and *cat*, for example, can be considered different forms of a single word, where we choose which form we want to use based on the number of the items we want to REFER to, not based on what kind of items we want to refer to. An even more obvious case is *propiada* and *propiado* in the earlier Spanish examples; these are simply different forms of the word that means 'appropriate.'

But considering the Spanish examples one more time can lead us to a third reason for claiming inflection yields another form of the same word. Look at what makes us choose to use *propiada* vs. *propiado*: the linguistic context. We chose the form that agreed with the modified noun. **Often inflectional affixes are conditioned by nonsemantic linguistic factors outside the word they attach to but within the phrase or sentence**. The choice of using a derivational affix, instead, is more often based on simple meaning distinctions: For example, do we want to talk about the property wise *(wise)* or do we want to talk about the state of being wise *(wisdom)*?

Just using these criteria, can you find other inflectional affixes in English? Think about verbs. Are there any affixes that attach (relatively) productively to verbs, contribute no or very specific meaning, and do not change category? For English there are a few candidates you might have come up with:

the *-ed* of simple **past tense**: He *walked* home.
the *-s* of simple **present tense**: He *walks* home.
the *-ing* of **progressive aspect**: He is *walking* home.
the *-ed* of **perfect aspect**: He has *walked* home.
the *-ed* of **passive voice**: That dog is *walked* too often.

You will learn more about these in Problem Set 3.5 of this chapter and in Problem Set 4.3 of Chapter 4 (additionally you can look closely at *-ing* in Problem Set 4.4, where you will see that this morpheme can, in fact, change category, contrary to what you might have expected).

What about English nouns: Are there any inflections that attach to nouns other than the plural morpheme? First, you might ask yourself if English has any affixes that mark gender, like Spanish does. Pairs such as the following might come to mind:

steward stewardess   dominator dominatrix

Such pairs, however, are few. Thus neither *-ess* nor *-(atr)ix* shows the kind of productivity that we'd expect of an inflectional morpheme. Furthermore, such suffixes often carry information other than mere gender (compare whom a governor governs to whom a governess governs), so their meaning is not as precisely limited as we'd expect of an inflectional morpheme. Neither of these can be considered inflectional today, although perhaps both of them can be argued to have come from inflectional sources. (*-Ess* came into English via French, where the suffix descended from a Late Latin suffix that had been borrowed into Latin from the Greek ισσα. The other affix came from Classical Latin, where it had limited productivity as a feminine ending.)

We do have another candidate for an inflectional ending that attaches to nouns: the genitive, as in

the *dog's* tail

You will explore some phonological details of this morpheme in Problem Set 3.5 and you will discover a major complication in the description of this morpheme in Problem Set 4.4 of Chapter 4.

Do we have any candidates for inflectional morphemes in English that attach to adjectives? Promising candidates are the COMPARATIVE *-er* and the SUPERLATIVE *-est*:

tall   taller   tallest

Make a list of adjectives to which the comparative affix can attach. Keep going. When you get to twenty (which should take you only a minute), stop. Now make a list of adjectives to which the comparative affix cannot attach, such as:

*beautifuler   (cf. more beautiful)

When you get to twenty (again, a quick task), stop. In Problem Set 3.5, you will discover the factor(s) relevant to whether or not an adjective can take the comparative *-er*. These factors are phonological. Typically, if an adjective satisfies the phonological context required, *-er* can attach. So the comparative is productive in the way we expect inflectional affixes to be. It also contributes to meaning in a precise way and it never changes the category of the word it attaches to. The same remarks can be made of the superlative affix.

Now try to come up with some derivational affixes of English, just using the criteria we've discussed thus far. Here are some:

Prefixes:

*a*moral   *ante*room   *anti*war   *auto*matic   *circum*vent   *con*sent
*contra*diction   *counter*vailing   *dis*regard   *en*treat   *hemi*sphere
*in*solvable   *inter*vene   *pro*nounce   *un*zip

Suffixes:

read*able*   ver*acity*   prim*acy*   parent*al*   pedl*ar*   bin*ary*
emascul*ate*   bureau*cratic*   preserv*ative*   thick*en*   dream*er*   spac*ious*
self*ish*   dogmat*ism*   san*ity*   magnet*ize*   govern*ment*

You could have kept going and going. What can you notice about the number of derivational affixes as opposed to the number of inflectional affixes? **The derivational set is relatively large and potentially open.** That is, we might very well add new derivational affixes to our language over time. **But the inflectional set is small and relatively closed.** We add new inflectional affixes to our lexicon much less freely than we add new derivational ones. So we have now discovered one more difference between these two types of affixes.

The general statements we have made thus far about the differences between derivational and inflectional affixes hold across languages. But there are at least three more differences that are LANGUAGE SPECIFIC—that is, they hold for English, but they do not necessarily hold for other languages.

First, list some English words in which we have more than one derivational affix. This is easy to do. We can find examples with a prefix and a suffix:

unconscionable   dismemberment   entreaty

We can find examples with multiple suffixes:

governmental   musicality   hopefulness

It is harder to find examples with multiple prefixes, but, still, it is possible, especially with words that also have suffixes:

unpremeditated   unpronounceable   inadvisable

Now list some words in which we have more than one inflectional affix. Can you think of any? Certainly the verbal ones cannot co-occur. You couldn't have the simple past morpheme and the simple present morpheme in the same word for obvious semantic reasons: Two tenses wouldn't make sense. But it is also impossible to get any other combination of verbal inflectional suffixes, such as both a passive morpheme and a perfect morpheme on the same verb stem, for reasons you will discover in Problem Set 4.3.

Likewise, the adjectival comparative and superlative cannot co-occur in a single word, for obvious semantic reasons. So let's look only at the inflectional affixes that attach to nouns.

It is definitely conceivable that a plural and a Genitive could co-occur. Yet the regular plural (the productive one, written as "s" or "es") generally does not co-occur with the regular Genitive (and in Problem Set 3.5, you will look at some instances in which you expected to find such examples).

That covers all the possible combinations. So we must conclude that **in English we allow only one productive inflectional affix per word, whereas we allow multiple derivational affixes**. Many other languages allow multiple inflectional affixes per word, including most of the Indo-European languages, where notions like tense, aspect, and mood (notions we'll discuss later) are handled by affixes on verbs, as well as person and number of the Subject of the verb.

A second difference for English is apparent from the data above: **Derivational affixes can be prefixes or suffixes, but inflectional ones are only suffixes**. Many other languages allow inflectional prefixes, such as the Na-Dene language family Athapascan of western Canada and Alaska, in which the person and number of the Subject of a verb are typically given in a prefix and various notions having to do with the time frame are also given in a prefix.

And, finally, in English where does the inflectional suffix come in a word? What happens if we have both derivational suffixes and an inflectional suffix? What order do they come in? **The inflectional suffix will always be word final**.

The boldfaced statements in this section help us to distinguish between these two types of affixes. Actually, none of these distinctions alone can make a clear determination in every case. For example, while inflectional morphemes generally attach productively across the whole category and derivational ones don't, the adverb-deriving affix -*ly* attaches quite productively across the whole category of adjective. And while inflectional morphemes generally contribute either nothing or a very precise sense to the meaning, the adverbial -*ly* can be argued to contribute nothing to the meaning. But once we turn to the issue of changing categories, we see that adverbial -*ly* is arguably derivational and not inflectional. So when we go to classify a morpheme, we need to consider all of its properties. Even then it will not always be clear whether a given morpheme is best classified as inflectional or derivational. My advice to you is to use these classifications if they are useful, but never to let them stand in the way of your being able to adequately and accurately describe the properties of a given morpheme.

Evaluative Affixes

We are now ready to analyze the last word on our original list: *pamphlet*. Are there any obvious subparts to this word? Compare it to *booklet, froglet, piglet, owlet*. What does the morpheme -*let* mean? It indicates smallness, and it is called a DIMINUTIVE. Can you think of other diminutives in English? Consider words like:

doggy   duckling   operetta

Is a diminutive affix inflectional? Support your answer.
If you're having trouble getting started, all you have to do is look back at the list of

distinguishing characteristics we just developed. Let's take them in order, each time considering -*let* first, and then other diminutives if they shed new light on the issue.

First, is -*let* widely productive? Certainly not. It occurs on a handful of words at most. -*Ling* and -*etta* are also very limited in the number of words they can attach to. The only diminutive that is strongly productive is the -*y*. Notice that we can even attach this diminutive to names *(Johnny, Danny)*, although not to all names *(*Merly/*Merlie, *Grahamy/*Grahamie)*. In general, then, the diminutives behave more like derivational than inflectional affixes with regard to productivity.

What about with respect to sense? Diminutives certainly do carry sense and the sense in English varies somewhat. So in *booklet* and *boomlet* the diminutive simply indicates that the book probably has few pages and the boom probably wasn't very loud, whereas in *owlet* and *piglet* the diminutive indicates the young of the species. Diminutives can also be used to show affection on the part of the speaker, as in the sentence *You little sweetie, you.* (The connection between smallness and endearment is apparent here, and is common in languages that have diminutives.) And diminutives can be used to show a negative evaluation, as in *How's your wifey?* (The connection between smallness and distain is apparent, and is common among languages.) Again, the diminutives exhibit behavior more like derivational than inflectional affixes.

What about the ability to change category? Diminutives don't change the category of the word they attach to. Certainly there are some derivational affixes that do not, either, but no inflectional affixes do. So what does this criterion tell us? You might say, "Nothing," and you'd be logically correct. However, diminutives are part of a larger set of affixes that we call EVALUATIVE affixes, a set that includes, as well, AUGMENTATIVES (indicating large size), PEJORATIVES (indicating negative evaluation), AMELIORATIVES (indicating positive evaluation), and others. So let's look at some of the other evaluative affixes and see how they behave with respect to this criterion before we decide whether this criterion is informative in this instance or not.

Can you think of any affixes that indicate large size or negative or positive evaluation? If you're having trouble, don't worry. English does not seem to express these notions with affixation (although, as we noted above, diminutives can carry an ameliorative or pejorative sense). The only type of example anyone has offered me is -*alicious*, used sometimes in advertisements as an ameliorative. *(It's cinnamonalicious!)* In fact, English has no productive way of handling these notions with anything other than lexical morphemes (but you'll meet a suggestion of a nonproductive way in Problem Set 3.1), although prosody can kick in as an intensifier. So, for example, *tiny* said with extra loudness and, perhaps, duration, can have the sense of "very tiny," just as *huge* said in the same way can. The prosody, however, may not be reliable, since the same loudness and duration can indicate a contrastive situation. For example, if someone misheard me and said that Paul was tidy, I might correct that person by saying that Paul was tiny, with extra loudness and, optionally, duration, on *tiny*.

Italian, on the other hand, makes liberal use of evaluative affixes. Here are some representative examples.

Diminutive:

V→V attorcere 'to twist'   attorcinare 'to sidle'

Augmentative:

N→N ragazzo 'boy'   ragazzone 'big boy'

Pejorative:

A→A dolce 'sweet' dolciastro 'sickly sweet'

Ameliorative:

N→N Elena (a girl's name) Elenuccia 'dear Elena'

In each case here the addition of the evaluative suffix did not change the category. This pattern, of evaluative affixes not changing category, is typical of Italian (with scattered exceptions) and of Romance languages in general. I don't know if it is typical across other languages and language families. If it were to be shown to be, then we might conclude that evaluative affixes as a group share the property that they don't change category. In this way, they would be more like inflectional than derivational affixes.

While evaluative affixes don't appear to change category, they can change features of a lexical item. In Dutch and German, for example, there are a variety of diminutives (for example, German -*chen*, -*lein*, -*el*) which determine not only the gender of the noun but the choice of plural inflection. In this regard these affixes are more like derivational affixes than like inflectional ones.

Returning to English, we can now ask if the set of evaluative affixes appears to be large and open (like derivational affixes) or small and closed (like inflectional affixes). English has only a very few evaluative affixes, and they are diminutives. Could you imagine English coming up with a new evaluative affix? Surely it wouldn't be that hard to do. If I told a child that we were going to play a language game, in which the name of everyone who was large got *lul* added to the end of it and the name of everyone who was small got *lil* added to the end of it, I doubt the child would have much trouble converting:

Daddy gave baby Sue a bath.

to

Daddylul gave baby Suelil a bath.

And even the idea of adding *lal* at the end of words that mean things you, the speaker, like and *lol* at the end of words that mean things you don't like isn't hard for a child to grasp. So:

Mamma served liverwurst and then cake.

easily gets transformed to

Mamma served liverwurstlol and then cakelal.

As you might expect, then, languages do add new evaluative affixes with relative ease. So even though this is a small class, it is open. On this criterion, then, the evaluatives waffle.

Do we ever get more than one evaluative affix per word in English? Could you say something like *pigletty* for a dear little pig? I could. If you can, then evaluative affixes are more like derivational than inflectional affixes by this criterion.

Do we ever get evaluative prefixes in English? We haven't seen any thus far and I don't know of any. If they are always suffixes, then they are more like inflectional affixes in English.

Does the evaluative suffix always come last in a word? In *pigletty* the *-y* does. But that is a sequence of two evaluative suffixes. Can an evaluative suffix ever be followed by a nonevaluative suffix? Think of the plural *ducklings*. So evaluative suffixes are followed by inflectional suffixes, just as derivational suffixes are.

But is the location of evaluative suffixes identical to that of derivational suffixes? We have seen that derivational suffixes can occur in sequence. Can evaluative suffixes, likewise, both precede and follow derivational suffixes?

In order to answer this, we need to examine words in which both an evaluative suffix and a derivational suffix co-occur. What about *pigletlike*? Here the derivational suffix *-like* follows an evaluative one, just as derivational suffixes may follow other derivational suffixes.

Italian, however, presents a different situation. The diminutive *-in* in Italian, for example, is extremely productive for nouns; you can add it to just about any noun and people will understand you, although the result may not be colloquial. Consider the noun *quercia* 'oak tree.' There is a derivational affix that can be added to the name of a tree to yield the sense of a grove of such trees. For example, *querceta* means 'oak grove.' Now let's try adding both the diminitive and this derivational suffix to the root of the word *quercia*, in both orders:

> querc + in + et + a → quercineta 'a grove of small oaks'
> querc + et + in + a → quercetina 'a small grove of oaks'

Italians I have asked strongly prefer the second word to the first. I have tested with other words and found the same preferences regardless of which derivational and which evaluative suffixes I have used. So in Italian it appears that evaluative suffixes tend to follow derivational suffixes. And, like in English, evaluative suffixes always precede inflectional suffixes. In other words, in Italian, evaluative suffixes have a linear slot of their own.

In sum, evaluative suffixes may well be a separate kind of morpheme from either derivational or inflectional ones. This conclusion is strong for Italian, where these suffixes have their own slot (coming after derivational suffixes and before inflectional ones) and a little weaker for English. (Both derivational and inflectional suffixes can follow them.) And this conclusion is not totally unwelcome. Notice that unlike the grammatical affixes, evaluative suffixes do not seem to have any grammatical effect. They never change category, unlike most other derivational suffixes in English (in contrast to prefixes); they never respond to nonsemantic linguistic factors of the phrase a word is found in for either English or Italian, unlike many inflectional affixes (as in agreement processes). On the other hand, they are certainly not root morphemes, so if we persist in identifying root with lexical morphemes, then evaluative morphemes cannot be classified as lexical morphemes, either. I suggest that evaluative morphemes are a third kind of morpheme, which, like the lexical morphemes, always carry sense, but like the grammatical morphemes, are affixes. This suggestion is louder for Italian than for English.

Beyond English, or, the World of Affixes

A discussion of affixes limited to English words can only bring us so far. But if we look at other languages, we find other types of affixes. Let's proceed logically to see if we can predict the range of affixes that occur. In English we have seen that affixes can attach to the front of a root; these are prefixes. And they can attach to the end of a root; these are suffixes. What other logical possibilities are there?

For one, they might attach inside a root somewhere. That is, a morpheme might interrupt another morpheme. Such morphemes are called "INFIXES," and they do, indeed, occur. In Ulwa, a language of Nicaragua, the morpheme which indicates that a noun is possessed can be infixed into the root:

Root	Possessed form	
su:lu	su:kalu	'dog'
ana:la:ka	ana:kala:ka	'chin'
kuhbil	kuhkabil	'knife'

(Actually, the affix -ka- sometimes appears as a suffix, as well. You will explore this in Problem Set 3.7. The rubric "possessed form" comes from the literature source of these data. This form corresponds to the possession sense of our Genitive, as in *the dog's tail*. So the rubric doesn't indicate some form possessed by demons. Morphology is fun, but not that fun.)

Does English have infixes? I don't think so. But English does do two things that you might consider similar to infixation of an affix.

First, notice the irregular plurals that involve a change internal to the lexical morpheme, as in:

foot feet   goose geese   mouse mice

and the irregular past tenses that involve a change internal to the lexical morpheme, as in:

run ran   take took   ring rang

This is not infixation of an affix, however. Instead, the root vowel(s) changes, and this change indicates the inflection (of plurality or past tense). This process is called ABLAUT (a term that comes to us from German). Ablaut has been a productive way to handle inflection over the history of German, so perhaps the appearance of it in English goes back to a productive stage in Proto-Germanic (given that English and German are related languages). Today, however, we have to memorize the nouns and verbs that use it. (We will return to a discussion of ablaut in the section "Process Morphology.")

Ablaut is an example of what is known as a PORTMANTEAU (a term that comes to us from French). In a portmanteau two or more morphemes have merged to create a single form. In French, for example, the preposition meaning 'to' (*à* [a]) merges with the masculine singular (MS) definite article (*le* [lœ]) and with the plural definite article (*les* [le]):

au [o] 'to the' (MS)   *aux* [o] 'to the' (plural)

We can contrast this to *à* followed by the feminine singular (FS) definite article (*la* [la]):

à la 'to the' (FS)

Merging of this sort is very different from infixation. Here no part of the final form can be singled out as being one morpheme while the remainder is a different morpheme. In true infixation, the infix interrupts another morpheme—it doesn't merge with the other morpheme.

The second thing that English does that we can compare to infixes is a much closer candidate. English allows whole words (rather than just affixes) to interrupt other words, as in:

> fanfuckingtastic

You can see that here *fucking* interrupts the root *fantas* (of the morphologically complex word *fantastic*). Only a handful of expletives can do this, and since their function is largely to emphasize, one could argue that a word like *fucking* has been semantically reduced in this position to mere emphasis, in which case its sense/function is much more like that of an affix than that of a lexical word. Perhaps we can see here an incipient infix—an evaluative one at that.

What would be the opposite of an infix? An affix that surrounds the root it attaches to, right? That's called a CIRCUMFIX. There is controversy over whether circumfixes really occur in language. Some morphologists argue that instances of what look like circumfixes are really simultaneous attachment of a prefix and suffix, which conjointly express a single morphological property (semantic or categorial). Consider the following verb PARADIGM from Chukchee of north east Siberia (often called a Paleosiberian language, although this rubric does not indicate a genetic class):

təkətgəntatgʔak	'I ran'	məkətgəntatmək	'we ran'
kətgəntatgʔe	'you (S) ran'	kətgəntattək	'you (P) ran'
kətgəntatgʔe	'he ran'	kətgəntatgʔat	'they ran'

Is any sequence of sounds common to all the forms? *kətgəntat*. Certainly, then, we expect this to be the root for 'run' (and perhaps some other morpheme, as well, that is present throughout this paradigm, such as the past tense morpheme, so that this sequence would mean 'ran'—we will return to this). Now can you tell me what the affix is that means 'I'? Before you can answer that, we have to analyze all that goes into 'I.'

Person, Number, Gender, and Verbal Inflection

Up to this point we have used the term "person" a few times without defining it. For people who are monolingual speakers of English, the notion of person is not obvious insofar as a discussion of affixation goes. But still, you are familiar with the notion. In any given speech act, what are the various participants? Certainly there is a speaker. We call the speaker FIRST PERSON. Often there is a listener or hearer distinct from the speaker. We call the hearer SECOND PERSON. And often there is something or someone spoken about that is distinct from both speaker and hearer. We call this the THIRD PERSON.

In English a speaker may present himself or herself as speaking as a representative of a larger group. Thus it's possible for us to have both singular and plural first persons, which are embodied in the pronoun systems of *I*/*me* vs. *we*/*us*. (And, of course, if two people or a group of people speak simultaneously, they could well refer to themselves as *we*/*us*.) Even more obviously, the hearer can be singular or plural, as can the something(s) or some-one(s) spoken about. So we make distinctions of NUMBER in each of the three persons seen in our pronominal system, and our two numbers are singular and plural.

What is the distinction between singular and plural? In English we use the singular for precisely one and the plural for any number larger than one, and we mark our nouns accordingly *(one pig, two pigs)*.

Our verbs can also show both number and person, by a process of agreement with the Subject. Our verbal system, however, is quite deficient in showing sensitivity to the persons and numbers that English pronouns and nouns distinguish. Still, we can see that both person and number are important when we decide to say *walk* vs. *walks* (and you will follow up on this in Problem Set 3.5). An important point is that the *-s* here gives us three separate pieces of information: singular, third person, and present tense.

Let's take a very brief aside for a moment and look more closely at the verbal *-s* of *walks*. How would you classify this affix? Is it derivational, inflectional, evaluative? Is it a portmanteau? It is inflectional and, since it carries three pieces of information but we cannot point to three particular parts of the *-s* and say that those parts correspond to each of the three pieces of information, it is also a portmanteau. However, the term "portman-teau" is not typically applied to inflection of this sort. Rather, we reserve it for instances in which we would expect a discrete sequence of morphemes but instead find one unanalyz-able form (as in the French example I gave when I introduced the term earlier). In English we do not find a discrete sequence of morphemes for person, number, and tense in the normal situation (or ever); thus, this *-s* is an inflection but we will not call it a portmanteau.

English has three persons and two numbers. This is a very common person and number arrangement among the world's languages, but some languages demonstrate different arrangements. The number 2 is often singled out, so that languages have a DUAL number. Attic Greek, for example, made a morphological distinction among singular, dual, and plural (where plural means three or more) on nouns; many of the Semitic languages have singular, dual, and plural agreement marking on verbs in the various persons (although the Semitic languages generally do not have a dual in the first person); Hopi (a Uto-Aztecan language spoken in northern Arizona) has the singular, dual, and plural distinction in both nouns and verbal agreement. Some languages even distinguish the number 3 from all others, adding a TRIAL, as in the verbal agreement system of Kiwai, a language of New Guinea, and of American Sign Language.

Furthermore, many languages will distinguish a polite or HONORIFIC person, sometimes only for reference to the listener (as in many Romance languages), but sometimes also for reference to someone spoken about (as in Japanese). The morphological shape of the predicate shows the (degree of) honorific. And sometimes the very choice of lexical items used (both nouns and verbs) can indicate an honorific.

And languages can distinguish an INCLUSIVE from an EXCLUSIVE person. Fijian, an Austronesian language spoken on the island of Fiji, distinguishes in the plural first person between a 'we' that includes both speaker and hearer and a 'we' that includes only the speaker and not the hearer.

Beyond person and number, languages may distinguish gender. Is there anywhere in English where we can hear a gender distinction? In our third-person singular pronouns: *he/him, she/her*, and *it*. So besides masculine and feminine, English pronouns distinguish a neuter. The third-person-singular possessive adjectives and Genitive nouns also show gender *(his, her/hers*, and *its)*. Do our verbs agree with their Subjects for gender? No.

Many languages make much fuller use of gender than English does (when what we mean by "gender" is morphological classes of nouns). In the Romance languages, for example, every noun has a gender (masculine or feminine) and adjectives that modify the noun will agree for gender (as well as number). But in the vast majority of cases, there is no relationship between morphological gender and real-world sex type. Instead, the assignment of gender is arbitrary. (The arbitrary assignment for the Romance languages was made long ago in their ancestral past.)

In Hindi-Urdu (spoken in India and Pakistan) verbs agree with their Subject for person, number, and gender. Furthermore, there is an honorific (HON—it does not distinguish for number) in both the second and third persons, as in:

ghumega	'you (MS) take a walk'
ghumegi	'you (FS) take a walk'
ghumoge	'you (MP) take a walk'
ghumogi	'you (FP) take a walk'
ghumenge	'you (M HON) take a walk'
ghumengi	'you (F HON) take a walk'

In the Dravidian language Tamil, spoken in southern India and Sri Lanka, there are two major genders (or noun classes), which correspond roughly to the distinction of human/nonhuman, and the human class breaks down into feminine and masculine. In the Bantu languages of southern Africa several genders (often more than ten) can be found. Some nouns are arbitrarily assigned to a particular class. Others are assigned to a particular class based on a variety of factors, such as physical shape of the object referred to by the noun (long and thin, for example), or whether the object referred to by the noun tends to come in pairs or larger groups (such as hands or grapes), or whether the object referred to by the noun is human or animal.

Furthermore, when we look at agreement processes that involve verbs, we find that agreement is not limited to features of the Subject. In many languages, verbs can agree with various Objects. In Kubachi (a dialect of Dargwa, a Caucasian language spoken in Russia and Europe) we find agreement with both Subject and Direct Object. For the TRANSITIVE verb (a transitive verb is one that takes a Direct Object) meaning 'to praise,' the paradigm for a singular Subject in each of the three persons is shown in Table 3.1. (Here the number indicates person. My source does not give information about what happens if the Object is 3SF. We can see that the verbal form is agreeing not only with the person and number of the Subject, but with the gender, as well, of the Object, at least for 3SM.) So the verb form you would use with a third-person singular Subject and a third-person-singular masculine Object would be w-$\bar{a}q$-aj. Number and person are relevant for both Subject and Object, but gender is relevant only for the Object. But INTRANSITIVE

Table 3.1. Kubachi Agreement in Transitives

Subject	Object Class			
	3SM	1P	2P	3P
1S	w-āq' a-d	d-āq' a-d	d-āq' a-d	b-āq' a-d
2S	w-āq' a-t:e	d-āq' a-t:e	d-āq' a-t:e	b-āq' a-t:e
3S	w-āq' aj	d-āq' aj	d-āq' aj	b-āq' aj

verbs behave differently. There is no Object to agree with. But the Subject agreement is sensitive to person, number, and gender now, where three gender classes are distinguished:

Table 3.2. Kubachil Agreement in Intransitives

	Subject Class		
P/N	M	F	Nonhuman
1S	li-w-da	li-j-da	li-b-da
2S	li-w-de	li-j-de	li-b-de
3S	li-w	li-j	li-b

(P/N = person/number. We see here a morphological sensitivity to the PREDICATE-ARGUMENT STRUCTURE—often called simply "argument structure"—of a predicate. We will return to a discussion of this sort of phenomenon in the section "Valency and Argument Structure.")

Besides this sort of agreement system, we even find languages in which the verb sometimes agrees with the gender of the person addressed, as happens in Basque (spoken in the western Pyrenees of southern France and northern Spain). Basque also has agreement of the verb with an Indirect Object.

Back to Chukchee

Consider again the Chukchee verb paradigm, repeated here for the sake of convenience:

təkətgəntatgʔak	'I ran'	məkətgəntatmək	'we ran'
kətgəntatgʔe	'you (s) ran'	kətgəntattək	'you ran'
kətgəntatgʔe	'he ran'	kətgəntatgʔat	'they ran'

Can you figure out now what morpheme means 'I'? Your job is to figure out how the first-person singular is indicated. Let's begin by breaking down that job into trying to isolate number and trying to isolate person.

Comparing all the singular forms to the plural forms of the same person (that is, Column 1 to Column 2), can you see any morpheme that indicates plurality? You might have thought that *-ək* in final position indicated plurality, looking at the "we" and "you (pl.)" forms. But the "they" form is inconsistent with this analysis. You might have thought the *-gʔ-* sequence indicated singular, but the "they" form is inconsistent with this analysis. In other words, there doesn't seem to be any identifiable morpheme that indicates number only.

Comparing the first-person forms to all the other forms (that is, Row 1 to the other two rows), can you see any morpheme that indicates only first person and not number, as well? Again, the answer must be no. Person and number are inextricably mixed and handled by a single morpheme in Chukchee (just as they are in English *walks*).

So we really are looking for a morpheme that means 'I'—that is, a morpheme that indicates simultaneously both first person and singular. What is it? It could be the prefix *tə-*, and an examination of other verbs in the first person singular confirms this:

təpelarkən 'I leave (something)'

But then we are left with the question of what the suffix -gʔak means. Can it by itself mean past tense? No, for it is not carried consistently throughout the paradigm. Thus we are left with two possibilities. Either the sequence common to all the verbal forms here, kətgəntat, represents the lexical root plus the past-tense morpheme, and the circumfix tə . . . gʔak means first-person singular; or the sequence kətgəntat represents only the lexical root, and the circumfix tə . . . gʔak represents first person, singular, and past tense, all three at once.

In fact, morphologists tend to say that tə- alone means 'I.' But with this analysis, we must admit that the proper choice of the suffix for tense is dependent upon the person and number of the Subject. Thus this analysis could be argued to be only terminologically different from calling the discontinuous sequence tə . . . gʔak a circumfix giving person, number, and tense all at once. (In fact, the story is even more complex. We find that with other verbal roots in the past tense with a first-person-singular Subject, we do not always get the suffix -gʔak, as in:

təwakʔok   'I sat down.'

So the proper choice of the tense morpheme may depend on the choice of the root, as well.)

Does English have any circumfixes? I think not. Those few instances in which it looks like we have circumfixes turn out to be open to other analyses. For example, consider the be . . . èd seen in:

belovèd   belatèd   benightèd

However, this is not a true circumfix. Instead, in Old English we had a verbal prefix be- that attached to a stem to create a new verb that could occur in the range of tenses, including the past. Thus this be- and the past -ed could co-occur, and it is that co-occurence that we witness in examples like these.

Thus far we have prefixes, suffixes, infixes, and, possibly, circumfixes. What other kinds of affixes might you expect to find? For words that contain only a single lexical morpheme, these four types of affixes may cover the logical possibilities. But if we have two lexical morphemes in a word, then another logical possibility comes up: the INTERFIX, which occurs between two lexical morphemes. Ancient Greek had such an interfix; it is called "omicron" and seen in compounds (words with more than one lexical morpheme— we met them in Chapter 2 and worked on them in Problem Set 2.9) such as:

σωματ-ο-φύλαξ   [sɔːmatopʰýlaks]   'bodyguard'

Does English have interfixes? While interfixing does not really play a significant role in English morphology, we can find a handful of cases. The omicron, in fact, occurs in some words where the second stem is of Greek origin, such as:

speedometer   historiography   Italophile

and it enjoys a limited productivity, as in the new word:

Veg-o-matic

The epenthesis of "t" in fantastic (fantas + ic) and of "v" in Peruvian (Peru + ian) might also be instances of a kind of limited interfixation, but between a lexical and a grammatical morpheme.

If you think back to our remarks on tone languages in Chapter 2 (in the section "Geometric Phonology"), you might be able to come up with one more possible type of affix: a SUPERFIX. A superfix could be a certain tone or change of tone, or a certain pitch or change of pitch that carries with it a lexical, derivational, or inflectional sense. Perhaps even a displacement of a stress that has affixal-type sense could be considered a superfix. In Quiotepec Chinantec, an Amerind language spoken in Oaxaca, Mexico, tone can be a superfix, I believe. It can express a Genitive. I indicate falling tone across two syllables, falling tone on one syllable, a drop in tone between two syllables, and a severe drop in tone between two syllables in these examples:

[Mm ⟍ M] 'water' [Mm · M] 'my water'

And it can express person and number:

[ʔmʔm] 'I pinch' [ʔmʔm] 'you (sg.) pinch'

However, tone as an inflection is not common. Much more common is tone that carries with it an evaluative or AFFECTIVE sense. In Bini, a Kwa language of Nigeria, adverbs have a uniform tone, either high or low. For around 90% of these adverbs there is an iconic relationship between tone and semantics. The high tone goes with tall, thin, tight, bright, or open senses, while the low tone goes with short, thick, loose, dull, or closed senses. Here is one example to represent each group:

High-tone adverbs	*Low-tone adverbs*
gadagba: 'long and lanky'	giɛ:ghɛgiɛghɛ 'short'
gilɔgilɔ 'tall and slender'	gbankangbankan 'big and thick'
kanka:nkan 'tight'	panpa:npan 'slack'
giɛ:rlɛn 'bright and clear'	muɛn 'faint and dull'
gboo 'wide open'	kuku:ku 'closed'

(These are not accurate phonetic transcriptions. And I have indicated tone only by putting the examples in lists since my source didn't mark the tones.) We can even find a few minimal pairs, where tone is the only difference, such as:

	High tone	*Low tone*
bɛtɛ:	'big and fat'	'short and fat'
gidigbi:	'tall'	'husky'

If you are full of questions about what kind of morpheme the tone is here, in terms of our classifications of lexical, inflectional, and derivational, you are right to be disturbed. The traditional classification is as unhelpful here as it is with evaluative affixes.

With respect to languages that use stress placement to indicate morphological distinctions, Basque may be one. Thus we find pairs like these:

mutíla	'boy'	Nominative Case
mutilá	'boy'	Vocative Case
gizónen	'of man/men'	Genitive Case, indefinite
gizonén	'of the men'	Genitive Case, plural

(These are not phonetic transcriptions. We will get into Case briefly later, where the terms NOMINATIVE and VOCATIVE will be handled. We will also spend a large part of Chapter 4 on matters of Case.)

Does English seem to have any superfixes? Not in any obvious sense. We do, however, have at least one melody that carries a lexical sense with it. Sing the child's taunt:

[ɲæ̃: ɲæ̃ ɲæ̃ ɲæ̃: ɲæ̃]

Now add that melody over these words: "You have an old dog." Suddenly the sentence becomes a taunt. So melodies can have senses in English, this one having a pejorative sense much like an evaluative affix or the affective use of tones in Bini. This melody differs from a superfix in an important way, however. Its domain is the full utterance, rather than the word or root.

Another melody you might consider is the vocative melody, used for calling people from a distance: *Ma--ry*. (By the way, Italian makes use of the same vocative melody.) While names are the typical lexical items used in this melody, the melody is not defined only on that domain. Thus we can say, for example, *little sis--ter*. Again, the domain is the full utterance (where the utterance must be able to serve as a vocative, so it is automatically syntactically limited).

In sum, English seems to lack true superfixes.

You might suggest at this point that English sometimes uses stress to distinguish between morphosyntactic categories, pointing to pairs like the noun *récord* vs. the verb *recórd*. If you transcribe these two words, you'll see that stress is not the only difference between them. Because we reduce unstressed vowels and because we often drop those unstressed vowels and let sonorant consonants slide into the nucleus of the syllable (or, rather, the syllabicity is stable and is reassociated with the sonorant consonant after the vowel deletes), these two words differ in a few ways. But one could easily argue that before stress assignment, they are identical. Thus stress could be a superfix, telling us category here.

In our discussion of English stress in Chapter 2 (in the section "English Stress"), we pointed out that the final syllable of nouns is extrametrical, and this difference, naturally, correlates with the difference in stress placement between N and V. Now we can look again at this account and see that it differs only terminologically from a superfix account.

There are also language-particular special uses of other aspects of prosody that can be thought of as rather limited and specialized superfixes. In Hebrew, for example, many words have special shapes when they come at the end of a sentence. They are called PAUSAL shapes, and they often involve lengthening of a syllable nucleus and sometimes a change in stress or other types of sound changes. The pausal shape itself could be thought of as a type of inflectional morpheme, perhaps, indicating a major syntactic break. (This sort of phenomenon would fall in the realm of process morphology, which we'll talk about later.)

Are there any other kinds of affixes? Once we've introduced the idea of compounds, other logical possibilities for affixes may well present themselves, such as an affix that is discontinuous in three parts (instead of two, like a circumfix), where one part comes before the first member of the compound, one part comes in between, and the last part comes after the second member. And I'm sure you can think of other possibilities. So far as I know, these other possibilities do not occur in language.

Inventory of Morphological Types

We've noted at least two ways to classify words thus far. One is to distinguish between words which contain only one morpheme, SIMPLEX WORDS or monomorphemic words, and words which contain more than one, COMPLEX WORDS or polymorphemic words. We have also made a distinction between words that contain only one lexical morpheme and compound words, which contain more than one lexical morpheme. Noncompound words can be simplex or complex (having derivational and/or inflectional affixes). Compound words are, of course, complex. There is at least one other distinction in classifications of words that we should make. Consider this sentence:

Ida gave a box of crackers to my friend.

Are there any words here that seem somehow to be less full semantically than others? Any for which you feel uncomfortable calling them lexical morphemes? The words *a*, *of*, and *to* might well be bothering you. While the other words here are called CONTENT words, words like *a*, *of*, and *to* do something other than give you content. Try to isolate what each does. *A* introduces the box of crackers, telling us that this box is new to the discourse. If we were going to follow the sentence above with a question about the box, we would no longer use *a*, but, instead, a different DETERMINER, perhaps the DEFINITE ARTICLE *the*, as in:

Is this the box of crackers Ida gave her?

So determiners tell us something about the roll of a noun phrase in the discourse as a whole.

What about *of*? It tells us that there's a relationship between the crackers and the box. Does *of* give us any specifics about what that relationship might be? You might be tempted to say that *of* tells us that the crackers are in the box. But consider these other instances of *of*:

I thought of that issue, but I decided to ignore it.
Would you like a piece of cake?
She went out of her mind.

Can you see that there is no single sense, precise or vague, that you can attribute to *of*? How, then, do we know that in *a box of crackers* the crackers are in the box, but in *a piece of cake*, the cake is not in the piece but instead the piece is a part of the cake? I would suggest that here the *of* is semantically VACUOUS and pretty much a kind of SYNTACTIC GLUE (a term I'm coining right now and I hope catches on), allowing us to put these words in this sequence. But our understanding of the content words (*box*, *crackers*, and *piece*, *cake*) plus our understanding of how the world works (crackers often go in boxes but boxes are not typically made of crackers, for instance) act together to help us interpret the sense of the phrase. Small words that act as syntactic glue occur much more extensively in some languages, such as the Tsimshian languages (of the Penutian branch of the Amerind phylum, spoken in western Canada).

What about the *to* of the phrase *to my friend*? Here we could get into a rather long debate, but we won't. Instead, you can face this debate in Problem Set 4.9 of Chapter 4.

For now, we'll say that this *to* helps us to know the PARTICIPANT ROLE or THEMATIC ROLE of the noun phrase *my friend* in the sentence. It tells us that my friend is the one who receives the box of crackers: the BENEFICIARY.

Determiners and certain prepositions (*of* and the *to* seen above, at the least, but not prepositions that indicate spatial or temporal relationships, such as *under* or *after*) along with a handful of other kinds of words are called "function words". In many languages, there are no independent function words; instead, affixes do the job of English function words.

Tell me, do function words in English participate in morphological processes that build new words? Can you add affixes to them, for example? Do they take inflections? Can they appear as a member in a compound? Generally not. We pointed out above in passing that *unless* in English looks like it might be composed of *un-* plus the function word *less*. But this analysis is debatable and this example is isolated. So for English, function words are uninteresting from a morphological point of view. They are morphologically inert. We will, therefore, not concern ourselves with them further.

We can also talk about a TYPOLOGY of morphemes. We have seen that morphemes can be classified as roots or affixes, as free or bound, as lexical or grammatical. We have seen that affixes can be classified further as derivational or inflectional, and that they can be prefixes, suffixes, infixes, cirumfixes, interfixes, and superfixes.

Typology of Languages by Morphology

Linguistics books often classify languages with respect to their morphological characteristics. We will do that here. Consider this sentence from the Sino-Tibetan language Běijīng Mandarin:

> wǒ bu cháng kàn diànyǐng
> I   not often see movie
> 'I don't see movies often.'

What is the relationship between words and morphemes? Each word here is a single morpheme. Mandarin (as well as other languages of China) is often claimed to be ISOLATIVE or ANALYTIC—that is, to express each morpheme as a separate word. In fact, however, there are a handful of affixes even in Mandarin:

> qiáng-shàng guà-zhe   yǐ-fu   huà
> wall-on   hang-DUR one-CL painting
> 'There is a painting hanging on the wall.'

(DUR = duration; CL = classifier. A hyphen between morphemes here and later indicates that one morpheme is affixed to the other. I have put spaces between roots and affixes sometimes just to make it easier to see the gloss for each morpheme.) The three suffixes here are *-shàng*, which indicates location much as a preposition does in English, *-zhe*, which indicates duration, and *-fu*, which is a CLASSIFIER (a morpheme indicating the class of a noun—we will talk about classifiers in the section "Classifiers" of Chapter 5). In Chinese, referential nouns occur with determiners (such as numerals, quantifiers, demonstratives) and a classifier will accompany the determiner. Here *-fu* is suffixed to the numeral *yĭ*. Additionally, Mandarin has many bimorphemic words, which might well be compounds.

In my search through books on various languages, I have found no language which appears to be completely isolative. But certainly the Chinese languages come closer than many.

Now consider this sentence from Turkish:

> Kitap-lar masa-lar-dan   yer-e   düş-tü
> book-PL   table-PL-ABL   floor-DAT fall-PAST
> 'The books fell from the tables to the floor.'

What can you say about the relationship between words and morphemes here? Is Turkish isolative? Certainly not. Turkish has many suffixes. Do you notice anything about these suffixes? Contrast them to the suffix *-o* in this Latin verb:

> Amo.
> am-o
> love-1S Pres Active
> 'I love.'

What is the sense of each of the suffixes in Turkish and what is the sense of the suffix *-o* in Latin? Do you see a difference? Some have claimed that Turkish is an AGGLUTINATIVE language, in which each morpheme carries only one sense, in contrast to Latin, which is an INFLECTIVE or SYNTHETIC language, in which a morpheme may carry more than one sense (the *-o* carries the senses of first person, singular, present tense, active voice).

Please be very careful here. We have an unfortunate overlapping of terminology. We have used the term "inflectional" to describe a certain kind of morpheme—one that does not change the category of the stem it attaches to, but instead gives us another form of the same word, adding either no semantic information or a restricted and precise bit of semantic information. But now we are talking about an "inflective" language as one that uses inflectional morphemes that are complex in features. Agglutinative languages can have inflectional morphemes in the first sense (morphemes that indicate person, number, gender, tense, and so forth), but those morphemes will carry only one meaning (person or number or gender or tense, and so forth).

And now, while I've just made this clean distinction for you, I must, again, qualify it. While Turkish is pointed to repeatedly as an example of a canonical agglutinative language, we can find a few inflectional suffixes that carry more than one meaning:

> (Ben) bu   makale -yi   yarin   bitir -eceğ -im
> I   this article-ACC tomorrow finish-FUT -1 SG
> 'I will finish this article tomorrow.'

Which of the three suffixes here is a complex inflection (carrying more than one feature or piece of information)? The *-im*, for it indicates both person and number at once. There may well be languages that are purely agglutinative and contain no complex inflections. But usually when someone classifies a language as being agglutinative, the claim is not

Table 3.3. Pashto Case

	Direct	Vocative	Prepositional	Oblique
MS	pox	póxa	póxa	pāxə
MP	pāxə	paxó	paxó	paxó
FS	paxá	paxé	paxá	paxé
FP	paxé	paxó	paxó	paxó

that every single morpheme will conform, but that those that don't form a small set of exceptions.

We have already pointed out a third type of language, inflective languages, like Latin. Where do you think English falls? Certainly the -*s* on *walks* in the sentence *John walks home* is a complex inflection, so some have called English an inflective language. But, actually, English is rather impoverished with respect to inflection because distinctions in inflection that used to have a phonetic realization at an earlier period in the history of English have been NEUTRALIZED over time (and many linguists have, indeed, claimed English is more neatly classified as an analytic language).

Many languages have a much richer inflectional system than English, such as the Iranian language Pashto, spoken in Afghanistan and northwestern India. Pashto distinguishes two genders (masculine and feminine) and two numbers (singular and plural) in both the nominal and verbal systems. It further distinguishes CASE in the nominal system, whereby a noun phrase gets a different suffixal ending based on its grammatical and/or hierarchical role in the sentence (see Problem Set 3.4, and we will talk much more about Case from various perspectives in Chapter 4), and it distinguishes three persons in the verbal system. Adjectives agree with nominals (unlike in English). Thus, for instance, consider the forms of the adjective meaning 'ripe, cooked', in Table 3.3. I have put a Case heading each column and the rows vary by gender and number.

Vocative is the Case used for direct address (and we met this term earlier—as in the discussion of the vocative melody). You might be familiar with a use of the vocative in Latin, for example, in the famous sentence from Shakespeare's *Julius Caesar*:

Et tu, Brutē?   You, too, Brutus?

Brutē is the Vocative form that corresponds to the Nominative (or Subject) form of *Brutus*. Direct is the Case used for Subjects and Direct Objects. Oblique is the Case used for Indirect Objects. Prepositional is the Case used for Objects of Prepositions. (Please hold off on your questions about Case until Chapter 4.)

As you can see, in the plural, for both masculine and feminine, the three Cases Vocative, Prepositional, and Oblique have been neutralized into one form. Beyond that, however, the system is quite rich.

It is important to notice that so-called inflective languages allow grammatical morphemes that carry only one meaning (the plural being an obvious instance in several languages), as well as complex inflections. English, for example, has many, if we look at derivational morphemes (as in our analysis of *unfriendliness*). Thus when a language is classified as inflective, the classification means only that complex inflections are not rare in the language, not that agglutination doesn't occur.

A fourth type of language distinguished by morphology is one that INCORPORATES words for the participants of the ACTION or STATE and for various modifications of the action or state into one word with the action or state word. This example is from Tuscarora, an Iroquoian language of North Carolina, New York, and Ontario:

Ae-hra-taskw-ahk-hwa?   ha? tsi:r.
PRE-3M-domestic animal-pickup-ASP PRT dog
'He regularly picks up dogs   [he is a dog-catcher].'

(PRE = prefix; ASP = aspect marker; PRT = particle.) Incorporating languages are also called POLYSYNTHETIC, and while the Iroquoian languages and the Inuit languages are typically cited, many Amerind languages are incorporating, as are some Bantu languages and some Australian languages. Furthermore, even languages that we don't think of as belonging to the incorporating type may have incorporation processes to greater or lesser extents. And, as you can see in this one example from Tuscarora, incorporating languages also have morphemes that are typical of inflective languages (like the *hra* that means 3M) and of agglutinative languages (like the *ae-* prefix). Thus classifying a language as incorporating is claiming that it typically forms word-sentences that have ARGUMENTS and modifications of the predicate all in one word with the predicate, not that the language doesn't have other kinds of morphemes as well.

I should warn you that the terms "polysynthetic" and "incorporating" have been used in the linguistic literature in varying ways, so any use of them is likely to open the door to all sorts of confusion. If you are familiar with these terms from elsewhere, please, as you read this book, employ the terms in a sense compatible with the senses demonstrated in this section.

English can incorporate in at least two ways. One is to form compound verbs, where an argument of the verb (that is, a participant in the action or state denoted by the verb) is the first member:

I'm going spearfishing.

The instrument for fishing, the spear, has been incorporated into the new verb *spearfish*. Another method of incorporation in English is to take a nominal that would normally serve as the argument for a verb and create a verb out of it, sometimes a compound verb:

She bottled the wine.
She redpenciled my paper.

With *bottle* as a verb, we have taken the action of putting something into a bottle and expressed it as a single word. The senses of both action and location are incorporated in the newly formed verb, even though phonetically all we hear is *bottle*. With *redpencil* as a verb, we have taken the action of writing with a red pencil and expressed it as a single word. But here we have a compound, with two morphological roots.

We will meet yet a fifth kind of language, based on morphological type, later.

While this kind of typology can give one a general sense of how the morphological processes of a language work, very few languages (if any) fall strictly into one class. The classifications of isolative and agglutinative tend to be somewhat exclusive, but even languages in these classifications will probably have some morphemes of other types, as well. The classifications of inflective and incorporating, on the other hand, are not exclusive. Rather, they indicate the language has a certain morphological possibility that may exist side by side with other kinds of word-formation processes.

Verbal Inflections and Affixes

Thus far we have run across a range of nominal affixes, indicating person, number, gender, class (as in the classifiers of Chinese), and Case. And we have realized that many of these have counterparts in the verbal system, often due to agreement with the Subject of the sentence. Thus if the Subject of a sentence is first person plural, in Portuguese, for example, the verb will have a suffix indicating this person and number. We also noted that languages can have honorific systems that affect the morphological shape of the predicate.

But there is a wide range of inflections that belong to the verbal system in many languages and this range goes well beyond agreement and honorific inflections. So let's meet some of them.

Be warned: This section goes very rapidly through a large number of new ideas and you may feel bombarded by terminology. Please try to read with a certain resilience of spirit. A precise understanding of each of the ideas here is not the point and, indeed, is not easily accomplished without extensive reading. (Some of the bibliography can help you there.) My goal is to show a representative sampling of possible meanings that can be expressed through verbal inflections. That's all. Okay?

Make a list of several random sentences of English. Then consider the actions or states described in those sentences and think about all the different kinds of information about those actions or states that the sentences give you. Try this one for a starter:

We wondered if Bill would get arrested.

What do we know about the act of wondering as contrasted to the act of arresting? The wondering actually happened; the arresting might or might not have. **The contrast is between reality and possibility, and we say this contrast is one of MOOD.** Many languages distinguish mood inflectionally, using one kind of marker for REALIS actions (actions that take place in the real world) and another for IRREALIS ones (actions that take place in a hypothetical world, perhaps actions we hope for or dream about or believe). In English we generally use a single mood form, called the INDICATIVE, for both realis and irrealis actions, although we do have a few instances in which we use a different form, the SUBJUNCTIVE, for irrealis actions. An example is the form of the verb *be* in:

Joan demands that you be here on time.
(cf. You are here on time.
and: Joan knows that you are here on time.)

Most of the time, in order to express irrealis action, English uses the indicative form of AUXILIARY verbs that show MODALITY, like the *would* of the sentence *We wondered if Bill would get arrested.* Other MODAL verbs include *may, might, will, can,* and others you'll meet in Problem Set 4.3 of Chapter 4. Thus the English approach to irrealis mood is to get across the idea ANALYTICALLY (that is, with a separate form, here a separate modal verb to show irrealis sense) rather than SYNTHETICALLY (that is, with a special form of the word, such as having an inflection on the verb denoting the main action).

Italian is a language that indicates indicative and subjunctive mood with inflection. In the second sentence here the italicized verb is subjunctive in contrast to its counterpart in the first sentence:

Marina dice che Iole *mentisce*.   'Marina says that Iole lies.'
Marina pensa che Iole *mentisca*.   'Marina thinks that Iole lies.'

Other moods include the IMPERATIVE (for orders), the OPTATIVE (for wishes), and the HORTATIVE (often translated into English with let's . . .). Ancient Greek, for example, has inflectional morphemes to show indicative, subjunctive, optative, and imperative moods.

Going back to our English sentence about Bill getting arrested:

We wondered if Bill would get arrested.

we see another contrast between the two actions. The action of wondering is in the ACTIVE VOICE, but the action of arresting is in the PASSIVE voice. English has at least two ways of expressing passive voice: with the auxiliary verb *be* or with the auxiliary verb *get*, both followed by the PASSIVE PARTICIPLE of the main verb:

Bill was arrested.   Bill got arrested.

Here our way of dealing with the passive is mixed; we add an auxiliary verb (an analytical strategy), but we also add a suffix to the main verb (a synthetic strategy).

Latin is a language that handles voice entirely with inflection:

portamur   'we are carried'   vs. portamus   'we carry'

(Latin, like Italian, Spanish, Portuguese, and many other languages, need not have a Subject expressed in the sentence. Thus a form like *portamur* can stand alone in a sentence, without need of any pronoun meaning 'we.' We will talk about such languages in the section "The Null Subject Parameter" of Chapter 4.)

A third voice, MIDDLE, is also often handled with inflection. Greek uses the middle when the Subject of the sentence and another argument of the verb are coreferential or when the Subject somehow acts in his or her own interest. Only in certain tenses is the middle inflectionally distinct from the passive, one of them being the future:

παιδεύσομαι 'I will learn' (literally: 'I will educate (mid.)')

(I used the Greek alphabet here and a few times earlier just for fun. Throughout this book, examples from other languages are transliterated into the Roman alphabet or transcribed into the IPA and we almost never get a chance to look at other writing systems—with the exception of Problem Set 1.2 of Chapter 2, where we looked at a Japanese syllabary. So I thought I'd sneak in a little Greek, which I hope isn't too jarring, given that the Greek alphabet and the Roman alphabet have much in common.)

Other languages handle the sense of middle with a reflexive CLITIC (a phonetically weak pronoun—we study clitics in a section by that title later) that is phonologically attached to the verb (although orthographic conventions may represent the clitic—CL— as separate from the verb). French is a case in point:

Les maisons se	vendent	facilement	à	Paris.
the houses themselves (CL)	sell	easily		in Paris

'Houses sell easily in Paris.'

You can see from the English translation of the French that English uses neither an inflection nor a clitic to indicate middle voice. Instead, in the English middle we find a Subject (here *houses*) that corresponds to what we expect as the Direct Object in the active sentence (which might be: *People sell houses easily in Paris*), but no special morpheme for middle occurs on the verb or anywhere else in the sentence.

Besides mood and voice, the most common verbal inflections found in languages involve factors of the time frame of an action or state. In English we handle simple present tense and simple past tense inflectionally:

She walks.   She walked.

But we have no other inflections that by themselves give us information about the time frame. Morphologically speaking, then, English has only two inflectional tenses: past and present.

This does not mean that our ability to express nuances in the time frame is limited. We deal with other complications in the time frame in an analytical way, adding auxiliaries. Thus we use the modal *will* to show future time and the modal *would* to show future time from a past perspective:

Mary will leave.   I knew Mary would leave.

Besides conveying whether an event takes place in past, present, or future time, we can also convey the ASPECT of an event. Aspect has to do with the way we look at an event, whatever its time frame might be. We can look at an event from the inside, so to speak, and talk about its duration or habitual nature or repetition or continuity and so on, or we can look at it from the outside and talk about the fact that it is completed or it is punctual and so on. Aspect is often conveyed by affixes, but sometimes by auxiliary verbs and sometimes by main verbs.

English uses the auxiliary *have* to show perfect aspect (conveying the notion of completion), and we accompany this *have* with an inflection on the following verb that turns that verb into a perfect participle. (This is similar to our use of the passive auxiliary *be*, which turned the following verb into a passive participle.) We can express the perfect aspect in the present or past tense:

present tense, perfect aspect: Mary has left.
past tense, perfect aspect: Mary had left.

We use the auxiliary *be* to show progressive aspect (conveying the notion of continuity), and again we accompany this *be* with an inflection on the following verb that turns that verb into a progressive participle. Both present and past tenses are found in this aspect:

present tense, progressive aspect: Mary is leaving.
past tense, progressive aspect: Mary was leaving.

We can combine all these and have, for example, a future modality in the present tense with both progressive and perfect aspect:

present tense, perfect-progressive aspect, future modality:
Mary will have been studying for at least an hour by the time you get there.

(We will return to a precise study of the English verbal string in Problem Set 4.3 of Chapter 4.)

Other languages can show a wide range of inflections that can convey both time and aspect. Italian is one:

present: parlo 'I talk/I am talking'
imperfective: parlavo 'I was talking'
preterite: parlai 'I talked'
future: parlerò 'I will talk'
conditional: parlerei 'I would talk'

Notice that what we called progressive aspect in English is handled with an inflection that also shows tense in Italian. (The simple present can be understood progressively and the imperfective is a past progressive.) But what we called perfect aspect in English is handled in Italian with an auxiliary verb plus a participle form of the main verb, just as in English:

present perfect: ho parlato 'I have spoken'
past perfect: avevo parlato 'I had spoken'

The preterite tense also needs comment. This is a form that indicates past time and often is used when that past time is looked at as REMOTE or PUNCTUAL. Many languages make use of a special inflection for remote or punctual time. And English may still have a vestige of that in contrasting irregular and regular past tenses:

She spilled the milk.   She spilt the milk.

If the milk came slowly, one is unlikely to use the form *spilt*. But if the milk came all in a gush, one might use either form or perhaps even prefer *spilt*. (If you don't have *spilt* in your speech, perhaps this distinction is alive for you in the contrast between *leaped* and *leapt* or *dreamed* and *dreamt*.)

Still other distinctions in the verbal system can be made. Some of them are elaborations and refinements of the kinds of things we have already talked about. For example, many languages make fine aspectual distinctions, marking verbs differently for whether the action is habitual, continuous, repeated, repeated at intervals, inchoative (that is, inceptive, beginning, or becoming), and more. (Mapudungan, the language of the Mapuche poeple of

Chile, has such an aspectual system.) But other distinctions in verbal systems can be quite new and different from those we've discussed thus far.

Otomí verbs, for example, have an elaborate set of prefixes that indicate many things, including factors of time, participant reference, and the realis/irrealis distinction, but also things such as the spatial location or direction of an event. Affixes that point to a location are DEICTIC (or INDEXICAL). Any verb which doesn't show at least this much information (time, reference, mood, spatial deixis) is considered to be dependent upon the linguistic context for the missing information. That is, we will interpret the missing information in a given sentence from the corresponding given information in another sentence of the discourse.

Deixis is not limited to verbal inflections. In English we see a two-way deictic distinction that is LOCATIVE (having to do with physical or psychological space) in the demonstratives:

> this   that   these   those

In Japanese we see a four-way deictic distinction that is again locative. It is evidenced in the pronouns and in demonstratives:

Pronouns:

*ko*re 'this thing'   *so*re 'that thing near you'
*a*re 'that thing over there'   *do*re 'where?'

Demonstratives:

*ko*no zisyo 'this dictionary'   *so*no konpyuutaa 'that computer'
*a*no teepu 'that tape over there'   *do*no hon 'which book?'

In a sense, agreement processes are all deictic. That is, when a verb, for instance, agrees with its Subject and/or its Object, the agreement itself helps us to pick out the Subject or Object; it points to the Subject or Object. Pronouns are also, often, deictic. If I say, "He stole the cookie," the pronoun *he* points either to a referent that has been mentioned in the discourse or to some referent that is obvious from the nonlinguistic situation (where we are at the time of the utterance, what time it is, who is in sight, and so forth). Pronouns are therefore often called REFERENTIAL INDEXICALS.

Returning to our examination of the range of types of verbal morphemes languages exhibit, let's look at Yaqui, an Uto-Aztecan language spoken in Arizona and Sonora, Mexico. In Yaqui we find morphemes that indicate PROPOSITIONAL ATTITUDES. Some are affixes that attach to the verb. In these examples I indicate a morpheme boundary with "-" and I gloss the propositional attitude morpheme with the appropriate abbreviation:

Reportative: ʔa:po yeʔe-tea
                  ʔa:po dancing-REP.
                  'They say ʔa:po is dancing.'
Inferential: ʔa:po si:m-neme-ta-vena
                  ʔa:po leave-FUT-OBJ-INFER
                  'Looks like ʔa:po will leave.'

(The Object affix *ta* presumably indicates the place left.) Others are affixes that attach to the first word of the clause in a statement, but to the final word in a question:

Consequential: ʔa:po-su   yeʔe-ka
ʔa:po-CONS dance-PAST
'Because (since) ʔa:po danced'
ʔa:po yeʔe-k-su
ʔa:po dance-PAST-CONS
'What if (suppose) ʔa:po danced?'

While the variable position of the consequential affix is remarkable, in fact, many languages have propositional affixes that attach in clause final position (such as Japanese).

These are just a selection of the propositional attitude morphemes of Yaqui. Yaqui also has a range of morphemes that indicate particular aspects of an event, including affixes on the verb that are quotative (as in "X said . . . "), directive ("X told Y to . . . "), causative ("X made Y . . . "), desiderative ("X wants to . . . "), inclinative ("X feels like . . . "), and others.

There is much more that could be said about the various functions of different types of morphemes among the world's languages. I hope here only to have sensitized you to the subtleties of the possibilities so that you can be on the alert as you investigate additional languages.

New Word Formation

Up to this point we have looked at a variety of ways in which the addition of an affix can derive a new word. We also briefly mentioned the fact that compounding can result in new words. (We'll have much more to say about compounding later.) These two processes are the major sources of new word formation in English. However, there are many less pervasive ways to coin a word. We noted that new words can enter the language as borrowings from other languages (as in the case of *crayfish*). And, while we talked about onomatopoeia in regard to animal sounds, we can now note that it is probably responsible for scattered words of other types, such as the verb *buzz*. We also mentioned that proper names can enter the lexicon as ordinary nouns and verbs associated with that proper name somehow (as in *pasteurize*).

At this point let's take a moment to consider several other types of processes that can result in new words.

First, what has happened in forming these words:

prof (=professor)   cig (=cigarette)   synch (=synchrony)

Clearly we have made a one-syllable word from a polysyllabic word, but how? This process is often called CLIPPING. We have clipped off the end of the word so that only one syllable remains. What is that one syllable? Is it the first syllable of the polysyllabic word? To answer this, syllabify the words *professor* and *cigarette*. In these words the initial syllable is open. But the clipped form is a closed syllable. Now syllabify the word *synchrony*. The first syllable has three segments. But the clipped form has four. So how did we decide how much of the polysyllabic word to clip off? What we are doing is using a TEMPLATE to determine the final clipped form. (And you will learn how to formally deal with templates when we talk about prosodic morphology.) The final clipped form typically includes the first syllable of the polysyllabic word plus as much more segmental material as can fit within the rules of English syllable formation. In other words, we make the largest possible syllable out of the initial segments of the polysyllabic word and clip off the rest. That is our target template: the maximal syllable.

There are exceptions to this template (as there are exceptions to most templates in phonology and morphology). Thus the clipped form of *professional* is *pro*, which contrasts with *prof* above. Also, some clippings require additional suffixation, such as *Philly* < *Philadelphia*. (We indicate that one word or form is derived from a second word or form by putting < between the two words.) In German this kind of additional suffixation on clippings is productive: *Vati* < *Vater* 'father'; *Mutti* < *Mutter* 'mother'; and so on. Indeed, if you're looking for a paper topic in morphology, clippings in many languages are begging to be studied.

How did we form the following words?

AIDS   SIDS   NATO   OPEC   MADD   UNICEF

It's easy to see that we took the first letter of the words that made up a phrase; for example, we looked at the phrase *acquired immune deficiency syndrome* and formed *AIDS*. These are ACRONYMS.

What did we do in forming these words?

Kleenex (for 'tissue')   Xerox (for 'photocopy')

With *Kleenex* the name of a particular brand of tissue has become generalized to mean any brand of tissue. With *Xerox* the name of the corporation that made the first widely distributed photocopy machine has been generalized to mean the very act of photocopying (and, by zero-morpheme derivation, the corresponding noun). This is very similar to the sort of process that goes on when an individual's name is used to form a new word.

Where did we get this word?

enthuse

The word *enthusiasm* predated the occurrence of the word *enthuse*. How did we get from *enthusiasm* to *enthuse*? This is called BACK-FORMATION (and the very word *back-formation* is a back-formation). We pulled out the first part of the word *enthusiasm* and analyzed it as a root, even though no such root occurs elsewhere in the language and even though *-iasm* does not occur elsewhere as a derivational suffix changing verbs into nouns. Back-formation does not always call for such complexity of analysis, however. We might just take a word of a given category and form a new homophonous word of a different category. Thus *whitewash* the verb is a back-formation from *whitewash* the noun.

Do you know the source of these words?

smog   motel   brunch

Smog is a BLEND of *smoke* and *fog*. You can go to a dictionary and find out what *motel* and *brunch* are blends of, if it isn't apparent to you.

To see another kind of word-formation process, consider these two words:

napkin   apron

Do you think they share a morpheme? Unless you know something about the history of English, probably your answer is no. In fact, however, the occurrence of *ap* in both of them is no accident. At one point in English the word for *apron* was *napron*. (That means the shared morpheme was at least *nap*. So, just by the way, can you guess what -*kin* and -*ron* are historically? Diminutives.) How could an initial "n" get stolen away from a noun? How is the consonant "n" relevant to nouns? Consider these phrases:

a book   an oath
a history book   an honorable oath

Look across the top row first. When do we use the INDEFINITE ARTICLE *a* and when do we use the article *an*? I hope it's clear to you that *an* is used when the following word begins with a vowel and *a* is used elsewhere. What does the second row tell us about this particular rule of the distribution of *a* vs. *an*? Is the rule sensitive to orthography or is it sensitive to phonetics? Both *history* and *honorable* are spelled with an initial *h*; but the first starts with [h] and the second starts with [ɑ]. So the first starts with a consonant and the second with a vowel. You can see from this that the rule is sensitive to phonetics, not to orthography.

Now look again at the historical derivation of *napron* to *apron*. Put the indefinite article in front of *napron*. What do you think happened? Of course, the initial "n" got RE-BRACKETED (that is, reanalyzed) as being part of the article rather than of the noun:

[a] [napron] → [an] [apron]

Why didn't rebracketing occur with *napkin*, you might ask? No one I've asked knows the answer to this, nor does any book I've consulted offer an explanation. Indeed, morphological processes can seem (and be) capricious. Many linguists have called the lexicon (which is the place where many morphological rules arguably take place, as you learned in Chapter 2 when we talked about Lexical Phonology) the repository of irregularities. Both phonology and syntax are much more regular, in comparison.

Rebracketing in the opposite direction is responsible for the breaking down of the word *another* into a phrase in the playful *a whole nother thing* ([an+other] → [a] [nother]).

In the discussion of the distribution of the indefinite-article allomorphs *a* and *an*, I pointed out that the distribution is based on sound, not on orthography. But that doesn't mean that orthography is never involved in new word formation. Consider computer jargon, known as Techspeak. A bit is the smallest unit of information (a 1 or 0). A *byte* is (usually) 8 bits. Werner Buchholz, an employee of IBM, coined this spelling in 1956. The playfulness is orthographic: we relate the word *bite* with a sense concerning eating to its Techspeak homophone but, importantly, not homogram, *byte*. Can you guess what a half byte is called? A nybble.

Another way to form new words is seen in the following. Consider the child who says:

I brang home my lunchbox.

Where did this verb form *brang* come from? This is an irregular past, based on ANALOGY with rhyming verbs that exhibit this irregular past:

sing sang   ring rang

While this child's example is not considered standard speech, analogy can result in new inflected forms of a range of words that may enter the standard speech. Analogy can also play a part in compounds. My youngest son, when he was eight years old, said,

I'm late cause I took the longcut.

The reasoning seems to be: If *short* can be the first member of a compound with *cut*, then why can't *long*? Again, this form has not crept into the standard language (and there may be semantic reasons for this one, given that a cut results in shortening, not lengthening), but other instances of analogy may find their way into standard speech.

And, finally, we can form new words just by arbitrarily coining them. The word *byte*, used in computer talk, is an example. New technologies offer one the best sources for finding such examples.

While there is more to say about all of these kinds of word-formation processes, we will focus our attention in this chapter on derivation, inflection, and compounding.

Theories of Morphology

So far we've been amassing a good deal of data, but we haven't talked much about how to account for these data. It's time to go into theories of morphology. The rest of this chapter may feel like bits and pieces stuck together. Unfortunately, that is largely the state of morphological theory at the moment. There is debate over whether morphological processes take place exclusively in the lexicon, or exclusively in the syntax, or exclusively in some postsyntactic level, or partly in the lexicon and partly in the (post-) syntactic level, or even whether there is a component of the grammar called morphology that can be distinguished from phonology and syntax. Nevertheless, there are many topics that we should cover and can enjoy covering, even without a clear theoretical framework to hang them on. So that's what we'll do. (You will get a chance to reflect further on theoretical approaches to morphology in Problem Set 4.4 of Chapter 4.)

You are already quite familiar with one theory of morphology, because it is inseparable from a particular theory of phonology. LEXICAL MORPHOLOGY goes hand-in-hand with Lexical Phonology, studied in Chapter 2. Recall that in this theory phonological rules and morphological rules are interspersed within a level or stratum. Let's look at some data in this framework to refresh your memory.

The three verbs here come from Palauan, an Austronesian language spoken on the islands of Palau in the Western Caroline Islands.

P-M	FP-A	FP-B	Gloss
mətábək	təbəkáll	təbákl	'patch'
mədáŋəb	dəŋəbáll	dəŋóbl	'cover'
məŋétəm	ŋətəmáll	ŋətóml	'lick'
məʔárəm	ʔərəmáll	ʔəróml	'taste'

(P-M = present middle; FP-A = future participle A; FP-B = future participle B. FP-A is an innovative form; FP-B is a conservative form.) Stress is on the final vowel if there is a suffix. Otherwise it is on the penultimate syllable.

Can you isolate the morpheme for P-M? (the prefix *mə-*) Can you isolate the morpheme for FP-A? (the suffix *-all*) Can you isolate the morpheme for FP-B? (the suffix *-l*)

So what's interesting here? Take a good look at the vowels across the three columns. What is the interaction between stress and vowel quality? A stressless vowel is reduced to [ə]. That means that only when a vowel is stressed can you tell what its underlying representation is. Given that, identify the lexical morphemes for 'patch,' 'cover,' 'lick,' and 'taste' *(tabak, daŋob, ŋetom, and ʔarom).*

All right, now we need to make an inventory of the rules involved and figure out how they interact. We have three rules that add affixes. We have a rule that assigns stress. And we have a rule that reduces vowels.

Is stress assigned before or after vowel reduction? It has to be before vowel reduction. Why? If we reduced to [ə] before stress assignment, then we'd have nothing to tell us whether the stressed vowel should be [a] (as in *mədáŋəb*), or [o] (as in *dəŋóbl*), or [e] (as in *məŋétəm*), or any other vowel that occurs in Palauan.

Is stress assigned before or after suffixation? To figure this out, consider the phonological shape of words ending in roots in comparison with the phonological shape of words ending in suffixes. If these data are representative (and I hope they are), it would appear that words ending in a root end in a single consonant. But words ending in a suffix end in two consonants. Now words ending in a root have penultimate stress, but words ending in a suffix have final stress. Can you make sense out of these facts? Think back to Classical Arabic (studied in the section "Unbounded Feet" of Chapter 2 and examined in Problem Set 2.7), in which stress is on the rightmost heavy syllable, discounting the final syllable, with the exception that if the final syllable is superheavy (that is, if the rhyme contains three or more segments), then it receives stress. Palauan is quite similar.

So let's propose that Palauan has a quantity-sensitive foot and that the final consonant of the word is extrametrical. That way in a word that ends in a root, the final syllable is light, but in a word that ends in a suffix, the final syllable is heavy. What kind of foot is consistent with stressing a final heavy syllable, otherwise the penultimate syllable? A moraic trochee, right? And what direction do we form feet? R-L.

This whole analysis is based on suffixation preceding stress assignment. If suffixation followed stress assignment, we'd need both a stress-assignment rule and a second rule to attract stress onto the final vowel of the word. Without even considering what that rule would look like, we can see that this analysis is more complicated and hence to be eschewed, given that we have a simpler analysis available.

Do prefixes attach before or after stress assignment? With no information on secondary stress, we cannot answer this. So simply for the sake of having all affixation take place at one point in the grammar, I will assume that prefixation takes place before stress assignment, as well. (Absolutely nothing hinges on that assumption, however.)

Okay, now let's go through the derivation of the P-M and the FP-B for 'cover.' Recall that angled brackets around segmental material indicate extrametricality. I will put parentheses around feet. And I will allow degenerate feet, although we have no evidence here whether degenerate feet are banned by the metrical rules or not.

	P-M	*FP-B*
root:	daŋob	daŋob
add affix:	mədaŋob	daŋobl

assign stress: (mə)(dáŋo)\<b\>   (da)(ŋób)\<l\>
reduce vowels: mədáŋəb   dəŋóbl

Not every morphological problem, however, lends itself this nicely to a handling with Lexical Phonology-Morphology. So let's look at a different kind of problem. In Egyptian Arabic (EA), for example, many nouns have long vowels:

[taag] 'crown'   [diin] 'religion'   [nuur] 'light'

But when the suffix -*na* 'our' is added to these nouns, the vowels are short:

[tagna] 'our crown'   [dinna] 'our religion'   [nurna] 'our light'

The immediate question before us is whether the vowel is long underlyingly, and shortens when this suffix is attached, or short underlyingly and lengthens in the absence of the suffix. Either analysis can handle the data. But empirical adequacy isn't our only concern. A major point of Chapter 2 was that our analyses should be motivated—they should shed light on the true nature of the linguistic process we are dealing with.

So let's think about what kinds of rules we'd be dealing with in each analysis. Consider the analysis that involves vowel shortening first. If the vowel is long underlyingly, why should it shorten before the suffix? Is there anything fundamentally ill-formed in EA about a word such as the nonexistent [ta:gna]? We would want there to be, in order to motivate the vowel shortening.

In fact, we never find a long vowel followed by two consonants in EA so far as I know. In Old Arabic, we did find such sequences, but EA has clearly shortened the vowels in these cases—not just when the long vowels occur before our -*na* suffix; in other places as well:

Old Arabic   *Egyptian Arabic*
[bi:rna]   [birna]   'our well'
[da:rkum]   [darkum]   'your (pl.) house'
[ti:nha]   [tinha]   'her figs'
[jiħu:ʃni]   [jiħuʃni]   'he prevents me'

(My sources do not use the IPA consistently. I apologize if I have interpreted those sources in such a way as to lead to an incorrect transcription. The point of interest, however, is clear, regardless of errors in transcription I may have made.) Thus it is possible that this historical vowel shortening rule persists in EA today.

Now consider the second analysis, in which the vowel is short underlyingly. Why should it lengthen in these bare roots? Is there anything fundamentally ill-formed in EA about a word such as the nonexistant [tag]? Again, we would want there to be, in order to motivate the vowel shortening.

Take a look at these data:

[bint] 'girl'   [ħibb] 'love'   [zurt] 'you (masc.) visited'
[falla:ħ] 'peasant'   [zurti] 'you (fem.) visited'
[xabbarkum] 'he told you (pl.)'   [ħamalhum] 'he carried them'

Where do we find syllables of the form consonant-vowel-consonant (CVC—like our nonexistent word [tag])? They can be first syllables (as in [zurti]), second or third syllables (as in [ħamalhum]), even all syllables (as in [xabbarkum]). But the three monosyllabic words given here are not of this form. All of them are of the form CVCC.

So the first question we need to ask is whether the form CVC is ever found in a monosyllabic word in EA. So far as I know, it is not for words that are lexical category words (nouns, verbs, adjectives). Furthermore, we don't find monosyllabic nouns, verbs, or adjectives of the form CV, either.

Is CVCC the only possible type of monosyllabic word in EA? No. If we go searching, we can find words like:

  [ʃaːf] 'he saw'   [ʔuːm] 'stand up!'   [saːb] 'he left'

Here we have CVVC. And we can even find words of the form CVV:

  [maɪ̯] 'water'

How do CVC and CV (the two syllabic shapes that do not occur in EA monosyllables) form a natural class in EA, separate from CVCC, CVVC, and CVV (the three syllabic shapes that do occur in EA monosyllables)? If we assume that in EA the final consonant of a word is extrametrical (and this turns out to be the case), as in Classical Arabic, then we can see that monosyllabic words of the form CVC and CV are monomoraic as far as the metrical rules are concerned, whereas monosyllabic words of the form CVCC, CVVC, and CVV are all bimoraic as far as the metrical rules are concerned.

What all this means is that lexical category words in EA are required to have at least two moras. If we had a rule that lengthened the root vowel to yield a word like [taːg], for example, this rule would simply be supplying a second mora. We have, thus, discovered that EA has a minimal word constraint. And many languages do (as we noted in Chapter 2).

Which analysis will we opt for? The first analysis (of vowel shortening) has in its favor that we know it existed as a diachronic (that is, historical—we met this term in Chapter 2) rule. Furthermore, the application of a vowel-shortening rule would prevent the sequence V:CC, a sequence that does not appear to occur in EA.

The second analysis (of vowel lengthening) has in its favor that it can relate the vowel lengthening to the minimal word size (that is, to the requirement that monosyllables be bimoraic).

Prosodic (or Templatic) Morphology

Perhaps a scholar of EA could offer additional empirically based arguments that would help us choose between the two analyses. I cannot. Instead, I want to help you to see that the second analysis calls for a new way of looking at morphology, and then I will argue on theorical grounds that this is the superior analysis.

With the second analysis, we recognize that the language adds vowel length in order to match a template. It has been proposed that templates will always be statable in terms of prosodic units above the segment. The units that have been identified to be relevant to templates are:

Pw   prosodic word
F   foot
σ syllable
σ_μ light syllable (monomoraic syllable)
$\sigma_{\mu\mu}$ heavy syllable (bimoraic syllable)
σ_c core syllable

You are already familiar with all of these prosodic units. The only new terminology here is CORE SYLLABLE, which has the form CV (to be contrasted with σ_μ, in which an onset is optional and is not limited to a single C). This is the most common syllable type across languages, as you learned in the section "Syllable Types" of Chapter 2. And in languages which do not require an onset, V also qualifies as a core syllable.

Core syllables and light syllables are quite similar: Both can consist of (C)V. But a light syllable can have more than one element in the onset and, in some languages, a light syllable can even have an element in the coda. Generally, if you are talking about a language that is quantity sensitive, you will probably want to talk about light vs. heavy syllables. And if you are talking about a language that is not quantity sensitive, you might have occasion to contrast core syllables to all others.

How can we state the template for Egyptian Arabic in terms that use only one of these units? We can say that the minimal word in EA is a bimoraic syllable. Then in order for a root such as [tag] to meet that template (that is, to be an acceptable word), the vowel must spread to fill two moras. But let's not stop there. Let's ask ourselves why this particular requirement—of at least two moras—should be the threshold for a minimal word in EA. What do you know about lexical category words regarding stress? In stress languages, lexical category words almost invariably receive a primary stress. Stress is a property of syllables, but it is assigned by looking at foot structure. Thus in order for a word to receive primary stress, it must constitute at least one foot. Now let me tell you a fact about EA: The foot is a moraic trochee. Can you explain why the minimal word requirement is two moras? A moraic trochee consists of two moras. In other words, the minimal word in EA must be a foot. We can show the effect of the template, using the root [tag] for an example:

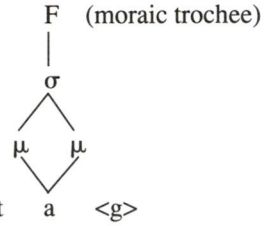

Indeed, in stress languages, the minimal word is generally a foot.

The vowel-lengthening analysis, then, is not simply a rule specific to EA. This analysis draws upon the much more general fact, cutting across languages, that lexical category words in stress languages have a minimal size equivalent to their foot size. Thus the vowel lengthening is expected; the rule is motivated by a universal principle. The alternative vowel-shortening rule, on the other hand, would have to be stated as a language-specific rule, arbitrary to EA. No one looking at the general phonological or morphological parameters of EA would have predicted this rule. Thus the first analysis is strongly to be preferred.

At this point you can go back to our examples of clipping in English. Give a derivation of *prof* from *professor* using templatic morphology.

Reduplication

While problems like those posed by the EA data can be handled with or without the templates of prosodic morphology (with varying degrees of insightfulness, however), other kinds of phenomena are markedly more effectively handled by templates than by other approaches to morphology. One such type of phenomenon is seen in these examples from Ilokano, a Malayo-Polynesian language spoken in the Philippines:

Verb base	Progressive	
/basa/	/agbasbasa/	'be reading'
/dait/	/agdadait/	'be studying'
/takder/	/agtaktakder/	'be standing'
/trabaho/	/agtrabtrabaho/	'be working'

Describe what constitutes the progressive aspect of a verb. It consists of the root plus material preceding the root. Part of that material is invariable: the prefix *ag-*. But part of that material varies for each verb: the segmental material that comes between the *ag-* and the verb root.

Let's focus on this variable material. Can it be described in terms of a fixed number of segments? Certainly not. In these examples alone the variable material ranges from as few as two segments (in /agdadait/) to as many as four segments (in /agtrabtrabaho/). This shouldn't surprise you, given the claim of prosodic morphology that templates should be statable in terms of prosodic units. So let's try to see if we can describe the variable material in terms of a prosodic unit.

Must the variable material be a certain fixed kind of syllable? We can eliminate σ_c and σ_μ with examples like /agbasbasa/. (Do you see how? The syllables *ag* and the first *bas* are heavy, closed syllables.) We can eliminate $\sigma_{\mu\mu}$ with examples like *agdabait*.

Well, then, can we just say the variable unit must be a syllable? Indeed, it always is. But what accounts for the fact that this syllable can vary in shape? Where are the segments that make up the syllable coming from? Clearly, they are the initial segments of the verb root. For that reason this type of phenomenon is called REDUPLICATION. Reduplication can be of a variety of prosodic units from the phoneme on up to the entire morpheme, and it can be to the left (as in the Ilokano data), to the right (as in Chukchee), or even internal (that is, infixed, as in many Semitic languages).

Are the reduplicated segments identical to the initial syllable of the verb root? No. Consider just the fourth root above. It syllabifies like so: /tra.ba.ho/. Yet the syllable that precedes it in the progressive form is /trab/ not /tra/. What strategy does Ilokano seem to be following in forming this syllable, then? The progressive takes segments from the initial part of the root until it has formed the largest possible syllable. Does this remind you of anything we've already discussed? Look back at clipping in examples like *prof* for *professor*. A similar strategy applied there.

We can talk of the SEGMENTAL MELODY of the verb root, and we can say that the syllable that comes between *ag-* and the verb root takes as much of the segmental melody as possible to form another syllable, like so:

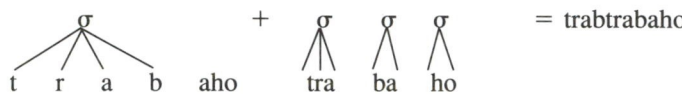

We then prefix *ag-* and we have the correct progressive form. Prosodic morphology handles reduplication in a simple and insightful way. Any theory that did not recognize and make use of prosodic units would be incapable of capturing the same insights.

Uses of Reduplication

Before going on with our discussion of prosodic morphology, let's take a moment longer to look at reduplication in American Sign Language. ASL uses reduplication in a number of ways. To pluralize a noun, for example, one can make the sign for that noun repeatedly in different places in the signing space. To show that an action has been performed by multiple individuals separately (that is, several separate instances of the same action have been performed), one makes multiple iterations of the verb sign. More could be said about both noun and verb reduplication, but I won't do that here. Instead, let me focus on adjectival predication.

When an adjective like SICK is reduplicated, five other factors come into play in interpreting the reduplicated form. (Please recall that all ASL signs are rendered by capitals in English. That's why SICK is all in capitals.) We ask whether the reduplicated form is:

1. Even: Is the tempo even throughout a cycle of the sign movement?
2. Tense: Are the hand or arm muscles extra tense?
3. End-marked: Is there a stop or hold at the end of a cycle of the sign movement?
4. Fast: Is the rate of movement increased in relation to the signs that preceded?
5. Elongated: Is the size of the movement elongated (covering more space) in relation to the ordinary size of that sign?

These factors interrelate to produce great subtlety in the interpretation of the sign. If SICK is reduplicated, even, tense, end-marked, fast, and elongated, the sense is frequentative (that is, getting sick easily and often). See Figure 3.1A. If SICK is reduplicated, even, fast, and elongated (but not tense or end- marked), the sense is one of predisposition (that is, 'sickly' as a general characteristic). See Figure 3.1B. If SICK is reduplicated, tense, and elongated (but uneven, not end-marked, and not fast), the sense is continuative (that is, being sick over a long period of time). See Figure 3.1C. If SICK is reduplicated, tense, end-marked, and fast (but uneven and not elongated), the sense is incessant (that is, getting sick without respite). See Figure 3.1D. And there are other nuances still, including reduplication for the simple purpose of emphasis.

While I have read of no oral language that uses reduplication (in concert with other factors) with as wide a range of interpretive effects as ASL, the kinds of inflectional and semantic effects noted here for ASL reduplication are quite similar to the kinds of effects reduplication has in oral languages. With respect to verbal reduplication, we find reduplication to add the sense of "quickly" (as in the Australian language Warlpiri spoken in the Northern Territories), the sense of "in many places" (as in Agta, a Malayo-Polynesian

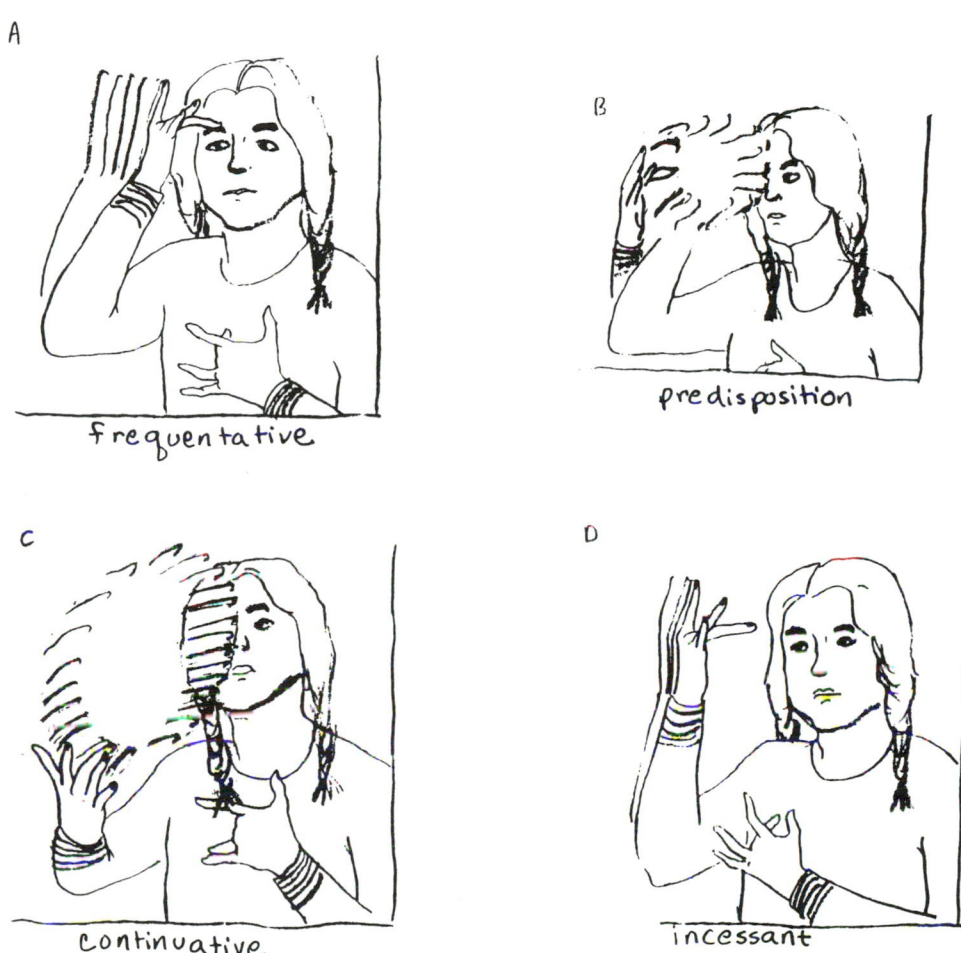

Figure 3.1 Four uses of reduplication in ASL.

language spoken in the Philippines), the sense of simultaneity (as in Temiar, a Malacca language spoken in Malaysia), the sense of plurality (as in Samoan, a Polynesian language spoken in Samoa), the sense of repetition (as in Karok, a Hokan language of northwest California), and many others. With respect to nominal reduplication, we often find reduplication to add the sense of plurality— as in Agta, Madurese (a Malayo-Polynesian language spoken in northeast Java), Yidin^y (a Pama-Nyungan language spoken in Queensland, Australia), and others. But it can also add other senses such as wholeness (as in Temiar).

But reduplication in oral languages can also be a simple indicator of a grammatical process. For example, it can be used to derive nouns from verbs (as in Tagalog, a Malayo-Polynesian language of the Philippines, and Yoruba, a Niger-Congo language of Nigeria); it can mark a particular modality or aspect (such as future in Tagalog or perfect in Classical Greek); and it can mark Subject-Verb agreement in certain persons and numbers (as in the Chukchi-Kamchatkan language Itel'men of northeast Siberia).

Back to Prosodic Morphology: Infixing

Now that we have been introduced to prosodic morphology, we can discuss a fifth typological classification for languages based on morphology (in addition to isolative, agglutinative, inflective, and incorporating languages): INFIXING or TEMPLATIC languages. We discussed the kind of affix that is known as an infix above in relation to Ulwa. But when we speak of infixing-templatic languages as a morphological classification, we mean something much more pervasive than just the presence of some infixes. Please pay close attention as you read this section, for the issues that come up in templatic languages are complicated and need to be pondered. And you might want to review the notions of tiers from Geometric Phonology in Chapter 2 before reading this.

The Semitic language family is probably the best-known group of infixing-templatic languages. Let's look at Classical Arabic. We find there some rather ordinary infixes (as well as the more flamboyant ones we will get into below), such as the reflexive morpheme *-t-*, which affixes to verbs. Verb forms in Arabic can be partitioned into derivational classes called "*binyānîm*" (singular *binyān*), which is actually a Hebrew term, but which linguists have applied to the Arabic verbal system. In the eighth binyān, this *-t-* appears as an infix, the first "t" in *ktatab*, which is the uninflected form of the perfective active:

> ktatab 'write, be registered'

The other consonants, *ktb*, all belong to the root meaning 'write.' In fact, the discontinuous sequence of the three consonants *ktb* constitutes the entire root and it is called a TRI-LITERAL root (a root consisting of three consonants). This root never occurs free, however. It is always accompanied by vowels interspersed among the consonants. It is the particular vowels and their placement that determine whether the final word is a verb or noun and which particular verbal or nominal form we have. Consider these examples:

> **nouns**: kitaabun 'book (NOM)'
> **verbs**: kataba 'he wrote'
>   kaataba 'he corresponded' (habitual)

(NOM indicates the Nominative form.) Arabic has a rich set of affixes that can add consonants as well as vowels to the triliteral root. The reflexive *-t-* is one, but there are others, as in these examples:

> **noun**: kitaabatun 'act of writing (NOM)'
> **verb**: kattaba 'he caused to write'

The extra "at" in the nominal form here makes the difference between 'book' (just shown as *kitaabun*) and 'act of writing.' The extra "t" in the verbal form here makes the difference between 'he wrote' (just shown as *kataba*) and 'he caused to write.'

If we extract away the morphological material that makes a noun Nominative Case, we find *kitab* for 'book.' If *ktb* is the root, then it is the discontinuous sequence of "i" and "a" that make this form a noun. And the "i" and "a" must come in just that order, not in the reverse order. Furthermore, we can't just add "i . . . a" anywhere we want to the root *ktb*; instead, these vowels must be added after the first and second consonant, respectively. We are therefore talking about how to integrate a VOWEL MELODY with a consonantal root, which could be called a CONSONANT MELODY. What we find is that there are restrictions on the final shape of the newly created word. In other words, we have a template that both the vowel melody and the root must be mapped onto.

We are now dealing with NONCONCATENATIVE morphology in that we can't simply say that we take one morpheme and add things to it (that is, concatenate) on one side or the other or both. This sort of process is probably the strongest evidence we have for the existence of templatic morphology. To get the form *kitab* we do this mapping:

$$\mu \quad (= \text{noun})$$

The CVCVC template is the PROSODIC tier. The root tier for the lexical morpheme *ktb* and the affixal tier for the derivational morpheme *ia* are associated with that prosodic tier.

The mapping here is quite simple. But when we look at other forms, we can get into more and more elaborate mappings. In the fourth binyān the vowel melody for the active perfective verb form is *a*, the prosodic template is CVCCVC, and there is a prefixed glottal stop. Let us assume that affixal tiers are associated with the prosodic tier before root tiers are. Let us assume further that association in Classical Arabic goes left to right. We will then associate the lexical root *ktb*, the prefix *ʔ-*, and the perfective active vowel melody of this binyān to the prosodic template CVCCVC thus:

$$\mu \quad \mu$$

$$\text{CVCCVC} \quad = \text{ʔaktab}$$

The template has two vowel slots, so the vowel melody must spread left to right to fill those slots. Since the glottal stop is an affix, it associates first, taking up the first C of the prosodic template, so that the root morpheme begins on the second C.

In other binyānîm we find different prosodic templates. Sometimes the number of consonants is such that elements on the root tier must spread to fill all the C slots. Rules that erase association lines, followed by automatic spreading, can result in new associations. Rules that FLOP an association line from one slot on the prosodic tier to an adjacent slot of the same kind (that is, C or V) can also result in new association lines. There are many complexities to the Classical Arabic verbal system (and to the nominal system, as well). Add to all this the fact that beside triliteral roots, there are also QUADRILITERAL roots (with four consonants making up a root) and a few BICONSONANTAL roots, and that there are fifteen binyānîm, and you come up with an array of data that might seem wildly arbitrary without the recognition of prosodic templates.

Process Morphology

Taking a morpheme and affixing another morpheme is one kind of word-formation process. We've seen several examples of that from many languages. In this sort of morphological process we can point to a certain phonetic reality and identify it as a morpheme with such-and-such properties.

Taking a vowel and/or consonantal melody and matching it up with a template is another, quite different, kind of word-formation process. And, again, we've looked at a range of examples of that. Here we have various melodies and various templates we can point to and identify as (parts of) morphemes with such-and-such properties.

But there are other word-formation processes that occur in natural language for which it is quite difficult to point to any phonological construct (whether a template or a melody of segments) and identify that construct as a morpheme. Instead, a morphological process occurs and the very process itself is meaningful in the way that morphemes can be meaningful.

We've actually looked very briefly at one such instance already, English ablauting in irregular noun plurals and in irregular verbal forms, such as:

   foot feet   run ran

Here the substitution of one sound for another carries the sense of plurality (for nouns) or past tense (for verbs). (Actually, the vowel alternation in the noun plurals is historically distinct from ablauting. While ablauting in verbs was a change in vowel quality to indicate a morphological change, the vowel change in the root of a noun was a vowel-fronting rule triggered by the presence of a front vowel in the next syllable. In other words, the noun vowel change was an instance of vowel assimilation (or spreading of features among vowels). But today there is no following syllable in the plural of *foot*, so as far as the speaker is concerned today, this is a phonologically unmotivated vowel change, indistinct from ablaut.)

You might object that this is not really a morphological process—that, instead, speakers of English memorize these irregular plurals and past tenses. With this analysis both *run* and *ran* would occur in the lexicon and there would be no ablauting process in English.

This is a well-taken objection, for such irregular plurals and irregular verbal forms behave exceptionally when we contrast them to regular plurals and regular verbal forms. For example, we learned earlier that an inflectional morpheme is always external to a derivational morpheme in English:

   kingdoms   *kingsdom

Yet derivational morphemes can sometimes follow irregular inflections:

   Jack's a *goner.*

Lexical Phonology-Morphology accounted for this, of course, by placing irregular inflection on an earlier level than derivation, which would be on an earlier level than regular inflection. But simply saying that *gone* occurs in the lexicon side by side with *go* is an alternative worthy of consideration. In fact, if we consider the irregular form *went* and the kind of magic morphology we'd need to turn *go* into *went*, this alternative looks better and better.

When we talk about a paradigm that contains such totally different forms as *gone* and *went*, we are talking about suppletion, as we mentioned earier. The form *went* is suppletive in this paradigm because the ordinary rules of morphology would not have produced *went* as the past-tense form of *go*. Proposing particular morphological rules to handle suppletion of this sort *(go* vs. *went)* is obviously folly.

Nevertheless, there may be value to maintaining an ablaut rule in English. For one, in the verbal system, the phenomenon affects a number of verbs, so an ablaut process allows us to group those instances together. But, more important, if *ran* is not a combination of *run* plus the past morpheme, we need to account for the absence in our grammar of the regular past:

   *runned

That is, why can't the regular past morpheme come along and attach to *run*?

Lexical Phonology-Morphology would account for the absence of **runned* by what is known as the ELSEWHERE CONDITION. The Elsewhere Condition states that if two rules can apply to a single form, if one of the rules has a less extensive domain, then it gets priority and the other rule cannot apply. (In other words, the more restrictive rule applies first, and the less restrictive one applies "elsewhere.") Since the ablaut rule is lexically conditioned (only a limited list of verbs undergo the rule), the ablaut rule has priority over the regular past-tense morpheme rule, and we can get *ran* but not **runned*.

If we don't have an ablaut rule, then we must BLOCK the formation of **runned* another way. There is another way, in fact. Many linguists have argued that **there is a general condition which blocks a derivation if there already exists a word with the same stem and the same meaning**. Blocking would be responsible for the failure, for example, of derivations such as:

   music + ed → *musiced

in contrast with

   talent + ed → talented

because of the existence of *musical*. Likewise **talental* would be blocked because of the existence of *talented*.

However, we can only appeal to blocking to account for **runned* if, in fact, the lexicon can recognize the same stem in *run* and *ran*. But do we need to recognize the validity of ablaut to recognize that the same stem (here root) is present in both words? We may be caught in a circle here.

Even if we omit ablaut from the morphology of English, however, we have to admit stem changing as a morphological process in our theory of morphology because it occurs in other languages. Many languages have stem changes that indicate an aspectual distinction either alone or in concert with an affix. Among these languages are Nahuatl (an Aztecan language of Central America), Burushaski (an isolate spoken in northern Pakistan and India), Kiwai (spoken in New Guinea), Pawnee (a Caddoan language spoken in northcentral Oklahoma), Sierra Miwok (a Penutian language spoken in California), Serbo-Croatian (a South Slavic language spoken in Serbia), Temiar, and Touareg (a variety of Berber spoken in southern Algeria and Niger), all of which exhibit verb stem differences in connection with the imperfective vs. perfect aspect distinction. Nahuatl also has stem changes associated with tense for some irregular verbs. And Sierra Miwok also has stem changes associated with the aspectual distinction of habitual/continuous.

Let's take a look at a particularly intractable example of verb-stem changes to indicate morphological changes. In the Wakashan language Kwakw'ala, spoken in British Columbia, verbs can exhibit three different kinds of plural agreement. One plural agreement indicates that the Subject is plural—just as verb agreement does in other languages we have already talked about. Another plural agreement indicates that the action occurs at the same time in different parts of a unit. And a third plural agreement indicates repeated action.

a	mədə́lqʷəla	'it is boiling'
b	miʔmədə́lqʷəla	'many are boiling'
c	maʔə́mdəlqʷəela	'it is boiling in all its parts'
d	mədə́lχʷmədə́lqʷəla	'it is boiling repeatedly'
a	tə́nkəla	'it is sizzling'
b	tíʔtə́nkəela	'many are sizzling'
c	tə́ntənkəla	'it is sizzling in all its parts'
d	tə́nxtənkəla	'it is sizzling repeatedly'

(Look at those beautiful labialized uvular stops and fricatives. Be sure to consult the appendix to Chapter 1 so you can hear these words.) Clearly we have some affixation here in the final -əla. Just as clearly we have some partial reduplication (in the (b) forms), some full root reduplication (in the (d) forms), and some irregular reduplication (in the (c) forms). But we also have some changes in the stem. If we assume that reduplication happens leftward, then there are times when stem vowels seem to be lost (the [ə] that we expected to follow the second [m] in (c) for the first verb) and times when stem consonants seem to be lost (the [l] that we expected to precede the [qʷ] in (d) for the first verb).

The kinds of stem changes found here differ from instances of vowel assimilation, in which a feature of an affixal vowel spreads to a stem vowel (which we saw for Turkish vowel harmony in the section "Underspecification Theory in Lexical Phonology" of Chapter 2). But even in vowel-assimilation instances, we can see a process as being meaningful: The feature spreading carries the information of the inflection just as much as the affix does. German UMLAUTING is a typical example of a vowel assimilation that can be found in many linguistics texts. But the process is common in the Romance languages, as well, so much so that Romance linguists have given the process their own name: METAPHONY. For example, in the Italian dialect Northern Salentino, stem vowels on adjectives raise when the inflectional affix is high:

MS	FS	MP	
frisku	freska	friski	'cool'
russu	rossa	russi	'red'

(Each column differs by gender/number distinctions.)

Another type of process that can bear morphological sense is metathesis. In the Malayo-Polynesian language Hanunóo of the Philippines, the prefix *ka-* is added to a numeral to form the corresponding ordinal. Two concomitant effects are found in the stem. If the first vowel of the stem is [u], that vowel deletes. And if the stem begins with [ʔ], the [ʔ] appears following the next consonant, like so:

Ɂusa 'one'   kasɁa 'once'

In sum, we have seen morphological stem alterations of four types: addition of segments, loss of segments, substitution (or change) of segments, and permutation of segments. We could add to that a fifth type, blending, which we mentioned in our discussion of coining new words. Thus in *brunch*, the phonological blending of two stems into one carries with it the morphological blending of the senses of the two stems *breakfast* and *lunch*.

Compounding

Compounds are words that contain more than one lexical morpheme. By considering them now we will uncover more issues for morphological theory.

Limiting yourself to the lexical categories noun, verb, adjective, and preposition in English, try to come up with a list of compounds that have two roots, with every logically possible combination of category types for the two roots. For the moment limit yourself to roots that have no affixes attached. Here are some examples:

N + N:	teapot	(N)
N + V:	globetrot	(V)
N + A:	headstrong	(A)
N + P:	chin-up	(N)
V + V:	stir-fry	(V)
V + N:	swearword	(N)
V + A:	speakeasy	(N)
V + P:	turn-off	(N) (as in: *His breath was a turn-off.*)
A + A:	white hot	(A)
A + N:	high school	(N)
A + V:	dry-clean	(V)
A + P:	blackout	(N)
A + N:	within	(P)
A + N:	outhouse	(N)
A + N:	overthrow	(V)
A + N:	underripe	(A)

(Don't let spelling throw you off. Our orthographic conventions are somewhat capricious when it comes to compounds. We write some as a single word, we hyphenate others, and we simply put ordinary spaces between others.)

It would appear that every combination is possible, although examples come readily to mind for some of these and only with great difficulty for others.

Tell me, why did I limit you to considering only lexical categories? Can you think of compounds in which one of the members belongs to a FUNCTIONAL CATEGORY (also often called a MINOR category), such as a determiner (like *the*) or a conjunction (like *and*)? Words like these might come to mind, where *the*, *as*, *much*, and *so* are all members of functional categories:

nevertheless   inasmuch as   insofar as

But we do not typically call these compounds. Instead, these are lexicalized phrases, similar to:

what's-his-name   (as in: *What's-his-name is at the door.*)
how-do-you-do   (as in: *That's a fine how-do-you-do.*)
know-it-all   (as in: *Mr. Know-it-all is here again.*)

True compounding is limited to only lexical category words. In fact, the very participation of prepositions in compounding (as in *love-in* and *upstage*) is one reason why many linguists consider preposition a lexical category in English. And the lack of participation of prepositions in some other languages is one reason why linguists consider preposition a functional category in those languages.

Going back to our lists of compounds, label each example as to what the category of the whole is. I have put that category label in parentheses beside each example. Compare my list to yours. Almost undoubtedly we will have some compounds of a given combination that belong to a different category. For example, for P+V you might have given the example *outcry*, which is a N, as contrasted to my *overthrow*, which is a V. Go through your list and mine now and everywhere that we both came up with compounds of the same category, try to find another compound with the same types of components that belongs to a different category.

I expect that you cannot do it for some combinations (such as P+P) and you have great difficulty doing it for other combinations, and that these two groups together cover most of the possible combinations. Look at the combinations that resist (either absolutely or very strongly) an outcome that is anything other than one fixed category. What determines what that category is? Look carefully. Do you see that the category of the second member of the compound more often than not determines the category of the whole compound?

Now looking at only those resistant combinations, consider the sense of the compound in comparison to the sense of the component members. For example, a teapot is a kind of pot, not a kind of tea. To globetrot is to do a kind of trotting, not to be a kind of globe. If you are headstrong, you are stubborn—you are in some sense strong in the head; you are not a kind of head. And so on. In other words, usually the right-hand member not only determines the category of the whole compound, but it determines, as well, the major part of the sense of the compound.

For these reasons we say that most compounds in English are right-headed. **The right member acts as a head, just as suffixes usually act as heads.** And the morphosyntactic category of the head percolates up to the word level, just as it does in noncompound words. We can see this in the compound *blackboard*, which consists of an adjective and a noun:

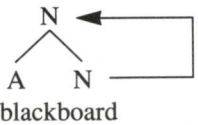

blackboard

What about in the other cases? Instead of searching through every combination, let me ask you whether it's possible to have the most extreme cases. First, can you find a compound whose category is not identical to the category of either component member? And second, can you find a compound whose sense is not mainly determined (in a way parallel to the headed compounds) by either of the component members?

Indeed, both extreme cases are possible. In *speakeasy*, for example, we have a verb and an adjective combining to form a noun. In *pickpocket* we find the sense of a person who picks pockets, not the sense of a kind of pocket or of a kind of picking. So some compounds are not headed.

Headed compounds are called ENDOCENTRIC. Unheaded compounds are called EXOC-ENTRIC. (These terms are often applied to syntactic constructions, as well, as we mention in passing when dealing with structural ambiguity in the section "Ambiguity" of Chapter 5.)

The Interaction of Compounding with Other Morphological Processes

Many interesting questions come up in the analysis of compounds and we will only very briefly touch on them. Just about everything we do here will be controversial in the sense that there are often multiple explanations for the data we will look at, and depending on one's explanation, the impact of such data on morphological theory varies. My goal is simply to expose you to the kinds of questions that come up so that you can recognize how important the analysis of compounds is for determining a theory of word formation.

Let's look first at questions that have to do with the interaction between compounding and other types of morphological processes. Given that we have two component stems plus a final resulting word, we have three possible sites for affixation: the first stem or the second stem—that is, affixation INTERNAL to the compound—or the compound as a whole—that is, affixation EXTERNAL to the compound. Do we get derivational affixes in all three sites? Try to find examples. You might come up with compounds like these: I have added in the possibility of affixation internal to both members of the compound in the third example here:

first member: decen*cy* clause
second member: language require*ment*
both members: decen*cy* require*ment*
compound: daredevil*ness*

A context for the (quite unusual) fourth compound might be:

I don't know when she's going to get over her *daredevilness*.

(If you don't get that compound, you might try *pickpockethood*. Also, all of these examples involve suffixes. In Problem Set 3.8 you will try to fill in comparable examples involving prefixes.) *Daredevilness* refers to her quality of being a daredevil, not to her quality of daring "devilness." So the *-ness* has SCOPE over the entire compound and is therefore external from a semantic point of view (but we will consider instances in which semantic considerations for bracketing are not consistent with other kinds of consider-ations for bracketing in the section "Bracketing Paradoxes").

The trees and bracketings for these examples are:

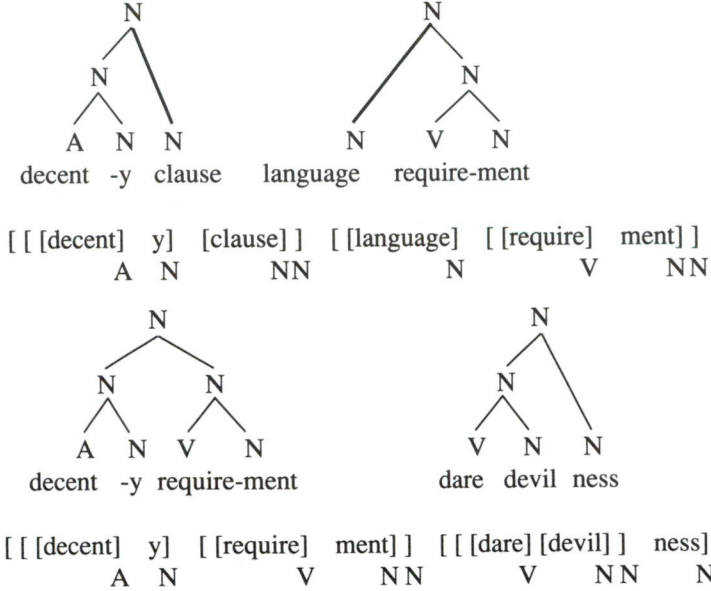

[[[decent]   y]   [clause]]   [[language]   [[require]   ment]]
         A   N   NN   N   V   NN

[[[decent]   y]   [[require]   ment]]   [[[dare] [devil]]   ness]
         A   N   V   NN   V   NN   N

What do these data tell us about the interaction between compounding and derivation? We must allow derivation to both precede and follow compounding. Do you see that? We must add the -y to *decent* to produce *decency*, for example, before we form the compound, because once we have formed the compound, the Strict Cycle Condition (of Chapter 2) will prevent us from going inside the compound and performing a morphological process on just a subpart of the compound. And we must allow derivation to follow compounding in order to produce words like *daredevilness*.

Do both Level I and Level II derivational affixes attach before compounding? (Recall from Lexical Phonology in Chapter 2 that Level I affixes can affect word stress, but Level II affixes generally cannot. Also, Level I affixes can attach to bound roots, but Level II cannot.) Yes. The -y of *decency* is a Level I affix (witness the fact that it can attach to a bound root, as in *fancy*); the -ment of *requirement* is a Level II affix.

Do both Level I and Level II derivational affixes attach after compounding? Our only example has a Level II affix attaching after compounding. For now, let us assume that no Level I affixes can attach after compounding.

If this description of the interaction of compounding with derivation is correct, where would Lexical Phonology-Morphology order compounding? In Level II. Do you see that? That way no Level I affixes could attach after compounding, but Level II affixes could attach before and after compounding.

Can we find compounds with inflectional affixes on either member and on the whole compound? Try to find examples.

first member: sales receipt
second member: sawbones (a derogatory term for "doctor")
compound: speakeasies

(I have found no example of the plural on both members for which I am convinced the plural on the second element does not have scope over the whole compound.) Again, it appears that this kind of affixation can both precede and follow compounding.

What about irregular inflection, such as irregular plurals or irregular past tenses? Can these occur in compounds? Again, test all the logically possible sites.

first member:	teethmark
second member:	timeworn
both members:	data driven
compound:	postmen

Given that we don't have a compound *timewear*, *timeworn* cannot be a past participle form of that nonexistent verb. (Contrast it to *forego/forwent/foregone*.) Instead, we have compounded *time* with the irregular past-participle form *worn*.

Still, even though we found some examples with regular or irregular inflection internal to compounds, you probably had trouble coming up with examples in which, for example, only the first member was pluralized or in which only the second member was pluralized without the plural having scope over the whole compound. In fact, even when our knowledge of the world tells us the first member should be plural, we use a singular:

toothbrush   eyeglasses   footwear   nail clippers

And even when our knowledge of the world tells us the second member should be plural, we use a singular:

scarecrow   tattletale   pickpocket

(Be careful here: we are talking about internal inflection. Surely, we say *scarecrows*, but that indicates more than one *scarecrow*. The point is that we don't say *scarecrows* to indicate a single object that scares more than one crow.) Because of this fact, some morphologists claim that regular inflection has to follow compounding. We can see, though, that that claim has exceptions.

Nevertheless, we want an explanation for the strong tendency to use the uninflected rather than the inflected stem in forming compounds. I'd like you to think about that. And in your ruminations, I'd like you also to consider the fact that inflections in English are always the last affixes to be added to simplex words. In fact, it has been argued that inflectional affixes universally have a tendency to attach farther from the root than derivational ones do. So please keep that fact in mind, as well.

What makes us decide whether to use inflection and which inflection to use? Some instances of inflection are based purely on what meaning we want to convey: Are we talking about a single object or more than one? Are we talking about a past event or a present one?

Other instances of inflection are based on linguistic relationships between words within an utterance, such as agreement and Case assignment. This second type of instance is, therefore, strongly related to the syntax in that we need to have the word in its syntactic context before we can know which agreement morpheme and/or Case to assign it. It could be that inflection of this sort should apply after the syntax—and, that means, of course, that it would apply after the other kinds of word-formation processes we have discussed thus far. Still, that wouldn't explain why even the first type of instances of inflection (based on semantics) also seems to apply late in word-formation processes.

Exactly how to deal with inflection in general and peculiarities of inflection such as those described here are among the many issues being debated in morphological theory today. Some people argue that all word formation takes place in the lexicon, so the morphological component of the grammar feeds the syntax. Others argue that morphology is not a discrete component of the grammar, but instead some morphological processes take place in the lexicon and others take place much later, perhaps after some or all syntactic rules.

The Interaction of Compounding with Syntax and Semantics

We have arrived quite naturally at questions that will relate more to issues in chapters to come than to the material we have already covered in this book. That is, we've arrived at questions regarding the nature of the relationship between morphology and both syntax and semantics.

Consider these compounds:

leg man   cake baker

What does *leg man* mean? If we're at a furniture factory and one man makes the table legs and another makes the table tops, we might call the first one the "leg man." If we know a pirate with a peg leg, we might refer to him as the "leg man." If we know a boy who prefers the drumstick at a chicken dinner, we might call him the "leg man." If we know a casting director who chooses dancers by their legs, we might call him the "leg man." I'm sure you can think of other instances in which you might use the compound *leg man*. In other words, without a context, all we know is that we have a man who has some relationship toward a leg or toward legs that is salient enough to characterize him by mentioning legs.

Now what does *cake baker* mean? In most situations, it's the one who bakes cakes, right? It's not the baker of bread who just happens to love cakes. It's not the baker of bread who just happens to wear an apron with pictures of cakes all over it. It's simply the one who bakes cakes. An endocentric compound whose head is a N or A that is derived from a V (that is, whose head is DEVERBAL) is called a VERBAL COMPOUND or a SYNTHETIC COMPOUND. All other compounds are called ROOT COMPOUNDS. *Baker* is a N derived from the V *bake*, so *baker* is deverbal and *cake baker* is a verbal compound. Here are some others:

Nouns	Adjectives
housecleaning	eye-catching
surface adherence	germ-resistant
self-deception	heat-sensitive
troop deployment	hand washable
trash removal	disease inhibitory
schoolteacher	sunbaked

What can you notice about their interpretation? It is quite specific, right? This is true of verbal compounds in general, as opposed to any of our other endocentric compounds. In contrast, nominal endocentric compounds as a rule are notoriously capricious with respect to their interpretation.

Let's look closely at the ordinary interpretation of these verbal compounds. Focus on the verb that forms the stem of the right member. Think of the action denoted by that verb. What do you notice about that action with respect to the sense of the first member of the compound? The first member is an argument of that verb. That is, when we do housecleaning, we clean the house; when a product is disease inhibitory it inhibits disease. We say that in verbal compounds the nonhead member must SATISFY an argument of the deverbal head.

What this all means is that in our lexicon, when we learn a word like *bake*, we learn that it takes two arguments: an AGENT (the person who does the baking), and, optionally, a THEME (the thing that gets baked). Syntax uses this information when it forms sentences such as:

Suzanna baked the cake.

Rules of morphology, syntax, and semantics all can be fed by this lexical information.

This is not to say that these are the only readings for verbal compounds. Many verbal compounds have readings similar to those for root compounds. So in contrast to *cake baker* we find *prison baker*, although *prison* does not satisfy an argument of the verb *bake*. Also, bizarre readings for verbal compounds can occur side by side with the ordinary reading. For example, a *cake baker* could be a baker made of cake (in a world of edible characters), although you might stress this differently from the way you stress it with the ordinary reading. So even verbal compounds can show variation in meaning. Nevertheless, the ordinary interpretation takes the first element of the verbal compound to be an argument of the verb root.

We see another very clear instance of the relevance of the argument structure of a predicate to compound formation when we consider the exocentric nominal compounds consisting of V+N which we've mentioned, and which I'll exemplify again:

killjoy breakwater cutthroat

Similar to these are V+N exocentric adjectives:

breakneck (He did it at breakneck speed.)
lackluster (What a lackluster comment!)

as well as V+A exocentric nouns and V+P exocentric nouns:

blowhard breakthrough

In all these instances the nonverb member either satisfies an argument of the verb or modifies the verb or is a verb PARTICLE (as with *breakthrough*—you will learn about particles in Problem Set 4.11 of Chapter 4). But something even more precise can be said about the relationships here. Which argument of the verb is the noun in the V+N exocentric compounds? It is the theme, not the agent. It has been claimed that in both verbal compounds and in these exocentric compounds, if one member is an argument of the other, it must be an argument internal to the verb phrase. (Agents are external and themes are internal.) You will learn about verb phrases in Chapter 4, and you can come back then and reread this section. But let me just point out that there are exceptions to this claim for both verbal compounds and our exocentric compounds. Here are some exceptional adjectives:

verbal compound: henpecked (He is a henpecked guy.)
V + N exocentric: hangdog (He has a hangdog look about him.)

The sense of the verbal compound is not that he pecks hens, but that hens peck him. So *hens* is the agent argument of *peck*, not the theme argument. The sense of the exocentric compound is not that he has a look of someone who hangs dogs, but that he has the look of a dog that hangs (its head). So *dog* is the agent argument of *hang*, not the theme argument.

Because some compounds show relationships that are relevant to the syntax we need to consider whether some compounding is actually done in the syntax. That is, while we can straightforwardly generate root compounds other than our special exocentric ones by simple concatenation of words in the lexicon, it is possible that we need a syntactic operation to generate verbal compounds and our special exocentric compounds. And, of course, once we allow a mechanism that allows compounding in the syntax, then we could as well use it to generate all compounds in the syntax (not just our special ones). So we could argue that if any compounding is done in the syntax, all compounding should be done in the syntax—and the lexicon should not have a compounding mechanism at all.

The trouble with discussing a possible syntactic source for some compounds, of course, is that we haven't studied syntax yet, so it would be difficult for us to pursue this line of questioning in any detail at this point. Once you've completed Chapter 4, you might want to return to this issue. For now, we will do only a cursory comparison of compounding and syntactic operations, noting some similarities and differences.

First, as you've seen, some compounds display the same kinds of argument-predicate relationships we find in the syntax.

Second, compounding, at least in English, is recursive (a term you met in Problem Set 2.9). That is, compounds are words which can be compounded with other words (which might themselves be compounds), over and over again, yielding words like:

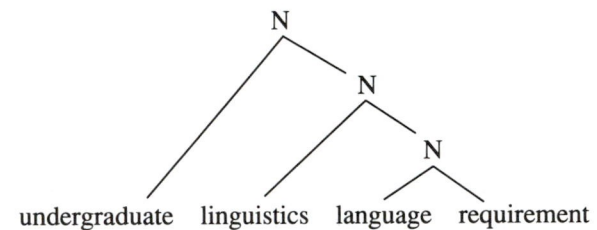

undergraduate   linguistics   language   requirement

[[undergraduate] [[linguistics] [[language] [requirement]]]]
     N   N   N   NNNN

and:

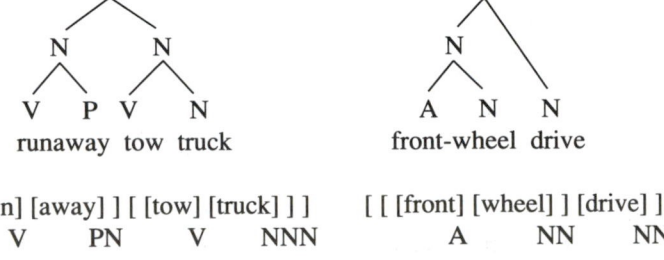

runaway tow truck   front-wheel drive

[[[run] [away]]] [[tow] [truck]]]   [[[front] [wheel]] [drive]]
   V   PN   V   NNN   A   NN   NN

These representations give us an internal breakdown of the compounds. An undergraduate linguistics language requirement is first of all a type of language requirement. Which type? A linguistics language requirement. That's what the different nodes on the tree tell us. And a car with front-wheel drive has a certain kind of drive. What kind? Front wheel. (If you are troubled by my calling *front-wheel drive* a compound, please trust me for now and I hope to answer your troubles later in the discussion of the compound *transformational grammarian*.)

Did anything in the above bracketings surprise or confuse you? Why would I have labeled *drive* a N and not a V in *front-wheel drive*? Certainly there is a V *drive*. But notice that we also have a N *drive*, as in:

Let's go for a drive.

Still, this N *drive* is different in sense from the *drive* in our compound. This one means "ride"; the one in our compound has to do with where the drive shaft goes. There are at least three reasons to posit that *drive* in the compound is a N that has the sense of driveshaft.

First, this analysis is possible. In English we allow zero-morpheme conversion between N and V easily:

V→N: Let's go for a {run/ walk/ ride/ drive/ swim/ . . . }.

In fact, the conversion goes both ways:

N→V: I have to **chair** that meeting.
I'll **table** the motion for now.
You better **hound** him about showing up on time.

Make a list of V's that can be used as N's and another list of N's that can be used as V's. Now make a second list of V's that strongly resist being used as N's (such as *evacuate*) and N's that strongly resist being used as V's (such as *destruction*). Do you notice any correlations? You might have noticed that **short words, that is, words of one or two syllables, are more likely to undergo zero-morpheme conversion than long words**. Or you might have noticed a related fact, that monomorphemic words are more likely to undergo zero-morpheme conversion than polymorphemic words. This would be a nice paper topic—determining which of the two hypotheses (or some third) is (more nearly) adequate. So I won't pursue this line of questioning here. (And please note that this observation, whatever its correct formulation, holds for English, but it is not a language universal by any means.)

Second, this analysis is the more theoretically preferable in that if *drive* is a N in *front-wheel drive* we have an endocentric compound. In fact, we have a verbal compound (since the N *drive* would be derived from the V *drive*). Since most compounds are endocentric, we'd favor any endocentric analysis over an exocentric one. Furthermore, this particular compound behaves as we expect verbal compounds to behave, since *front wheel* would be an internal argument of the verb *drive* (from which the N *drive* is derived).

Third, and conclusive, we do, in fact, use *drive* by itself with the same sense it has in the compound:

Cars come with different kinds of **drive**. I prefer front wheel **drive**, don't you?

At this point you may have asked why I didn't simply bring up Point 3 to start with and thus resolve the issue immediately. I could have. But I wanted to take the opportunity to point out to you both theoretical issues made in Points 1 (that zero-morpheme conversion is possible and you should be on the lookout for it) and 2 (that an endocentric analysis is, all other things being equal, taken as theoretically superior to an exocentric analysis). So we can now proceed with agreement over the labeling in *front-wheel drive*.

The extravagant recursiveness of English in compounding is part of our Germanic heritage, by the way. Thus both Dutch and German, our sisters, have the same feature:

Dutch: brandweerladderwagenknipperlichtinstallatiemonteurs
              'fire department ladder truck blinking light installation mechanics'
German: Donaudampfschifffahrtgesellschaft
              'Danube Steam Ship Company'

In fact, our extravagant use of zero-morpheme conversion between N and V is likewise due to our Germanic heritage.

Syntax is also recursive. We can take one CLAUSE and EMBED it inside another clause indefinitely (although multiple embeddings test the memory and we generally limit our embeddings accordingly):

Mary knows [Paul said [Bill expected [that Sue wanted rice]]].

The structure of clauses will be handled in depth in Chapter 4.

Third, when I did the trees for *undergraduate linguistics language requirement*, *runaway tow truck*, and *front-wheel drive*, I used the interpretation to figure out the structural relationships. The meaning of the whole was built up compositionally from the meaning of the parts. This is not always true in word-formation processes, as we have seen for derivation. Thus, for example, a *recital* is not just an act of reciting, but probably a public performance, and neither the *recite* nor the *-al* alone is responsible for this unexpected part of the interpretation.

In contrast to derivational processes and like certain kinds of compounding, the meaning of syntactic phrases is generally compositional from the meaning of the component words. Thus we understand *all big dogs* by putting together the senses of the three words. (Of course, the relationship between syntax and semantics is much more complex than this, as you will learn in Chapters 4 and 5.)

Fourth, over time many compounds whose sense was originally compositional lose that compositionality, sometimes to such an extent that they may no longer be recognizable as compounds. An example is the word *cupboard*, in which we no longer even hear the morpheme *cup*. The compound has been LEXICALIZED into a simplex word. Syntactic phrases are, of course, much more variable than compounds in that we speak many original sentences every day, but we don't make up new compounds every day. It is the repeated use of a given compound that makes it susceptible to lexicalization. So to make a comparison here, we must focus on syntactic phrases that occur in great frequency— phrases that have become relatively fixed, either because they are somehow idiomatic or because their pragmatic context comes up frequently. When we do that, we find that phrases, like compounds, tend to be reanalyzed over time, so that two words can become one and sometimes a word can even eventually become an affix to another word in the original phrase. *Because* is an example of a phrase becoming a single word.

But compounds also differ from syntactic phrases in several ways. First, although the verbal compounds and certain exocentric compounds have a predictable semantics, the nominal endocentric compounds have sometimes-wildly-unpredictable semantics (as we saw with *leg man*).

Second, agreement processes take place between syntactically defined entities (for example, adjectives that modify nouns—as in Pashto, or verbs that agree with their Subjects—as in the Semitic languages or English for that matter). But agreement processes often fail to take place between the members of a compound (but see Problem Set 3.8). Thus in Dutch the uninflected form *groot* 'wide' occurs in the compound *groothoek-lens* 'wide-angle lens,' but the non-neuter form (Dutch makes a gender distinction between neuter and nonneuter only) *grote* must be used when it modifies the non-neuter noun *hoek* in the noun phrase *grote hoek* 'big angle.' A similar situation holds in German. The noun *Maul* 'mouth,' for example, is masculine and in an NP a modifying adjective agrees for gender and number: *ein grosser Maul* 'a big mouth.' But in a compound with this N as head, the same adjective appears without inflection: *ein Grossmaul* 'a loud mouth.'

Third, the component parts of a compound are not referential. So I cannot say,

The horsethief was hung, so I rode it home.

and expect you to understand *it* as referring to some horse. But the component parts of a sentence or phrase are typically referential (though not necessarily; you will learn about the functions of modification and predication in Chapter 4):

I saw a horse by the river, so I rode it home.

Fourth, words in a syntactic phrase can be interrupted by parentheticals. Here *get a load of this* interrupts the phrase *your best friend*:

John said he's **your**, get a load of this, **best friend**.

But the members of a compound cannot be likewise interrupted:

*I met a horse, and you're not going to believe it, thief.

Fifth, there are phonological rules that apply to compounds but not to syntactic phrases. We know that the stress rule for compounds in English, for example, is different from that for phrases (as in our *bláckboard* vs. *black bóard* examples from Problem Set 2.9 of Chapter 2).

After you've done Chapter 4, you may find more similarities and differences between compounds and syntactic phrases. But even now there are certain words in English that a total novice to syntax can still recognize as being phrasal in their source. These words are not compounds (which are so thorny to analyze), but lexicalized phrases as we pointed out earlier:

What's-his-name is on the phone again.
He's got that employee-of-the-month smile.

And just as the members of compounds can become phonologically distinct from their sources over time, so the parts of lexicalized phrases can become distinct from their sources over time:

Where did you put my whatchamacallit?

A word like *whatchamacallit* is so far from its phrasal source that we can even pluralize it: *whatchamacallits*. Thus syntax can definitely feed word-formation rules, at least in this limited way. You will explore another example of a process in which syntax feeds word-formation rules in Problem Set 4.4 of Chapter 4.

So what's the upshot of all this? There is no transparent answer at the present stage of linguistic theory. The important thing is what evidence you can bring to bear on the issue. So if your appetite is whetted, I invite you to join the feast.

Bracketing Paradoxes

The discussion of compounds has brought us to another important issue in morphology. When I did the trees of *undergraduate linguistics language requirement*, *runaway tow truck*, and *front-wheel drive*, I appealed to the interpretation of the compounds to figure out the internal structure. While this method is generally useful for all words, it encounters a number of problems in the analysis of not only compounding, but also derivation.

Let's look at a problem involving compounding first. Consider this compound:

transformational grammarian

First, let me ask you why this is a compound and not simply an adjective that modifies a noun, as in:

stubborn grammarian

Do you see the difference in interpretation? A stubborn grammarian is a grammarian who is stubborn. But a transformational grammarian is not a grammarian who is transformational. So *transformational grammarian* is a single word—a compound. (If you had the analogous question on your mind regarding the *front* of *front-wheel drive*, I hope you can now lay it aside.)

Now what is the interpretation of this compound? A transformational grammarian is a person who studies or works in transformational grammar. Semantically, then, the suffix *-ian* takes the compound *transformational grammar* and attaches to it, like so:

[[[transformational] [grammar]]-ian]

But morphologically speaking, we know that the *-ian* is a Level I affix, and all Level I affixation precedes compounding (which is ordered in Level II). So we have the bracketing:

[[transformational] [[grammar]-ian]]

This result, of two different bracketings for one word (here a single compound word), is known as a BRACKETING PARADOX. In this example, semantics vs. level-ordering resulted in a bracketing paradox.

Many different kinds of bracketing paradoxes occur in language. Let's look at one involving derivation now, rather than compounding. Consider the word *ungrammaticality*. Based on the kind of category that *un* selects, what bracketing would you assign it? This *un-* selects adjectives (with a few exceptions like *uncola* and *unless*). *Grammatical* is an adjective, but *grammaticality* is a noun. So *un-* must attach before *-ity* attaches, like so:

[[un[grammatical]]ity]

(I am ignoring the bracketing internal to *grammatical*, since it is irrelevant here.) However, *-ity* is a Level I affix, while *un-* is a Level II affix. Thus *-ity* should attach before *un-*, giving the bracketing:

[un[[grammatical]ity]]

So now selection vs. level-ordering has resulted in a bracketing paradox. (If you have been won over by Optimality Theory, discussed at the very end of Chapter 2, you might be unhappy with my continued reference to level-ordering. In that case, simply convert what I've said to the distinction between prosodic word and lexical word. Thus *grammaticality* forms a prosodic word—the domain for stress assignment—and *un-* is outside that domain. Therefore, prosody tells us that *un-* is the most externally bracketed affix in the lexical word *ungrammaticality*.)

There is much controversy over how to resolve bracketing paradoxes. A prevalent idea is to allow one bracketing for the morphophonology (the bracketing relevant to prosody) and to convert that into a different bracketing for semantic interpretation. But this approach has problems dealing with similar paradoxes of analysis that involve either substitution of a morpheme or loss of a morpheme, rather than differences in bracketing.

substitution: moral philosophy → moral philosopher
loss: theoretical linguistics → theoretical linguist

A moral philosopher is one who studies moral philosophy. Thus one compound is formed from the other, but not via addition of a morpheme; instead, by substitution of *-er* for *-y*. Yet the *-er* has scope over the whole compound. A theoretical linguist is one who studies theoretical linguistics; thus, again, one compound is formed from the other. But now it is via the loss of the morpheme *-ics*. And, again, the change, the very process of the loss itself, has scope over the whole compound. Surely the issues of analysis raised by such examples are similar to the issues raised by bracketing paradoxes. But these types of problematic examples cannot be resolved by allowing two bracketings at two points in the derivation.

This kind of issue is being debated today, and we cannot go further in that debate here if we are to have a finite book.

Valency and Argument Structure

In our discussion of compounds, another very important issue for morphological theory came up. We recognized that certain kinds of compounds (verbal compounds and our exocentric compounds of the form V+N) involve requirements regarding predicate-argument structure. (In these two instances, the nonverbal member of the compound must satisfy an internal argument of the verbal member.) Derivational morphology is also concerned with argument structure in at least two ways.

First, many languages will make morphological distinctions based on how many arguments a predicate (typically a verb, but other categories can be predicates, as you will learn in the section "Predicates" of Chapter 4) takes. The question of how many arguments a predicate takes is the question of VALENCY. We say a verb with one argument has a valency of 1; a verb with two arguments has a valency of 2; and so forth.

We already saw one instance of a morphological distinction based on valency in the Kubachi Dargwa verbal inflection earlier (in the section "Person, Number, Gender, and Verbal Inflection"), where transitive verbs displayed different agreement morphemes from intransitive verbs. This is a common type of distinction.

Case Systems

Another way in which morphology is sensitive to valency has to do with Case assignment. In most languages of the world that have a morphological Case system the Subject of a tensed verb (as opposed to a tenseless verb form, such as an INFINITIVAL—as in *to run*) gets a particular Case (often dubbed Nominative, a term we've used several times already) regardless of the valency of the verb, and this Case differs from that given to a Direct Object (often dubbed ACCUSATIVE). Such languages are called Nominative-Accusative languages. You are very familiar with such languages because English is an example of one, although since English shows Case almost exclusively in the pronominal system, you might not have paid much attention to it before. Consider this pattern:

> He likes her.
> He runs.
> *Her runs.
> *Everyone saw he.

We use the form *he* in Subject position of transitive and intransitive verbs, but never in Object position. We use the form *her* in Object position (in fact, not just in Direct Object, but in Indirect Object and Object-of-a-Preposition position, as well) but never in Subject position. List the other Subject pronouns of English. List the other Object pronouns of English.

Latin is a more satisfying language to look at Case in, for the Latin system is morphologically rich. We see the same pattern in Latin on nouns that we see in English on pronouns with regard to Subjects and Direct Objects:

> Virī   equum   amant.
> man-NomMP horse-AccMS love-Pres3P
> 'The men love the horse.'
> Equus   virōs   amat.
> horse-NomMS man-AccMP love-Pres3S
> 'The horse loves the men.'
> Virī   invictī   sunt.
> man-NomMP invincible-NomMP be-Pres3P
> 'The men are invincible.'

(Nom = Nominative; Acc = Accusative; Pres = present tense; numbers indicate person; M = masculine; S = singular. In Latin adjectives agree for Case, number, and gender with the nominal they modify or are predicated of. That is why the adjective for "invincible" has these features. We will talk at length about Latin Case in Chapter 4.)

But ERGATIVE-ABSOLUTIVE languages (also just called ergative languages) have a different Case system. Dyirbal, a Pama-Nyungan language of Queensland, Australia, presents this pattern in nouns:

Object	Subject	Verb	
	ŋuma	banaganʸu	'Father returned.'
	yabu	banaganʸu	'Mother returned.'
ŋuma	yabuŋgu	buṛan	'Mother saw Father.'
yabu	ŋumaŋgu	buṛan	'Father saw Mother.'

Can you find the groupings? The Case of the Subject of an intransitive verb is identical to the Case of the Object of a transitive verb. This Case is absolute. The Case assigned to the Subject of transitive verbs is ergative. Pronouns, however, do not behave like nouns for Case:

Subject	Object	Verb	
ŋana		banaganʸu	'We returned.'
nʸura		banaganʸu	'You returned.'
nʸura	ŋanana	buṛan	'You saw us.'
ŋana	nʸurana	buṛan	'We saw you.'

What is the pattern for pronouns? They have the Nominative-Accusative pattern. So Dyirbal is called a SPLIT ERGATIVE language. (And notice that Nominative pronouns come before Objects in Dyirbal, so the word order in our second data set on Dyirbal is different from that in the first data set.)

Many other Australian languages are ergative, as are many Amerind languages and scattered other languages in the world. But probably almost all the so-called ergative languages are really split ergative. (Basque may be the true exception here.)

Adding and Subtracting Arguments

Derivational morphology is also concerned with argument structure in a second way—in that affixal morphemes can actually change the valency of a predicate. One of the most common such morphemes is known as the causative (which I mentioned in passing with respect to Yaqui—and we talked briefly about the causative sense for the transitive use of verbs like *break* early in this chapter). In English we often express the idea of causation analytically, through a separate verb of causation:

Hasan {made/let/had} the butcher cut the meat.

Many of the languages of Europe have analytical causatives with special syntactic properties, similar to English. But other languages will use a causative affix on the main verb, so from a morphological perspective there is only one verb in the sentence. From a semantic perspective the argument that does the causing belongs only to the causative affix and the argument that does the cutting (or whatever other action the verb describes) belongs only to the root verb. But the syntax usually does not allow a single morphological form (the complex verb made of the causative affix and the verb root) to have two syntactic Subjects. So the syntax maps the agent argument of the causative affix into the Subject position of the complex verb.

Sometimes linguists use a shorthand way of talking when describing this kind of causative. They will say that every argument present is an argument of the one and only (morphological) verb. That means that the argument analogous to "the butcher" in the English example here would have to be an argument of the same verb that "Hasan" (or its counterpart) would be an argument of. So, in this way of speaking, the causative morpheme increases the number of arguments of the verb it attaches to. We find such a morpheme in Turkish. Compare the noncausative to the causative sentence:

Kasap   et-i   kes-ti.
butcher meat-ACC cut-PAST
'The butcher cut the meat.'
Hasan kasab-a   et-i   kes-tir-di.
Hasan butcher-DAT meat-ACC cut-CAUSE-PAST
'Hasan had the butcher cut the meat.'

(ACC = Accusative Case, the Case normally given to Direct Objects; DAT = DATIVE Case, the Case normally given to Indirect Objects.) The verb for 'to cut' has a valency of 2: It takes an agent and a theme argument. But when we add the causative morpheme *tir*, the causer (the one who instigates the cutting) is added to the argument structure, so now the newly formed causative verb has a valency of 3.

Affixation can also result in the loss of an argument. The most common example of this is the passive morpheme. Consider the English verb *discuss*. In the active voice, it is obligatorily transitive, having two arguments, which are boldfaced here:

We discussed **that issue** all night.
(cf. *We discussed all night.)

But in the passive voice, only one argument need appear, the agent argument being optional.

That issue has already been discussed (by **us**).

(Actually, while I have put *us* in boldface, it is debatable whether the Object of *by* in a passive sentence has argument status.) And there are languages, such as Latvian (a Baltic language spoken in Latvia), in which the agent argument must be suppressed when the verb has a passive morpheme on it:

Es tieku mācīts (*no mātes).
'I am   taught (*by mother).'

So we can say that the passive morpheme causes the verb it attaches to to lose an argument.

And, finally, morphemes can change the types of arguments that verbs take. In English we see this behavior with the prefix *mis-*. The verb *manage*, for example, can be followed by a nominal or an infinitival:

She managed [the company].
She managed [to make a million dollars].

But when we add *mis-*, the possibility of an infinitival following the verb is removed:

She mismanaged [the company].
*She mismanaged [to make a million dollars].

The second sentence could only be said as a kind of linguistic joke.

Clitics

The final issue of morphological theory that we're going to touch on and the one that interacts most undeniably with the syntax is the analysis of clitics. We've mentioned clitics many times, but we haven't yet defined them. What are clitics? Say the following English sentence in a formal style and then in a casual style:

Put them down.
formal: [pʰʌt ðɛm daʊn]
casual: [pʰʌɾ m̩ daʊn]

Them, whether it is pronounced as in the formal style or the casual style, is a lexical item, like other words and unlike affixes. But in the casual style it has a phonologically reduced allomorph which has one very special property. Consider the question:

Put what down?

If you wanted to answer, "Them," would you use the full allomorph or the reduced allomorph? Certainly only the full allomorph, regardless of what style of speech you were using. **The reduced allomorph cannot stand alone, just like an affix, and unlike most words. This is an essential property of clitics.**

Notice, by the way, that we do not normally indicate clitics with any special writing conventions in English. This is true of many languages. And some languages are inconsistent, using a particular writing convention for clitics in one context but not in another. So please do not let writing conventions confuse you here and as you do Problem Set 3.9. Writing conventions can be misleading (as you know, from having compared English orthography to the sounds of the words).

When can you use the reduced allomorph [m̩]? Give a list of at least five utterances in which you can use it, such as:

I saw them.   I gave them to her.   Who wants them?
She left with them.   I wrote to them.

Is there any position in the utterance that the allomorph [m̩] never occurs in? Sure: initial position. That's because this allomorph must CLITICIZE onto a preceding HOST.

Clitics like [m̩] are **SIMPLE CLITICS. They are phonologically reduced allomorphs of full lexical items, and, as in most instances of allomorphy, clitics and their corresponding full forms display complementary distribution. Clitics further have the property that they must be phonologically attached to a host.** Using that definition, can you think of other simple clitics in English? What about the reduced allomorph of *not* that occurs in:

He isn't very nice.

How can you test whether this is just a reduced allomorph or a genuine clitic? A crucial question is whether it can stand alone, as in:

—Is he very nice or not?
—*[n̩t]. (cf. —Not.)

(The initial dash on these sentences indicates a change in speaker in a discourse. That is, the first line is said by one person and the next line is said by another person.) So it certainly looks like a simple clitic. Since we know that the simple clitic [m̩] requires a host to precede it, we might further ask whether the simple clitic [n̩t] needs a preceding host (as opposed to a following one). We should therefore test whether it can come in the initial position of an utterance, as in:

—Is he nice?
—*[n̩t] very. (cf. —Not very.)

In sum, [n̩t] has all the properties of a simple clitic in English. (And now you can recognize that what you learned in grammar school to call "contraction" results in a clitic.)

Other languages have simple clitics as well, although they may vary on whether the clitic finds a host to its left or its right. Other languages may also have other kinds of clitics different from simple clitics. Consider these Italian sentences:

Elena torna, e trova proprio me a casa.
'Elena returns, and finds indeed me at home.'
Elena torna, e mi trova a casa.
'Elena returns, and finds me at home.'

Compare the two words for 'me' in these sentences: *me* [me] and *mi* [mi]. Does one look like a phonological reduction of the other? They both start with [m], but there is no sense in which either vowel is a reduction of the other. These are simply two different forms that mean 'me,' but one is not a reduced form of the other.

Furthermore, they have a different distribution. The form [me] occurs in the sentence in the same linear slot where a nonpronominal noun would occur:

Elena torna, e trova proprio l'amica a casa.
'Elena returns, and finds precisely her friend at home.'

But the form [mi] occurs to the left of the finite verb. [mi] and [me] cannot exchange places in the sentences above:

> *Elena torna, e me trova a casa.
> *Elena torna, e trova proprio mi a casa.'

It certainly looks like the [mi] form is cliticized to the verb.

We can test whether either form is a clitic by asking if it can stand alone. And we find, as we might have suspected, that [me] can stand alone in an utterance, but [mi] cannot:

> —Chi hanno visto? 'Who did they see?'
> —{Me./*Mi.} 'Me.'

So [mi] is a clitic. This kind of clitic is called a SPECIAL clitic, because the sense of 'me' has two forms, neither derived from the other—one for when it is not cliticized to a host and a special one for when it is cliticized. The uncliticized form is often called a STRONG or TONIC form (*tonic* means able to bear word stress) precisely because it can bear word stress (as it must when it stands alone); the cliticized form is often called a WEAK or ATONIC form precisely because it cannot bear word stress (which is one reason why it cannot stand alone). Both simple clitics and special clitics are generally atonic, although I will return to this point directly below.

In:

> Elena mi trova a casa.   'Elena finds me at home.'

the clitic [mi] is a PROCLITIC on the verb—that is, it attaches on the left end of its host. In the English examples we had ENCLITICS, which attach on the right end.

Both simple clitics and special clitics can be proclitic or enclitic. The choice of whether to attach to a host on the left or the right is one parameter of a clitic system. Italian has a mixed system with respect to this parameter. While we find proclitics with tensed verbs (as above), we find enclitics with nontensed verbs, such as infinitivals and participles:

> Elena vuole   trovarmi.
> Elena want-Pres3S find-INF-1SAccCL
> 'Elena wants to find me.'
> Vedendomi,   sciupi   tutto.
> see-PRT-1SAccCL ruin-Pres2S everything
> 'By seeing me, you ruin everything.'

(INF = infinitival; CL = clitic; PRT = participle.) And there are other complications to the placement of Italian special clitics, as well—complications we won't go into here.

Look at the words we've discussed thus far which can be simple or special clitics in English and Italian. They are pronouns and a negative marker. Such lexical items are often clitics. Other typical types of lexical items that can be clitics include auxiliary verbs and adverbial PROFORMS (analogous to pro-nouns). In Italian there are two such adverbial proforms:

> —Vai al cinema?   'Are you going to the movies?'

—Sì, ci vado   ora.   'Yes, I'm going there now.'
    yes CL go-Pres1S now

The *ci* here is a locative adverbial, which goes with either a fixed location or movement toward a location. The other is seen in:

—Vuoi delle caramelle?   'Do you want some candies?'
—Grazie. Ne prendo   una.   'Thanks. I'll take one (of them).'
    thanks CL take-Pres1S one

The *ne* is understood in this sentence as a PARTITIVE, where *ne* plus *una* expresses a part of the whole (here, one from the group of candies). In other sentences *ne* can be understood as a locative which goes with movement from a location:

Ne vengo 'I'm coming from there.'
CL come-Pres1S
Ne trasse la pistola.   'He took out (from there) the gun.'
CL pull-Remote3S the gun

(The remote tense in the second example is a past that often carries a punctual sense.)
    Given that there is such a wide semantic range of clitics, we might well expect more than one to occur in a given sentence. And, in fact, they can co-occur stacked up on a single host, giving a CLUSTER of proclitics or a cluster of enclitics. This example from Bulgarian (a Balto-Slavic language spoken in Bulgaria) shows about as wide a semantic range of clitic types stacking together as occurs in language:

ne   si   li   mɨ   go   dala?
Neg Aux2S Q   3SDat 3SAcc give-PartF
            CL CL   CL   CL
'Didn't you (feminine) give it to him?'

(Neg = negative marker; Aux = auxiliary verb; Part = participle; Q = question marker.)
You will discover other properties of special clitics in Problem Set 3.9.
    Before leaving special clitics, there is one complication I'd like to point out. In Italian we find enclitics on certain imperative verbs:

Daglielo.   'Give it to him.'
(da-glie-lo   'give-Dat3SM-Acc3SM,'   literally: 'Give him it.')

The stress rule in Italian (whatever it may be) operates from right to left. That fact leads us to ask how the addition of enclitics interacts with the placement of stress. In the standard language, the stress of a verb falls on a certain syllable without regard to the presence of a clitic. Thus the stress always falls on the root, as in the verb above, transcribed here:

[dáʎ:ɹelo]

One way to account for this fact is to say that clitics attach after word stress is assigned. Alternatively, we could say that clitics do not form part of the prosodic word with the verb.

But in many dialects of Italian, particularly those spoken in the south, the relevant data are different. The same sentence in one dialect of Calabrese, that spoken in Cipolla, is:

Dannillu. 'Give it to him.' (literally: 'Give him it.')
[dan:íl:u]

Does this mean that clitics are tonic in Cipolla, contrary to our claim above that clitics are atonic? Certainly not. The clitic does not carry a lexical stress of its own. Instead, the clitic is part of the prosodic word headed by the verb, and as a result, when word stress is assigned to the entire prosodic word, that stress may just happen to fall on a clitic. We can maintain our original idea of clitics, then, as not having word stress of their own.

There is yet a third kind of clitic. Consider this sentence from Serbo-Croatian:

Dolazite li često ovamo?
come-2 Q often here
'Do you come here often?'

The morpheme *li* marks the sentence as a question. It is encliticized onto *dolazite* in this sentence. Unlike simple clitics and special clitics, however, it does not have a nonclitic counterpart. It is therefore called a BOUND WORD (which differs from a bound root, since it does not demand affixation in order to result in a well-formed word). Many languages have bound-words, and, in fact, bound-word question markers are common (as in Japanese and Chinese).

The Serbo-Croatian *li* exhibits behavior that is different from English or Italian clitics, but that is quite typical of clitics in many languages. Take a look at these sentences:

Hoćeš li doći?
Aux2S Q come
'Will you come?'
Jeste li joj se predstavili u sali?
Aux2P Q 3SFDat Refl-Acc introduced in hall
'Did you introduce yourselves to her in the hall?'
Da li mi ih je dao Jovan?
Comp Q 1SDat 3PAcc Aux3S give Jovan
'Did Jovan give them to me?'

(Refl = reflexive; Comp = a clause introducer called a COMPLEMENTIZER.) Is there anything you can say about the placement of *li* that holds true for every sentence you've seen it in? *Li* occurs encliticized to the first word. You could say that it appears as the second CONSTITUENT in the sentence. Language after language marks the second position (P2) of a clause as a special position. It is in fact called WACKERNAGEL POSITION after the nineteenth-century scholar who first wrote about this sort of phenomenon. The Australian language Warlpiri of the Northern Territories, the Uto-Aztecan language Luiseño of California, the Penutian language Alsea (spoken on the Oregon coast), and many other unrelated languages also place clitics in P2.

While the sentences with *li* made the issue look transparent, in fact the question of what constitutes P2 is often quite difficult to discern in a language. What might the position of second constituent in a sentence be? What are the constituents of a sentence? You will learn about the constituents of sentences in Chapter 4. But even now there are some logical possibilities that you can entertain. For example, we could define P2 as after the first word, or as after the first phrase, or as after the first word with a certain characteristic, or as after the first phrase with a certain characteristic. And all these possibilities and more are exercised by the world's languages. In fact, Serbo-Croatian can define P2 variably, allowing the position after the first stressed word or after the first stressed phrase. So we get the clitic *mi* (Can you guess what it means? Serbo-Croatian is an Indo-European language like English and Italian, and *mi* means 'me') allowed in two different positions in a single sentence:

[Taj pesnik] mi je   napisao knjigu.
[that poet]   me AUX wrote   book
'That poet wrote me a book.'
Taj mi je pesnik napisao knjigu.
'That poet wrote me a book.'

Just looking at these two sentences, can you tell me whether *je* is a clitic or not? It certainly looks like a clitic in that it appears to be in a clitic cluster with *mi*; notice its variable position. Furthermore, it is an auxiliary and we know that auxiliaries are among the types of word that are often clitics.

All along in this discussion you may have been plagued by the question of what precisely the line is between clitics and words, on the one hand, and between clitics and affixes, on the other. The distinctions between clitics and words are multiple. Both have a range of senses, but clitics are more likely to be limited to senses that involve functions or relations or bundles of features (such as the nominal features of person, number, and gender), whereas words are completely unlimited in their types of senses. Both can have a range of phonological shapes and can undergo a range of phonological rules, but clitics are never independent prosodic units (that is, the domain for metrical rules—they are either extrametrical or part of a metrical domain with their host), nor is any subpart of them an independent prosodic unit, whereas lexical words are or contain prosodic units. Both can have a range of syntactic functions, but the syntactic distribution of clitics is predictable, whereas the syntactic distribution of most words is not.

The distinctions between clitics and affixes may be harder to see. Both must occur bound. And while affixes do not have nonclitic counterparts, bound word clitics do not either (though simple clitics and special clitics do). In many ways pronominal clitics seem very similar to agreement markers with Subjects or Objects. What, then, are the differences that we can count on?

There are at least five major differences between clitics and affixes. One is that clitics can often move to a fixed position in the sentence, typically P2, and take as a host whatever precedes or follows that position, even words which might otherwise be morphologically inert, such as prepositions, complementizers, determiners, and the like. Affixes never do that. Instead, affixes attach to a fixed category or categories of word, regardless of where the word is located in the sentence. So affixation can occur without reference to the syntax. But cliticization is always a syntax-sensitive process.

Second, clitics can attach to words or phrases, but affixes attach to words only (although we will explore this further in Problem Set 4.4 of Chapter 4).

Third, enclitics can follow an inflectional suffix in languages that do not allow derivational suffixes to follow inflectional ones and in which each word has at most one inflectional affix, such as English. You can see this with the simple negative clitic [n̩t] that we looked at. In fact, while it is not a universal, most languages order inflection after derivation, yet enclitics can come after inflectional suffixes in language after language. Conversely, I have not read of any language in which inflectional suffixes can follow enclitics.

Fourth, affixes often exhibit idiosyncracies, both phonological and semantic, and are subject to lexical vagaries (recall the contrast of *arrival* vs. **derival* in Problem Set 2.8 of Chapter 2). Clitics, instead, have a generally constant phonological form (although when clitics cluster together on a single host, they may well influence each other's phonological shape) and a consistent semantic value, plus they attach to a syntactically appropriate host without fail.

Fifth, sandhi rules that take place between two words can take place between a clitic and its host, but not between an affix and the stem it attaches to. One such rule in Italian is Raddoppiamento Sintattico (RS), which we looked at in the section "Postlexical Rules" in Chapter 2. This is the rule that causes lengthening of an initial consonant of a word when the word that precedes it ends in a stressed syllable and the two words stand in a particular syntactic relationship to one another. Here we see that RS applies between a preposition and its Object, between a verb and a clitic, but not between a prefix and a stem:

a Roma [ar:óma] 'to Rome'
da + mi → dammi [dám:i] 'give me'
a + tono → atono [átono] 'atonic'

All the same, the line between clitics and affixes is not always distinct and over time this is one line that is often crossed. A typical diachronic pattern is for a word to become a proform (auxiliaries have some properties that make them qualify as pro-verbs), then a simple clitic, then a special clitic, and finally an affix.

This is all we will do with morphology in this chapter. As you can see, we have come to the point where we are constantly making reference to issues of syntax. So it's time for us to move on to that topic.

Problem Set 3.1: Arbitrariness or not?

1. The relationship between sound and meaning is generally arbitrary in oral languages. I'd like you now to consider what the analogue of this claim would be for manual/visual languages, such as ASL. In Figure 3.2 we see six signs of ASL. Let me verbally describe the signs to you to aid these drawings.

A. A closed fist with the thumb extended moves from the cheek forward in an out, slight in, out movement. (The handshape here is known as handshape [Á]. [A] alone indicates the fist shape, and the dot indicates that the thumb is extended. I give this information for those of you who want to go on to read about ASL. This information is not necessary to do the problem.)

B. Both hands in a fist with the first two fingers extended (in the [H] handshape), start with the dominant hand on top and move both hands outward, slightly in, and then outward.

C. A hand with the tips of thumb and index finger coming together and the other three fingers extended and separated (in the [F] handshape) moves from the corner of the mouth outward.

D. One arm rests on top of the other. The top hand forms a fist with the index and

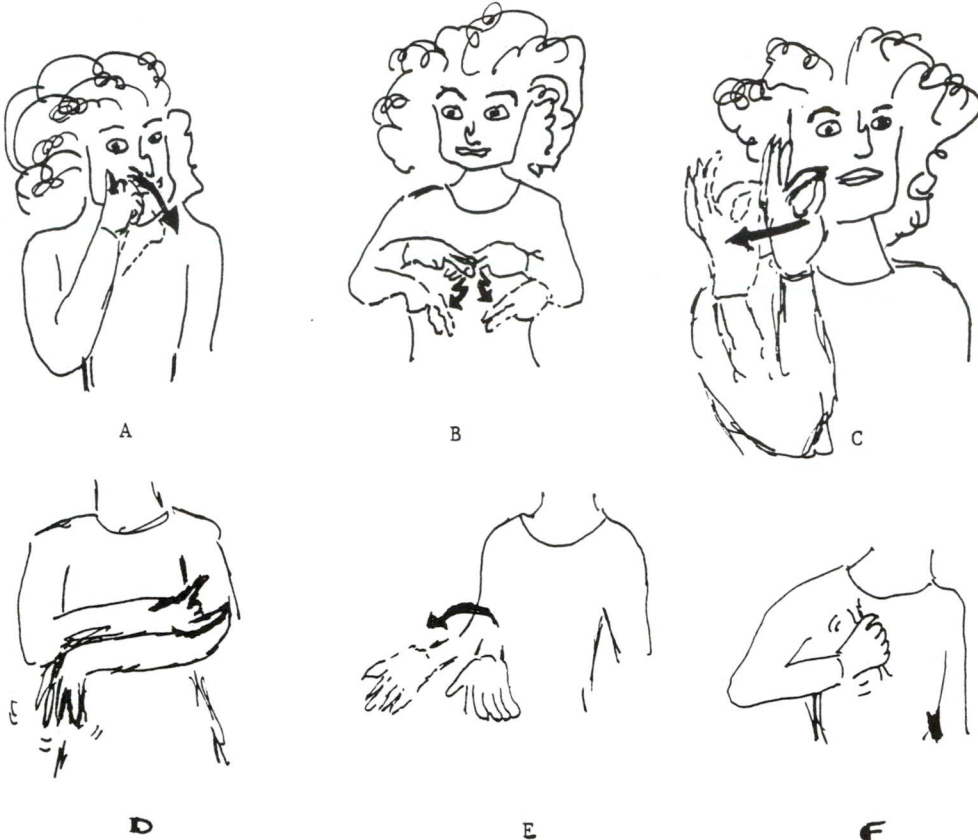

Figure 3.2 Six signs of ASL with attention to the issue of iconicity.

pinky fingers extended (in the handshape represented by a block capital Y, for which I will use the symbol [Ÿ]). The bottom hand has all the fingers dropping downward and wiggling.

E. A flat hand with the fingers together and the thumb extended (the handshape [Ḃ]; the dot indicates the extended thumb) oriented with palm turned upward moves from in front of the waist outward to the side.

F. A fist with an extended thumb [Å] grabs the shirt on the chest and yanks gently.

These six signs mean (in alphabetical order according to their English gloss): BULL-SHIT, CANADA, CAT, EGG, GIRL, THING. Try to match the senses with the signs. Can you? Discuss the degrees to which these signs are ICONIC (that is, mimicking their sense).

2. Now let's take another look at a set of signs from ASL (Fig. 3.3). These signs are (in alphabetical order): CLIMB, JUMP, KNEEL, SIT, STAND. Match the sense of each sign to the sign. The task is much easier now than it was in 1. Why? Draw an analogy with oral-language words whose sense is easy to guess at.

3. In ASL inflectional processes generally divide into two basic groups.

One group affects the rhythmic and dynamic qualities of the movement. These changes include, among other things, variations in tenseness of the muscles in the hands and arms, the evenness of movement, pausing, and the rate of movement. In this group are the

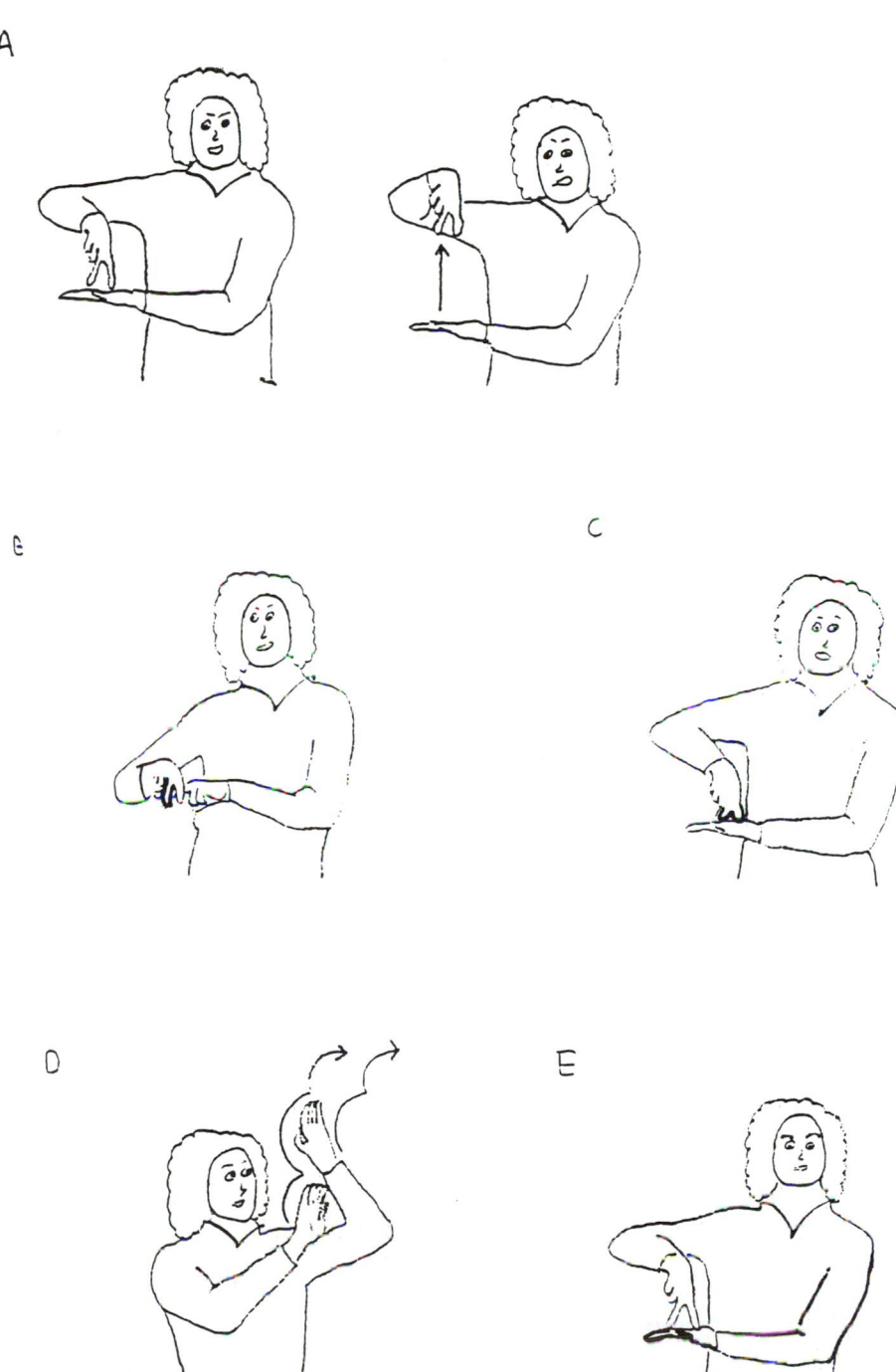

Figure 3.3 Five signs of ASL with attention to the issue of iconicity.

morphemes indicating temporal focus (for distinctions such as 'starting to,' 'resulting in,' 'increasingly'), temporal aspect (for distinctions such as 'regularly,' 'continuously,' 'over and over again'), degree ('very,' 'approximately'), and manner ('with ease').

The other group affects the spatial arrangement of the movement. These changes include, among other things, differences in geometric pattern, direction of movement, use of a second hand to mimic or double the first, and planar focus (whether the movement is horizontal or vertical). In this group are the morphemes indicating number, referential indexing (that is, the reference of pronouns), reciprocals ('each other'), and distribution ('each').

Comment on these two groups with respect to the question of whether there is an arbitrary relationship between a sign and its meaning. Is one group more (nearly) iconic than the other? Does the placement of certain morphemes in one group as opposed to the other make any sense in iconic terms? (Without a video, this problem may seem too abstract to you. It may help to hold your hands in front of your chest and make a given movement—any movement. Then do it again varying the factors in the first group— tenseness, evenness, pausing, rate. Then do it a third time varying the factors in the second group—geometric pattern, direction, second hand, planar focus.)

4. In the text we saw that words that begin with "st" in English often have a vague, slow, or negative sense associated with them.

(a) Another initial cluster that has a vague sense typically associated with it is "fl." Give a group of words that show what that typically associated sense is. Now give another group of words that do not have this sense but begin with "fl."

(b) Find a third initial cluster that has some vague sense typically associated with it. Give two lists of words, one exemplifying that sense and another showing that that sense need not be associated with that cluster.

5. Consider the words:

   bang   bong   bing

Someone might claim that in *bang* the [e] vowel (with or without a diphthong) or the [æ] vowel (depending on how you say this word) gives a sort of rude sense; in *bong* the [ɔ] vowel gives a sense of large size; and in *bing* the [i] vowel (with or without a diphthong) gives a sense of small size. Try to find other triplets or pairs that show this same range of senses associated with these three vowels. (This is not easy to do. If you can't find any triplets, then try to find pairs that use two of these vowels. If you can't do that, forgive me.)

Now find other triplets or pairs that do not have this range of senses associated with these three vowels.

Find any other pair of words that differ in the quality of the vowel, in which either a sense of size difference or perhaps politeness/rudeness difference is associated with the contrast in vowel quality. (Again, this is hard, since there are few examples, but I think you can do it.)

Now compare:

   bing   ping

What is the effect of the contrast in voicing of the initial consonant? Can you find other pairs of words differing only in the voicing of a consonant that show this same effect?

(Don't limit yourself to only word-initial consonant contrasts. Consider also pairs like *crumble* and *crumple*.)

6. In Korean we find pairs of words that have the same consonant melody, but different vowel melodies, in which the difference in vowel quality corresponds to a difference in semantics. In general, the words in the first column here, traditionally called "dark," are augmentative, and the words in the second column, traditionally called "light," are diminutive:

Dark	Light	
sukun	sokon	'whispering'
kel kel	kæl kæl	'exhausted'
kɪtɪlmək	katɪlmak	'almost full'
hyhy	høhø	'round about'
pipi	pæpæ	'twisting'
səpək	sapak	'crunching'

(These transcriptions are not accurate with respect to the obstruents. Korean voiceless obstruents come in three types: laxed, tensed, and aspirated (for the stops). The tensed ones are produced with more glottal tension than the laxed ones, although they are not ejectives. This fact will not affect your ability to do this problem.)

(a) If someone were to claim that in data like those here the sounds had an iconic relationship to the meanings—in other words, that we are dealing with IDEOPHONES— what correlation between sound and meaning would they point to here?

(b) How does the Korean pattern seen here compare to the English pattern in 5 (*bing*, *bang*, *bong*)? Comment on this difference with respect to the claim that sounds are arbitrarily related to meaning.

7. Consider these pairs:

ass arse   cuss curse

What is the effect of the [ɹ] in these words in contrast to their counterpart without the liquid? (If you don't see the point here, think of the people you might use the word *ass* with and the people you might use the word *arse* with. Then look at why you would choose *arse* with the second group.) Can you find other pairs of words that show this same use of [ɹ]?

Can you find any other pair of words in English in which one has a consonant that is missing from the other and only a vague meaning difference is associated with that consonant difference? If so, give it.

8. In Korean we find a three-way distinction among obstruents in syllable-initial position: A voiceless stop can be lightly aspirated (with no special diacritic), or unaspirated (indicated here with the diacritic '), or heavily aspirated (indicated with the familiar superscript). Consider this data set:

Simple	Intensive	Paraintensive	
piŋ piŋ	p'iŋp'iŋ	pʰiŋ pʰiŋ	'round and round in circles'
təl təl	t'əl t'əl	tʰəl tʰəl	'rumbling, rattling'
kam kam	k'am k'am	kʰam kʰam	'in the dark; uninformed'

The second column here has intensified sense as compared to the first column, and the third column has the greatest intensity of sense.

Can this paradigm be considered an example of ideophones? Go back to what you know about aspiration from our discussion of articulatory phonetics in Chapter 1 in answering this.

9. In Japanese, reduplication in the form of repetition of an entire root can be found in various constructions.

A. Onomatopoetic words are often reduplicated, as in:

> Inuga **wan wan** hoete-iru.   'The dog is barking.'
> dog   woof   barking-is
> Darekaga too   **ton ton** tataita   'Someone tapped at the door.'
> someone door tap   tapped
> (literally: 'Someone tapped tap tap at the door.')

(I have not glossed many complexities in the morphology since that is not our point of interest here.)

B. Reduplication on some nouns can indicate plurality:

> ki 'tree'   kigi 'trees'   hito 'person'   hitobito 'people'

C. Reduplication can indicate repeated actions in verb forms:

> yasumi yasumi hataraku 'to work taking a break now and then'
> rest   rest   work

D. Reduplication can indicate emphasis in adjectival forms:

> waka-i 'young'   waka-waka-shii 'very young'

E. Some baby words exhibit reduplication:

> me 'eye(s)'   meme 'eye(s)'   te 'hand(s)'   (o)tete 'hand(s)'

Now consider these sentences:

> (1) Darekaga aruiteiru. 'Someone is walking.'
> (2) Darekaga koto koto to aruiteiru.
> (3) Darekaga karan koron to aruiteiru.
> (4) Darekaga peta peta to aruiteiru.
> (5) Darekaga dosun dosun to aruiteiru.

NOTE: There is no typographical mistake in 3: The vowels in *karan* differ from the vowels in *koron*, so this is not exact reduplication.

Number 1 is the ordinary way to say, "Someone is walking." Number 2 might be said if the walking person is wearing leather shoes. NOTE: Not all speakers find 2 acceptable. I am relying on the source in the bibliography here. Number 3 might be said if the person is wearing wooden clogs. Number 4 might be said if the person is barefoot or wearing a beach sandal. Number 5 might be said if the person walks heavily or is heavy.

If the examples of reduplication in 2–5 had to be classified into one of the traditional groups exemplified in A–E above, the most likely group would be onomatopoeia. Why? Why is this not a perfect fit? That is, how is the reduplication in 2–5 different from the other instances of onomatopoeia that we discussed in the text?

Now use the examples in 2–5 to briefly discuss the difference between onomatopoeia and ideophones. (Look back to question 6 of this problem set for an example of ideophones in Korean.) Take a stance as to whether onomatopoeia or ideophones are present in each of sentences in 2–5.

10. In Italian we find an alternation in roots of [n] vs. [ɲ] in many words, such as:

[víno] 'wine'   [víɲ:a] 'vineyard'
[káne] 'dog'   [kaɲ:olíno] 'lap dog'

and between [ʎ] vs. [l]:

[famíʎ:a] 'family'   [familiáre] 'domestic'
[fíʎ:o] 'son'   [filiále] 'filial'

Just on the basis of these words, do you think either alternation is an example of onomatopoeia or ideophones or any other type of iconic alternation? If this isn't an iconic alternation, what might be responsible for the alternation? (With so few words to judge from, you are largely guessing here. But there are certain alternatives you should be able to eliminate just from looking at these examples.)

Problem Set 3.2: Sources of new words

1. Look up the etymology of *riding coat* or *Mayday* (as a cry of distress). Discuss what their etymology tells us about the borrowing of words from one language to another.

2. Look up the etymology of *attack* and *attach*. Now look up the etymology of *owe*, *ought*, and *own*. Before you looked them up, did you consider the first pair to share the root morpheme? Do you now? Before you looked them up, did you consider the second group of three to share the root morpheme? Do you now?

Use the etymologies of these words as a focal point for briefly discussing some complexities of the issue of how native speakers of a language recognize morphemes.

3. In the text we noted that the regular plural morpheme in English cannot attach to several nouns, such as:

*foots   *oxes   *sheeps   *phenomenons   *alumnuses   *seraphs

Give the plural form for *foot*, *ox*, *sheep*, *phenomenon*, *alumnus*, and *seraph*. Look up their etymology and explain why these words have irregular plurals.

4. Consider the word *fridge*. What is the process we used to form this word? How does it differ from a similar process described in the text?

Now consider the word *vamp*. Is this word morphologically related to any other words of English? If so, what process formed this word? What semantic effects did this process have?

5. Look up the etymology of the word *snafu*. What is the process by which we formed this word? What practical factors might have come into play in encouraging people to form this short word instead of saying the longer source it came from? What sociological factors might have come into play, as well?

6. In Italian the definite article *lo* introduces masculine singular nouns that begin with certain sounds or sound sequences. Among these sound sequences are [s] and [z] followed by a consonant:

[sf]: lo sfagno 'the bog moss'   [zv]: lo svago 'the amusement'
[sk]: lo scoglio 'the rock'   [zg]: lo sguardo 'the glance'
[sp]: lo specchio 'the mirror'   [zb]: lo sbirro 'the cop'
[st]: lo stile 'the style'   [zd]: lo sdegno 'the distain'
[str]: lo strame 'the hay'   [zdr]: lo sdrucio 'the rending'

Actually, this is really one type of sound sequence, not two. Collapse the two into one by positing a single rule of Italian phonology. (If you did Problem Set 2.4, you can simply refer to it now.)

Okay, now in Italian the word for hospital is the masculine noun *ospedale*. But once I was in a rural part of Italy and at a crossroads I saw a sign with an arrow that read: "Lo Spedale". Explain what the maker of that sign did in deriving *spedale* from *ospedale*.

7. The British have dubbed the new tunnel that goes under the English Channel the "chunnel." What type of word formation is this an example of?

8. In the late 1800s Italy politically unified from several small city-states into the country it is today. In that process, Italy went from having many kings to having a single king. Vittorio Emmanuele II, who had been the king of Sardinia and Piedmont, became the first king of all Italy. He was a popular political figure at the time, partly because of his anti-Austrian sentiments, and many people wanted him to be the king of Italy before he actually became it *(re d'Italia)*. At the same time, the composer Verdi was popular in Italy. The supporters of Vittorio Emmanuele, who had to be subversive in their activities, took up the saying, "Viva VERDI," charcoaling it on walls. The *VERDI* part of it was always in capitals. Can you guess why they wrote *Viva VERDI*? That is, what could *VERDI* have meant? What process that is typical of new word formation did they employ here?

9. Consider these Italian nouns and verbs:

Noun	Verb
favol+a 'tale'	favol+eggi+are 'make up tales'
padron+e 'master'	padron+eggi+are 'boss'
rumor+e 'noise'	rumor+eggi+are 'make noise'

I have used + to indicate a morpheme boundary. In the nouns the boundary is between the root and the inflectional ending that tells number and gender. In the verbs we have the order root morpheme, then *eggi*, then the inflectional ending that tells the conjugation class and the fact that this is the infinitival form.

(a) What kind of morpheme is *eggi*, lexical, derivational, or inflectional? What is its function (based on just these data)?

Now consider these Italian nouns and adjectives:

Noun	Adjective
pecor+a 'sheep'	pecor+esc+o 'sheeplike'
bambin+o 'child'	bambin+esc+o 'childish'
animal+e 'animal'	animal+esc+o 'animallike'

Here the morphemes in the adjectives come in the order of root, then *esc*, then the inflectional ending for number and gender, which varies according to agreement. I have given the masculine singular inflectional ending here, which is the citation inflection that is used in dictionaries.

(b) What kind of morpheme is *esc*—lexical, derivational, or inflectional? What is its function (based on just these data)?

Now, Italian has three great authors of the Renaissance that are known to most literate and even illiterate people: the poets Dante and Petrarca, and the storyteller (novelist) Boccaccio (who wrote in a fixed metrics, but without rhyme). We find these verbs in Italian:

    danteggiare   petrarcheggiare

and these adjectives:

    boccaccesco   dantesco   petrarchesco

(c) Guess at the meaning of each of these five words.

(d) What kind of word-formation process are these five words an example of?

(e) The adjective *boccaccesco* can mean 'licentious.' What do you think a frequent topic of Boccaccio's famous work the *Decameron* was, just based on this one fact?

10. Consider these Italian words:

ragazzo 'boy'	ragazza 'girl'
ragazzi 'boys'	ragazze 'girls'
gatto 'male cat'	gatta 'female cat'
gatti 'male cats'	gatte 'female cats'
padrone 'male boss, owner'	padrona 'female boss, owner'
padroni 'male bosses'	padrone 'female bosses'

(a) What inflectional ending added to a noun root indicates feminine singular? What inflectional ending added to a noun root indicates feminine plural? (Please base your answers on these data only. There is another feminine singular ending in Italian, but we are not concerned with it here.)

Now consider these irregular male-female counterparts in the singular and plural:

male: [káne]/[káni] cane/cani 'dog/dogs'
female: [káɲ:a]/[káɲ:e] cagna/cagne 'female dog(s), bitch(es), bad actress(es), or singer(s)'

(b) What is the irregularity here in contrasting the masculine forms to the feminine forms? (Please look carefully at the phonetic transcriptions.)

Now consider these noun phrases:

un ragazzo italiano 'an Italian boy'
dei ragazzi italiani 'Italian boys'
una ragazza italiana 'an Italian girl'
delle ragazze italiane 'Italian girls'

(c) What are the four inflectional endings added to an adjective root to indicate the four possible combinations of the two genders of masculine and feminine and the two numbers of singular and plural?

Now consider the senses of these words:

italiano 'Italian' or 'Italian boy'
pazzo 'crazy' or 'crazy male person'
povero 'poor' or 'poor male person'

(d) What is one way of deriving nouns from adjectives in Italian that is exemplified in these data?

Okay, now we are finally ready for the point of all this. In the summer of 1993 I saw this sign painted on the wall of a university building in Venice:

americani americagne

which would be pronounced:

[amerikáni] [amerikáɲ:e]

The adjective root for 'American' is *american-*.

(e) What would the normal feminine plural of this adjective be?

(f) What morphological process that is common to new word formation was employed in producing *americagne*?

(g) Do you think this sign displayed a favorable or unfavorable attitude toward American women? Why?

11. Consider these Japanese words:

[desuku] 'desk'
[supo:tsuka:] 'sportscar'
[kuri:mu] 'cream'
[te:buru] 'table'

(a) How (where) do you think Japanese got these words?

(b) Based only on these words, what do you think the structure of syllables is in Japanese?

(c) What would you say is the unmarked vowel in Japanese? Why do you say that?

(d) What do you think the Japanese borrowing of the English word *golf* would be? (Be careful. Take a good look at the word for 'table' and look back at Problem Set 1.2 of Chapter 1.)

12. Consider these English pairs of verbs and nouns:

    use   utilize   drunk   drunkard

Are you surprised that English allows both members of each pair to exist side by side? Discuss whether these pairs constitute violations of the principle of Blocking.

Problem Set 3.3: Types of Morphemes: English

1. At one point morphologists argued about the value of identifying *cran* (as in *cranberry*) as a morpheme. In those days we did not have the juices *Cranapple* and *Cranraspberry*. If *cranberry* were the only word of English that used this *cran* (just as *strawberry* seems to be the only word today that uses that particular morpheme *straw*), would you want to claim the existence of a morpheme *cran*? Why or why not? (Look back to the discussion of *stub* in the text if you don't know where to begin.) Given the existence today of words like *Cranapple*, do you now want to claim the existence of a morpheme *cran*? What would that morpheme mean and what would the morphemic analysis of the word *cranberry* be? If we didn't claim *cran* was a morpheme by itself, what else could it be in a word like *Cranapple*? Discuss the possible role of clipping here.

2. What problems for morphological analysis does the word *peppercorn* bring up? (Hint: The issues here are similar in some ways to those you just discussed in 1.)

3. Analyze the following words into component morphemes:

    ridiculous   inconsistent   walked   happy   morbid

(a) Classify each morpheme as lexical, derivational, or inflectional.

(b) Classify each morpheme as free or bound.

(c) For each bound morpheme you identify, give at least two other words in which the same morpheme occurs.

4. Analyze the following words into component morphemes:

    frenzy   linguist   shepherd   raspberry   geese

(a) Classify each morpheme as lexical, derivational, or inflectional.

(b) Classify each morpheme as free or bound.

(c) For each bound morpheme you identify, give at least one other word in which the same morpheme occurs.

(d) This group of words is more complicated to discuss than the group in 3. Pick one of these words and discuss the complexities involved in identifying its lexical morpheme.

(e) Pick another of these words and discuss the complexities involved in identifying its inflectional morpheme.

(f) Pick another of these words and discuss the complexities involved in identifying its derivational morpheme.

(g) Two of these words can be analyzed as consisting of two lexical morphemes. That is, two can be seen as compounds. Discuss whether or not their stress patterns give evidence one way or the other.

5. In the text we saw that the reversal *un-* can attach to verbs, but not to nouns or adjectives. We see this *un-* in examples such as:

untie/tie   undress/dress   unburden/burden   unlearn/learn

Consider the word *unhand*, as in:

Unhand that child!

With respect to semantics, what complications does this verb present?

6. Consider the *-en* of *kitten* and *vixen*. What does it indicate in each word? Do you believe this is a single suffix, or two different, homophonous suffixes? Why? Classify this (these) suffix(es).

7. Discuss one nonlexical and nonevaluative morpheme of English for which classifying it as inflectional or derivational is not very helpful. (It's your job to find an appropriate morpheme. This is not an easy task, since you will probably have to go through several morphemes before you come upon one that fits the bill. So perhaps you'd like to do this as a paper topic rather than as part of a problem set.)

8. Consider the discourse:

—Where's Paul?
—He's coming.

In casual speech the second sentence might be reduced to:

—'s comin'.

In the text, I claimed that within a prosodic word, lexical morphemes cannot have a zero phonetic realization, and I suggested furthermore that this generalization follows naturally from the fact that we need lexical morphemes in order to interpret our words. How does this second answer to the question about Paul's location challenge my claim? What strategies do we use to interpret the zero lexical morpheme in such cases? NOTE: *-'s comin'* also presents an interesting question for the theory of clitics, which is taken up in Problem Set 3.9.)

9. Analyze the word *exotic* into its component morphemes. Why is this word interesting from a morphological point of view?

10. Consider the irregular past verbs:

   leapt   dreamt

How is past tense conveyed here? (Be careful: These verbs present a complication that goes beyond our discussion of irregular pasts in the text. You might need to transcribe them into IPA to see it.) What issues for our classification of affix types (prefix, suffix, infix, circumfix, interfix) are raised by such irregular pasts?

11. Consider the first stanza of the poem "Jabberwocky":

> 'Twas brillig, and the slithy toves
> Did gyre and gimble in the wabe:
> All mimsy were the borogoves,
> And the mome raths outgrabe.

   Identify the appropriate category (noun, verb, adjective, adverb, preposition) for each of the following words:

   slithy   borogoves   outgrabe

Give at least one argument based on morphology for each of your answers.

12. Consider the suffix -*ward*, as in:

   backward   upward   heavenward   homeward   eastward

   (a) Make a list of as many words that use -*ward* as you can.
   (b) If you can, state a morphosyntactic restriction on the stem to which -*ward* can attach. If you can't, explain why you can't.
   (c) Now look at the sense of the stems to which -*ward* can attach. Come up with a semantic generalization about them.

13. Consider these pairs of words:

   flammable inflammable   peel unpeel

and some people even allow both of these:

   regardless   irregardless

What's the issue here? What do the prefixes *in-*, *un-*, and *ir-* contribute to the sense of the words they appear in here? Why do you think this can happen?
   Consider now the following pairs of words:

   dress undress   strip unstrip

Which pair do you think is a likely candidate to become SYNONYMS and which is not? Why?

Now consider the pair:

ravel   unravel

Look them up in a dictionary. *Ravel* is ambiguous and its two meanings are ANTONYMS (the opposite) of each other. Discuss how this situation might have come about. (You will be conjecturing here, but given what you've learned from the rest of this particular problem, your conjecture should be an educated one.)

14. Consider the word *whosever* in this sentence:

Tell whosever on the phone that I'm not home.

Not all speakers of English can say this, but many can. For those who can, discuss the morphological status of the "s."

14. Give at least one argument for and one argument against analyzing the -*th* of *depth* as a morpheme. (Hint: Remember the claim that within morphemes the sonority hierarchy is a metric for syllable organization.)

Problem Set 3.4: Basic Issues of Word Formation: Other Languages

1. In Figure 3.4 you see the ASL signs for (A) FARMER, (B) DENTIST, (C) POSTAL CARRIER, (D) GROCER, (E) BARBER, and (F) SANITATION WORKER.

(a) Isolate a morpheme that is common to all these signs. What does that morpheme mean?

(b) What effect does that morpheme have on the category of the sign(s) it "attaches to"?

(c) Guess at the signs for FARM, HAIRCUT, TEETH, LETTER, and FOOD. (You will probably not be exactly right on some or maybe any of them, but I bet you will come close.)

(d) Can the morpheme you isolated in (a) attach to both verbs and nouns or to only one? Argue for your answer.

(e) Do you think the morpheme you isolated in (a) is an affix or a root? (In other words, is a sign like FARMER a compound or not?) Give at least one argument for your answer. If you say this morpheme is an affix, is it derivational, or inflectional? Support your answer with at least one argument. (NOTE: I am not suggesting it is an affix. I am merely asking you to expound on whatever answer you give.)

(f) In fact, the morpheme you isolated in (a) can appear as an independent sign meaning PERSON. Given this fact, does your answer in (e) still hold? Explain why or why not.

NOTE: Not all varieties of ASL use the morpheme in (a) for all the six signs given in Figure 3.4. If you know some other variety of ASL, you might want to analyze the signs for TEACHER, PREACHER, INTERPRETER, HUNTER, COUNSELOR, STUDENT, and THERAPIST, instead.

2. Spanish has a range of evaluative affixes, just as Italian does (discussed in the text). Consider just these two suffixes:

Augmentative -ot:

N: angel 'angel'   angelote 'sweetie'
V: bailar 'to dance'   bailotear 'to dance around informally'

Diminutive -et:

N: aro 'hoop'   areta 'earring'
V: correr 'to run'   corretear 'to run around/loiter'

How do they offer a challenge to the Unitary Base Hypothesis?

3. Here is a list of Nominative singular and plural nouns in one variety of Bulgarian (the data in this section of the problem are due to Roumyana Izvorski, who kindly discussed the issues presented by them with me):

Data Set A:

Singular	Plural	
cvjat	cvetové	'flower'
grad	gradové	'town'
glas	glasové	'voice'
noʒ	noʒóve	'knife'
most	mostóve	'bridge'
dvor	dvórove	'yard'
slon	slónove	'elephant'
pən	pənove	'log'
pop	popóve	'priest'
bor	bórove	'pine tree'
vjátər	vetrove	'wind'

(a) What is the plural morpheme? Where does it attach? (Please don't concern yourself with any root-internal vowel alternations.)

(b) Propose a rule to deal with the loss of the last root vowel in the plural for 'wind.'

Now consider these Nominative singular nouns:

Data Set B:

cvetʧé	'small or sweet or tender flower'
gradʧé	'small or pretty or boring town'
glasʧe	'small or tender or sweet voice'
noʒʧe	'small knife'
mostʧe	'small bridge'
dvorʧe	'small or cute yard'
slonʧe	'small or sweet elephant'
pənʧe	'small log'
popʧe	'very young or inexperienced priest'
borʧe	'small pine tree'

(c) Compare Data Sets A and B. What type of morpheme is *-ʧe* in terms of its sense? Where does it attach? What does it attach to? (If you have trouble figuring out what this

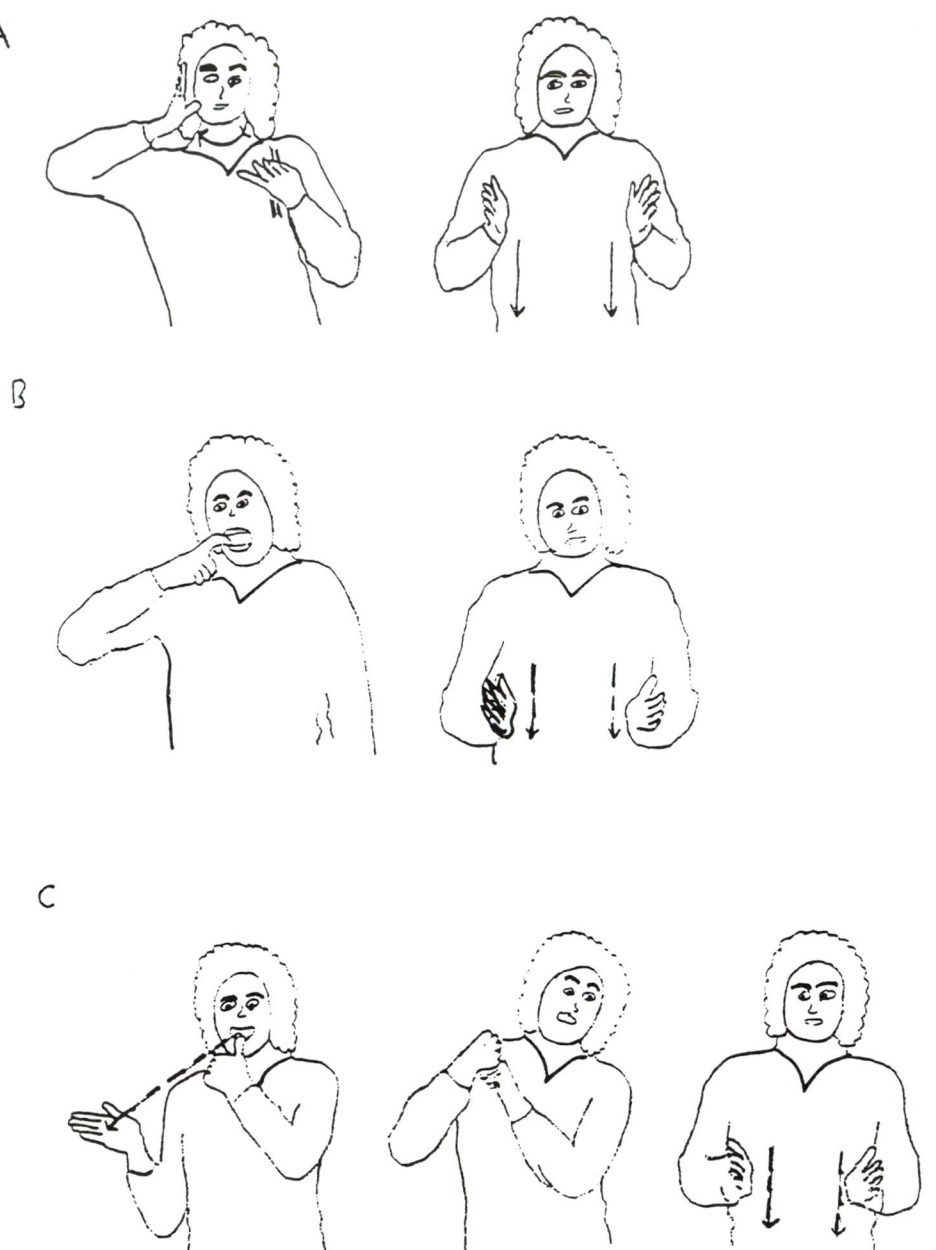

Figure 3.4 Six signs of ASL, with attention to morphological makeup.

last question is getting at, look at the word for 'flower' in the singular and plural. Consider the stem in each form. Which stem does -*tfe* attach to?)

(d) For your information, the forms with -*tfe* in Data Set B are all neuter, even though these nouns are masculine without this suffix. What might this fact suggest about which element, the root or the suffix, is the head of the word?

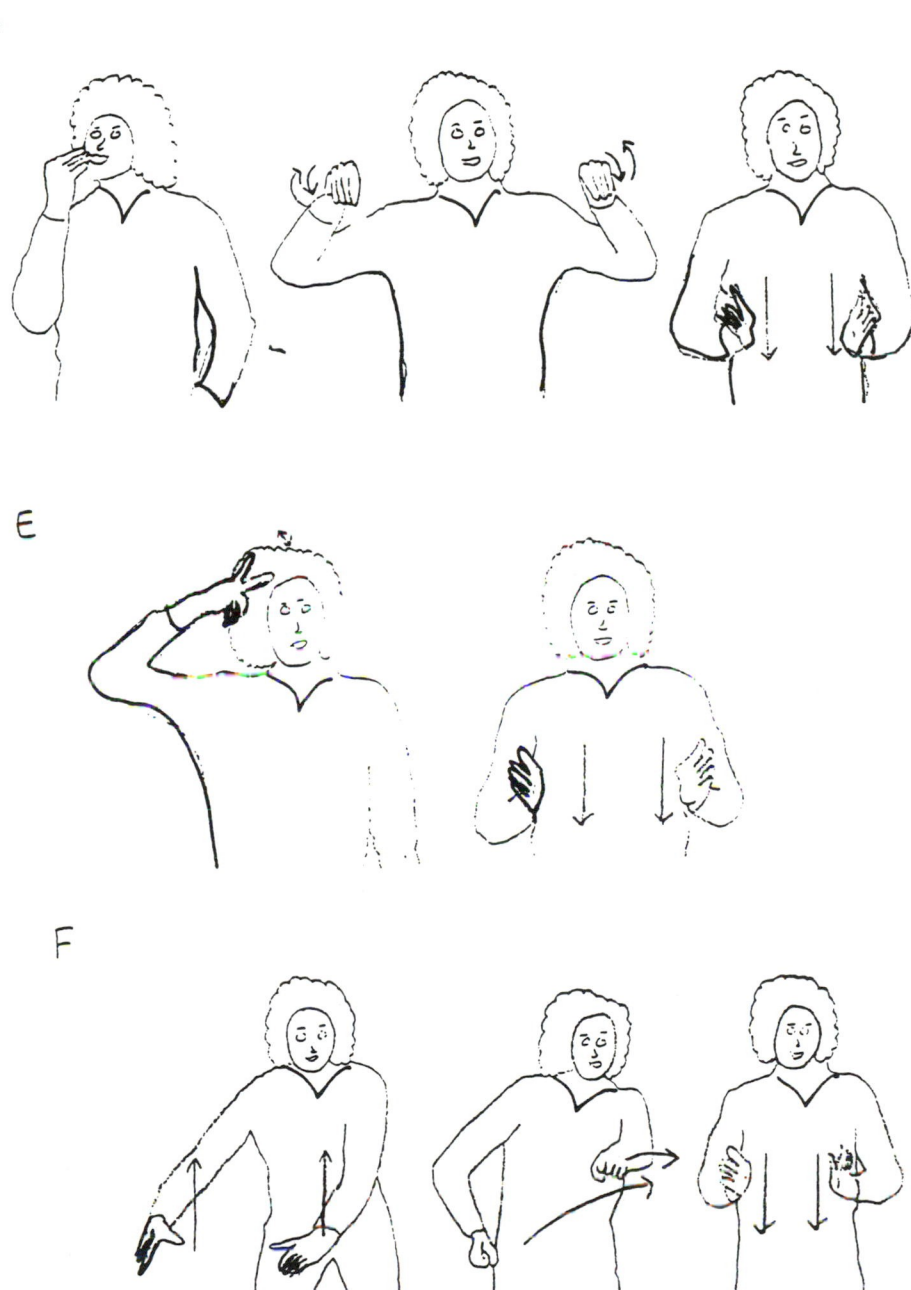

Figure 3.4 (continued).

Now consider the Nominative plural forms of the nouns in Data Set B:

Data Set C:

cvetʧeta
gradʧeta
glasʧeta
noʒʧeta
mostʧeta
dvorʧeta
slonʧeta
pənʧeta
popʧeta
borʧeta

(e) The roots here have had two morphemes attached. What are they? What might be responsible for the difference between the plural morpheme in the first data set and the plural morpheme here?

(f) What order do the morphemes you identified in (e) come in? Did you expect this order? Explain your answer. (If you don't know where to begin here, go back and look at the generalizations in the text about typical differences between derivational and inflectional affixes. I am not suggesting that you shouldn't have expected the order here; this is not a trick question. I'm just asking you to try to develop some expectations.)

Now consider these other nouns, which form their simple plurals (in the second column) differently from the nouns in Data Set A. All of these forms are Nominative again:

Data Set D:

Singular	*Plural*	*Singular*	*Plural*	
bonbon	bonboni	bonbonʧe	bonbonʧeta	'candy'
kon	kone	konʧe	konʧeta	'horse'
brat	bratja	bratʧe	bratʧeta	'brother'

(g) Would you have predicted the forms in Columns 3 and 4? Why or why not?

Now consider this paradigm for a different variety of Bulgarian, reported in Cowan and Rakušan (1987:116):

Data Set E:

cvet	cvetove	cvetec	cvetovce	'flower'
grad	gradove	gradec	gradovce	'town'
veter	vetrove	vetrec	vetrovce	'wind'

As in Data Set D, Column 2 gives the plural forms for Column 1, and Column 4 gives the plural forms for Column 3.

(h) Will the rule you proposed in (b) account for the forms *vetrove* and *vetrec*? If not, revise it so it will. If it already does, show how it does.

(i) The roots in Column 4 have two morphemes attached. Many questions arise as to the correct analysis of the forms here. Discuss at least two possible analyses for the forms in Column 4. Do we need to add a new kind of affix to our list of prefix, suffix, infix, circumfix, interfix, and superfix?

(j) Contrast the data in Column 4 to the data in Data Set C and to the data in Column 4 of Data Set D. In this regard consider again question (f). What major difference do you find between this variety of Bulgarian and the variety seen in Data Sets A–D? What principle of morphological theory is at issue here?

4. Consider these forms of the Japanese verbs for 'cut' and 'read':

Data Set A:

kire 'cut!'	yome 'read!'
kiru 'cuts'	yomu 'reads'
kitta 'cut' (past)	yonda 'read' (past)
kiraseru 'causes to cut'	yomaseru 'causes to read'
kirareru 'is cut'	yomareru 'is read'
kiraseta 'caused to cut'	yomaseta 'caused to read'
kirareta 'was cut'	yomareta 'was read'
kiraserareta 'was caused to cut'	yomaserareta 'was caused to read'

(I translated with the third-person singular form in English, but, actually, the Japanese forms have no person or number morpheme on them.)

(a) List two allomorphs of the past-tense morpheme. (There are eight verb forms in the past tense here. Please consider all eight.) What is the UR of this morpheme? Give one argument for your answer.

(b) List two allomorphs of the passive-voice morpheme. (There are six verb forms in the passive voice here. Again, please consider all six.) What is the UR of this morpheme? Give one argument for your answer.

(c) Just based on these data, what is the causative morpheme? (There are six verb forms in the causative here. Please consider all six.)

Now consider these data:

Data Set B:

miru 'sees'
mita 'saw'
mirareru 'is seen'
misaseru 'causes to see'
misaserareru 'causes to be seen'

(d) In light of these new data, what are the two allomorphs for the causative and what is the UR of this morpheme? Give one argument for your answer.

(e) Go back now and make sure that your answers to (a) and (b) are consistent with the data in Data Set B. If they aren't, change them now to make them consistent.

(f) What is the UR of the present-tense morpheme? (Be sure to consider all the data here.)

(g) Give the root morphemes meaning 'cut,' 'read,' and 'see.'

(h) In general, what happens to an affix-initial [r] when it is preceded by a C? Give the derivation of one verbal form in Data Set A or B in which this rule takes place.

(i) In general, what happens to an affix-initial [s] when it is preceded by a C? Give the derivation of one verbal form in Data Set A or B in which this rule takes place.

(j) What keeps you from being able to collapse the rules you described in (h) and (i) into a rule applying to any affix-initial C preceded by a C?

(k) Given the data here, classify Japanese as isolative, agglutinative, inflective, incorporating, or infixing-templatic.

5. In Tamil there are eight different Cases in the nominal system. The Nominative is generally used for Subjects; the Accusative for Direct Objects; the Dative for Indirect Objects; the Sociative for accompaniment; the Genitive for possession; the Instrumental for causes or instruments; the Locative for location; and the Ablative for a range of other senses such as purpose, goal, reason, etc. Consider these paradigms for the noun meaning 'man':

	Singular	*Plural:*
Nominative:	maNitaN	maNitarkaḷ
Accusative:	maNitaNai	maNitarkaḷai
Dative:	maNitaNukku	maNitarkaḷukku
Sociative:	maNitaNōṭu	maNitarkaḷōṭu
Genitive:	maNitaNuṭaija	maNitarkaḷuṭaija
Instrumental:	maNitaNāl	maNitarkaḷāl
Locative:	maNitaNiṭam	maNitarkaḷiṭam
Ablative:	maNitaNiṭamiruntu	maNitarkaḷiṭamiruntu

(The symbol "N" here is used to mean a nasal which is fully determined by its context.) Compare the paradigm for 'man' to the paradigm for the noun meaning 'flower':

	Singular	*Plural:*
Nominative:	pū	pūkkaḷ
Accusative:	pūvai	pūkkaḷai
Dative:	pūvukku	pūkkaḷukku
Sociative:	pūvōṭu	pūkkaḷōṭu
Genitive:	pūvuṭaija	pūkkaḷuṭaija
Instrumental:	pūvāl	pūkkaḷāl
Locative:	pūvil	pūkkaḷil
Ablative:	pūviliruntu	pūkkaḷiliruntu

(a) Give the morphemes for these Cases: Accusative, Dative, Sociative, Genitive, and Instrumental.

(b) What is the relationship between the Locative and the Ablative morphemes? What are the two Locative morphemes?

(c) In Tamil, many scholars say the singular uses one stem and the plural uses a different stem. Please take that approach for a moment. Give the stem for each of these two nouns in the singular. Give the stem for each of these two nouns in the plural.

(d) If I were to claim that the stem for each number is either the root of the Nominative or of the Accusative form, which one would it have to be (Nominative or Accusative)? Why?

(e) Now assume instead that there is one root for both singular and plural and that there is a plural morpheme. What is the plural morpheme?

(f) With the analysis in (e), what is the root for the noun meaning 'flower'? Account for the distribution of the forms *pūv* and *pūk*.

(g) When more than one Case morpheme is added to the root, what order do they come in?

(h) Just based on these data, classify Tamil as isolative, agglutinative, inflective, incorporating, or infixing-templatic.

Now consider the paradigm for the noun 'tree':

	Singular	*Plural*
Nominative:	maram	maraŋkaḷ
Accusative:	marattai	maraŋkaḷai
Dative:	marattukku	maraŋkaḷukku
Sociative:	marattōṭu	maraŋkaḷōṭu
Genitive:	marattuṭaija	maraŋkaḷuṭaija
Instrumental:	marattāl	maraŋkaḷāl
Locative:	marattil	maraŋkaḷil
Ablative:	marattiliruntu	maraŋkaḷiliruntu

(g) Are your answers to (b) and (d) consistent with these new data? If not, change them now to make them consistent.

Problem Set 3.5: Issues in English morphology

1. Consider the English verbs *walk*, *giggle*, and *clash*. In your head, go through their paradigms for all persons and numbers in the simple present tense (for example: *I walk*) and the simple past tense (for example: *I walked*).

(a) In what person(s), number(s), and tense(s) do we hear an agreement morpheme (agreement being between the Subject and the verb)?

(b) There are three allomorphs of the morpheme you identified in (a). What are they? What phonological factors condition the appearance of each one? (That is, give the environment for each one.)

(c) Argue for an UR of the morpheme you identified in (a). Give the rules which will produce the other two allomorphs.

(d) Consider the simple present and simple past paradigms for the verb *be*. In what person(s), number(s), and tense(s) do we hear an agreement morpheme?

(e) In light of (d), would you say that the person(s), number(s), and tense(s) that do not exhibit a phonetically audible agreement morpheme in regular verbs such as *walk*, *giggle*, and *clash* actually do not have any agreement going on, or that the agreement morpheme here just turns out to be phonetically null? Why?

2. Consider the regular agreement morpheme you identified in (1c) with all its allomorphs—which you listed in (1a). There are two other morphemes in English that are homophonous with this morpheme and that have the same range of allomorphs in the same phonological contexts.

(a) What are they? Give example words to show the three allomorphs of each.

(b) There is potential for two of the homophonous morphemes you identified in (a) to co-occur in the same word. What happens when they do? Give three example words to make your point, in which the three words supply the different contexts for the different allomorphs —which you discussed in (1b). Did you expect this? Why or why not?

(c) English has a range of irregular plural forms, some of which you looked at in Problem Set 3.2. Can any of these irregular plurals co-occur in a word with another inflectional affix? If so, give examples.

(d) Consider the word *series* as in *There's a new series on TV*. The plural of this word is still *series*, as in *There are two new series this season*. Discuss the implications of this fact. Can you think of any other nouns in English that behave the same way? If so, give them. If not, contrast how *series* behaves in comparison to how *scissors* or *shorts* behaves with respect to number. (If you don't see the contrast, put these words in sentences where you are referring to one object and then in other sentences where you are referring to two objects. You'll see the difference.)

3. English does not have irregular Genitive nominal forms except in the pronominal system, where we find nouns like *mine* and *his*, as in:

Mine is in the drawer. His is on the table.

(a) Is *hers* an irregular or a regular Genitive nominal form? That is, did you expect this form if you had simply added the productive Genitive affix to the pronominal root? Explain your answer by giving the pronominal form you take to be the stem for affixation and discussing why you think that form is the proper one. (We did not discuss this issue in the text of this chapter, so you are on your own here. But if you did the question on Tamil in Problem Set 3.4, you may already have some sense of which Case form of a nominal is likely to show us the root that is used in derivation.)

(b) Is a form like *theirs* or *yours*, as in:

Theirs is older than yours.

irregular in any way? That is, is this the form you'd expect if the productive Genitive had attached? Make sure your answer here is consistent with your discussion in (a).

4. Discuss whether the "s" in the compound *bullseye* is a plural marker or a Genitive marker or neither. Is there a way to distinguish between the two? If it were a plural or Genitive marker, why would this compound be unusual?

5. You are going to try to figure out when we use *-er* to form a comparative adjective in English, and when we instead put the word *more* in front of the adjective. Begin by studying these four lists:

List A:

taller   bluer   nicer   sicker   wiser   sweeter   smarter   younger
rounder   wider   longer   swifter   fatter

List B:

prettier   smellier   yellower   sallower   littler   narrower   brittler
giddier

List C:

*insaner	*jejuner	*lambenter	*risquér	*decenter	*gnarleder
*privater	*liquider	*sanguiner	*ribalder		

List D:

*beautifuler	*intelligenter	*interestinger	*phenomenaler
*ridiculouser	*provocativer	*proteaner	*insipider

(a) What do all the words in List A have in common before we add on *-er* that distinguishes them from the words in the other three lists? What do all the words in List D have in common before we add on *-er* that distinguishes them from the words in the other three lists? Give a statement about when we use *-er* and when we use *more* that will cover the adjectives in these two lists only. (Don't worry about Lists C and D yet.)

(b) What do the words in Lists B and C have in common before we add on *-er* that distinguishes them from the words in Lists A and D?

(c) What factors of their phonological shape do the words in Lists B and C differ on? You should state this in terms of a description of the words in List B that will exclude the words in List C. (Be careful to look closely at all the words. Note that *risqué* is on List C, not List B. Make sure your statement takes account of that fact. If you are having trouble, remember that English is quantity sensitive for stress assignment, and the foot is the moraic trochee.)

(d) Using the theory of prosodic morphology, give a statement about when we use *-er* and when we use *more* that will generally cover the adjectives in all four lists. Your statement may well not cover every example to your satisfaction. Note the problematic cases for your statement and explain briefly why they are problematic. (And don't feel bad about the lack of neatness here. Most of morphology is not perfectly neat.)

(e) Why are the adjectives in List E problematic for your statement in (d)?

List E:

*butcher	*righter	*wronger	*flyer

If you aren't familiar with the first and last words on this list, consult a teenager. Here are example sentences using them:

Rachel's more butch than Susan.
Their newest CD is more fly than their last one.

(Actually, some people can say *butcher*, but others can't. So answer this question considering the speech of those who can't.)

(f) Is either or both of the adjectives in List F problematic for your statement in (d)?

List F:

*cleverer	*silverer

(I expect one of them to be.) If either (or both) is (are), can you offer an account of why adjectives like *clever* and *silver* can't take *-er*? (It may help if you first transcribe the ill-formed words on List F.)

(g) Is the adjective in List G problematic for your statement in (d)?

List G:

stupider

If you can, indeed, say *stupider* (as I can), and if you have any idea of why *stupid* can take *-er*, please offer that idea for your teacher's scrutiny.

(h) Consider the adjectives in List H:

List H:

*lithesomer   awesomer

Did you expect *lithesome* and *awesome* to form their comparative in the same way? If so, did you expect them to take *-er* or to be preceded by *more*? If you're not sure which, transcribe these two words without *er* to see if they match the statement you came up with in (c) for the phonological shape of words on List B. Many young people can say *awesomer* today (although everyone can, I believe, also say *more awesome*). If you can find someone who says *awesomer*, listen to that person and see if that person's pronunciation would place *awesome* in List B or List C.

6. One might try to account for the fact that *-er* can occur with words like those in Lists A and B, but not with words like those in Lists C and D, with a Lexical Phonology-Morphology solution along the following lines. *-er* would be a Level I suffix. Therefore it could not follow the addition of a Level II suffix. Hence, it could not attach to *beautiful*, for example, since *-ful* is a Level II affix.

Give at least two (and, if you can, three) ways in which such a Lexical Phonology-Morphology account of the distribution of comparative *-er* is empirically inadequate.

7. The comparative in 5 is not the only type of comparative we use. Sometimes even the words on Lists A and B must be preceded by *more*. Compare these two sentences:

Milton is slimmer than Susan.
Milton is more slim than skinny. (Cf. *Milton is slimmer than skinny.)

We call the the comparative in the second example a METACOMPARATIVE. Come up with three other pairs of sentences in which one uses the regular comparative and the other uses the metacomparative. Give a brief statement of what the general meaning difference is between a regular comparative and a metacomparative.

8. How does *unhappier* present a bracketing paradox? Give the two bracketings and the reasons for each. Please make use of the information you have learned in this problem set.

9. Consider these words:

cats   rips

(a) Transcribe these words.

(b) The sonority hierarchy can be thought of as a principle for syllable organization. Is the sonority hierarchy operative only within a morpheme or across morpheme boundaries? Why? Support your answer with additional examples of your own.

(c) Now argue whether written "th" in words like the following is a morpheme or not:

fifty-ninth   one-hundredth   one-thousandth

(d) Consider the words:

ripped   kicked

Transcribe them. These monosyllabic words violate a phonotactic constraint on syllable structure that we have not yet discussed. State that phonotactic constraint informally. Why can that constraint be violated in words such as these?

10. In the text we looked at several properties of suffixes. Here I'd like you to look at prefixes.
(a) What are the heads of the following morphologically complex words?

empower   indiscreet

Argue for your analysis. Give several other words that use the same prefixes as part of your argument.
(b)   How is the word *denude* problematic? (If you don't see the point, consider the fact that we have many words like *devalue* and *deregulate*, but we do not find words like *depretty* or *declever*.)
(c) Consider these words:

disregard   disrespect

They are categorially ambiguous. What does that tell you about the prefix *dis-*? Given that, does this word surprise you at all?

dishonest

And given all the data on *dis-* here, are you surprised at:

discourage

Why?
And, finally, discuss the use of *diss* as a verb by itself as in:

You dissin' me again?

Does anything you've learned about the properties of this prefix help to account for the fact that it has been freed (whereas, it was a bound morpheme before)?
(d) Some have claimed that prefixes do not select the category to which they attach, unlike suffixes. Argue that this claim is false and give counterexamples, using some prefix other than negative *un-*.
(e) What new issues do examples like these raise for morphological theory?

encapsulate   encounter   endive   embolden

(NOTE: *Endive* is a joke. Sorry.) Do examples like these have any impact on the Adjacency Condition?

11. In English we have a prefix *out* that attaches to verbs, like so:

> Paul ran.
> Paul outran Peter.
> Paul ate pizza.
> Paul outate Peter.

But notice that we don't say:

> *Paul outate pizza Peter.

Discuss the effect that *out-* has on the argument structure of the verb stem it attaches to.

12. Consider the italicized words in these sentences:

> (1) Mind your *elders*.
> (2) She does childcare and *eldercare* right in her house.

Is the *-er* of *elder* a derivational or an inflectional affix? Give at least two reasons for your answer. (If you don't know where to begin, consider two facts. First, in the word *elders*, the *-er* is followed by the affix *-s*. Think about the type of affix this *-s* is and ask yourself how English behaves in general when it has more than one suffix in a single word. Second, in the word *eldercare* we have two lexical roots. Consider what kind of word *eldercare* therefore must be. Then consider the typical restrictions we have in English on that kind of word.)

Problem Set 3.6: Typological Distinctions and Incorporating Languages

1. Just based on the very slight data here, classify these languages as isolative, agglutinative, inflective, incorporating, or infixing-templatic.

> (A) Rumanian: Om-ul   spal-ă   cal-ul.
>   man-MSDef wash-3SPres horse-MSDef
>   'The man washes the horse.'

(Def = definite; M = masculine; S = singular; Pres = present tense; 3 = third person)

> (B) Vietnamese: đêm qua ra đú'ng bò'   ao
>   night last go stand edge pond
>   'Last night I went to stand on the edge of the pond.'

> (C) Onondaga: Hati-hnek-aets   o-v:ta:k-iʔ
>   3MP-liquid-gather PRE-syrup-SUF
>   'They gather maple syrup.'

(PRE = prefix; SUF = suffix)

    (D) Tigré: qatla 'to kill'
               qa:tala 'to do some killing'
               ʔaqa:tala 'to cause to do some killing'
               qata:tala 'to kill now and then'

Rumanian is a Romance language spoken in Romania. Onondaga is an Iroquoian language spoken in southern Ontario. Tigré is a Semitic language spoken in northern Ethiopia. For the last verb in D, my source did not give a gloss. I am guessing at the gloss based on the translation of other verbs in the source.

    (E) Ecuadorian Quechua: maqa-chi   naku-rka-n
                              beat-CAUSE Rec-P-3
                              'They let each other be beaten.'

(Rec = reciprocal; CAUSE = causative)

2. Consider these two sentences from Basque:

    Edalontzi-a   apurtu   da.
    glass-DefCASE break-Perf 3SAux
    'The glass has broken'
    Jon-ek   edalontzi-a   apurtu   du.
    Jon-CASE glass-DefCASE break-Perf 3SAux
    'Jon has broken the glass.'

(Don't worry about the difference between *da* and *du*; it doesn't concern us here.) The suffixes *-a* and *-ek* are Case markers on nouns. Based on just these two sentences, would you classify Basque as a Nominative-Accusative or Ergative-Absolutive language? Why?

3. Give a sentence of English that would make someone who didn't know English believe it was isolative.
    Now give another sentence to make that person believe English is agglutinative.
    Now give another sentence to make that person believe English is inflective.
    Now give a fourth sentence to make that person believe English is incorporating.
    Now give a paradigm to make that person believe English is infixing-templatic.

4. Consider these two sentences from Nahuatl:

    Neʔ ø-panci-teteʔki ika kotʃillo.
    he   3S-bread-cut   with knife
    'He cut the bread with a knife.'
    Yaʔ ki-kotʃillo-teteʔki panci.
    he   3S-knife-cut   bread
    'He cut the bread with a knife.'

(The ø in initial position of *ø-panci-teteʔki* represents a zero morpheme indicating third person singular agreement.)

(a) Just based on these sentences, classify Nahuatl as isolative, agglutinative, inflective, incorporating, or infixing-templatic.

(b) What does the choice of the pronoun for 'he' seem to depend on?

(c) What does the choice of the Subject-Verb agreement morpheme seem to depend on?

5. Give a sentence of English in which the verb seems to have incorporated into it the theme argument.

Give a sentence of English in which the verb seems to have incorporated into it the instrument argument.

Give a sentence of English in which the verb seems to have incorporated into it the locative argument.

6. Consider these word-sentences from Ahtna, a northern Athapascan language.

(1) natadghitaan 'Water dripped down.'
(2) nixałnitaan 'He stopped the sled.'
(3) qetajdeztaan 'Water caused it to drift ashore.'

In 1 *na* = 'down'; *ta* = 'water.' In 2 ni = 'cessation'; xał = 'sled.' In 3 *qe* = 'ashore.' (These are not pure IPA transcriptions, but they are as close as I know how to translate from my sources. I believe the "aa" is [a:].)

(a) Assume that *taan* is an uninflected verb stem—without prejudice yet as to whether it is monomorphemic or polymorphemic: we will discuss that in (j)—and the same verb stem in all three sentences. What do you think it means?

(b) If you think of this word-sentence as having slots for different morphemes, what type of morpheme goes into the first slot on the left? Be sure to consider the effect of this morpheme on the sense of the verb.

(c) What type of morpheme goes into the second slot on the left? What does this tell us about the classification of Ahtna?

(d) Give the sense of the phonetic material in brackets:

   nata[dghi]taan   nixał[ni]taan   qeta[jdez]taan

If this material in each case were to be a single morpheme (a different morpheme in each word, of course), what kind of morpheme would it be: lexical, derivational, or inflectional? Please give a short discussion; don't just give a single-word answer.

(e) How is your answer to (d) surprising, given what you know about the normal ordering of different kinds of morphemes within a word?

Now consider these additional word-sentences:

(4) nik'aji'aan 'He lifted it up.'
(5) ilaq'ejghi'aan 'He handed it to him.'

In 5 *ilaq'e* = 'Into the hand of.'

(f) Assume both of these sentences use the same verb stem *'aan*. What do you think *'aan* means?

(g) Assume *j* is a morpheme with a constant meaning in 4 and 5. What might *j* mean?

Give an argument for your answer. Do you think this is the same *j* we saw in 3? Why or why not?

(h) Assume *nik'a* is a single morpheme. What might *nik'a* mean?

(i) Now compare the two verb stems *taan* and *'aan* from the two sets of sentences. What do they have in common semantically? What distinguishes them semantically from one another?

(j) Do you think each of these verb stems might be polymorphemic? If so, why? Refer to your answer in (i).

NOTE: Question (j) is asking for conjecture, and it may well be leading you to an incorrect proposal, given that the *n* at the end of each verb is actually of different status. The verb *taan* ends in "n" and in this sentence a suffix *-n* is added, but that suffix deletes after a verb that ends in "n". The verb *'aa* ends in a vowel and in this sentence the same suffix *-n* is added. But now that suffix is not deleted.

Nevertheless, I ask for your conjecture because this is the sort of thing you should be sensitive to as you delve into the morphology of any language.

*Problem Set 3.7: Prosodic Morphology

1. In the text we learned that in the Nicaraguan language Ulwa, the morpheme *-ka-* indicates that a noun is possessed, and it can occur as an infix, as in:

Root	Possessed form	
siwanak	siwakanak	'root'
su:lu	su:kalu	'dog'
ana:la:ka	ana:kala:ka	'chin'
kuhbil	kuhkabil	'knife'
karasmak	karaskamak	'knee'

But it can also occur as a suffix, as in:

Root	Possessed form	
bas	baska	'hair'
sana	sanaka	'deer'
sapa:	sapa:ka	'forehead'
al	alka	'man'
ki:	ki:ka	'stone'
amak	amakka	'bee'

Here I'd like you to come up with a single statement of where *-ka-* attaches, by going through the following steps.

(a) Syllabify all the roots and all the possessed forms.

(b) Must the phonological material preceding *-ka-* be taken into account in your statement of where *-ka-* attaches? Must the phonological material following *-ka-* be taken into account in your statement of where *-ka-* attaches? Explain your answers.

(c) Make a list of the syllables that can precede the *-ka-* affix. What is the lower limit on the number of syllables that can precede *-ka-*? What is the upper limit on the number of syllables that can precede *-ka-*?

(d) Mark the syllable or syllable sequences that can precede -*ka*- as light or heavy. You should come up with three possible sequences in terms of syllable types that can precede -*ka*-.

(e) What prosodic unit covers the three possible sequences you identified in (d)?

(f) What do you guess is the foot type used in assigning stress in Ulwa?

(g) Give a statement of -*ka*-'s placement that makes use of the prosodic unit you identified in (e).

2. Below we find verbs in Mokilese (an Oceanic language of Micronesia) in which the progressive aspect form (the form for 'be V-ing') is derived from the root:

Root	Progressive aspect	
/podok/	/podpodok/	'plant'
/mʷiŋe/	/mʷiŋmʷiŋe/	'eat'
/kaso/	/kaskaso/	'throw'
/wadek/	/wadwadek/	'read'

(a) What kind of word formation process is this an example of?

(b) Is the newly formed prosodic material attached to the left or right of the root?

(c) Based on just these four examples, state the two possible prosodic units that the newly formed material could be characterized as in terms of a syllable type. (That is, is the newly formed material a core syllable, a light syllable, a heavy syllable, or a syllable that gathers all the segmental material it can?)

(d) Consider the proposals that the prosodic unit that the newly formed material is characterized as is (1) a foot or (2) a prosodic word. Can you evaluate the validity of these proposals with only the information I've given you here? If so, evaluate them. If not, what other information would you need in order to evaluate them?

Now consider these additional data:

Root	Progressive aspect	
/pa/	/pa:pa/	'weave'
/wia/	/wi:wia/	'do'
/diar/	/di:diar/	'find'

Assume (as always) that every short vowel is syllabic unless it is marked as nonsyllabic.

(e) Explain how these data are significantly different from the first set of data.

(f) How does the second set of data eliminate one of the two possible prosodic units you identified in (c)? What, then, is the correct prosodic unit for characterizing the newly formed material?

(g) What is the process by which we arrive at the long vowels in the progressive forms of the verbs in the second set of data?

(h) Give the derivations of /kaskaso/ and /di:diar/. (Look back to the derivation of *agtrabtrabaho* in the text for a model.) NOTE: There are other complications in the progressive in Mokilese that I have chosen to overlook here.

3. Consider these instances of reduplication in Luiseño:

ʔváva	'be red	ʔaváʔvaš	'pink'
máha	'to stop'	mahámhaš	'slow'

Here phonological rules have interacted with the reduplication process. Do not let that throw you off. The issue I want you to address is the semantic effect of reduplication that you can see in just these two examples. What is that effect? Discuss this effect in light of the types of effects that you know reduplication can have based on this problem set and on the remarks in the text of this chapter.

4. Consider these verb forms from the Semitic language Amharic, which is spoken in Ethiopia:

	'Dress'	*'Open'*
perfect:	läbbäsä	käffätä
imperfective:	yɨläbsal	yɨkäftal
gerund:	läbso	käfto
jussive:	yɨlbäs	yɨkfät
infinitive:	mälbäs	mäkfät

(a) Identify the consonantal roots for 'dress' and 'open.'

(b) Identify one circumfix.

(c) Identify two prefixes.

(d) Identify one suffix.

(e) Argue that the vowel [ä] (regardless of how many times it occurs in a given form) is not part of the lexical roots, but instead goes with all the tense morphemes.

(f) The template for the infinitive is:

mä + CCVC

(NOTE: If you had analyzed the prefix as simply *m-*, with the vowel here being the same vowel that goes with all tenses, that's okay. There is no information here that would have indicated otherwise. So don't worry. Likewise, the final [ä] of the perfect form could be analyzed as a suffix or as the vowel that goes with all tenses. In fact, scholars of Amharic analyze this [ä] as a suffix. But nothing here could have told you that. I have not given you the information necessary to have analyzed these examples in only one way with respect to these two matters. So don't worry about it.) Give the templates for the other four tenses.

(g) Here I give the mapping of the consonantal root and the tense marker -*ä*- onto the template for the infinitive, with the prefixation of *mä*-, for the verb 'dress':

$$
\begin{array}{c}
\mu \quad \text{(tense marker)} \\
| \\
ä \\
| \\
\text{mä + CCVC} \\
| \ | \ / \\
\text{l b s} \quad \text{('dress')} \\
\text{\Large\vee} \\
\mu \quad \text{(infinitive root)}
\end{array}
$$

(An infinitive is a tenseless form. So when I call [ä] a "tense marker" here, I am merely drawing a parallel with the other verbal forms in the verb paradigms already given. The second [ä] in *mälbäs*, for example, does not indicate a specific tense; its mapping into this particular template in this particular way indicates that the verbal form is infinitival.) Give the mappings for the tenses of imperfective, gerund, jussive, and infinitive for the verb 'open.' (Do not give the mapping for the perfect yet, please.)

Now consider these forms for a third verb:

	'Like'
perfect:	wäddädä
imperfective:	yɨwäddal
gerund:	wäddo
jussive:	yɨwdäd
infinitive:	mäwdäd

(h) What is the consonantal root for 'like'? (Be sure to make use of the Obligatory Contour Principle of Chapter 2 (see the section "Comparing Linear with Geometric Phonology"), which has the effect of blocking from UR a sequence of identical segments.)

(i) Given your answer to (h), how will you account for the presence of more than one "d" in the final verbal forms for 'like'?

(j) Given your answers to (h) and (i), is the mapping in Amharic of a consonantal root onto a template from left to right or right to left?

(k) If the mapping went in the other direction, what is the gerund form we would have expected for the verb 'like'?

(l) Now look at the perfect forms of the first two verbs. There is a disturbing question about the mapping from the consonantal root onto the template here. What is that question?

(m) It has been proposed that the template for the perfect is actually:

CVCVC + ä

and that there is a rule which geminates the perfect, to change this template to:

$$\underset{\displaystyle \vee}{CVCCVC} + ä$$
$$\vee \quad = \text{gemination}$$

How would that proposal solve the problem you identified in (l)?

Problem Set 3.8: Compounds

1. In the text we listed English compounds with derivational suffixes on either member, on both members, and on the compound itself. Can you find comparable compounds with prefixes? List them, if you can. (This is very hard to do. Just give it a good try and don't go crazy if you can't find examples.)

2. How does *carpetbagger* present a bracketing paradox? Give the two bracketings and the reasons for each.

3. How is *woman driver* problematic for the claim that the non-deverbal member of a verbal compound must satisfy an internal argument of the verb? Try to find at least one other such example.

4. Consider these compounds from Vietnamese and from Breton:

Vietnamese:	[N V]$_N$	nguòi	ó	
		person	be located	'servant'
	[N V]$_N$	nhà	thuong	
		establishment	be wounded	'hospital'
Breton:	[N A]$_N$	korn boud		
		horn low-pitched		'low-pitched horn'
	[N N]$_N$	gavr-venez		
		goat mountain		'chamois'

(Breton is a Celtic language spoken in western France.)

For each of the four compounds, say whether it is right- or left-headed and explain how you know.

5. Consider the following English compounds:

verb:	slam-dunk	jump-start
	stir-fry	blow-dry
adjective:	deaf-mute	bittersweet
preposition:	into	onto
	upon	
noun:	gentleman farmer	producer-distributor
	poet-linguist	fighter-bomber

Are these compounds right-headed or left-headed? Why is this question hard to answer?

6. Consider these Italian compound nouns, all of which are masculine and for which I have given the singular form:

tergicristallo 'windshield wiper'
portamonete 'changepurse'
reggiseno 'brassiere'

We also have these verbs in Italian:

tergere 'to wipe'   portare 'to carry'   reggere 'to support'

and these nouns:

cristallo (M) 'windshield'   moneta (F) 'coin, money'
seno (M) 'breast'

(a) The first member of the compound is a verbal stem. The second member is a noun. Consider the semantic relationship between this verb and this noun. Did you expect this relationship? Why or why not?

(b) Is this kind of compound endocentric or exocentric? Explain your answer.

(c) Compare the second elements of the compound words *portamonete* and *reggiseno* (that is, look at *monete* and *seno*) with respect to the question of whether inflection can take place internal to a compound or not. Discuss whether the presence of inflection internal to this type of compound seems to be based on semantic-pragmatic considerations, or instead, seems arbitrary to you. Explain your answer.

Now consider one more compound of this type:

girasole 'sunflower' < gira- 'turn' + sole 'sun'

(The < indicates that the first word, *girasole*, is derived from *gira-* plus *sole*.)

(d) How is the meaning of this word problematic for claims about compound structure? Look back at (a) of this question and at Question 3.

7. Consider these Italian compounds:

Data Set A:

duramadre (F) 'tough membrane that envelops the brain and spinal cord'
    < duro 'hard' + madre (F) 'mother'
pellerossa (M) 'redskin, Native American'
    < pelle (F) 'skin' + rosso 'red'
purosangue (M) 'thoroughbred'
    < puro 'pure' + sangue (M) 'blood'
altopiano (M) 'plateau'
    < alto 'high' + piano (M) 'plain, flat land'

(I have given the masculine singular form of the adjectives in the sources because this is the citation form.)

Look back at what you learned about gender/number agreement inflections in Italian in Problem Set 3.2. What process is going on internal to these compounds that doesn't ordinarily happen within compounds?

Now consider the contrast in these two words:

Data Set B:

terracotta 'terra cotta, pottery made of clay'
    < terra (F) 'earth' + cotto 'cooked'
terremoto 'earthquake'
    < terre (FP) 'earths' + moto 'moved'

Does the process you saw operating in Data Set A behave consistently? Does this fact surprise you or did you expect it? Why? (In syntactic phrases agreement is entirely consistent in Italian.)

8. Consider these words of Italian:

zucchero 'sugar'   zuccheriera 'sugar bowl'
pattume 'garbage'   pattumiera 'garbage container'
uccello 'bird'   ucelliera 'bird cage'
te 'tea'   teiera 'teapot'

(a) What sense does the morpheme *-iera* contribute to the stems here?

Now consider these words:

> balena 'whale'   baleniera 'whaling ship'
> sabbia 'sand'   sabbiera 'sandbox'
> gamba 'leg'   gambiera 'legging'
> banda 'gang, band'   bandiera 'flag'

(b) How do these examples contrast with the examples in the first data set with respect to meaning? How is this contrast typical of derivational processes?

Now consider these words:

> guardaroba (F) 'linen room, cloakroom'
>   < guarda- 'watch' + roba (F) 'dress'
> guardarobiera 'linen maid, cloakroom attendant'

(*Guardaroba* is a compound of the type you studied in Question 4 made of a verbal stem plus a noun. There is no noun **robiera*.)

(c) Give a bracketing for *guardarobiera*.

(d) If Italian has a level-ordered morphology, what does the analysis of the word *guardarobiera* tell us about the level-ordering of the suffix *-iera* with respect to compounding?

Now consider these words:

> acqua (F) 'water'   santo 'holy'
> acquasantiera (F) 'holy water font'

The way you say 'holy water' in Italian is generally 'acqua benedetta' (literally: 'blessed water') or, less typically, 'acqua santa.' For many Italians there is no compound word **acquasanta*, although I have found one dictionary that lists it. Normally, when I ask speakers if there is a word *acquasanta*, they either say no or they are very unsure.

(e) Give a derivation of *acquasantiera* (which is a word Italians easily recognize). What is so striking about this word? (Consider the scope of the suffix *-iera*. What does it attach to?)

9. Consider these compounds of Italian:

> capostazione (M) 'station master'
>   < capo (M) 'head' + stazione (F) 'station'
> arcobaleno (M) 'rainbow'
>   < arco (M) 'arch' + baleno (M) 'flash'
> pescecane (M) 'shark'
>   < pesce (M) 'fish' + cane (M) 'dog'
> porcospino (M) 'porcupine'
>   < porco (M) 'pig' + spino (M) 'thorn (bush)'

These are all NN compounds.

(a) Are these compounds endocentric or exocentric?

(b) Given these, would you say compounds in Italian are right- or left-headed?

Problem Set 3.9: Clitics

1. What is the morphological status of *'ll* in:

I'll leave, if you want me to.

Is this an affix or a clitic? If it's a clitic, what kind of clitic is it? Give arguments for your analysis.

2. Consider these French sentences:

Data Set A:

Marie me voit. 'Marie sees me.'
Marie ne voit que moi. 'Marie sees only me.'
   (literally: 'Marie doesn't see except me.')
Marie voit Pierre. 'Marie sees Pierre.'
Marie ne voit que Pierre. 'Marie sees only Pierre.'

But these sentences are ungrammatical:

*Marie moi voit.
*Marie ne voit que me.

(a) On the basis of these data alone, what is the difference between *me* and *moi*? Which is the clitic? Is this a simple clitic or a special clitic?

Consider a second data set:

Data Set B:

*Jean me et te voit. 'Jean sees you and me.'
Jean l'a acheté pour moi et toi. 'Jean bought it for me and you.'

Assume that *te* is a clitic and *toi* is not.

(b) What new property of clitics can you see illustrated in these data?

Now consider these data:

Data Set C:

Jean, paraît-il, me préfère. 'Jean, it seems, prefers me.'
*Jean me, paraît-il, préfère. 'Jean, it seems, prefers me.'
Jean l'a acheté pour moi, paraît-il, hier soir.
'Jean bought it for me, it seems, last night.'
Jean l'a acheté, paraît-il, pour moi hier soir.
'Jean bought it, it seems, for me last night.'

(c) What new property of clitics can you see illustrated in these data?

And, finally, consider a fourth data set:

Data Set D:

(1) Jean me le donnera. 'Jean will give it to me.'
    Jean me it give-Fut3S

(2) *Jean le me donnera. 'Jean will give it to me.'
(3) Jean donnera le gateau à moi. 'Jean will give the cake to me.'
(4) Jean donnera à moi le gateau. 'Jean will give to me the cake.'

Assume that *le* in 1 and 2 is a clitic. (In 3 and 4 *le* is a definite article, not a clitic.) The 3 sentence here has the unmarked word order, whereas the 4 sentence calls for special circumstances in the speech context in order to be appropriate. The 4 sentence would most likely be uttered with contrastive stress on the phrase *à moi*. But both 3 and 4 are grammatical. However, among 1 and 2, only 1 is grammatical, not 2.

(d) What new property of clitic clusters can you see illustrated in these data?

(e) Consider the properties of clitics you stated in (b)- (d). Do affixes in English have any or all of these same properties? Give data to support your answer.

3. In the text you learned that *mi* is a special clitic and *me* is the tonic pronoun (nonclitic) in Italian. Now consider these data:

(1) Sergio mi dice tutto. 'Sergio tells me everything.'
(2) Sergio lo dice a me. 'Sergio tells it to me.'
(3) Sergio me lo dice. 'Sergio tells me it.'

Assume that *lo* is a clitic (and that here it is coreferential with 'everything'). Sentences 1 and 3 are unmarked. Sentence 2 calls for special circumstances in the speech act in order to be appropriate, but it is grammatical.

(a) Why are these data disturbing?

Now consider these data:

(4) Sergio ti dice tutto. 'Sergio tells you everything.'
(5) Sergio lo dice a te. 'Sergio tells it to you.'
(6) Sergio te lo dice. 'Sergio tells you it.'

Assume that *ti* is a clitic. Again, sentences 4 and 6 are unmarked and sentence 5 is marked, but all are grammatical.

(b) Given both sets of data, what analysis can you offer? Do you think that the *me* of sentence 3 is a clitic or not? Why?

4. In Problem Set 3.3, Question 6, you met the sentence *'s comin'*. Consider the status of *'s* as a clitic. What is problematic about the grammaticality of *'s comin'*?

Now consider these other sentences:

—Seems to have understood, doesn't she?
—Seen Tom?
—Can't sing a note, can he?

Compare their intonational pattern to the sentences:

—She seems to have understood, doesn't she?
—Have you seen Tom?
—He can't sing a note, can he?

If the rule operative here is sensitive to phonology, what particular phonological fact is it sensitive to?

Would that account for the absence of *he* in *'s comin'*?

Would that account for the persistence of *'s*?

5. In the text we learned that in some languages clitics are part of the prosodic word that their host is part of. Thus, in a northern variety of one dialect of Calabrese, that spoken in Cipolla, we find examples like:

Dannillu. 'Give it to him.' (literally: 'Give him it.')
[dan:íl:u]

Here the verbal root is followed by a series of two clitics.

In the theory of Lexical Phonology, what kind of rule is the rule that attaches clitics to their host in this Calabrese dialect: lexical or postlexical? If it is lexical, which level must it be? (Look back at the section "Lexical Phonology" of Chapter 2 or at Problem Set 2.8. What does Lexical Phonology claim about a word-formation process that yields a new morphological form to which the stress rules apply?)

Discuss briefly why your answer to the last question above is problematic, given what you know about clitics.

4

Syntax

Chapter Organization—for the Instructor

This chapter focuses on syntax, but we take a needed tangent early in the chapter and discuss a descriptive vs. prescriptive approach to grammar. We then approach phrase structure, starting with one-word utterances and building up a uniform structure for both lexical and functional category phrases, distinguishing along the way between elliptical utterances and gapped utterances. Developing Case Theory drives our emerging knowledge of phrasal and sentence structure, primarily because Case Theory in English introduces us to hierarchical structure and to the crucial relationship of government. Many concepts are introduced bit by bit, as the various modules of the grammar grow, including grammatical functions (GFs), predication, and constituency. The goal is to give an outline of English syntax, but other languages are brought in to illustrate various points, as in the discussion of word-order typology and lexical Case. Modules covered include Theta Theory, X-Bar Theory, Case Theory, and Control Theory. Other modules touched upon include Binding Theory and Trace Theory. In particular, movement is treated as controversial, rather than given, even though the overall approach is Government and Binding (GB). The chapter ends with a brief introduction to the Minimalist Program.

Okay, let's go

We started out at the beginning of this book looking at individual sounds. Then we looked at the interaction of sounds when they were put together to form syllables, words, and phrases. Then we looked at the interaction of morphemes when they were put together to form words. We are now ready to look at another structural unit of language: the sentence. And in doing that, we will look at the phrases that make up sentences. This study is called SENTENCE SYNTAX (as opposed to DISCOURSE SYNATX or DISCOURSE ANALYSIS), and most people simply call it syntax.

I should tell you that for about twenty years I was completely a syntactician. Then I recognized the magnificence of phonology and morphology and the dizzying spin of semantics and now I consider myself a general linguist, ready to jump into any sort of linguistic puzzle (and at the slightest provocation). Nevertheless, my greater knowledge of and affinity for syntax show in this book (as the students who have been troubleshooting the text as I write it tell me) in that the syntax chapter feels like a never-ending story. I apologize for length, but, believe it or not, it was painful for me to keep it this short. Given that warning, I suggest you spend more time on this chapter than on the others of this book simply because there's more covered here.

Syntactic theory, more than any other area of linguistics, is rife with controversy. Syntacticians often describe themselves or others as belonging to particular theoretical camps, and there has been a history of debate bordering on fights and name-calling in our less-admirable moments. Thus if you were to ask linguists which syntactic theory or theories should be included in an introductory text such as this, you would not find consensus.

Furthermore, syntactic theories are comprehensive; they often lead one to a unique analysis of any given syntactic phenomenon. Contrast this with phonological theories, which are often more limited in scope. For example, metrical theory has much to say about stress patterns but may offer little insight on a phenomenon of assimilation, whereas geometric theory has much to say about assimilation but may offer little insight into a given stress pattern. Thus, in order to have some idea of how to approach many different kinds of phonological phenomena, you must get a sense of the various phonological theories current today. But to give a complete understanding of the various syntactic theories current today, I would have to show how they each approach a wide range of the same syntactic phenomena. The result would be a book on syntax, not a chapter.

So what will I do? Syntax is a theoretical field—and a discussion of syntactic problems requires knowledge of theory because the theory defines the problems. So I must offer a single theoretical approach and still aim for as general an introduction to syntactic issues and methodology as possible. The particular theory presented here is known as GOVERN-MENT AND BINDING (GB). It is the theory that frames most of the syntactic literature of the past fifteen years. However, even while using that one theory, I will do my best to point out some types of phenomena that have been fundamental to developing contrasting theories of syntax.

So let's begin.

You are already familiar with three types of issues that may arguably involve syntactic matters. One is sandhi rules, those rules with a phonological effect which take place across word boundaries and are possibly dependent upon the syntactic relationship of the two relevant words—such as French liaison and Italian raddoppiamento, both mentioned in Chapter 2. (See the section "Postlexical Rules" and Problem Set 2.9.) (If you don't remember why I say "possibly" here, it's because some have argued that sandhi rules are dependent upon prosodic relationships at the level beyond the prosodic word.)

Another type of issue concerns rules of inflectional morphology, such as Subject-Verb Agreement and Case Assignment. We talked about such inflectional processes in Chapter 3 and we will talk more about them in this chapter. The reason syntax is relevant to them is that the very notion of Subject is defined relative to structure, so we must have our words together in a sentence before our relevant rules can identify the Subject and correct predicate (for English, the first element of the verbal string) and check that the inflectional morpheme is the appropriate one; likewise it is only at a syntactic level that our grammar can check whether a given NOMINAL (a noun with or without paraphernalia—and we'll be discussing what the paraphernalia might be), for instance, has the appropriate Case.

The third type of issue we have discussed for which syntax may be relevant is the analysis of clitics, since, again, we are dealing with the interaction of words in a larger context. For example, in language after language (though not in all languages) clitics will take as their host the second word or phrase in a sentence—but we cannot know which word or phrase will be second in the sentence until we have arranged our words into phrases and sentences.

All the same, we will not begin our study of syntax by picking up any of those three issues. Instead, we'll begin at a more basic level.

Let me warn you from the start: This chapter may drive you crazy with frustration. Syntax is not the type of thing that lends itself to study of discrete parts, because the various parts are not discrete. The approach I'll be using in this chapter is a MODULAR one, in which the various modules of the grammar interact in simple ways to produce a complex range of data. Because of the interaction of the modules, it is not possible to study first one module completely, then the next, and so forth. Instead, we have to begin looking at one, then shift over to another, then perhaps go on to a third, then maybe we'll be ready to hop back to the first for a while, and so forth—building up our picture of each module bit by bit, until we manage to have something close to a complete outline of a syntactic system. (I say "outline" because that's as much as we can hope for in a single chapter.) So if you're the type of person who likes things to come at you in a neat package with a recognizable organization, I cringe at the thought of your frustration as you read this and I ask your forgiveness. There is an organization here, but you may not be able to discern it easily. Good luck.

We will start by going through a rather detailed buildup of basic phrase and sentence structure, looking primarily at English. But then we will step back and take a more sweeping look at some common syntactic constructions in a variety of languages.

One-Word Utterances

Make a list of three one-word utterances that you can easily imagine yourself using in a discourse—one-word utterances preceded and/or followed by (noninterrupting) utterances from another speaker so you can feel sure these one-word utterances are a complete syntactic unit. You might have come up with utterances like:

Mow!   Apples.   Under.

(If you can't think of a context for *Mow*, consider a mother talking to her teenage son and pointing at the lawnmower.) It was easy, right? If you speak another language, do this same exercise. Let me do it for Italian here:

Mangia! 'Eat!'   Roma. 'Rome.'   Sopra. 'Above.'

I made the Italian examples syntactically parallel to the English ones on purpose. Can you tell me how the first example of each language is similar? What is the function of each of these utterances? They look like orders. Do orders always have to be single words? Certainly not:

Give me that toy, right away.
Dammi quel giocattolo, subito subito.

Okay, then, is there anything else special about *mow* and *mangia* that makes it obvious they are orders? Unless you know Italian, you cannot answer this for *mangia*. But you certainly can answer it for English *mow*. What kind of word is *mow*? Think about it in terms of morphological categories. Is it a noun? A verb? An adjective? A preposition? How do you know?

Categories

Identifying categories is to a great extent a morphological matter, as you know from having worked your way through Chapter 3. Yet the import of identifying categories plays a crucial part in understanding the syntactic system of a language. So what do you think *mow* is? If you don't know where to start, consider the use of various inflections of this word, as in sentences like these:

> I mow grass. John mows grass.
> Sally's mowing the lawn. Sally mowed the lawn.
> Sally wants to mow. Sally may mow.

Each line here has two sentences in it and each line is making a different point.

Consider the first line. Compare *mow* to *mows*. What's the difference? When do we use *mow* and when do we use *mows*? If you read Chapter 3, you know the answer right off. But let's pretend like you didn't read Chapter 3, because by doing that we'll be able to demonstrate how one investigates such a question, and, more importantly, we'll be led to a tangent that we need to take.

Say many different sentences with *mows* and see if you can figure out what factors in the sentence are crucial to your selecting *mows* over *mow* in those sentences. You might notice that changing what follows *mow(s)* doesn't matter:

> John mows {lawns/on Sunday/with a pushmower/unwillingly}.

(The braces indicate that you are to select only one of the options within them. The example above represents four separate sentences.) But changing what precedes *mow(s)* can matter very much:

> {Pete/Annie/Someone} mows grass.
> *{You/We/Those boys} mows grass.
> {You/We/Those boys} mow grass.
> *{Pete/Annie/Someone} mow grass.

The asterisk indicates that a sentence sounds strange to a native speaker. Thus we can surely understand a sentence like *You mows grass*, but the native speaker of what we might call standard English would not produce that sentence in a linguistically unselfconscious context.

Standard Language

A lot of ideas are coming at you at once, and if you balk at them, join the club. The issues here are not simple, but they must be understood at the outset, for only by facing them can you recognize what the job of syntax is. A syntax is a description of the utterances of a native speaker, and not of the nonutterances. A syntax can describe a standard speech or a nonstandard speech. But the important thing, is that **it describes, not prescribes.**

We're going to go on a much-needed tangent here, and it's long. So try to keep in mind that we started out on the path of figuring out the category of the word *mow* and that we will return to that path once we've reached the end of our tangent.

Let's begin with a fundamental question: What is a so-called standard language? Certainly there are native speakers of English who say:

I's mowin'.

while others of us have to say:

I'm mowin'.

And there are native speakers of English who say:

Don't dare do that!

while others of us have to say:

Don't you dare do that!

And there are native speakers of English who say:

There's the fellow stole my lunchbox.

while others of us have to say:

There's the fellow who stole my lunchbox.

I could go on and on. Native speakers of a language don't all speak the same way. So what do we mean by a standard language, and why would such a notion even be useful?

You tell me: If you can remember a time when someone corrected your speech in your native language, who was that person? Did that person explain why what you said was in need of correction? Did that person explain why the alternative offered was better? Compare these two sentences:

Ain't nobody here.
There isn't anybody here.

Which one do you think is standard? The second is. Why?

Up to this point in this book we haven't spent a lot of time dealing with variation. We have merely pointed it out and gone on to other matters. For example, in the section "Vowels and Diphthongs" in Chapter 1 we pointed out that some speakers have a diphthong in *beat* and others don't. But we didn't label either pronunciation as standard. Surely, though, you've been in situations where people have pronounced words in a way that you felt was odd and that you perhaps even felt was somehow substandard. In fact, the film *My Fair Lady* (and the Bernard Shaw play *Pygmalion* that it derives from) is built on the idea that how you speak, particularly your phonology, can indicate your social class and education. And the film wasn't wrong.

Yes, indeed, those factors as well as others, such as where we grew up, gender, race, ethnicity, age, and sexual orientation, can all be reflected in our speech. The point I want to make is different, however. I want you to focus on the question of what factors we use to determine which variety of speech is the standard.

Some of those factors are relatively innocuous. For example, many American English speakers pronounce the word *often* with a medial [t], but many more have no [t] in that word. We might well say the pronunciation without the [t] is standard, whereas that with the [t] is a variant, and the relevant factor here might have been simple frequency: More speakers say the word without a [t].

But other factors are far from innocuous. Why do some people say that *ain't* is not only substandard, but not even a word? It most certainly is a word, and it's used by many native speakers of English (and it has a fascinating syntax—when you finish reading this chapter, you might want to research the syntax of *ain't*). So what could anyone mean to call it a nonword? Why would someone want to ban this word from speech?

I raise such questions now because variation in syntax is a pervasive basis for labeling a language variety substandard. Certainly, we can smile or frown at variation in phonology, but that variation is limited to speech. Variation in syntax, on the other hand, is apparent in writing, as well: Syntactic variation can affect a person's self-presentation on written material, such as a job application. So it's time to face facts.

The facts we have to face are undoubtedly more complex than I will represent here, but in the interest of getting us onto the right track in thinking about syntax, I want to state things in the baldest way possible. **We choose a standard language based on looking at how those who have the cultural power speak.** (When I say "we" here, I mean whatever authority does the choosing.) If you look across time in any literate country I know of, you will find that until the very recent past, literacy has been a privilege of the rich because education was a privilege of the rich. Today in America we think of education as every-one's right—it is guaranteed to us in our constitution. But this is a relatively new right, and even today not every public school has the resources to deliver the same quality of education as all other public schools. (And if you're enraged at that fact, again, join the club.)

But let's stick to the history of things for a moment. What all this means is that we choose a standard variety of language by considering issues of power—cultural, econom-ic, whatever. We do not say, "Hey, that variety of English has a phonological rule that calls for spreading of two features so I'll prefer this other variety, which just has a deletion rule," or anything like that. **Our reasons for choosing a standard have nothing, in fact, to do with the structure of language per se.** So they have nothing to do with any of the areas of linguistics we have discussed thus far. Our reasons are purely sociological.

From a linguistic viewpoint, which would be better: a rule that voiced a consonant between vowels or a rule that made a consonant a continuant between vowels? The question, I hope, makes no sense to you. Voicing a consonant in that context is a simple feature spreading rule, just as is making a consonant continuant in that context. Neither rule is better. We can talk about one formulation of a rule being better than another in that it can offer more insight into what's truly going on. We can talk about one theory of rules being better than another in that that theory can allow a formulation of rules that offers more insight into what's truly going on than the other theory can. We can talk about one derivation being more optimal or economic (in senses we'll discuss later in the section "The Minimalist Program"). But we do not talk about one rule being better than another if both are sanctioned by the principles of the grammar.

Given that, since the differences between varieties of a given language amount mostly to differences in the rules applied, **all varieties of a given language are equally good so far as linguistics is concerned.** Oh, some may have marked rules and some may have more typical rules. But none are better than any others. In fact, when linguists come across a language with rules that seem highly marked, we don't discount the language. Rather, we are quite likely to review our theory to see whether and where we goofed. New data often precipitate changes in theory.

So when I ask you whether a sentence is grammatical in your speech, I want you to ask yourself whether you think you'd say such a sentence spontaneously in the appropriate context. I'm not asking you whether you think you should say such a sentence or whether you think it is correct in any judgmental way to say such a sentence. I'm simply asking you how this sentence sounds to you ear—is it something that you feel comfortable saying in ordinary speech or not?

The Language Mechanism

Why am I doing this? Why should I care about what you really say or what you really would say rather than about what you think you should say or have been taught you should say? I care because this book is about the structure of language, it is not about the structure of society. Language is one convention of society, and certainly we make conscious choices when we speak. So some of us would never say *ass* to a respected elder of our community, but instead, if we had to, we'd say *arse* or *bottom* or some other lexical item that seems more polite (and if you did Problem Set 3.1, you may have already thought about this sort of choice). Probably none of us would use the word *lambent* with a small child, and we might well not use it in ordinary conversation, but we could use it if we were giving a lecture or talking with someone in an academic or literary context. We make these choices all the time. But most of our linguistic choices are not made consciously. In fact, sometimes people can report what we said and we can honestly respond with an amazed, "I said that?"

Normally, however, we aren't amazed at our own words. Nor, are we aware of the choices that make us say, for example:

I have to leave.

rather than:

*To leave I have.

The study of syntax is almost entirely the study of an organization of language that we do not have conscious control over. Indeed, if we attempt to learn the syntax of a language after we reach a certain maturity (typically the onset of puberty), no matter how closely we study it, we will probably never have the same competence in that language as a native speaker—that is, as someone who grew up speaking it. The same can be said for the other components of the grammar discussed in this book.

But why?, you might ask. Why study this LANGUAGE MECHANISM that is outside our conscious control? The reasons are many and I refer you to the introductory chapter of most textbooks in linguistics. I will mention only two here. One is scientific in the traditional sense: If language is the product of this language mechanism in our brain, then surely the analytical study of language will lead to an understanding of this mechanism and, thus, to an understanding of how at least part of our brain works. In other words, linguistics falls within the domain of cognitive science, and studying linguistics is studying one aspect of our cognition.

Another reason, and one that is pertinent to more people, is social: If we take a close look at the structures of what people actually say, we cannot help but realize that **there is no linguistic standard by which to judge one language better than another.** We have already looked at the systems of phonology and morphology and if you aren't convinced that the phonology and morphology of Japanese are just as good as the phonology and morphology of English (or any other language), then I've failed and you should burn this book. I hope to convince you of the same proposition for syntax in this chapter. This is a major finding of modern linguistics because it impacts our world today. You, the person who reads this book, are no longer linguistically naive. You can be the one who hires someone who can do the job well, even when that person speaks a variety of language that is labeled substandard. You can be the one who disabuses people of their ignorance when they judge others to be stupid based on linguistic differences. You have knowledge now, and with it comes power and responsibility. So welcome to the crusade.

Once we've decided to look at how people actually do speak, however, our job of describing linguistic systems becomes much more difficult—because we have much more data to consider. And, while I have just convinced you (I hope) that all those data are important, I will now, perhaps paradoxically, not consider them. Instead, I will leave the job of considering variation in language to linguists who specialize in precisely that, and I hope that in your class discussions you will take the time to consider variation among the speakers in your own class.

Undoubtedly, readers will disagree with each other about the grammaticality of sentences brought up for discussion in this chapter. So what am I going to do? As I said, I will not pursue the variations. I will mention some and ignore others. And I will move ahead, deciding to focus on a single corpus of data without regard to the variations. That's because a major goal of syntacticians is to construct a syntactic theory that is internally consistent. You may not yet realize what I might mean by "consistency" in syntactic theory, but you soon will. An empirically adequate syntactic theory should be able to account for the data of a given speaker of the language—the variety of language peculiar to that one speaker—or the IDIOLECT of that speaker. But since different speakers speak differently, taking data about one type of construction from one speaker and data about a second type of construction from another speaker might well wind up leading us to a distorted picture of the syntax of either speaker. We might then come up with a syntax that, in fact, describes no one's speech. For that reason, when we look at data from English, we will use the data from a single speaker: me. We could as easily have picked any other native speaker of English since all varieties of English are equal in the eyes of the linguist. But we are using my speech since I'm writing this book and my speech is available to me. Once you've finished this chapter, if you like, I invite you to come back and reconsider all the theoretical points we bring up here in light of your own analysis of data from your idiolect. (And for the sociolinguists among you, if you want to know the linguistically potentially relevant facts about me, write and I'll tell you.)

Our very long tangent has now ended.

Back to Recognizing Categories: Agreement

Let's return to the question I posed earlier when we were asking what category the word *mow* belongs to. That question was: When do we use *mow* and when do we use *mows*? We looked at the sentences:

I mow grass. John mows grass.

As you learned in Chapter 3, in many languages the verb agrees with the Subject. In English we have Subject-Verb Agreement. What features of the Subject does the verb agree for in English? Person and number. Do you see that? That's what the *-s* of *mows* tells us: that the Subject of this verb is third-person singular, as well as telling us that the tense is present. **So the presence of the agreement morpheme identifies *mow(s)* as a verb in these sentences.**

English is poor when it comes to agreement inflections. The third person singular of the present tense is the only place we hear an agreement morpheme, except with the verb *be*, which is slightly more richly inflected. Japanese is even poorer than English: It has no Subject-Verb Agreement at all. Italian, on the other hand, is rich in this regard, agreeing for person and number:

Parlo. 'I speak.'   Parliamo. 'We speak.'
Parli. 'You speak.'   Parlate. 'You (all) speak.'
Il ragazzo parla lentamente.
'The boy   speaks slowly.'
I ragazzi   parlano lentamente.
'The boys speak slowly.'

Despite the poverty of the agreement inflection in English, we say that there is agreement between Subject and verb in English in all combinations of person, number, and tense. Why should we do this?

Think of the alternative. If we were to say that English had a rule of Subject-Verb Agreement that occurred only when the Subject was third person singular and only in the present tense, we would be putting strange and arbitrary conditions on the agreement rule. Instead, since we know that zero morphemes exist anyway (as we learned in the section "Morphemes: Phonetic Realization" of Chapter 3), we posit a productive and regular rule of agreement, and we can say that the inflectional morpheme has been neutralized to a phonetic zero in all persons, numbers, and tenses, except the third person singular present.

Please be carcful here. The assumption that certain verbal forms in English have a zero morpheme marking agreement with the Subject (you will figure out exactly which verbal forms in Problem Set 4.3) is based on the fact that we do find an overt agreement marker for person and number in one instance: the third-person singular present. However, even though some languages exhibit Verb-Object Agreement (as we learned in the section "Person, Number, Gender, and Verbal Inflection" of Chapter 3), we do not posit zero morphemes for Object agreement on English verbs. Why not? Given that we find agreement for third person singular present tense, we need the whole apparatus that gives us that agreement, regardless of whether that agreement is realized by a zero morpheme in most instances. However, given that we never find overt agreement with an Object, we have no motivation for adding the costly apparatus of Verb-Object Agreement to our grammar of English.

The tack just taken (of assuming the Subject-Verb Agreement rule applies for all combinations of persons, numbers, and tenses) is a common one in syntax. One of the basic premises of syntax is that **syntactic rules should obey principles that are sensitive to syntactic structure only** (and this whole chapter will introduce you to syntactic structures). Thus a rule such as Subject-Verb Agreement, which is arguably a syntactic rule since it is sensitive to the syntactic relationship between a Subject and its verb, should apply regardless of which particular Subject and which particular verb we have in a given syntactic structure.

Morphological rules, on the other hand, are notorious for lexical lapses and suppletion. So we can leave to morphology the rule that spells out the proper morphological form of a verb with a given agreement marker on it—a rule that we know has an impoverished paradigm. That means we have two rules: Subject-Verb Agreement (S-V Ag—a syntactic rule that copies features from one syntactic entity to another—that is, from the Subject to the V), and an inflectional spell-out rule (a morphological rule that takes the features supplied by agreement—person and number—and realizes them with a morphological form).

An Agreement Rule for English

Let me go through this analysis for the agreement in the two English sentences we've been looking at. Here S-V Ag will COPY the person and number of the Subject into the feature matrix of the verb. Then the morphological spell-out rule will give us a zero morpheme or -*s*.

	[I]$_{Subject}$	[mow]$_V$ grass.	[John]$_{Subject}$	[mow]$_V$ grass.
S-V Ag:		[1S]		[3S]
spell-out:		[mow]		[mows]

We call the level of structure before any syntactic rules have applied to it the D-STRUCTURE, known as DS for short. We call the level of structure after all syntactic rules that are going to apply have applied the S-STRUCTURE, known as SS for short. DS is the level that reflects information given by the lexicon, including the predicate-argument structure of *mow* and other information. (You are familiar with the concept of argument structure from the sections "Person, Number, Gender, and Verbal Inflection" and "Valency and Argument Structure" of Chapter 3.) SS is the level that feeds phonological rules. We will talk more about both levels (and about predicate-argument structure) throughout this chapter.

Let me make a quick aside. You might ask why "D" and "S" have been chosen in the labels *D-Structure* and *S-Structure*. These letters hark back to a time in the 1950s through 1970s when syntacticians talked about "Deep Structure" and "Surface Structure". Today those terms are not used and have almost become taboo. Indeed, there were certain ideas about Deep Structure and Surface Structure that have been discarded and, thus, are not associated with the new DS and SS. This book does not deal with the history of linguistics except in a few scattered and passing remarks, so I won't go into those differences. I just thought you might want to know that the choice of "D" and "S" is not arbitrary.

Returning to the analysis of agreement given above, we need to discuss a problem. You tell me, with this analysis, where must all spell-out agreement rules be ordered in a Lexical Phonology? Clearly in the postlexical level, since they must follow the syntax. However, in some languages it looks like the morphological spell-out rules for agreement are not postlexical, but lexical. (For example, in Icelandic, a Germanic language spoken in Iceland, there is a u-umlaut rule that appears to be a cyclic lexical rule, but it can follow a deletion rule that applies after morphological spell-out rules involving Case endings on nominals and agreement on verbs. We will not go into the details here, since that would take us on a long tangent through phonology again. Instead, I ask you to believe me on this point.)

So what can we do? An alternative is to allow inflectional morphology to take place in the lexicon. If that happens, when we get to the point in the syntax where we are ready to do S-V Ag, we already have an inflected verb. Then S-V Ag will apply, copying onto the verb the person and number features of the Subject. At that point a FILTER will compare, or CHECK, the features that have been assigned by S-V Ag to the features that the inflected verb form already has. If the features match, the verb form passes through the filter (that is, the verb is marked as grammatical) and the sentence is acceptable (all else about the sentence being grammatical). If the features don't match, the filter blocks that verb form (that is, the verb is marked ungrammatical) and the sentence is marked ungrammatical. (Alternatively, we could say that S-V Ag is itself a filter that checks the features of the verb against the features of the subject.)

This alternative solves the ordering problem. It is costly, however, in two ways. First, it introduces a new grammatical mechanism, the filter. We would hope to find independent evidence that we need such a mechanism in other constructions before we could feel justified in proposing it here. Second, it means our syntax OVERGENERATES, so that many more sentences are generated and then abandoned along the way in our syntactic derivation than actually make it to the level that feeds the phonology (the level we're calling SS). (And you've already seen overgeneration in phonology, as in Optimality Theory.)

We will not take a stance on this issue (although we'll discuss it a little further when we talk about the Minimalist Program at the end of this chapter). My goal in this chapter is not so much to lead you into particular views of syntax as to sensitize you to the fact that any given analysis raises its own set of issues. If this approach frustrates you, all I can do is repeat that syntax is an area of the grammar that is fraught with controversy. And the data rarely settle the controversy for long. The most useful thing I can do is help you to see some of the basics of syntax that most syntacticians of a more modern ilk agree about, point out a wide range of options for the other points (also often basic points) that syntacticians disagree about, and focus on giving you rudimentary skills for entering the debate.

Back to Recognizing Categories

We learned in Chapter 3 that in English (as opposed to many other languages, including ones of the Romance family) agreement inflections show up only on verbs. Thus agreement helps us identify the word *mow(s)* in our sentences as a verb.

Now let's reconsider other sentences I gave that had different forms of *mow* in them:

Sally's mowing the lawn.   Sally mowed the lawn.

What about the suffixes *-ing* and *-ed*? What morphological information do they carry? One is the progressive aspect marker and one is the past-tense marker, and both attach only to verb stems. (If you don't remember what aspect is about, look back at our discussion in the section "Verbal Inflections and Affixes" in Chapter 3.) So again these data confirm our proposal that *mow* in its various forms in these sentences is a verb. And again we can see that the presence of an inflectional morpheme is an invaluable aid in identifying the category of a word.

What about the third pair of sentences I gave earlier, repeated here:

> Sally wants to mow.   Sally may mow.

Here the two forms of *mow* are without any audible inflection. Yet there are reasons for wanting to call these instances verbs, as well. Ask yourself: If we have only one word following *to* or *may* in a sentence, what can that one word be? To make life simpler, let's start with *may* and approach infinitival *to* later. You can say,

> Sally may {mow/talk/smile/eat/ . . . }.

but not

> *Sally may {books/under/intelligent/quickly . . . }.

Do you agree with my judgments here? Try to find a context in which the sentences I have starred are acceptable. It's not that hard to do for some of them. For example, consider this snatch of discourse:

> —Let's close the account. After all, John will never order magazines.
> —(Oh, but) Sally may books.

What does the second sentence mean? Surely that Sally may order books. The second sentence here is called a GAPPED sentence, because we have a gap where we might have expected to have a word (in fact, in this sentence we have a gap where we expected to have a particular kind of word—which is the point we're trying to get at) or a STRING of words.

Gaps and Ellipsis

Often in discourse we will accept sentences that in isolation are judged ungrammatical. Make a list of three. See how easy that was? You could have come up with examples like these, where I have put an appropriate preceding context in parentheses:

> (When is she coming?)   I hope the eighth of May.
>   Paul thinks never.
>   John guessed soon.

All of these sentences are interpreted in the same way as corresponding expanded sentences. So we interpret *I hope the eighth of May* in this context (that is, following the question in parentheses) the same way we interpret *I hope she is coming the eighth of May*. Sentences like these, which are missing parts, are called ELLIPTICAL. Context helps us to interpret them, but in isolation they may be (close to) uninterpretable.

When we judge whether a sentence is grammatical in this chapter, I am asking you to make that judgment of the sentence in isolation. Do not consider its possibility as an elliptical utterance unless I ask you to do so. The rationale here is that if we limit ourselves to looking at sentences in this very rarefied (and, indeed, unnatural, with respect to ordinary usage) way, we can hope to get close to the mechanisms that are operative within a sentence without terribly much interference from the mechanisms that are operative across utterances within a discourse. (That's why I told you at the outset that this chapter is about sentence syntax, not discourse syntax.) This hope might be ill-founded, but it is nevertheless the motivation for our approach.

Okay, so what does that mean about the words that can follow *may*? They must be verbs. Can you see that? So the fact that *mow* occurs after *may* is another argument that this word is a verb. (Recall that the first argument was that *mow* undergoes Subject-Verb Agreement.)

And now I should point out a distinction for you between gapped sentences and elliptical ones. Gapped sentences are a particular kind of elliptical sentence, and the gapped sentence we looked at above was particularly interesting because **the gapped element was a verb**—that's why we looked at it when we were trying to figure out the category of *mow*. I'll repeat that example in context, with the gapped element in brackets:

—Let's close the account. After all, John will never order magazines.
—(Oh, but) Sally may [order] books.

Elliptical sentences occur in many structures, but gapped sentences occur typically in COORDINATE STRUCTURES (structures connected by *and*, *or*, or *but*—we'll discuss them later in the section "Coordination and Subordination"). Here the *but* in parentheses is what let's us know this is a gapped sentence.

Homophony and Polysemy

You can see that the argument involving *may* can be made just as easily for the *to* of *Sally wants to mow*, what I have called infinitival *to*. That is, this *to* must be followed by a verb. So why did I hold off on talking about *to*? Why did I begin with *may*? What is the extra complication that *to* brings up? Consider this sentence:

Mary walks to the store.

Is this the same *to* as the *to* in the following sentence?

Mary wants to mow.

And what about the *to* in the following sentence?

Mary gave a book to Bill.

This question is not small. In the section "Homophony" of Chapter 3 we talked about homophony vs. polysemy (and we'll talk about it again in the section "Semantic Uses of Lexical Decomposition in Comparing Words" of Chapter 5). Homophonous words sound the same, but their meanings are different. Polysemous words are single lexical items that have a range of related meanings. So do we have a single polysemous *to* or do we have two or maybe three homophonous *to*'s?

You might feel sure that all three *to*'s are distinct. The *to* of *Mary walks to the store* is locative; the *to* of *Mary gave a book to Bill* is dative (that is, introduces an Indirect Object); and the *to* of *Mary wants to mow* is infinitival. In fact, the third one can occur in a sentence with a verb that has nothing to do with location or with Indirect Objects:

Mary wants to breathe.

If meaning alone can convince you that we have different *to*'s here, fine. But in case the meaning difference doesn't seem that clear to you, I'd like to add another way to distinguish homophonous items from polysemous ones: SYNTACTIC DISTRIBUTION. **The syntactic distribution of a lexical item is part of its identity.** Infinitival *to* is followed by a verb phrase (and we will get to an understanding of what a phrase is). Locative and Dative *to* are followed by a noun phrase. (And we already used a syntactic distribution argument when we talked about the relevance of the fact that *mow* can follow *may*.)

This reasoning may seem circular to you. We might just as well argue that we have one *to* and that if that *to* is followed by a noun phrase it is interpreted locatively or datively (and we'd need a way to distinguish between the two, which we will find when we discuss the Double-Object construction in a later section)—otherwise, it is infinitival *to*. So let me add yet another type of diagnostic.

In Chapter 2 we talked briefly about sandhi rules (see the section "Postlexical Rules" and Problem Set 2.9). It is debatable (as we noted there) whether that sensitivity is to prosodic phrase structure or to syntactic phrase structure, but that debate need not concern us now. The fact is that there exists a sandhi rule of English that distinguishes between Locative and Dative *to*, on the one hand, and infinitival *to*, on the other. Thus we can say *I want to win* as:

[aɪ̯ wɑnə wɪn]

often written as *I wanna win*, and *I'm going to win* as:

[aɪ̯m ɡɑnə wɪn]

often written as *I'm gonna win*. That is, infinitival *to* can appear reduced and cliticized onto a preceding verb. But Locative and Dative *to* do not undergo this rule. So *I'm going to Bill's* cannot be pronounced as:

*[aɪ̯m ɡɑnə bɪlz]

In sum, then, infinitival *to* can also help us to identify *mow* as a verb.

Back to One-Word Utterances

Let's go all the way back to our one-word utterances, where we claimed that *Mow*! and *Mangia*! were orders. We now know that the English word is a verb. The Italian word is also a verb. (Trust me.)

Now compare these one-word utterances to the others we saw earlier, repeated here:

English		*Italian*	
Apples.	Under.	Roma. 'Rome.'	Sopra. 'Above.'

Are these also verbs? Again, we'll look at English and figure it out and then I'll tell you for Italian.

What category does the word *apples* belong to? I hope you have a few types of tests in your head to try. You should consider both morphological information and syntactic distribution right off. What does morphology tell you? Can you recognize this -*s* suffix? It's the plural suffix, and while it is homophonous with the third-person-singular present-tense agreement morpheme on verbs, it is semantically distinct and it attaches only to noun stems. So *apples* looks like a noun.

What does syntactic distribution tell you? If we were to put this word into other multiple-word utterances, we'd find phrases like:

    the apples   those apples   all apples

If we limit ourselves to just a single word following *the*, what sort of word must it be? Consider:

    the {dog/idea/milk}   *the {put/under/delightful}

The introduces a noun. The same can be said for *those*. (*All*, on the other hand, can introduce a variety of types of words, including nouns, but also adjectives and prepositions, as in *all dirty*, *all over*.) So the data on syntactic distribution support our contention that *apples* is a noun.

What about *under*? What category does it belong to? Here morphology can't provide positive tests, because we cannot affix anything to *under*. But it can provide a negative test. We learned in the section "Unitary Base Hypothesis" of Chapter 3 that prepositions typically resist affixation. However, function words such as determiners (like *the*—we met this term in Chapter 3) and conjunctions (like *and*, which we will discuss in our section on conjunction) do, as well. So we can propose that *under* is either a preposition or a function word.

The *Right*-Test

Syntactic distribution can help further. Consider the use of the word *right* that means 'directly,' as in:

    She went right under.

We cannot say:

    *She loves right books.
    *That book seems right red.
    *They speak right quickly.

Can you say anything about what *right* introduces? Yes, a preposition. So the fact that *right* can introduce *under* tells us *under* is a preposition.

Let me make an aside here about language variation. The claim I just made, that this use of *right* introduces only a preposition, holds for most varieties of English but not all. Examine the distribution of *right* in your own speech. Can you say:

> She's right crazy.

Many people can. With adjectives, particularly adjectives that denote quantifiable properties, *right* can be used for these speakers. However, so far as I know, no variety of English uses *right* to introduce nominals.

Returning to our one-word utterances with the new knowledge that *under* is a preposition, we can conclude that one-word utterances in English can be verbs, nouns, or prepositions. And since *Roma* is a noun in Italian and *sopra* is a preposition, the same can be said for Italian.

Can one word utterances in English be adverbs? Sure:

> Quickly!

Do you guess they can in Italian? If you guessed yes, you're right (for example: *Rapidamente!* 'Rapidly!'). Can one-word utterances in English be function words? What would be a context for:

> The.

It's difficult to think of one, but perhaps if you consider a situation that is linguistically self-conscious, such as one in which someone is teaching someone else how to speak, you can come up with a context. The same is true for Italian.

But now I want you to step back and look across the one-word utterances we have considered. Is there any way in which the order *Mow!* stands out from *Apples*, *Under*, *Quickly*, and (if you allow it) *The*? Think back to our distinction between elliptical utterances and utterances that have a full interpretation in isolation. Can you make any similar distinction here?

Fragments

Most one-word utterances are FRAGMENTARY. Unlike elliptical sentences, they don't just have recognizable holes; they are so partial that we aren't sure where and how many holes are present. For example, if a parent walks in the door with a full bag and calls out, "Apples," are we to expand that to "I've bought apples," or "Come eat apples," or "Here are apples," or any number of other possibilities that you might think of? We can't say for sure. Neither the context nor the syntax tells us.

But orders like *Mow!* in English or *Mangia!* in Italian are completely interpretable. They are not fragmentary, since fragments are open to many interpretations; they are not even elliptical, since we don't need context to fill in any holes. We know what they mean when we hear them, even if we're on the other side of the wall and we haven't heard prior context and we can't see any elements of the context.

For this reason, I will call these orders full sentences, as opposed to elliptical sentences like *I hope the eighth of May* and fragments like *Apples*. Sentences, whether full or elliptical, have a certain semantic integrity that fragments don't have. Sentences give us an event and the role players in the event (terms you are familiar with from the section "Inventory of Morphological Types" in Chapter 3). Fragments typically give us only a REFERENT.

Okay, now we can continue without being derailed by any confusion among full sentences, elliptical sentences, and fragments. But before going on with our discussion I want to correct a misperception we've been dealing with all along.

Phrases

Can you think of any two-word utterances of English that are fragments? This should be easy. You might have come up with examples like:

Big apples.   Tall children.

Can you come up with any three-word utterances? Again, it should be easy. Examples include:

All big apples.   Five tall children.

And you can go on to four-word and five-word and even longer fragments, such as:

all the big apples
all the big apples that Bill told you to buy and I want to make pie from

What you are doing is expanding your phrases. We have now met the misperception I referred to above: **The one-word utterances we looked at were not just nouns or prepositions; they were noun phrases or prepositional phrases.** It's just that these phrases consisted of only a single word—they were, in a sense, UNEXPANDED. We say that every lexical category word used in an utterance HEADS a phrase. The head is called the LEXICAL PROJECTION of that category. The phrase is called the MAXIMAL PROJECTION of that category. So *apples* by itself is a noun that heads a noun phrase; *big apples* is also a noun phrase headed again by *apples*; *all big apples* is likewise a noun phrase headed by *apples*. We schematize this analysis with labeled brackets, like so:

[[apples]$_N$]$_{NP}$ [big [apples]$_N$]$_{NP}$ [all big [apples]$_N$]$_{NP}$

You might be rebelling here. I said that every lexical category word heads a phrase. Now in *big apples*, we have two lexical category words: the adjective *big* and the noun *apples*. So each should head a phrase, right? Yes, you're right. And we'll go into that very soon. But first, consider the utterance *big apples* as a whole. Why would we want to call the whole utterance an NP (like I did) as opposed to an Adjective Phrase (AP)? Can you see that when we say "big apples," we are talking about a kind of apples, not about a kind of bigness? If meaning is any sort of indication (and it is a relatively good indication much of the time, although not a perfect indication, as we'll learn in Chapter 5), we'd want to analyze *apples* and *big apples* as the same kind of syntactic phrase. Indeed, the phrases *apples* and *big apples* have similar syntactic distribution. That is, they can appear in the same places in larger utterances, such as:

{Apples/Big apples} grow on that tree.
I eat {apples/big apples} with peanut butter.
I make pie from {apples/big apples}.

But the phrase *apples* and the phrase *big* (by itself) do not have similar syntactic distribution:

*Big {grow/grows} on that tree.
*I eat big with peanut butter.
*I make pie from big.

That's why *big apples*, as a whole, is an NP. (And now you can convince yourself that *all big apples* is also an NP.) **In general, a phrase consists of a head and all its paraphernalia** (and we are working now on learning what that paraphernalia is). In the NP *big apples*, *apples* is the head of the NP and *big* is the paraphernalia—even though *big*, by itself, heads an AP.

Let's pursue this. If every lexical category word is a head, and if the lexical categories are N(oun), V(erb), A(djective or adverb), and P(reposition), then the NP *all big apples* contains an AP headed by the adjective *big* and, in fact, consisting entirely of *big*:

[all   [[big]$_A$]$_{AP}$ [apples]$_N$]$_{NP}$

What, then, do we do with *all* in this phrase? Is *all* a lexical category word? *All* is a QUANTIFIER, and there is controversy over the analysis of both quantifiers (like *all*, *some*, *few*) and NUMERALS (like *one*, *ten*, *a thousand*). Some people argue they are lexical categories. Others argue they are functional categories, more like determiners. (We introduced the distinction between functional and lexical categories in the section "Compounding" of Chapter 3. Essentially words with minimal sense of their own which function largely to give information about the words they introduce—as determiners like *the* do— are function words. Later in the section "Functional Heads with Verbal Phrases: Another Look," we will learn about other types of functional categories.) So what are we to do?

In fact, we won't enter that controversy because there are many linguists today who would argue that every word heads a phrase, not just lexical words, and we will take this approach. But before we can add our labeled brackets regarding the quantifier, we need to think about the paraphernalia that goes with each head.

Functional and Lexical Categories

When I asked you to come up with one-word utterances belonging to the various lexical categories, you easily found ones for V, N, P, and A. But we noted that a one-word utterance that consists of a functional category word, such as *the*, is either impossible to find or calls for a linguistically self-conscious context—so that we have, actually, a kind of metalinguistic use of the word. This is a fundamental difference between lexical categories as a whole and functional categories as a whole. Lexical category words can head one-word phrases (although not every lexical item that is a lexical category word—like V, N, P, and A—can do so, as we will see); but no functional category words can head one-word phrases. (You now have a criterion by which to judge whether numerals and quantifiers are lexical or functional categories. You will apply this criterion in Problem Set 4.1.)

Functional category heads require a companion, called a SISTER. If we think of the functional word as a kind of OPERATOR or FUNCTOR, then its sister is what it operates over, what we will call a COMPLEMENT (and the term "complement" is also used to cover sister phrases that are arguments of a lexical head). The complement of a numeral is an NP. The complement of a determiner (another functional head) is also an NP. And the complement of the quantifier *all* in our phrase is an NP (although you know *all* can take complements of other category types too). We will look at functional heads with complements other than NPs later. We can now give a revision of the labeled bracketing for *all big apples*. In this book I will lump numerals and quantifiers under the single label of Q(uantifier). The entire phrase is then a QP, and only the subpart *big apples* is the NP:

$$[[all]_Q \quad [[[big]_A]_{AP} \quad [apples]_N]_{NP}]_{QP}$$

Tree Analyses

Labeled bracketing like this takes up little space and gives the relevant information, but the same information is often more easily seen in the schema known as SYNTACTIC TREES, like so:

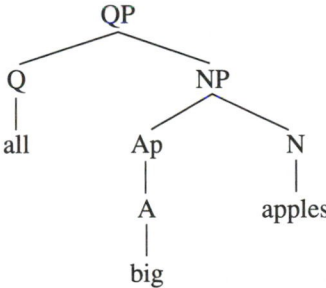

(So now you've seen metrical trees in Chapter 2, morphological trees in Chapter 3, and syntactic trees. In Chapter 5 you will meet semantic trees. **Every component of the grammar makes use of trees.**)

You almost assuredly have major questions in your mind about the contrast between the analysis of *big* and *all* in this tree. You understand why *big* alone is an AP (we went through that above), but you might have expected that *all* alone would also constitute a QP. Please wait on this question, and let us get some terminology down first, so we can talk sensibly about these trees.

When we talk about trees, we have a fixed terminology. Much of it you met already in the section "Bounded Feet" of Chapter 2. But since some readers may not have gone through Chapter 2 and since many others may need a little refresher, we'll go through it again.

Each label on the tree, other than the lexical items at the very bottom, is called a node (a term from Chapter 2). So Q is a node; A is a node; N is a node; AP is a node; NP is a node; QP is a node. We say that a node dominates (another term from Chapter 2) all the nodes below it in the tree that are connected to it by downward branches (again, a term from Chapter 2). So QP in this tree dominates every other node in the tree, but AP, for example, dominates only A, and N dominates no other nodes. We say that nodes immediately dominated by another node are DAUGHTERS to that node, and that that node is the MOTHER. So NP, for example, is mother to AP and N, who are daughters to NP. We say that daughters of the same node are sisters (a term we have met). So Q and NP, for example, are sisters. We call the lexical items along the bottom of the tree the terminal string (just as in phonological trees). Every node in the tree is also called a CONSTITUENT. So A is a constituent, as is AP, as is NP, and so forth.

When talking about a tree analysis of a phrase, we speak of two relationships: IS A and IS ANALYZABLE AS. For example, AP and N together **are an** NP. Q, N, and A all together **are a** QP, because the single node that dominates all and only the terminal string that Q, N, and A together dominate **is a** QP.

On the other hand, NP **is analyzable as** [AP N] in this tree. But NP **is also analyzable as** any combination of nodes that dominates the same terminal string that NP dominates. So NP **is also analyzable as** [A N]. How many ways is QP analyzable? That is, how many string analyses does QP have? If we include QP as an analysis, then QP has four analyses:

[QP]   [Q NP]   [Q AP N]   [Q A N].

We will find reason to complicate the analysis of phrases later on. But for now, let's work with this simple type of analysis.

Functional Phrases Pattern Like Lexical Phrases

One important point is that while we have called *all big apples* a QP, what we are dealing with here is a quantified noun phrase. And QPs of this sort have the same syntactic distribution and properties as nonquantified NPs. The important differences between quantified NPs and nonquantified NPs are more semantic than syntactic. (We will discuss quantification in the section "Quantified NPs" of Chapter 5). So for our purposes in this chapter, thinking of this kind of QP as a type of noun phrase is a perfectly reasonable and sensible thing to do. In fact, I will feel free to call such QPs noun phrases whenever I am not focusing attention on the fact that they are quantified. And, **in general, a functional phrase will pattern syntactically like the lexical phrase that is the complement of the functional head.** So unless I am focusing attention on the functional head, I will generally treat functional phrases as though they are lexical phrases.

And now let's get back to the question you may have had in your head when I gave the very first syntactic tree above: Why isn't *all* by itself a QP (just like *big* by itself is an AP)? There are several reasons why, but you aren't prepared yet to go through any of them. Still, this is too important a point for you to be asked to simply believe me without any justification. So I will outline one for you, and when you have finished reading this chapter and the next, you can come back and reconsider this argument critically.

The Q *all* is understood to **quantify across** *big apples*, so we say *all* has **scope** over *big* *apples*. (You'll consider scope in a precise way in Chapter 5, see particularly the sections "The Universal Quantifier" and "Ambiguity of Scope", as well as Problem Sets 5.5 and 5.6.) For many reasons, linguists have proposed that a quantifier has scope only over those constituents that it C-COMMANDS. We'll formally define the notion of c-command in the section "Interpretation: Anaphors and Binding Theory" later; for now all you need to know is that it is a hierarchical relationship defined between nodes on a syntactic tree. In the tree given above, *all* c-commands *big apples*. But if we had a tree in which *all* formed its own QP by itself, something like:

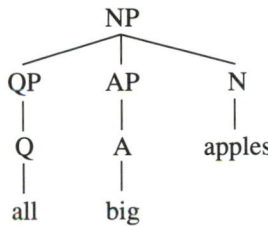

all would not c-command *big apples*. So please accept the first tree and return to it much later, when you are better prepared to understand this argument and when you can yourself bring more facts and arguments to bear on this issue.

Uniformity of the Structure of Phrases

We've touched on the analysis of quantified NPs. Before going into more detail, let's look at other types of phrases, asking ourselves the same kinds of questions that led us to our analysis of NPs. We can begin with PP (prepositional phrase). Find two-word, three-word, and multiple-word utterances headed by P. You might have come up with examples like:

    after lunch
    right after lunch
    after the important lunch that I told you about

What is the structure of these phrases? We have a P followed by an NP in all of them. But in one of them we have an initial *right*, as well. What is that *right*? This is the 'directly' sense that we identified earlier, where we claimed that the slot following *right* must be filled by a P. What kind of word is *right* in this usage? Does it seem more like a functional or a lexical category?

This is hard for you to answer. The only functional categories you have dealt with so far are numerals, quantifiers, and determiners (*the*, *a*, and various demonstratives such as *that*, *this*, *these*, *those*, mentioned in Chapter 3). What differences do you know between functional category words and lexical category words?

First, we pointed out explicitly that functional category words require a sister. Does *right* require a sister? Try using this sense of *right* alone in a sentence:

    *She went right. (cf. She went right out the door.)
    *She left right. (cf. She left right after lunch.)

So by this test *right* could be a functional category. (I say "could be," since some lexical heads cannot occur without a sister, either, as we'll see.)

What other contrasts can you notice between the two types of categories? Look at NPs for a moment:

[the boys]   [the tall boys]   [all boys]   [all tall boys]

The functional word always comes at the very beginning of the phrase. One way to look at that is to say that **in English functional categories take sisters on their right.** This is true, even when we have more than one functional word in an NP, such as both *all* and *the*:

[all the boys]   [all the tall boys]

Try to make a tree analysis of *all the boys*. Let the phrase headed by *the* be called a DP (determiner phrase).

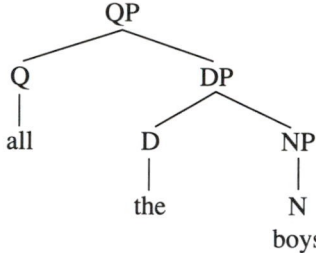

This is a quantified determiner phrase. Remember, however, that throughout this chapter we will refer to various kinds of nominal phrases (including quantified determiner phrases) as simply NPs unless our specific interest is the quantification. That's because all nominal phrases have a great deal in common syntactically.

Contrast the position of *all* and *the* to the word order of other types of words that can occur in an NP, such as adjectives:

smart girls
girls smart at math

In English an AP can precede or follow the N (and in Problem Set 4.1 you will explore the factors relevant to this choice of word order). So in English lexical categories can take right or left sisters (although this is not a free choice—and some categories take only right sisters).

How does *right* stack up by this test? *Right* always occurs in initial position of a PP:

right up my alley   *up right my alley   *up my alley right

So once again *right* looks like it could be a functional category word.

Is there any other difference you can find between the two types of categories? Think of their sense. In general, nouns have a sense that is somehow self-contained. Prepositions do as well. That is, when we hear *up*, we have a sense of direction that persists in the phrase *up the stairs*. Determiners, on the other hand, have very little self-contained sense. Think of what *the* means. Can you give it a sense? When would you use these two sentences, for example:

A man came into the room.
The man came into the room.

The first one could start a conversation. But the second one presumes some prior, appropriate knowledge on the part of the listener. In the second one, the speaker is counting on the listener assigning to the NP *the man* the very referent that the speaker intends. But in the first one, the speaker is introducing the NP *a man* into the discourse (and I don't mean introducing in person—I mean introducing as a topic for discussion in the discourse), which from that point on in the conversation will have an agreed-upon referent (the one the speaker just introduced). Numerals and quantifiers, on the other hand, can be argued to have some self- contained sense. (Let me remind you that there is controversy over whether numerals and quantifiers are lexical or functional.)

What about *right*? Does it have a self-contained sense of this sort? When you say:

She went right home.
She left right after lunch.

does *right* have a constant sense? In the first it means something close to "straight." In the second it means something close to "immediately." You might well feel this is, indeed, two aspects of a single, rather well-defined, sense. Or you might feel that *right* is more like *the*, in having a sense that is more discourse dependent. But I hope that you can at least see that the semantics of *right* are not inconsistent with an analysis of it as a function word. In fact, *right*, *straight*, *immediately*, and *directly* could all be argued to fill the role of functional head introducing PP in phrases like:

{right/immediately} after lunch
{straight/directly} to the library

Intensifiers

I like to call *right* an INTENSIFIER and call the phrase it heads an IntP. Assuming that, please give a tree analysis of *right after lunch*:

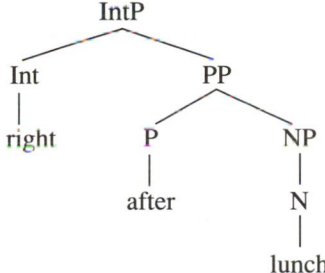

Think now about adjectives and adjective phrases. Take the adjective *smart*. Can you think of any word that looks like a functional word that could introduce *smart*? If you're having trouble, ask yourself what kind of words for APs might be comparable to *all* or *the* for NPs and *right* for PPs. I hope you came up with examples like:

{very/so/too/that} smart

And notice that, like with NPs (but unlike with PPs), these function words can stack up:

so very smart
all that smart (as in: *He isn't all that smart.*)

Some of these functional words you can recognize as quantifiers *(all)* or demonstratives *(that)*. The others we will lump together under the term "intensifier" again. Now draw the tree for the AP *so very smart*.

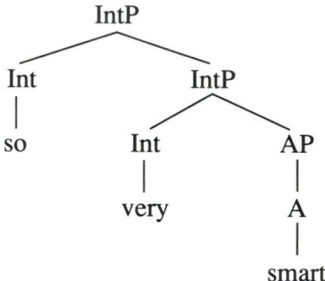

I should point out that many linguists categorize words like *right*, *so*, and *very* as adverbs. However, syntactic differences are significant. Thus, we can often repeat intensifiers for emphasis *(very very cold)*, but we do not do this with adverbs. *(*She talked loudly loudly.)* Furthermore, intensifiers always precede the head they intensify in English, but adverbs can precede or follow the head. *(She quietly left. She left quietly.)* For these and other reasons, I will maintain a syntactic and categorial difference between intensifiers and adverbs.

Looking at these various trees, what can you say about phrases in general? Can you see that the NP and PP phrases are very similar? Indeed, **phrases have a lot in common structurally, regardless of what their head is.** So NPs are headed by N and they might or might not have APs that are sisters to the N (as in *(big) dogs*), and they might or might not be sisters themselves to functional nodes (as in *(all) dogs*), and they can both be sisters to functional nodes and contain an AP at once *(all big dogs.)* And PPs are headed by P and they might or might not be sisters themselves to functional nodes as in *(right) after lunch.* But we haven't yet talked about whether P can take an AP sister and we haven't talked at all about either N or P taking an NP sister (though our tree for *right after lunch* shows an NP sister to P).

AP and More on PP

Let's consider APs next, since they are quite similar to NPs in many regards. APs are headed by A and the AP itself may or may not be a sister to a functional head—as in *(so) smart*. Now can an AP contain another AP that is a sister to the head A? Try to think of examples. Remember that AP includes both adjective phrases and adverb phrases. So now can you think of any? What about:

[shockingly yellow]   [laughably absurd]   [remarkably smart]

So an A head can have a sister AP, just as an N head can have a sister AP. Is it possible for an AP both to be the sister to a functional head and to contain another AP at once? What about:

so remarkably smart

What is the meaning of this AP? Does it mean smartness that is so remarkable or does it mean remarkable smartness that is to a high degree (the degree denoted by *so*)? The issue is whether the functional head *so* here takes the AP headed by *smart* as its sister, or the AP headed by *remarkably* as its sister:

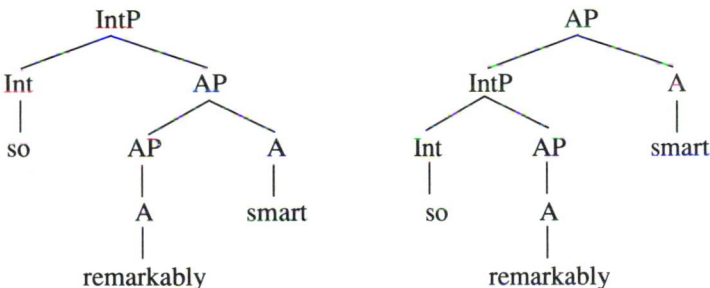

I feel unsure about the fine semantic distinction we should be able to discern between the readings associated with these two analyses. But everything we've done thus far would suggest that both analyses should be available to us. So, given no clear evidence to the contrary, I will assume both analyses are possible. And that means that I answer yes to the question of whether an AP can both be the sister to a functional head and contain another AP at once.

And, finally, as we know, PPs are headed by P and the PP itself may or may not be a sister to a functional head (as in *(right) over*). But can a P take an AP sister? The only types of potential examples I've been able to come up with involve adverb phrases that are open to other analyses, such as:

obviously up

I do not believe that *obviously* is a sister to the head P here, together under a PP node. First, notice that if PPs behaved in a parallel fashion to NPs and APs, we'd expect that if a functional head introduced the PP, that head would precede an AP sister to the P. But, in fact, if a functional head occurs with this P, it follows the AP:

obviously right up   *right obviously up

So the structure would be:

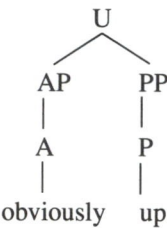

(Here I used the node label "U" for "utterance," without taking a stand as to what the overall phrase category should be.) It appears that PP differs from both NP and AP on this point: P does not take an AP sister.

Modification

This last fact is interesting. Let's pursue it a moment longer. What function do APs inside NPs and inside other APs have? What is *sallow* doing in the NP *sallow skin*? What is *comfortingly* doing in the AP *comfortingly warm*? *Sallow* describes the skin, just as *comfortingly* describes the warmth. We say that these APs MODIFY the head N or A. Modification is the most common function an AP can have.

And at this point I can ask you another question, one that may have been on your mind since Chapter 3. Why do we lump adjective phrases and adverb phrases together into one category called AP? What do they have in common? Well, certainly, you've just learned that the most common function of both is modification. But what else do you notice about them? Is there any morphological relationship between adjectives and adverbs? Yes. In many instances, an adverb is an adjective stem plus the suffix *-ly*.

What kind of head does each modify? Look back at the examples we've just analyzed. Adjective phrases modify nouns. Adverb phrases modify adjectives. This is generally true. And even though we haven't yet looked at phrases of other category types, I'm sure you can tell me another category that adverb phrases modify. I hope you thought of verbs, as in *run quickly*. But can you think off the top of your head of any other categories that adjective phrases modify? It is harder to come up with examples here. In fact, **in general, when an A modifies a noun, the form we find is an adjective; and when an A modifies anything other than a noun, the form we find is an adverb.** This sort of complementary distribution allows us to gather them together into one larger syntactic category that we call A. (You might well be thinking of problems for the claim that adjectives modify only nouns. If so, please hold on to them, and I will return to this issue.)

Now let's consider the fact that APs cannot modify a head P. Why would that be? What is it about a P like:

under   through   after   with   off   out   beside   behind

that makes it unable to bear modification, in contrast to an N like:

dog   love   wisdom   pig   house   tree   cloud   star   lie

I hazard the conjecture that it has to do with the sense of most P's. P's are relational words and, indeed, the function that is carried out by P's in English is carried out in many languages by affixes, instead (as we noted in the sections "Lexical and Derivational Morphemes" and "English Case" of Chapter 3). These relations are of a limited semantic type—in comparison to the seemingly limitless semantic types of nouns or adjectives. Perhaps P's are simply not semantically rich enough to bear true modification. That is, P can be quantified *(almost out; all over; halfway in)*, but beyond talking about the degree of a P's sense, we don't modify P. This is an important difference between PPs on the one hand and NP and AP on the other.

One final point can be made now: **every word in a phrase or sentence needs to be LICENSED.** That is, every word in a syntactic structure must have a function that allows it to be there. A P can occur inside a PP because it is the head of the PP. But an N cannot occur inside a PP unless it is the head of an NP that occurs inside that PP, as in:

PP: over [the **rainbow**]$_{NP}$

Likewise, phrases must be licenced. An AP cannot occur as a sister to a P because it cannot function to modify that P. But an AP can occur as a sister to an N or a V or an A because it can function to modify that N or V or A. Phrases can be licenced by a variety of functions, not just modification. You will learn about these functions immediately following, and throughout this chapter.

Objects

P differs from N and A in at least one other way beyond the fact that it cannot take an AP sister. Make a list of several PPs. You might have come up with examples like:

[with a friend]   [to the bank]   [out the back]   [off the roof]

In all of these examples we have an NP inside the PP. What is that NP doing there? What is its function? Probably in some English class somewhere in your education you came across the term "OBJECT OF A PREPOSITION," and, indeed, we will call these NPs Objects of the P, or OPs.

PPs as Modifiers

We have just said that the GRAMMATICAL FUNCTION (GF) of an N like *hesitation* in:

Mary opened the door with hesitation.

is OP. But what function does the PP *with hesitation* have in this sentence? It is a modifier—here it modifies the verb *opened*, just as an adverb phrase like *quickly* would.

Are all PPs modifiers? Consider a sentence like:

Mary opened the door with a key.

Does *with a key* modify anything here? You might think that it does, but even if you think that, you should be able to recognize that there's an important difference between *hesitation* in the first sentence and *a key* in the second sentence. For one, we cannot say:

*Hesitation opened the door.

But we can say:

A key opened the door.

We will discuss the function of PPs such as *with a key* when we discuss arguments. And we will see other functions for PPs when we talk about different types of predicates. For now the important point is that you recognize that while OP is a GF, a PP (that contains that OP) can play a variety of functions in a sentence.

Back to Objects in General

We just learned above that P can take an Object. Can N or A take an Object? Search around. The answer you should come to is no. And this is another significant difference between P on the one hand and N and A on the other. We will offer an account of this difference later.

First, however, let's talk about one more type of phrase. But to see this type of phrase, we'll need to put it into the larger context of a sentence. Consider this sentence:

The little boy eats fried potatoes.

What phrases do you recognize in this sentence? There are two NPs, which you should be able to bracket:

[The little boy] eats [fried potatoes].

(Notice that I'm calling the DP (determiner phrase) *the little boy* an NP, since the fact that it is introduced by the functional head determiner is not of interest to our present discussion.) The obvious question is how to analyze *eats*. You know it is a verb. And you know it has to head a phrase, which, of course, we'll call a VP. But is it a phrase all by itself, or does it take an NP sister—and, if so, which NP is its sister, or are both of them its sisters?

All these questions are about the CONSTITUENCY of the sentence—the recognition of the various nodes in an analysis of the sentence—and questions of constituency are among the most pressing questions in syntax. We call the NP *the little boy* the Subject of the sentence. (And you already have one way to recognize Subjects—they are the NP that the V agrees with. Actually, we will see later tenseless clauses in which no Subject-Verb Agreement takes place. But for tensed clauses, agreement can help us identify the Subject.) We call the NP *fried potatoes* the DIRECT OBJECT (DO) of the V, or simply the Object of the V. So the question is whether the sentence is analyzed as having the three separate subparts, SVO (Subject-Verb-Object), or whether the first two or the last two of those subparts group together to form constituents:

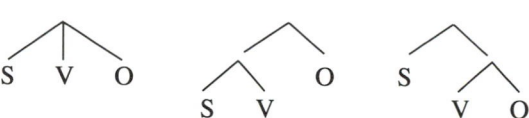

Movement as a Test for Constituency

Probably the most relied-upon tests for constituency in syntax have to do with movement (or, more simply, distribution—as I will discuss). Consider these sentences:

John will buy those same shoes.
Those same shoes John will buy.

The first sentence has unmarked word order for English (SVO). The second has a marked word order for English (OSV). Many linguists would argue that in the second sentence the DO has moved from its canonical position after the V to the front of the sentence. One of the basic assumptions of syntax is that **movement applies to a node, never to a string of words that don't form a node.** The words *those same shoes* form an NP (actually, a DP, given the presence of the DEMONSTRATIVE *those*), so we can move these words as a unit. But we can't move just *those same* since there is no single node that dominates all and only those two words:

*Those same John will buy shoes.

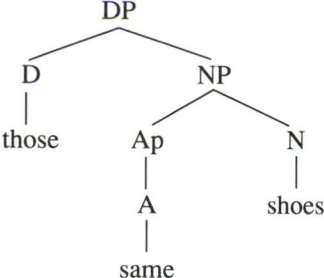

Do you see that? D and AP together do not form a constituent. (There is no node that dominates only D and AP.) However, we also cannot move *same shoes*, even though they do form the constituent NP:

*Same shoes John will buy those.

That's because English does not allow us to STRAND certain functional nodes, of which D is one. The word *those* in this ungrammatical sentence is stranded in that it has been left behind when the rest of its phrase moved away.

Movement vs. Distribution

We need to interrupt the present discussion. Not all theories of syntax allow movement rules, and the issue of whether or not movement rules exist is a hotly debated one.

However, we don't really need to get into that debate here because this discussion about constituency can be rephrased entirely in terms of distribution, without assuming movement at all. For example, we could say that the fact that *those same* cannot appear separately from *shoes* and the fact that *same shoes* cannot appear separately from *those* are distributional facts that tell us about constituency. So if you find yourself adopting a syntactic theory that does not admit movement rules, you can still use distribution facts as evidence for constituency. I will therefore continue this discussion without getting into the debate and I will persist in talking about "movement," but you can interpret the discussion as being about distribution (that is, about which elements can occur in which contexts).

Back to Constituency and VPs

Now let's see if we can use movement to discover the proper constituency of VPs. Look again at the sentence:

John will buy those same shoes.

Try to front the V along with its DO:

Buy those same shoes, John will.

This may not sound terrific to you. But in a larger context, I believe it is acceptable:

John said he would buy those same shoes, and **buy those same shoes, he will.**

How could we account for the movement here? There are at least two logical possibilities. First, we could have moved the V and its DO together in one movement. Second, we could have moved the V and its DO separately, in two movement rules. Can you think of a way to test which of these proposals is right? With the second proposal, we are claiming that movement of the V alone is allowed, as is movement of the DO alone. Are those claims true? Test them. We've already seen above that movement of the DO alone is licit, in the example:

Those same shoes John will buy.

Is movement of the V alone licit? No:

*Buy John will those same shoes.

And this is so whether we try to move just the V or the V plus the auxiliary:

*Will buy John those same shoes.

So the second proposal is wrong.

We can conclude that the V and the DO moved together (the first proposal). And since movement is of constituents only, we can now propose that a V and its DO form a constituent headed by the V—a VP. The structure we will assign to *The little boy eats fried potatoes*, then, is:

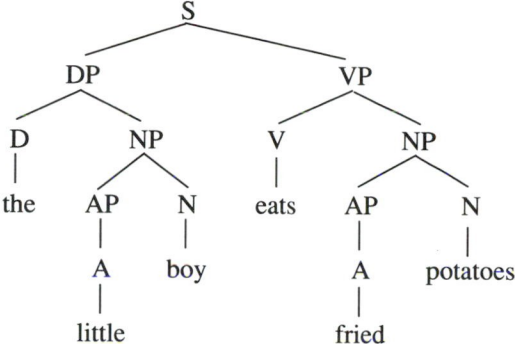

I have used S to indicate the node that dominates the whole sentence. This is just a shorthand for the moment—we will get into the proper categorial status of sentences later. The important thing to keep in mind for the moment is that S is like other phrasal projections, not like lexical projections—that is, **S must be a maximal projection.** So don't be led astray by the fact that I've represented it as just a single letter.

Before going forward, please take a moment to get a little facility with drawing trees. Draw the tree for *My best friend lost important races.* Is it structurally identical to the tree above? I hope so. The only difference is that instead of a determiner on the first nominal, we have a possessive adjective. But in English, possessive adjectives and determiners are mutually exclusive (we say *my sister* and *the sister*, but not *the my sister), so they might very well be the same kind of syntactic animal. Now let's make a little change: Draw the tree for *Every boy eats three hot meals.* *Every* is a quantifier, so *every boy* is a QNP. And in this chapter we are treating numerals as quantifiers, so *three hot meals* is also a QNP. You should have:

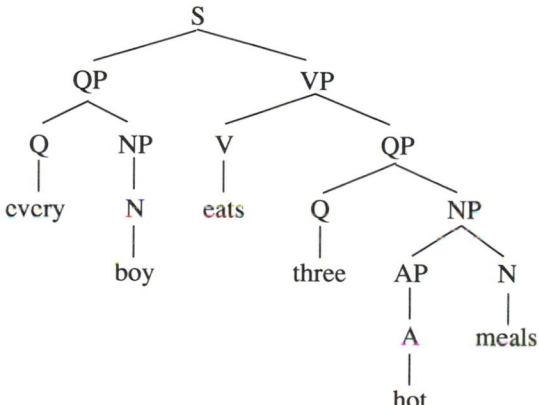

If you didn't get this pretty quickly, slow down and play with trees a little longer before continuing.

The important thing about these trees with respect to the question we raised above is that the verb heads a phrase, a VP, and that VP is like PP in that its head can take an Object. In fact, some Vs and some Ps require Objects. That is, they are obligatorily or strictly transitive (a term you met in Chapter 3). Other V's and P's optionally take an Object (they are optionally transitive). And still others cannot take an Object (they are obligatorily or strictly intransitive—another term you met in Chapter 3). We SUBCATEGOR-IZE lexical items according to whether or not they must, may, or cannot co-occur with other items. So, for example, transitive verbs are a subcategory of verbs—they are verbs subcategorized to take Objects. You can explore some issues of subcategorization in Problem Set 4.7.

Do you expect V to be able to be modified by an AP? Given that N and A can be and that one probable reason P cannot be is that it is not strong enough semantically to support modification, you should expect that V can be modified by an AP. And, indeed, it can, as you very well know from our discussion of adjectives vs. adverbs:

John [eats [quickly]$_{AP}$]$_{VP}$.

And now let's stop a moment and return to a point we brought up earlier. We said that adjective phrases typically modify only nouns. But in fact in ordinary speech today in America, we can find adjective phrases (not just adverb phrases) modifying verbs. Can you think of examples? There are many:

Mary plays **rough.**
Please drive **slow.**
Don't work so **hard.**

Perhaps not all the examples I've listed here sound good to your ear, but I bet at least the third one does. We seem to be expanding the syntactic environments for adjective phrase.

A Restriction on Fronting

Let's now address a question that may well have come to mind as you were looking at the movement possibilities in the sentences about eating potatoes and buying shoes: Why can't we move just the V alone to yield:

*Eats the little boy fried potatoes. (Cf. the little boy eats fried potatoes.)
*Buy John will those same shoes. (Cf. John will buy those same shoes.)

The answer may not come to mind right off. So let's approach it step by step. First, is this restriction (whatever it is) only on V? To test that, let's look at other sentences in which we have fronted elements of different categorial types, such as:

[Into the woods]$_{PP}$ John ran.
[Abuse of children]$_{NP}$ I simply can't understand.
[Fond of John]$_{AP}$ she definitely is.

Can we front just the P or just the N or just the A alone? No:

*Into John ran the woods.
*Abuse I simply can't understand of children.
*Fond she definitely is of John.

We noted earlier that English doesn't allow stranding of certain functional nodes. Can that restriction be responsible for the ungrammaticality of these three sentences? No. The items stranded by movement here are not functional nodes; they are whole phrases. (*The woods* is an NP; *of children* is a PP; *of John* is a PP.)

We can conclude that not one of our lexical category nodes can be fronted alone, leaving behind the rest of the phrase it heads. Indeed, **this particular fronting rule moves only phrases, not heads.** But not all movement rules are like this. We will encounter a head movement rule later, in the section "Functional Heads with Verbal Phrases: Another Look."

Functional Heads with VP: A First Look

Let's return now to our analysis of verbal phrases. Can VP be the sister to a functional head? This question is harder to answer. VPs aren't generally introduced by words like quantifiers or intensifiers. However, there do appear to be instances in which an intensifier of sorts can introduce a VP, such as the *well* in this sentence:

Mary might [well win].

We might call this use of *well* a positive operator (and you'll see a way to handle it in the section "Functional Heads with Verbal Phrases: Another Look").

Are there other types of functional heads that can take VP sisters? What about the *might* here? What is *might*? This is an auxiliary verb (a term you met in Chapter 3), and you will learn about the range of auxiliary verbs in English in Problem Set 4.3. Probably most linguists consider English auxiliary verbs to be lexical heads (V's, which take VP complements), although they are certainly a closed set and of limited semantic sense, so their category type is debatable (much like the category type of P is debatable). However, there are other potential candidates for functional heads that can introduce VP, and we need to discuss them.

Loose Ends

At this point there are two phrase-structure issues that we've brought up but haven't yet discussed satisfactorily. One we just raised: the determination of the full range of functional heads that can take VP as sister. The other we raised earlier (in the section "Back to Objects in General"): the question of why V and P can take Objects but A and N can't. We'll now discuss these issues, which turn out to be related, but we'll begin in a rather indirect fashion. You might want to outline the argument as we go in order to see the logic of it.

Case and Phrase Structure: A Look at Latin

If we sidestep into other languages for a moment, we can learn more about phrase and sentence structure that will help us understand syntax in general as well as the syntax of English in particular. We're going to look at Latin here because the morphology of Latin illustrates several important concepts in an obvious way.

Consider this Latin sentence:

Gallī   urbem   expugnāverant.
gaul-II-P-Nom town-III-S-Acc take by storm-3P-Pluperfect
'The Gauls had taken the town by storm.'

(P = plural; S = singular; 3 = third person; II = second declension; III = third declension. A DECLENSION is a noun class, and membership in a declension determines the Case endings for singular and plural, as we will discuss.) This sentence consists of the string NP$_1$-NP$_2$-V. If we take this string and permute its parts, we still get the same reading for the resulting sentences. Thus all these sentences mean the same thing:

Urbem Gallī expugnāverant.
Gallī expugnāverant urbem.
Urbem expugnāverant Gallī.
Expugnāverant Gallī urbem.
Expugnāverant urbem Gallī.
'The Gauls had taken the town by storm.'

I am not claiming that word order in Latin is free. There were indeed many constraints on word order, and the most typical place for the V was clause-final. The point I'm making is that, so far as I know, all the word orders I've just given were possible in appropriate contexts, and all had the same TRUTH CONDITIONS. That is, the conditions under which any one of these sentences is true are identical to the conditions under which any other of these sentences is true. But these sentences may well have differed with respect to their non-truth-functional meanings—that is, with respect to what the sentence is focusing on or who the speaker is empathizing with or other such matters.

Contrast that situation to the English sentences:

John noticed Paul.
Paul noticed John.

The different word orders here correspond to drastically different meanings: these sentences are not truth-functionally equivalent. (You can easily imagine a situation in which the first sentence is true but the second is false and vice-versa.) Word order in English, then, plays quite a role in helping us figure out the grammatical functions (GFs) of Subject and DO. But word order is not playing that same role in the Latin sentences.

Grammatical Functions

Let's stop a moment to inventory our GFs. We have Subject and DO. But there are two others we've already met. First, consider the GF of the Object of *to* in:

Ralph told everything to Bill.

We call *Bill* the Indirect Object (IO), and we will talk more later about ways of recognizing IOs. (What GF does *Ralph* play? Subject. What GF does *everything* play? DO.)

Now let's augment this sentence like so:

Ralph told everything to Bill for only five dollars.

What type of syntactic phrase is *for only five dollars*? A PP. So what role does the NP *only five dollars* play? Yes, it is an Object of a Preposition (OP). These four GFs are the only GFs we will talk about to any significant extent in this chapter.

You might well look at *Bill* and notice that it is an OP, as well. That's true. But *Bill* is different from other OPs in important ways that we will discuss. So we will be careful to call IOs that are OPs by the rubric of IO to distinguish them from OPs that don't have the properties that IOs have.

NPs in GFs

At this point we've talked about NPs, APs, PPs, and VPs and we've noted that NPs can occur inside PPs and VPs in the GFs of OP, DO, and IO. NPs can also occur as the Subjects of sentences. NPs can occur in other positions, as well. But what I'd like to ask you to consider here is whether the range of NP types we have talked about thus far can occur in all these GFs. Recall that we can have NPs that consist of just the head N (such as *houses*) or of the head N plus a modifier (such as *big houses*). Furthermore, the NP can itself be the sister to a functional head, giving us a larger nominal phrase—perhaps a Determiner Phrase (a DP, such as *the big houses*) or a Quantifier Phrase (a QP, such as *all big houses*).

Can all of these types of NPs occur as OPs? Yes:

Back yards are [behind **houses**].
You often find fancy roofs [on **big houses**].
The realtor has information [about **the big houses**].
[In **all big houses**] you find multiple bathrooms.

Can all of these types of NPs occur as DOs? Demonstrate to yourself that the answer is yes. Do not feel restricted to using only NPs with *houses* as the head N. Use whatever NPs come to mind that have the requisite forms.

Can all of these types of NPs occur as IOs? Again, it should be easy for you to convince yourself that the answer is yes.

Can all of these types of NPs occur as Subjects of sentences? Show it.

So, while our focus thus far has been on the structure of particular types of phrases, we can now see that phrases can build together into larger and larger phrases and into sentences. We will learn later that sentences are, really, another kind of headed phrase.

Back to Latin GFs

Let's return now to the Latin sentences we were discussing. What tells us which NP is Subject and which is DO in the Latin sentences? To figure this out, compare the earlier

Latin sentences to this new one (and I repeat one permutation of the earlier Latin sentence here for your convenience):

Old sentence

Gallī   urbem   expugnāverant.
gaul-II-P-Nom town-III-S-Acc take by storm-3P-Pluperfect
'The Gauls had taken the town by storm.'

New sentence

Urbs   Gallōs   expugnāverat.
town-III-S-Nom gaul-II-P-Acc take by storm-3S-Pluperfect
'The town had taken the Gauls by storm.'

All the other five sentences that result from permuting the two NPs and the V in the new sentence have the same reading. Take a close look. What differs between the new sentence and the old one?

You should realize that morphology is playing an enormous role (and you might remember that we looked at some of this morphology in the section "Case Systems" of Chapter 3). The suffixes on the NPs differ, and the suffixes on the V differ. The suffixes on the NPs indicate declension membership and number (as I've glossed them), as well as Case. The suffixes on the V indicate tense and person–number agreement with the Subject. Two different pieces of information help us to identify the Subject—the Case and the agreement on the V.

However, if both NPs have the same person and number, the agreement on the V will not distinguish which NP is the Subject. In such an instance, Case alone can do the job of telling us which one is the Subject, as in:

Gallī   feminās   expugnāverant.
gaul-II-P-Nom woman-I-P-Acc take by storm-3P-Pluperfect
'The Gauls had taken the women by storm.'

Here both *Gallī* and *feminās* are third person and plural. Yet no matter what order these three words come in, the sentence will always mean that the Gauls acted upon the women, not vice versa. If we wanted to say that the women acted upon the Gauls, we'd use the following sentence or any permutation of these three words:

Gallōs   feminae   expugnāverant.
gaul-II-P-Acc woman-I-P-Nom take by storm-3P-Pluperfect
'The women took the Gauls by storm.'

So the fact that *Gallī* is Nominative Case but *Gallōs* is Accusative Case tells us that *Gallī* is the Subject of its sentence, but *Gallōs* is the Object of its sentence.

Written Classical Latin has five declensions and each of them has particular suffixes for five separate Cases in the singular and five separate Cases in the plural: Nominative, Accusative, Dative, Ablative, and Genitive. (There was a sixth Case, the Vocative, used for direct address. But it was largely moribund even in writing by the Classical period, and we often find the Nominative where we would expect the Vocative.) Nominative Case is typically assigned to the Subject of a tensed clause *(Gallī* is a Nominative form, as are *feminae* and *urbs)*; Accusative to the DO *(Gallōs* is an Accusative form, as are *feminās* and *urbem)*; Dative to the Indirect Object (IO), as in this sentence (where *servō* is Dative):

Amīcus   servō   pecūniam   dedit.
friend-II-S-Nom slave-II-S-Dat money-I-S-Acc give-3S-Perfect
'The friend gave money to the slave.'

Beyond that, prepositions typically assign their Object Ablative Case, as in:

ā   militibus
by soldier-III-P-Abl
'by the soldiers'

or Accusative Case, as in:

propter   fluctūs
because of wave-IV-P-Acc

And the Genitive Case has many uses, including showing possession:

virī   cquus
man-II-S-Gen horse-II-S-Nom
'the man's horse'

Furthermore, the Ablative Case can show up on nominals that play a variety of roles, such as showing means, manner, time, cause, and many others.

However, there is quite a bit of variation on these general rules. For example, some verbs assign Dative Case to their Object, even when they take only one Object, so this Object is presumably a Direct Object:

Puer   suō   patrī   pāruit.
boy-II-S-Nom his-SM-Dat father-III-S-Dat obey-3S-Perfect
'The boy obeyed his father.'

(Here the adjective *suō* is showing masculine gender in agreement with the noun *patrī* that it modifies.) When a particular lexical item assigns a fixed Case to its Object and that case is different from the Case normally found on that GF in that structure, we say we are dealing with LEXICAL CASE ASSIGNMENT. Lexical Case assignment in Latin is not limited to just a few verbs assigning Dative to their DO. Other verbs assign Ablative Case to their only Object, such as the verbs *ūtor* 'use,' *fruor* 'enjoy,' and *fungor* 'perform' (all of which are DEPONENT verbs—that is, verbs which appear with the morphological suffix that shows passive voice, but which do not have a passive sense associated with them). A rare verb assigns Genitive Case to its only Object, such as *egeo* 'lack.' Which prepositions assign Ablative Case to their Object and which assign Accusative Case is also largely lexical assignment, although sometimes a given P can take either Case with differing meanings:

with Ablative: in Italiā 'in Italy'
with Accusative: in Italiam 'into Italy'

And there are other less common variations.

Furthermore, adjectives assign Case to their Objects, typically Dative:

inimīcus   matrī
hostile-MS-Nom mother-III-S-Dat
'hostile (to the) mother'

but also Genitive:

capax   imperiī
capable-MS-Nom order-II-S-Gen
'fit for the order'

And sometimes adjectives can take an Ablative Object or even an Accusative Object (particularly if the adjective is morphologically built on a verbal root). So adjectives are like verbs and prepositions in being able to assign both STRUCTURAL CASE (the typical Case given to a certain GF in a given structure) and lexical Case (the exceptional Cases assigned by particular lexical items to their Objects).

English Case

Before continuing with our picture of Latin, let's take a moment to compare it to English. Some linguists have talked about English Case using terminology borrowed from Latin. Thus they have talked of Nominative, Accusative, Dative, Genitive, and Ablative Case. You tell me, does that make sense? First of all, when do we have a phonetically audible Case in English? Say a group of sentences and look for morphological indications of Case. You might have come up with sentences like:

Christine eats meat.
Meat is wonderful.
I saw Christine and the new boy's sister.
Christine saw me.

No matter what sentence you say a full NP in, with only one exception that NP is not phonetically distinguishable for Case: the Genitive, indicated by 's (as in *the new boy's*). Thus our Case system is best studied by looking at sentences in which the various GFs are played by pronouns.

Okay, look at sentences with lots of pronouns. What do you find? When, for example, do we use *I*? For Subjects (but only of tensed clauses, as we'll see). When do we use *me*? Say lots of sentences with *me* until you can see the pattern. We use *me* for everything except Genitives and Subjects of tensed clauses.

In other words, English makes only a three-way distinction: Subjective Case, Objective Case (whether DO, IO, or OP), and Genitive Case.

Different languages make use of fewer Cases (some languages have no audible Case system—such as Chinese) and of more Cases. Finnish uses fifteen: Nominative, Accusative, Genitive ("of" or "to"), Essive ("stationary"), Partitive ("away from"), Translative ("to/toward"), Inessive ("in"), Elative ("from (outside)"), Illative ("into"), Adessive ("at/near"), Ablative ("from (outside)"), Allative ("to/toward"), Instructive ("with" in an instrumental sense), Comitative ("accompanied by"), and Abessive ("without"). Many of these have senses that English renders via prepositions, as some of the glosses indicate. We will now return to our discussion of Latin, with the realization that this discussion is quite language-specific (as opposed to universal).

Nouns: Objects and Case

Now while V, P, and A take Objects in Latin, N does not take Objects except via the aid of a preposition (unless we consider the Genitive an Object of the noun, a proposal you can consider for yourself after you have done Problem Set 4.4). In this regard, Latin is very much like English. So there are N's that occur with PPs that have Objects, like the English *a book about war*, and there are N's that occur with Genitive NPs, like the English *the city's destruction*. But there are no N's that take an Object. (Please be sure not to confuse compound nouns like *lighthouse* and *apple pie* with noun phrases. Go back to Chapter 3 and reread our discussion in the section "Compounding" if this issue troubles you.)

I am assuming a distinction here that we need to talk about explicitly. Compare these NPs:

a discussion about the war
a moment of horror

Consider the semantic relationship between *discussion* and *the war* in the NP *a discussion about the war*. We call *the war* an argument of the N *discussion*. That is, in the event of discussing, the war is a participant (a passive participant, to be sure, but nonetheless a participant). (All these terms were introduced in Chapter 3.)

Compare this semantic relationship to the semantic relationship between *moment* and *horror* in *a moment of horror*. Is it the same? Surely not. *Horror* in the NP *a moment of horror* is not a participant in any event denoted by *moment* because *moment* does not denote an event, but a time. So *horror* is not an argument of *moment*. What is the function of *(of) horror* in this NP? We've already talked about this function above: It is modification. The PP *of horror* modifies the head noun *moment*, just as the AP does in *a horrible moment*.

So the single structure $[(D) \ N \ [P \ NP_1]_{PP}]_{NP}$ in English (an NP introduced by an optional Determiner and containing a PP) can correspond to two very different readings: one in which the OP (here NP_1) is an argument of the head N, and one in which the PP modifies the head N. Only if an NP is an argument of a head N, not if it is a modifier of the head N, do we ask whether that NP is an Object of the N. In the English NP *a discussion about the war*, *the war* is an argument of the head N but it is an Object of the P *about*. So we say that in English N cannot take an Object except in a kind of indirect way via a P.

When I say that nouns in Latin do not take Objects, I mean that they do not take NP arguments except via a P, just like English. However, they certainly do occur with NPs that modify them (similarly to *a moment of horror*) without those NPs being introduced by a P, as in:

flūmen magnā   altitūdine
river   great-Abl depth-Abl
'a river of great depth'

The Case of the modifying NP *(magnā altitūdine)* here is Ablative, and that Case is not assigned by the N *flūmen*. Instead, this NP is always in the Ablative Case when it modifies a N, regardless of which particular noun it modifies. **The Case of these modifying NPs, then, is linked to their function, not to the particular lexical items they appear with in a phrase or sentence.** This makes this instance of Case Assignment special and we will return to it when we talk about Genitives in English.

Okay. Now consider once again our conclusion: P, V, and A in Latin can take Objects, but N can't (at least not without the help of a P). Can you guess why that is? What else can P and V in both English and Latin do that N can't do? And what can A in Latin do that A in English can't do? We have now circled back to the question we faced a little earlier, just adding in Latin along the way: Why can V and P in English take Objects, but A and N can't? Let me try to lead you to the answer many linguists have proposed.

Think about Case assignment in Latin. What kind of category gets Case? Look at this sentence, in which I've labeled the morphemes for Case:

Ōlim in longinquā terrā   habitābat potēns   rēx.
once in distant-Abl land-Abl lived   powerful-Nom king-Nom
'Once upon a time in a faraway land there lived a powerful king.'

We see Case endings on adjectives and nouns here, but not on the adverb *ōlim* or on the verb *habitābat*. Indeed, only adjectives and N's can take Case endings in Latin. But there is more to it than that: All adjectives and N's do have Case endings in Latin. So we can conclude that **all adjectives and N's must be assigned Case in Latin.**

Can you tell me what determines which Case an adjective gets? Look at the Latin sentence just displayed and ask yourself what the function of *longinquā* is. Now ask yourself what the function of *potēns* is. Both of these are modifiers of nouns. Adjective phrases in Latin agree for Case with the head N that they modify. In fact, they agree for the features of number and gender as well. *(Longinquā* is feminine singular, in agreement with *terrā*; *potēns* is masculine singular, in agreement with *rēx.)* So the Case on an adjective phrase is determined by the Case on the head N that it modifies. Think of it is this way: Something assigns Case to the NP. That Case gets spelled out on the head N and on all modifying APs of that head N that are located inside the NP.

So the real question is: What determines the Case on the NP as a whole? We have learned that the Case of a nominal (leaving aside Subjects and leaving aside the use of the Ablative on modifying NPs such as in *flūmen magnā altitūdine*) in Latin is assigned by the V, P, or A that it is an Object of. So let us propose that **V, P, and A are the only lexical categories that are structural Case assigners in Latin.** What this means is that if an NP were an Object of an N, it would be in trouble. Every nominal must get Case (as we said), but if an NP were the Object of a N, it couldn't get Case since N is not a Case assigner. That's why N doesn't take an Object in Latin. Do you see this reasoning? If not, please reread this paragraph.

Exactly the same argument would be made for English, accounting for why N in English cannot take an NP Object, so long as we assume that all NPs in English must be assigned Case (just as in Latin). This argument is consistent with the fact that whenever an N takes a nominal argument following it, that argument must be introduced by a P that gives it Case:

a desire [for success]
my response [to the letter]
the obvious dependency [on flattery]

Sometimes that P seems to have no semantic value; all it does is assign Case to the Object of the head N:

the thought [of failure]
her hatred [of poetry]

Of is often called a vacuous preposition here. (Recall that we saw a vacuous P when we discussed the syntactic-glue use of *of* in the section "Inventory of Morphological Types" of Chapter 3.)

Assume this argument is correct. Now how could you account for the fact that A can take an NP Object in Latin but not in English? All we need to do is claim that A in Latin, unlike in English, is a Case assigner. It then follows that A in Latin can take a nominal Object, but A in English cannot. Can A in English take a nominal argument? Try to find such adjectives. You might have come up with examples like:

similar to Bill
familiar with my problem
different from Italy
fond of Catherine

Once again a P appears to introduce a following NP argument following the A, and vacuous *of* is employed as a default.

Clauses and Case

Our understanding of Case, which we have arrived at by looking only at phrases so far, can be enriched in at least two ways by looking at sentences. The discussion that follows is a bit intricate, so take your time reading it, and I suggest that if you haven't been outlining up to this point, you should begin now.

First, we have looked at Objects of V and P (and of A, for Latin) that are NPs. But these are not the only kinds of Objects we can find. Consider this pair of sentences:

Mary expected a visitor.
Mary expected that Bill would come home.

In the first sentence the verb takes an NP Object. But what is its Object in the second sentence? Here it is the whole string *that Bill would come home*. What is that string? It isn't V or P or A or N or any other category we have talked about. It is a clause (a term you met in Chapter 3), here a sentence within a sentence, known as an embedded clause (a term you met in Chapter 3, also called a DEPENDENT or SUBORDINATE clause). The clause whose verb is *expected* (that is, the entire sentence) is called the MATRIX (or MAIN, or ROOT, or TOP, or INDEPENDENT) clause.

Coordination and Subordination

This brings us to one of the major differences in sentence types. Almost all of the sentences we've discussed thus far in this chapter contain at most one verb string (such as *buys* or *may have bought*), and they are called SIMPLE SENTENCES. But the sentence

Mary expected that Bill would come home.

contains more. How many? Two: *expected* and *would come*. We say that the clause *that Bill would come home* is a subordinate clause because it plays a role in the structure of the clause whose verb string is *expected*—that is, this clause is subordinate syntactically to the matrix clause. As we noted, that role is the GF of DO, so the subordinate clause here is a SENTENTIAL OBJECT of the matrix verb. Later we will find other GFs that subordinate clauses can play.

Is filling a GF the only kind of role a subordinate clause can have? What's going on in this sentence:

Mary left home [because her sister cried].

Is the clause *because her sister cried* a Subject, DO, or IO of the verb *left*? No. Is this subordinate clause an OP? One might argue that it is, if one could argue that *because* is a P. And certainly P's can take sentential Objects, as we will see. But it is by no means clear that *because* is a P. Assuming it is not, this subordinate clause has no GF. What is it doing in this sentence, then? You've already met the function that this clause has: It is modification. What is this subordinate clause modifying? The predicate of the matrix clause. Give other examples of sentences that contain a subordinate clause which modifies the predicate of the matrix clause. You might have come up with examples such as:

Mary left home [after her sister cried].
Mary left home [although her sister cried].
[If her sister cries], Mary will leave home.

Such clauses are often called ADVERBIAL CLAUSES, although their structure is certainly not that of an adverb. Be careful to distinguish between the term "adverb," which is the name of a morphosyntactic category (and is exemplified by words like *quickly* and *fast*—the latter of which is homophonous to an adjective), and the term "adverbial," which refers to the function of modifying a predicate.

Notice that the embedded clause following *after* in the sentence *Mary left home after her sister cried* is an OP, since *after* is a P. (Show that this *after* is a P. Did you use your *right* test? You should have.) That the embedded clause is an OP and that the whole PP *after her sister cried* is a modifier should not be surprising to you. We have learned that PPs are often modifiers (when we discussed the PP *with hesitation*).

Can you think of a sentence that contains a modifying subordinate clause in which the clause modifies not the predicate of a higher clause but some nominal in that higher clause? You might have come up with examples such as:

The girl [who left town] is named Mary.
I noticed the cat [that John carried].

Clauses that modify nominals are called RELATIVE CLAUSES.

Sentences that contain subordinate clauses are called COMPLEX SENTENCES. Is every sentence that has more than one verb string a complex sentence? That is, can you think of a sentence in which one clause neither has a GF with respect to the other nor modifies any constituent of the other clause? This is actually quite hard to do (and you'll learn why as you do Problem Set 5.4 of Chapter 5), but you might have come up with examples like:

[Mary is tall] and [Bill is short].

These two clauses are syntactically independent of one another. They are called COORDINATE CLAUSES (the sentence they make up together is called a COORDINATE SENTENCE) and the connector *and* is called a COORDINATOR. This particular coordinator is a CONJUNCTION. Can you think of a different coordinator? We already mentioned two others when we talked about gapping: *Or* and *but*.

Mary is leaving or Bill is leaving.
Mary is leaving but Bill isn't leaving.

Or is called a DISJUNCTION. And I don't know of any special name for *but*. These three words are often listed as the only coordinators of English. (You might consider whether or not they are, indeed, all coordinators in all their uses and whether or not there exist other coordinators in English when you do Problem Set 5.4 of Chapter 5.)

Back to Verbs and Their Objects

Many V's are like *expect* in being able to take nominal or sentential Objects. Other verbs require only nominal Objects. Can you think of any? There are many, such as *drink, touch, eat*. Why can't we eat a clause? Think about meaning here. NPs can refer to tangible objects, some of which are edible. But clauses refer to PROPOSITIONS—that is, to events made of actions or states and participants in those actions or states. We don't eat propositions, so *eat* cannot take a sentential Object.

Some verbs require only sentential Objects and don't allow NP Objects. Can you think of any? They are harder to find, but they do exist—for example, *hope*:

*We hoped [candy].
We hoped [that someone would give us candy].

Is this for semantic reasons, also? No, for we can say:

We hoped [for candy].

So there is nothing about the meaning of *hope* that precludes an NP Object. Instead, following the same line of reasoning we used earlier, we can conclude that **some verbs simply lack the ability to assign Case,** and *hope* is just such a verb—that's why it cannot take a nominal Object. Can you think of other such verbs? *Insist* and *think* are good examples. Give example sentences to make the same point for these verbs that we just made for *hope*. It was easy, right? You might have come up with examples like:

> *We think [problems].
> We think [of problems].
> We think [that there are problems].

Notice that our vacuous P *of* appears when we try to give *think* a nominal Object, just as it does when certain nouns and adjectives (try to) take nominal Objects.

Is P similar to V in these ways? Can we find P's that can take either an NP or a sentential Object? There are many good examples, including *after*, *before*, and *in*:

> I cried [after the movie].
> I cried [after my sister left town].
> Be here [before noon].
> Be here [before it rains].
> Mary was wrong [in her expectation].
> Mary was wrong [in that Bill didn't come home].

Are there P's that take only NP Objects and never sentential Objects? These are a little harder to find. *Into* is an example:

> Bill went [into the house].
> *Bill went [into (that) there are problems all around].

Try to find others. Be careful. Not all embedded clauses are introduced by *that*; *whether* can also introduce them—and some of them take no introducer. So while we cannot say:

> *Mary thought [of that John was wrong].

we can say:

> Mary thought [of whether John was wrong or not].

And that means that *of* can take both sentential Objects and NP Objects, as in:

> Mary thought [of problems with his analysis].

Are there P's that take only sentential Objects and never NP ones? Yes; *while* is one:

> *Bill left [while the halftime show].
> Bill left [while the halftime show was going on].

You might be seriously unhappy now. Why on earth did I just assume *while* is a P? Here you were, working your way happily through examples that all made sense to you, and I just plopped in something totally foreign. But, actually, you can give me a reason for labeling *while* a P. Look back at our discussion about the use of *right* that means 'directly' or 'immediately.' This *right* is a functional head that takes a PP complement. Not all PPs can appear with *right*, but only PPs can appear with *right*. So *right* provides a sufficient, but not necessary, test for a PP. Now can you use the *right*-test to show me that *while* is a P? I hope you can. If *right* can introduce a phrase headed by *while*, then *while* is a P. So, can it? In my speech it can:

They make your pizza [right while you wait].

So by this test *while* is, indeed, a P, heading a PP in which the P has a sentential Object. (You can work more on this kind of question in Problem Set 4.7.)

Okay, now let's bring the discussion back to issues of Case. Do embedded clauses get assigned Case? In Latin, clauses do not have any Case marker for the whole clause, so unless Latin is allowing an embedded-clause Case marker that is a zero morpheme (a concept we met in the section "Morphemes: Phonetic Realization" of Chapter Three), we can conclude that clauses in Latin don't get Case marked. However, it is certainly possible for clauses to get Case marked in other languages. Hopi (an Uto-Aztecan language spoken in northern Arizona) and Quechua (an indigenous language of Peru and Bolivia), for example, both exhibit Case marking on embedded clauses:

Hopi:

Ni? [mimiy totimhoymiy pima timala?yyin] qa   t   namoti?yta
I   that boys   they work   Nom Obl know
'I know that the boys are working.'

Quechua:

[[xwan papa-ta   mikhu] sqa   n ta]   yacha ni
  Juan   potato-Acc eat   Nom 3 Acc know I
'I know that Juan eats potatoes.'

The suffix *-t* in Hopi indicates that the clause is an Object of the verb (Obl = Oblique Case, which in Hopi is the appropriate Case here). The suffix *-ta* in Quechua indicates that the clause is an Object of the verb (and here the Case is Accusative). So despite the lack of evidence for clauses getting Case in Latin (or a lack of evidence so far as we can discern with our present knowledge of Case), grammars can allow Case to be assigned to clauses.

So do English clauses get Case? When do we hear Case distinctions in English? We already discussed this in the section "Case Systems" of Chapter 3, but let me remind you. In English we do not hear Case distinctions on nouns (*the dog* sounds the same whether it is the Subject, DO, IO, or OP in a sentence), with the exception of the Genitive (*the dog's*). Instead, only on pronouns do we hear a range of Case distinctions (*he* vs. *him*, for example). So English definitely allows zero morphemes for Case and, accordingly, the fact that our ears don't hear Case on clauses is not a reliable indicator that clauses don't get Case in English. We must admit that we don't have enough information to be sure that no embedded clause in English gets Case. However, we do have enough information to claim that **not all embedded clauses have to get Case.** Think about it. We said that *hope* and *think* are not Case assigners. Yet both of them can take sentential Objects. So their Objects are examples of embedded clauses that don't have Case assigned to them.

There is an alternative to this conclusion. We could revise our claim about verbs like *hope* and *think* to say that they are Case assigners, but that they can assign Case only to clauses and not to NPs. Then we could conclude that all clauses in English might very well require Case. While this alternative is logical, it certainly complicates CASE THEORY (the theory we've been developing, about which items get Case and how they get it), for we now have to claim not just that the ability to assign Case is lexically determined (some verbs can do it and some can't, which is the distinction between transitive and strictly intransitive verbs), but also that the ability to assign Case is split into two parts—the ability to assign Case to NPs and the ability to assign Case to clauses—where each of these abilities is lexically determined.

We will opt for the simpler theory. So some verbs are not Case assigners and, therefore, not all embedded clauses have to get Case. (And it is possible that no embedded clauses get Case. We have not yet found any evidence to the contrary.)

Given that at least some clauses in English do not have to have Case assigned to them, we might expect that if the only reason N and A can't take NP Objects in English is that they are not Case assigners, then there might be some Ns and some As that can take sentential Objects since sentential Objects don't require Case. Can you think of any? Start with adjectives. Can you come up with an adjective that is immediately followed by a sentential complement? Sure, there are many:

Mary is [afraid that Bill will come visit].
(cf. *Mary is afraid Bill.
     Mary is afraid of Bill.)

Others you might have thought of include *sorry*, *angry*, *hopeful*. Can you see anything in common in the group with respect to meaning? In general adjectives that concern psychological states are good candidates for taking sentential complements.

What about nouns? Can you come up with nouns that are followed by sentential complements? Actually, while I'm sure lots of nouns are coming to your mind, this is a difficult question to answer. That's because there is controversy over the proper analysis of examples like the following:

[The idea that flies are mammals] is absurd.
(cf. *The idea flies is absurd.
     The idea of flies is absurd.)

NPs like *the idea that flies are mammals* have been analyzed in a variety of ways and I will not go into them in this book. Only under an analysis in which *idea* takes a sister clause do we have a potential instance of an N taking a sentential Object. We will leave this question open.

We can see from the AP example, though, that our analysis of how Case works in English is supported by the fact that some adjectives can take sentential Objects.

Case and Subjects

Sentences also raise another interesting point about Case Theory. Consider this example:

Susan eats pizza in the park.

There are three NPs in this sentence. List them and tell how each gets its Case. *Pizza* gets its Case from the V *eats*, whose Object it is. *The park* gets its Case from the P *in*, whose Object it is. That should have been easy for you. But what does *Susan* get its Case from? *Susan* is not the Object of any V or P; it is the Subject of the sentence. How do NPs in Subject position get Case? We will have to do some work to answer this question (and we won't, in fact, arrive at an answer for several more sections), so hang on tight and let's get there.

Functional Heads with Verbal Phrases: Another Look

First, we need to look at the structure of sentences as a whole. And to do that, we need to look at the structure of verbal phrases. We will begin by looking back once more at Latin. Consider again the verb form that we saw in the first set of sentences on Latin: *expugnāverant*.

> Gallī   urbem   expugnāverant.
> gaul-II-P-Nom town-III-S-Acc take by storm-3P-Pluperfect
> 'The Gauls had taken the town by storm.'

This verb consists of a verb stem *expugnā* (which is itself morphologically complex, consisting of the prefix *ex-*, the root *pugn*, and the theme vowel *-ā-* identifying this verb stem as belonging to a class of verbs called "the first CONJUGATION"—there are four conjugations (or verb classes), with distinct inflectional suffixes), plus *-vera-* indicating pluperfect (which arguably is analyzable itself as consisting of a *-v-* indicating perfect aspect, plus *-era-* indicating the past), plus *-nt* indicating third-person plural agreement:

> expugnā + v + era + nt

Some linguists have argued that **each morphological suffix here (except the theme vowel *ā*) is the spelling out of a functional head onto a verbal stem.** With this approach, the verb *expugnāverant* would have three functional heads realized in it as suffixes. The functional head structurally closest to the verbal stem *expugnā* is the perfect-aspect one; the next closest is the past-tense one; the farthest is the agreement one. The analysis would be:

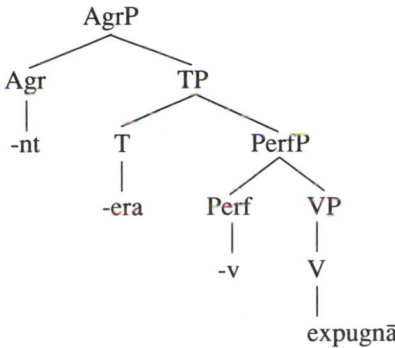

(AgrP = Agreement phrase; TP = Tense phrase; PerfP = Perfect phrase.) The claim is that the V moves up into the Perf head slot, suffixing the perfect marker-*v*. Then this new stem *(expugnāv)* moves up into the T head slot, suffixing the tense marker *-era*. Then, finally, this new stem *(expugnāvera)* moves up into the Agr head slot, suffixing the person/number marker *-nt*, yielding the complete verbal form, and there the verb stays, like so:

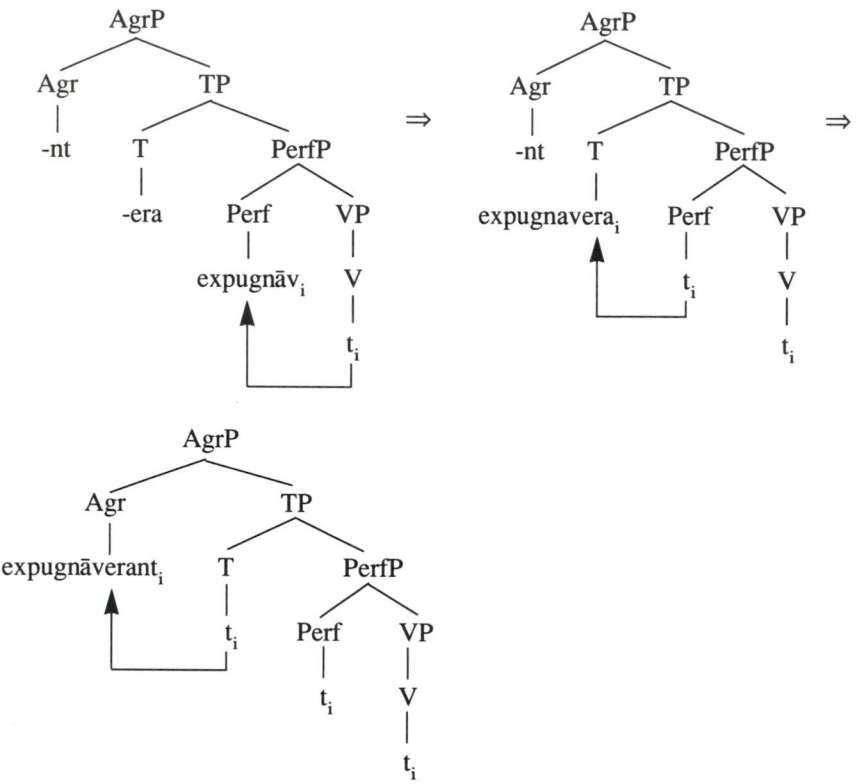

I have left a little TRACE behind in each head as movement emptied that head, indicated with a "t." Subscripts co-index the "t"'s and the final verbal form. Recall that we looked at a different type of movement rule earlier in the section "Movement as a Test for Constituency"—the fronting movement in sentences like:

Those same shoes John will buy.

While we did not give a tree analysis for sentences like this, if we were to give such a tree, this movement would also leave behind a trace. **All movements leave behind traces.**

The movement of the head verb up through the functional heads of T and Agr is called HEAD-TO-HEAD MOVEMENT. Head-to-head movement contrasts with the fronting movement in that fronting moves only phrases (as we argued earlier in the section "A Restriction on Fronting"), but head-to-head movement moves only heads.

Look carefully at the tree just displayed. What is the relationship between the arrangement in the tree of the various functional phrases and the final order of the morphemes in the word? Can you see that this arrangement reflects the final order, with the outermost morpheme being the head of the highest functional phrase in the tree? The hierarchical configuration and the linear order of the morphemes follow what is known as the MIRROR

PRINCIPLE. You can think of this principle as arranging the morphemes so that the one attached closest to the root of the verb is lowest in the structural tree, and each successive morpheme in a linear sense is higher in the tree, with the morpheme farthest from the root being the highest in the tree.

While English does not have so rich an inflectional system as Latin, the claim is that a similar analysis applies to the English verb. English does not use inflection to show verbal aspect, unlike Latin. Instead, for perfect aspect it uses the auxiliary verb *have* with a perfect participle suffix (*-ed* or *-en*, typically) on the verb form following *have*. It also uses auxiliary verbs to show progressive aspect, modality, and passive voice. (You can learn about the English verb string in Problem Set 4.3.) But English does use inflection to show tense and agreement, as we already know. So we could analyze the verb *mows*, for example, like so:

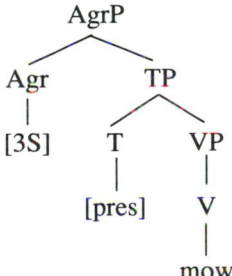

I have put features under the Agr head and T head rather than suffixes, since the English *-s* is a single form indicating person, number, and tense all in one (and recall our discussion in the section "A Typology of Languages by Morphology" of Chapter 3 of so-called inflective languages). There is debate, for reasons that we won't go into here, over whether in English the material in Agr head and in T head moves downward in an example like this one, to attach (as a suffix) to the verb stem in V head, or upward, as in Latin. Since nothing we do will be crucially tied to this decision, we will assume English head-to-head movement is upward, like Latin's:

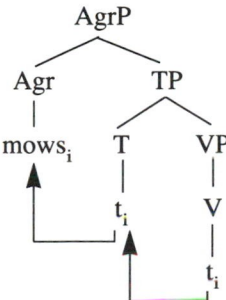

We will return to a brief discussion of a difference between languages like Latin and languages like English when we talk about the Minimalist Program at the end of this chapter.

The important point for us now is that in both languages, the inflectional endings on the verbs are the spelling out of functional heads in the syntactic tree. And in both languages additional functional heads could be proposed. For example, it's been proposed that there is a functional head for POLARITY, which can be either AFFIRMATIVE/POSITIVE (Pos) or NEGATIVE (Neg) (comparable to the fact that Tense in English can be either present or past), so positive and negative sentences will differ on their polarity head. If such a polarity functional head existed and could be argued to be located between the projections of Agr and the projections of T, we'd have trees like these:

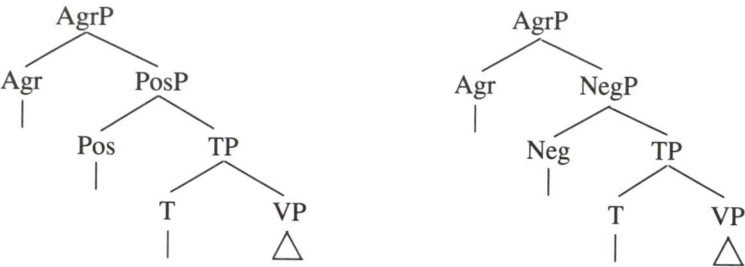

The heads Pos and Neg would be filled either with features that get spelled out as affixes (like the heads Agr and T) or with lexical items. (*Not*, in English, might be a candidate for Neg, for example, and the *well* we discussed in the earlier section "Functional Heads with VP: A First Look" might be a candidate for Pos.)

A language with an even richer inflectional system than Latin would, presumably, have an even more elaborate syntactic tree with regard to the functional heads that occur in the underlying structure (the structure at DS) of a verbal form. In fact, this is one of the criticisms of this particular analysis of verbal forms. The Mapudungan language of the Mapuche people of Chile, for example, has nearly forty verbal suffixes and several of them can co-occur on a single verb. Many of them indicate information about various arguments of the verb. But many others indicate information relevant to the action or state, such as moods, tenses, and aspects—the sort of information that we might expect a functional head that takes a verbal complement to give. If we were to analyze all of these affixes as functional heads, we'd have an elaborate D-Structure, indeed.

Despite this sort of objection (and others—including the fact that many theories of syntax preclude all movement rules; thus head-to-head movement is precluded), much of the current linguistic literature assumes this kind of analysis for verbal forms in English, as will we (although we will talk about a shorthand way of representing the functional projections in the tree later on). Our phrase structure, then, is fairly complex. And in order to account for the Case of Subjects which is our eventual goal), we will have to make it even more complex. So let's do that now.

Infinitival Clauses

All of the embedded clauses we have considered thus far have been tensed. And while all matrix clauses must be tensed in English, we allow a few types of tenseless embedded clauses. One type is the infinitival clause, which has a *to* as the first element in the verb string, as in:

I expected [Sue to give the job to Joan for a bribe].
(cf. I expected [that Sue would give the job to Joan for a bribe].)

A close examination of the distribution of infinitival clauses will lead us to an understanding of the position of Subjects in clauses, which is our present goal. So, while we will now examine infinitival clauses, know that we will eventually tie the following discussion into that goal.

In the clause *Sue to give the job to Joan for a bribe* what GF (grammatical function) does *Sue* play? Subject. What GF does *the job* play? DO (Direct Object). What GF does *Joan* play? IO (Indirect Object). What GF does *a bribe* play? OP (Object of a Preposition). **Infinitival clauses in general have all the internal GF possibilities that tensed clauses have.**

Now let's not consider the internal structure of the infinitival clause for a moment, but instead look at it as a whole and consider how it relates to the higher clause. What function can an infinitival clause play in a higher clause?

Look first at the example we have given: *I expected [Sue to give the job to Joan for a bribe]*. What function does this infinitival have in the matrix clause? It is the DO of the V *expected*.

Is that the only function infinitival clauses can have? Try to find examples in which an infinitival clause follows something other than a V. Perhaps you came up with an example like:

I hoped for [Sue to get the job].

What function does the infinitival clause here play? It's the Object of *for*. **So infinitival clauses can be OPs as well as DOs.**

What other function can an infinitival clause have? Can you find an example in which an infinitival clause follows something other than a V or a P? We noted earlier that adjectives can take sentential Objects in English. Can adjectives take infinitival clauses as their Objects? Consider this contrast:

He is afraid [that Sue will leave].
*He is afraid [Sue to leave].

Adjectives cannot take infinitival Objects (or at least not this type of infiniitival Object) in English, even though they can take tensed sentential Objects. We need to find an explanation for this fact. But let's get a larger inventory of the functions infinitivals can play before we search for an account.

We know that infinitivals can be DO or OP. What are the other GFs? Subject and IO. Can infinitival clauses be Subjects? We need to test with the kind of predicate that could take a proposition as its Subject, such as *be true* or *means nothing*. Both of these predicates can have tensed sentential Subjects:

[That Sue got the job] is true.
[That Sue got the job] means nothing.

But they reject the corresponding infinitival Subjects:

*Sue to get the job is true.
*Sue to get the job means nothing.

(If you noticed that a slight alteration on the second sentence here makes it grammatical, please bear with me. We will get to that fact soon.) So infinitivals cannot be Subjects.

Predicates

I just asked you to think about the kind of predicate that can take a sentential Subject. You are very familiar with the term "predicate" from various discussions in Chapter 3, but we never explored any of the syntactic correlates of the semantic notion of predication. It's time to do that.

You know that the predicate of a clause is the word or words that give the action or state of the event. And you know that a predicate takes arguments, which are role-players in that action or state. When you think of predicates, what is the first category that comes to your mind? Probably V, for verbs are our typical predicates, as in:

Mary loves tomatoes.
Jack prowls at night.

But we have many sentences in which categories other than V can tell us the action or state. Can you think of any in which an AP is the predicate? Sure:

Mary is [noisy].
Mary is [intelligent].
Mary is [remarkable].

What is the *is* doing here from a semantic point of view? If you compare these three sentences, you can see that the *is* doesn't supply a lot of information beyond tense (and in Problem Set 4.2 you will see other languages that would translate these sentences without any form of *be*). Thus the AP is doing the work of a predicate. Can you think of any sentences in which a PP is the predicate? It should be easy.

Mary is [in the kitchen].
Mary is [out of her mind].

Can you think of any in which an NP is the predicate? Again, it should be easy.

Mary is [the best doctor around].
Mary is [a fine football coach].

Identification vs. Predication

These sentences with the copula raise the question of whether the noun phrase following the copula is a predicate or, instead, an alternative identification of the Subject. Certainly, an NP like *the best doctor around* assigns a property to the Subject in the sentence just given, so it is a predicate. But what about the NP following the copula in:

Mary is Miss Jackson. (Didn't you know her last name?)

Here someone might have heard of both Mary and Miss Jackson and not have known that both names referred to the same individual. The speaker is then simply informing the listener of this coreference. The NP *Miss Jackson* doesn't have any properties associated with it; it is just a name. On the other hand, we might use this same sentence in the context in which someone has referred to the boss as "Mary" and the speaker wants to remind that person that the boss should be referred to with the formal title "Miss" and her last name. In that case, *Miss Jackson* might be understood to assign the property of higher social or economic or power status to the Subject, and *Miss Jackson* can be considered a predicate.

Okay, now we can return to our discussion of phrase structure.

Indirect Objects

Before our aside about predicates and identification, we were asking what GFs infinitival clauses could have. We had learned that an infinitival clause can be a DO or an OP, but not the Object of an Adjective nor the Subject of a clause.

Now we turn to the remaining GF: IO. Can an infinitival clause be an IO? To answer that, we need to have a better sense of what an IO is. Generally we call the Object of *to* or *for* in sentences such as these an IO:

> I gave the book to Bill.
> I bought the book for Bill.

In English we have a handy test for recognizing IOs. Look at these two sentences. Can you think of other ways to say them—ways that use almost all the same words and give (nearly) the same information, but change word order? Sure:

> I gave [Bill]$_{NP}$ [the book]$_{NP}$.
> I bought [Bill]$_{NP}$ [the book]$_{NP}$.

In most instances, a sentence with a DO and a following IO that is the Object of *to* or *for* has a corresponding sentence with two NPs following the V (and no P in front of either NP), in the opposite order from that in which those Objects would occur in the sentence that contains the P *to* or *for*. This second construction is called the DOUBLE-OBJECT construction. (You may be coming up with problems for this diagnostic for recognizing IOs. Please hang on a moment longer and I'll address some of them soon and in Problem Set 4.9.)

There is more than one *to* in English (as we noted earlier in the section "Homophony and Polysemy," when talking about infinitival *to*, Locative *to*, and Dative *to*) and there is more than one *for* in English. Locative *to* is followed by an NP, just like Dative *to* is, but a Locative phrase never corresponds to the first NP in the Double-Object construction:

> I walked my dog to school.
> *I walked school my dog.

Likewise, a variety of non-Dative *for*'s can be followed by NPs, just like Dative *for* is, but these *for* phrases never correspond to the first NP in the Double-Object construction:

I bought the book for a dollar.
*I bought a dollar the book.
I tested the water for the baby.
*I tested the baby the water.

So the existence of a corresponding sentence in the Double-Object construction helps us identify IOs that are Objects of *to* or *for*.

Now ask yourself if you see any coherency to the type of participant or argument role (called thematic role, as you know from Chapter 3, or THETA-ROLE) that IOs (the Object of *to* or *for* in the first pair of sentences, the first NP after the V in the second pair of sentences) have. Think in terms of who does what to whom and for whose benefit. Can you see that IOs are the beneficiary (a term we met in Chapter 3, also called BENEFACTEE or RECIPIENT or GOAL) of the action? We will discuss theta-roles in a separate section later (and in Problem Set 4.8). For now, noticing that IOs are beneficiaries is enough.

So do we expect infinitival clauses to be able to be IOs? Probably not. We don't expect tensed clauses to be able to be IOs, either. The sense of a clause, infinitival or tensed, is a proposition, and propositions are not usually the sorts of things that can be beneficiaries. People and animals and institutions can be beneficiaries. Abstract ideas and propositions generally cannot be. Thus the failure of a sentence like this is due to semantic anomaly:

*I gave my trust to [that children should go to school].
*I gave my trust to [children to go to school].

You might object strenuously at this point, for we certainly allow sentences like:

I gave my life to [the proposition that all humans are created equal].

Here the NP object of *to* is headed by the N *proposition*. You might conclude from this that from a semantic point of view propositions can, in fact, be fine candidates for beneficiaries. After all, the denotation of the NP *the proposition that all humans are created equal* must be a proposition. So the problem with our ungrammatical sentences looks like it's syntactic: Clauses (whether tensed or infinitival) can't be IOs, but an NP whose referent is a proposition can be an IO. However, note this contrast:

I gave my life to that proposition.
??I gave that proposition my life.

The Double-Object sentence is decidedly odd. This suggests that the sentence *I gave my life to that proposition* may not really involve an IO, but, instead, an OP of some other sort (and you can explore this issue further in Problem Set 4.9).

If you don't agree with my conclusion about why clauses can't be IOs, that's okay. We don't need to agree about why. All we need to agree on is the facts: Clauses can't be IOs. And this is equally true for tensed clauses and infinitivals. Therefore, this fact does not shed any light on the difference between tensed clauses and infinitivals and this is the last we will say about it.

How Subjects Get Case

We are now ready to take an overview of what we've discovered. Tensed clauses can appear as Subjects, DOs, OPs, and Objects of A. Infinitival clauses can appear as DOs and OPs, but not as Subjects or Objects of A. This distribution should ring a bell—we've seen it somewhere else. What lumps DO and OP position together and separates them from Object-of-A position? DO and OP are in a position to get Case from the V and the P, respectively. But the Object of A cannot get Case from the A.

Infinitival clauses, then, seem to be occurring only as sisters to Case assigners, but tensed clauses have wider distribution, occurring also as Subjects and the Objects of A (and perhaps the Objects of N). Why would that be? Look at this infinitival clause:

Sue to give a book to Bill

We know already how the NPs *a book* and *Bill* get Case, but we don't know how the Subject *Sue* gets Case. Now compare to the tensed clause:

Sue gives a book to Bill

If the infinitival clause can appear only as the Object of a Case assigner, but the tensed clause can appear in other places, as well, we would hope to find a difference between infinitival and tensed clauses that was relevant to Case somehow.

What is the structural difference between tensed and infinitival clauses? One difference, of course, is that infinitivals either don't include a functional head T(ense) or lack a value for T. That is, instead of T being marked as present or past, T would be marked as lacking tense altogether, perhaps with the feature [−tense] (or, simply, [−]). The two choices are:

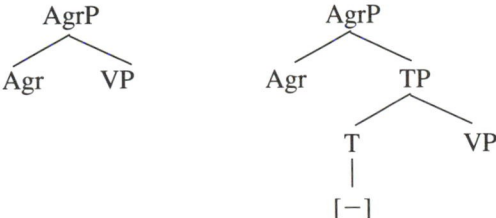

We could say that T in the tree on the right has a negative value.

The whole idea of a [−] feature may seem like a terminological fudge to you. How can having [−] be any different from just not having any projections of T in the tree at all? But, in fact, there is a difference. Some linguists have argued that certain kinds of elements are sensitive to whether there's a TP node above them in the tree. These elements cannot occur in tenseless clauses that have no projections of T. But these same elements can occur in tensed clauses and in tenseless clauses that have a value of [−] for T. We will not get into those sorts of arguments here, but just be aware that the choice above is not merely terminological.

Another difference between tensed and infinitival clauses is that infinitivals either don't include the functional head Agr(eement) or have a negative value for Agr (that is, lack a value for Agr). Notice that whether we have a singular or plural Subject of an infinitival clause, the verbal string shows no different inflection:

the child to give a book to Bill
the children to give a book to Bill

The tree analysis for this verbal string then would be (if we take the position that we have a negative value for these functional heads, rather than no functional heads):

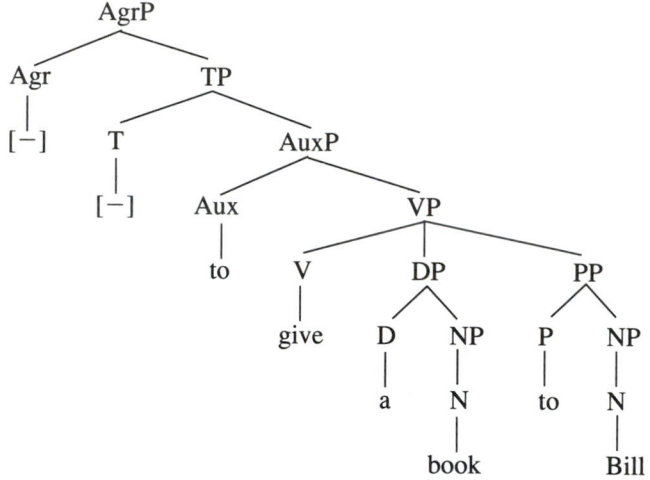

(I have labeled infinitival *to* an auxiliary verb. You can consider the advantages and disadvantages of analyzing *to* as a verb in Problem Set 4.3. Actually, many linguists would argue that even if *to* is part of the verbal string, it shouldn't be under Aux in the tree, but under T or Agr. That debate, however, will not affect the argument here.) The proposal that I hope is coming to your mind is that the functional heads that are responsible for the verbal inflection in the tensed clause are relevant to Case. Indeed, this is what has been proposed: **[+ Agr] is a Case assigner; [− Agr] is not. And the Subject gets its Case from [+ Agr].**

Alternatively, you will find proposals that talk about [+T] as the Case assigner, or that conflate Agr and T and talk about [+Infl]—Infl = Inflection—as the Case assigner, with a simplified tree like this:

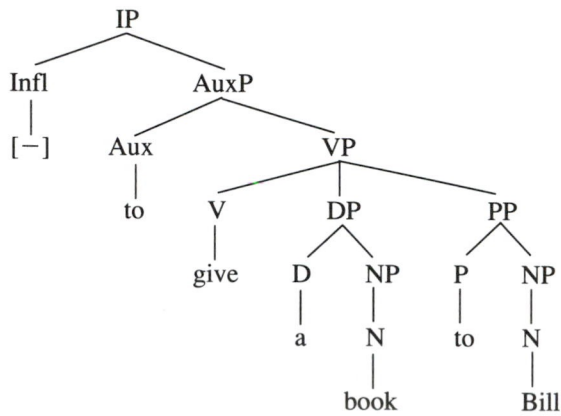

(IP = Inflection Phrase.) **All the literature in syntax before the late 1980s uses Infl and IP and quite a lot of the literature since uses Infl and IP as a shorthand, considering AgrP and TP to be expansions of the same structure.** Please remember this so that you won't be lost when you face IP in other works.

For English the difference between these proposals is hard to see, since one inflectional suffix carries both tense and agreement (which is why conflating T and Agr into Infl is so common in the literature on English syntax, particularly). For other languages, however, the difference matters, as you will discover in Problem Set 4.10.)

We need to discuss exactly how [+Agr] assigns Case to the Subject. But first let's just assume that Case does get assigned, and let's see how this proposal explains the data. If [+Agr] is a Case assigner and it gives Case to the Subject of the sentence, then the Subject of a tensed clause will get Case from the [+Agr] within its clause. That means that all the NPs inside a tensed clause are assigned Case from a Case assigner within the tensed clause, so the tensed clause is in no way dependent on anything in the context outside itself with respect to Case. Thus a tensed clause shouldn't be sensitive to whether it is the Object of a Case assigner or not. And, indeed, it isn't.

But if [−Agr], on the other hand, is never a Case assigner, then the Subject of an infinitival clause will not get Case from anything inside the infinitival clause. Given that every NP (so far as we yet know) must get Case, this means that the Subject of an infinitival clause will have to get Case from outside the clause. And now it suddenly makes sense that **infinitival clauses should be able to appear only as Objects of Case assigners—for those Case assigners are needed to assign Case to the Subjects of the infinitivals.** Let's see this in a tree. Consider the sentence:

I expect [Bill to leave].

The VP of the matrix clause will have this analysis:

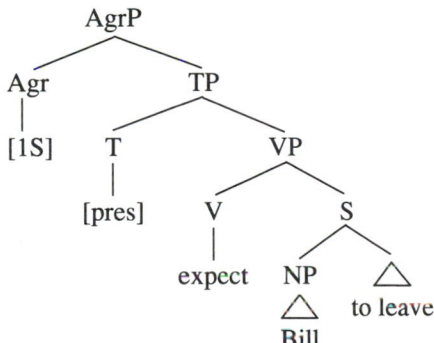

(I have not filled in a label on the right branch of the embedded S because that part doesn't interest us yet.) A triangle under a node indicates that the material dominated by this node could be analyzed further (for example, *Bill* is not just an NP, but an N).

Exceptional Case Marking and Government

You might well be flustered. So far we have said that V and P assign Case to their Objects, which are sisters to them. But the NP *Bill* is neither the Object of *expect* (the whole embedded S *Bill to leave* is the Object of *expect*) nor a sister to *expect*. (The embedded S node is the sister of the V.) You are right to object here. We are doing something tricky, and this thing we are doing is among the messiest points in modern grammatical theory. We are allowing the **V to EXCEPTIONALLY assign Case to a following NP that is not its Object, but is instead the Subject of its Object.** (Reread that sentence. S is the Object of the V. And the NP *Bill* is the Subject of this sentential Object.)

Let's word this as formally as we can by defining the structural relationship of GOVERNMENT.

For any head X, we say that X GOVERNS everything within its maximal projection (that is, everything within XP) that is not dominated by another phrase node YP contained in XP. In other words, government is blocked by another maximal projection. So, for example, in this hypothetical tree:

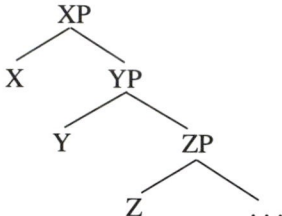

X governs YP since YP is contained in XP. But X does not govern Y or ZP or anything dominated by ZP. It can't govern Y or ZP or anything dominated by ZP because all those nodes are contained within YP.

You tell me: Does a head govern its sister? Look at the tree. I hope you said yes. In fact, given what we know so far, the only thing a head governs is its sister (but we will see later that a head can also govern one other position). So V governs its Object, as does P. We can now rephrase our structural Case assignment to say that **a Case assigner gives Case to an NP it governs.**

Now consider a head V that has a sentential Object as its sister. Does that head V govern the Subject of the sentential Object? Look at the relevant section of the tree:

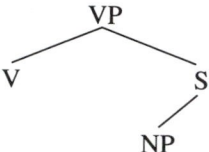

So long as S is a maximal projection, it will be a BARRIER to government of anything it dominates from any head outside the S. When I first introduced the symbol "S," I told you that it was to be understood as a maximal projection. We will justify that position in a later section. So please assume that now. Tell me: Does V govern the NP in this tree? No.

Consider the parallel instance with a P that takes a sentential Object. Draw the relevant section of the tree. Does the P govern the Subject of its sentential Object? Again, the answer is no.

Nevertheless a V can assign Case to the NP in this configuration, and a P can assign Case to the NP in this configuration. That's why we call these two instances exceptional

Case assignment. We can now think of the exceptional Case assignment from a V or P onto the Subject of its sentential Object as being an instance of exceptional government; that is, a **V or P can exceptionally govern the Subject of its sentential Object.**

Finally, if Case assignment by [+Agr] also depends on the relationship of government (a proposal we haven't yet advanced, but will), and if [+Agr] governs the Subject of its clause (another proposal we haven't yet advanced, but will), we can say that [+Agr] differs from V and P in being unable to exceptionally govern. So [+Agr] cannot assign Case to the Subject of a sentential Subject.

The argument here is complex and the proposal is more abstract than anything else we've talked about yet in this book. We need to discuss additional support for this analysis of Case assignment. But first let me tell you that appealing to something exceptional in order to account for Case assignment to the Subject of an infinitival is not really as disturbing as you might think. In fact, few languages appear to allow infinitivals with expressed Subjects. Thus the English sentence:

I want [Bill to leave].

would have a translation in most languages that included a tensed embedded clause, not an infinitival. In Italian, for example, the translation is:

Voglio   [che Guglielmo se   ne   vada].
want-1S   that Bill   self from-here go-3S-Subjunctive
'I want that Bill should go away.'

If the construction is truly marked in language, then it is not unreasonable that exceptional syntactic mechanisms should account for it, rather than the ordinary mechanisms that we might expect to occur in language after language.

Okay, now let's go searching for support for our account of why infinitivals like *Bill to leave* occur as sentential Objects of V and P but don't occur in Subject position. One bit of support is easy to find. If the problem with the example we brought up earlier (in the section "Infinitival Clauses"):

*Sue to get the job means nothing.

is, indeed, that *Sue* fails to get Case, then if we can adjust the syntax of this sentence in such a way as to supply a Case assigner for *Sue*, the result should be grammatical. Can you think of a small adjustment that would render this sentence grammatical? Perhaps you can say:

For Sue to get the job means nothing.

The matrix clause here takes a PP as its Subject. And the P *for* takes a sentential Object. So here *for* exceptionally governs *Sue* and, thus, assigns it Case. Are you happy? I hope so. This kind of explanatory value is what makes one syntactic analysis superior to another.

Indeed, we can find even more evidence for our account of why infinitivals occur as sentential Objects of V and P, but don't occur in Subject position. To do this, we have to consider additional data.

Subjects and pro

All tensed clauses in English have an audible Subject. In fact, if the predicate does not take any arguments, we will supply a so-called DUMMY SUBJECT, like the *it* in:

It rains in autumn.
It's two o'clock.

English is not alone in having dummy Subjects: French and German do, among other languages:

French: Il pleut. 'It's raining.'
German: Es regnet. 'It's raining.'

But many languages do not. In instances where a dummy Subject would occur in English, these languages have no phonetically audible Subject. Italian is such as language, as are Spanish and many other languages:

Italian: Piove. rain-3S-Present 'It's raining.'
Spanish: Llove. rain-3S-Present 'It's raining.'

And in sentences where we would use a pronominal Subject in English, Italian will often (though not necessarily) have no audible Subject:

Voglio   un bacio.
want-1S-Present a kiss
'I want a kiss.'
Non ha   detto   la verità.
not   have-3S-Present say-PerfPart the truth
'(S)he hasn't told the truth.'

There are at least two possible explanations for these facts. First, English might have only one structural breakdown for sentences, that in which we have a Subject and a predicate. And Italian might allow two structural breakdowns for sentences, one like English and the other with simply a predicate. The second explanation is that both English and Italian require a Subject in every sentence, but Italian allows phonetically null Subjects in tensed clauses, whereas English does not.

Look back at the two Italian sentences above that have no audible Subject. Can you think of any reason to claim that these sentences really do have a Subject, just a phonetically null one? Consider the morphological endings on the verbs. Subject-Verb Agreement has applied here. If this is a syntactic rule (similar to that for English we outlined earlier in the section "An Agreement Rule for English"), then we must have a syntactic Subject present for the V to agree with. For this reason (and many others), syntacticians have argued that the structure for Italian sentences includes an obligatory Subject, just as the structure for English sentences does. The Subject slot in sentences like *Voglio un bacio* is filled with a phonetically null pronoun called **"pro"** (always written in lowercase letters, and talked about as "little pro"). Little pro will have a set of features just like any other pronoun, so S-V Agreement can take place between little pro and the V, just like it can between any other pronoun and the V. And in sentences like *Piove* 'It's raining,' little pro is a dummy pronoun—and it has the features of singular and third person by default, since these are the unmarked number and person for Italian. (This is not the only way to analyze a sentence like *Piove*, but it is a way consistent with the other assumptions we've made thus far.)

The big difference between English and Italian, then, is not in sentence structure, but, rather, in where little pro is allowed. English does not allow little pro in Subject position of tensed clauses, but Italian does. Languages that allow little pro in Subject position of tensed clauses are often called pro-DROP languages or NULL SUBJECT languages.

The Null Subject Parameter

You might ask why English is not a Null Subject language but Italian is. Actually, you already saw relevant data when I gave you Italian sentences with the verb *parlare* 'speak.' But let me give data again, this time contrasting the paradigms for the verb *walk* and its Italian translation *camminare* for the present tense of the three different persons in the singular and plural:

	Singular	*Plural*
1:	walk/cammino	walk/camminiamo
2:	walk/cammini	walk/camminate
3:	walks/cammina	walk/camminano

If you just heard the verb alone, what would you know about the Subject of the sentence in English? In Italian? In English, you wouldn't know the person or number unless the verb form you heard was *walks*. But in Italian, you know the person and number for every verb form you hear in this paradigm. It has been proposed that only languages with a rich-enough inflectional system to identify crucial features (here, number and person) of the Subject can be Null Subject languages.

However, in some languages, such as Chinese and Japanese, no agreement takes place between Subjects and verbs, yet Subjects need not be audible in tensed sentences. You can explore relevant data for Japanese in Problem Set 4.6, where you will consider methods of interpreting Subjectless sentences. An example sentence is:

Sasimi-o taberu.
sashimi   eat
'{I/You/He/She/We/They} eat sashimi.'

(I have purposely left off a gloss for the particle *o* on *sasimi-o*. You can fill in this gloss after you have done Problem Set 4.4.)

Because of the existence of languages like Japanese, many linguists believe that **only languages with morphologically uniform inflectional paradigms can be Null Subject languages** (although they need not be). This is known as the NULL SUBJECT PARAMETER because it gives us a parameter by which languages can vary. Italian has a uniform inflectional paradigm since each verbal form has an audible agreement affix. Japanese has a uniform inflectional paradigm since no verbal form has an audible agreement affix. But English does not have a uniform inflectional paradigm since one form in the paradigm (the form for 3S) has an audible agreement affix and the others don't. So Italian and Japanese are possible Null Subject languages (and, indeed, they are Null Subject languages), but English is not a possible Null Subject language.

PRO in Infinitivals

Now that we've proposed the existence of null pronominals, we can ask where else null pronominals might occur in a sentence other than Subject position of a tensed clause. Rather than pursue every possibility, let me ask you to focus on the fact that so far the only internal difference we have uncovered between tensed clauses and infinitival clauses is that the former show a tense morpheme on the verb and the latter do not. In fact, we have noted that infinitival clauses have the same range of internal GF possibilities that tensed clauses do. That is, infinitival clauses can have Subjects, DOs, IOs and OPs. So we expect the possibility of null pronominals appearing in Subject position of an infinitival, given that they can appear in Subject position of a tensed clause.

We will call such a null pronominal PRO (written in capitals and often called "big PRO"). It is very important to keep big PRO (the phonetically null Subject of an infinitival) distinct in your head from little pro (the phonetically null Subject of a tensed clause), because they have different properties, as we are about to discover.

Do infinitivals, in fact, allow null Subjects (that is, big PRO Subjects) in English? Try to find a sentence in which an infinitival verb string (that is, a verb string starting with *to*) is not immediately preceded by an audible NP that is understood as its Subject. Can you find any? Let's be more specific. Try to find such an infinitival which immediately follows a matrix verb and serves as the sentential Object of that verb. Can you do it? Easily, I hope. You might have come up with examples like:

I want to leave. = I [[want]$_V$ [PRO to leave]].

Let's call an infinitival with big PRO as its Subject, like the one here, a "PRO-infinitival." (This is usually called a Control-infinitival; we'll see why when we turn to the section "Control Theory.")

Can we get PRO-infinitivals as sentential Objects of P? What you're looking for is a verbal string that starts with *to* and that immediately follows a P. Can you find one? In most varieties of English today, the answer is no. But in some varieties we find these infinitivals after *for*, as in the folksong "Oh, Susanna" (by Stephen Foster, 1848):

(I'm goin' to Louisiana,) my true love for to see
my true love [[for]$_P$ [PRO to see]]

So whatever rules are responsible for phrase structure should allow this kind of structure, and some other mechanism should be taken to be operative in most varieties of English to block this structure. In fact, some have argued that this is another instance where a filter can help. The filter would mark as ungrammatical any sentence in which a preposition takes a sentential Object that begins with infinitival *to* (that is, the filter will block the audible sequence of P + *to*).

Can we get PRO-infinitivals in places where full infinitivals (that is, infinitival clauses with audible Subjects) cannot appear, such as in Object position of an A or an N, or in Subject position of a higher clause? The answer is yes for all three positions:

Object of A: I'm [[afraid]$_A$ [PRO to leave]].
Object of N: It's [[time]$_N$ [PRO to leave]].
Subject: [PRO To leave now] would be a great pity.

If you had trouble finding examples of your own, now that you've seen these examples, find additional ones for each of the three positions.

Think a minute about the distribution of PRO-infinitivals. They occur as sentential Objects, Objects of A, Objects of N, and sentential Subjects. We also said that we should allow them to be generated in OP position (but in most varieties of English a filter will then mark them as ungrammatical). Where else have you seen this distribution? Yes: PRO-infinitivals have the same distribution as tensed embedded clauses, with the one difference that a filter blocks PRO-infinitivals after a P.

Let's rephrase that fact: **Tensed clauses and clauses without an audible Subject have the same distribution** (with one difference, caused by a filter).

How can we account for this? We accounted for the limited distribution of full infinitivals by noting that they were dependent upon the larger context they found themselves in for Case assignment to their Subject. And we accounted for the contrasting wide distribution of tensed clauses by noting that they were independent of the larger context with regard to Case assignment to their Subject. So now PRO-infinitivals appear to be, likewise, independent of that larger context with respect to Case.

Why? What relevant difference is there between big PRO and other NPs? Since we have said big PRO is a pronoun (so it can have a feature bundle, like other pronouns), the most obvious difference is that big PRO has no phonetic matrix. If we alter our Case Theory to say that **only NPs with a phonetic matrix must get Case,** then big PRO need not get Case. And if big PRO need not get Case, then the wide distribution of PRO-infinitivals follows.

Review of Phrase Structure thus Far

The phrase structure we've developed thus far has a phrase made up of a head and, possibly, a sister phrase (which might precede or follow the head, depending on the category of the head and other factors you can study in Problem Set 4.1), like so:

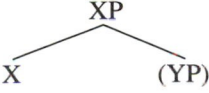

Notice that the head position is a LEXICAL POSITION—it is to be filled by a single lexical item, whereas the sister position is a PHRASAL POSITION—it is to be filled by a phrase (which can be a single lexical item or can be a string of lexical items). We've arrived at this structure by studying a variety of categories. Thus, the sister phrase can be a modifier of the head (the head is italicized here) for a head N, V, or A:

[Intelligent *women*]_{NP} run this college.
They want to [*talk* intelligently]_{VP}.
My voice is [remarkably *loud*]_{AP}.

or it can be an argument (or contain an argument) of the head for N, V, or A:

[*Discussions* about war]_{NP} depress me.
She made us [*discuss* the war]_{VP}.
Aren't you [*fond* of John]_{AP}?

The category of P is a little more tricky. It's very difficult (perhaps impossible?) to find an instance in which a head P is modified by some other phrase within the PP (as we discussed above). And there is debate over whether the Object of a P is an argument of the P itself or whether the P is merely TRANSMITTING the theta-role from some predicate to the OP. I think both happen. So in a sentence like:

Mary is [*into* Greek art]_{PP}.

the PP contains a P that is itself a predicate and, thus, gives a theta-role to its Object (the NP *Greek art*). But in a sentence like:

I'm depending [*on* you]_{PP}.

the PP contains a P that is not a predicate. Rather, this P is lexically selected by the verb *depend* (we depend on others, not in them, or for them, or with them, or anything else). So here the V assigns a theta-role to the OP. Nevertheless, we can see that P can take an OP that is an argument of something (whether of the P or of some other head).

And, finally, we've seen this same structure for phrases headed by functional categories. Thus *the*, for example, takes a nominal phrasal sister, and [+Agr] takes a Tense Phrase sister which in turn takes a VP sister:

[*The* boy]_{DP} enjoys liver.
Mary [*walks*]_{AgrP}.

Are you surprised by my italicizing the verb *walks*? Did you realize that this verb is the head of the AgrP? Certainly in underlying structure, the head Agr contains no phonetically realized material. But head-to-head movement results in a convergence of the Agr head, the Tense head, and the Verb head. So our SS of the AgrP is:

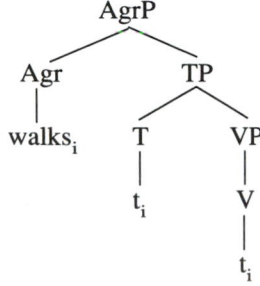

In sum, all categories, lexical and functional, appear in this very simple phrase structure:

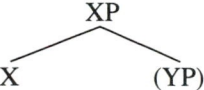

(although you might argue that some of them appear in more complex structures, as well).

[+Agr] as a Case Assigner and X-Bar Theory

We are now ready to return to the question of exactly how [+Agr] assigns Case to the Subject of its clause. If [+Agr] really is a Case assigner, like V and P, then we might expect [+Agr] to assign Case only to an NP it governs. But in the structural analysis we've given for AgrP, an Agr head governs only another phrase that is part of the verbal structure (such as Tense Phrase). We need to rethink our analysis of AgrP, then, to allow a head Agr to govern the Subject.

It's been proposed that we need more LEVELS or projections than just heads (the lexical projection) and phrases (the maximal projection). We need an intermediary projection. We will call the intermediary projection X' (to be read "X bar," and often written as X̄), and the maximal projection X" (to be read "X double bar," and often written as X̄). So we have three levels for any category: X, X', and X", where X is the lexical level (it dominates a lexical item) and X" is the maximal level (the phrasal level):

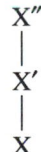

(If you are chomping at the bit for independent justification for the X' level, please have patience. We'll get to that in the section "Coordination, Genitives, and X'." For now, let's try to finish our argument without interruption.) It's been further proposed that the intermediary projection, X', can take a sister phrase, what has been called the "SPECIFIER" of X. And you know that X can take a sister. So a phrase of category X would have the structure:

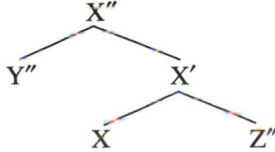

Here Y" is the (optional) sister to X' and Z" is the (optional) sister to the head X. The proposal that all phrases have this form is the mainstay of what is known as X-BAR THEORY, or the theory of phrase structure. Notice that the only lexical position in any phrase XP is the head X. In particular, the sister to X is always a phrasal position, as is the sister to X' (the specifier position).

We can then propose that the Subject of a sentence is a sister to the X′ level (that is, Subjects sit in specifier position). So a sentence like *I swim* has the structure at DS:

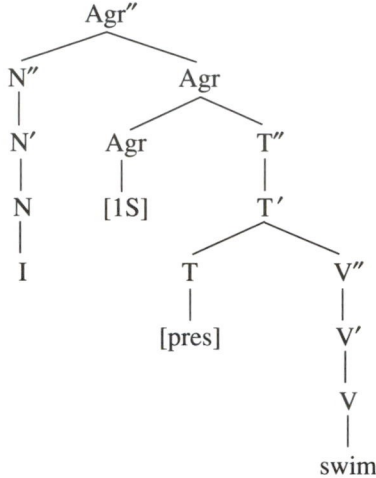

Since a head governs everything within its maximal projection that is not contained within another maximal projection dominated by that head's maximal projection, Agr now governs the Subject. And since the Agr here has an inflection, it qualifies as [+Agr] and it can assign Case to the N″.

While there is a lot of disagreement over the details I've presented to you here, something like this general outline of phrase structure is common to mainstream theories of syntax today. And an important theoretical issues is whether or not the intermediary level with a sister specifier phrase is motivated for all categories. Above we've seen one example of the use of a specifier position: specifier of Agr—this is the position that Subjects of clauses sit in. Very soon we will discuss the specifier position for nominal phrases. And in a later section, when we discuss the DS position of Subjects, we will briefly touch on motivation for a specifier position for other types of phrases.

Definitions of GFs

Notice that in the theory we are developing here, the GF of Subject is hierarchically defined: A Subject is the sister phrase to Agr′.

Can you define DO hierarchically? This is a little harder. Certainly the DO is a sister phrase to a head V. But if modifiers of a V are also sisters to the head V, then we need to complicate our definition with remarks about function, to the effect that we exclude modifers of V from consideration as DOs. We won't do that here; I brought it up just so you would be aware of the issue.

Can you define IO hierarchically? Again, this is tricky. We could say the IO is a sister phrase to a head P *to* or *for*, but only when we have the right kind of *to* or *for*. (While defining the right kind of *to* or *for* is complex, for now you can simply use the test of whether or not there is a corresponding sentence with the Double-Object construction.)

Can you define OP hierarchically? Sure: The OP is the sister phrase to the head P.

Not all theories of syntax define GFs in hierarchical terms. In the theory known as RELATIONAL GRAMMAR, Subjects, DOs, and IOs are taken as primitives and thus they are not defined via any other constructs. In that theory rules are written as manipulations of GFs. We will not even begin to evaluate the advantages of one theory with respect to the other, since any fair evaluation could fill a book. I bring this up solely so that you know alternatives exist.

Genitives in English

It's time to examine one more detail of Case in English that we haven't yet handled: We have not offered a rule to account for the Genitive Case, as in *the boy's book*. Let's do that now.

Tell me: Will the rule involve Case assignment by a head to an NP it governs? The only available head is N and we have based a lot of our Case Theory thus far on the claim that N is not a Case assigner in English (or in Latin). Instead of questioning everything we've done so far, we will just assume that what we've done is on the right track and try to account for Genitives in a way consistent with the rest of the theory that we've developed. Thus the Genitive rule will not involve a head that assigns Case.

What's the alternative? It seems to be an arbitrary fact of English that when an NP occurs in specifier position of N, that NP gets Genitive Case. So let's admit the arbitrary nature of the rule and write it simply as:

Genitive Case: Assign Genitive Case to NP_1 in the structure $[NP_1\ N']_{NP_0}$.

This may feel foreign to you. We have tried very hard to motivate the rules of Case Theory. Why should we suddenly be satisfied with a statement of the Genitive rule that makes it look as though it's capricious? Well, capriciousness may not be totally out of place here, for, you see, the Genitive of English is rather unusual. If you know another language, ask yourself how you say *the boy's book* in that language. Often a Genitive in English corresponds to an OP in another language similar to *the book of the boy's* (as in the Romance languages). But there are many languages with Genitive Case where the Case depends on the function of the NP, not strictly on its syntactic location (such as Latin and Finnish). In English, however, syntactic location is the key, not function (and if you're not convinced of this claim, you will be after you do Problem Set 4.4). So the fact that English has a rather arbitrary statement for the Genitive Case rule corresponds to the fact that English Genitives are rather arbitrary when compared to Genitives in other non-Germanic languages.

Notice that Genitive NPs sit in specifier position of N, just as Subjects of clauses sit in specifier position of Agr. Can you find any times when Genitives seem to be parallel to Subjects of clauses in other ways beyond this structural one? You might have thought of examples like:

John lectured on AIDS.
[*John's* lecture on AIDS] was good.
The panelists debated the difficult issues.
[*The panelists'* debate of the difficult issues] continued.

Sometimes the specifier of a nominal seems to play the same argument role that the specifier of Agr plays in the corresponding sentence. This fact might help you feel more reassured about proposing a specifier slot for nominal phrases (although in Problem Set 4.4 you will find that not all genitives are open to a Subject-like interpretation).

A final point should be made here. We learned earlier that in Latin an N could be modified by an NP in the Ablative Case; recall our example *flūmen magnā altitūdine* 'river of great depth.' As with the Genitive in English, we have an instance in which there is no Case assigner for the NP *magnā altitūdine*, given that N's in Latin could no more take Objects than N's in English can. So Ablative Case here is assigned by a rule as specialized as the Genitive rule in English. Still, I believe that the Latin rule was functionally driven: The Ablative NP modifies the head N in a few rather narrowly confined ways. In contrast the English rule is structure driven and the semantic relationship between the Genitive NP and the head N in English is broader than the relationship between the Ablative NP and the head N in Latin. (Again I refer you to Problem Set 4.4).

Coordination, Genitives, and X'

Another point can be made now. We can use our new understanding of genitives in English to justify the intermediary level of X' in our tree analyses. Consider this coordinate NP:

Joan's big dogs and cats

It is multiply ambiguous. Give some of its readings. On one reading the cats are not big nor do they belong to Joan. That reading is equivalent to the reading of the NP:

cats and Joan's big dogs
(as in: I'm allergic to cats and Joan's big dogs.)

What constituent does *cats* form on this reading? It is an N and it is also an NP, right? The coordination, then, is of NPs. So we have:

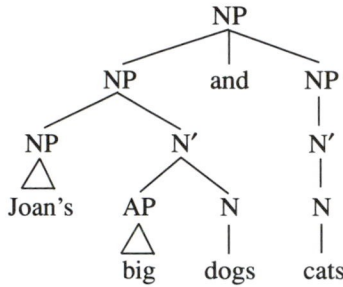

(I have left *and* dangling between the two NPs it conjoins. This is not the whole story on *and*, but the proper positioning would not affect our argument and would muddy the water unnecessarily.)

On another reading the cats are big and they do belong to Joan. So the coordination is of N's, and we have:

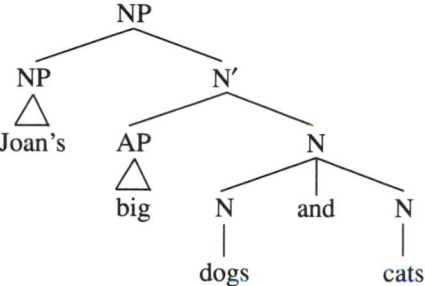

But there is also a third reading, in which the cats belong to Joan but they are not big. This reading is equivalent to:

Joan's cats and (her) big dogs

So the coordination is of the intermediary level—of the N' 's. The structure is:

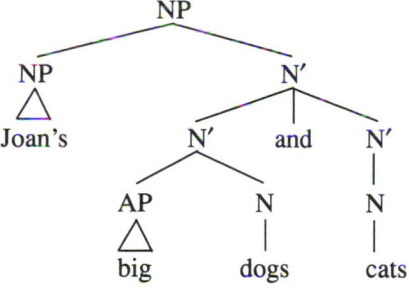

In order to account for all three readings of this NP, we needed to appeal to three different levels that coordination could take place at. Coordination, then, gives strong evidence for the existence of the X' level.

Phrase Structure and Other Languages

We built up our picture of X-Bar Theory by looking at English, but this theory is intended to account for phrase structure in all natural languages. What should be maintained from language to language are the three projections of X, X', and X''. What can vary is the order of constituents at each level in the projection.

Indeed, in the world's languages there is much variation in the word order of the constituents of a phrase. Some linguists have argued that at DS, all languages have the same order of branching in syntactic trees; in particular, branching is rightward, so heads precede their phrasal complements. Then various movement rules will account for word order at SS.

As you know, however, not all theories of syntax allow movement rules. So it is useful for us to consider word order variation from a different perspective. We will do that now by discussing parameters that have been proposed. Our discussion will have a pedagogical purpose beyond the exploration of word order parameters, however, so please pay attention to the argumentation.

One parameter is where the head of a phrase falls with respect to its complements (both for lexical and functional phrases), giving us two types of languages: those in which the complement to a head is on its right—HEAD-INITIAL languages—and those in which the complement to a head is on its left—HEAD-FINAL languages.

Another parameter is where the specifier of a phrase falls, giving us two types of languages: those in which the specifiers are left sisters to X′ (and thus precede the head and complement and are PHRASE-INITIAL), and those in which the specifiers are right sisters to X′ (and thus follow the head and complement and are PHRASE-FINAL).

A third parameter is where modifiers of the head fall with respect to the head and complement. An interesting fact is that modifiers of a head, as a general rule, do not intervene between a head and its complement.

> *I [ate rapidly pizza].   (cf. I rapidly ate pizza.)

Still, you might well know languages in which modifiers can easily intervene between a head and an argument, such as the Romance languages. The French translation of that English sentence, for example, is grammatical:

> J'ai mangé rapidement la pizza.

Nevertheless, when we look across the languages of the world, this behavior is not common. Some linguists claim that modifiers will always have the same parameter setting as specifiers. So if specifiers are left branches of X′, modifiers will fall to the left of the head, and if specifiers are right branches of X′, modifiers will fall to the right of the head. If that is so, then the position of modifiers does not offer us a third parameter for word order within phrases, after all. But the question is still open today as to whether the parameter about modifier position is an independent one or not.

NPs in Thai

Let's begin looking at these various parameters by considering noun phrases in Thai the Austroasiatic language of Thailand:

dèk sǎam khon	'three boys'
dèk lɔɔ sǎam khon	'three handsome boys'
dèk lɔɔ sǎam khon níi	'these three handsome boys'

Dèk means 'boy.' Given this one fact, describe the order of elements inside a nominal phrase. In particular, where does the lexical head come and where do the functional heads come with respect to their complements and modifiers? It looks like lexical heads in Thai are on the left, but functional heads are on the right, like so:

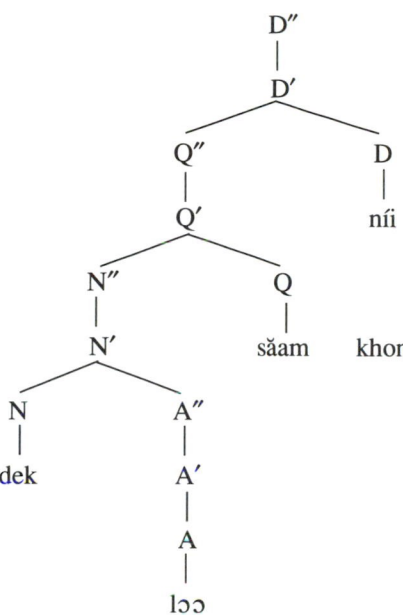

So lexical phrases would branch rightward and functional phrases would branch leftward—a rather complex picture.

However, not all linguists believe that determiners and numerals are really heads themselves (contrary to the analysis we gave of them for English). Instead, one could argue that determiners and numerals occur in specifier position of the phrase. Now specifiers could be initial or final, regardless of whether the head takes a right sister or a left sister. With this approach, the third Thai nominal phrase just given could be analyzed like so, allowing us to say that nominal phrases are head-initial in Thai:

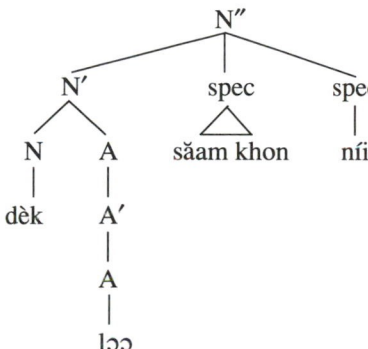

(I have used the label "spec" in this tree, but specifier is not the name of a category and, strictly speaking, it should not, therefore, occur as the node in a syntactic tree. I should have put the category labels of numeral and determiner, instead. But you will find the term "spec" used in trees frequently, so you should learn how to interpret it.)

This tree raises a point we've overlooked thus far. The N″ branches three ways: to N′

and to two specifier slots. Ternary branching like this is eschewed by many linguists. In fact, some have proposed that **all syntactic branching is at most binary.** If you'll think back to your phonology, you'll remember that when talking about metrical feet, we must admit binary and unbounded feet, but many linguists claim there is no need for ternary feet. And if you'll think back to your morphology, you'll remember that when we analyzed words into morphological trees, our branching was always binary. This is true even for compounding. Language clearly likes binarity. Ternary branching is equally clearly marked. However, the issue is still open as to whether or not we need ternary branching in syntax (as it is in metrical phonology and, perhaps, even in morphology).

Some people argue that we need ternary branching for several constructions in English, including sentences like:

I pressed the flower flat.

In the V″ here we have a V *(pressed)*, a DO *(the flower)*, and an AP *(flat)*. What is the function of this AP? What is it doing in this sentence? It tells us the state of the flower as a result of the pressing. In other words, it is a predicate. *Pressed* is the PRIMARY predicate of this sentence; *flat* is the SECONDARY predicate. There are various kinds of secondary predicates in language, classified mainly for their semantic value. The secondary predicate *flat* in this sentence is called a RESULTATIVE predicate, for obvious reasons.

By the way, not all sentences allow secondary resultative predicates. For example, I cannot say:

*I ripped the shirt shabby.

(which is intended to mean 'I ripped the shirt with the result that it wound up shabby'). There is a debate in the linguistic literature over exactly what factors license a secondary resultative predicate. Is it the lexical choice of the primary predicate? (That is, *press* licenses a resultative, but *rip* doesn't.) Or is it a more conceptually based restriction, having to do with types of primary predicates? Or is it some complex interaction of the primary predicate and the secondary predicate? Or what? Indeed, it's been argued that a particular grammatical mechanism is at play in the interpretation of secondary resultatives and that some languages simply lack this mechanism and, thus, secondary resultative predicates are never licensed in those languages. This is an area I encourage you to do research on (mainly because it's an area in which I find the literature less than enlightening, so there's lots of room for you to come up with a better account).

I will leave open the question of whether or not we need ternary branching in syntax (and you will undoubtedly return to this question on your own if you do research on resultatives). Certainly, if we were to take the position that all branching must be at most binary, and if we were further to take the position that functional phrases couldn't branch in a different direction from lexical phrases, then we would be forced into analyzing *dèk lɔɔ săam khon níi* in some new way.

One way is to say that heads have more than three projections. There is the head and there is the phrasal level. But in the middle, we can have more than one intermediary level. I'll label all such levels X′, but I could as easily have decided to indicate each level with one more bar than the next level down. The structure might then be:

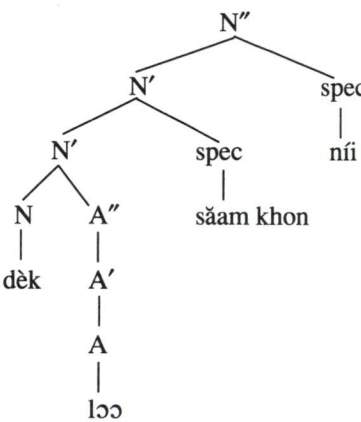

In Thai the V″ likewise branches rightward (and I will give a ternary branching in the next example, but I could as easily have allowed two V′ levels and restricted myself to binary branching), having both the complement and a modifier following the head:

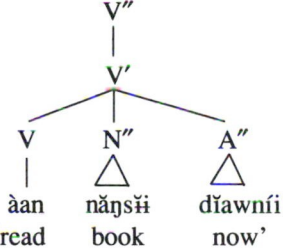

At the sentence level, what do you think the order of Subject, verb, and Object will be? Well, first you know that the Object is part of the V″ and since V″ is head-initial, the Object will follow the V. So the remaining question is where the Subject should come. Will we have SVO, VSO, or VOS?

While we talked earlier in the section "Movement as a Test for Constituency" about English as having SVO order, you may not have felt completely comfortable with that claim then. And now that we are talking about trying to make an analogous claim for Thai, you might want to object to the whole approach. So let's take a closer look at why we said English has SVO order.

Surely in English we allow several word orders. Give some sentences that show a variety of word orders in English. You might have come up with examples like:

SVO: I love you.
OSV: You I love./I wonder [[what]$_O$ [you]$_S$ [saw]$_V$].
VS: Will you?

If you speak another language well, you probably realize that that language allows some variation in word order, as well. Yet linguists call English an SVO language and linguists probably classify any other language you might speak as having a certain word order.

Can you figure out why? What standards do we use to decide which of the various word orders that occur in a language is "the" word order? Essentially what I'm asking you to do is figure out how we pick out the unmarked word order. Why are English SVO sentences unmarked, but VS and OSV marked? First tell me: When do verbs precede Subjects in English? In questions and a few other constructions—that's all. When do Objects precede SV in English? In what we have called topicalization sentences and in certain questions (the embedded clause of *I wonder what you saw* is an embedded question). In general, DECLARATIVE sentences (as opposed to INTERROGATIVE or imperative sentences) will have the unmarked word order, because declarative sentences are the most frequently used type of sentence. So when you consider the sentence structure of a language, you might want to look first at declaratives. And declaratives in English tend to use SVO—so SVO is the unmarked word order for English.

Okay, now let's return to Thai. This language has head-initial phrases. Does that fact help us to predict which of SVO, VSO, or VOS will be the order of constituents at the sentence level? Given an analysis of Subjects as being the specifier of Agr, if this language puts specifiers on the right branch (as we saw it did for the specifiers of nominal phrases), then we might expect the order VOS. But, in fact, **very few languages have an unmarked word order in which the Object precedes the Subject.** So just based on that fact, we can limit our expectations to SVO and VSO. We have no information thus far to help us determine which of these two is correct.

Thai's sentential word order turns out to be SVO. And many other languages which have phrases that are head-initial are also SVO languages, including Vietnamese, Hausa (spoken in Nigeria), and Hebrew. But other languages which have phrases that are head-initial are VSO, such as Classical Arabic, Irish, and Welsh. Still, not many languages of the world allow the S to intervene between the V and the O—and you can certainly see that such intervention would raise important questions about the structure of V″ in such a language. (I'll return to this issue.) The claim that this intervention is unfavored is supported by the fact that in Modern Standard Arabic as well as in colloquial Arabic dialects, the word order today is SVO.

Now we have a new problem. If we are right in our analysis, the specifier of a phrase in Thai is on a right branch. So if Subjects sit in the specifier slot for Agr″, we'd expect Subjects to follow the V″, like so:

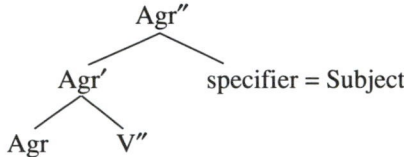

But Subjects precede the V″. So we have a real problem for our X-Bar Theory here. Thai does not, however, inflect its verbs for agreement (or for tense, for that matter). So it may make no sense to analyze a sentence as an Agr″. If that is so, then either Subjects are a left sister to some projection of V and, consistently, V″ would then be equivalent to the whole sentence, or Subjects are left sisters to V″ and, therefore, some other node dominates the whole sentence. (Let's arbitrarily call this node B, since we don't know anything about this category other than that it's the big guy dominating everything.) The structure of a sentence like the following would be one of those given here:

Khăw síi aahăan.
he buy food
'He buys food.'

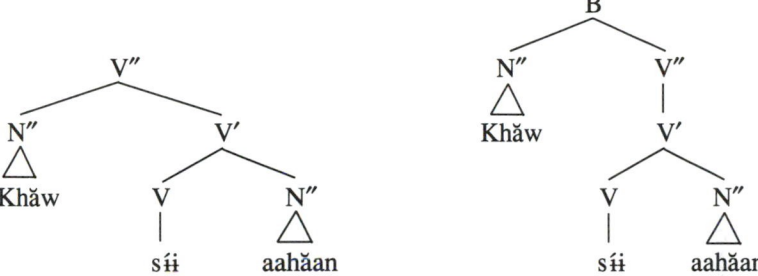

Either structure raises additional questions about sentence structure, which we won't go into here. But you can see that we might be no worse off if we had simply gone with our initial analysis of the nominal phrases in which we found that functional heads took a left sister, in contrast to lexical heads. That's because with that analysis we could still accept the specifier position as being the left sister of X'. So Subjects would naturally appear before the V'', and we'd predict SVO order.

As I said, however, some languages with head-initial phrase structure have the unfavored VSO order, such as Classical Arabic. This structure raises the interesting question of what the verb phrase looks like. If we assume that the O is inside the V'' (as it is in most languages), then the (intervening) S is also inside the V'', and we have a structure like this (if we allow ternary branching):

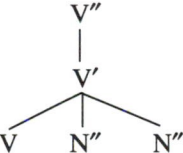

or, perhaps, this (if we restrict ourselves to binary branching):

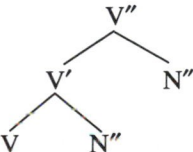

The major point of this rather complicated and certainly speculative discussion of Thai word order is to show you the importance of theoretical consistency in your analysis of any construction. Each choice potentially limits other choices you might make. **Internal consistency is essential to linguistic analysis.** As someone who does not work on Thai and who purposely picked Thai to use here because I have not read about its phrase structure, I could still look at sentences and note how various assumptions limited their potential analyses.

Arguments and the DS Position of Subjects

The final two structures just proposed for VSO languages are interesting in that they put all the arguments of V inside V″ (whereas in our trees of English sentences, the Subject argument was outside the V″ proper, being the specifier of the Arg). Some have argued that all arguments of a head X should be located within X″ at DS. (Recall that DS is the structure before any rules of syntax have applied.) That is, they want THETA THEORY (the theory that concerns the assignment of thematic roles, or theta roles, to arguments) to call for a particular (and confined) syntactic relationship between a theta assigner and its arguments, that of government.

With that approach, the English sentence structure we developed earlier would have to be considered the structure at SS only. But at DS, the Subject would be in specifier position of V, and a syntactic rule would move it out of the V″ and up into specifier of Agr position. Here are the DS and SS of the sentence *John swims* with that analysis. The Subject moves from inside the V″ up to specifier of Agr; the V undergoes head-to-head movement, first into T and then into Agr, picking up the person/number/tense inflection:

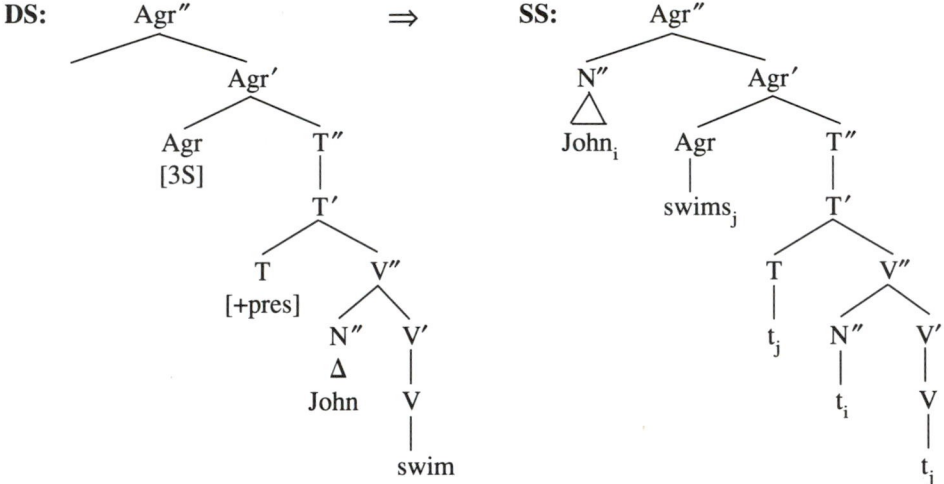

I have located the Subject argument of *swim* in the specifier position of V at DS since we have become accustomed in this chapter to finding Subjects in specifier position (as developed in the sections "[+Agr] as a Case Assigner and X-Bar Theory" and "Genitives in English").

While there are many advantages to this approach, it is more abstract than the approach we gave earlier and it calls for a new syntactic movement rule (into Subject position). We will briefly discuss this analysis further in the section "minimalism", and you should be aware of this approach as you read current articles in syntactic theory.

Head-Final Languages

Languages with head-final phrase structure are also not hard to come by. Turkish is one. Here is an example N″ and V″:

N″: üç   ilginç   kitap
    three interesting books
    'three interesting books'

V″: çocuğa   elmayı   verdi
    child(Dat) apple(ACC) gave
    'gave the child the apple'

(Turkish has a rich Case system and many PPs in English correspond to Case-marked NPs in Turkish.) You can see that Objects precede verbs in Turkish.

What word order do you expect at the sentence level? Will we have SOV, OSV, or OVS? Since I've already told you that it is rare for Subjects to follow Objects in unmarked word order, you should have guessed that the word order is SOV. And, indeed, it is:

Adamlar heykeli   kırdılar.
men   statue(ACC) broke
'The men broke the statue.'

Many languages have SOV order, including Hopi, Hindi-Urdu, American Sign Language, and Burmese (a Sino-Tibetan language spoken in Burma).

What do you think the order is in Turkish if we have a sentential Object? Take the English sentence *Hasan told me that you passed the exam* and reorder the words the way you think they will come in the Turkish equivalent. Okay, now let me tell you that verbs are highly inflected for person and number in Turkish. Given this fact, is Turkish a potential pro-drop language or not? It is. And, in fact, Turkish is a pro-drop language. The Turkish translation of this English sentence comes out as:

Hasan bana   [intihanı   geçtiğin]i   anlattı.
Hasan 1S(Dat) [exam(ACC) passed-2S](ACC) told
'Hasan told me that you passed the exam.'

The only real question you should have had in your mind was whether the IO preceded or followed the DO (here a sentential DO), but if you looked at our earlier example of a V″ in Turkish (*çocuğa elmayı verdi* 'child apple gave'), you might have guessed that IOs generally precede DOs in Turkish.

It is not necessarily so that IOs precede DOs in SOV languages, however. Japanese is an SOV language, but IOs easily follow DOs and this may be the unmarked word order:

Taroo-ga Hanako-ni hon-o watasita.
Taroo   Hanako   book handed
'Taroo handed the book to Hanako.'

(No glosses are given for the particles *ga*, *ni*, and *o* on the NPs here. After you have done Problem Set 4.4, you can fill in the glosses for yourself.)

Mixed Systems

While Thai is head-initial for both N″ and V″ and while Turkish is head-final for both N″ and V″, some languages have mixed systems. In Finnish, for example, N″ is head-final, but V″ is head-initial. And the word order at the sentence level is SVO:

Kaksi nuorta miestä istui huoneessa.
two   young men   sat   room
'Two young men were sitting in the room.'

Relating Sentence Pairs

In our discussion of word order, we said that declarative sentences are generally where linguists look to find the unmarked word order of a language. Indeed, sometimes word order looks like the only syntactic distinction between a declarative sentence and an interrogative sentence in English. Can you give me such a sentence pair? Examples are easy to find:

John is very nice.
Is John very nice?

The difference between these sentences, however, has been argued to be not merely one of word order, but of the hierarchical arrangement of the words in the tree.
    To see this, consider for a moment this complex sentence:

I know [that she's nice].

Look at the *that* that introduces the embedded clause. Do you recognize it as belonging to any other grammatical classification we have talked about? Is there any GF or any other function (such as modification or predication) that it seems to be playing? I hope you said no. This use of *that* is termed a complementizer (a term we met in Chapter 3), and its job is to introduce a clause (just like determiners can introduce NPs and intensifiers can introduce many kinds of phrases).
    Now follow closely where your X-Bar Theory leads. If *that* is a C(omplementizer), then what node is the whole embedded clause? Think about it. Every lexical node heads a phrase. So the C here heads a C″. We can then analyze embedded clauses as having the form:

The embedded clause in *I know that she's nice*, then, would have the analysis:

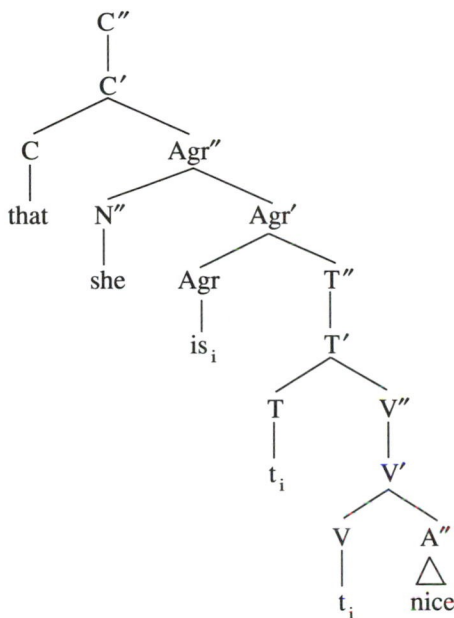

(The verb *is* (which started out as *be*) undergoes head-to-head movement through T into Agr (which is why there are traces in V and T).) In other words, embedded clauses are really COMPLEMENTIZER PHRASES (C″).

All other things being equal, do we want embedded clauses and matrix clauses to have the same structural configuration or not? You might not feel sure about this. That is, all other things aren't equal. Indeed, many kinds of embedded clauses do not sound good if they are used in isolation like matrix clauses. For example, infinitival clauses are odd except in embedded position:

    *Betsy to move across town.
    (cf. I expect Betsy to move across town.)

Likewise, tensed clauses introduced by *that* are strange except in embedded position:

    *That Betsy will move across town.
    (cf. I think that Betsy will move across town.)

And clauses like the following one in the subjunctive mood are strange alone:

    *(That) Jeff be here on time.
    (cf. I demand that Jeff be here on time.)

Nevertheless, the structural similarities between all clauses, whether embedded or not, are great. List some of them. You might have noted that all clauses allow the same range of GFs to be filled, word order in clauses of all types in English is SVO, the verb string has the same components in the same order in all types of clauses (and see Problem Set 4.3), and so on. All of these things are configurational in nature. For this reason we might indeed want a single configuration for both types of clauses. And notice that one configuration for all types of clauses would surely be the simplest analysis—the one that calls for the least new apparatus in X-Bar Theory. So let's propose that matrix clauses are also C"s. And that means that in the sentence:

I know [that she's nice].

the C of the matrix clause is not audible. But after our discussion of little pro and big PRO, you are aware of benefits of proposing null items, so this type of approach shouldn't be terribly alien to you. The higher complementizer (the C node) would take an Agr" as its complement, just as in embedded clauses. The structure of our sentence *I know that she's nice* at SS would be:

Does this astound you? It may seem like a lot of structure for just a dinky little string of five words (plus a contraction). So I'm going to try hard to convince you that this tree structure is needed.

First, we justified the existence of a null C and its higher projections (C′ and C″) on the basis of having an identical expansion for all kinds of phrases. But you might feel a lot more confident of this if you could see some empirical support for C. After all, the other null items we've talked about, little pro and big PRO, both fill structural positions that are not always phonetically null. Thus Italian allows either a full NP or little pro in Subject position of tensed clauses:

(Maria) viene.   '{Maria/(S)he} is coming.'

and English allows either a full NP or big PRO in Subject position of infinitival clauses:

I want (Bill) to leave.
[I want [{Bill/PRO} to leave].]

Indeed, proposing a structural node that is always phonetically empty is suspect. What evidence is there that such a node really exists? So if we want to say that matrix clauses have the structure C″, we would hope to find times when a matrix clause could have a phonetically filled C position.

That brings us back to the example question above:

Is John very nice?

What position does *is* fill here? As you probably have guessed, it's been proposed that the fronted auxiliary *is* fills the C position. That is, it's been claimed that in questions in English, the first auxiliary moves up into C position. So at SS the analysis of *Is John very nice* would be as in the tree on the next page. The movement of *is* into C is another instance of a head moving into a head slot (although this movement differs from the other instances of head-to-head movement since it is across the intervening Subject NP).

So the C position can be filled at SS for both matrix and embedded clauses. However, matrix and embedded clauses differ in that the C position is always empty at DS for matrix clauses. That is a fact that we have not accounted for (and we will not account for it in this book).

Let's stick with our X-Bar Theory and see where else it leads us. Once we propose the existence of a C″, with a head C, we are also admitting the possibility of a specifier position for C, which can be filled by a phrase (since specifier of any X is a phrasal position). Again, linguists have argued for precisely this structure and again interrogative sentences have been cited as crucial evidence, since they can begin with an interrogative phrase preceding the C position:

[Where] is John?
[What] are you reading?
[Why] did Bertha leave?

These initial question phrases are often called WH-PHRASES because so many of our interrogative words have an initial "wh", like *what, when, which, why*; but this group also includes *how*.

In all three of these sentences, the wh-phrase is filled by a single lexical item, yet I'm calling these lexical items phrases. Can you show me that the initial position that *where*, *what*, and *why* occupy in questions like these is really a phrasal position? Look for questions that begin with wh-phrases that consist of more than just a single word. They are easy to find:

[How nice] is John?
[Which book] are you reading?
[What on earth] did you do to him?

So the rule that moves *what* or *why* and so on into the specifier position of C cannot be movement of a head; it is a phrasal movement rule. (You will meet another phrasal movement rule in Problem Set 4.14.)

Wh-Movement

The interrogative sentence *How nice is John?* would have the SS structure:

```
                        C″
              ┌──────────┴──────────┐
             X″                     C′
          ┌──────┐            ┌──────┴──────┐
        [how nice]ⱼ           C            Agr″
                              │        ┌────┴────┐
                             isᵢ      N″        Agr′
                                       │      ┌───┴───┐
                                     John   Agr     T″
                                             │       │
                                            tᵢ      T′
                                                 ┌───┴───┐
                                                 T      V″
                                                 │       │
                                                tᵢ      V′
                                                     ┌───┴───┐
                                                     V      Int″
                                                     │       △
                                                    tᵢ      tⱼ
```

The Int″ (which is the wh-phrase *how nice*) would start out at DS in the same position it fills in the corresponding declarative sentence—that is, inside the V″. This questioned Int″ would then move up to specifier of C position, leaving behind a trace. The *is* would likewise move from Agr up to C, leaving a trace (which is co-indexed with traces in T and V, since this verb passed through those positions, as well).

The movement of the Int″ into specifier position of C is called WH-MOVEMENT. Wh-movement has been argued to be operative not just in questions but also in the sentences we noted with fronting earlier (sentences like: *Those same shoes John will buy*) and in a variety of other types of sentences.

The proposal of a rule of Wh-movement is controversial, just as all movement in syntax is controversial. It is significant, however, that, by and large, even theories that do not allow movement rules in the syntax still recognize the need for a syntactic structure similar to that above for questions. That is, whether *how nice* (or any other wh-phrase) gets moved to the front of the clause in *How nice is John?* or whether it is generated in initial position at DS, we still need to relate this phrase to the Int″ that is the sister to the V in order to be able to interpret the sentence properly. Do you see that? We are questioning whether a degree of niceness is correctly predicated of John—and predicates are normally found within the V″.

The upshot is that, regardless of the issue of syntactic movement, sentences which look rather simple in terms of their linear string at SS are generally agreed to have a complicated hierarchical structure. This is the major point that I hope you draw and keep from our discussion of questions in English.

We will assume the movement approach to wh-questions, since it is consistent with everything else we've done and will do in this chapter. And you need a good understanding of certain issues related to wh-movement in order to read any of the literature on questions written since the mid 1970s. So let's now look at those issues.

Islands and Subjacency

The issues related to wh-movement are complex, but they are important. Yet this book has to come to an end in due course. Given those facts together, I can neither lead you step by step through all the issues nor can I omit some of the issues without cheating you. So I am going to change approach here and present to you a lot of things without argumentation. I apologize. I don't believe this is an effective way for anyone to learn any area of linguistics, but I don't see another choice.

The wh-questions we looked at were all simple sentences. The phrase we questioned moved up to the front of its own clause. Can complex sentences be wh-questions? In particular, can a questioned phrase moved out of a sentential Object clause up to the front of the matrix clause? Sure. Examples are easy to come up with:

> Who did Mary say Paul invited?
> (cf. Mary said Paul invited someone.)

Where did the wh-phrase start out in this question? Can you see that the initial *who* must be co-indexed with the DO position of the verb *invited*? So we posit a trace in DO position of the sentential Object:

> who$_i$ did Mary say [Paul invited t$_i$]

The movement at this point looks like it went two clauses up. Can wh-movement go three clauses up? That is, can an initial wh-word be co-indexed with a trace in a clause that's embedded inside another embedded clause? Please look for examples in which all the embedded clauses we are dealing with serve as sentential Objects. Again, examples are easy to find:

> Who did Mary say Bill predicted Paul would invite?
> who$_i$ did Mary say [Bill predicted [Paul would invite t$_i$]]
> (cf. Mary said Bill predicted Paul would invite someone.)

Now give an example in which the wh-word is co-indexed with a trace four clauses down. You might have come up with something like:

> Who did Mary say Bill predicted Susan would insist Paul invite?
> who$_i$ did Mary say [Bill predicted [Susan would insist [Paul invite t$_i$]]]
> (cf. Mary said Bill predicted Susan would insist Paul invite someone.)

Five?

> Who did Mary say Bill predicted Susan would insist Ralph should announce Paul would invite?
> who$_i$ did Mary say [Bill predicted [Susan would insist [Ralph should announce [Paul would invite t$_i$]]]]
> (cf. Mary said Bill predicted Susan would insist Ralph should announce Paul would invite someone.)

The examples get more and more farfetched, but the point is that they are possible, right? Practical limitations stop us from speaking like that—but the grammar itself doesn't.

So that makes it look like wh-movement is unbounded. But, actually, there are several reasons not to believe that is true. For example, there are various kinds of constructions that don't allow wh-movement. Here's one:

John spoke after Mary bought the peaches.
*What did John speak after Mary bought?
what$_i$ did John speak [after Mary bought t$_i$]

What function does the clause *after Mary bought the peaches* play in the sentence *John spoke after Mary bought the peaches*? It modifies the time of the event of the matrix clause, right? So this is an adverbial clause. Give me at least three other sentences that have adverbial clauses introduced by something other than *after* and test to see if an initial wh-word can be co-indexed with a position inside the adverbial clause. You might have come up with examples like:

John spoke {because/before/even though} Mary bought the peaches.
*What did John speak {because/before/even though} Mary bought?
what$_i$ did John speak [{because/before/even though} Mary bought t$_i$]

None of them is grammatical. In general we find that **adverbial clauses are ISLANDS for movement.** What that means is that an adverbial clause behaves as though it is an island, isolated from the rest of the sentence it is contained it, with respect to EXTRACTION (that is, movement of anything out of it). This fact is known as the ADVERBIAL ISLAND CONSTRAINT. If wh-movement was an unbounded movement, we wouldn't expect it to care about the structure that intervenes between the starting point of the movement—what we can call the FOOT of the movement CHAIN—and the LANDING SITE of the movement— what we can call the HEAD OF THE CHAIN. But wh-movement is sensitive to this intervening structure.

We could look at more types of constructions that lead to the same conclusion, but we won't for considerations of time and space. So let me tell you that it turns out that wh-movement out of an embedded clause is allowed only when all the relevant clauses between the foot and the head of the wh-chain are either sentential DOs or sentential OPs, where the DO or OP receives a theta-role from the predicate of the next higher clause. Adverbial clauses, being modifiers, are not arguments.

This finding is fascinating and it is the foundation behind the claim that **maximal projections that aren't LEXICALLY MARKED (that is, that don't receive a theta-role) from the V and that don't also fall inside the VP are barriers to movement.** Let me here give you a the definition of a useful term: L-GOVERNMENT. We say that **a head L-governs everything within its maximal projection that it assigns a theta-role to. So only L-governed clauses allow extraction.** There are matters that complicate this statement, but on the whole, this statement covers the facts. And this statement is the heart of what is known as the SUBJACENCY PRINCIPLE (generally referred to as Subjacency).

What does Subjacency predict about extraction from a sentential Subject? It should be blocked, right? That's because the sentential Subject does not fall inside the VP, even though it receives a theta-role from the V. So sentential Subjects are not L-governed— they are not governed by a lexical head that assigns them a theta role. And, indeed,

sentential Subjects form an island (and this fact is known as the SENTENTIAL SUBJECT CONSTRAINT):

That John likes Mary upsets Paul.
*Who does that John likes upset Paul?
who$_i$ does [that John likes t$_i$] upset Paul

The wh-question is pure garbage, right? So Subjacency is a useful principle.

Now let's look at another kind of construction out of which extraction is blocked. Can you find me a sentence in which it looks like we have wh-movement inside an embedded clause? What you're looking for is a sentence in which the wh-phrase has moved up to the front of some embedded clause, rather than up to the front of the matrix clause. An example is:

Sally wonders who Bill will invite.
Sally wonders [who Bill will invite t$_i$]

The embedded wh-question *who Bill will invite* is called an INDIRECT QUESTION. Find me a sentence that contains an indirect question in which something other than the DO of the embedded verb has been questioned. You might have come up with examples like:

Sally wonders who will invite Ralph.
Sally wonders who Bill gave the ring to.

and various other types. In the first one we have questioned the Subject of the embedded clause. In the second one, we have questioned the IO of the embedded clause. Now, can we turn these sentences into DIRECT QUESTIONS (that is, matrix questions) by questioning the DO of the embedded clauses? Try it.

*Who does Sally wonder who will invite?
*What does Sally wonder who Bill gave to?

They sound awful. **Indirect questions form another island.** This fact is known as the **WH-ISLAND CONSTRAINT.** Again, we see wh-movement being sensitive to the structure that intervenes between the foot and the head of the wh-chain.

Tell me, are indirect questions barriers to movement, given the statement we gave above about theta-marking? The indirect questions in the examples given here do serve as DOs to the verb *wonder*. And they are theta-marked by that V. So they are L-governed and they are not barriers to movement (so far as we know in this book). We should, therefore, be able to extract from them. Why can't we? There must be something more we need to know about how wh-movement proceeds in order to account for wh-islands. We will learn that something else now and we will see how it accounts for wh-islands at the very end of the next section.

Strict Cyclicity

The fact that wh-movement is sensitive to the structure that intervenes between the foot and the head of the wh-chain can be accounted for if wh-movement is a bounded movement—and that's what we will now propose. **A wh-phrase moves into the specifier of the C of its own clause. From there it hops up to the specifier of the C of the next higher clause, and so on, until it ends up in the specifier of the relevant C.** The relevant C for a direct question is the matrix C. The relevant C for an indirect question is the C of the highest clause of the indirect question. That is, in wh-questions we will have a trace in spec of C for all intervening C's between the foot and the head of the wh- chain.

Wh-movement has been called a SUCCESSIVE CYCLIC MOVEMENT, where we can think of each clause here as being a CYCLIC domain for movement. So the wh-phrase moves to the front of its cyclic domain, then up to the front of the next higher cyclic domain, and so on, successively. (Notice that each movement is bounded within the domain of the cycle, so movement is local. We saw this type of local restriction on movement in the Locality Constraint discussed in the section "Metrical Grids" of Chapter 2.)

The movement of a wh-phrase into spec of C is required by details of the Subjacency Principle that we haven't gotten into. If a wh-phrase that started out in an embedded clause did not move into spec of C of its own clause and, instead, tried to move in one fell swoop, so to speak, into the spec of the C of the matrix clause, it would cross too many barriers. So spec of C is, in a sense, an ESCAPE HATCH for movement. By going into spec of C of its own clause, a wh-phrase manages to circumvent barriers to movement.

Let me give an example analysis of wh-movement for a direct question and then for an indirect question.

Who did Mary say Paul invited?

(The tree for this sentence is on page 376.) Three different movements took place in this derivation. Look at the wh-movement first. The wh-phrase *who* started out in DO position of the lower clause. It moved up into spec of C of its own clause. Then it hopped from there into spec of C of the matrix clause. Had there been any other clauses in between, it would have hopped into the spec of C of each of those clauses, gradually making its way up the tree. So in a question like:

Who did Mary say Paul wanted Bill to invite?

we will have traces in the lowest DO position and in the spec of C position of both embedded clauses, all co-indexed with the *who*, like so:

who$_i$ did Mary say [t$_i$ Paul wanted [t$_i$ Bill to invite t$_i$]]

The other two movements we see in our tree are head-to-head movements of the verbs *did* and *invited*.

Embedded questions would go through a similar derivation. Let's look at the derivation for:

Mary wondered who Paul thought Bill invited.

(The tree for this sentence is on page 377.) Again, there are several instances of head-to-head movement (the verb *invited* moves up through T to Agr of its clause; the verb *thought* moves up through T to Agr of its clause; the verb *wondered* moves up through T to Agr of its clause). The wh- movement is from the DO position of the lowest V into spec of C of the lowest clause, and from there into spec of C of the next higher clause. Wh-movement stops at that point because that is the front of the indirect question.

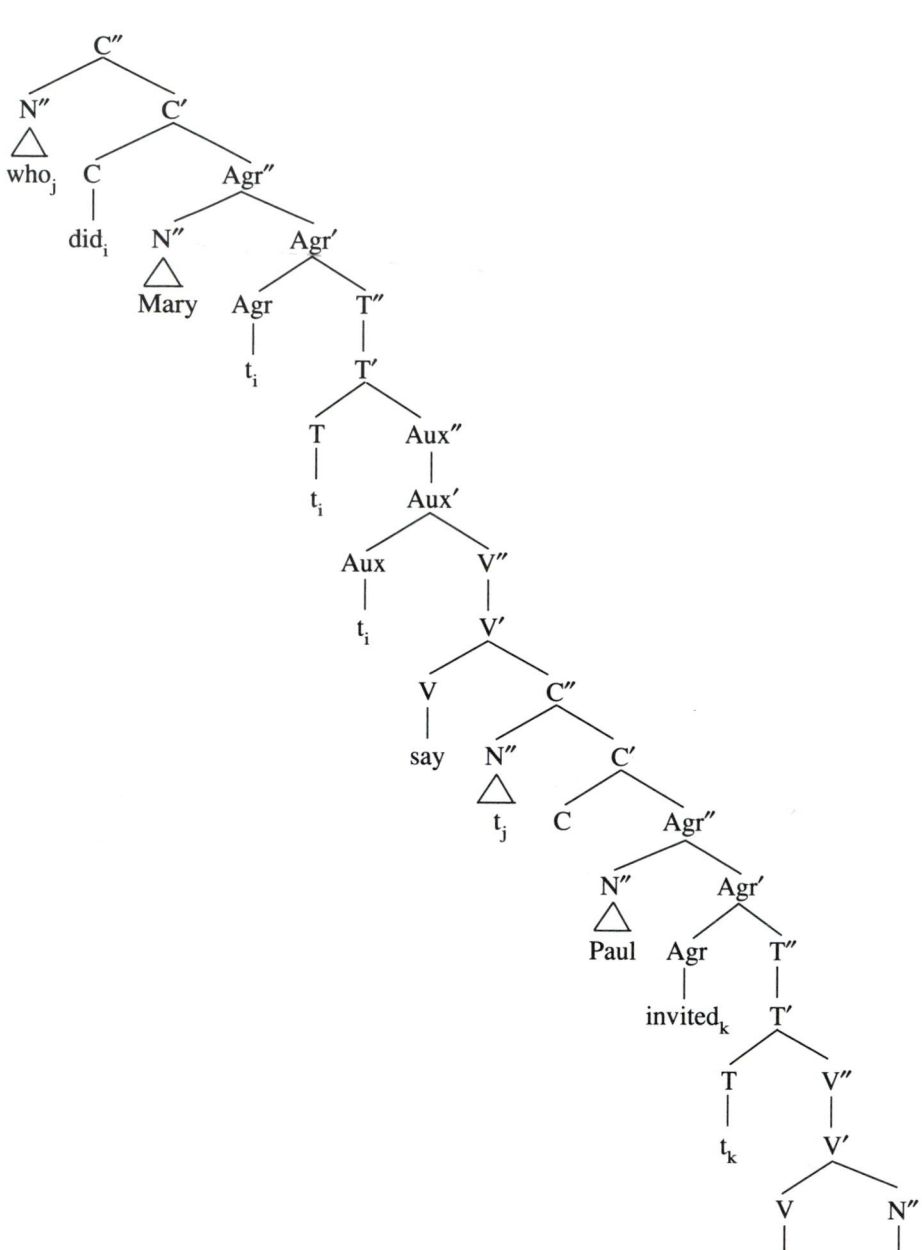

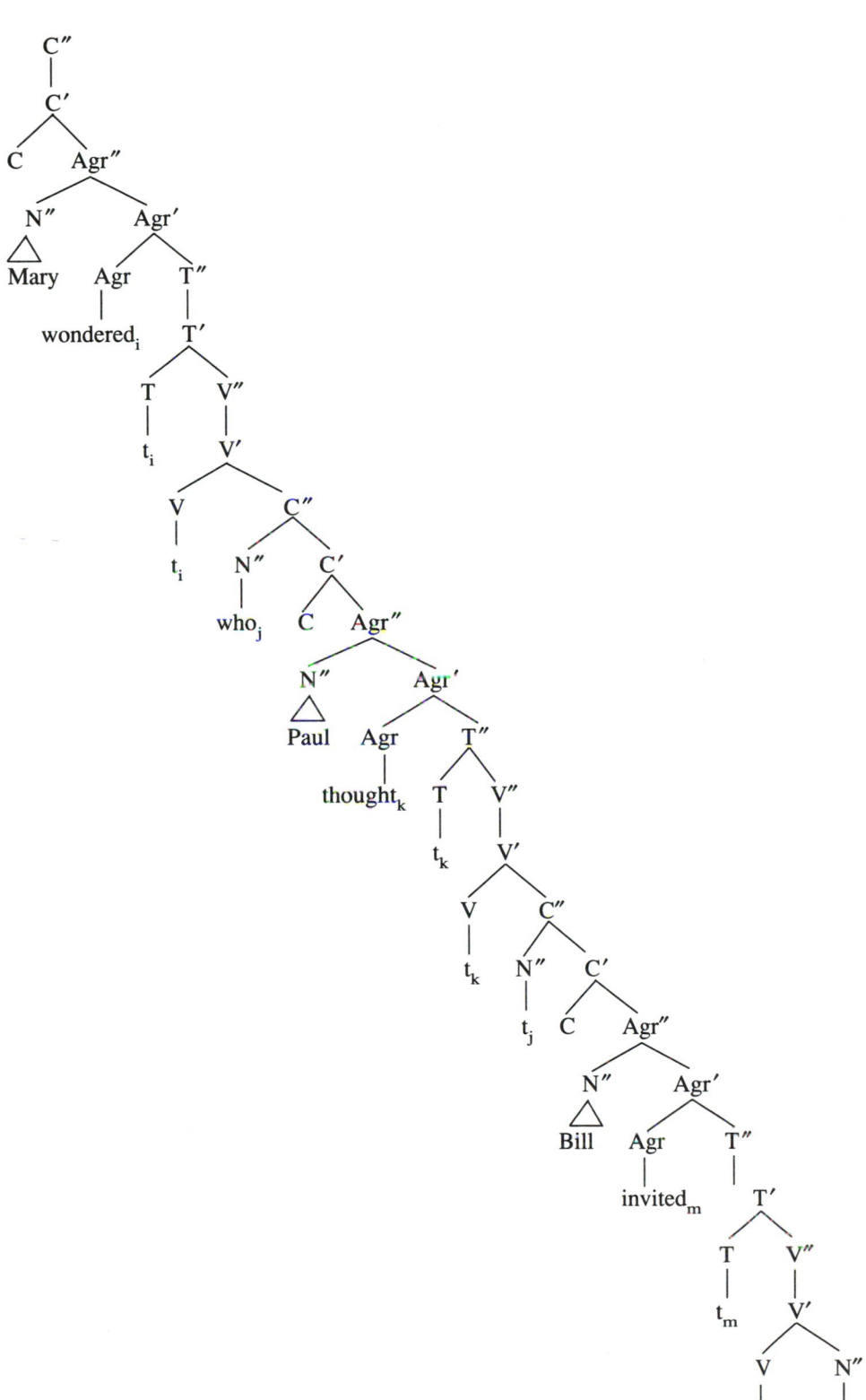

Given this analysis of wh-movement, we can now go back and account for the wh-island constraint. Consider again this sentence:

Sally wonders who Bill gave the ring to.

We noted above that we can't do wh-movement out of this (or any other) embedded question:

*What does Sally wonder who Bill gave to.

Why not? Go through the steps involved in the wh-movement here. The *what* starts out as the DO of the verb *gave*. Where does it move? Well, it should move into spec of the C of its own clause. So what's the problem? That spec of C is already filled with *who*. That's the problem. **A node cannot be doubly filled.** So *what* is blocked from moving into spec of C of its own clause, and the derivation is thwarted. (And wh-movement out of an embedded clause turns out to be a VIOLATION of Subjacency after all.)

There is a potential problem with this analysis. Let's look again at the structure of the ungrammatical question *What does Sally wonder who Bill gave to?* before any wh-movement (but I will position the verbs in their SS locations, to avoid confusion):

[_____ does Sally wonder [_____ Bill gave what to who]]

The empty slots indicate where the specifier of C positions are for both clauses. Okay, now we know that both *what* and *who* have to get moved into a specifier of C position. We want *what* to wind up in the matrix clause and *who* to wind up in the embedded clause. And we know that all wh-movement is successive cyclic. So let's move *what* first into the spec of C of the lower clause, then into spec of C of the higher clause, like so:

[what$_i$ does Sally wonder [t$_i$ Bill gave t$_i$ to who]]

Now we can move *who* into spec of C of its own clause, to yield:

*What does Sally wonder who Bill gave to?

What's wrong with that derivation? Something has to be, because the result is ungrammatical.

We could suggest that t$_i$ fills the lower spec of C after the movement of *what* up the tree, so that *who* cannot move into there because nodes can't be doubly filled. But, in fact, there are other instances (which we won't go into) in which it appears that moved items can land in a position that a trace occupies and cover that trace, so to speak.

Instead, the explanation given is that the movement of *who* cannot follow the movement of *what*, since the movement of *who* involves only the lower cycle, while the movement of *what* involves both the lower and the higher cycle. The idea is formalized in the following principle:

STRICT CYCLICITY: No rule may affect only the members of a given cycle once that cycle has already been passed.

This syntactic principle takes its place beside the phonological principle of the Strict Cycle that we met in the section "Cycles and the Strict Cycle Condition" of Chapter 2 and the morphological principle of the Adjacency Condition that we met in the section "Lexical and Derivational Morphemes" of Chapter 3. So both *what* and *who* must move into spec of the lower C during the same cycle. Then *what* would move on to the spec of the higher C during the next cycle. But the problem is exactly what we just identified: *what* and *who* can't coexist in the same specifier slot, even temporarily.

Wh-movement and movement in general raise many more issues for the theory of syntax than those we've touched on here. Some of the most important of those issues have to do with restrictions on traces. If you are intrigued, I urge you to consult an introduction-to-syntax book or to go directly to the sources in the bibliography of this book. It's time for us to move on to other issues.

Transformations

Besides declarative/interrogative pairs, there are many other sentence pairs that have similar meaning but differ in word order and, possibly, structural hierarchy. Can you think of other such pairs? Limit yourself to considering only declarative sentences here. We've already mentioned one such pair, the sentence in which a DO is followed by an IO, paired with the sentence in which we have a Double Object:

John gave milk to the kitty.
John gave the kitty milk.

What other difference beside word order do we have here? The first sentence has a *to* which the second sentence lacks.

Another classic example that most syntax textbooks handle is the PASSIVE. In English, for example, we find active, and passive counterparts, such as:

John stole the necklace.
The necklace was stolen by John.

Again, there are more differences than just word order and hierarchical structure. List them. The passive sentence has a form of *be* and the P *by*, as well as having a verb in the participle form *(stolen)*.

A third type of example is seen in what are often called the *spray/load* sentences. Here are two such pairs:

Joan sprayed paint on the wall.
Joan sprayed the wall with paint.
I wrapped the child in a blanket.
I wrapped a blanket around the child.

Again, you can see another difference beside just word order and hierarchical structure. What is it? The P used in each sentence of a given pair is different *(on* vs. *with*; *in* vs. *around)*. And you might also note that while the meaning differences between the pairs involving a DO and an IO and between the active/passive pairs are slight, the meaning differences between the various *spray/load* pairs are more robust.

In the past some linguists argued that some or all of these pairs should be syntactically related to each other by rules called TRANSFORMATIONS. For example, they argued that the Double-Object sentence was DERIVED FROM the sentence with a DO followed by an IO in a *to*-phrase via a movement rule often called DATIVE MOVEMENT. But you can see that any movement rules you might propose to relate any of these pairs would involve more than simple movement.

Stop right now and ask yourself what else would have to happen if the Double-Object sentence was derived from the sentence I have paired it with. If there really were a Dative Movement, the grammar would also have to allow us a way to DELETE the P *to* and all the hierarchical structure that that P entailed (the P′ and P″ level) without deleting the Object of the P (the IO).

Now consider the active and passive pair. Let's assume there is a movement rule called Passive that derives the passive sentence from the active one by moving around noun phrases. Again stop and ask yourself what else the grammar would have to do to allow this derivation. Here we'd have to INSERT a form of *be* and insert the P *by*, plus we'd have to BUILD all the hierarchical structure that is entailed by the addition of this verbal form and this P. Then we'd have to make sure that the N″s we moved around got positioned correctly (the old Subject, for example, would have to become the Object of the *by*). It would be quite an undertaking.

Finally, consider the two pairs of the *spray/load* sentence type. What would we need to do besides just movement? Here we'd have to delete a lexical item (a P) and replace it with a different lexical item (another P). But the lexical item we are deleting can vary (in these examples we find both *on* and *in*) and the lexical item it gets replaced with can likewise vary. (In these examples we find both *with* and *around*.) And the replacement is not random—thus we don't find pairs like:

>   Joan sprayed paint on the wall.
>   *Joan sprayed the wall around paint.
>   I wrapped the child in a blanket.
>   *I wrapped a blanket with the child.

Instead, we must choose *with* for the second sentence and we must choose *around* for the fourth sentence. So we must look at the other words in the sentence to decide which P to replace the old P with. In other words, our supposedly syntactic rule is looking at lexical information of a nonstructural sort. Our syntax, then, is not AUTONOMOUS—it is sensitive to nonsyntactic information. This certainly muddies the syntactic waters.

Today few theories of syntax would relate any of these pairs. Deletion, insertion, replacement (also called SUBSTITUTION), and structure building rules are pretty much taboo in modern theories of syntax, and you have at least some inkling of why from this discussion.

What about the head-to-head movement rules and the wh-movement rule we've discussed—are they subject to the same criticisms as the putative transformations discussed in this section? They do not involve deletion of any lexical items (unlike the zapping of *to* from an IO in a Double-Object sentence). They do not involve the insertion of any lexical items (unlike the insertion of *by* and *be* in the derivation of passive sentences discussed in this section). They do not involve the replacement of any lexical items with other lexical items (unlike in our *spray/load* pairs).

Do these movement rules involve structure building? Since no lexical items are inserted, no structure building is called for. And the moved items wind up in SS slots that are justified on independent grounds. For example, we know that the C head must exist independently of movement considerations, since that's where the *that* of a sentence like *I know that Mary's nice* is located. And if all phrases have the same structural expansions, as X-Bar Theory would tell us, then C' must be able to take a specifier phrase as its sister—therefore wh-movement does not require any structure building. In sum, movement of a head into another head slot and wh-movement are not subject to the criticisms we leveled at other types of proposed transformations.

Modern theories of syntax, then, have very few and very restricted types of transformations. Indeed, as I've said before, even movement is not allowed by some theories. Instead, the job of the linguist in modern theories would be to account for the similarities in meaning between sentence pairs of the types we've looked at without appealing to transformations of any sort.

Theta Theory

Appeals to the theory of thematic relations, Theta Theory, have been very helpful in accounting for such similarities. Recall that Theta Theory is the theory concerned with how predicates assign thematic roles to their arguments. Consider again the active/passive pair:

> John stole the necklace.
> The necklace was stolen by John.

What do we understand these sentences to mean in terms of event structure? What action took place? Stealing, right? Who was the agent of that stealing (the one who initiated and/or controlled the action—a term we met in Chapter 3)? John. What was the PATIENT or theme of that stealing (the one affected by the action in terms of being moved or manipulated—another term we met in Chapter 3)? The necklace. Okay—we can now see that the similarities between these sentences are of this thematic sort. We have the same predicate in both sentences: *steal* (though the morphological form of that predicate differs). All predicates are listed in our lexicon as taking a certain predicate-argument structure. This particular predicate can have an agent argument and a theme argument, like so:

Predicate-Argument structure:

steal: agent, theme

What the active and passive sentences show us is that we need ways to account for the variety of SS positions that these arguments can occur in. **Theta Theory comes in here; it tells us how to MAP from predicate argument structure into syntactic structure.** If we do not allow movement rules, we can say that there is flexibility in the rules that LINK arguments to grammatical positions. For example, the theme argument of *steal* can be mapped into DO position (as in the active sentence) or Subject position (as in the passive sentence). And the agent argument can be mapped into Subject position (as in the active sentence) or OP position (as in the passive sentence). (Actually, some linguists argue that the OP in the passive sentence is not really an agent. But that argument is relatively esoteric from our present stance. I just want you to know that almost any statement one can make about syntax is open to attack.) The mapping choice is not arbitrary, of course. We need to have the passive auxiliary *be* in order to map the theme into Subject position, for example.

If we do allow movement rules, we can map the theme argument of *steal* into DO position in both the active and passive sentences and then move it into Subject position in the passive sentence. (However, movement rules won't allow us to take a Subject and move it into OP position, for reasons we will not discuss in this book.)

Likewise the dative sentences and the *spray/load* sentences can be accounted for by looking at the argument structure of the predicates and considering how the arguments get mapped into GF positions. For the *spray/load* sentences this is a particularly useful approach, since lexical selection of the P's is, appropriately, handled in the lexicon.

Theta-Roles

Let me make an aside here about theta-roles. You've been introduced to agents, themes, and beneficiaries. But linguists have argued for many additional and often subtle distinctions in theta roles. Let's take a quick look at Kichaga, a Bantu language spoken in Tanzania. Here a verb can have a morphologically derived form which is known as the APPLICATIVE. The applicative form allows a verb to add an extra argument to its ordinary argument structure. The verb for "eat," for example, normally takes only a theme. But in the applicative construction it can take a range of other arguments, including a beneficiary or, its opposite, a MALEFICIARY:

> Náílyìíà **m̀kà** kélyà.
> eat   wife food
> 'He is eating food for/on his wife.'

(All the words in this and other examples from Kichaga are polymorphemic, but I have not indicated the morphemes here.) The argument translated as "wife" is understood to be the one to whose benefit or detriment the eating took place. (You might compare the maleficiary sense in this example to the sentence *My dog got lost on me*, where the Object of *on* is understood to be adversely affected by the loss of the dog.) That is, this sentence is ambiguous.

There is also an INSTRUMENT theta-role:

> Náílyìíà **m̀àwòkǒ** kêlyâ.
> eat   hand   food
> 'He/She is eating food with his/her hands.'

And there is a LOCATION theta-role:

> Náílyìíà **m̀r̠ìnyì**   kélyà.
> eat   homestead food
> 'He/She is eating food at the homestead.'

And there is a MOTIVE theta-role:

Ná̯́lyìí!à **njáá**   kêlyâ.
eat   hunger food
'He/She is eating the food because of hunger.'

If you start thinking about English sentences, of course you will realize that we, too, recognize distinctions in participant behaviors in any event. And the more sophisticated we are about matters like psychology, the more distinctions we might recognize. So should we, too, talk about a motive theta-role for English, for example? And should we perhaps have a reluctant theta-role that contrasts with an eager theta-role?

If you are using this book as part of a course, gather a small group of classmates and try to decide precisely how many and which theta-roles you can distinguish for English using only your sensitivity to semantic nuances. It shouldn't take long before you realize that consensus is probably an impossibility.

Indeed, linguists do not limit themselves to only semantic factors when deciding how many and which theta-roles to talk about with regard to any given language. Instead, we demand that the language exhibit morphological and/or syntactic behavior that correlates with the semantic factors. If the language morphologically distinguishes a theta-role, then we list that theta-role for the language. Look again at the Kichaga examples. You can see that in the first three examples the verb form is identical, but the form of the word for "food" varies as the theta-role of the other argument (the Beneficiary/Maleficiary, Instrument, or Location) varies.

Likewise, if the language has syntactic constructions that require a certain theta-role on one of the arguments in order to be grammatical, we list that theta-role for the language.

You might now be confused about why we distinguish a Beneficiary from a Maleficiary in the Kichaga sentence, given that the two readings do not correlate with other grammatical differences. Perhaps in this language there are other types of constructions in which the Beneficiary/Maleficiary distinction correlates with a syntactic or morphological or phonological difference. If not, then I would suggest that we instead say Kichaga has a theta-role called "seriously affected" or something like that, which is open to a positive or negative interpretation about the nature of the affect.

For English the debate over how many and which theta-roles we have is ongoing. In Problem Set 4.8 you will get a chance to see some of the syntactic factors that are relevant for distinguishing theta-roles in English.

Interpretation: Anaphors and Binding Theory

While today's theories of syntax concern themselves primarily with issues of word order and constituency and do not typically talk much about transformations, you will also find extensive discussion of the interpretation of sentences, and not just matters involving theta-roles. Here I'd like to talk briefly about two such matters, one in this section and the next and the second in the section after that.

Consider these sentences:

I like myself.
*John likes myself.

Why can't *myself* occur in the second sentence? Give ten good sentences with *myself* in them. You might have thought of sentences like:

> I talk to myself.
> I expect myself to win.

Now give ten more that sound bad to your ear with *myself* in them. You might have thought of sentences like:

> *Sally won't talk to myself.
> *They never leave myself alone.

Can you see that *myself* requires another coreferential NP to be present in the overall sentence? *Myself* simply won't occur without another first-person singular NP in the same sentence. Words that must be interpreted as coreferential with some other phrase in the overall sentence, like *myself*, *yourself* and the other REFLEXIVE PRONOUNS, are called ANAPHORS.

How does a discussion of anaphors pertain to a chapter about syntax? To see that, consider these sentences:

> The psychiatrists introduced Joan to herself.
> *The psychiatrists introduced herself to Joan.
> I like myself.
> *Myself likes me.

Can you guess why the second and fourth sentences are not acceptable? You might notice that in the good sentences the anaphor follows the NP it is understood as coreferential with. You might also notice that in the good sentences the anaphor is lower in the tree than the NP it is understood as coreferential with. Which one of these structural factors, if either, is crucial to the proper interpretation of the anaphor?

In fact, determining which factors are crucial for the interpretation of anaphors is difficult. But linguists have argued that the crucial notion involves tree structure. They have defined the notion of *c-command* (which we raised briefly in the section "Functional Phrases Pattern Like Lexical Phrases"):

> **Any node X c-commands every node dominated by the first branching node that dominates the X.**

This is to be understood in such a way that X does not c-command itself or anything it dominates. The claim is that the coreferential NP must c-command the anaphor.

Let's make sure you have a grasp on the notion of c-command before we look at this claim. Consider this tree:

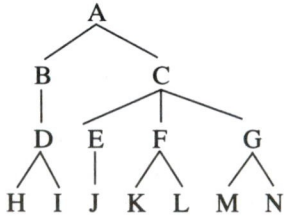

What does A c-command? Nothing. There is no node dominating A, so A does not c-command anything. What does B c-command? C and everything dominated by C. That's because the first branching node that dominates B is A, and A dominates the whole tree. (Remember that I said that no node c-commands itself or anything it dominates. So B does not c-command D, H, or I.) What does C c-command? B and everything dominated by B. What does D c-command? C. Do you see that? The first node dominating D is B, but the first branching node dominating D is A. So D and B have the same c-command domain. Probably now you can successfully go on to talk about the c-command domain for every node on the tree by yourself. (What can you say about M and N, for example? They mutually c-command each other.)

All right, now consider a Subject NP. What does it c-command? The first branching node that dominates the Subject is the Agr″. And the Agr″ dominates all lower nodes in the tree. So Subjects c-command every node in the V″—which means they c-command all other arguments of the V in sentences with ordinary tree structure. Therefore Subjects are good candidates as BINDERS for anaphors that occur in the V″. We say that the NP *I* BINDS the anaphor *myself* in *I like myself*. (**An NP binds another NP that it c-commands and is coreferential with.**)

If this approach is correct, then the DO c-commands the IO in *The psychiatrists introduced Joan to herself*, but the IO does not c-command the DO, accounting for the ungrammaticality of **The psychiatrists introduced herself to Joan*. Does this make sense to you? Draw the tree for this sentence without filling in the lexical items in the DO and IO positions.

The first branching node above NP_1 is V′, and NP_2 is dominated by V′, so NP_1 c-commands NP_2. Therefore, if NP_1 is coreferential with NP_2, it will bind it. But the first branching node above NP_2 is P′ and P′ does not dominate NP_1, so NP_2 does not c-command NP_1 and, therefore, NP_2 cannot bind NP_1 even if it is coreferential with it.

There are lots of complications to the proper interpretation of anaphors that go beyond the notion of binding, and you may already be champing at the bit with problematic examples, particularly if you noticed pairs like:

I expected myself to like Bill.
*I expect Bill to like myself.

In both sentences *I* binds *myself*. But in the second sentence this binding does not license the anaphor, whereas in the first sentence it does. The NP *I* is somehow LOCAL enough to the anaphor in the first sentence but not in the second. There is much discussion over how the relevant notion of locality should be formulated, but in general it seems that when two NPs are CLAUSEMATES (within all and only the same clauses) they are local to one another, and when NPs are not clausemates, they are usually not local to one another except when the lower NP is the Subject of a tenseless clause and the higher NP is in the very next clause up (the ADJACENT clause).

BINDING THEORY is the theory of types of NPs, and it divides NPs up into those that must be locally bound (anaphors), those that must be locally FREE (or not bound—which includes pronouns), and those that must be free everywhere, not just locally (full referential NPs). Thus a pronoun may or may not be interpreted as coreferential with an NP that binds it but is not local to it:

John knows that Sue likes him.

Here *him* may be interpreted as coreferential with *John*, but it need not be. Contrast this to:

John likes him.

Here *him* cannot be interpreted as coreferential with *John*, because if it were, the pronoun would be locally bound (*John* is local to *him* because the two NPs are clausemates) and pronouns must be locally free.

Likewise, consider the interpretation of these sentences:

He likes the boy.
He knows that Sue likes the boy.

The boy is a full referential NP and it cannot be understood as coreferential with *he* in either sentence. Thus neither local binding (in the first sentence) nor nonlocal binding (in the second sentence) is allowed.

Because binding is a notion defined in terms of tree structure and because locality is also arguably defined (at least partially) in terms of tree structure, the interpretation of anaphors, pronouns, and full NPs is considered an area of syntax.

Reflexives

Before I go on to a second main issue of interpretation that is of concern to syntacticians, I want to make an aside regarding reflexives across languages. In English reflexives are anaphors and many languages have anaphors that carry a reflexive sense. But the notion of reflexivization need not be carried by an anaphor. Consider incorporating languages, in which a single phonological word can tell us an entire proposition, complete with predicate and arguments and sometimes even modifiers. For such a language talking about a configurational condition such as binding might well be irrelevant. Mohawk, a northern Iroquoian language spoken in New York, Quebec, and Ontario, uses the morpheme *-atat-* to indicate coreference of two arguments of a predicate:

> waʔkátathleneʔ 'I cut myself.'
> waʔ-k-átat-hlen-eʔ
> fact-I-REFL-cut-aspect

(The accent over a vowel indicates a high tone. Please do not concern yourself with the location of tones in this discussion.) The same morpheme can also indicate a variety of other senses, including reciprocity:

> waʔkyakyatátkwahteʔ 'We two bumped into each other.'
> waʔ-k-yaky-atát-kwaht-eʔ
> fact-dual-1 dual exclusive-REFL-bump-aspect

And the morpheme *-(a)t(e)-*, called the SEMIREFLEXIVE, can be used to show senses such as greater involvement of an argument:

> tesatohtáhlos kʌʔ 'Are you cleaning up?' (implies a big job)
> te-s-at-ohtáhlo-s kʌʔ
> dual-2 S-SEMIREFL-clean-aspect intensifier

or the middle voice (used to show an activity that occurs spontaneously without indicating any agent or cause):

> waʔkutehyá:luʔ 'They all grew up.'
> waʔ-ku-t-ehyá:l-uʔ
> fact-3PF-SEMIREFL-grow-aspect

If you recall from the section "Verbal Inflections and Affixes" of Chapter 3, French also uses the reflexive morpheme (a clitic) to show not just reflexivization, but also middle voice. And this French clitic (in the third person, *se*) can also indicate reciprocity. In fact, in language after language, from the Romance family to the Slavic family, (for example, Russian) to the Amerind family (for example, Quechua), we find a single morpheme indicating reflexivization and other notions such as spontaneity of an event and, often, passivization. Some have argued that the reason for this convergence lies in semantics, not in syntax. The middle and passive voices and the reflexive and reciprocal constructions all share the fact that they refer to events in which their Subjects are affected by the action. In nonreflexive, nonreciprocal active sentences, the Subject need not be affected by the action at all.

The point of this aside was to sensitize you to the fact that languages can handle a single notion with drastically differing syntactic mechanisms. Thus, while you might hope to find anaphors (that is, NPs that must be locally bound) in languages other than English, you should not expect that the anaphors of English will necessarily have anaphor counter-parts in those other languages and viceversa.

Control Theory

A second issue of interpretation that is of interest to syntacticians involves something we have already discussed, the interpretation of big PRO, the null Subject of certain infinitival clauses. Consider this sentence (where I put the structure with big PRO beneath the sentence for clarity):

> Bill expected to cry.
> Bill expected [PRO to cry].

We interpret the missing argument of *cry* as coreferential with *Bill*. Compare that sentence to:

> To cry is appropriate.
> [PRO to cry] is appropriate.

How do we interpret the missing argument of *cry* now? This means that anyone crying would be appropriate. But in *Bill expected to cry*, we do not understand that Bill expected just any person to cry, but only that he expected himself to cry. In the first sentence we have what is called CONTROLLED PRO; that is, the interpretation of big PRO is controlled within the sentence—big PRO is coreferential with another NP within the sentence. In the second sentence we have what is called ARBITRARY PRO (or PRO$_{arb}$); that is, we interpret the big PRO as being GENERIC and not as being coreferential with any other NP in the sentence.

CONTROL THEORY is the theory of how we interpret controlled PRO. To my mind, Control Theory is problematic. But there is at least one claim of Control Theory that I think is relatively sound and that you should be able to come up with yourself. Consider this sentence:

> *To cry was expected by Bill.
> [PRO to cry] was expected by Bill.

Why is this sentence bad? Sketch a tree for it. What do you notice about the relative positions of big PRO and *Bill*? In the good sentence with controlled PRO above, big PRO is bound by the NP it is coreferential with. But in this bad sentence, *Bill* does not bind big PRO. Thus binding is relevant to the control of big PRO, and, in fact, Control Theory can be viewed as a subtheory of Binding Theory.

Conclusion to GB

This is all we will do with the Theory of Government and Binding. However, the picture we have drawn of this theory is disturbingly incomplete; you have seen only a partial sketch of the various modules of the grammar. In particular, TRACE THEORY, the theory that deals with the licensing of traces, has hardly been touched on at all. There are many important conditions on the binding of different types of traces, conditions that bring to light a typology of empty categories. Nevertheless, we must proceed to other matters that press on us.

Let me now offer a brief summary of the Theory of Government and Binding (GB) that we have developed. We have a lexicon that lists all our words. Some of our words have a predicate-argument structure and are listed with this structure in the lexicon. Our Theta Theory tells us how to link the arguments of a given predicate to GFs in the syntactic structure. Our X-Bar Theory tells us how to place our words together into phrases and sentences in a syntactic tree. Our first syntactic tree is called our D-Structure. Some theories (including GB) allow movement rules to operate on that DS to derived the S-Structure. There are at least three types of movement rules in the theory we've developed: head-to-head movement, wh-movement, and NP-movement (which you will meet in Problem Set 4.14). All movement obeys the Subjacency Principle. Our Case Theory operates on SS-Structure to assign Case to all the phonetically realized NPs. The S-Structure is also operated on by our phonological rules to derive Phonological Form (PF). The S-structure is likewise the structural level at which we consider matters of co-indexation (binding and control phenomena) and the structure operated on by rules that raise quantifiers (as you will learn in the section "SS vs. LF" of Chapter 5) to derive a representation called Logical Form (LF), which is used in assigning a semantic interpretation. All this can be seen on our map:

A Map Through GB

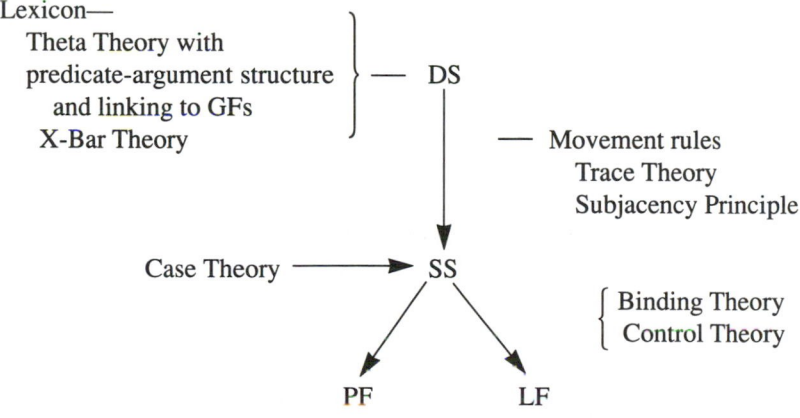

Minimalism

Although GB is without a doubt the theory that frames most of the syntactic literature of the 1980s and of the 1990s thus far, a successor theory has arisen: MINIMALISM. As I write this, Minimalism is more a program for research than a real theory. With that caveat, I'll try to lead you through some of the current ideas.

The source of the name for this theory is the theory's major goal: minimizing the syntactic apparatus needed to generate sentences. Look back at our map of GB. Certain parts of this map are needed independently of syntax. Which ones? Well, definitely the part of the lexicon that gives predicate-argument structure. The information supplied by the predicate-argument structure of lexical items must be checked for coherence with the final semantic structure of sentences. If they are consistent, the sentence is well formed and is said to CONVERGE. If they aren't consistent, the sentence is not well formed and is said to CRASH. So that means we also need an LF, the input level for our semantic rules.

PF is also needed: We must have an input level for our phonological rules, given that utterances have a phonetic realization. Both the PF and LF levels are INTERFACE **levels, levels where one component of the grammar feeds or otherwise interacts with another.**

The rest of the map is up for grabs. Clearly, both DS and SS are purely syntactic levels. So let's first try to do away with them and see what we come up with.

If we said there was no DS, what would that amount to? We'd be saying that there is no initial tree into which all the syntactic elements of the sentence are placed. This seems patently wrong, since we know that we do have a syntactic tree, and it must have been formed somewhere along the way, so there must, in fact, be some initial tree somewhere in the derivation of every sentence. Still, it could be that there is no one level we can point to as the level at which LEXICAL INSERTION (that is, the inserting of elements from the lexicon into the syntactic structure) takes place. Indeed, in the new theory, which we will call the MINIMALIST PROGRAM (MP), there is no such level. Instead, we have nodes that come together into phrases, and phrases that come together into clauses, and clauses that come together into sentences, all via GENERALIZED TRANSFORMATIONS that insert already-formed trees into other trees. I like to think of it from a baker's point of view. You have the flour, the eggs, the baking powder, the cocoa, the butter, the sugar, the salt, the milk. You mix them together into a wet batter. It bakes, and, lo and behold, you have red devil's food cake. The ingredients are somewhat different for angel food cake, the batter is somewhat different, the final product somewhat different. The batter of devil's food cake and the batter of angel food cake take on solid form at different points. So it is with the points at which sentences have a form that the phonological rules apply to, according to the MP.

We call the mechanism that allows us to build up trees and insert them into other trees the COMPUTATIONAL SYSTEM. If a tree has an empty node in it, this node could be filled by another tree in the batter, so to speak, via a generalized transformation. For example, a tree that contains a V followed by an empty node might by combined with another tree that is dominated by an NP node, and the second tree fills the empty node in the first tree (as in the case of transitive verbs—since a transitive verb would project a structure in which V takes an NP sister). But a tree that contains an N followed by an empty node will not be combined with a tree dominated by NP in the same way (since we have no transitive nouns). (I'll return to the question of the projection properties of lexical items when we look at a syntactic tree.)

If, instead, we fill the empty node with another node from within the same tree, we have a SINGULARY TRANSFORMATION, which is essentially equivalent to syntactic movement. However, in the new theory, there is no real movement per se. Instead, one node is copied into another node. Hence there are no traces in this theory, but, rather, a principle that tells us that in PF only the highest of a chain of copied nodes, the head of the chain, receives a phonetic matrix. The other node(s) in the chain is phonetically empty.

We can see that some principles are relevant only to the PF (such as the one spelling out only the head of a chain) and you know from our study of GB that other principles are relevant only to the LF (principles such as those involved in Control Theory). So we must

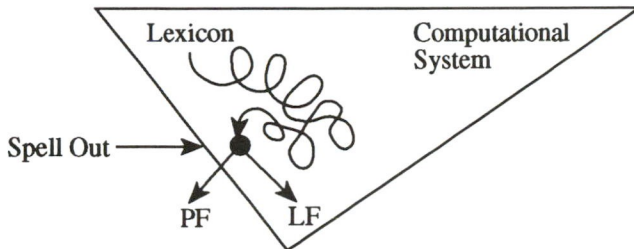

Figure 4.1. Model of the grammar with the Minimalist Program.

allow a point in our derivation where whatever structure we have come up with diverges along two paths, after which point principles relevant to PF operate separately from principles relevant to LF. In our old theory this was, of course, SS. In the new theory we call that point SPELL OUT, and we do away entirely with the old syntactic level of SS.

The difference between SS and Spell Out is not merely terminological; it is conceptual. No conditions or constraints apply to Spell Out, so in that sense, it is not a syntactic level. In the MP the computational system operates from the lexical resources to produce the LF. Along the way, a certain point in the derivation is reached beyond which these computational operations are relevant only to the LF and not to the PF. At that point, our Spell Out point, a path leading to PF diverges. Thus Figure 4.1 is the picture of the theory.

So, let's see where we've arrived. We have eliminated DS and SS. We have replaced movement with copying, although **we will continue to talk about "movement," since the literature in the MP does that—and it is to be understood as "copying."** (Indeed, when we talk about principles of the MP, we will find the term "move" used repeatedly, even as part of the name of one of the principles.)

Now what about Case Theory? If you step back and try to look over our chapter as a whole, you might be able to discern that **the development of Case Theory was the driving force behind much of this chapter. That's because within GB, Case Theory offers some of the strongest arguments for the relevance of hierarchical relationships. In particular, our Case Theory was built on the syntactic notion of government:** In structural Case assignment a Case-assigner assigned Case to those items it governed. But if in the MP we want to minimize syntactic mechanisms, then we might try a different approach to Case Theory—an approach that doesn't depend on government.

So let's do away with structural Case-assignment altogther. How? What if we started with lexical items that already have Case markings? In fact, we could start with lexical items that already have all morphological inflection. Then our job would be to check those features. A structure whose features check appropriately converges at PF and LF. A structure whose features fail to check (because something fails to meet an interface condition) at PF and/or LF crashes.

We already met this kind of approach very early in the chapter (in the section "An Agreement Rule for English") when we talked about the possibility of viewing agreement processes in precisely this way. At that time we pointed out that letting inflectional morphology take place in the lexicon spared us problems in our syntax concerning rule ordering. However, it was costly in that it required us to have a mechanism to check the inflectional features.

But how costly is that mechanism, really? Well, that depends on what the mechanism is. Consider verbal inflection first. We have already argued for head movement of a verb up the tree, through the functional heads of T(ense) and Agr(eement). Let's say that each functional head already has a set of features. For example, T might be marked as having the verbal feature past and Agr might be marked as having the verbal feature third-person plural. Let head movement, then, take the verb and ADJOIN it (or, rather, a copy of it) to each functional head up the tree. By adjoin, I mean that we will attach a copy of the verb as a sister to the functional head under a new functional head of the same category, like so:

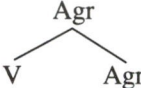

If the features of the verb match the features of the functional head it adjoins to, the verb's features would then "be checked." **So we know feature-checking can take place between adjoined elements in a head.**

Now let's assume that Subjects arise inside VPs (a possibility we discussed earlier in the section "Arguments and the DS position of Subjects"). Subjects then move into specifier of Agr position. Assume that the head Agr has not only verbal, but nominal features. If the features of the Subject match the Agr nominal features, the features of the Subject would then be checked. **So we know feature-checking can take place between a head and its specifier.**

Notice that in both of these instances stating the conditions on checking features was simple because movement (that is, copying) resulted in either of two structures: adjoined heads or a specifier-head relationship. We could say that the position adjoined to a head and the specifier of a head make up the LICENSING or CHECKING DOMAIN of the head. Now let's consider the relevance of that fact. We could pursue the idea that all movement is feature-driven. In other words, **constituents move because they have unchecked morphological features that need to get into the checking domain of a functional head.** Certainly this statement is metaphorical to some extent: Syntax doesn't really make choices of this sort (at least not the non-anthropomorphic syntax I conceive of). If a constituent didn't move and it had morphological features, the derivation would simply crash. Instead, this statement helps us to understand the relationship between types of constituents and landing sites for movement. If a constituent is of a type that has verbal or nominal morphological features that must be checked, in a convergent derivation it will end up in a position from which those features can be checked (that is, **as sister to a functional head if it has verbal features or as specifier to a functional head if it has nominal features**).

An important point of the MP is that morphological features can be checked at either the PF or the LF levels, although some features, called STRONG FEATURES, must be checked off at the PF level. If movement takes place before Spell Out, then that movement will be apparent at PF. If movement takes place after Spell Out, then that movement will not be apparent at PF, but movement might still take place after Spell Out, so that morphological features can be checked at the LF level. This discussion is abstract, I know. We'll return to this idea after we learn a bit more about the theory.

As I said, every movement is really copying in the MP. So when we say that movement is motivated by the need to have features get checked, you might object. After all, only the head of a chain will end in a position in which its features will be checked off. The other constituents in the chain will have unchecked morphological features. In order to accommodate that fact, we need to understand our theory as allowing the checking off of the morphological features of the head of a chain to count for the entire chain.

Okay, now sentences have other nominals beside Subjects, so let's consider another. How could we handle Case assignment to a DO in English, for example? If we wanted to check the nominal features of an NP, we'd move it into specifier position of the relevant functional head. What is the relevant head for DO? There isn't one in the tree as we know it. So we need to propose a new functional projection above VP whose specifier position the DO can move into and whose head has the appropriate nominal features (which, for English, will be the Case markings). This functional head is very similar to Agr, but instead of checking the features of the Subject, it will check the features of the Object. So let's redub Agr as AGR_S (for AGR-Subject), and we can call the new functional node AGR_O (for AGR-Object). Our sentence structure after movement will be:

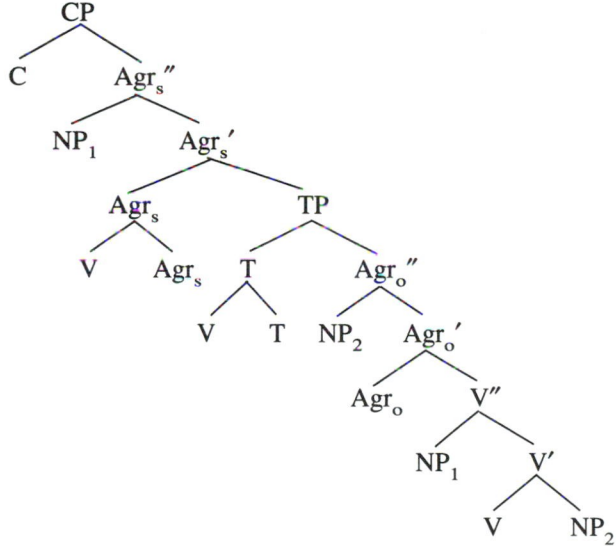

(You will have a chance to argue for the hierarchical location of Agr_O in syntactic trees in Problem Set 4.15.) The NPs with the same subscript form a chain, and only the head (that is, top) of the chain will receive a phonetic matrix. All the V's, likewise, form a chain and only the head of the chain is phonetically realized at PF.

Notice that I projected three levels for Agr_S, Agr_O, and V, but not for T or C. Since we no longer have X-Bar Theory, there is nothing to tell us that all phrases should have the same structure. Instead, each kind of head might project differently in different sentences. Each lexical item is the minimal projection and it can constitute a phrase by itself. The largest phrase that is of type X is the maximal projection of the word of type X. Some phrases might have many levels within them. Others might have only one. And it's possible that some kinds of words do not project at all—such as clitics. So in the tree I gave no unnecessary projections—that is, every nonterminal node branches.

You might well ask why we maintain projections of C. Certainly in many matrix clauses and in some embedded clauses C will not be lexically filled. But remember that other movement rules might fill the head C in a matrix clause (such as movement of the auxiliary in a question) or the specifier (spec) of C in a matrix or embedded clause (such as wh-movement), so these nodes are, indeed, lexically filled in the trees of some sentences. Here I gave the tree for a sentence whose C would be filled, but whose spec of C would not be.

You might be asking yourself how movement of an auxiliary in a question could be for feature checking and how wh-movement could be for feature checking. While I don't see an immediate answer to the first question, I think we can successfully approach the second. Surely, a wh-word has a feature associated with it that marks it as a question word. The very fact that we call question words "wh-words" is a recognition of this morphological fact. To propose that the C of a question also has this question feature is entirely reasonable. So movement of the wh-word into specifier of C would allow checking of the feature, after all.

At this point we have an overgenerating syntax (since many structures will crash), just as in Optimality Theory we had an overgenerating phonology. So we need principles to help us sift through all the possible derivations. We hinted at some of those principles when we said that a derivation would crash if it didn't meet conditions of the PF or LF interface. The relevant conditions are, as yet, only beginning to be explored in the MP. However, there are some metrics for comparing derivations. That is, some derivations are more nearly optimal than others.

The metrics consist of ECONOMY PRINCIPLES, all of which are motivated by the idea that the syntax prefers the minimal way of doing whatever has to be done. Exactly what consitutes minimal in this sense is a bit murky, but a notion of least effort is part of it. So if there are two derivations that converge, grammaticality will depend on comparing these derivations and choosing the one that is minimal. Grammaticality, then, is TRANSDERIVATIONALLY dependent. We can think of the economy principles as being GLOBAL FILTERS, as opposed to the various local filters we've discussed above (such as the one blocking the sequence of a P followed by infinitival *to*, which we mentioned in the section "PRO in Infinitivals").

The three economy principles that have been most written about in the literature thus far are: SHORTEST MOVE, PROCRASTINATE, and GREED.

Shortest Move tells us that a constituent must move to the first position—that is, the hierarchically closest position in an upward direction—of the right kind from its source position. Shortest Move prevents movement from passing over an intervening node of the right kind, whether that intervening node is lexically filled or empty. Thus a verb could not move directly into Agr_S, for example, skipping over the head T. Instead, it must move into T and from there into Agr_S. Notice, however, that if a verb were to move directly into Agr_S, its tense feature would not be checked and the derivation would crash in PF. As you can see, sometimes violations of Shortest Move can result in ungrammaticality even without comparing alternative derivations. So Shortest Move is not always a global filter.

You might be wondering about nominal movement now. Why can't a Subject, for example, move into specifier of Agr_O? The move from original Subject position (that is, from specifier of V) to specifier of Agr_O is shorter than the move from original Subject position to specifier of Agr_S, so we might expect the first move to be preferred. However, the Subject must check off Subject features (Subjective Case, that is), and only Agr_S has the requisite kind of features. So Agr_O is not the right kind of landing site for a Subject.

Procrastinate tells us to prefer derivations that hold off on movements until after the Spell Out point. In other words, movements that do not affect PF are preferred over movements that do affect PF. In this chapter we have not talked about any movements that do not affect PF. That's because we made some oversimplistic assumptions about how the English verbal system works. In Chapter 5 (in the section "SS vs. LF"), you will encounter the proposal that quantifiers undergo a movement rule that has no affect on PF. Once you have read Chapter 5, you might want to come back and reconsider the Procrastinate principle. But right now, let's look a little more closely at verbal systems.

We adopted the analysis earlier (in the section "Functional Heads with Verbal Phrases: Another Look") that verbs in both Latin and English undergo head-to-head movement, so they pick up the tense and agreement morphemes in the functional heads above them. However, I mentioned at that point that there was controversy over exactly how the process worked in English in contrast to Latin. Let's look now at a particular difference in how the process might work—a difference that involves issues of word order. It won't suit our purposes here to contrast Latin to English, since word order in Latin is extremely varied. Instead, the same sort of analysis could be made for many languages, including the Romance languages, and the Romance languages have less flexibility in word order than Latin. So we will use French (which has a more rigid word order than, say, Italian or Spanish) to contrast to English here.

First, ask yourself what our analysis of the verbal system predicts about the relative order of the V and an adverb that modifies it. Will the adverb be inside the VP or not? It will be inside the VP, since modifiers are typically inside the phrase of the head they modify. Now, what about the V? In PF will the V be inside the VP or not? Well, that depends on when head-to-head movement takes place, right? If the V moves up the tree before Spell Out, then in PF the V will not be inside the VP; instead, it will precede all constituents contained in the VP—including, of course, any adverbs that modify the V. If the V moves up the tree after Spell Out, then PF will not be affected by that movement and the V will be inside the VP in PF. In that case, adverbs that modify the V might precede or follow it, depending on the type of adverb and what its location was at Spell Out.

We find that in French, adverbs that modify a V follow it:

> Marie se   lave   souvent les mains.
> Marie REFL washes often   the hands
> 'Marie washes her hands often.'
> *Marie souvent se lave les mains.

(*Se* is a reflexive clitic.) So the V undergoes head movement before Spell Out.

But in English, adverbs that modify a V can precede the V, and, in fact, never come between the V and a following constituent that is inside the VP:

> Marie often washes her hands.
> *Marie washes often her hands.
> (cf. Marie washes her hands often.)

So in English the V undergoes head movement after Spell Out. Do you see that? The V is inside the VP in the PF; otherwise we couldn't account for the failure of an adverb to occur linearly between the V and the DO in the PF.

Why can the languages have this difference in ordering? It's been claimed that the verbal features in French are strong (an idea I mentioned above), so they are VISIBLE at PF unless they are checked off (which can only happen via head movement), while the verbal features in English are WEAK, so they are invisible at PF even if they aren't checked off.

This claim may seem vacuous to you. That is, it begs the important question of what makes features strong in one language and weak in another. It could be that mere morphological robustness is at stake. That is, English has audible agreement on the verb only in one person and number and in one tense. But French is different.

If you speak French, you might well object: While the orthography of French indicates a rich agreement system, when we listen to French verbs, the audible agreement is relatively impoverished. (For the first conjugation present tense, for example, all persons sound the same except the first and second plurals.) Nevertheless, French is richer than English regarding agreement inflection. Furthermore, English has only a past vs. present morphological distinction for tense, but French has a range of morphologically realized tenses. So French is much richer than English regarding tense inflection.

Now, while the derivation would crash in French if the V did not undergo head movement before Spell Out, is it also true that the derivation would crash in English if the V did undergo head movement before Spell Out? Certainly nothing we have talked about in the MP suggests it would. That is, if the V moved up into the T head and then into the Agr$_S$ head before Spell Out, its features would be checked off and the derivation should converge. Yet, sentences in which the relevant adverb intervenes between the V and the DO are ungrammatical (as we saw). What would account for this fact? Procrastinate. Procrastinate tells us that since English can hold off on head movement until after Spell Out, it must do that.

The third principle, Greed, says that a constituent may not move to statisfy the needs of another constituent, but only to satisfy its own needs. For example, a constituent can move in order to check off its own features, but not in order to make it possible for another constituent to check off its features. Giving an example for this principle is tricky, because what counts as an example depends on a wide range of other assumptions about the theory. So I will leave this principle unexemplified.

Both Procrastinate and Greed appear to come into play only when choosing between alternative converging derivations (unlike Shortest Move). So they are always global filters.

The discussion here is short and partial. Indeed, there are two additional structural positions that are within the checking domain of a head that we haven't mentioned here; there are other principles of economy; there is a more complicated notion of distance for the Shortest Move principle than the one I gave above; and so on. But from this discussion, I hope you have a sense of the distinctly different nature of the Minimalist Program. And I hope that you can see **how similar it is in spirit to Optimality Theory.** Both overgenerate—although the GEN(erator) of Optimality Theory is less constrained than the Computational System of the Minimalist Program. Both employ metrics of comparison in determining optimality/minimalism—although Optimality Theory compares input/output pairs and the Minimalist Program compares derivations and outputs.

One other thing you might have noticed from this discussion is the paucity of data. The literature on the MP right now consists largely of debates over theoretical issues that do not look to data for confirmation. Instead, these issues concern the standards for determining what kind of theory is superior, if two theories are equally empirically adequate. That's partly because of the nature of the theory and partly because the theory is nascent yet. As more scholars working in more languages explore this new framework, we should be seeing discussions that pull in data as crucial evidence.

Conclusion

This chapter may have left you dangling in the air because of the nature of the argumentation. But, toughen yourself; if you go on with syntax, you've got a lot of air travel ahead of you. This is a theoretical field where much of the work is argumentation that carries you further and further from the data.

Despite the rapidity with which we have covered the material here, I hope the problem sets convince you that you have, indeed, learned some syntax. All of the problem sets assume the GB theory unless they explicitly mention some other theory (as in Problem Set 4.15). So dig into them (for as long as they take—which could be months) and then go eat a hearty meal and get a good night's sleep so that you're ready for the next chapter, which is on the area of the grammar that, historically, is most discussed by nonlinguists: semantics.

Problem Set 4.1: Phrase Structure in English

1. In the text we found the claim that lexical category words can head one-word utterances (as a group, although there are lexical category words that cannot because they are obligatorily transitive) but that no functional category words can head one-word utterances.

(a) By this criterion, are numerals in English lexical or functional categories?

(b) By this criterion, are quantifiers in English lexical or functional categories?

(Don't be confused. If a single numeral can head a one-word category, then numerals are lexical category words by this test. The same goes for quantifiers. That some quantifiers might be obligatorily transitive, so to speak, doesn't affect this diagnostic.)

(c) Compare *no* and *not* by this criterion. (Be careful here. In a discourse such as:

—Is he coming or not?
—Not.

you need to consider whether this is ordinary speech or linguistically self-conscious speech. Contrast to:

—Is he coming or not?
—No.

Who would say the first discourse and who would say the second and what would be the stylistic effect of saying *not* vs. *no*?)

(d) Now consider the more recent development exemplified here:

—He's coming. Not.

Could this be taken as evidence that *not* is changing the type of category it belongs to? Why or why not?

2. Match these phrases to the appropriate tree analyses:

very talented at chess
gave plums to Mary

the teacher's discussion of every paper
right up my arm

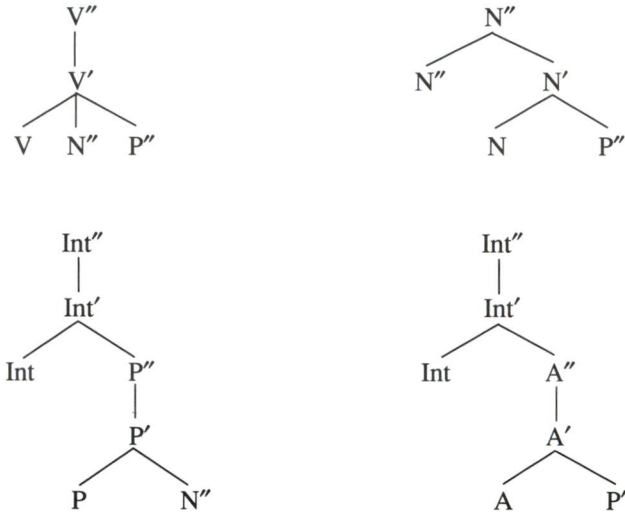

3. We noted in the text that in English APs modifying a head N can be found both preceding and following the N. Some examples include:

a [very talented] child
a child [talented at chess]
those [ridiculously old] books
those books [yellow with age]

Make a statement in terms of tree structure about modifying APs that follow the head N. Be sure this statement will distinguish them from modifying APs that precede the head N. (It is up to you to figure out the relevant factor in the tree structure. Begin by treeing the NPs given in the list here. Step back and look at the general shape of the tree. What can you notice about the tree shape of the APs that precede as opposed to those that follow the head N?)

Now notice that when a PP modifies a head N, the PP always follows the N:

the boy [in the car]
a moment [of truth]

Would you have expected this word order, given what you know about the placement of modifying APs inside NP? Why? (Hint: You should have expected it.)

Where do modifying relative clauses come in English, before or after the head N they modify? Give two examples to support your answer. Did you expect that word order? Why?

4. Consider the conjoined (that is, using the conjunction *and*) phrase:

quickly eating and drinking

This phrase is ambiguous. State the two readings. Then explain why these two readings emerge. (That is, what leads to the ambiguity? Think about the different projections of V that *and* could possibly conjoin.) Give two tree analyses for this VP, and tell which reading each corresponds to.

5. Consider the relative clauses:

(1) Whales that live in the North Sea are small.
(2) Whales, which are mammals, have blowholes.

The relative clause in 1, *that live in the North Sea*, is called a RESTRICTIVE relative clause. The relative clause in 2, *which are mammals*, is called a NONRESTRICTIVE. Do you see the semantic difference? Paraphrase each of these sentences in such a way as to make the restrictive/nonrestrictive difference clear.

Classify the following examples as to whether they contain restrictive or nonrestrictive relatives:

(3) The boy that I met last night is very nice.
(4) I'd like to climb Mt. Everest, which is exceedingly high.
(5) I'd never speak to any person who would do such a thing.

In 1 and 2, *that* introduces a restrictive clause and *which* introduces a nonrestrictive clause. Is this just by chance or is it a necessity in your speech? To test this, try to find a sentence with a relative clause introduced by *that* that is nonrestrictive. If you can, give it. If you can't, say you can't. Now try to find a relative clause introduced by *which* that is restrictive. If you can, give it. If you can't, say you can't.

What kind(s) of relative clauses can *who* introduce: restrictive, nonrestrictive, or both? Give examples to support your answer.

If you found that restrictives and/or nonrestrictives can be introduced only by *that*, *which*, or *who*, or, alternatively that *that*, *which*, and/or *who* can introduce only a certain kind of relative, do you think this fact should be reflected in the syntax? That is, do you think such a fact would suggest that there is a syntactic difference between restrictives and nonrestrictives? This is not a question for you to answer on paper but rather to think about and to discuss with your class.

Problem Set 4.2: Structural Configuration Issues: Copular Sentences in Egyptian Arabic and Negation in Korean

(NOTE: Question 2 is more difficult than 1.)

1. A sentence that uses the copular verb *be* in English often corresponds to a sentence without *be* in another language. This is true of languages as different as Hopi, Russian, and Egyptian Arabic (EA):

Hopi:	Pooka qöösa.	'The dog is white.'
	dog white	
Russian:	Viktor studént.	'Victor is a student.'
	Victor student.	

In this problem set we will take a look at phrase structure issues that this fact brings up by examining EA, but we could as easily have used Hopi or Russian (or dozens of other languages).

Part 1

Consider these sentences from EA:

> (1) ?il-bent zakeyya
>   the-girl intelligent
>   'The girl is intelligent.'
> (2) ?il-mudi:r   hina
>   the-director here
>   'The director is here.'
> (3) wald-i   mudarris
>   father-my teacher
>   'My father is a teacher.'
> (4) ha:ni fi l-be:t
>   Hani in the-house
>   'Hani is in the house.'

(There is no word for *a* in EA. Do not let that confuse you. Assume that *mudarris* is an NP in 3.)

What is the analysis of 1–4 at SS in terms of categories? Just give a string analysis; that is, a string of categories, such as NP-VP (but none of these consists of an NP-VP string).

Part 2

There are also noncopular sentences of EA that have verbs in them:

> (5) nadya ra:Hit   is-sinema
>   Nadia she-went the-movies
>   'Nadia went to the movies.'

The *it* on the verb in 5 is a RESUMPTIVE pronoun (it is a copy of the NP *Nadia*). Ignore it for the sake of this problem set. Write a single string analysis for surface structures of simple sentences in EA that will cover 1–5. You can use parentheses to indicate categories that are optional.

Part 3

One question you should consider is whether equational sentences like those in 1–4 have no Inflection and no V, or whether they do, in fact have Inflection and a V, where the V is phonetically empty and, therefore, the Inflection is also not heard.

Let me use the label Infl″ to denote an inflectional phrase headed by an inflectional node Infl, without taking a stand on whether that node is Agr or T. (In other words, I am conflating Agr″ and T″ here, since there are no data given to you in this problem set that would allow you to distinguish between the two.)

If there is no Infl″ and thus no Infl, do sentences like 1–4 present any problem for Case theory? (Assume that in EA, just as in English, all phonetically realized NPs must get Case.)

Part 4

Now look at other equational sentences in EA:

(6) ?il-bent   ka:nit   zakeyya
    the-girl   was   clever
    'The girl was clever.'

(7) ?il-mudi:r   ha-yku:n   hina.
    the-director will be   here
    'The director will be here.'

(8) wald-i   ka:n   mudarris
    father-my   was   teacher
    'My father was a teacher.'

(9) ha:ni   ha-yku:n   fi   l-be:t
    Hani   will be   in the house
    'Hani will be at home.'

And consider the contrast in meaning between 10, with the copular verb phonetically expressed and 11, without it:

(10) ?ana   ca:yez   ?ibn-i   yeku:n   muhandis
     I   want   son-my   he-be   engineer
     'I want my son to be an engineer' (when he grows up . . .)
     (compare to: ?ibn-i   muhandis
                  son-my   engineer
                  'My son is an engineer.')

(11) ?ana   ca:yez   ?il-ba:b   madhu:n
     I   want   the-door   painted
     'I want the door painted.' (now—this is an order of sorts)
     (compare to: ?il-ba:b   madhu:n
                  the-door   painted
                  'The door is painted.')

When does a form of the copular verb show up?

Part 5

Now in EA there are two ways to negate. One is with *ma* attached to a verb:

(12) ka:nu   il-ciya:l   naymi:n
     they-were the-children   asleep
     'The children were asleep.'

(13) ma-kanu:-š   il-ciya:l   naymi:n
     not-they-were the-children   asleep
     'The children were not asleep.'

The other way is with *miš* attached to a nominal:

(14) ?abilt   il-kuba:r   miš il-ciya:l

(I) met the-grown-ups not the-children
'I met the adults, not the children.'

But *miš* cannot attach to a form of the copular verb:

(15) *il-ciyal:l   miš ka:nu naymi:n
the-children not were asleep
'The children were not asleep.'

Now, neither *ma* nor *miš* can occur in an equational sentence that has no phonetically audible verb:

(16) *ma il-ciya:l   naymi:n
not the-children asleep
'The children are not asleep.'
(17) *miš il-ciya:l   naymi:n
not the-children asleep
'The children are not asleep.'

Do the facts on negation help us to determine whether or not equational sentences in EA that lack a phonetically audible V really have an (empty) Infl and V? If yes, how?

Part 6

In English we have a single schema for all expandable categories:

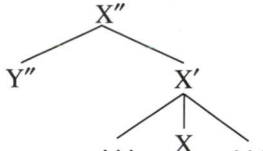

The dots on either side of X may be filled with other phrases.
   In particular, the schema for a sentence is:

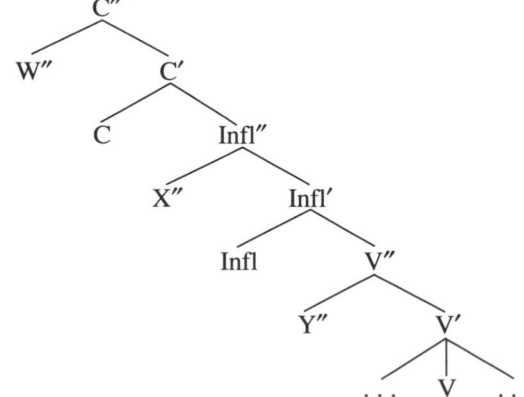

(I have used Infl″ instead of Agr″ and T″ here so as to make the parallel with EA as easily discernible for you as possible. I have labeled the specifier nodes as W″, X″, and Y″ to indicate phrasal projections of any category. I could as easily have put X″ for all three of them.) From all you have done on EA here, what do you think the schema for EA sentences is? In other words, take a stance on the issue of whether or not all equational sentences have an Infl (and, thus, an Infl″) and a V (and, thus, a V″).

2. There is a use of the word *anyone* in English that is called a NEGATIVE POLARITY ITEM. It occurs only when a negative is also present and in a particular structural configuration with respect to *anyone*. For example, when a VP is negated, *anyone* can occur as a DO, IO, OP, or Genitive inside an NP that is inside that VP, as well as in a range of GFs inside a sentential Object:

(1) I do**n't** love **anyone.**
    I did**n't** give the book to **anyone.**
    I would**n't** go there with **anyone.**
    I did**n't** invite **anyone's** mother—this was a gathering for fathers only.
    I did**n't** think [**anyone** would come].
    I did**n't** think [Bill had invited **anyone**].

But *anyone* cannot be licensed in Subject position by a negative VP in its own clause:

(2) ***Anyone** doesn't love me.

However, it can occur as a Subject when a negative phrase of a certain kind precedes it. The negative phrase in 3, for example, licenses *anyone*, but that in 4 doesn't:

(3)   **Not for five minutes** did **anyone** hesitate.
(4) ***Not long ago anyone** hesitated.
      ***Not long ago** did **anyone** hesitate.

There are debates over exactly what the required structural configuration for the licensing of *anyone* is in English and we will not take a position here.

Part 1

Consider the two structural configuration relationships of government and c-command. Let me remind you of how those relationships work:
    A head governs everything within its maximal projection, and a maximal projection is a barrier to government.
    A node c-commands all nodes dominated by the first branching node that contains it. Now consider this statement:

Anyone is licensed only by a governing negative.

Point out at least one sentence in 1–4 that disconfirms this statement and explain why it disconfirms this statement. (You do not have to make any assumptions about whether *not* in English is a head (an X) or a phrase (an XP) in order to do this problem. Just try to find a sentence in 1–4 in which *anyone* is not governed by a negative.)

Part 2

Now consider the following data on the Korean word *amwuto* 'anyone.'

    (5) Sam-i   amwuto ani-cohaha-n-ta.
        Sam-Nom anyone neg-love-Pres-Dec
        'Sam doesn't love anyone.'
    (6) Amwuto Sam-ul   ani-cohaha-n-ta.
                Sam-Acc
        'Anyone doesn't love Sam.' (='No one loves Sam.')
    (7) *Na-nun [amwuto-uy   hyeng]-ul   ani-po-ess-ta.
        I-Top   [anyone-Gen brother]-Acc neg-see-Past-Dec
        'I didn't see anyone's brother.'
    (8) *John-un [Mary-ka   amwuto po-ess-ta-ko]   sangkakha-ci
        John-Top Mary-Nom anyone see-Past-Dec-Comp think-Inf
        ani-ha-n-ta.
        neg-do-Pres-Dec
        'John doesn't think Mary saw anyone.'

(Dec = declarative; Top = topic; Comp = complementizer; Inf = infinitive.)

Just based on the data in 5–8, do you think that government or c-command is the relevant structural relationship to the licensing of *amwuto* in Korean? That is, is *amwuto* licensed by a governing negative or by a c-commanding negative? Explain your answer by pointing out at least one sentence in which you would expect that licensing might occur if c-command were involved, but in which you expect that licensing would not occur if government were involved, and, indeed, licensing does not occur, or at least one sentence in which you would expect that licensing might occur if government were involved, but in which you expect that licensing would not occur if c-command were involved, and, indeed, licensing does not occur.

Problem Set 4.3: English

(Note: Part 7 is more difficult.)

Parts 1 through 6 of this problem set are due (in altered form) to Joan Maling and Ray Jackendoff, who I thank.

Answer all parts of this problem set, even if the questions seem trivial to you. Each succeeding question depends on your having answered the ones before it. So please do not read through the whole problem set before beginning.

There are several words in English that function as auxiliary (helping) verbs and occur between the Subject and the main verb in declarative sentences.

    (1) Modals: My frog *will* eat your lizard.
                 can
                 may
                 . . .
    (2) Perfect Aspect: My frog *has* eaten your lizard.
    (3) Progressive Aspect: My frog *is* eating your lizard.

Part 1

What effect does each kind of auxiliary verb have on the morphological form (not the meaning) of the main verb? That is, state whether or not a special morpheme appears on the main verb in each of the three contexts (after a modal, after the perfect *have*, and after the progressive *be*) and, if one does, give that morpheme. If no special morpheme appears in that context, say that the main verb is uninflected.

Answer separately for each of the three kinds of auxiliaries just given. Consider sentences in which you have only a single auxiliary followed immediately by the main verb. Your answer should have the form:

After a modal the form of the main verb is . . .
After a perfect aspect the form of the main verb is . . .
After a progressive aspect the form of the main verb is . . .

Part 2

Suppose we try to use more than one auxiliary in a single sentence. Think of all the combinations you can. Think of some ungrammatical combinations.

Consider bad sentences such as:

*The lizard has will eat my supper.
*The sky is have fallen.
*No one may will leave this room.

as well as good combinations like:

That course of action may have proven unnecessary.

Give an example of a sentence with three auxiliaries.

Now state a general rule that describes which combinations are possible. (A really good general rule—that is, one that truly captures a generalization—will not just list the lexical items. Instead, you need to figure out if certain classes of auxiliaries behave in the same way with respect to how they can combine with other classes of auxiliaries.) Your answer should start out:

When there are three auxiliaries before the main verb . . .

Part 3

Consider again Part 1. Does your answer generalize to sentences with more than one auxiliary? Why or why not? Which verb (whether auxiliary or main) does each auxiliary constrain the form of? State a general rule which will cover sentences with a string of auxiliaries.

Part 4

Consider the *be* we find in passive sentences, such as:

Mary was ignored by her classmates.

This *be* is also an auxiliary. Specify precisely its linear order with respect to the other auxiliaries (that is, where does it come in the auxiliary string?).

How does the passive *be* affect the form of the other verbs in the string? Is your answer consistent with your general rule from Part 3? It ought to be. Consider sentences like:

The lizard has been eaten by the frog.
*The lizard is have eaten by the frog.
No one will be permitted to leave.
*No one is will permitted to leave.
The U.S. is being attacked by Fredonia.
*The U.S. is been attacking by Fredonia.

as well as other sentences you think of to test your theory.

Now give a sentence with four auxiliaries.

Part 5

Which element in the auxiliary string carries the tense inflection? (Please do not confuse time frame with tense here. The entire verb string, including the auxiliaries, helps us to interpret the time frame, as do other elements in the sentence and in the discourse. What I'm looking for is which element carries tense, in particular—where tense in English is realized by an inflectional suffix.)

Part 6

An auxiliary *do* turns up in negative statements *(Newts don't eat goldfish food)*, in direct questions *(What do newts eat, then?)*, in tag questions *(They eat brine shrimp, don't they?)*, and in emphatic sentences *(Newts DO like bagels, though)*.

How does this *do* affect the form of the main verb that follows it?

What are the rules governing its occurrence in the same sentence with other auxiliaries?

Give at least one way in which the *do* in *Fred might have done the dishes* differs from the auxiliary *do*?

Part 7

Consider embedded clauses in which the verb string is not tensed, as in:

(1) John wants *to leave.*
(2) John expected *Bill to have left by noon.*
(3) I arranged *for Bill to leave.*
(4) John broke the dish *to upset his mother.*

In 1 *to leave* has the GF of DO of the main verb *wants.* In 2 *Bill to have left by noon* has the GF of DO of the main verb *expects.* In 4 *to upset his mother* is an adverbial modifier (telling purpose) of the main clause. In 3 it is debatable whether *Bill to leave* is the Object of the preposition *for* or whether, instead, *for* is a complementizer and *for Bill to leave* is the DO of the main verb *arranged* (but that debate does not concern us here).

State a general rule which describes the full range of possibilities of the verb string in an embedded tenseless clause like those in 1–4. (Be careful not to consider other types of tenseless clauses, such as those with a verb form ending in *-ing* where there is no progessive aspect *be* around to account for that *-ing*.] Your rule should tell the order of the auxiliaries and the affect each auxiliary has on the form of the following verb.

In doing this, ask yourself whether or not any of the modals can occur in these infinitival verb strings, and if they can, where they occur. Then ask whether or not perfect *have* can occur, and where. Then ask whether or not progressive *be* can occur and where. Do not forget to cover the possibilities of a passive *be* and the *do* of Part 6, if these possibilities arise in these tenseless clauses.

Is *to* in these clauses an auxiliary? Give one argument for your answer. Why can this *to* and the *do* of Part 6 not appear in the same verb string?

Problem Set 4.4: Syntax and Morphology

1. Consider these compounds:

> **Set A:** punch-in-the-stomach effect
> bad-hair day
> employee-of-the-month program
> **Set B:** over-the-fence gossip
> off-the-rack dress
> around-the-world flight
> **Set C:** easy-to-sew pattern
> black-and-blue mark (=bruise)
> (a) chilled-to-the-bone look
> **Set D:** (a) slept-all-day look
> (a) drank-too-much headache
> (a) thinking-about-it wink
> **Set E:** how-are-you letter
> stick-it-in-your-ear attitude
> I-told-you-so look

(I put an optional article (the *a*) with some compounds to help you interpret them.)

(a) What category is the whole compound in all these sets of data? Is the compound right- or left-headed?

(b) What category is the element that is not the head? Give a separate answer for each of the five data sets.

(c) What projection of that category is the element you identified in (b): X, X′, or X″? In answering that consider these additional data:

> **Set F:** (a) bird's-eye view
> (a) too-hot-to-handle sense
> (a) right-to-the-bottom plunge
> (a) didn't-eat-enough look
> (a) who's-the-boss wink

(d) How is Data Set G a problem for your answer in (c) and which category is it is a problem for?

Set G: *those a salad and some soup suppers
            (cf. those salad and soup suppers)
            *that a dirty old man look
            (cf. that dirty old man look)

(e) Set aside the problem in (d) now and consider only your answers to (a)–(d). How do these compounds offer evidence as to the ordering of morphological rules with respect to the syntax? In particular, consider these three hypotheses:

I. All morphological rules take place in the lexicon.
II. Some morphological rules take place in the lexicon and some take place in the syntax.
III. All morphological rules take place in the syntax.

Can you use these compounds to eliminate one or more of these hypotheses? If so, which one(s) can you eliminate and why? (Your discussion should be very brief. I'm not asking for a treatise here.)

(f) In the text we proposed that modifiers precede the head in English, but complements follow the head. We made that generalization about syntactic phrase structure. However, if at least some morphological rules take place in the syntax (as Hypotheses II and III state), one might expect to find that this generalization holds for word-internal structure, as well. That is, the head of a word would be preceded by elements that modify it but followed by elements that are arguments of it.

Assume that the compounds studied here are single words with a head (and if you feel uncomfortable with that assumption, go back to Chapter 3 and look again at our discussion of compounds). Are the compounds studied here consistent with the generalization that modifiers precede a head and arguments follow a head? If so, how? If not, why not? Did you expect them to be? Why or why not?

2. Consider the morpheme written as *'s* in:

the boy's book (as in: This is the boy's book.)
the-boy-who-went-out's book
(as in: This is the-boy-who-went-out's book.)

(a) Does this morpheme attach at the end of an N or at the end of an NP? Justify your answer.

(b) What does this morpheme add to the semantics of a nominal? Consider nominals like:

Sally's brother
last-night's party
the new-kid's desk
Bill's lecture about health care
John's untimely death
Mary's photo of Bill that Jim owns

(Be careful not to give an answer that you may have been taught in grade school without first making sure that the data support that answer. In particular, do not simply say that this morpheme always indicates possession. There is much more to it than that. Consider all these examples and any others that come to mind. Then, even if you have tons to say, limit your answer to one half of one page.)

Given this, do you think it would make sense to call the Genitive NP an "argument" of the head N?

(c) Discuss whether the Genitive morpheme identified here is an affix or a clitic. (Look back to Chapter 3 for a discussion of the different properties of affixes and clitics. This is not a simple matter and it could well serve as a topic for a term paper. But I'd like you to just identify some of the major issues here.)

3. Consider the boldface morphemes in these Chinese sentences (I have left off all the tone marks since they are not relevant to this problem):

    (1) Yuan-ding jiau-**shi**-le hua
        gardener water-wet-ASP flower
        'The gardener watered the flowers wet.'
    (2) Shu zhang-**xie**-le.
        tree grow-slant-ASP
        'The tree grew and became slanted.'
    (3) Taiyang shai-**hong**-le tade lian.
        sun burn-red-ASP his face
        'The sun burned his face red.'

(ASP = aspectual marker)

Question 1

What is the function of these boldfaced morphemes? In particular, do they fill a GF or are they modifiers or are they predicates? Explain your answer.

Question 2

Notice that the aspectual marker attaches to the end of these boldfaced morphemes. Does this fact support your answer to 1 or not? How?

Question 3

Assume the simple morphemes connected with hyphens form a single morphologically complex word. Describe the morphological structure of that word. (Think in terms of lexical, derivational, and inflectional morphemes.) Is this word a compound? Why or why not?

Question 4

Consider these isolated Chinese words:

    ta '(s)he'   la 'pull'   men 'door'   kai 'open'

Now translate this English sentence into Chinese:

    (4) He pulled the door open.

(Please use *-le* as the aspect marker here, as in 1–3. Your only real question is what order these words come in.)

4. Besides the progressive aspect marker *-ing* that you studied in Problem Set 4.3, there are at least two other *-ing* morphemes in English, exemplified here:

    a. I enjoyed [reading Shakespeare].
    b. I enjoyed [those readings of Shakespeare].

Give at least three reasons for claiming that the word that contains the *-ing* suffix in (b) is a noun. (Hint: One argument can be built by considering Case Theory. Which types of heads can assign Case and thus take DOs? Another argument can be built based on what types of categories demonstratives like *those* can introduce (that is, an argument based on syntactic distribution). And a third argument can be built based on restrictions on what the plural morpheme can attach to.)

5. Consider these English sentences:

    (1) Jack gave Pete Sally.
          Jack gave Sally Pete.
          Pete gave Jack Sally.
          Pete gave Sally Jack.
          Sally gave Pete Jack.
          Sally gave Jack Pete.

In order to allow for a good context for these sentences, you may have to think of Sally, Pete, and Jack alternately as pets, perhaps. That is, in the first sentence Jack is giving Pete a pet named Sally; in the second sentence Jack is giving Sally a pet named Pete; and so on. These sentences do not mean the same thing.

    Now consider the Japanese sentences:

    (2) Toshio-ga Hitomi-ni Hanako-o yatta.
          Toshio-ga Hanako-o Hitomi-ni yatta.
          Hitomi-ni Toshio-ga Hanako-o yatta.
          Hitomi-ni Hanako-o Toshio-ga yatta.
          Hanako-o Toshio-ga Hitomi-ni yatta.
          Hanako-o Hitomi-ni Toshio-ga yatta.
          'Toshio gave Hanako to Hitomi.'

All of these sentences can be used to describe the situation in which Toshio gave Hanako to Hitomi, as the gloss at the end of 2 shows (although some of them are more peculiar than others and call for certain restrictions on the contexts in which they can be appropriately used). Again, in order to have a pragmatically suitable situation, we might allow *Hanako* to be the name of a pet in 2.

    The important point for us in this problem set is that 2 contrasts sharply with 1. In 1 all the sentences were sharply distinct in meaning. They described different situations and they would be true in different situations. But the sentences in 2 are similar in meaning. They describe the same situation and they are true in the same situations. (The differences in meaning are of a subtle sort, having to do with issues such as what is old and new information in the sentence, where our sympathies lie, and other factors of the discourse.)

In both 1 and 2 the verbs remained in a fixed position, but the noun phrases were arranged differently from sentence to sentence. Rearranging the order of the noun phrases in English resulted in drastic changes for the semantics. But rearranging the order of the noun phrases in Japanese did not.

Why? (Hint: I am asking you to guess at the function of the PARTICLES *ga*, *o*, and *ni* in Japanese.]

Problem Set 4.5: Hopi Questions

Consider these wh-questions in Hopi:

(1) Pam haki? 'Who is he/she?'
(2) Hak tohot mu'a? 'Who shot the leopard?'
(3) Hak kwuhut qöhikna? 'Who broke the wood?'
(4) Pam maana haki? 'Who is that girl?'
(5) Hakim taavok öki? 'Who (all) arrived yesterday?'
(6) Um hakiy kuntuva? 'Who did you kick?'
(7) Ina hakumuy maamatsi? 'Who (all) did my father recognize?'

What is the root of the word for "who"?

Is there wh-movement in Hopi or does the question word stay in situ (that is, does the question word sit in the same position at DS and SS)?

What is the word order in Hopi? (VSO, SVO, or SOV?)

Does Hopi have audible Case marking on NPs?

Give a statement of when the form *haki* is used. (Hint: Look at the sentences that use *haki* and ask yourself what function *haki* has in those sentences.)

Translate the following two Hopi sentences into English, using the vocabulary below and what you learned from looking at 1.7.

(8) Nu' hakiy tuwa?
(9) Hakim songohut tukuya?

tuwa 'find'   nu' 'I'
tukuya 'cut (plural)'   songohut 'reed' (plural)

Problem Set 4.6: Agreement Processes

(NOTE: The last part of Question 3 is very difficult here.)

1. This question has several parts, all connected to agreement processes in Italian.

Part 1

The color words in Italian typically show a morphological ending that indicates agreement with the item the color word modifies inside the noun phrase, as in:

(1) la macchina nera   'the black car'
    the car (FS)   black (FS)

le	macchine	nere	'the black cars'
the	car (FP)	black (FP)	
il	piatto	nero	'the black plate'
the	plate (MS)	black (MS)	
i	piatti	neri	'the black plates'
the	plate (MP)	black (MP)	

(FS = feminine singular, FP = feminine plural, MS = masculine singular, MP = masculine plural.) In this way, the color word in 1 behaves like an ordinary adjective of Italian. Other color words that behave identically include *bianco* 'white,' *giallo* 'yellow,' *rosso* 'red,' and several more.

On the basis of 1, for what features do the color words agree with the noun they modify in Italian? What are the four morphological endings seen in the color word and what are the features associated with these endings?

Part 2

A few color words, however, are invariable. One type is exemplified in:

(2) la macchina rosa   'the pink car'
    le macchine rosa   'the pink cars'
    il piatto rosa   'the pink plate'
    i piatti rosa   'the pink plates'

Rosa in Italian has more than one meaning. Just on the basis of your knowledge of English, suggest a second meaning for *rosa* beside "pink". Consider the semantic and pragmatic relationships between these two meanings for *rosa*. Why do you think *rosa* is invariable for agreement? Guess at another color word that might possibly be invariable, based solely on your knowledge of color words in English. (Consider objects whose name is their color.)

Part 3

A second type of color word that is invariable for agreement is exemplified in:

(3) la macchina blù   'the blue car'
    le macchine blù   'the blue cars'
    il piatto blù   'the blue plate'
    i piatti blù   'the blue plates'

The accent marks in 3 indicate stress on the final vowel. Consider the four morphological endings you came up with in Part 1. Now consider the root for the word which means black to which these endings were attached in 1. If the color word here were to make use of these endings in agreement processes, what morphological questions would arise? (Hint: Consider what the root for the word that means blue might be. How does it differ from the root for black in Part 1? Could this difference be the source of the impossibility of adding the agreement suffix in 3? You don't have much to go on here, so just make a stab at it.)

Part 4

Tensed verbs agree with their Subjects in Italian. Consider:

(4) Io canto.
  'I sing.'
(5) Tu canti.
  'You sing.'
(6) Il ragazzo canta.
  'The boy sings.'
(7) La ragazza canta.
  'The girl sings.'
(8) Noi cantiamo.
  'We sing.'
(9) Voi cantate.
  'You (plural) sing.'
(10) I ragazzi cantano.
  'The boys sing.'
(11) Le ragazze cantano.
  'The girls sing.'

Whether the speaker is male or female, whether the person spoken to is male or female, 4, 5, 8, and 9 are all grammatical. While 5 and 9 have the same translation in English, the difference in Italian is that 5 is understood to say that a single person sings, whereas 9 is understood to say that more than one person sings.

On the basis of 4.11, for what features do verbs agree with their Subjects in Italian?

Part 5

As I said in Part 1, the agreement phenomenon exemplified in 1 is typical of adjectives in Italian. Compare, then, the features for which adjectives agree in Italian (which you discovered in Part 1) with the features for which verbs agree (which you discovered in Part 4). What feature is reflected in both agreement processes?

What feature is reflected in only adjective agreement?

What feature is reflected in only verb agreement?

If you are doing this problem set as part of a course, you might want to discuss in class the differences you find in these two agreement processes.

2. This problem has two parts, comparing Japanese to Italian.

Part 1

The following are some brief conversational exchanges in Japanese. No word-by-word gloss is given. Instead, following each exchange is a loose translation.

(12) —Wakarimasu-ka?
  —Ee, wakarimasu.
  —Do you understand?
  —Yes, I understand.
(13) —Tukurimasita-ne?
  —Hai. Kinoo tukurimasita.
  —You made it, right?
  —Yes. I made it yesterday.

In 13 *kinoo* means 'yesterday.' In 12 *ee* means 'yes' and in 13 *hai* means 'yes.' These two words are not equivalent, however. They differ with regard to the level of politeness and with regard to style. We will not concern ourselves with these differences here.

Looking at these sentences, what category do you think the words *warakimasu* and *tukurimasita* belong to? (Think of the categories of N, V, A, and P we discussed in this chapter.) Why? What functions do these words perform in these sentences? (Think of the functions we discussed—referring, modifying, and predicating.)

Ka in the question sentence in 12 and *ne* in the question sentence in 13 are called sentence particles. Based solely on these examples, what functions do you think these two sentence particles play?

What semantic difference is there between them?

Is there any single word or part of a word (that is, morpheme) in 12 or 13 that you can point to and say means 'I' or 'you'?

Now consider one more exchange:

(14) —Asita kimasen-ne?
      —Iya, kimasu-yo.
      —You're not coming tomorrow, right?
      —No, I AM coming.

Asita in 14 means 'tomorrow.'

Based on 12–14, what category do you think *kimasen* and *kimasu* belong to?

Note that in 12 and 13, the words *wakarimasu* and *tukurimasita* are absolutely identical phonologically and morphologically in the question and the answer. But in 14, in the question we have the form *kimasen* and in the answer we have the form *kimasu*. To what do you attribute the difference in phonological and morphological forms in 14?

Based on 12–14 what function do you think the sentence particle *yo* in the answer in 14 plays?

Given all of 12–14, can you point to any word or morpheme and say it means 'I' or 'you'?

Part 2

Consider the following Italian conversational exchanges:

(15) —Capisci?
      —Si, capisco.
      —Do you understand?
      —Yes, I understand.
(16) —Lo fai, no?
      —Si, lo faccio ora.
      —You are making it, right?
      —Yes, I'm making it now.

Ora in the answer in 15 means 'now.' The *lo* in both question and answer in 16 means 'it.'

Compare 15 and 16 in Italian to 12 and 13 in Japanese in Part 1. In Japanese the questions and answers were identical except for the particles and the interjections meaning 'yes.' In Italian, the questions and answers differ in other ways. Can you point to any one word or morpheme in 15 or 16 that you think means 'I'? Can you point to any one word or morpheme in 15 or 16 that you think means 'you'? If so, give those words or morphemes.

(NOTE: You might feel confused by these Italian sentences, given the Italian sentences in Question 1-Part 4 of this problem set. While sentences 4, 5, 8 and 9 of Question 1-Part 4 are grammatical, the exchanges in 15 and 16 of the present question are also grammatical and are, perhaps, more colloquial in more contexts than the sentences 4, 5, 8, and 9 of Question 1-Part 4 are.)

Now consider,

(7) —Non vieni domani, vero?
    —No. Vengo di sicuro.
    —You're not coming tomorrow, right?
    —No. I'm coming for sure.

Domani in the question in 17 means 'tomorrow.' *Di sicuro* in the answer in 17 means 'for sure.'

Again, compare the Italian exchange in 17 to the Japanese exchange in 14. Are your ideas about the morphemes that mean 'I' and 'you' confirmed here or not?

Assume that both Japanese and Italian have phonetically null (that is, inaudible, or nonovert) pronouns in Subject position in all these sentences. If your answers to whether or not the language has audible morphemes in these examples that indicate 'I' and 'you' differ for Japanese and Italian, how could you account for this difference?

Discuss whether any evidence in this problem set can support the claim that one or the other or both of these languages have nonovert Object pronouns.

Finally, briefly discuss interpretation strategies that you might expect, based on common sense alone, to come into play in sentences that have no overt Subjects in Japanese. For example, just based on 12 and 14, if a question is asked out of the blue (without previous context), and its Subject is not overtly expressed, how do you think that Subject is to be interpreted? Now guess at how a missing Subject is to be interpreted for a statement made out of the blue. Now guess at how a missing Subject is to be interpreted for a statement when there is previous context. In contrast, guess at how a missing Subject is to be interpreted for a question when there is previous context.

3. In colloquial Russian there is a fair amount of freedom in word order, often referred to as SCRAMBLING. Typically this scrambling is among members of a single clause. But sometimes a phrase from an embedded clause can be located separated from the rest of its clause, both preceded and followed by words from higher clauses. This is known as LONG-DISTANCE (LD) scrambling. LD scrambling yields sentences that vary in acceptability from fully acceptable to totally unacceptable. Here are five sentences whose acceptability gets progressively worse as we go down the list:

(1) Ty   Mašu   dumaeš' Andrej   ljubit.
    you(Nom-2S) Masha(Acc) think-2S Andrej(Nom) loves
    'Do you think that Andrej loves Masha?'
(2) ?Vy   Maša   dumaete ljubit Andreja.
    you(Nom-2P) Masha(Nom) think(2P) loves Andrej(Acc)
    'Do you think that Masha loves Andrej?'
(3) ??Olja   Mašu   dumaet Andrej   ljubit.
    Olja(Nom) Masha(Acc) think(3S) Andrej(Nom) loves
    'Does Olja think that Andrej loves Masha?'
(4) ?*Ty   Maša   dumaeš' ljubit Andreja.
    You(Nom-2S) Masha(Nom) think(2S) loves Andrej(Acc)
    'Do you think Masha loves Andrej?'

(5) *Olja   Maša   dumaet ljubit Andreja.
    Olja(Nom) Masha(Nom) think(3S) loves Andrej(Acc)
    'Does Olja think Masha loves Andrej?'

(a) Which word has been scrambled away from its clause in every example sentence?

(b) Consider the features of person, number, gender, Case. Which of these features do you know NPs in Russian must have, given these sentences? (Do not use information about Russian that isn't available from these sentences alone, please.) How do you know that?

(c) There are three NPs in each of these sentences. List the NPs and give the feature bundle for each NP. For example, for 1, you will list the NPs *ty*, *Mašu*, and *Andrej*. And for *ty* you will give the feature bundle [2-S-Nom].

(d) Look closely at the feature bundles you gave in (c). Now formulate a proposal about what factors are relevant to the declining acceptability as we go from sentence 1 to 5 above. (Certainly there are other data you'd like to have before making an entirely precise proposal. However, even with just these data, you should be able to take a stab at a generalization. Don't drive yourself crazy. The interaction of the factors is complex and I'm not asking you to figure that out. I'm merely asking you to guess which factors interact to affect declining acceptability.)

Problem Set 4.7: Subcategorization in English

Read this problem set through to the end. Then go about your business and let it brew in the back of your mind. Come back to it every few hours and you'll find that examples will come to you.

Part 1

You know of four grammatical functions: Subject, Direct Object, Indirect Object, and Object of a preposition. Now think about the different verbs of English and answer the following questions.

(a) Give one verb in English that must occur without a DO and also without an IO. Do not use *be* or a passive sentence.

Be careful here and in the following. A verb like *run*, for example, can be used transitively in a sentence like *She runs marathons*. You must find a verb that can **never** occur with any DO or IO, such as *elapse*. Note also that some intransitive verbs allow so-called COGNATE OBJECTS:

(1) She slept the sleep of the weary.
(2) He lived {a life of leisure/a fantasy}.

Try to find a verb which disallows even cognate Objects.

(b) Give one verb in English that can optionally occur with a DO but must never take an IO. An example is *eat*. Now find an example of your own.

(c) Give one verb in English that must occur with a DO.

(Again, be very careful. There are many verbs that are typically transitive but in common contexts can be used intransitively. For example, *buy* is typically transitive, but we can easily understand a sentence like *Are you buying again today?* said in the context of one person asking if the other will pay for lunch. Make sure the verb you give doesn't lend itself to easy comprehension when used intransitively. An example is *confuse* as in *Mary confuses the issues*, but not **Mary confuses on most days, so I'll do the confusing today*. Watch out for variations in tense and aspect that affect whether or not an Object is required. You want examples where the DO is required in all tenses and aspects.

(d) Give one verb that must occur with a DO and also requires some other element (beyond the Subject) to be there—perhaps an IO, perhaps a PP, perhaps something that is locative (telling a place or position or direction), perhaps something that modifies the action of the verb. This verb must be different from the one you used in (c). (I am not giving you an example here, because if I do, I will give away the class of verbs for you, since they tend to be quite similar. Instead, let me give you an example of an intransitive verb that requires a locative in my speech: *lurk*, as in *She lurked in the bushes*, but not **She lurked all day*. Now you need to find a verb that requires both some other phrase plus a DO.)

Part 2

Prepositions, like verbs, can occur in different environments and we can subcategorize them according to these environments. For example, like most verbs, most prepositions are only optionally transitive:

(3) Susie went <u>in</u> <u>(the house)</u>.
            P   NP

Compare to an optionally transitive V:

(4) Susie <u>drank</u> <u>(the beer)</u>.
          V   NP

Also, prepositions, like verbs, can introduce another PP rather than only an NP Object.

(5) Susie fell <u>down</u> <u>[through the hole]</u>.
            P   PP

Compare to a V introducing a PP:

(6) Susie <u>fell</u> <u>[down the stairs]</u>.
         V   PP

And prepositions, like verbs, can introduce clauses rather than just NPs or PPs.

(7) <u>In</u> <u>[that there's nothing left to say]</u>, I'm leaving.
    P   clause

    I wouldn't cry just on account <u>of</u> <u>[his mother yelled]</u>.
                         P   clause

You may not find the second sentence of 7 grammatical, but many people do and this is an ATTESTED (that is, actually heard) example. Compare to a V introducing a clause:

(8) I <u>think   [that there's nothing left to say]</u>.
     V   clause
I   <u>noticed   [his mother yelled]</u>.
     V   clause

There are lots and lots of prepositions in English, once you recognize that you do not have to have an NP Object in order to be a preposition. As you learned in this chapter, one diagnostic for a P is whether or not it can be introduced by *right* or *directly* (or other similar words). Thus for most speakers of English, these specifiers do not introduce any category other than P:

(9) She went {right/directly} [into]$_P$ the house.
*She's {right/directly} [intelligent]$_A$.
*She {right/directly} [cried]$_V$.
*It fell {right/directly} [quickly]$_A$.

The *right*-test for P is sufficient, but not necessary. That is, if an item can be introduced by *right*, it is a P. But not all Ps can be introduced by *right*:

(10) *She bought a basket [{right/directly} of peaches].

In 10, *of peaches* is surely a PP, but *right/directly* cannot introduce it. Now try to answer the following questions.

(a) Give one preposition that can never take an NP Object (although it is okay if your example can introduce another PP). Use it in a sentence.

(b) Give one preposition that must take an NP Object. Use it in a sentence.

(c) Give one preposition that must introduce only a clause. Use it in a sentence. (Hint: Look back in the chapter. We discussed one of these.)

(d) What is the category of each of the bracketed phrases here? Give an argument to support each of your answers.

(11) Mary ran [back].
(12) Mary went [home].
(13) Mary found it [there].

(I expect this to make you unhappy. Try to follow your *right*-test and forget your preconceived notions about categories. If you know other languages well, you might try to see if you can find similar examples in the languages you know.)

(e) Some verbs cannot take DOs, most can optionally take DOs, and a few must take DOs (as you found out on Part 1). No category other than V and P can take an Object. However, nouns and adjectives can take complements which are PPs. Usually, these PPs are optional:

(14) destruction (of the city)/the rumor (about Pete)
     sick (of milk)/dependent (on Pete)

Find one adjective of English that requires a PP when it is used predicatively.

There are only a handful, but if you bring this up at the dinner table, maybe your friends can help you find one. I will give you an example just so you believe there are some.

(15)   Joe is fond of Sue
          *Joe is fond.

(Notice that the subcategorization frame of an adjective may vary between its use as a modifier and its use as a predicate:

    a fond look
??Her look was fond.
    my fondest memory
  *That memory is fondest.

For this reason, please demonstrate with a predicative use of an adjective.)

Problem Set 4.8: Theta-Roles in English

(NOTE: This problem set is as much on semantics as on syntax.)

This problem set may seem tough at first. Try to relax. Read it through. Think about it. Determine which example sentences seem relevant to which questions. Then dig in. I am sure you will see the point after you have thought a little while. And try to remember that in syntax (in life?) there are no clean answers—so do not try to force any. State what you see.

Assume for the purposes of this problem set that the only GFs are Subject, DO, IO, and OP.

In this chapter we discussed the thematic roles that arguments of a given predicate (usually a verb) may have. These are typically called theta-roles.

They concern the semantics of a sentence.

For example, in

(1) John threw a ball to Susie.

John has the GF of S, and the theta-role of agent; *Susie* has the GF of IO, and the theta-role of beneficiary (also called recipient, also called benefactee, also called goal—but various linguists make various distinctions between these different labels—do not worry about it for now); *a ball* has the GF of DO, and the theta-role of theme (also called patient).

Another theta-role is EXPERIENCER. So in,

(2) John went crazy.

John has the GF of S, and the theta-role of experiencer.

A fifth theta-role is instrument (which we met earlier when looking at Kichaga). So in,

(3) This key opens that door.

This key has the GF of S, and the theta-role of instrument.

There are no clear definitions for the various theta-roles and there's no easy way of determining how many theta-roles a given language makes use of. For the sake of this homework, consider only the five theta-roles of **agent, beneficiary, theme, experiencer,** and **instrument** exemplified.

Diagnostics for Agent

There are several diagnostics for agent. First, an agent can license the occurrence of the adverbial *voluntarily*. A theme, a beneficiary, an experiencer, and an instrument cannot:

> Joan ate the meat voluntarily.
> *The meat burned to a crisp voluntarily.
> ??Joan received the gift voluntarily.
> *Joan slipped a disk in her back voluntarily.
> *The key opened the lock voluntarily.

Thus if a sentence has no agent, it cannot have the adverbial *voluntarily*. And if a sentence can have the adverbial *voluntarily*, it does have an agent. In other words, the ability of *voluntarily* to occur in a sentence is a necessary-and-sufficient test for whether the sentence has an agent. (This is generally taken to be true for most speakers.)

There is another diagnostic for agent, but the use of this test requires some judgment calls. Consider:

(4) I promise to come home on time.
(5) *I promise to be five feet tall.

Certainly the first promise is just fine. But the second one is odd. Still, in spite of the fact that I have starred it, it actually might occur. For instance, let us assume it is fall tryouts for the basketball team. But the team will not actually start playing until late winter. Let's further assume that anyone on the team must be five feet tall. Now if a seventh grader is trying to convince the coach to allow her/ him to be on the basketball team, but that seventh grader is presently too short, she/ he might say, "I promise to be five feet tall by Christmas." No, it is not a real promise. It is more like a declaration of hope or belief in the pediatrician's words that you will keep growing. Nonetheless, the sentence might be said. If we can distinguish the non-promise sentences with *promise* from the true promises, we can say that true promises with an infinitival (like "I promise *to come home on time*"), have an agent (the guy that is going to perform the event of the infinitive—that is, the one who is going to come home on time).

Another diagnostic for agent is progressive aspect. Consider:

(6) I'm talking to you.
(7) *I'm understanding French.

If the Subject is an agent, then it has potential control over the event, so the progressive is possible. This test, while necessary (that is, every verb with an agentive Subject can be in the progressive so long as the extrasentential context of the particular sentence permits), is not sufficient. Thus, even experiencers can occur as the Subjects of verbs with the progressive aspect:

(8) You've gone and left—and I'm so blue—*I'm hurting* over you.

And a fourth possible diagnostic for agent involves RATIONALE clauses: they can occur only with an agent present.

(9) She shouted in order to make everyone look.
(10) *She had good reflexes in order to impress everyone.

(NOTE: Rationale clauses are distinct from PURPOSE clauses, which do not require an agent: *I know a book [to read to the kids]*.) So far as I know, this test is both necessary and sufficient. However, it is tricky, too, because we have another use of *in order to* that is a conditional, and that use is not a test for agent:

(11) We need money in order to impress his mother.
(similar to: If we are going to impress his mother, we need money.)
(cf. *We are needing money.
*We need money voluntarily.
*I promise to need money.)

(You might have noticed that you can say:

I promise not to need money.

In English we seem to allow ourselves to treat (linguistically, at least) lack of necessity as controllable, but necessity as uncontrollable.)

Diagnostics for Theme

There is at least one test for theme. A resultative AP can be predicated of a theme, but it cannot be predicated of an agent, a beneficiary, an experiencer, or an instrument. For example, consider:

(12) John scrubbed the floor clean.

The reading in which John scrubbed the floor until it became clean is called resultative (a term we met earlier in this chapter). With that reading, we understand only *the floor*, the theme, to wind up clean—not *John*, the agent. Of course there is the reading in which John scrubbed the floor while he was clean, parallel to:

(13) John came home clean.

Here the adjective *clean* is predicated of *John*, but *clean* is not a resultative. (We don't come home until we wind up clean.) The resultative test is only a sufficient test, however, not a necessary test. That is, if a resultative can be introduced into a sentence, then the sentence has a theme. But if a resultative cannot be introduced into a sentence, we cannot conclude that no theme is present. Instead, there may be extraneous interfering factors that prevent the resultative.

For example, *the paper* is the theme in:

(14) John saw the paper.

but no resultative can be added here:

(15) *John saw the paper flat.

Why do you think that is? If you give it just a moment's thought, you will realize that just seeing some inanimate object does not typically result in some change happening to that inanimate object. So it is likely that one problem with *John saw the paper flat* is that it could never happen, not that there is no theme here. (Contrast to: *John pressed the paper flat.*) Of course, there may be other problems with 15, as well.

Diagnostics for Instrument, Beneficiary, and Experiencer

Some have proposed a diagnostic for instrument. If an NP is an instrument and it is not the Object of *with*, there is often another parallel sentence very close in meaning in which the relevant NP shows up as the Object of *with*:

(16) The key opened the door.
(17) Someone opened the door with the key.

However, this is not always the case:

(18) The medication made me sick.
(19) *I got sick with the medication.
       (cf. I got sick from the medication.
             I got sick with the flu.)

Furthermore, an agent in one sentence might occur as the Object of *with* in a sentence with similar meaning:

(20) John and Mary left the party.
(21) John left the party with Mary.

Here we have a sense of accompaniment, rather than instrument. Because of problems like these, *with* is not considered a good diagnostic for instrument.

I know of no good test for beneficiary or experiencer, either. If you can think of one that works for any of these, write it up and give it to your professor or send it to me.

Now answer the following questions using the example sentences that follow to support your answers with arguments.

Part 1

Is there any GF that always gets a fixed theta-role? If so, which?

Part 2

Is there any theta-role that always goes with a certain GF? If so, which?

(NOTE: the answers to Parts 1 and 2 are not dependent upon each other. That is, Part 1 asks if GFx can have only theta-role y, where theta-role y might also be allowed with GFz. But Part 2 asks if theta-role x can be allowed only with GFy, where GFy might allow theta-role z.)

Your answers to Parts 1 and 2 should have the following form. Set up a matrix in which the columns are the GFs and the rows are the theta-roles, as in Table 4.1. Now if one of the example sentences that follows has an agentive Subject, put the number of that sentence in

Table 4.1. Relationships of GFs to Theta-Roles

	Subject	Direct Obj	Indirect Obj	Object of P
Agent				
Theme				
Beneficiary				
Experiencer				
Instrument				

the proper grid. Then if an example sentence has an agentive DO, put the number of that sentence in the proper grid. And so on. If you find that a certain column is empty except for an entry in one row, then that GF has only one theta-role associated with it. If you find that a certain row is empty except for an entry in one column, then that theta-role has only one GF it can fill.

Do not try to assign every sentence to a grid (Theta Theory is, indeed, a lot more complex than this grid can accommodate). Just one example in each grid is enough to show that that grid is not empty.

You can answer this using only my sentences (I think). But if you think you have an example of your own that fills in a grid that would otherwise remain empty, please write that sentence and show where it fits in the grid. Note that each sentence may appear in the grid more than once—it can appear one time for each NP it contains.

Hold on, there are two more questions.

Part 3

Some people have proposed that each GF in a sentence can have at most one theta-role and that the theta-roles for all the various GFs in a given sentence must be different. (This is known as the THETA CRITERION.) Since you have seen that arguments are generally linked only to GFs, it follows, then, that each argument of a given predicate has a unique theta-role. (That is, you cannot have two experiencers; you cannot have two instruments; etc. Be careful here: a conjoined DO, for example, is still a single DO with a theta-role that goes for the whole DO:

I bought milk and spaghetti.

Here the conjoined NP *milk and spaghetti* is the theme.)

Do sentences like 16 which follows present problems for this claim?

Be sure that if you say there are two GFs with the same theta-role in 16, you check to make sure that both pass whatever diagnostic tests you have for that theta-role.

Limit this discussion to one half of one side of a page.

Part 4

Discuss briefly (limit: half of one side of a page) the issues that pairs of sentences like the following raise for an approach to meaning in which we talk about predicates and theta-roles as distinct entities.

John buttered the bread.
John put butter on the bread.

Give another pair of sentences that demonstrates the same kind of problems.

And here, finally, are the example sentences (in no particular order). As I said above, I think it is possible to answer the questions considering only these data. But so long as you consider all these data, if you want to consider others, you are welcome to. If you disagree with my grammaticality judgments, please nonetheless use my judgments to arrive at an answer to the questions. Then if you want to go through the questions a second time using different judgments, you can do that.

Some of the sentences here present questions that are, strictly speaking, irrelevant to this homework, because they do not speak to the particular questions asked here. Other sentences present contradictory evidence regarding the relationship between GFs and theta roles. I include such sentences with the hope of tantalizing you into taking a syntax course.

Please do not spend countless hours trying to identify the theta-role of every word with a GF in these sentences. Remember, first of all, that not all words are participants in some event, so not all words will get theta-roles. And remember that linguists have argued for years about precisely which theta-role some GF in a given sentence may have. So do not force yourself to do the impossible. Simply identify the theta-roles of enough words to answer the questions. Then stop.

1. John broke the window with a hammer.
2. John understood the theorem.
3. We drew a picture for Mary.
4. Mary was shot down by the police in order to restore law and order.
5. We regaled Mary with jewels.
6. Mary was knocked down by accident.
7. Mary was given a diamond ring.
8. We surprised Mary.
9. John caught a cold.
10. We feted Mary with fine foods.
11. We feted Mary nude. [We or Mary or both can be nude.]
12. *We feted Mary fat. [There is no resultative reading here.]
13. The floor was scrubbed clean.
14. *John understood the theorem voluntarily.
15. Mary was chosen by fiat.
16. Bill exchanged books with Mary.
17. We paid John.
18. We paid John the money.
19. We paid John with money.
20. John used the hammer to open the door.
21. This piece was written by Mozart in order to please his wife.
22. Mary got arrested by the police voluntarily. [Only Mary's will is expressed.]
23. John helped his parents.

Problem Set 4.9: Similarities and Differences in Meaning: Double Object Sentences

(NOTE: This problem set is as much on semantics as on syntax.)

In the section "Transformations" of this chapter I pointed out that earlier theories of syntax often derived active and passive sentences from a single DS, and Double-Object sentences from the same DS as the corresponding non-Double-Object sentences, and, finally, *spray/load* sentence pairs from a single DS. One of the rationales for doing this was claimed synonymy between the sentence pairs. In fact, though, there are semantic differences between the members of these pairs. I believe that for active and passive pairs those semantic differences are subtle and are most easily understood through study of discourse (that is, related sentences in a conversation). Thus sentence grammar doesn't have much to say about these differences. I also believe that for *spray/load* pairs the differences are gross and you will have no trouble seeing them. So we won't deal with active/passive pairs or with *spray/load* pairs.

Instead, in this problem set I'd like you to examine dative sentence pairs, where the differences in meaning are, indeed, slight, but, nevertheless, able to be discerned by looking at sentences in isolation. Let's limit ourselves to pairs that involve *to* in the non-Double-Object sentence. Try to state what factors make a *to* appropriate or inappropriate introducing an IO. In doing this, you should uncover subtle semantic differences between sentences with a *to* and sentences with the Double-Object construction. Please expect exceptions to arise. The point is to come up with a generalization that holds for most of the sentences you can think of. Then list all the exceptions you have come across and perhaps you will find motivation for their exceptional behavior (but perhaps not).

(1)   Jack gave Mary a book.
      Jack gave a book to Mary.
(2)   Jack gave Mary the creeps.
      *Jack gave the creeps to Mary.
(3)   Measle germs give you measles.
      *Measle germs give measles to you.
(4)   Max gave linguistics his all.
      *Max gave his all to linguistics.
(5)   The judge spared John the ordeal.
      *The judge spared the ordeal to John.
(6)   *We left chance the outcome.
      We left the outcome to chance.
(7)   *Cast the wind your fate.
      Cast your fate to the wind.
(8)   *I donated charity money.
      I donated money to charity.
(9)   *Sock me it. (Compare: Hand me it.)
      Sock it to me.

Once you have an idea of what's going on, consider the contexts in which you might choose to say 10 and those in which you might choose to say 11:

(10) Jack told the commission everything he knew.
(11) Jack told everything he knew to the commission.

There is a difference, though delicate. You might want to consider whether you'd be more likely to use one than the other in reporting that Jack was a whistle-blower with a negative evaluation of his behavior. Would one of them be more likely if the speaker is backing up Jack and trying to confirm for the listener that Jack really did his best to answer the questions put to him? Will the generalization you just came to regarding 1–9 account for this difference?

Now can you see a difference between:

(12) Sue paid Mary the rent.
(13) Sue paid the rent to Mary.

Is one of them more likely if Mary isn't the person we normally expect to receive the rent? Why?

Account for the marginality of 14 in contrast to 15:

(14) ??Bill gave a little squeeze to Mary.
(15)   Bill gave Mary a little squeeze.
         (compare to: So Bill turns around and gives a hug to the wrong lady.
         So Bill turns around and gives the wrong lady a hug.)

Do you now see any difference between:

(16) Just give some food to your children.
(17) Just give your children some food.

Does your analysis account for the fact that we have the following fixed order on certain idioms?

(18)   I gave him the boot. (= I kicked him out.)
         *I gave the boot to him.
(19)   Mary showed Oscar the door. (=Mary kicked Oscar out.)
         *Mary showed the door to Oscar.

(The asterisks on the second sentences in 18 and 19 are for the idiom reading only. In other words, these sentences have only a literal reading.)

Make your discussion as clear as you can, but please limit yourself to at most one side of one page. (This problem set is not intended to ruin your life.) If you can think of other pairs that make your point better, please offer them.

NOTE: I'm not saying that your analysis must account for all the data. I'm just asking if it does (and if it does, that's interesting and nice). If it doesn't, you should comment on what you think is going on in the data that fall outside your analysis. (That is, please offer some sort of account.)

In the idioms in 18 and 19 only the Double-Object construction is allowed. Can you think of any idioms for which only the [NP-V-NP-to-NP] construction is allowed? Give them if you can. If you can't, does your analysis of this type of sentence pair predict this lack of occurrence?

*Problem Set 4.10: Portuguese Case Assignment

In this chapter we developed a rudimentary picture of Case Theory by looking primarily at English. Let me review that quickly.

(A) Every NP with a phonetic matrix must get Case.

(B) The Case assigners for English are V and P, and in tensed clauses either T or Agr (which gives Case to the Subject). We also pointed out that not all verbs are Case-assigners. In general, it looks like only verbs that can be followed by a nominal DO can assign Case.

(C) A Case-assigner gives Case to an NP it governs (that is, to an NP within its maximal projection that is not separated from it by any other maximal projection).

(D) The rule of Genitive Case-Assignment marks as Genitive an NP in specifier of N position.

(E) The rule of Exceptional Case-Assignment (ECA) is responsible for a V or P giving Case to the Subject of an infinitival. ECA operates with only some V's and with only some P's. Thus *expect* can exceptionally assign Case to the Subject of an infinitival Object, but *say* cannot:

> I expect [the boy to leave].
> *I say [the boy to leave].

Here we are going to look at European Portuguese (EP), a Romance language spoken in Portugal. Assume that the Case Theory outlined for English holds for EP on Points A– C (but not D and E; EP does not have a Genitive Case rule nor does it have ECA).

Now in English all and only tensed clauses exhibit Subject-Verb Agreement. Thus it is not possible for us to be sure on purely empirical grounds which of [+T] and [+Agr] is the true Case-assigner for Subjects. But in EP some tenseless clauses do exhibit Subject-Verb Agreement. So in EP it is possible on empirical grounds to determine which of [+T] and [+Agr] is the true Case-assigner to Subjects. You will now make this determination. But I will lead you to it through a series of questions.

Part 1

How does Case of a Subject correlate with agreement on a verb in EP? Base your answer on the data in 1–7 which follow.

Let me now help you to sort through those data before you attempt to answer the question. In EP a finite verb agrees with its Subject in person and number (as in English) and its Subject is Subjective Case (as in English). In each example, the first gloss under a verb is V (for "verb"), followed by person and number features, while pronouns and nouns have only person and number features on the first gloss. (NOTE: Only those items relevant to the question have a first gloss. Also, while pronouns vary for person, in EP, as in English, nouns do not vary for person: All are third person. Still, I mark nouns for person here to help you focus on the issues.)

(1)	Carolina	tomou	óleo-de-rícino.	(*tomaram,	*tomamos,	etc.)
	3s	V3s		V3p	V1p	
		[+tense]				
	Carolina	took	oil-of-castor			
	'Carolina	took	castor oil.'			

(*Rícino* is the name of the castor oil plant.) **In EP, like in English, Case is audible only on pronouns, not on full NPs.**

In EP (but not in other varieties of Portuguese) an infinitival verb may agree with its

Subject in person and number under certain conditions. We are not concerned in this problem set with what the conditions are for agreement. Take the fact that agreement does or does not occur as a given. Do not try to account for agreement. Instead, use the facts on agreement to help you answer the following questions.

(2) Julio   disse   para   nós não   sairmos de casa.
    3s   V3s   1p   V1p
        [+tense]   SUBJ   [−tense]
    Julio   said   for   we not   [leave from home
    'Julio said we shouldn't leave home.'

(3) Vi-os   assaltar   a velha.
    V1s-3p   V-unmarked
  [+tense]-DO   [−tense]
    saw-them   assault   the old lady

    '(I) saw them assault the old lady."

The single Portuguese word *velha* is translated 'old lady' here. In 3 the Portuguese example does not have an overt Subject pronoun. Portuguese, like Italian, is a pro-drop language. Do not let that throw you off. It does not complicate anything in this part of the homework. The pronoun *os* in 3 is also found in 4:

(4) Vi-os   regar   o jardim.
    V1s-3p   V-unmarked
  [+tense]-DO   [−tense]
    saw-them   water   the garden
    '(I) saw them water the garden.'

While the pronoun *nós* in 2 is a Subjective pronoun, the pronoun *os* in 3 and 4 is an Objective pronoun. (By the way, the pronoun in 3 and 4 is a clitic—it forms a phonological word with the verb it follows. Objective pronouns in Portuguese may or may not be clitics. Do not worry about this. It will not affect your answers.)

In 2 *sairmos* is an infinitival form (it is not tensed), yet it agrees for person and number with the pronoun *nos*. In 3 and 4 *assaltar* and *regar* are infinitival forms and they have no agreement markers on them. (They are in the unmarked form.)

Consider the data in 2–4 and those in 5–7.

(5) *Julio   disse   para   os   meninos   não   sair   de casa.
                        3p   V-unmarked
       [+tense]   [−tense]
    Julio   said   for   the   boys   not   leave   from home
    'Julio said the boys shouldn't leave home.'
    (cf. Julio disse para os meninos não sairem de casa.)
                        3p   V3p
      [+tense]   [−tense]

(The *os* in 4 is an Objective clitic pronoun. But the *os* in 5 is the third-person-plural masculine definite article that introduces the NP headed by *meninos* 'boys.')

(6) *Vi-os   assaltarem   a velha.
      3p   V3p
  [+tense]-DO   [−tense]
  saw-them   assault   the old lady

   '(I) saw them assault the old lady.'

   (cf. 3 and: Vi   eles   assaltarem   a velha.
                3p   V3p
          [+tense] SUBJ   [−tense]
            saw   them   assault   the old lady
          '(I) saw them assault the old lady.')

(7) *Vi-os   regarem   o jardim.
     3p   V3p
  [+tense]-DO   [−tense]
  saw-them   water   the garden
  '(I) saw them water the garden.'
   (cf. 4 and: Vi   eles   regarem   o jardim.
                3p   V3p
          [+tense]   SUBJ   [−tense]
           saw   them   water   the garden
          '(I) saw them water the garden.')

Okay, you should now be able to answer the question, which I'll repeat: How does Case of a Subject correlate with agreement on a verb in EP? The only verbs you have had are the verbs for 'take,' 'say,' 'leave,' 'see,' 'assault,' and 'water.' But these verbs are entirely representative of how verbs in general behave in such structures.

Does your statement cover both finite (that is, [+tense]) and nonfinite (that is, [−tense]) verb forms? Try to make it do that.

(NOTE: Even if you know EP, do not bring data beyond those given in this problem set to bear in your answers. You may well arrive at different answers if you consider more data—particularly if you consider the informal REGISTERS or styles of the language. Make sure that the answer you give is justified by the data given to you here. At the very end if you speak EP and you think that the actual answers are different from those that these data lead you to, you should write up the problem set again, using the data you know.)

Part 2

As you saw in 3 and 4, Portuguese, unlike English, allows sentences to have no expressed Subject. That is, it is a pro-drop language. But even when the Subject is not overt, we have agreement with it, as in 3 (where the top clause has a missing 'I' Subject) and in 8, following.

(8) Tomaram   óleo-de-rícino.
    V3p
  [+tense]
  took   oil-of- castor
  '(They) took castor oil.'

Again, unlike English, there are no dummy Subjects in Portuguese. So parallel to the *it* of *It seems that things are hot in Belfast*, we find:

(9) Parece   que   as   coisas   estão   quentes   em   Belfast.
    V3s   3p   V3p
    [+tense]   [+tense]
    seems   that   the   things   are   hot   in   Belfast
    '(It) seems that things are hot in Belfast.'

In 9 both verbs are tensed (*parece* and *estão*).
Now keeping the facts that 8 and 9 demonstrate in mind, why is 10 good but 11 bad?

(10) Parece   estarem   as   coisas   quentes   em Belfast.
     V3s   V3p   3p
     [+tense] [−tense]
     seems   be   the things   hot   in Belfast
     '(It) seems things to be hot in Belfast.'
(11) *Parece   estar   as coisas quentes   em Belfast.
     V3s   V-unmarked   3p
     [+tense]   [−tense]
     seems   be   the things hot   in Belfast
     '(It) seems things to be hot in Belfast.'

Your explanation for 10 vs. 11 should present no new problems for the Case system you have developed thus far for EP. If it does, revise your system to account for 10 vs. 11.
    Hint: In doing this, assume *parecer* is similar in its predicate argument structure and in its subcategorization to our *seem*. Notice that our *seem* is not a Case-assigner:

(12) *It seems [John]$_{N''}$.
      *It seems [John to be nice].

Furthermore, our *seem* takes a complement that is sentential and that is its only true argument.

(13) It seems (that) John is nice.

Do not consider the structure that *seem* occurs in in:

(14) John seems to be nice.

This has a different analysis which we will not discuss in this book.

Part 3

Now translate the following sentence into EP:

(15) It seems that the boys are assaulting the old lady.

There should be only two ways that you know of to grammatically translate 15 into EP— one way parallel to 9 and another way parallel to 10. You can give one translation just from the data on this homework. However, you cannot give the other translation. Why not? (What information are you lacking that keeps you from being able to do the other translation?)

[NOTE: The progressive aspect in the embedded clause in 15 should be translated into EP by a simple form of *assaltar* without any auxiliary verb. Your job is to figure out whether or not the form of *assaltar* should appear with agreement.]

Part 4

So, tell me: is the real Case-assigner for Subjects of tensed clauses [+Agr] or [+T]? Revise statement B of Case Theory in such a way that it will cover both all the EP data given here and English, as well.

Problem Set 4.11: The Cleft-Test for Constituency

One of the most relied-on tests for constituency in English is the cleft-test, which you will meet here. So even though this test is language-specific, it is important for you to be familiar with it. And when you look at the syntax of other languages, you should keep your eyes open for parallel tests.

Sentences like:

(1) It was Mary that my friend saw.
(2) Who my friend saw was Mary.

are called CLEFT-SENTENCES. The cleft in 1 is an *it*-cleft, and the cleft in 2 is a wh-cleft (because the one in 1 begins with *it* and the one in 2 begins with a question word, where most question words in English begin with *wh*—it also called a PSEUDOCLEFT).

It is possible to invert the wh-cleft around the form of the verb *be*:

(3) Mary was who my friend saw.

Let us take the liberty of calling the sentence in 3 a cleft sentence also. And let us call *Mary* the clefted item. This is the kind of cleft we will use in this exercise. So whenever I refer to cleft sentences below, I mean sentences with the form:

(4) clefted item + form of the verb *be* + wh-word + clause

(I am purposing using the vague term "clefted item" rather than any precise term that deals with structural entities we have discussed since one of your jobs in this problem set will be to figure out what kind of structural entity the clefted item can be.) In the clause at the end of the cleft sentence, we have a hole that corresponds to the clefted item:

(5) Mary is who my friend saw _____.

That is, we understand *saw* to have a Direct Object but the DO is missing. Furthermore, we understand the missing DO to be coreferential with Mary.

Do not make any assumptions about how we form cleft sentences, please. Just note that all cleft sentences have a corresponding noncleft sentence. The noncleft sentence corresponding to 3 is:

(6) My friend saw Mary.

Cleft sentences always contain a form of the copula (the verb *be*) with material both preceding and following (although not all sentences that contain a copula are cleft sentences). So examples like those in 7, which have fronted (or topicalized) items, are not cleft sentences:

(7) Mary my friend saw.
    Beans I like.
    That guy Sue just swears you're going to like.

Please do not consider topicalization sentences as you do this problem set. Instead, stick to clefts of the type seen in 3.

There may be a number of restrictions on the various parts of cleft sentences. But the clefted item in examples like 3 at first looks as if it has no restrictions on it with regard to category, although many people are not perfectly comfortable with clefted verbal items:

(8) Quickly is how she went.
    Out is where Mary went.
    Intelligent is what she is.
    ?Run is what Mary did.

Quickly is an adverb. *Out* is a preposition. *Intelligent* is an adjective. *Run* is a verb. And in 3 we found *Mary*, which is an N.

Actually, there is an important restriction on the type of category that the clefted item can be. Consider the following examples, where a line indicates the hole.

(9) The girl is who my friend saw _____.
(10) *Girl is who my friend saw the _____.
(11) Those exact dogs over there are what I'd like to buy _____.
(12) *Dogs are what I'd like to buy those exact _____ over there.

Part 1

If the clefted item is a nominal, is it an N or an NP? Support your answer with relevant data.

Part 2

In Problem Set 4.4, you learned that the Genitive marker attaches to the end of an NP. Use that fact now.

Are the following sentences consistent with your answer to Part 1 of this problem set? Why or why not? (Do not worry about where the hole is in 13 and 14. That is not the point of this question.)

(13) Jack's is whose book I saw on the table.
(14) Your brother's is whose car needs washing.

(Not all speakers get 13 and 14 easily. If you do not, treat this question as though it is asking about a variety of English that you do not speak, and simply answer the question for the grammar of the variety in which 13 and 14 are good sentences.)

Part 3

Now consider prepositions and prepositional phrases. P's are words like *in*, *out*, *after*, *with*, *to*, etc. PPs are made of a P plus its Object. Let us use the term prepositional item as a cover term for both P and PP (just like "nominal" is a cover term for both N and NP). If the clefted item is a prepositional item, is it a P or a PP?

(15)   Into the house is where she ran.
(16)   *Into is where she ran the house.

Part 4

Are the following sentences consistent with your answer to Part 3? Why or why not?

(17)   In is where she ran (not out).
(18)   Up is where Dukakis hoped to be headed.

(Hint: Recall that an NP can consist of simply an N sometimes, as in **Dogs'** *ears can be floppy*. This fact will, I hope, open up your mind as to the possibilities with prepositional items.]

Part 5

A word like *pretty* is an adjective. A string like *very pretty* is an Adjective Phrase (AP, or here AdjP).

A word like *quickly* is an adverb. A string like *too quickly* is an Adverb Phrase (also AP, or here AdvP to distinguish it from AdjP).

A word like *eat* is a verb. A string like *eat the pizza* is a VP.

Give a cleft sentence in which the clefted item is adjectival. Is it Adj or AdjP that we find here? Support your answer. (Hint: Look at the contrast in 9 vs. 10, 11 vs. 12, and 15 vs. 16. Use that as a model.)

Do the same for adverbials that have the category Adv or AdvP.

Do the same for VERBALS (where the term verbals covers V and VP).

Part 6

What is the general restriction on the category of the clefted item of a cleft sentence? (Do not talk about specific categories, like N, V, etc. Just state what type of category this initial item must be. Try to think in terms of heads vs. phrases.)

Part 7

Looking back at 8, what category does the clefted item in each sentence belong to? Be sure to make use of the answer you just gave in Part 6 and to consider whether the clefted items are heads or phrases.

Part 8

Is the string of words *up the ladder* a PP in 19?

(19)   She climbed up the ladder.

Give an argument using what you know about the clefted item of cleft-sentences to support your answer.

Part 9

Is the string of words *up the number* a PP in 20?

(20) She looked up the number.

Give an argument to support your answer.

Part 10

Some languages have POSTPOSITIONS (like Japanese). Here is an example, just for interest's sake:

Toshio-ga   [Hitomi-to]   [kuruma-de] [Kobe-ni] itta.
Toshio-SUBJ Hitomi with car   by   Kobe to   went
'Toshio went to Kobe by car with Hitomi.'

(The *ga* following *Toshio* tells us that *Toshio* is the Subject of this sentence.)
    Some languages, including all the Romance languages, have only prepositions (and no postpositions). Here is an Italian example:

Daria   andra   [con Tonino] [al negozio] [dopo cena].
'Daria will go with Tonino   to the store   after dinner.'

And some have both. Included here are Dutch and German. The following examples are from Dutch.

Prepositional Phrase:

Joop heeft [aan haar] nog vaak gedacht.
Joop has   of her   often   thought
'Joop often thought about her.'

Postpositional Phrase:

Kom   mee, [het bos   in].
come with, the forest into
'Come along, into the forest.'

    Now the question for you is whether English has any postpositional phrases. A potential candidate is *the number up* in:

(21) I can look the number up.

Is the string of words *the number up* a PP in 21 (where PP stands for postpositional phrase here)? Give an argument to support your answer.

Part 11

Compare 20 to 21. Please list three other combinations besides *look . . . up* that can have this same kind of varying word order. (This is not complicated. It should not take you more than a few minutes to find them.) These are generally called VERB-PARTICLE combinations.

Problem Set 4.12: ASL Highlighting

American Sign Language makes use of a number of structures to highlight information. One of them consists of a clause that contains a final wh-word, followed by a single phrase. The signer raises his or her eyebrows as he/she signs the wh-word (but not elsewhere in the structure). The wh-word is followed by a blink, a head nod, or both. Sometimes a short pause precedes the final phrase. I will indicate this structure in the following way:

br   hn

LEE PAINT WHAT,   CHAIR

(br = brows raised; hn = head nod or blink. A comma indicates a possible pause.)

Two analyses have been proposed for this structure, which I will call by the neutral name of HIGHLIGHTING.

In one analysis we have a rhetorical question followed by an answer. This would be equivalent to the English:

What did Lee paint? A chair.

said by a single speaker.

In the other analysis we have a single sentence that consists of a clause plus a phrase. This would be equivalent to the English wh-cleft structure, as in:

What Lee painted was a chair.

(If you didn't do Problem Set 4.11, please look at it briefly now to learn a bit about clefts.)

In this problem set I'd like you to argue for one analysis over the other. In doing that, you should consider all of the following information (which is organized into four points). Some of this information is clearly indicative. Some of it is more problematical. It is your job to try to see the connections. Be sure to discuss each of the four points separately.

First, particular brow movement appears in questions. In true wh-questions and *yes/ no* questions, the brows are raised or squinted throughout the question. Often the eyes are wide. The body may tilt forward (and generally does so in *yes/ no* questions) and the shoulders may raise. The head is usually tilted to the side or back. All of these facial and body movements together are indicated by wh-q (for question marker), as in the question:

wh-q

ARRIVE WHEN

(Although I wrote *wh-q* at the end of the construction, you are to interpret these facial and body movements as being continuous throughout the construction.)

In rhetorical questions (whether *wh-*, such as *Oh, what will become of me?*, or *yes/ no*, such as *Does a bear shit in the woods?*), on the other hand, the brows are furrowed throughout the entire question and often the head tilts. These facial and body movements together are indicated by rhq (for rhetorical-question marker).

Second, head nods appear in certain focusing constructions. For example, the following structure has been labeled topicalization, where a whole VP is fronted:

$$\underline{\qquad\text{br}\qquad}\qquad\underline{\;\text{hn}\;}$$

CHASE CAT,   DOG

Additionally, the fronted elements in a topicalization structure can be accompanied by raised brows and are optionally followed by a short pause (as indicated in the structure here). The example here is roughly equivalent to the English sentence:

As for chasing the cat, the dog did it.

Head nods do not generally appear in true or rhetorical questions.

Third, the signer (or speaker) does not expect an answer to a rhetorical question (by either the signer/ speaker or the addressee), although one is possible.

Fourth, in true wh-questions the position of the wh-word varies. Typically it appears in final position (as shown in the wh-question preceding) or in situ:

$$\underline{\qquad\qquad\text{wh-q}\qquad\qquad}$$

WHO GIVE$_2$ BOOK

This corresponds to the English question:

Who gave you a book?

(The subscript on the V indicates agreement with a second person Object.) But very commonly the wh-word can be repeated, appearing in both initial and final position, in what is called BRACING:

$$\underline{\qquad\qquad\qquad\qquad\text{wh-q}\qquad}$$

HOW HAPPEN DEAF HOW

This corresponds to the English sentence:

How did you become Deaf?

Likewise, WHEN and WHO in the other two questions shown earlier can appear on both ends of the structure.

Problem Set 4.13: Five Quicky Questions on a Variety of Topics

1. In Problem Set 4.7 you learned that resultatives in English can be predicated only of theme arguments. Consider the following Japanese sentences that contain resultatives. Does the same restriction appear to hold for Japanese or not? Explain your answer.

    (1)   Taroo-ga uti-o siroku nutta.
            Taro   house white painted
            'Taro painted his house white.'
    (2)   *Taroo-ga kutakutani hasitta.
            Taro   dead tired ran
            '(intended meaning) Taro became tired as a result of running.'

(3) Pan-ga makkuroni kogeta.
     bread   black   burned
     'The bread burned black.'

(4) Hune-ga suityuu   hukaku sizunda.
     ship   in water deep   sank
     'The ship sank deep in water.'

2. Many languages have special syntactic structures for handling notions like causation, as in the English:

I made Mary read Latin.
I had Mary read Latin.

The causative construction in Romance languages has received a lot of attention because it raises important questions about the relationship between argument structure and syntactic structure. Here is a grammatical causative sentence in Catalan, spoken in the area of Barcelona.

(1) Els   faré   dormir junts.
    them I-will-make sleep   together
    'I will make them sleep together.'

Els is a clitic Object, cliticized to the verb *faré*. It is not grammatical to say instead:

(2) *Faré   dormir-los junts.
    I-will-make   sleep-them together
    'I will make them sleep together.'

Here *los* is a clitic Object (the form we would expect attached to an infinitive), but it cannot be attached to the infinitive verb *dormir*.

Normally in Catalan (as in other Romance languages) a clitic must attach to the verb of its own clause.

What is the argument status of the word translated as "them" in these examples? How is its attachment to *faré* problematic?

3. In Problem Set 4.3, you learned that English has a verb string that allows four different types of auxiliaries: modals, the perfect *have*, the progressive *be*, the passive *be*. We analyzed them in this chapter as being of the category V and as taking VP complements, so that the verb string *may have spoken* would have the analysis:

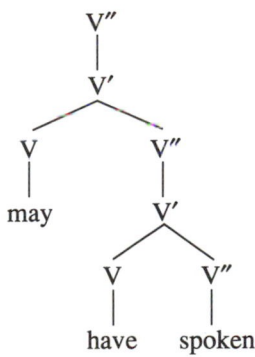

We distinguished auxiliary verbs, which take V″ complements, from main verbs that take sentential complements. In English this is quite easy to do since even if a sentential complement has a null Subject (that is, big PRO), the verbal string will be distinguishable since it will always begin with *to*. Thus while:

Mary may leave.

has a V *(may)* that takes a VP complement *(leave)*, the sentence

Mary expects to leave.

has a V *(expects)* that takes a sentential complement *(to leave)*, like so:

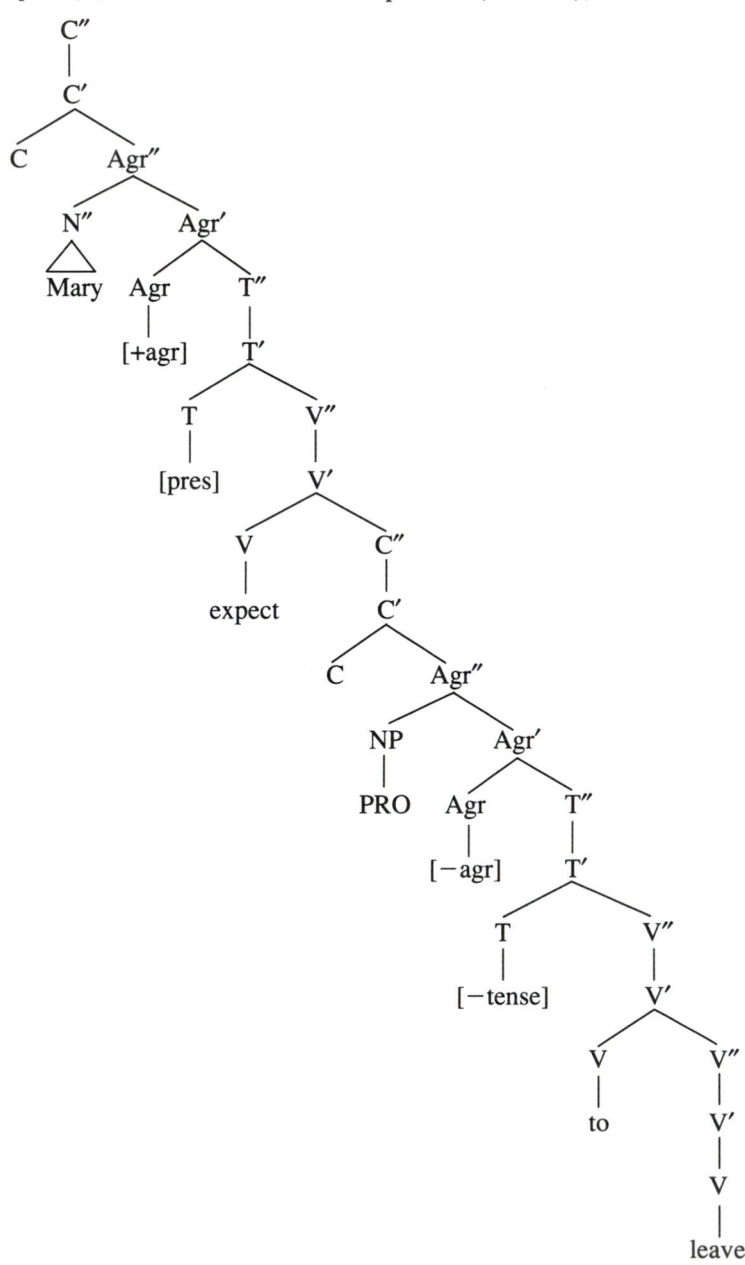

(Actually, there is debate over details in this tree, particularly regarding the position of *to*—which some generate at DS under one of the inflectional nodes—but those debates don't concern us here.)

In other languages, however, it is more difficult to distinguish between V's that take VP complements (that is, auxiliaries) and V's that take infinitival sentential complements, since there may be no flag parallel to our *to* that signals the difference. Hausa, a Chadic language spoken in Nigeria, presents relevant data. Consider these examples:

(1) Aabù tā sō   wankè tukunyā.
    Aabù   like wash pot
    'Aabù wanted to wash a pot.'
(2) Aabù tā tàfi wankè tukunyā.
    Aabù   go   wash pot
    'Aabù went to wash a pot.'
(3) Aabù tā dainà   wankè tukunyā.
    Aabù   stop/cease wash pot
    'Aabù stopped washing the pot.'
(4) Aabù tā fārà   wankè tukunyā.
    Aabù   start/begin wash pot
    'Aabù started washing the pot.'

Other verbs that pattern the same way concern notions like doing to an excessive degree, being bothered or annoyed at doing, postponing or failing to do, being capable of doing, finish doing, return to or resume doing, be about to do or almost do, be unable to do, not do as usual, manage or succeed to do, do often or do a lot, share doing, take steps toward doing, persist in or persevere in doing, keep doing.

The question I'd like you to discuss (briefly, a half page should do it) is whether these Hausa verbs take a VP complement or a sentential complement. In this discussion, please consider the following facts.

First, none of these verbs can take tensed sentential complements. Thus, while *may* cannot take a tensed complement in English, *expect* can:

*Mary may [that she will leave].
Mary expects [that she will leave].

But *fārà* 'start/begin,' for example, cannot:

(5) *Audù yā fārà [(pro) yā aurē tà]
    'Audù started marrying her.'

(Hausa is a pro-drop language; thus there is no audible pronoun in the tensed embedded clause here, and I have signaled that fact by putting in little pro in parentheses.) *Yā* is the morpheme that indicates the past tense (in both clauses).

Second, the majority of these verbs do not allow lexical Subjects in their complements. Thus, while *may* cannot have a lexical Subject in its complement, *expect* can (even in a tenseless complement):

*Mary may [Sue leave].
Mary expects [Sue to leave].

But *dingà* 'keep on,' for example, cannot, even if its complement is a tenseless subjunctive:

(6) *Audù yā dingà [Bàlā tàfi].
    'Audù kept on [Bàlā to leave].'
(7) *Audù yā dingà [Bàlā yà tàfi].
    'Audù kept on [that Bàlā should leave].'

In 7 *yà* is the morpheme that shows subjunctive mood (as well as showing that *Bàlā* is masculine).

Now complicate your discussion a bit further (another half-page at most) by noting the relevance of the fact that English has verbs like *try*, which take a complement that begins with infinitival *to*:

Mary tried to leave.

but which cannot take tensed sentential complements:

*Mary tried that she should leave.

And which cannot have lexical Subjects on their complements:

*Mary tried herself to leave.

4. Consider the following ungrammatical question.

*Who did Sally get angry because Paul hated?
 (cf. Sally got angry because Paul hated someone.)

What is the name of the constraint that this question violates? What is the name of the principle that that constraint is an example of?

5. The rule responsible for the position of the auxiliary verb in questions such as:

Has John left?
What will you do now?

is traditionally called Subject-Auxiliary Inversion. How is that name a misnomer? What rule is really responsible for the position of the auxiliary verb here?

*Problem Set 4.14: Five Not-so-Quicky Questions on a Variety of Topics

1. In Japanese the word for 'self' is *zibun*. It has two uses in which it can occur without a linguistic antecedent.

One use is when *zibun* refers to the speaker—first person singular, as in:

(1) *Zibun*-wa gakusei desu.
    self-TOP student be

'Self be a student.'
"I am a student."

(2) Butyoo-ga   zibun-ni soo iimasita.
    captain-SUBJ self-IO   so   said
    'The {captain/division manager} told self so.'
    "The {captain/division manager} told me so."

This use is limited to some dialects, such as the Kansai dialect.

The other use is when *zibun* refers to the person spoken to—second person singular only—and this use is rather recent in the spoken language, as in:

(3) *Zibun*-ga matigatteru-yo.
    self-TOP   wrong
    'Self be wrong.'
    "You are wrong."

(4) Taroo-ga *zibun*-o suki-da -to   itte-ita-yo.
    Taro-TOP self-DO   like   -Comp saying-was
    'Taro said (he) likes self.'
    "Taro said he likes you."

(Not all speakers accept 4 with the reading here. In fact, this is a rare usage. Note that for all speakers 4 also has the reading in which *zibun* is coreferential with the Subject of its own clause.)

We are going to ignore the uses in 1–4 (which are, indeed, unusual) and concentrate only on the use of *zibun* that has a third person referent. Let me give you some facts about this *zibun*, which has been claimed to have some properties of anaphors.

Part 1

First, neither 1 nor 3 can be interpreted to mean that some other third-person not mentioned elsewhere in the sentence is a student (as in 1) or is wrong (as in 3). The verb is not inflected for person or number agreement in Japanese. Therefore the absence of this reading cannot be due to any problems with verb agreement. Given that, what property does *zibun* with a third person referent have in common with the vast majority of uses of English anaphors?

Part 2

In some ways *zibun* with a third person referent is more restricted than English third-person anaphors. Identify one way, given the data here:

(5) Taroo$_i$-ga Michi$_j$-ni zibun$_{i/*j}$-no koto nituite hanasita.
    Taro-SUBJ Michi-IO   self- GEN   matter about talked
    'Taro$_i$ talked to Michi$_j$ about self's$_{i/*j}$ matter.'
    "Taro talked to Michi about his (only Taro's) matter."

(In 5 the *no* particle is comparable to a Genitive marker within an NP, like the *'s* of English.) The important point is that 5 is not ambiguous. We understand *zibun* to be coreferential with *Taroo* only.

You will have to make a stab at it, since there are not many sentences I can give you to make the point. If you have no idea after looking at all the Japanese sentences given to you on this problem set, then just skip this question.

Part 3

In other ways *zibun* with a third-person referent is less restricted than most uses of English anaphors. Tell me one way, given the data here:

(6) Taroo$_i$-ga   Michi$_j$-ni   [Hitomi-ga   zibun$_{i/*j}$-o   suite-iru]-to   itta.
Taro-SUBJ Michi-IO Hitomi-SUBJ self   -DO liking-is -Comp said
'Taro$_i$ said to Michi$_j$ [that Hitomi likes self$_{i/*j}$].'
"Taro told Michi that Hitomi likes him (Taro only)."

Comp = complementizer. (NOTE: The use of *zibun* in 6 is often called a LONG-DISTANCE anaphor use. Many languages have long-distance anaphor uses, including Mandarin Chinese, Icelandic, and Italian.)

2. The verb *melt* appears in a transitive-intransitive alternation:

(1) Floyd melted the glass.
(2) The glass melted.

Notice that *melt* differs from an optionally transitive verb like *eat*:

(3) Floyd ate potatoes.
(4) Floyd ate.

How? State the difference between alternating verbs like *melt* and optionally transitive verbs like *eat* in terms of which argument in their predicate structure is missing from the intransitive sentence.

Give five other verbs that participate in transitive/ intransitive pairs like *melt* in 1 and 2, with example sentences for each.

Verbs like *melt* have been labeled UNACCUSATIVES (also called ergatives—but that term, as you know from Chapter 3, is also applied to languages with a particular morphological pattern in their Case system) and a sentence like 2 has been claimed to involve syntactic movement.

With this analysis we have only one verb *melt*, which can be used in both transitive and intransitive sentences. *Melt* is semantically analyzed as involving the change of state from a solid to a liquid, with the possibility of a varied number of participants in this change of state. The essential participant is the item which actually changes state (the glass in 1). But *melt* has the option of also taking another participant which is understood as an agent— someone who brings about the change of state (Floyd in 1). So the predicate-argument structure of *melt* requires one and allows up to two arguments. The argument which undergoes the change of state is linked to Direct Object position:

(5) _____ melted the glass.

Now if there is an agent present, the agent will be linked to Subject position, as in 1. But if there is no agent present, the Subject slot will be empty at DS (as in 5).

English, however, does not permit empty Subject positions at SS and 5 is not a good sentence at SS. In order to generate 2, a syntactic rule takes the Direct Object in a DS like 5 and moves it into Subject position:

(6) [The glass]$_i$ melted t$_i$.

Many arguments have been given to support the proposal of a movement rule in unaccusative sentences like 2, but in my opinion the strongest arguments are based on data from languages other than English. English, instead, presents a number of problems for this analysis of 2. Using the data that follow, discuss one of those problems.

(7) The man rang the bell.
   The bell rang.
   The bell rang the hour of the Mass.
(8) The butcher bled the cow.
   The cow bled.
   The cow bled all her blood out.

3. Sentences 1 and 2 have very similar strings of words:

(1) John wants to understand math.
(2) John seems to understand math.

However, they are syntactically and semantically quite different.

Think first about predicate-argument structure. Is John in 1 an argument of *want*? Certainly. It is the agent argument. Is John an argument of *understand*? Again, the answer is yes. He's the experiencer.

Is *John* in 2 an argument of *seem*? If you aren't sure, go through the types of arguments we know about (agents, themes, beneficiaries, instruments, experiencers) and ask whether John is playing any of these participant roles. Do you see how John doesn't nicely fit into any of these classes? What really 'seems'? The whole proposition that John understands math, right? So John is not an argument of *seem*. Is John an argument of *understand*? Yes, of course.

Given that we will link our arguments to GFs at DS, the DS of 1 and 2 will, accordingly, be different, since the argument structures of *seem* and *want* are different. You already know the DS of 1: This is a sentence that involves control:

John wants [PRO to understand math].

The DS that has been proposed for 2 is:

_____ seems [John to understand math]

That is, the Subject position for *seem* is empty at DS (which I have indicated with "_____").

The SS of 1 is identical to its DS. *John* controls the interpretation of big PRO, allowing us to correctly understand John to be an argument of both *want* and *understand*.

The SS of 2, however, is different from its DS. *John* is moved from Subject position of the lower clause to Subject position of the higher clause, leaving behind a trace, like so:

John$_i$ seems [t$_i$ to understand math].

This movement rule has been called RAISING, since a constituent of a lower clause is raised up into a higher clause. Unlike wh-movement, it moves a phrase into an argument position. For this reason, it is often referred to as NP-MOVEMENT (since the landing site for movement is a typical NP-slot).

The first question for you is whether NP-movement is a good movement rule or a bad movement rule, judging by the standards we discussed in the text when contrasting the so-called good movement rules of head-to-head movement and wh-movement to the so-called bad movement rules of Dative Movement and Passive (the version of Passive that derives passive sentences from the corresponding active sentences). Explain your answer by discussing those standards.

Second, is NP-movement a head movement or a phrase movement rule? Give examples to support your answer.

Third, give at least one other verb of English beside *seem* that at DS takes an empty Subject, but at SS can have a derived Subject.

Fourth, discuss why 3 is a bad sentence but 4 is a good sentence by going back to the predicate-argument structure of *want* and *seem*:

(3) *It wants that John understands math.
(4)   It seems that John understands math.

4. Consider this sentence:

Mary loves madrigals and Paul loves sonnets.

Form a direct question that corresponds to this sentence in which instead of the NP *madrigals* we have the wh-phrase *what*. Give that question. Is it grammatical?

Now form the direct question that corresponds to this sentence in which instead of the NP *sonnets* we have the wh-phrase *what*. Give that question. Is it grammatical?

Does the wh-movement in either of the two questions you formed violate the Adverbial Island Constraint, the Sentential Subject Constraint, or the Wh-Island Constraint? Explain your answer.

Does the wh-movement in either of the two questions you formed violate the Subjacency Principle as we stated it in the text? Explain your answer.

If you said that none of the constraints nor the principle was violated, what do you think makes extraction from only one of the conjuncts here ungrammatical? Don't just guess wildly. Make a hypothesis and test it. (And this last question of the problem set should not be graded by your instructor, but only commented on.)

5. In all the wh-questions we looked at in this chapter, the wh-phrase started out in some position other than Subject. Indeed, wh-phrases can start out in DO, IO, and OP position, as well as in an adverbial position:

What have you written?
Who have you written to?

What have you written about?
Why have you written that letter to Paul?

And this is true for direct and indirect questions:

I wonder what you wrote.
I wonder who you wrote to.
I wonder what you wrote about.
I wonder why you wrote that letter to Paul.

But when a wh-phrase starts out in Subject position, the linear order of the words at PF does not exhibit movement in an obvious way:

Who wrote that?
I wonder who wrote that.

It's been proposed that even when a wh-phrase sta..s out in Subject position, it undergoes wh-movement into specifier of C. How does the following sentence bear on that issue?

(1) Who did Mary say left?

And, now, how does 2 bear on that issue?

(2) *What did she wonder who saw?
    (cf. She wondered who saw what.)

Problem Set 4.15: Minimalism

1. Consider the derivation of this sentence in the Minimalist Program:

(1)   John said that Bill left.

Give at least two reasons why the alternative derivation in which *Bill* moves from specifier of the V of the embedded clause into specifier of Agr_S in the higher clause crashes:

(2)   *Bill said John that left.

(In 2, *John* is in spec of V of the matrix clause and *Bill* is in spec of Agr_S of the matrix clause.)

One reason should concern a problem with leaving *John* in the position of specifier of the matrix clause's V. Another reason should concern a problem with the movement of *Bill* from the specifier of the embedded clause's V to specifier of the Agr_S of the matrix clause (past the empty specifier of the Agr_S of the embedded clause). If you can come up with additional reasons, great.

2. Consider sentences that have fronted elements other than wh-phrases, such as:

(1) Into the woods ran the little boy.
(2) Quickly she snatched the eggs.

Give a brief discussion of what issues such sentences raise for the MP. Do they involve movement (that is, copying)? If so, what motivates the movement?

3. In this problem I'd like to lead you to an argument for locating Agr_O in the tree as we have done—that is, with the maximal projection being a sister to T and the head taking the maximal projection of V as its sister, like so:

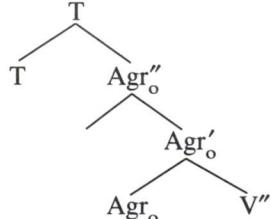

First, assume that a V and its DO are syntactic sisters in all languages.

Second, assume that branching is universally rightward. So before any movement (that is, copy) applications, a complement will always follow its head in every language. What does this mean about the relative order of a verb and its DO before any movements?

Third, assume that there is a universal arrangement of all functional heads with respect to lexical heads in the tree. That is, if Agr_O takes VP as its complement in one language, it will take VP as its complement in all languages.

Fourth, assume that in both French and Italian, head movement of the verb occurs before Spell Out (as discussed in the chapter text). Assume, likewise, that the DO moves into spec of Agr_O before Spell Out.

Now, the ordinary word order in both languages is SVO, as in:

Marie lit le roman.
Maria legge il romanzo.
'Maria reads the novel.'

What does that tell us about the location of Agr_O in the tree with respect to Agr_S? Does it tell us anything about the location of Agr_O in the tree with respect to projections of T? Does it tell us anything about the location of Agr_O in the tree with respect to projections of V? Be sure to state which assumptions you are making crucial use of in your answers.

Okay, now in Japanese the ordinary word order is SOV, as in:

Taroo-ga Mieko-o mita.
'Taroo saw Mieko.'

Does movement of the DO into spec of Agr_O take place before or after Spell Out? How do you know? Does head movement of the V take place before or after Spell Out? How do you know?

What does Japanese show us about the location of Agr_O in the tree with respect to projections of V?

At this point you should be able to locate Agr_O in the tree with respect to both Agr_S and projections of V. So what is the only question remaining to you in order to justify the precise arrangment of Agr_O between projections of T and projections of V?

4. Again, assume that all languages have identical tree arrangements, given here (where no movement has yet taken place).

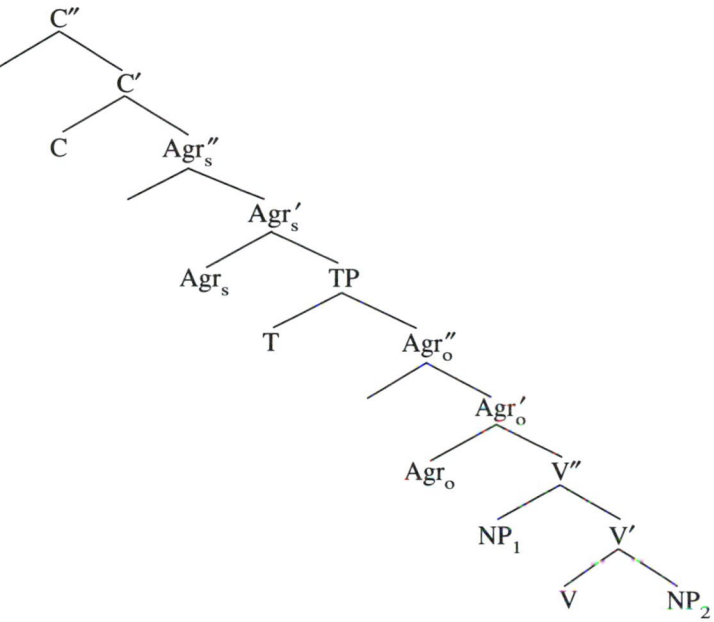

(I drew a left branch in spec position for both Agr projections to indicate where the NPs will move if they move. I projected C and spec of C to allow for sentences that fill those positions.) After movements of the head V and of both NPs, we'll have:

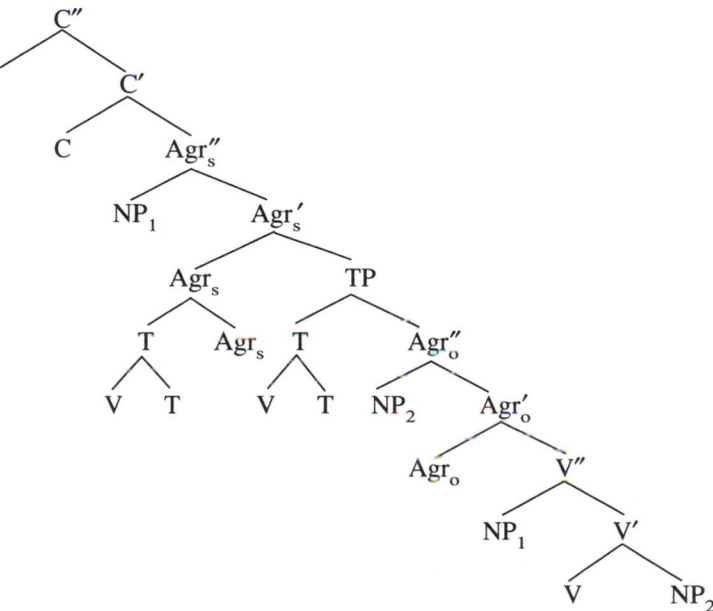

In this tree the copy of V is an adjunct of T, and the copy of the newly formed T (which now branches) is an adjunct of Agr$_S$.

Okay, now some languages have VSO order at PF, such as Irish and Welsh. In these languages, what movement(s) takes place before Spell Out and how do you know?

Other languages have SOV order at PF, such as Japanese. In these languages, what movement(s) takes place before Spell Out and how do you know?

Now give a very simple characterization of the difference between VSO, SVO, and SOV languages in terms of the relative ordering of certain copying rules with respect to Spell Out.

5

Semantics

Chapter Organization—for the Instructor

We take one sentence and approach it from varying points of view. This one sentence leads us from a speech-acts-based semantics to a conceptual semantics to a lexical semantics. From there we move into a model-theoretic semantics. We discuss those rudimentary points of logic that help in understanding the formal semantics model at issue. We therefore concern ourselves with different sentences in the second half of this chapter, focusing on sentences with quantifiers.

Okay, let's go

Consider this sentence:

George Washington entered the church.

What does it mean?

While that may seem like a simple enough question (and my husband just said, "It means the guy entered the church"), there are many different ways one could go about answering it.

Speech Acts

Certainly the meaning of a sentence is at least partly composed of the meanings of the words in the sentence. However, a sentence also has a meaning that goes beyond the words in the sentence—meaning that is related to context. We will begin our discussion by looking first at that contextually dependent meaning.

For example, consider the context in which I have commissioned someone to paint a picture of George Washington on a Sunday. If I uttered the sentence to the painter, how might the painter interpret it? What I'm asking you to do is analyze this utterance as a SPEECH ACT, that is, within a given context.

Certainly, the painter is going to understand the undeniable part of the act, the uttering of the statement that George Washington entered the church. Any speech act has as one of its parts this LOCUTIONARY ACT. But in this context the speech act could be taken as not only a statement but a direction or order from me to the painter, equivalent in PRAGMATIC force to a variety of other utterances, such as *Paint him entering the church, not just standing outside it.* This part of the act is called the ILLOCUTIONARY ACT. It is the intention of the locutionary act. Illocutionary acts can be orders or warnings or advice or acts of persuasion, and so on.

Now consider the context in which I am the mother of a girl for whom George Washington is a great idol and we are visiting the church he used to attend. If she refuses to enter the church and I say the sentence, how might you interpret it? The locutionary act is, of course, the same. That's because the locutionary act is not dependent upon the context. But the illocutionary act here differs, since illocutionary acts are dependent upon context. This speech act could be taken as having as one of its parts the illocutionary act of persuading. A PARAPHRASE for that particular force of the utterance might be *If you want to be like George Washington, you should enter the church.*

Find a third context for our same utterance that constitutes yet a different illocutionary act.

What we're talking about here is meaning as social or pragmatic use. And there is quite a literature on this approach to meaning. (In fact, it's been argued that every speech act constitutes not just a locutionary and an illocutionary act, but a third kind of act that you will meet in Problem Set 5.1.) No adequate theory of meaning can ignore the ways in which we use language to convey messages and illocutionary acts are of major importance in communication. So let's look a bit more at these acts.

Tell me: Can you think of contexts in which uttering *George Washington entered the church* necessarily constitutes the illocutionary act of ordering the painter to paint him entering? I hope you got convinced pretty quickly that you couldn't (unless you did something like redefine the particular lexical items in the sentence). Thus, regardless of context, it is not a CONTRADICTION to say:

George Washington entered the church, but don't paint him entering it.

But it is a contradiction to say:

→←Paint George Washington entering the church, but don't paint him entering it.

(Two arrows meeting head on are the symbol for a contradiction.) So while the determination of the locutionary act of any utterance is something we should all agree on, the determination of the illocutionary act might well be controversial. That's because when we talk about language use, we are talking about cooperative social interaction that is based on real-world experience.

Thus, an extremely agorophobic person who has had few experiences outside the home might interpret the illocutionary act of an utterance such as *It's going to rain tonight* differently from the person who has plans to go to a play this evening. The agorophobe could take the sentence as a simple description of facts that might indeed not be of much interest. But the person who plans to go to a play might take the sentence as a warning to take suitable precautions against the weather (such as bringing along an umbrella).

Performatives

Now consider these two sentences:

Father Pagliari baptized my son.
I baptize you.

What is the illocutionary act of the first utterance? I hope this question stumped you. We can't even begin to guess without knowing the context for the utterance, right? What is the illocutionary act of the second utterance? If we assume that the APPROPRIACY CONDITIONS for this utterance are met—that is, that someone who has the authority to baptize others is the speaker of this sentence—then the illocutionary act is, indeed, a baptism.

Sentences like *I baptize you*, in which **the locutionary act is equivalent to the illocutionary act** (here the utterance is itself an act of baptism) are called PERFORMATIVES and the verb *baptize* is a performative verb. The very saying of the sentence *I baptize you* is the act of baptizing itself. Is every sentence that uses the verb *baptize* a performative sentence? Of course not. The sentence we just saw, *Father Pagliari baptized my son*, is not a performative, because the utterance of this sentence is not the act of baptizing.

Which of these four sentences is performative?

John and Sue married each other.
I now pronounce you husband and wife.
The rabbi married John and Sue.
The rabbi pronounced John and Sue husband and wife.

The second, right? Because the very act of uttering it is an act of marriage. Can you think of other performative predicates? Give at least one, and use it in two sentences, where one is nonperformative and the other is performative.

Performatives differ from nonperformatives (also called CONSTATIVES) in a variety of ways. Can you notice anything about their form that seems to be constant? If the Subject of a performative sentence is overtly expressed (that is, audible), what must it be; is it limited to any specific person? Almost always the Subject of a performative is first person, although there are times when a passive sentence can be a performative. For example, if at the end of a trial a judge announces:

The defendant is sentenced to ten years.

the utterance is equivalent to the sentencing.

What about the time frame of a performative utterance; is it limited in any way? Compare:

I baptize you.
I am baptizing you.

Are both performatives? Think about this a moment. There's a significant difference between the simple present and the present progressive. The present progressive is a description of the act of baptism; the utterance does not constitute an act of baptism. Only the sentence in the simple present is a performative. Indeed, quite generally performatives with an overt Subject are limited to the simple present tense.

There are also additional meaning differences between performatives and constatives that we haven't yet discussed. Consider these two sentences:

> I wish you wouldn't leave.
> I order you not to leave.

Is either a performative? The second is, because the locutionary act is the order and the very utterance of this sentence constitutes the order, so the locutionary act and the illocutionary act are identical.

Now, is the first sentence *Father Pagliari baptized my son* true or false? Well, that depends, right? We need to look at the context in which the sentence is uttered and find out if it's true. That is, we need to ascertain whether Father Pagliari actually baptized the son of the speaker of that utterance. But certainly it is either true or false. What about the second sentence, the performative? Is it true or false?

What about the performative sentence *I baptize you*? Is it true or false? Will looking at the context of the utterance help us to decide this? If you're confused, that's fine. Some have said that performatives simply don't have truth values. They are merely FELICITOUS or INFELICITOUS, where a felicitous utterance is one whose appropriacy conditions are met. That is, they are either used appropriately or not. For example, if I, being a lay person, were to say to you, "I baptize you Jonathan," the sentence would be inappropriate under the ordinary reading of *baptize*.

Others have said that peformatives are true when their felicity conditions are met but false when they aren't. So if I am a priest in the situation of baptizing a child and I say, "I baptize you Jonathan," the sentence is true. But if I am not a priest (or some other appropriate member of the clergy) and/or if I'm just walking down the street with you and I say that same sentence, the sentence is false.

Assertions and Presuppositions

Since we've brought up the issue of truth, let's explore it a bit more to see another meaning and form difference between performatives and constatives. Consider these two sentences:

> Jeff's a painter.
> Jeff isn't a painter.

Let's say that in a given context, the first sentence is true. What does that mean about the truth value of the second sentence in that same context? It's false. Negation changes the truth value of an ASSERTION. The first sentence asserts that Jeff has the property of being a painter. But is that the only information that the speaker of the first sentence has committed himself to the truth of? What else is this speaker taking as true? Compare that sentence to:

> If there's a boy in that class, he might be a painter.

Now you can see that the first sentence *(Jeff's a painter)* PRESUPPOSES that Jeff exists, while the third sentence *(If there's a boy in that class, he might be a painter)* does not presuppose that such a boy exists.

Okay, go back to our original sentence about Jeff and its negated counterpart. Does negation affect presuppositions, like it affects assertions? No. When we say *Jeff isn't a painter*, we still presuppose the existence of Jeff.

Factives

Before we return to performatives, let's explore this assertion/presupposition difference a little more. We can presuppose a lot more than just the existence of referents of noun phrases. Consider these two sentences:

Mary said that Jeff failed the exam.
Mary is angry that Jeff failed the exam.

What does each assert in terms of propositions? (We have been using the term "proposition" since Chapter 4—**propositions are the semantic entities that correspond to the syntactic entities called sentences.**) That is, what does each assert in terms of complete events, with an action or state and participants in that action or state? What does each presuppose? To see this, try negating both sentences:

Mary didn't say that Jeff failed the exam.
Mary isn't angry that Jeff failed the exam.

Now can you see? The *say* sentences assert that Mary did or didn't say that Jeff failed the exam, but the speaker is not giving any information as to the truth or falsity of whether or not Jeff failed the exam. But the *be angry* sentences assert that Mary was or wasn't angry that Jeff failed the exam, and, furthermore, they tell us that the speaker is taking as a truth that Jeff did, indeed, fail the exam. We say that predicates like *be angry* presuppose the truth of their complement sentences (that is, *be angry* presupposes the truth of its sentential Object).

Another test for presupposition is questioning. Consider this pair:

Did Mary say that Jeff failed the exam?
Is Mary angry that Jeff failed the exam?

Again, the speaker is not making any commitment toward the truth or falsity of Jeff's failing the exam in the first question. But in the second question the speaker takes as a given that Jeff did, indeed, fail the exam.

Predicates like *be angry* are called FACTIVE predicates. While most predicates are nonfactive, several are factive. In these two sentences, which has a factive predicate?

Sally was surprised she convinced the principal.
Sally tried to convince the principal.

The *surprise* sentence, right? The speaker takes as a truth that the principal was convinced by Sally. (You can demonstrate that to yourself by doing the negation and question tests.)

Can we ever deny or dissassociate the presuppositions of a factive sentence? Sure we can.

Mary isn't angry that Jeff failed the exam because he didn't, in fact, fail. He got the lowest passing grade.

But notice that we have to deny the presupposition explicitly (as we did here), or the hearer will understand us to be committing ourselves to the truth of the embedded proposition.

Back to Performatives

All right, now let's look at what happens to performatives when we negate them:

I promise I'll buy anything Jeff wants.
I don't promise I'll buy anything Jeff wants.

The first sentence is a performative because the act of uttering it is, in itself, the promise. But what about the second sentence? The utterance of the second sentence is no longer a promise, and negation here has changed a performative into a constative. In general, performatives are positive, not negative.

What about the presuppositions of the performative? Do they hold constant even under negation? Sure, they do: Jeff is presupposed to exist in both sentences.

The Cooperative Principle

I have said that in order for an utterance such as *I baptize you* to be understood as a performative, the speaker must be someone with the authority to perform the ceremony of baptism. That was an appropriacy condition of the utterance. And, in general, performatives have certain appropriacy conditions that are specific to the individual performative predicate.

Let's take the idea of appropriacy conditions to heart and ask a far-reaching question now: Are there any assumptions we make about the speaker and/or hearer of all utterances (not just performatives) pretty much regardless of context? To answer this, let's look at a speech situation.

A friend walks in the front door. I say to her:

There's a pot of coffee on the stove.

How might she interpret that utterance? Unless my friend thinks I've simply gone bananas, she will assume that my utterance has a RELATION to the context. In other words, my utterance has to be interpreted as somehow relevant. What would the illocutionary act here be? An invitation to have a cup of coffee, right?

Okay, now let's follow the friend into the kitchen. She looks around and sees the coffee pot on the stove, but also a plate piled high with fresh doughnuts. I didn't mention that there were doughnuts in the kitchen, but I did mention the coffee on the stove. My friend wants a doughnut, but hesitates to take one. Why? What might she be assuming? That the doughnuts are for someone else, right? That is, my friend assumes that when I said, "There's a pot of coffee on the stove," I was saying all the relevant information—I was not holding back any information relevant to her. In other words, the QUANTITY of my utterance was appropriate.

Now she takes the coffee pot and fills a cup. Yikes! It's tea, not coffee. She's surprised. Why? Because my friend assumed the truthfulness of my utterance—in other words, she assumed the QUALITY of my utterance was good.

She is about to call out to me when she notices that there's another pot, a spaghetti pot, on the stove. She looks in it and, lo and behold, she finds coffee. Now she's annoyed at me. Why? Because she assumed that when I said, "There's a pot of coffee on the stove," I meant the coffee was in a coffee pot. People don't generally expect coffee to be in a spaghetti pot. So I should have told her there was a spaghetti pot full of coffee right from the start. The MANNER of my utterance was all wrong; I was being obscure.

Why did my friend make all these assumptions? What is the overall guiding principle that she had in mind as she interpreted my original utterance? That I was being cooperative, right? What we've just been talking about are called the four MAXIMS of Grice's COOPERATIVE PRINCIPLE. (H.P. Grice is the philosopher who developed these maxims.) I'll state them baldly, but you can interpret them more subtly.

Relation: Be relevant.
Quantity: Be as informative as required and not more informative than required.
Quality: Be truthful. Don't lie and don't say what you don't know to be true.
Manner: Be perspicacious. Avoid obscurity, ambiguity, disorderliness, rambling.

If you know another language well and that language goes with a culture quite different from the cultures in America, you might want to ask yourself whether these maxims hold of that language and whether that language exhibits other maxims.

These maxims are claimed to be the foundation for some of the ways we understand the IMPLICATURES of language—the things that aren't explicitly stated, but that the speaker and hearer assume to be understood if the discourse is to be cooperative. And these maxims have, accordingly, been appealed to in accounting for many types of language interaction. Consider the utterance:

If you mow my lawn, I'll give you fifteen dollars.

If I said this to you and you refused to mow my lawn, what would be your reaction if I then said, "Okay," and gave you fifteen dollars anyway? You'd be surprised, right? Why? What were you INFERRING from my utterance? That if you didn't mow my lawn, I wouldn't give you money, right? Does this inference (or implicature) follow necessarily from my utterance in a logical sense? That is, if my sentence is true, must it also be true that if you didn't mow my lawn, I wouldn't give you money? What I'm asking you is whether my sentence ENTAILS the sentence that you inferred. **Sentence A entails sentence B if whenever A is true, B must also be true.** The answer is no. It isn't illogical for me to give you money. It might be silly, but it isn't illogical. An inference like this is called an INVITED INFERENCE. How did I invite that inference? And why did you infer what you inferred? What maxim(s) were we both using? The key here is the use of *if*. I made the money conditional on the mowing. If the condition were not relevant to the money, then I shouldn't have said it. So the maxims of Relation and Quantity are violated here. I said something irrelevant and I gave more information than was necessary. All I should have said is, "I'll give you fifteen dollars."

There is much more that can be said about language use, what is called PRAGMATICS, and you can consult the references in the bibliography. But I'm going to stop here because there are many other matters that I want to take up in this chapter. That does not mean, however, that your consideration of pragmatics should stop at this point. Rather, you should use it to enrich your understanding of any speech act. In fact, you were asked to make use of your implicit knowledge of pragmatics when we talked about the interpretation of elliptical sentences in Chapter 4, so you probably do this almost automatically. On that sanguine note, I'll move us ahead to our next approach to meaning.

Mental Representations and Conceptual Semantics

Okay, so let's go back to our original sentence and start again:

George Washington entered the church.

What does this sentence mean? This time we are asking: What do we understand from this sentence out of context (or, equivalently, what is common to our understanding of this sentence regardless of changing context)?

In Chapter 3 we talked briefly about mental images. Along those lines, someone might answer that the meaning of this sentence is the mental representation we have when we hear it. You might want to go back now and reread the section "Mental Images as Concepts" in Chapter 3. Our discussion there may have made you doubt the viability of a mental representation approach based on actual images. I hope so.

But there are other, more promising, approaches to the mental representation of meaning. We can try to break down, or DECOMPOSE, sentences into conceptual PRIMITIVES. What would a conceptual primitive be? Let's answer this question as concretely as possible. We'll begin by trying to find the primitives with respect to the predicate-argument structure of our sentence about George Washington.

How can you decompose the action here? The verb is *enter* (we'll talk about verbs in the uninflected form). Can you think of a paraphrase for *enter* that involves another verb that seems somehow semantically less complex? Maybe you thought of the paraphrase *go into*. In what way is *go* less semantically complex than *enter*? Well, they both involve the notion of movement along a PATH that is encoded in *go*. But *enter* also encodes the notion of an endpoint or PLACE for that movement with the result of being inside a THING.

Now can you find a paraphrase for *go* that involves another verb that is semantically less complex? Perhaps you thought of *be in motion*. But once we start saying that the concept **BE** (and we'll capitalize *concepts* to distinguish them from lexical items and boldface them to distinguish them from terminology that I'm introducing for the first time—shown in *small caps*) is part of something as basic as *go*, we find that we'll have to say **BE** is part of any verb. That may make sense, but does it help us? Does it give us insight into the relationships between verbs? I don't think so. **There is no fixed standard**

for determining what the primitives of language should be. Instead, we demand that whatever primitives we settle on help us to understand the system we're trying to represent. For that reason we will accept **GO** as a primitive. And we will say that both *enter* and *go* involve the concept **GO**.

Can you think of other verbs that share the **GO** concept that the verbs *enter* and *go* encode? Sure, there are many, such as:

    run   visit   leave

and so on.

But **GO** is not the only concept encoded in *enter*. Can you think of other verbs that share the other concept or concepts in *enter*—that is, the concepts of the end Place and the result of being in a Thing? I'm asking you to look for an even more complex verb than *enter*, because a verb that involves an end Place with the result of being in a Thing will probably also involve **GO**. So now think of ways of entering. You might have come up with verbs like

    swallow   absorb   merge

and so on. These verbs encode the concepts involved in causing one thing to enter another (among other concepts).

But does that mean that the concept here is a primitive? The relevant issue is whether breaking down the notion of an end Place with the result of being in a Thing into semantically less complex notions is possible and insightful. Certainly it's possible. We can see that part of *enter* involves going to some Place and another part involves being inside a Thing. So we might propose that *enter* is decomposed into **GO (TO (IN))**.

Is that insightful? Well, it would be if we could find the concepts of **TO** and **IN** independently from one another in other verbs. Can we? Sure. We find **TO** without **IN** in these verbs as used in these sentences:

    arrive   visit   travel
    Mary arrived Tuesday.
    Mary visits relatives at Christmas.
    Mary travels widely.

and so on. One can arrive at a house, but not enter it, for example.

On the other hand, we find **IN** without **TO** in these verbs as used in these sentences:

    inhabit   occupy   fill
    A hermit inhabits that cabin.
    Semantics occupies my mind.
    Milk filled the glass.

and so on. You might want to contrast that last sentence to *John filled the glass with milk*. What additional concept(s) is present in this new sentence?

Thus decomposing *enter* into **GO (TO (IN))** is both possible and insightful. Indeed, this kind of decomposition may be very helpful in studying the lexicon in that we would hope that such an approach would allow generalizations across classes of verbs not otherwise statable. For example, we might find that all and only verbs that contain a particular concept, such as **TO**, have a certain set of properties.

We can say that *enter* is decomposed into three FUNCTIONS. The most internal one is **IN**, which takes only one argument, a Thing, and maps it into a Place that encompasses the interior of that thing. (In our George Washington sentence the Thing is the church and it is mapped into the Place that is the inside of the church.) The next one is **TO**, which again takes only one argument, here a Place, and maps it into a Path that terminates at that place. (In our sentence the Place is the inside of the church and it is mapped into the Path that is the trajectory that terminates at the inside of the church.) The most external one is **GO**, which takes two arguments, a Thing and a Path. It maps the Thing and the Path into an Event consisting of the Thing traversing the Path. (In our sentence the Thing is George Washington and the Path is the trajectory that terminates at the inside of the church.)

So now we have decomposed not just the action encoded in *enter*, but the whole event of the sentence *George Washington entered the church*. A schematization for this analysis looks like this:

George Washington entered the church.
$[_{\text{Event}}\textbf{GO}([_{\text{Thing}}\text{ G Washington}],[_{\text{Path}}\textbf{TO}([_{\text{Place}}\textbf{IN}([_{\text{Thing}}\text{ the church}])])])]$

Tell me: Are notions like Event, Thing, Path, and Place just the conceptual counterparts of the syntactic nodes of C″, N″, and P″? One might argue that. But there is no one-to-one mapping between conceptual structure and syntactic structure. Thus the sentence:

George Washington went into the church.

has the same conceptual structure as our original sentence, but its syntactic analysis differs.

One of the implicit claims of the kind of conceptual semantics we've been looking at here, in fact, is that paraphrases that are synonymous (a concept we met in Chapter 3), that is, entirely equivalent semantically, can occur. This may seem like an utterly obvious claim to you, but it is by no means believed by all linguists. In fact, some of us would take the extreme opposite position and argue instead that if two sentences differ in syntactic and/or morphophonological form, they likewise differ in meaning. Can you discern a meaning difference, no matter how delicate, between these two sentences? I have a hard time doing it—yet I tend to believe that with enough time and effort, one could.

I leave this matter open because, in fact, it's not necessary for us to enter the debate. It is possible to have a conceptual semantics that does not claim that synonymous paraphrases exist. For example, we might have a requirement in our semantics that only the optimal (where optimality would have to be defined) syntactic realization of a given conceptual structure could surface. Thus the issue of synonymy of paraphrases need not bear on whether or not conceptual semantics is a reasonable approach to language meaning.

There is still more decomposition to be done on our original sentence, however. We could decompose the two NPs into their primitives. For *the church*, I'm sure you can already begin to see possible primitives that would allow us to reveal what it has in common with other NPs such as *the library* (another building), *the cleric* (another entity associated with religion), and even with *the dog* (another individual material object).

For *George Washington*, you might at first feel stumped. How do proper names break down into concepts? Here our personal experience is relevant. For someone who has never heard of George Washington, the name itself may carry only the information that our referent is male. Indeed, if someone isn't familiar with the first name *George*, not even maleness would be associated with the name. On the other hand, someone who knows a lot about the referent might CONSTRUE this name as encoding primitive concepts that are shared by lexical items like *general*, others that are shared by lexical items like *president*, others that are shared by lexical items like *revolutionary*, and so on. This type of information would play a role in our understanding sentences like:

He's a real George Washington.
He's a Hitler at heart.

We will not go on to decompose the two NPs *George Washington* and *the church* here, because we will talk at great length about decomposition of NPs in the next section, which is on LEXICAL SEMANTICS. This, then, concludes our discussion of conceptual semantics, and we will not deal with any other MENTALISTIC theory of meaning in this book.

You might wonder why a conceptual semantics like the one we've been discussing should be called a mentalistic theory. After all, paths and places and things and maybe even events really exist in the world. However, in this theory the various uses of a given lexical item are assigned the same conceptual structure. Thus the conceptual structure just given for *enter* in the sentence

George Washington entered the church.

would be identical to the conceptual structure of *enter* in very different sentences, such as:

George Washington entered his access code into the computer.
George Washington entered puberty.

Obviously, there are significant differences between the types of paths, places, and things involved in our sentences here and the types of paths, places, and things involved in sentences like *George Washington entered the church*; that is not at issue. The claim I ask you to focus on is that the conceptual structure is the same. If there is truly an equivalence of structure here, it must be on the psychological level.

Conceptual semantics and other such mentalistic theories are about our internal language in terms of how we construe the world or how a speaker invites a hearer to look at the world. As such it belongs more in the tradition of meaning that psychologists (and some people in artificial intelligence) work in than in the tradition that linguists work in. Linguists tend to look at meaning more in terms of the relationship of language to objects in the world, a tradition that grew out of mathematical and philosophical logic.

Should linguists look more closely at mentalistic theories? Absolutely. And the theory of conceptual semantics we looked at was developed by a linguist. There may, in fact, be few linguists who wouldn't agree that conceptualization, in its broadest sense, is the foundation for meaning. So I urge you to read the literature in conceptual semantics, which you should now be able to approach on your own. (Some is listed in the section of the bibliography for this chapter.) And I urge you to consider conceptual matters throughout the rest of this book. Indeed, there is no doubt that conceptual semantics gives substance to the theory of lexical semantics, which we are about to deal with.

Lexical Semantics

One strength of conceptual semantics is that it helps to make obvious the semantic relationships between lexical items by decomposing them into conceptual primitives. Another approach to studying lexical networks that may be as helpful in this regard is to compare lexical items with respect to their LEXICAL FEATURES (and you're familiar with those lexical features that the morphology is often sensitive to from Chapter 3, such as person, number, gender). For example, consider these lexical items:

girl   woman   witch   governess   dominatrix

Is there one or more features that all these lexical items share? Sure, they all include in their sense the feature of [+female], and, depending on your understanding of witchcraft, they may also include for you the sense of [+human]. (And there are a range of other, more encompassing features you might have thought of here—such as [+concrete] as opposed to the abstract sense of a noun like *idea*.)

But aren't the notions of femaleness and humanness conceptual primitives? Are conceptual primitives and lexical features really the same things? Some might argue that they are (although I will argue against that), and, accordingly, that conceptual semantics is a lexical semantics. Yet there is a difference in the two approaches. The goal of decomposing lexical items into conceptual primitives is to offer a mental model of our understanding of utterances; in this way it is a psychological goal. The goal of decomposing lexical items into features is to make clear the relationships between utterances—purely a linguistic matter. With the second goal, we will not list all the features of a lexical item, but only those that are relevant to the linguistic construct under investigation. Indeed, you are quite familiar with this aspect of lexical decomposition because we did it at great length when we talked about morphology and to a lesser extent when we talked about syntax.

For example, as you know from Chapters 3 and 4, in many languages APs agree with the head N they modify. You learned in Problem Set 4.6 that one of the relevant features in this agreement process in Italian is gender. (And remember from the section "Person, Number, Gender and Verbal Inflection" of Chapter 3 that in the vast majority of cases, there is no relationship between morphological gender and real-world sex type.) Thus in order to describe this process, the linguist will make use of the feature [+female]. And in Problem Set 5.3 of this chapter you will discover a way in which Navajo makes use of the notion of humanness, which corresponds to the feature [+human]. For such reasons, these two features are often listed when linguists give lexical decompositions.

Do we have occasion to call upon the features of [+female] and [+human] in discussing the linguistic structure of English? Certainly we do when we are talking about the meaning of utterances, but what about beyond that? Are there any phonetic, phonological, morphological, or syntactic constructions that make use of either of these features? We first introduced the idea of features when we talked about morphology, so why not start there? Look again at our list of [+female] lexical items. Do you see that the suffix in *governess* carries the feature [+female]? Compare to:

lioness   stewardess   waitress

The same can be said of the suffix in *dominatrix*, although it is unproductive in modern English (compare to *aviatrix*).

Selectional Restrictions

What about [+human]? Consider these sentences:

Mary admires cubism.
#Cubism admires Mary.

Do either of these sentences strike you as odd? I hope the second does (and the "#" in front of it marks this sentence as semantically anomalous). We are now in the realm of SELECTIONAL RESTRICTIONS. We say that the lexical items in an utterance select one another as appropriate companions in the various roles that words can play (the grammatical functions, the predicate, the modifiers, and so on). Which lexical items in *Cubism admires Mary* just don't seem to go together in this particular arrangement of roles and why? The problem here is that cubism just isn't the sort of thing that can admire anything else. That is, *admire* can't select *cubism* as its Subject.

It's quite difficult to describe exactly which features are relevant in a nominal in order for it to be able to admire something, but let's try for a moment. Certainly, because I started this discussion with the issue of whether or not the feature of [+human] is relevant to the structure of English, you might suggest that this is the key to the distinction here: Only [+human] objects can admire things. And for many speakers this is a correct description. What about for you? Can you say, with a straight face, and without feeling like you are stretching the language:

My dog admires a good strong bark.

Some of you may allow that dogs are capable of admiration. Others may not. (And if you do a survey, you might also ask people if they own a dog.) For those of you who allow it, what do you think of:

That mouse admires Oreo crumbs.

I hope at least some of you are rejecting this. For those who allow it, how about:

An earthworm admires wet soil.

I expect you all to balk at this one, but if you don't, you might try a sentence with *amoebas* as the Subject. What we're talking about here is an ANIMACY HIERARCHY or cline or ranking (and you'll see effects of such a hierarchy in Problem Set 5.3). Somewhere along this cline we each draw our line, and things above it can admire and things below it can't. (And our experience with the world affects where we draw such lines—so pragmatics comes into play here.)

Classifiers

There are many lexical features that linguists list, some found in language after language and others quite particular to individual languages. In the section "Typology of Languages by Morphology" in Chapter 3 I mentioned that some languages (such as Chinese) use classifiers, which are morphemes that tell the class of lexical items, usually nominals. For example, in Thai, classifiers obligatorily appear in quantified NPs. The classifier *khon* is used for counting humans and the classifier *tua* is used for counting certain animals or certain inanimate objects:

> khru˙ lâ˙j khon 'teacher three person' = 'three teachers'
> mǎ˙ sí˙ tua 'dog four body' = four dogs'

So the classifier *khon* picks out [+human] nouns and the classifier *tua* picks out certain [−human] nouns.

American Sign Language uses classifers that are, essentially, information-rich pronouns. The classifiers are handshapes and, as such, they can often combine with verbs that consist solely of movements. Let's consider here only two (Fig. 5.1). The handshape of a relaxed fist with an extended index finger tells us that the referent is thin and straight. And the handshape of a closed fist (with the thumb wrapped across the knuckles of the other fingers) tells us the referent is round. If we wanted to indicate that a thin, straight referent did a certain action, we might hold our index finger extended throughout the motion of the verb; and if we wanted to indicate that a round referent did a certain action, we might hold our hand in a closed fist throughout the motion of the verb. Furthermore, we can add on other information by modifying these two handshapes. Thus if we extend the index and middle finger, the referent is narrow and straight. If we extend all four fingers, the referent is wide and straight. Likewise if we open our fist a little, the referent is round and large. If we open our fist until it forms a C, the referent is round and very large.

Many languages have classifiers that distinguish humans from nonhumans (like Thai) or that distinguish nominals by the shape and size of their referent (like ASL). In fact, if we look across languages, we find that classifiers fall into only a handful of main categories: material, shape, consistency, size, location, arrangement, and quantity. This fact has led some to suggest that classifiers pick out conceptual primitives. I'll return to this suggestion.

While English is typically not used to exemplify classifiers, we certainly have lexical items that select classes of other lexical items to go with. For example, we can say:

> a cup of tea   a cup of sugar   a cup of shortening

but not

> *a cup of meat   *a cup of soap   *a cup of book

For sure, if you diced your meat, you might be able to use *a cup of meat* to indicate *a cup of diced meat*. And if you meant detergent, you might be able to say *a cup of soap*. But without some added understanding of this sort, *cup* is not a good measure word for meat or soap. And I can't imagine a context for *a cup of book* (although I can for *a cup of books*, if the books are tiny enough). (I would guess that we must be able to pour an object or mold its shape in order to measure it in cups. Hence cups can measure milk and peanut butter, but are not generally used to measure amounts of ice cubes, for example, unless the ice cubes are so tiny they seem to fill the cup without big air pockets between them. What do you think?)

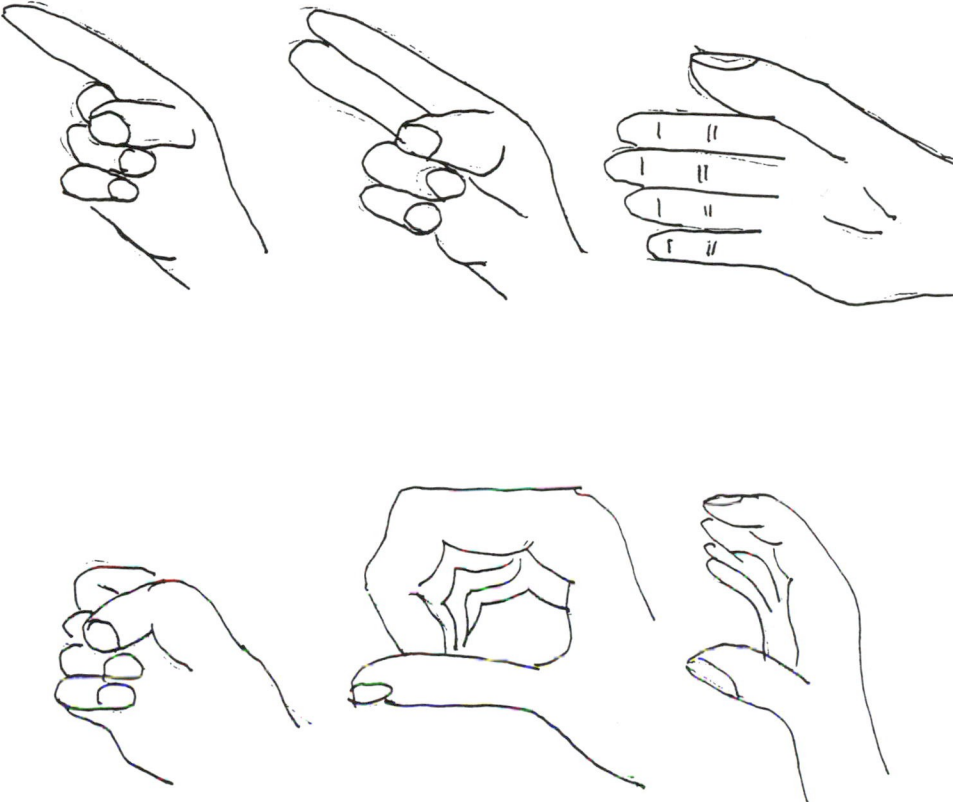

Figure 5.1. Modifications on two classifiers in ASL.

Lexical Features vs. Conceptual Primitives

One of the most important features for understanding the distribution of lexical items in English, and one that pertains to nominals, is seen in the contrast here:

> I heard two songs.
> *I heard two informations.

What's going on? We simply seem to be able to count songs but not information. The closest we can come is to count pieces or bits of information. That distinction is called the COUNT/MASS distinction. You can also see it here:

> I ate an orange.
> *I ate a meat.

I asterisked the second sentence. But, actually, it can be perfectly acceptable if put in the right context. What would *a meat* have to refer to in order for this to be a good sentence? Well, it could refer to a type of meat (a countable object—there's pork, beef, chicken, and so on—as in, "For a balanced diet, you should eat three breads, one meat, and five vegetables each day").

Now, I mentioned that the fact that classifiers across languages fall into only a few recurring groups might lead one to suggest that classifiers are picking out conceptual primitives. Do you think the count/mass distinction is reflective of a conceptual primitive? In Italian one can say:

> Ho sentito due canzoni.   'I heard two songs.'
> Ho sentito due informazioni.   'I heard two informations.'

Thus, both *canzoni* 'songs' and *informazioni* 'informations' are count nouns in Italian. Does this mean that Italian speakers conceive of information in a different way from the way English speakers conceive of it? Before you answer that, remember that if you say yes, you'll have to be saying that it isn't just Italians vs. Americans on this concept; it's all native speakers of Italian everywhere (including Australia, Canada, Tunisia, and elsewhere) vs. all native speakers of English everywhere (including Americans, Brits, Canadians, Australians, South Africans, Indians, and so on). And if you still feel inclined to say yes, ask yourself: Does an Italian who learns English have to learn a new conceptual structure for the lexical item *information*? And if you learned Italian, would you think of information differently once you found out that the Italian lexical item for it was [+count]?

Let's look at an even more drastic case. Consider the fact that *gravel* in English either has the feature [+neuter] or has no lexical feature for gender and we use the neuter pronoun *it* for the referent of this noun. But in Italian *ghiaia* 'gravel' is feminine. And in French *gravier* 'gravel' is masculine. If we were to equate lexical features with conceptual primitives, we'd have to claim that speakers of English, speakers of Italian, and speakers of French all conceived of gravel in extremely different ways with respect to gender. This seems ridiculous to me.

I'm not trying to argue that there is no relationship between conceptual primitives and lexical features. That would be absurd. There is a strong relationship. In fact, there is quite a lot of predictability about count vs. mass nouns as we move from language to language. And we might well be surprised when a noun phrase whose referent has real-world (that is, biological) sexuality (such as a witch, in contrast to the sea) has a lexical gender that differs from the referent's real-world's sex. However, this situation does arise: In Italian the word for tiger is *tigre*, a feminine noun always; the word for a big woman is *donnone*, a masculine noun; the word for a spy is *spia*, a feminine noun, regardless of the referent; and on and on. So the relationship between conceptual primitives and lexical features, while strong, is not a perfect one-to-one correspondence. Thus I believe it is worthwhile to talk both about conceptual primitives and about lexical features. The Italian word *tigre*, for example, would vary in the conceptual primitive assigned to it based on its biological sexuality, but would always have the lexical feature of [+female].

Paradigms

When decomposing lexical items, it can be helpful to set up paradigms that allow us to compare lexical items with respect to a particular component of the meaning. For example, if we want to compare the meanings of the lexical items:

aunt   niece   cousin   brother   nephew   sister   uncle

what components of meaning would we need to talk about? Look at *aunt* vs. *uncle*, for example. Yes, gender matters here.

Should we talk about the feature of [±male] or [±female]? This is not a political question (so please try not to let your ideas about societal structure influence your answer); it's a linguistic one. In English is there any reason to consider one gender the unmarked one? Certainly there used to be. When we needed to use a pronoun to refer to a referent whose gender was unknown, we used to use the masculine pronouns:

Everyone raised his hand.
Nobody likes his own lunch.
Someone should volunteer his time.

Today we are more likely to avoid the gender issue and simply use *their*. That is, the third-person plural pronouns, which are neutral for gender, are now often used as though they are neutral for number also. *Their, they, them* simply carry information about person now, not about number. So I no longer know whether we should talk about [±male] or [±female] for English. And I will therefore, arbitrarily (from a linguistic point of view), pick [±female].

Often the choice of which feature to pick is not arbitrary. For the count/mass distinction in English, which feature would you pick? Probably [±count], just based on the fact that there are more count nouns in English than there are mass nouns.

Okay, let's return to our list of lexical items. What other components of meaning need we talk about here? This is all about kinship. So we could set up a paradigm like that shown in Table 5.1. In English once we reach the kinship distance represented by *cousin*, we no longer make a gender distinction. We have an instance of neutralization for gender again (like the gender neutralization we are presently experiencing in the third-person pronouns).

Paradigms of this sort can reveal things about our lexicon. For example, consider the lexical items:

ice   carbon dioxide   dry ice   water   steam

Arrange them in a paradigm that makes sense to you (Table 5.2). What physical states are we dealing with here? Solids, liquids, and gases, right? And what substances are we dealing with here? Two types of molecules: H_2O and CO_2. There is a LEXICAL GAP in this paradigm: We seem to lack a word for the liquid state of CO_2. Can you figure out why this

Table 5.1. Kinship Terms

	[+female]	[−female]
Siblings	sister	brother
Parents' siblings	aunt	uncle
Sibling's children	niece	nephew
Parents' siblings' children	cousin	

Table 5.2.

	Solid	Liquid	Gas
H_2O	ice	water	steam
CO_2	dry ice		carbon dioxide

gap occurs? If you've ever done chemistry experiments with dry ice, you might know that it turns to a gas without passing through a liquid state. So the lexical gap here reflects a gap in the realities of the world.

Notice that the gender neutralization of *cousin* was not based on some neutralization in the realities of the world. Our cousins are male or female; in English we simply don't convey that information via the lexical item.

Can you come up with a paradigm that has a lexical gap where the gap does not reflect a gap in the realities of the world, but merely in our lexicon? Sure. Consider:

rooster   hen   pullet   chick

in contrast to:

brontosaurus

There were certainly male, female, young female, and baby brontosauruses (correspond- ing to *rooster*, *hen*, *pullet*, and *chick*, respectively), but we don't have lexical items that convey that information. Why not? Probably because we don't care about that information enough to go through the linguistic expense of having separate lexical items. Languages seem to (loosely) obey a principle of economy, which bans useless distinctions. Most of us really don't need to recognize genders and ages in brontosauruses. But we depend on hens for eggs and on roosters for fertilizing those eggs, and once chicks reach a certain size— for example, the size of pullets—they become useful to us as meat or for egg production. And if you didn't know the word *pullet*, you're probably in the majority of people who haven't visited a chicken farm. (Pullets are full-grown hens under a year old—they are often marked "fryers" in the grocery.)

Sometimes the relationships between lexical items don't lend themselves to neat para- digms that fit into matrices of the types we've just seen. The relationships may be a bit more idiosyncratic to the particular lexical items and they may reflect the beliefs and cultural attitudes of the speech community. This happens often when we are talking about types within a kind. For example, consider these words:

table   coffee table   stool   desk   couch   chair

What is the rubric all these fall under? Furniture. Do any of them seem to group together? Well, a coffee table is a type of table. What about a desk? Could you consider it a type of table? Some might and some might not. Is a stool a type of chair? I would say so, but someone else might feel that the lack of a back makes a stool unchairlike. We can represent the relationships here with a TAXONOMY tree.

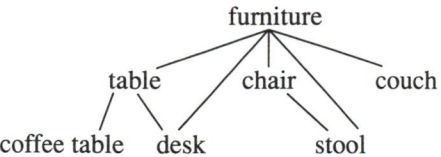

The particular lines connecting lexical items in a taxonomy tree will vary based on the speakers you interview.

Semantic Uses of Lexical Decomposition in Comparing Words

Decomposition of the type we've been talking about thus far is a tool used primarily for analyzing the semantics and other grammatical behavior of nominals. And it can help with some of the notions we've already talked about in other chapters and earlier in this chapter.

For one, it can be used to identify important relationships between lexical items. Our phonology allows us to recognize the form of lexical items. Our semantics, through lexical decomposition, allows us to recognize the meaning of lexical items. We have four logical possibilities in comparing the form and meaning of two lexical items.

1. The form and meaning of two lexical items can be the same. In this case the two lexical items are identical—for form and meaning are the essence of a lexical item.
2. The form of two lexical items can differ and their meaning can differ, as well. That's the case with most pairs of lexical items, of course.
3. The form of two lexical items can be the same, but the meaning can differ. We talked about this sort of relationship before, when we talked about morphology. We called morphemes that have the same phonetic shape but different meanings homophonous. Homophonous lexical items are called homonyms (as you well know by now in this book), and homonymy is common in language:

I like the color *red*.	Last night I *read* all night.
I've *led* a boring life.	Paint with *lead* is dangerous.
His *bare* bottom is pink.	In Michigan I saw a *bear*.
We fell *down* the stairs.	This jacket is stuffed with *down*.

(Be careful not to be led astray by orthography. When we speak of identical form, we are talking of the phonetic shape of a lexical item. Its spelling is irrelevant.)

While recognizing homonymy seems like a straightforward matter at first, it can be controversial, as we noted in Chapter 3 when we talked about polysemy (in the section "Homophony"). Let me remind you of our discussion there of *run*, as in these sentences:

We ran two miles.
Joshua ran the grocery store.
A woman runs a terrible risk.
The boss ran us ragged.

This car just doesn't run right.
Her stockings ran when she pulled them on.
The chocolate sauce ran all over my shirt.
Run these letters over to the mailbox, would you?

Whether there is one verb *run* that is appropriately varying in sense (that is, polysemous) so that it can occur in all these sentences, or whether there are two or even several verbs *run* is a matter you could argue about ad nauseam. I tend to think polysemy is rampant in language and that failure to recognize it leads not only to a cluttering of the lexicon with lexical items that have a lot in common and just happen to have the same form, but also to a failure to appreciate the fluid or shifting nature of lexical sense. What I mean by this will become clearer in the discussion on antonymy. For now, let's move on to the fourth way that we can match the form and meaning of two lexical items.

4. The form of two lexical items can differ but the meaning can be the same. We saw this relationship between sentences—when we talked about synonymous paraphrases. But now we're talking about single lexical items that are synonyms (a term we know from Chapter 3). Can you think of any such examples? It's hard to do. If you take a word like *couch* and a word like *sofa*, chances are many of us feel at least a delicate distinction between them, even if that distinction is one of register (and we met it in Problem Set 4.10).

We haven't talked about register yet, with the exception of a brief passing remark in Problem Set 4.10. Consider the following sentences:

I'd prefer that you lower the volume of your CD player.
Would you turn down your CD player?
Turn down that racket.

Can you see a difference in tone and style in these sentences? Which might you use if you were feeling snooty and wanted to keep a formal distance between yourself and your hearer? The first, right? When would you use the second? Probably in most situations— from formal to informal. When would you use the third? Probably when you are quite familiar with the hearers or have authority over them but don't need to treat them with respect. This kind of difference is called a difference in register—and we all use a range of registers in our daily speech acts.

For me, *sofa* belongs to a more formal register of speech than *couch*. I'd use *sofa* to refer to a fancy couch or to refer to a couch when I was talking to someone I considered to be fancy. So they aren't really synonyms in my speech, because their CONNOTATIONS (the subjective things they carry with them, like a feeling of fanciness or a feeling of pessimism or a feeling of silliness—whatever) are different, even if their DENOTATIONS (their actual senses) are the same. But you may well feel differently.

We can talk about connotations when considering any words or phrases, not just when considering words with the same denotation. For example, *roast turkey* for me has the connotation of holiday but *roast chicken* has no such connotation. I expect that if you are American, the same holds for you. That is, while the distinction I described above between *sofa* and *couch* may be idiosyncratic to my speech, usually differences in connotations are well agreed upon and vary little from person to person within a given culture.

Have you thought of any synonyms in your speech yet? Students I have asked in linguistics classes often bring up the names of household items as synoynyms in their speech. For example, to refer to that pan with low sides that we use for frying, I've heard:

frying pan   skillet   griddle   spider

If you have two or more of these in your lexicon and you use them interchangeably, then you may have a true instance of synonyms. For me some of these words belong to regional varieties of English and I either don't use them (as with *spider*) or I know that I'm using a word that really isn't natural to me when I do use them. Thus when I use *griddle*, I feel like I'm trying to present myself as a country kid. And when I use *skillet*, I'm either referring to an electric frying pan or I'm talking to someone I don't feel comfortable with so I've grasped for a word that seems a bit citified or sophisticated to me. The only one of these I really use unselfconsciously is *frying pan*.

In your search for synonyms, you might have noticed that often a word and a phrase seem identical in meaning, as in:

square
equilateral rectangle

Dictionaries clearly rely on this correspondence. However, isolated words are generally more polysemous than phrases. Thus we could use the word *square* when referring to an unhip person or a commercial area of a town or an equilateral rectangle, but we would use *equilateral rectangle* only in the last instance. This is true even of words like *uncle* in comparison to paraphrases like *parent's brother*. That is, we can call a good friend of the family by the title "uncle," but we wouldn't call that person our "parent's brother" unless he was, in fact, our parent's brother.

As you can see, I'm skeptical about the existence of synonyms (just as I'm skeptical about the existence of synonymous sentences). But every book on semantics I've ever opened takes synonymy as a given of language, and since paraphrasing is so often used in explaining the meaning of words or phrases, you can see why the concept of synonymy is important. You can make up your own mind now that you know what kinds of issues come up, and I encourage you to bring this matter up in class discussion. Delicate distinctions do matter—and their exploitation contributes much to the richness of conversation and literature.

Antonyms

The second of the four possible relationships between lexical items mentioned earlier was that in which the lexical items differ in both form and meaning. There are many possible ways in which lexical items can differ in both form and meaning. One of them is antonymy (a term we met in Problem Set 3.3). We call pairs like the following antonyms:

cold hot   long short   malignant benign

Such pairs are said to have opposite meanings—and you can immediately see how the concept of antonymy is appealing for semanticists in the same way the concept of synonymy is. It seems like a simple and helpful concept in illuminating the meaning of words. But, actually, the matter is more complex than it might appear at first.

You tell me: What's the antonym of *fat*? Let's narrow this and consider only the adjective *fat* (not the noun). If you think of meat, you might have said *lean*. If you think of fashion models, you might have said *skinny* or *thin* (at least if you're my age and getting wider every year). If you think of working out, you might have said *muscular*. And so it goes.

Now look back at the three pairs of antonyms I gave. Can you think of alternative antonyms for each of the words? For *cold*, if you think of typing animals by blood temperature, you might have said *warm*. For *hot*, if you think of spicy food, you might have said *mild*. I'm sure you can find alternative antonyms for *long* and *short* easily. But what about *malignant* and *benign*? These might be a little harder for you since I purposely gave the word *malignant* first. The word *malignant* is so often connected to the issue of cancer these days that you might have focused on that use exclusively and thus felt these two words truly are antonyms. But, in fact, if we are talking about someone's remark and we describe it as benign, the antonym would be *malicious*, not *malignant*, right? And if we are talking about a neighbor's attention to our family affairs and we describe it as benign, an appropriate antonym might well be *interfering* or *nosy*. Thus of this pair, at least the word *benign* can have different antonyms depending on context, even if it's hard to come up with different antonyms for *malignant* other than *benign*.

Try to give a definition of *cold*. It's hard to do, right? There are multiple ways that we use this word. Now try to give a definition of *malignant*. It's easier, right? *Malignant* means that something is cancerous or, perhaps by way of metaphor, very harmful.

Which word, *cold* or *malignant*, is an ordinary word of daily life? That question may seem dumb to you. Both could well be ordinary and used on a daily basis in your life if you have a lot to do with the medical profession or if matters of health are on your mind. But without that condition, probably *cold* is a more ordinary word than *malignant* for you. And *cold* is the one that's harder to define in a precise and brief way. Why is that?

We tend to use our ordinary words, our high-frequency words, in many different contexts, with slightly varying or even widely varying, though not unrelated, senses (as in *hot* for "spicy" and *hot* for "sexy"). That is, polysemy abounds in our high-frequency words. We are efficient about language. While our dictionary holds tens of thousands of words (Funk & Wagnall's *New Standard Unabridged Dictionary*, for example, has 450,000 entries, and rather short dictionaries routinely have 80,000 or more), even the more educated of us use only about 5,000 to 10,000 in typical speech in spite of the fact that we command about 13,000 by the age of six and about 45,000 to 60,000 by the time we've finished high school. (And in English about 85 percent of the words we use in speech are monosyllabic if we discount inflectional morphemes.) So the words we use in typical speech are used over and over again, even though the situations we find ourselves using them in are not identical. One reason common words are harder to define is that they have fewer limitations on their sense and they are therefore appropriate for more contexts. *Kill*, for example, is a relatively LOW-INFORMATION word, whereas *assassinate* is a relatively HIGH-INFORMATION word. In the contexts in which we would use *assassinate*, we could use *kill* and keep the truth value of the proposition constant (although we'd be giving less information about the action). Compare:

Someone assassinated J.F.K.
Someone killed J.F.K.

But there are many contexts in which we would use *kill*, but for which *assassinate* would not be appropriate, and a substitution would result in a change in truth value or even in a sentence that could never be true, as in:

Lack of food killed the cat.
#Lack of food assassinated the cat.

(I have marked the second sentence here as a violation of selectional restrictions, since *assassinate* calls for an agent argument and since the abstract NP *lack of food* cannot be agentive.)

We can see the shift in the senses of common words, like *cold* and *kill*, merely by putting them in shifting contexts. Infrequently used words, like *malignant* and *assassinate*, are appropriate for fewer contexts and thus their sense is more likely to seem fixed and circumscribed to us.

One way to account for the fact that a word like *cold* can have various antonyms is to say that it can be decomposed in multiple ways. And each decomposition might or might not have an appropriate antonym which differs from *cold* on one (or more) of the lexical features (or primitive concepts, as you will). But a word like *malignant* can be decomposed in only a few ways, and, accordingly, it has few possibilities for antonyms.

And now that we've looked at antonyms in this way, you can see that we could have (and should have) said entirely analogous things about synonyms. (If you want me to get you started, compare *brief* with *short*—and on it goes.)

Semantic Uses of Lexical Decomposition in Studying Sentences

Lexical decomposition can also be useful in helping us understand the semantics of sentences. For example, it can explain why the following sentence is always false (and if you think it isn't always false, please wait with your objection):

→←A woman is not a person.

Why is this sentence a contradiction (that is, always false)? Try to give your answer in terms of lexical features. Begin by decomposing the two nouns into features. *Woman* has the lexical feature [+human] (among other features). *Person* also has the feature [+human]. You might even say that [+human] is the only feature of *person*. But even if you think *person* has additional features, all the lexical features of *person* seem to form a proper subset of the lexical features of *woman*: A woman is a kind of person. Thus the sentence is a contradiction because *woman* is HYPONYMOUS to *person*, just as *tulip* is hyponymous to *flower*, *horse* is hyponymous to *animal*, *gold* is hyponymous to *mineral*, and so on.

You might object to this discussion because you know of or can imagine societies in which women are not considered persons. In those societies my putative contradiction would not be a contradiction. But notice that in those societies the very definition of *woman* is different from the definition I have assumed in that it would not contain the relevant feature (which I have termed [+human]). So maybe this objection is not damaging to the argument, after all.

Hyponymy also explains why the following sentence is always true—that is, why the following sentence is a TAUTOLOGY:

That bush is a plant.

Only if we changed the definitions of one or both of the lexical items *bush* and *plant* could this sentence have a chance of being anything but true regardless of context.

Again, you might be objecting, and this time rather vehemently. Certainly you can think of contexts in which you could say *That bush is a plant* and the sentence would be false. For example, if the bush were made of pipe cleaners and paper tissues, you might not want to call it a plant. Or maybe you would—an artificial plant. Well, what if the bush, upon closer inspection, was just a pile of old green rags? Would you then deem the sentence false? What if the speaker knew that it was just a pile of rags—and intended to say that the pile looked like a bush and it therefore made a nice house plant, so to speak? We don't have to agree on an answer here; I just want you to think about the issues.

The point of all this is, once more, efficiency: We use language efficiently. We don't have to say "artificial" when we say, "I like the flowers on your hat," even if the flowers are artificial. The context, the relationship that persists between the speaker and the hearers, the nature of the conversation, all of these things and many others allow us to use a rather small vocabulary to express a vast range of ideas. We play a lot of games with language—and an adequate theory of meaning in language should take those games into account.

All the same, as you might have suspected, we aren't going to do much with interpretations of language that are more metaphorical than literal and/or that depend on understanding some game or special relationship between the speech participants (although you will get a chance to think about metaphors a bit in Problem Set 5.9). A literal approach, while pitifully limited in terms of actual language use, will turn out to be far more than we can handle thoroughly in this chapter, as you'll see. So let's just proceed with our discussion, and you can keep objections of this sort under your hat.

Okay, try to use lexical features to explain why these two sentences seem to be (at least close to) synonymous:

I like that bachelor.
I like that unmarried man.

This should be easy: The definition of *bachelor* (or one of the definitions of this lexical item) is "unmarried man." So the two NPs *that bachelor* and *that unmarried man* will have the same lexical decomposition. (I have certain reservations about synonymy here—which you might well expect, since you know I'm skeptical about the whole notion of synonymy. For me the word *bachelor* and the phrase *unmarried man* do not carry the same connotations—although as I try to find examples to exemplify my point, I'm having trouble, so the distinction is delicate in my speech. I believe the phrase gives merely a description of a state—that of being unmarried. But the word *bachelor* can carry with it a sense pertaining to availability for marriage within the relevant context. If I were talking to a woman friend who wants to get married about a male friend who is gay, I might call him an unmarried man, but I doubt I'd call him a bachelor.)

Suddenly now we're talking about decomposing whole phrases. But this shouldn't come as a surprise; we did the equivalent when we had to talk about breaking down strings of words into conceptual primitives when comparing *enter* to *go into* in our George Washington sentence.

There is another issue, though, that phrases bring up—that of reference. We've mentioned reference and referents several times already in this chapter, and back in Chapter 3 we learned about the difference between sense and reference. A noun such as *dog*, for example, has sense by itself. If this noun heads an NP (even if it's the only word in that NP), then we say the NP has reference. What do you notice about the reference of the NPs *that bachelor* and *that unmarried man* in the pair of sentences? Can you argue that these sentences are not necessarily synonymous, even though the definition of *bachelor* is "unmarried man"? Of course you can—all you need to do is utter each sentence in a different context so that the referent of the NPs differs. So when we talk about synonymy of phrases and sentences we are usually talking about synonymy in a given context. The referent of a phrase and the truth of a proposition are relative to their context or WORLD.

Is this the same idea we discussed when we talked about the fact that words can have a variety of antonyms or a variety of synonyms? Look back at our discussion of antonymy. I hope you can see that the answer is no. Context is not the defining factor in those cases; it merely makes the range of senses obvious. But it is only in a context that *that bachelor* has a referent or that the sentence *I like that bachelor* has a truth value. Notice that the possible referents for *that bachelor* equal the number of bachelors in the world of the utterance, which could be very large. But the number of senses of a word like *cold* is much much more limited.

Now let's take a look at our sentences again:

I like that bachelor.
I like that unmarried man.

Which lexical item in this pair of sentences ties us to a given context? The indexical (or deictic) *that*, right? In the section "Verbal Inflections and Affixes" of Chapter 3 we talked about deixis and some of the ways language points to particular referents in terms of objects, locations, and times. What are the indexicals in these sentences?

She left it here.
He came yesterday.

All pronouns (including *she*, *it*, and *he* in these sentences) are indexicals in that we must link them to a particular referent in order to interpret them. *Here* is also an indexical. What does it point to? A position—a place close (relatively speaking) to the speaker. *Yesterday* is also an indexical. What does it point to? A time—the day before the time of the speech act.

Okay, so we have used lexical decomposition of nominals to reveal contradiction, tautology, synonymy, hyponymy, and antonymy.

Predicates and Arguments

Most work in lexical semantics, however, focuses more on the analysis of predicates and their arguments than on the analysis of nominals. Indeed, most work in conceptual semantics does the same. That may be because the study of predicate-argument structure reveals properties relevant to the morphological and syntactic realization of arguments, so the study of predicate-argument structure ties semantics to morphology and syntax. We have already done, then, quite a bit of lexical semantics in our discussions of both morphology and syntax. Indeed, Problem Sets 4.7, on subcategorization, and 4.8, on theta-roles, could as easily be viewed as problem sets in semantics as in syntax. And many of our problem sets on morphology in Chapter 3 concerned semantics in a direct way.

The Anticausative Alternation

Rather than repeat or summarize what we've done earlier, let's take a look at a particular way in which studying predicate-argument structure can give us insight into language. Consider these sentences:

> The ball bounced over the wall.
> Joan bounced the ball over the wall.

List a syntactic property of the verb *bounce* that you notice from comparing these two sentences. *Bounce* has both an intransitive and a transitive use. This is not surprising. If you did Problem Set 4.7, you know already that most so-called transitive verbs of English can be used intransitively. However, there is an important difference between *bounce* and a verb like *eat*. Compare the following pair of sentences to the sentences with *bounce*:

> Sally ate at the diner.
> Sally ate pork chops at the diner.

Compare the theta-roles of the various arguments of *bounce* and their GFs (grammatical functions) to the theta-roles of the various arguments of *eat* and their GFs. What can you notice?

In both the transitive and intransitive sentences with *eat*, the Subject is agentive. The only difference between these two sentences is whether or not a theme argument appears in Direct Object (DO) position. So a fixed semantic gap (the lack of a theme argument) corresponds to a fixed syntactic gap (the lack of a DO) in the intransitive sentence.

But the *bounce* sentences present a more complex situation. First tell me, what do both *bounce* sentences tell us? That the ball moved over the wall. In conceptual terms, we have a physical object that is moving along a path in a particular manner. What difference in meaning between the two sentences is there? The transitive one tells us the initiator or causer of the motion of the ball—the agentive argument of *bounce*. The intransitive one gives us no information at all about what caused the ball to move. For this reason, the transitive use of a verb like *bounce* is called a causative (a term we met in Chapter 3), and the intransitive use is called a NON-CAUSATIVE. The alternation exemplified in this pair of sentences is called the ANTI-CAUSATIVE ALTERNATION.

While both the causative and the non-causative uses of *bounce* require a theme argument (here, the ball) and the causative use also requires an agent argument (here, Joan), the directional or path complement (here, over the wall) is not required in either. Typically, verbs that participate in the anticausative alternation only optionally take goal, or source, or path complements.

The tricky thing is that the theme argument appears in Subject position in the intransitive sentence and in the DO position in the transitive sentence. So the relationship of the semantics to the syntax is complicated.

Is *bounce* unusual in this regard, or is it representative of a whole class of predicates? To answer this, find other verbs that enter into the anticausative alternation. Was it easy to do? Do the verbs that you found fall into any recognizable semantic classes? Indeed, many verbs that involve motion are in this class, including:

roll fly move drop turn rotate shift spin

But not all verbs that involve motion are in this class. Can you find any verbs that involve motion that are always intransitive? You might have thought of:

come go arrive fall stroll gambol rise

What do you notice about the theta-role of the Subjects of these verbs when you put them in sentences? They have theme Subjects, right? That is, the object in motion fills the Subject slot:

The elevator rose.
The tree fell.

However, sometimes an object in motion can have initiated its own motion and be in control of that motion for both the verbs that enter into the anticausative alternation and for strictly intransitive verbs:

anticausative: John moved as slowly as he could.
intransitive: The puppy gamboled through the flowers.

This raises an interesting question for Theta Theory (which you learned about in the sections "Theta Theory" and "Theta-Roles" and in Problem Set 4.8 of Chapter 4), by the way. Are these Subjects agents or themes? The *on purpose* test (which you met in Problem Set 4.8) tells us these Subjects are agentive:

John moved as slowly as he could on purpose.
The puppy gamboled through the flowers on purpose.

But a single argument of a given predicate cannot receive two theta-roles at once. So we must admit that objects in motion are the agent in some sentences and the theme in others.

Now can you think of any verbs that involve motion that are always transitive (or that at least lend themselves most easily to use in transitive sentences—but if they are used intransitively they participate in the kind of transitive/intransitive alternation that *eat* participates in, as we demonstrated)? You might have thought of:

bring take carry arrange raise put remove

What do you notice about the theta-roles of the Subjects and DOs of these verbs when you put them in sentences? The Subjects are agents and the DOs are themes:

Sue can arrange the flowers.
I'll raise the flag.
Jeff brought homemade pies.

Given what you learned about verbs that involve motion that are always intransitive (like *rise*) and verbs that involve motion that are always transitive (like *bring*), are you surprised at the linking between theta-roles and GFs that we find in the anticausative alternation with verbs like *bounce*? I hope you answered no. That is, we can see that when verbs that involve motion are used transitively, the argument that undergoes the motion is linked to DO position (and receives the theta-role of theme). And, of course, the agent is linked to Subject position—the canonical position for agents. When verbs that involve motion are used intransitively, the object that is in motion is linked to Subject position (and is either a theme or an agent, depending on whether it instigates and/or controls its own motion). So the linking between argument structure and GFs in the anticausative alternation does not have to be specified as part of the lexical entry for the verb *bounce* and other such verbs. **Once we see that a verb involves motion, we know quite a lot about its possible argument structure and about how that argument structure can be linked to GFs.**

Other Semantic Verb Classes

Verbs that involve motion form one semantic class of verbs, but there are many semantic classes. For example, consider these verbs:

carve   sew   weave   work   construct   build   mould

What concept do they have in common? They all involve creation (and they are called CREATION VERBS). How many arguments and what kind of arguments do verbs of creation take? To answer that, just pick one such verb and put it in various sentences, like so:

Joan formed a garland from the flowers.

Indeed, these verbs typically take three arguments: a creator, in the agent role; a product of the creative action, in a theme role; and the raw material from which the product is created, in what could be called a source role. Is the agent consistently linked to a particular GF? Sure, it fills the Subject slot. What about the theme and source? Consider:

Joan formed the flowers into a garland.

The verb *form* allows its theme argument to be linked to either DO or OP position. Accordingly, its source argument will be linked to either OP or DO position.

Do all verbs of creation work this way? Find a verb of creation that requires its theme argument to fill DO position. One is *construct*:

The third little pig constructed a house from bricks.
*The third little pig constructed the bricks into a house.

Now find a verb of creation that requires its theme argument to fill the OP position. One is *work*:

Nina worked the hemp into a rope.
*Nina worked a rope from the hemp.

So either there are finer distinctions to be made or the linking of arguments to GFs with verbs of creation is lexically determined. That is, we will have to specify that information as part of the lexical entry for each verb.

There's much more that we could say about predicates and classes of predicates, but you now have a handle on how to begin discussing such matters so I'll leave you to do that on your own. We will now move on to other matters.

The Importance of Reference

Let's once more look at our initial utterance, this time without decomposing the lexical items:

George Washington entered the church.

Could we begin a discourse with this utterance? Compare it to:

In the late 1700s there was a famous church in Boston.

Which one seems at first glance to be more likely to begin a discourse? The second, right? Why? What conditions would have to be met in order for the first utterance to be an appropriate opener for a discourse? And where does the problem lie?

Let's begin attacking these questions by looking at the various components of the sentence and seeing what we know about their use. Can you come up with a good discourse-opener that has *George Washington* in it? Sure:

Today we're going to talk about George Washington.

Can you come up with a good discourse-opener that has *entered* in it? Sure:

This morning I entered a new dimension.

Can you come up with a good discourse-opener that has the NP *the church*? You might have come up with sentences such as:

Look at the church.
The church is white.
Who's sitting in the church?

But could you use these as discourse-openers in a telephone conversation? Probably not. Why not?

The problem is the NP *the church*. Say several sentences with the NP *the church* and then substitute for that NP the NP *a church*. What do you notice about the situations in which you would use one NP as opposed to the other? Definite NPs—that is, NPs that use the definite determiners (such as *the*, *that*, *this*)—generally are used when the speaker assumes that the listener already has located the referent of the NP. (And see our discussion in the section "Inventory of Morphological Types" of Chapter 3.) When I say "located," I mean with respect to the discourse. So I wouldn't say,

I saw the teacher.

unless I was assuming that you knew what teacher I was talking about in that discourse. We say that definite NPs typically presuppose the existence of their referent. And we say that definite NPs give OLD INFORMATION to the discourse.

Stop for a moment, and take a look at definite determiners. I said that they are "generally" used to convey old information. Can you think of a sentence that contains a morphologically definite NP that is used to convey NEW INFORMATION? There is a highly informal usage of demonstratives that might have come to mind:

I saw this dog on the way to school, and you won't believe what it was eating.

This is morphologically definite (witness the *th-* that we see in *the*, *those*, *that*) but here it picks out a new referent. So the match between morphological definiteness and old information is not perfect. Still, it is a close match in most usages.

Now, earlier we talked about the sentences:

Jeff's a painter.
Jeff isn't a painter.

And we noted that in both sentences the existence of Jeff is presupposed. Proper names usually pattern like definite NPs. Thus, if I say:

I saw Jeff.

I assume the listener knows which Jeff I'm talking about. If the listener didn't, I have to properly introduce that NP into the discourse, as in:

I saw a guy named Jeff.

Generics

Is it really generally true that a definite NP gives old information? Consider this sentence:

The beaver is a four-footed mammal.

Could I use this sentence to start a discourse? Sure. Yet *the beaver* is a definite NP. What is the referent of this NP? It's difficult to state precisely what the referent is, but you can easily see that it is not some SPECIFIC beaver that the speaker assumes the listener can locate with respect to the discourse. So this is a different use of definite NPs from all those we've been talking about thus far. Here the sentence tells us a property of the class of beavers as a whole. We say this definite NP has a generic interpretation (and we met this term in Chapter 4).

Contrast our generic sentence to:

All beavers are four-footed mammals.

Is this sentence semantically equivalent to the generic interpretation sentence? While we don't have a formal standard for judging whether sentences are semantically equivalent yet, you should be able to answer this question. Tell me, is either of the sentences clearly true to you? I hope the generic sentence is. Even if you don't know much about beavers, you probably know that they are mammals and that they typically have four feet. Now is the sentence with *all beavers* a true sentence?

You may not know. Why not? What would you have to do to find out if this sentence is true? You'd have to go out and check each beaver. If you came across a beaver that was born with only three feet or that had lost a foot in an accident or fight, the sentence would be false, right? That is, the loss of a foot doesn't turn a beaver into a nonbeaver.

So a generic interpretation is not the same as a UNIVERSAL interpretation. Instead, a **generic is a statement of typicality and the existence of members of a class who do not have the property claimed of that class in a given generic interpretation sentence does not falsify the sentence.**

Now that we're talking about generics, let's explore them a moment more. Compare these two sentences:

The beaver is furry.
The beavers are furry.

Is either of these sentences open to a generic interpretation? The first one is, but the second one resists a generic interpretation. (Notice that the first sentence is ambiguous between a generic interpretation and a specific referent interpretation.) However, plural definite NPs can have a generic interpretation if we add more information to our NP:

The elephants of India are smaller than those of Africa.

This sentence can be true even if we find one colossal elephant of India that is larger than one dwarf elephant of Africa, so the plural definite NP has a generic interpretation here.

Is it only definite NPs that can have a generic interpretation? Consider:

A beaver is furry.

Contrast this to:

A beaver is coming to dinner.

The first sentence not only can be generic, it must be. The second one cannot. Why not?

Indefinite NPs can have a generic interpretation, but the predication must also be open to a generic interpretation. Is this true only of sentences with indefinite NPs? Certainly not. Look at:

The beaver is furry.
The beaver is coming to dinner.

The first is generic; the second is about a specific beaver. So when we talk about a generic interpretation, we may look at a variety of elements in the sentence, not just NPs.

Now that we've noticed that singular indefinite NPs can have a generic interpretation, we should ask whether plural ones also can (just as plural definite NPs can). Can they? Yes:

Beavers are furry.

Here the plural indefinite (which has no determiner on it in this sentence) has a generic interpretation. Must plural indefinites have generic interpretations? Of course not:

I saw beavers yesterday.

Here I saw specific beavers, not the class of beavers.

So both definite and indefinite NPs can have specific interpretations and generic interpretations. But on the specific interpretation, definite NPs represent old information, and indefinite NPs introduce new information.

Quantified NPs

Now that we've talked about indefinite NPs, we should talk a moment about the third and final type of NP, QUANTIFIED NPs (QNPs—and we looked briefly at QNPs in the section "Functional Phrases Pattern Like Lexical Phrases" in Chapter 4). QNPs raise another important point about the meaning of NPs. Consider these sentences:

Every beaver is furry.
No beaver is furry.

The initial NP in each of these sentences is quantified (by *every* and by *no*). What is its referent?

Maybe for *every beaver* you said something like *the class of beavers*. But this doesn't really work. We can say things about the class of beavers that don't make sense when said of every beaver:

The class of beavers comprises more than one hundred.
#Every beaver comprises more than one hundred.
The class of beavers is larger than the class of newts.
#Every beaver is larger than the class of newts.
The class of beavers typically has flat tails.
#Every beaver typically has {flat tails/a flat tail}.

For *no beaver* you may be truly stumped. Is this a class that contains no beavers? Is it, then, an empty class? If so, then *no beaver* would have the same referent that NPs like *no friend* or *no petunia* have and sentences like:

No beaver is furry.
No friend is furry.
No petunia is furry.

would all mean the same thing, which is an absurd conclusion.

Instead, QNPs don't really seem to have reference in the same way nonquantified NPs do. Rather, the semantic value of a QNP is best understood by looking at the entire utterance the NP occurs in. For example, in:

No beaver is furry.

the quantified NP *no beaver* combines with the predicate (the property of not being furry) to yield an event (here a state) in which no member of the class of beavers has that property. In this way, we can see quantified NPs as being OPERATORS which match properties to entities (we met the term "operator" in the section "Functional and Lexical Categories" of Chapter 4). That is, we understand the property of furriness to be attributed to members of the set of beavers, just as we do in ordinary sentences such as:

That beaver is furry.

but the operator *no beaver* in the sentence *No beaver is furry* tells us which members of the set of beavers this attribution holds for (in this case, none).

Back to Sentences

All right, now let's return to our initial sentence:

George Washington entered the church.

Part of the meaning of this sentence is that George Washington exists (in our history). What would happen to the meaning of the statement as a whole if we made a statement that presupposed the existence of someone we (the speaker and listener) know doesn't exist? That is, what would happen if we used a definite NP that had no referent? Consider this famous sentence:

The present king of France is bald.

There is no king of France presently. So baldness is predicated of a referent that doesn't exist. What does this sentence mean to you?

Some scholars have suggested that the meaning of a proposition is its truth conditions (brought up briefly in Chapter 4). That is, the meaning of a proposition (a semantic entity) is all the conditions that have to hold in order for the sentence to be true. Thus

Jeff is a painter.

would mean that Jeff exists, and that he has the property of being a painter and anything else that is a necessary condition for the truth of this proposition. On the other hand,

Jeff isn't a painter.

would still mean that Jeff exists (recall that presuppositions hold constant under negation) and that he does not have the property of being a painter.

Are you wondering about lies? What if I say *Jeff is a painter* and I know very well that he isn't? Is the meaning of my sentence different, just because it's a lie? Surely, not. The very reason lies can be effective is that they are interpreted the same way truths are. So whether the sentence is in fact true or false is irrelevant; in either case, we look at its truth conditions when figuring out its meaning.

With this idea of what meaning is, what would be the meaning of the following sentence spoken today:

The present king of France is bald.

Since the presupposition fails, we might want to say that the truth conditions aren't met so the sentence is false. Alternatively, since the presupposition fails, we might want to say that the sentence simply has no truth value in the real world. And scholars have proposed both answers.

Are you happy with either solution? Let's look at them a little more closely. Consider:

President Clinton is bald.

This sentence is false (at least in 1995 as I write it, it is). And the determination of that falseness is based on checking with the facts in the world as we know it. But the sentence about the present king of France is quite different. When we hear it, we recognize that the speaker is talking about someone who doesn't exist and for whom, therefore, the determination of baldness cannot be made. The speaker is speaking nonsense, not falsehoods, to my way of thinking.

So I feel more comfortable with the claim that the sentence about the present king of France has no truth value in the real world. We can certainly imagine a world in which France would have a king and in that world we could consider the truth conditions of the sentence. Whether or not you agree with my take on this issue, you should be able to see that there is room for discussion here—so the truth-conditional approach to meaning may still be able to be maintained.

On the other hand, there are other kinds of sentences that raise untenable problems for the claim that the meaning of a sentence is its truth conditions. Consider:

All squares are rectangles.
Two plus two equals four.

Both of these sentences are true in all worlds, under all conditions. So with a truth-conditional approach to meaning, these sentences would be synonymous. But they seem to have different meanings.

One might then conclude that the meaning of a proposition is not simply its truth conditions. Indeed, this has to be the case, for not all sentences have truth conditions. We know this, even if we discount for a moment sentences with failed presuppositions (like our king-of-France sentence). Think about it. Go back to what you learned in our syntax chapter. What types of sentences do we have other than declaratives? Yes, we have imperatives and interrogatives. What would be the truth conditions of:

Go home.
Who went home?

The question doesn't even seem applicable. We don't know what to do with it.

Nevertheless, truth conditions are relevant to understanding these sentences. In order to understand what is ordered or what is asked, we must know what sentences such as *You go home* and *Someone went home* mean. So we need to consider the truth conditions for those declarative sentences in figuring out the interpretation of the nondeclaratives.

In sum, truth conditions are definitely in the ball game, even if they don't comprise the whole game.

Logical Models for Meaning

Talking about notions like truth and operators brings us into the realm of logic, and if you go on to study in the area of semantics, you will need to have a rudimentary knowledge of symbolic logic, which is our next order of business. We will use the logic we learn here to investigate the semantic properties of sentences with quantifiers later. Here is one marvelously confounding sentence as an appetizer:

Mattie doesn't beat her donkey because she loves him.

Does she beat him or doesn't she? See the ambiguity? When you've finished reading this chapter, you'll know how to account for it and for many other types of ambiguous sentences.

We'll begin our discussion by looking at PROPOSITIONAL LOGIC. Part of our interpretation of language depends on decoding the relationships between propositions. Indeed, in ordinary conversation about various topics (not just linguistic topics), when we argue for a certain conclusion or position, we often rely on precisely those relationships. We will now look at five such relationships.

Operations on Propositions: Negation

Any argument in symbolic logic is made up of propositions (represented with small letters such as p, q, r) which are true (T) or false (F). So we could evaluate the truth value of these two propositions (call them p and q), for example:

Colombia is in South America.   T
Philosophy is a natural science.   F

We can operate on simple propositions, like these, in a variety of ways, to produce new propositions.

For example, we can do the operation of NEGATION on a single proposition p to get ~p, which can correspond to at least two different sentences, both of which are false if p is true:

Columbia is not in South America.   F
It is not the case that Columbia is in South America.   F

Do the two sentences here mean different things? As I said, whether or not exact paraphrases exist is a matter of controversy. But if we assume they do, then we need to make clear a distinction that we haven't really paid much attention to thus far: the distinction between sentences and propositions. **A sentence is a syntactic entity with a phonetic realization. A proposition is a semantic entity.** Sentences are to propositions as definite NPs are to referents. So when we do these operations in symbolic logic, we are operating on propositions, not on sentences. Thus there is only one result of negating p, and that result is ~p, regardless of how many sentences (paraphrases of each other) we might believe correspond to the proposition ~p.

Conjunction

We can also operate on two simple propositions to produce complex propositions. One such operation is CONJUNCTION, which means connecting two propositions with an *and* (although you will find in Problem Set 5.4 that the natural-language use of *and* is not always equivalent to logical conjunction). So we can take p and conjoin it to q, written as p $\wedge$ q, like so:

p: Paul is nice.
q: Susan is intelligent.
p $\wedge$ q: Paul is nice and Susan is intelligent.

Tell me, if one of the conjuncts (the elements joined by $\wedge$) is false, what happens to the truth value of the entire conjunction? It's false, right? That is, if Paul isn't nice, then whether or not Susan is intelligent, the conjunction as a whole is false. Indeed, a conjunction is true only if both its conjuncts are true.

Truth Tables

We can write a truth table (Table 5.3) for the operation $\wedge$ that reflects this fact. This table gives us the information that when both p and q are true (as in row 1), their conjunction is true; when p is true and q is false (row 2), their conjunction is false; when p is false and q is true (row 3), their conjunction is false; and when both p and q are false (row 4), their conjunction is false.

We're going to be forming a few more truth tables, so let me give you a strategy so that we'll be forming them the same way. Please set up a column for each ELEMENTARY proposition and for the complex proposition (column 3 in Table 5.3). Then set up 2^x rows, where x is the number of elementary propositions. (So in the truth table for conjunction we have $2^2 = 4$ rows, because we have only two elementary propositions, p and q.) Now

Table 5.3. Conjunction

p	q	p ∧ q
T	T	T
T	F	F
F	T	F
F	F	F

begin at the left and in the first column go halfway down assigning T to each cell of the matrix and then fill in F for the second half of the column. Now go to the second column and divide it into fourths, alternating T and F for each fourth. This method may seem overly technical right now, but if you do a truth table in which you are trying to evaluate a complex expression that includes several elementary propositions and may include several complex propositions, you will find that a systematic way of forming the truth tables will help you in checking your work.

Disjunction

Once we've connected propositions with *and*, you can easily think of other ways to connect them. Give some. You might have listed *or*, *but*, *if*, *although*, *since*, and many others. In our syntax chapter in the section "Coordination and Subordination" we made a distinction between coordination and subordination. We will maintain that distinction here. Symbolic logic makes use of the coordinators *and* and *or*, but not *but*. And it makes use of two kinds of subordinators. Let's first look at the disjunction *or* (symbolized by ∨). When is a sentence like the following true?

p: Mary smokes.
q: Bill drinks.
p ∨ q: Mary smokes or Bill drinks.

Here I'm asking you to go against the grain a bit. We don't ordinarily disjoin propositions that are totally independent of one another. You will have a chance to explore this fact in Problem Set 5.4. So for now, please let yourself interpret a disjunction as though the two propositions are independent of one another. Now can you answer the question? The disjunction should be true if either of the two elementary propositions is true, right? Make a truth table for ∨ now (Table 5.4). But this time use the numbers 1 for T and 0

Table 5.4. Disjunction

p	q	p ∨ q
1	1	1
1	0	1
0	1	1
0	0	0

Table 5.5. Exclusive Disjunction

p	q	p $\vee$ q
1	1	0
1	0	1
0	1	1
0	0	0

for F. (This is a convention that makes handwritten truth tables much easier to read.) If you compare the truth tables for conjunction and disjunction, you can see that they differ drastically. Conjunction is false unless both conjuncts are true; disjunction is true unless both disjuncts are false.

There is another disjunction that symbolic logic sometimes uses, called EXCLUSIVE disjunction, symbolized by $\vee$. Exclusive disjunction is true only if precisely one of the elementary propositions is true. It is similar to the use of *either . . . or* in natural speech (although probably not identical—you can check for yourself in your own speech after you have done Problem Set 5.4). Set up a truth table (Table 5.5) for exclusive disjunction.

The Conditional

Another operation that symbolic logic makes use of is called the CONDITIONAL or IMPLICA-TION, symbolized by →, and often spoken of with the words *if . . . then*, to which it roughly corresponds. When I say "roughly," I mean it. Consider this sentence of English:

If 2 plus 2 is 3, 2 plus 3 is 5.

Would you judge this sentence to be true, given the facts that 2 plus 2 is not 3 but 2 plus 3 is 5? Probably you either don't know how you'd judge it, or you'd judge it to be false. That is, you want the consequence of this implication to follow from the truth of the premise. If the premise is false, how can anything follow from it? And even if we were to allow a world in which 2 plus 2 does equal 3, we still don't expect 2 plus 3 to equal 5 in that world. That is, such a world would have different rules from ours, so we might have few expectations about how things work in that world. On the whole, then, this implication leaves us flummoxed.

Not so in symbolic logic. While negation, conjunction, and disjunction in logic are quite often similar to negation, conjunction, and disjunction in natural language with respect to the truth value of the complex proposition, the conditional is not. In symbolic logic, the statement:

If p, then q

written as

p → q

Table 5.6. Conditional

p	q	p → q
1	1	1
1	0	0
0	1	1
0	0	1

is true for all truth values of the ANTECEDENT p and the CONSEQUENCE q except the combination of a true p and a false q. That is, a false antecedent can imply anything and the resulting expression is true. But a true antecedent can imply only a true consequence in order for the implication to be true. So our sentence of English (about addition), when considered from the standpoint of symbolic logic, is true.

Give a truth table for the conditional (Table 5.6).

The Biconditional

The final connective I want to talk about is called the BICONDITIONAL, written as ⇔ and often talked about with the words *if and only if*, abbreviated as *iff*. (It is also often paraphrased as *just in case*—which may seem odd to you, but you should be aware of it when approaching the literature.) Consider this sentence of English:

I will leave tomorrow if and only if I get the car fixed.

What does this mean to you? If it means:

I will leave tomorrow if I get the car fixed and if I get the car fixed, I will leave tomorrow.

then the biconditional in your speech is a conjunction of two conditionals. (And that's what the *if and only if* sentence just given means for all speakers I have asked.)

That's exactly what the biconditional is in symbolic logic. Unlike negation, conjunction, disjunction, and implication, the biconditional is a complex connective—it is derived from conjoining two implications like so:

$$(p \rightarrow q) \wedge (q \rightarrow p) \equiv p \Leftrightarrow q$$

(This is to be read: The expression "p implies q," conjoined to the expression "q implies p" is equivalent to the expression "p biconditional q.") Can you tell me what the truth table for the biconditional looks like? Yes, because you can figure it out by making a truth table that has columns for the elementary propositions p and q, as well as columns for the complex propositions (p → q) and (q → p), as well as a final column for the conjunction of these two complex propositions (Table 5.7).

The values in the fifth column of Table 5.7 were obtained by conjoining the values in

Table 5.7. Biconditional

p	q	p → q	q → p	(p → q) ∧ (q → p) ≡ (p ⇔ q)
1	1	1	1	1
1	0	0	1	0
0	1	1	0	0
0	0	1	1	1

the third and fourth columns. Thus we can see that the biconditional is true when both the elementary propositions are true and when both the elementary propositions are false, but not when one is false and the other is true. This may be highly counterintuitive, but this is formal logic, not natural-language, we're talking about.

Tautologies and Contradictions

In evaluating the truth values of these complex expressions, we considered the truth values of the elementary propositions. But the truth value of a complex expression may be entirely independent of the truth values of the elementary propositions that make it up.

Can you think of a kind of proposition that would always be false? We've already talked about this kind of proposition: It is a contradiction. In propositional logic we have a simple definition of a contradiction: An expression whose truth value is false regardless of the truth values of its component elementary propositions is a contradiction. (The component elementary propositions of an expression are the elementary propositions that make up the expression—the p and q and r and so on.) And we've already discussed one such example:

→←It's raining and it isn't raining.

Represent this sentence as an expression in symbolic logic. I hope you came up with:

p ∧ ~p

Give a truth table for this expression to prove to yourself that the value is always false (Table 5.8).

Now, use a truth table to determine whether or not this expression is a contradiction:

p ⇔ ~p

(It is.)

Table 5.8. A Particular Contradiction

p	~p	p ∧ ~p
1	0	0
0	1	0

On the other hand, there are complex expressions which are always true, called tautologies. We talked about tautologies earlier in the section "Semantic Uses of Lexical Decomposition in Studying Sentences." However, we gave only one example, which I'll repeat here:

That bush is a plant.

Can you represent this sentence in symbolic logic in such a way as to make clear that this sentence is a tautology? Not with the logic we've been discussing thus far. The representation of this sentence in propositional logic is simply p, because this is a simple sentence. Propositional logic cannot deal with relationships internal to a simple proposition; it can deal only with relationships between (simple and complex) propositions.

But that won't stop us. Find a complex sentence that is a tautology and for which you can offer a symbolic representation that will make it easy to expose the tautology. You might have come up with something like:

It's raining or it isn't raining.

The symbolic logic representation of this would be:

p $\lor$ ~p

And it is a simple job for you to prove that this is a tautology by offering a truth table. So do that now, please.

And now please give me an expression of symbolic logic that uses the biconditional and that is a tautology. If you're having trouble, look back at our contradiction that used the biconditional. Can you do it now? (You may have come up with p $\Leftrightarrow$ p.)

Uses and Limitations of Propositional Logic

Why would we care to represent sentences of natural language in terms of propositional logic? It is true that the connectives of logic do not correspond perfectly to the connectives of natural language. And it is true that we have discussed just a few logical connectives, whereas natural language makes use of many more connectives. But it is also true that there are strong similarities between these particular logical connectives and relationships between propositions in natural language. So, for example, translating an argument into logical symbols can help us to see the form of the argument and, even though the determination of validity in natural language is sometimes different from the determination of validity in propositional logic, using the symbols can help to expose weaknesses and strengths of the argument (something crucial to logicians).

Talking about symbolic logic, particularly about logical implication, leads us, as well, to a discussion of the relationship of entailment in natural language. We defined *entailment* earlier, but let me remind you: We say that a proposition p entails another proposition q if the truth of p necessitates the truth of q. That is, if whenever p is true, q must also be true, p entails q. For example, consider the sentence:

She killed him, therefore he died.

If she did, in fact, kill him, then it must be the case that he died. So we can say that the proposition represented by *she killed him* entails the proposition represented by *he died*. Entailment is an important relationship to recognize, because it is fundamental to understanding the information of an utterance or discourse.

Notice that in the example sentence *therefore* is a connective that reflects entailment. Does *therefore* always reflect entailment? Give a perfectly natural complex sentence of the form "p therefore q" in which p does not entail q. You might have come up with examples like:

It's raining, therefore I'm bringing an umbrella.

The fact that it's raining does not mean that it must be true that I'm bringing an umbrella. So *therefore* here merely indicates a reason having to do with acting sensibly, not the reason of logical entailment. (And you will get a chance to evaluate whether or not other connectives of natural language are logical connectives in Problem Set 5.4.)

Still, propositional logic is a limited tool in semantics because it treats propositions as unanalyzable wholes. If we want to talk about the interpretation of a simple proposition itself rather than about the relationships between propositions, we need another model.

Arguments and Venn Diagrams

Consider the following argument:

Everybody loves a lover.
Peter loves Alma.

Therefore Jackie loves Paul.

The first two sentences of this argument are called the PREMISES. The final sentence, under the line, is called the CONCLUSION. If whenever the premises are true, the conclusion must also be true, we say the argument is VALID. Is this argument valid?

In ordinary conversation we would not find this argument valid. What has the aphorism about lovers and the statement *Peter loves Alma* have to do with Jackie and Paul's relationship? Nothing.

But in logic we could easily say this is valid, depending on what reading we assign to *Everybody loves a lover*. If we read *a lover* as meaning "any lover" in this sentence and if we define the N *lover* as "one who loves," then the first premise tells us that so long as there exists a single lover, all people are lovers. The second premise tells us that Peter loves Alma, so Peter is a lover, so there exists a single lover. From the two premises together, we can conclude that everyone loves Peter (since he's a lover and everybody loves a lover), so everyone is therefore a lover, so everyone loves everyone, and any particular instantiation of the love relationship holds—so, of course, Jackie loves Paul (and I love you).

I gave you this example just to have a fun way of pointing out the difference between what we consider logical (or valid) in ordinary conversation and what logicians consider valid in a formal system of symbolic logic. You may consider it a trick, since, even if you took *a lover* to mean "any lover," you probably did not define *lover* as merely "one who loves" for the aphorism *Everybody loves a lover*. And you're right. I tricked you. Forgive me, please. But I hope you had fun.

In many instances validity for ordinary conversation and for logical argument is identical. Consider these arguments:

(A)	All women are mortal.	(B)	All kangaroos are marsupials.
	Hillary is a woman.		All wallabies are marsupials.
	Hillary is mortal.		All kangaroos are wallables.

Only the one on the left is valid, right? How do you know that? This question is not a simple one to answer. If we used a propositional logic model for the argument in A, we'd have

$$(p \wedge q) \to r$$

which is by no means a tautology. So why do we all agree that A is a good argument? Let me reframe this question. Consider the sentence:

If all women are mortal and Hillary is a woman, then Hillary is mortal.

Is this sentence true? Again, I expect you to say yes. Why do we agree on its truth?

If you studied algebra at some point in your education, you may have studied SETS and their relationships and you may have drawn the relationships between sets with VENN DIAGRAMS. If you didn't, that's okay. The notions are simple and you can pick them up quickly. We're going to use Venn diagrams now to give us a way of representing and talking about why the argument in A is valid and that in B is invalid.

Draw a circle that represents the set of all mortals. Now draw a circle that represents the set of all women. Given the first premise in argument A, where should the second circle be located with respect to the first? Inside it, right? We say the set of women is CONTAINED IN or is a SUBSET of the set of mortals. Now make a dot that represents Hillary. Where should this dot be located? Inside the circle that represents women, which is inside the circle that represents all mortals. So Hillary is necessarily inside the circle that represents all mortals. That's why the argument is valid—because Hillary is contained in the set of women which is contained in the set of mortals:

where · = Hillary; ○ = the set of women; ◯ = the set of mortals.

Now consider the premises of argument B. Draw a circle that represents the set of all marsupials. Now draw a circle that represents the set of all kangaroos. What is the relationship between these circles? Again, kangaroos are a subset of marsupials. Now draw a circle that represents all wallabies. Where is it in relation to the other two circles? It is inside the circle of marsupials, given the second premise. But we know nothing about its relation to the set of kangaroos from these premises alone. Yet the conclusion is about the relationship of the sets of kangaroos, on the one hand, and wallabies, on the other. So the conclusion does not follow from the premises. Indeed, given these premises, it could easily be the case (and, in fact, it is the case) that the sets of kangaroos and wallabies are entirely separate from each other—they don't overlap (or INTERSECT) at all:

where one ○ = the set of kangaroos; the other ○ = the set of wallabies; and ○ = the set of marsupials.

All right, so now we have a graphic way of accounting for the validity of the argument in A (or, alternatively, for the truth of the sentence *If all women are mortal and Hillary is a woman, then Hillary is mortal*). Why couldn't propositional logic help us here? What does the validity of the argument rest upon? Look at the predicates of the elementary propositions—they involve womanhood and mortality. The argument relies on understanding the relationships between these predicates and the referents of which they are predicated—the set relationships that you just graphed with Venn diagrams. That's why propositional logic doesn't help here—it sees only the whole proposition, not the predicates inside it.

The Predicate Calculus

In order to represent the relationships pertinent to the argument in A with a symbolic logic, we need to have a way to distinguish the internal parts of a proposition. Look again at our example sentence:

If all women are mortal and Hillary is a woman, then Hillary is mortal.

What parts must we be able to distinguish in order to see the form of our argument? We already noted that the predicates of womanhood and mortality are relevant. What else? The INDIVIDUAL Hillary must be represented, also. Anything else? Can you see how you rely on the quantifier *all* in interpreting this sentence? That is, *all women are mortal* tells us that, for every member of the set of women, it is the case that that member is mortal. Now we are further told that Hillary belongs to the set of women. So let's represent each of these three types of entities (predicates, individuals, and quantifiers) in our PREDICATE CALCULUS.

Let M = be mortal, and W = be a woman. We have followed a convention here: typically capital letters are used to symbolize predicates.

Let h = Hillary. Again, we are following a convention: small letters typically symbolize individuals. We will let the statement $W(h)$ = Hillary is a woman. How would we symbolize the proposition *Hillary is mortal?* $M(h)$.

The Universal Quantifier

We are still missing one important part of the sentence. What other individuals do we need to distinguish besides Hillary? All women, right? But the quantifier *all* is mixed up in there. How do we separate out the quantifier from the woman part of the nominal?

Consider this sentence:

All women are mortal.

If we want to state this in terms of a relationship between sets, we might come up with something like: The set of women is a subset of the set of mortals. If you had to rephrase that in terms of an implication, could you do it? Sure:

If someone is a woman, she's mortal.

So when we say *all women*, we are quantifying over all individuals with the property of womanhood. We therefore need a symbol to represent an unnamed individual—a VARI- ABLE. We will use x for this, following the convention of using small letters from the end of the alphabet to represent variables. (If we needed two variables, we'd use x and y; if we needed three, we'd use x, y, and z; if we needed four, we'd add in w, and so on, drawing from earlier and earlier letters of the alphabet.) How would we symbolize the proposition *Everyone is mortal*? We are saying every individual has the property of mortality. The symbol $\forall$ is used to represent the UNIVERSAL QUANTIFIER *all*, and it is read "for all." So we write the proposition *Everyone is mortal* like so:

$$\forall x\ M(x)$$

which is read "for all x, x is mortal," and we say the quantifier binds the variable here (just as anaphors are bound by antecedents in Chapter 4).

Such a statement is interpreted with respect to a given UNIVERSE. So, for example, let's say that we have twenty-six members in our universe, and let's label each one with the letters of the Roman alphabet, like so:

$$U = \{a, b, c, d, \ldots, z\}$$

(Braces surround the members of a set. Here, the set defines the universe.) When we interpret a FORMAL EXPRESSION like $\forall x\ M(x)$, we evaluate its truth or falsity with respect to the universe as we've defined it for that expression. So with a universally quantified statement, we would go to the universe and check whether the predication holds true of each and every member of the universe. That is, we'd check to see if $M(a)$ is true, if $M(b)$ is true, if $M(c)$ is true, and so on, all the way to $M(z)$. If all of them are true, then $\forall x\ M(x)$ is true in the universe we've defined.

By convention, if we do not explicitly define a universe in which a formal expression is to be evaluated, the real world is taken as the relevant universe. (And if your mind rebels at the idea that we all agree on what the real world is, great. Start writing fantasy fiction.)

How would we represent the proposition *All women are mortal* (or, equivalently, *If someone is a woman, she's mortal*)? Try to say it in ordinary words first. We're saying that womanhood implies mortality for any given individual. So the quantifier has scope (a term we've used since Chapter 2) over the implication:

$$\forall x\ (W(x) \rightarrow M(x))$$

Here the parentheses around the entire implication are meant simply to help you see that the quantifier has scope over the whole implication. Read this aloud. You should have said, "For all x, if x is a woman, then x is mortal." Describe how you would evaluate the truth of this expression in the real world. You'd go from entity to entity in the real world checking to see if the implication holds. When you looked at women, you'd find that, indeed, all women are mortal. So the implication holds for those x that are women. But this formal expression says more than that. It says that the implication must hold for every x. So if we look at men, for example, we find that $W(x)$ is false when x is male. However, if you look back at your truth table for the logical connective $\rightarrow$, you'll find that a false statement can imply anything. So if $W(x)$ is false, then $W(x) \rightarrow M(x)$ is true. So for all nonwomen in our universe, $W(x) \rightarrow M(x)$ is true. And since for all women, $W(x) \rightarrow M(x)$ is also true, then it is true that for all x in our universe the implication holds.

All right, now let's take our original sentence again and write it in the predicate calculus, making use of our knowledge of the implication relationship that the quantifier *all* sets up:

Original sentence:

If all women are mortal and Hillary is a woman, then Hillary is mortal.
$((\forall x \, (W(x) \rightarrow M(x))) \wedge (W(h))) \rightarrow M(h)$

Here we have an implication that consists of a conjunction on one side $((\forall x \, (W(x) \rightarrow M(x)) \wedge W(h))$ and a simple statement $(M(h))$ on the other. The conjunction consists of an embedded implication $(\forall x \, (W(x) \rightarrow M(x)))$ and another simple statement $(W(h))$. Read this symbolic statement aloud. You should have said:

If for all x, if x is a woman, then x is mortal and Hillary is a woman, then Hillary is mortal.

Can you tell me now why this sentence is true? Since Hillary is an individual, and since the embedded implication falls within the scope of the universal quantifier, this implication must be true of all individuals and, in particular, it must be true of Hillary. So we can replace the variable with h, like so:

$W(h) \rightarrow M(h)$

Now, so long as Hillary is a woman (which we are told she is), we must conclude that Hillary is mortal by this implication.

The $\forall$ binds the x here. Does every quantifier need a variable to bind? Certainly it's hard to imagine how we could use a quantifier in a meaningful sentence and not give it a variable to range over.

The Existential Quantifier

Does every variable need a quantifier to bind it? That is, do FREE variables occur in language? What about the proposition:

Someone is a woman.

Does this merely assign the property of womanhood to a variable? Think about it. What else do we know from this sentence? We know that someone exists, right? This sentence is therefore also asserting the existence of an individual. The individual need not be known to the speaker or hearer, but the existence of the individual is asserted. Logicians use the symbol ∃ to represent the EXISTENTIAL QUANTIFIER, and it is read "there exists." So now let's give a symbolic representation of *Someone is a woman*. This is logically equivalent to *There exists a woman*:

$$\exists x \ W(x)$$

This is read, "There exists an x such that x is a woman." How would we represent the sentence *Some woman is mortal*?

$$\exists x \ (W(x) \wedge M(x))$$

Read it aloud. You should have said, "There exists an x such that x is a woman and x is mortal."

With this approach to existential quantification, we might conclude that free variables do not occur in natural language. However, some linguists have argued that the existential quantifier is not necessary in logical expressions corresponding to sentences like *Someone is a woman*. Instead, they use a sophisticated approach to discourse analysis in which a free variable would be used in such a sentence and a function in the discourse (the "assignment function") would bind it. We won't go into that way of handling quantification in this book because justification for it would take us farther into a technical discussion than is warranted for an introductory text. The chapter references can help you here if you want to read about this.

Ambiguity and Quantifiers

Now consider the sentence:

A woman is mortal.

Do you see two readings for that sentence? What are they? One is a generic sentence. But this particular generic sentence happens to be true of not just the typical case but of all cases. That is, this sentence is equivalent to *All women are mortal* not just because of the way our world works, but because of the definition of *woman*. If we found a female who was immortal in this world (as opposed to the next—I don't want to raise religious questions here), we'd label her something other than a woman—perhaps a goddess. (Maybe you disagree with me on that, if earthly mortality is not part of the concept of humanness to you. If so, please bear with me just for the sake of the argument. Thank you.) The other reading is a statement about a particular individual who is a woman; perhaps her name is Alice. Represent the two readings with the predicate calculus:

$$\forall x \ (W(x) \rightarrow M(x))$$
$$\exists x \ (W(x) \wedge M(x))$$

You have now seen a lovely fact: The symbols here make clear that we are not only dealing with different quantifiers in the two readings; we are dealing with different connectives. These symbols show us in a simple way how a sentence in which a property is assigned to a whole set establishes an implicational relationship between the two sets (a subset relationship), whereas a sentence in which a property is assigned to just an individual does not imply any such thing.

The Generic Operator

Most generic sentences, however, are not equivalent to universal statements, as you well know from our earlier discussion of generics. Give some examples using NPs introduced by the determiner *a*. You might have come up with sentences like:

A pig eats slop.

If we happen to find one pig that won't eat slop, does that falsify the sentence? No. The generic reading allows for aberration from the norm. So this sentence is not equivalent to *All pigs eat slop*, which would, in fact, be falsified by the existence of a slop-hating pig. For this reason, it is useful to introduce another operator: G, the generic operator. The representation of *A pig eats slop* would be:

$$Gx \ (P(x) \rightarrow S(x))$$

This is to be read: For the generic x, if x is a pig, then x eats slop.

Multiple Arguments

In this representation, I treated eating slop as a property of the eater. That is, I treated eating slop as a predicate taking the eater as its only argument. However, we know that in natural language, we often find reason to refer to all the various participants in an event and to distinguish the action or state from those participants. For example, in order to see the similarities between the sentences:

A pig eats slop.
A koala eats eucalyptus leaves.

we need to be able to separate out the action of eating from the thing eaten. And in order to see the similarities between the sentences:

A pig eats slop.
Her mother cooks slop.

we need to be able to separate out the thing acted upon from the action. So we need to allow our representations to distinguish all those participants and actions or states when useful. We can do this by allowing predicates that take more than one argument. *Her mother cooks slop*, for example, can be represented as:

C(m, s)

where C = cooks; m = her mother; s = slop. How could you represent *Ralph buys presents for Jane*?

B(r, p, j)

Here we have one predicate with three arguments.

Of course it is important for us to have a way to keep track of which argument each individual stands for in an expression with multiple arguments for the same predicate. What would you suggest as a convention? Think about natural language. What is the most prominent or salient argument in a sentence of English from the standpoint of syntax? The Subject, right? In fact, English tensed clauses demand overtly expressed Subjects, as do many languages (although many others do not, a fact you studied in the section "The Null Subject Parameter" of Chapter Four). For this reason, the first argument in a logical expression typically corresponds to the argument that goes in Subject position of the syntactic form corresponding to the proposition (that is, the sentence). The second argument typically corresponds to the Direct Object; the third to the Indirect Object. If oblique arguments are included in the logical expression, their order with respect to one another is not fixed by convention, but they will generally follow the Subject, DO, and/or IO arguments.

Binding

In the discussion thus far I have said that the quantifiers bind the variables. You are familiar with the concept of binding from the sections "Interpretation: Anaphors and Binding Theory" and "Reflexives" in Chapter 4. We talked about binding there in terms of the syntactic relationship of c-command. Let me remind you of the definition of that relationship:

> Any node X c-commands every node dominated by the first branching node that dominates the X.

We then defined binding of NPs like so:

> An NP binds another NP that it c-commands and is coreferential with.

It's been argued that the same structural relationship holds of binding with respect to quantification. That is, **a quantifier has scope only over those variables that it c-commands**.

Our semantic representation thus far consists of connectives (like $\rightarrow$ and $\wedge$) and parentheses as well as individuals, variables, predicates, and quantifiers, but no structure of the sort that the relationship of c-command could be defined over. So let's now add in structure.

How do you think we should begin? Keep in mind that you know quite a lot about syntactic structure and that we are talking here about the semantics of natural language. So a first stab might be to propose trees that locate the quantifiers appropriately with respect to their scope. Let's do this first for the sentence *Some woman is mortal*, for which we came up with the formal expression:

$$\exists x \ (W(x) \wedge M(x))$$

What semantic label corresponds to the syntactic label of C″ (for complementizer phrase—if you haven't read Chapter 4, you can just think of this as the label for clause)? Certainly, it is *formal expression* (which we'll symbolize with F). So our tree would be:

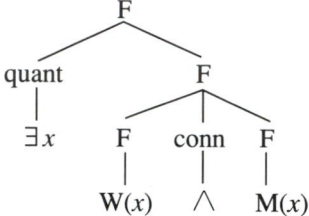

Here quant = quantifier; conn = connective. If we wanted to, we could break down the tree inside the lower F's, like so:

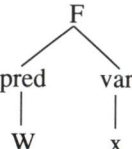

Here pred = predicate; var = variable. We did not break down the first tree in this way because the internal structure of the lower (or embedded) formal expressions is not of interest to us at the moment. The quantifier in the first tree c-commands both instances of the variable x since the first branching node that dominates the quantifier (the highest F of the tree) also dominates both instances of the variable x.

Now you give the tree for the sentence *All women are mortal*, for which we gave above the formal expression:

$$\forall x \ (W(x) \rightarrow M(x))$$

You should have come up with:

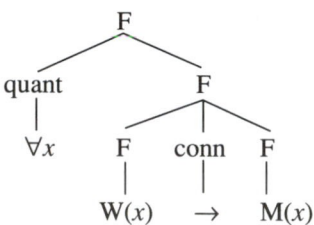

Ambiguity of Scope

We pointed out that formal representations of the meaning of sentences can give us insight into the ambiguity of a sentence like *A woman is mortal*. Other types of ambiguity can also be more easily understood with such representations. Consider the sentence:

Everyone loves someone.

This sentence can be read in at least two ways. Do you see the ambiguity? Following context can help reveal it:

Everyone loves someone, and her name is Sue.
Everyone loves someone, even if we all love different people.

Now that you see the ambiguity, try to paraphrase the two readings of our sentence. In one, there is a specific individual that everyone loves. In the other, everyone loves an individual, but the individuals can vary from person to person. Try to write the two readings in the predicate calculus making use of our universal and existential quantifiers. Since you will have two quantifiers in your expressions, let's agree to use x for the variable bound by the universal quantifier and y for the variable bound by the existential quantifier, just so that we all write the expressions in the same way. I hope you came up with:

$\exists y \; \forall x \; L(x, y)$
$\forall x \; \exists y \; L(x, y)$

The first expression says: There exists a y such that for all x, x loves y. So we pick out a y and all the x's love that y. The second expression says: For all x, there exists a y such that x loves y. So for each x, we pick out a y (which can be different for each x) that x loves. We say that the outer quantifier (the first quantifier in each expression) has WIDE SCOPE, while the inner quantifier has NARROW SCOPE. So the ambiguity of the sentence *Everyone loves someone* is a matter of scope ambiguity—it hinges on whether the existential or the universal quantifier has wider scope.

Draw the tree for the first expression. You should have come up with:

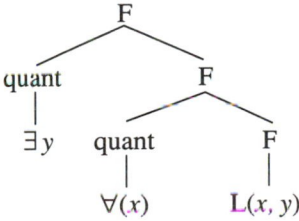

Draw the tree for the second expression. It should be identical in structure, the only difference being that the higher quantifier is now the universal one and the lower quantifier is now the existential one.

Not all ambiguities involving scope are as simple as that. Consider:

Every American loves a wonderful actress.

The ambiguity here is parallel to the ambiguity of the sentence *Everyone loves someone* with the added complication that the NP *a wonderful actress* can be interpreted as generic. So this sentence has three readings. Again, we can use context to help reveal them:

> Every American loves a wonderful actress, and her name is Emma Thompson.
> Every American loves a wonderful actress, and their names are Emma Thompson and Meryl Streep and Winona Ryder and . . .
> Every American loves a wonderful actress. It doesn't matter who: If she's wonderful, Americans love her.

Again, paraphrase the three readings of our sentence. In the first, there is a specific actress that every American loves. (In other words, we've got a given woman actress and if you're an American, you love this particular actress.) In the second, we are saying that every American has the property of loving a wonderful actress, where which actress varies from person to person (although we will obviously overlap quite a lot, since there are more Americans than actresses). In the third, for any wonderful actress we are told that every American loves her. (In other words, if anyone is a wonderful actress then anyone who is an American will love her.)

Now write the three readings in the predicate calculus. The first two should have presented no problem for you. I hope you came up with:

$$\exists y\ \forall x\ (W(y) \wedge (A(x) \rightarrow L(x, y)))$$
$$\forall x\ \exists y\ ((A(x) \wedge W(y)) \rightarrow L(x, y))$$

The first expressions says: There exists a y such that for all x, y is a wonderful actress, and if x is an American, x loves y. The second expression says: For every x there exists a y such that, if x is an American and y is a wonderful actress, then x loves y. So the ambiguity involves not just which quantifier has wide scope, but the relationship of the embedded expressions to the connectives. In the first expression, that y is a wonderful actress is conjoined to another expression that is an implication. In the second expression, the conjunction is inside the antecedent of the implication.

Coming up with a formal statement in the predicate calculus of the third reading may have been harder. You might have come up with:

$$Gy\ \forall x\ ((A(x) \wedge W(y)) \rightarrow L(x, y))$$

Or you might, instead, have put the two operators in reverse order:

$$\forall x\ Gy\ ((A(x) \wedge W(y)) \rightarrow L(x, y))$$

In fact, these two expressions are equivalent, because both quantifiers are universal. This expression says: For every x and for the generic y, if x is an American and y is a wonderful actress, then x loves y.

The moral is that you should look for scope ambiguities, but you should also be careful to check for other differences in the expression, as well. (And you might have been on the alert for such differences anyway, given the two analyses of sentences like *A woman is mortal.*)

Before leaving this example, there's one other point I'd like to make. Let's try to draw the tree for the first reading of *Every American loves a wonderful actress*, which we've represented with:

$$\exists y \; \forall x \; (W(y) \land (A(x) \to L(x, y)))$$

The existential quantifier has scope over everything else in this expression. The universal quantifier, on the other hand, has nothing whatsoever to do with the statement $W(y)$. Instead, it pertains only to the expressions involved in the implication. The universal quantifier, then, might be positioned c-commanding everything following it in the expression just given, or, instead, c-commanding only the implication expression. That is, the expression is equivalent to:

$$\exists y \; (W(y) \land \forall x \; (A(x) \to L(x, y)))$$

We will follow the convention of placing the quantifier in the lower position. The tree is then:

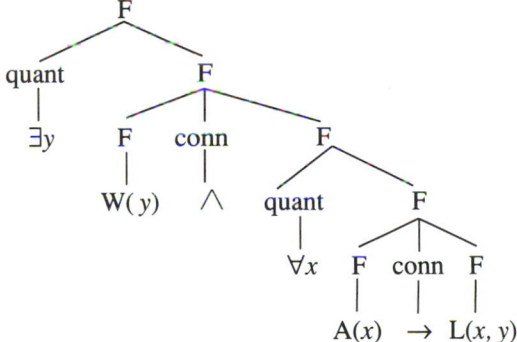

Ambiguity

The sentence *Everyone loves someone* is ambiguous, but the ambiguity is not represented in the syntactic tree at SS, only in the syntactic tree at LOGICAL FORM (LF). There is a difference between the two trees (and we'll talk about that). But the question I want to ask you now is whether we can ever have ambiguity arising from syntactic structures that don't involve quantifiers. Sure. Consider the famous sentence:

Flying planes can be dangerous.

Give two readings for this sentence. The issue is whether the activity of flying a plane can be dangerous or whether a plane that is in flight can be dangerous. In terms of syntactic structure, the issue is whether *flying* takes *planes* as its Direct Object, or whether *flying* modifies *planes*. Very simplified trees of these two readings are:

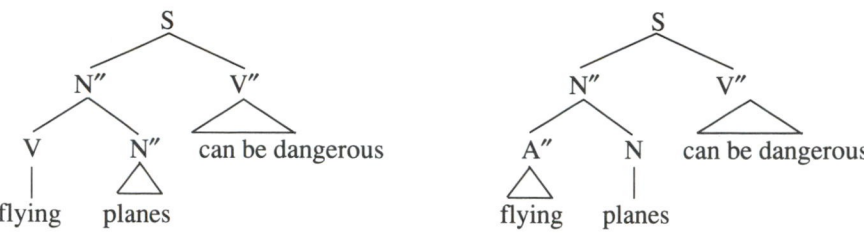

Here S = sentence; N" = noun phrase; V" = verb phrase; A" = adjective phrase. Recall from Chapter 4 that a triangle indicates that a node could be analyzed further, but we don't care to do it here. (If you are disturbed that a V can head an N" in the first tree, good. Given how we analyzed phrases in Chapter 4, you shouldn't have expected this. But if you look back at #4 in Problem Set 4.4, you should be able to convince yourself that *flying* in this sentence is best analyzed as a V. By the way, constructions like this are often called exocentric, a term we met when talking about nonheaded compounds in Chapter 3.)

Can other things beside quantifier scope and syntactic categories and branching be the source of ambiguity? Of course. Try to find a sentence in which a lexical item has more than one reading, so lexical ambiguity makes the sentence ambiguous. You might have come up with examples like:

I need bread.
Give me a line.

Bread could signify a food or money. So here we're into what might be called a literal vs. a slang definition. In the second sentence, the issue is what kind of line? A line of text (if I'm a printer), a fishing line, a series of romantic words, what?

Can a sentence ever mix two types of ambiguities? Sure:

I saw her duck.

If *duck* denotes an animal, I saw an animal, and *her duck* is the NP Object of *saw*. If *duck* denotes an action, I saw an event, and *her duck* is a sentential complement (although the particular syntactic structure of such a sentence is a matter of controversy). (You might also have noticed the lexical ambiguity in *saw*, in which case you got an additional (gruesome) reading for the sentence in which *duck* denotes an animal.)

SS vs. LF

Okay, now let's go back to the fact that a sentence like *Everyone loves someone* is ambiguous, but it has only one syntactic representation at SS, although it has two at LF. When we drew trees in LF, we made them very much parallel to trees at SS. And in general, there is a lot in common between the syntactic tree at SS and the syntactic tree at LF of a given sentence. However, scope ambiguities like those we've studied point out differences between the two types of trees. So how do we map from an SS representation into an LF representation (that is, into a logical form)?

This question looks simple, but its answer is among the most controversial in linguistic theory. It would be lovely, from the point of view of theoretical simplicity, if every syntactic structure could be mapped into a unique semantic structure and if every semantic structure corresponded to a unique syntactic structure. And the loveliest situation of all would be having an ISOMORPHISM between syntax and semantics.

We say that two systems are isomorphic if for each individual in one system there exists a corresponding individual in the other system, and if for each operation or relation in one system there exists a corresponding operation or relation in the other system, and, finally, if for the result of any operation or relation on a set of individuals in one system there exists a corresponding result of the corresponding operations or relations on the corresponding set of individuals in the other system. In simpler terms, we call two systems isomorphic if they are entirely parallel.

At various points in the history of linguistics people have proposed an isomorphism between syntax and semantics. I think such proposals are doomed, for reasons I've explained in articles and other books I've published. Let me give you just one example. Consider these two phrases:

a photograph of John
a prince of a man

All evidence I know of confirms that both phrases are NPs and that they have identical internal structure. (In particular, the head N takes a sister PP.) Yet in the first NP, *John* is arguably the theme argument of the head N *photograph*, whereas in the second NP, the head N *prince* is arguably a property predicated of *a man*. Thus a single syntactic structure is mapped into two very different semantic structures.

Nevertheless, the proposal that there is an isomorphism between syntax and semantics is at least partially the motivation for certain claims about LF. The idea is that LF should be the syntactic representation from which the semantics can be read. It should unravel, so to speak, all the ambiguities present at SS and give a unique LF for each reading.

How are we to get to LF from SS? Much of the time the mapping is straightforward. We have verbs that correspond nicely to predicates; we have noun phrases that correspond nicely to individuals; we have clauses that correspond nicely to formal expressions in the predicate calculus. The mapping question I want us to focus on then is the issue of quantifier scope. Consider once again the sentence *Everyone loves someone*, which has the two representations:

$\exists y \ \forall x \ L(x, y)$
$\forall x \ \exists y \ L(x, y)$

At SS, both the verb and the universally quantified NP (*everyone*) precede the existentially quantified NP (*someone*). But in these formal expressions, the predicate (L) follows both of the quantifiers. And the quantifiers come in different orders in the two expressions. It's been proposed that part of the mapping from SS to LF is carried out by a rule of QUANTIFIER RAISING, which takes each quantifier and moves it to an appropriate position (a position from which it c-commands those things that are within its scope).

The proposal of a rule of Quantifier Raising is very significant for linguistic theory in general. We have seen that movement rules are needed in the phonology (because of metathesis) and in the morphology (because of morphologically induced metathesis). And some have argued that movement rules are needed in the syntax (in particular, we discussed head-to head movement and wh-movement in Chapter 4 and we met NP-movement in Problem Set 4.14). If there is movement as we go from SS to LF, then, in a sense, there is movement in the semantics, as well. That is, while LF is strictly speaking a syntactic representation (given that a true semantic representation will be in terms of concepts), quantifier movement is entirely abstract and serves only to feed the interpretive component of the grammar. So all components of the grammar make use of the mechanism of movement.

Is there any other mechanism that we've seen all components of the grammar using? Yes: hierarchical structures (the tiers of phonology, the trees of morphology, syntax, and, again in a sense, semantics—because of LF trees). So we know that all the components do have certain things in common.

If we want to see all components of the grammar as making use of the same sorts of rules, principles, and parameters, then movement in LF is, indeed, welcome. I will leave this issue without further comment since you will surely discuss it at great length if you take a semantics course. And if you don't go further with semantics, at least you've been introduced to the concept.

Other Types of Quantification

Universal, existential, and generic quantifiers are by no means the only quantifiers we find in natural language. List some others and use them in sentences. You may have come up with examples like:

> Most dogs like potatoes.
> I know some intelligent crows.
> We'd give money to few charities.

While a predicate calculus approach to the semantics of sentences with universal, existential, and generic quantifiers can lead to many insights (as we've seen), such an approach to sentences with these other quantifiers is much more problematic. To see this, let's take a look at the semantics of *most* for a moment. If we allow a quantifier M for "most," we might want to propose for *Most dogs like potatoes* the formal expression:

$$M x \ (D(x) \to P(x))$$

This is to be read, "For most x, if x is a dog, then x likes potatoes," which seems like a reasonable paraphrase of the sentence. However, we have to look closely at the connector for implication in logic in order to evaluate how reasonable this representation of the sentence really is.

So let's check whether this gives us the right results when we compare it to the world. Let's say that, in fact, only one dog in our universe likes potatoes, even though there are many dogs. Our sentence, *Most dogs like potatoes*, is therefore false in the world we are considering. Is the formal expression also false?

When $D(x)$ is true, $P(x)$ is false in our universe except in one instance (that instance of the single dog that likes potatoes). So the implication is false most of the time for x is a dog. However, there are many things in our universe that are not dogs. So let's consider trees, of which there are many more than dogs. When x is a tree, $D(x)$ is false. But we know that a false proposition can imply anything. So $D(x) \to P(x)$ is true for all x that are trees. And, in fact, $D(x) \rightarrow P(x)$ is true for all nondogs. So for most x in our universe, $D(x) \rightarrow P(x)$ is true. But in the universe we just described, the sentence *Most dogs like potatoes* is false. Therefore, the formal expression $Mx\ (D(x) \rightarrow P(x))$ is a poor representation of that sentence, since it is true of our universe (and will automatically be true of any universe in which dogs do not make up more than half the entities in the universe).

You might then try some different formal expression as a representation of *Most dogs like potatoes*. But for any connective we have discussed (and you can fill them in, one after another, for ? below), the formal expression fails:

$$Mx\ (D(x)\ ?\ P(x))$$

For this reason (and others), linguists who make use of these quantifiers in a MODEL THEORETIC approach to semantics (like the one we are developing here) have to restrict the universe we consider appropriately. For example, we can say that

$Mx\ (P(x))$ **in the universe consisting of dogs only**

is a proper formal expression of *Most dogs like potatoes*. Quantifiers such as *most, some, few* are, accordingly, called RESTRICTED quantifiers.

There is at least one other characteristic of restricted quantifiers that we should mention. Consider these sentences:

All Latin verbs have rich inflection.
Few Latin verbs belong to the second conjugation.

When we speak of all Latin verbs, we understand that the entire set of verbs is being considered. The interpretation is absolute in this way. But when we speak of few Latin verbs, we understand only that a subset of verbs are being considered. We don't, in fact, know whether that subset is small or large. For example, there are approximately 130 verbs in the Latin second conjugation. That's quite a number of verbs. Yet it is few in comparison to the total number of verbs in Latin. On the other hand, if we said:

Many of the children in this classroom have siblings.

The number might be only nine, but if there are eleven students totally, the set that have siblings is many in comparison to the total number. In one instance 130 qualifies as "few"; in the other instance nine qualifies as "many." **The interpretation of restricted quantifiers is relative to context, unlike the interpretation of the universal and the existential quantifiers**.

You will have a chance to explore some of these quantifiers in Problem Set 5.5, where a variety of issues concerning the interpretation of natural-language quantifiers come up.

Anaphors and Pronouns

We have learned that quantifiers must bind variables. In Chapter 4 we talked about binding primarily with respect to anaphors and pronouns. In other words, anaphors and pronouns can be considered variables. **Anaphors are special in that they are variables that must**

be locally bound (Condition A of Binding Theory), as we saw with examples like:

John likes himself.
*John hopes the club likes himself.

Pronouns are special in that they are variables that cannot be locally bound (Condition B of Binding Theory), as we saw with examples like:

*John$_i$ likes him$_i$.
John$_i$ hopes the club likes him$_i$.

This approach to anaphors and pronouns can help us to account for certain facts regarding quantifiers. Consider this sentence:

All actresses love them.

Can this have a reading in which the actresses love themselves? No. Why not? You might feel very comfortable saying that *all actresses* cannot bind the pronoun *them* because of Condition B, the restriction against local binding of pronouns. (If you don't feel comfortable saying that, don't worry. We'll return to the source of your discomfort.) Give a formal representation of this sentence in the predicate calculus:

$$\forall x \ (A(x) \rightarrow L(x, y))$$

If x and y were identical (that is, coreferential), then we would see a violation of Condition B in the expression $L(x, y)$.

Now consider the sentence:

All actresses love themselves.

Can you account for the grammaticality of the anaphor here? Again, you may find this intuitively obvious: The anaphor is appropriate because it is locally bound. Give a formal representation:

$$\forall x \ (A(x) \rightarrow L(x, x))$$

We can see the local binding in $L(x, x)$.

While this example might have moved along smoothly for you, some sentences with quantifiers may disturb you. Consider:

No actress loves her.
No actress loves herself.

In the first sentence *her* and *no actress* cannot be co-indexed, and in the second sentence they must be. Here your intuitions probably fail you. Ask yourself, who would *no actress* refer to? We can see that *no actress* does not seem referential in the way *the actress I saw in a film last night* does. So why do we get only a non–co-indexed interpretation in the first sentence? And, along those same lines, why is the anaphor appropriate in the second sentence?

Let's give a formal representation of these sentences. We haven't yet talked about negation with respect to quantification and scope, but you can see that the sentence *No actress loves her* involves quantification. Paraphrase it trying to use either our existential or our universal quantifier. Perhaps you came up with something like, "It is not the case that there exists an actress that loves her." Okay, now let's give the formal expression:

$$\sim \exists x \ (A(x) \wedge L(x, y))$$

($\sim \exists$ = there does not exist. This can also be written $\not\exists$.) If the pronoun is really a variable, then we can see that y must not equal x (that is, must not be coreferential with x) if we are to conform to Condition B of Binding Theory.

For the sentence *No actress loves herself*, we have the same representation, but now $y = x$:

$$\sim \exists x \ (A(x) \wedge L(x, x))$$

So Condition A is satisfied.

Several things have come out of this discussion. First, you might now feel that all quantified NPs (like *every dog, few potatoes, each friend*) are not really referential in the same way definite NPs (like *Mary, my brother, the pig that lives out back*) are. Thus we needed our formal representations of *All actresses love them/themselves* to account for the interpretations and grammaticality of these sentences.

Second, you can now view negation as an operator over an entity such as an individual or an expression (even over an entire formal expression). Like quantifiers, negation has scope. Consider the ambiguity of this sentence you met earlier (the sentence I used as bait to help make you be willing to wade through all the logic):

Mattie doesn't beat her donkey because she loves him.

Do you see the two readings? Following context can help to reveal them:

Mattie doesn't beat her donkey because she loves him, and she never will.
Mattie doesn't beat her donkey because she loves him, but because he's a bad donkey.

In the first reading, the *not* (in its reduced form *n't*) negates the action of beating. So Mattie doesn't beat her donkey and the reason why is that she loves him. In the second reading, the *not* doesn't negate the action of beating. Rather, it negates the reason for the beating. So Mattie does beat her donkey, but not because she loves him. Once more the issue is scope, and the ambiguity arises from the interaction of two operators. Clearly, the negative is one operator. But what is the other? Can you see that the *because* clause, being a modifier, also has scope? Our two operators, then, are *not* and *because*.

Which one has wide scope in the first reading? You should be asking yourself whether *not* falls within the domain of *because*—in which case *because* has wide scope—or whether *because* falls within the domain of *not*—in which case *not* has wide scope. I hope you realized that *because* has wide scope in the first reading (in which Mattie doesn't beat her donkey), but *not* has wide scope in the second reading (in which she beats him, but not because she loves him).

If you're using this book as part of a course, talk with your classmates about the scope ambiguity, exploring the notions of wide and narrow scope. Can you find ambiguous sentences in which *not* interacts with another quantifier such as *all*? Can you find ambiguous sentences in which *all* interacts with a modifier like *because*? This may take a lot of discussion. If you are reading this book alone and you haven't yet started talking to yourself (miracle of miracles), start now.

Third, we can now answer a question we brought up much earlier: Does natural language allow free variables? The answer is yes. Pronouns are always locally free and often they are free even nonlocally.

Opaque Contexts

Talking about scope with quantification and negation leads us to the recognition of many kinds of operators and the domains (a term you met in Chapter 2) over which they operate. We can talk of a possibility operator that occurs in sentences such as:

Jay may play the trombone.

which we could represent as:

Mp

where M = may and p = Jay play the trombone. That is, the modal *may* sets up a hypothetical. So in some POSSIBLE WORLD Jay plays the trombone. We could also recognize a necessity operator in the modal *must*:

Jay must play the trombone.

Actually, this sentence is ambiguous. Do you see it? Let me add following context to help out:

Jay must play the trombone or he'll die of deprivation.
Jay must play the trombone; look at the pattern of indentation marks on the fingers of his right hand.

One reading deals with a necessity that stems from Jay. We call that the DEONTIC reading. The other reading deals with a strong probability. We call that the EPISTEMIC reading. Each reading uses its own operator.

In fact, now that you've seen the two readings for the *must* sentence, go back and try to see if you can find two readings for the *may* sentence: *Jay may play the trombone.* Can you? One deals with permission (perhaps he's allowed to play the trombone now because he's completed all his homework) and the other deals with probability (perhaps he's in a good mood and often when he's in a good mood he plays the trombone, so I say that sentence as a prediction of what he might do).

I won't here go into deontic (obligation and permission) and epistemic (knowledge and belief) logics, but you can easily find readings on them. And you can find readings on

BOULOMAIC (desire) logics and ALETHIC (logical possibility) logics, and others. In fact, it can be shown that even tense is an operator. For example, notice that tense can influence whether we read a sentence with a specific or a generic interpretation (and, certainly, other factors come in here, as well):

The dog bit mailmen.
The dog bites mailmen.

(The references for this chapter can get you started on relevant reading lists for all these kinds of logics.)

Instead of going into these other logics with their special operators, I want to briefly introduce you to what I consider to be one of the loveliest issues in logic for natural language, that of OPAQUE CONTEXTS. Consider this argument:

Oedipus married Jocasta.
Jocasta was Oedipus's mother.

Oedipus married his mother.

Is this valid? Sure. How do you know? Certainly, you can see that if Jocasta is Oedipus's mother, then we can subsitute in *Jocasta* for *his mother* in other statements of the argument. In particular, we can make that substitution in the conclusion and see that the conclusion has to follow from the premises, since the conclusion is the first premise after this substitution.

Now consider this argument.

Oedipus wanted to marry Jocasta.
Jocasta was Oedipus's mother.

Oedipus wanted to marry his mother.

Is this valid? No. Why not? What is so different about the two arguments? Why are we barred from making the subsitution of *Jocasta* for *his mother* in the conclusion of this argument?

Obviously, the addition of the notion of "want" changes things crucially. So think about worlds. Once we have introduced a want, we have set up a possible world, the world of Oedipus's wants. Keep a clear distinction in your head between the real world and the wanted world of Oedipus—the world that exists in that part of Oedipus's mind that deals with wanting. What parts of this argument are statements about the real world and what parts of this argument are statements about Oedipus's wanted world? Do you see that Jocasta's identity as Oedipus's mother is not part of Oedipus's wanted world? Her identity as his mother is part of the real world around him. He may know nothing about her identity in the real world (and, indeed, as the story goes, he didn't know she was his mother).

We say that the verb *want* has set up an opaque domain here. We cannot make subsitutions into that domain from other worlds. So long as we deal in a single world, all the domains are transparent to subsitution.

Extensions and Intensions

We made an implicit distinction in this argument that we need to make explicit now. Consider the sentence:

Oedipus saw his mother.

How do we understand the NP *his mother*? One way is to look at the referent of this NP in the real or actual world. We would then understand this NP to mean Jocasta. We are taking the EXTENSION of the NP as its meaning. So the statement is about seeing an individual.

But there are other times when such an approach to the meaning of an NP won't work. Consider:

The president of the United States is always an important world leader.

The president of the United States as I write this now is Bill Clinton. Does this sentence mean that Bill Clinton is always an important world leader? Certainly not. What does it mean? It means that anyone who holds the office of the president of the United States is an important world leader. So here we interpret the NP not to be its extension (the referent in the actual world), but its INTENSION (in this case the referent in the possible worlds of the past, the present, and the future). We have a statement that is about an individual concept rather than about an individual.

We could reframe our discussion of the Oedipus arguments above in these terms. Consider:

Oedipus wanted to marry his mother.

We read *his mother* not extensionally but intensionally here—he wanted to marry whatever person bore this familial relationship to him. But with that reading, we can see that the sentence is false as a conclusion to the premises. That is, Jocasta is the extensional equivalent of *his mother* in the actual world, but not the intensional equivalent. We cannot substitute extensions for intensions.

Let's dwell on the extension/intension contrast a moment longer. When we interpret the extension of an NP, we are mapping from a single world (the actual world) at a given time into the NP's extension. But when we interpret the intension of an NP, we are mapping from all possible worlds and times to all the extensions of the NP in those worlds at those times. We have a mapping from sets of world-time pairs into their extensions. The intension is the set of all the extensions in those possible worlds at those possible times. Intensional meaning, then, involves quantification over world-time pairs.

Can we apply this approach to meaning to words or phrases other than nominals? Try it. What would be the extension of the verb *run*, for example? *Run* is a predicate that takes only one argument. So we could think of the extension of *run* as being the set of things that run, where we ground this in our world—the actual world. The intension of *run*, then, would be the set of all the extensions of *run* in all possible worlds at all possible times.

Chapter and Book Conclusion

So much much more can and should be handled in a course on semantics. But my intention here was merely to give you a glimpse of the tip of the iceberg. I have been necessarily very selective and my choice of topics reflects my own tastes and idiosyncracies. Nevertheless, you have seen enough of a variety of approaches to meaning to know which direction you'd like to go off in from here.

There are two final thoughts I want to leave you with. One is that the various components of the grammar interact frequently and in essential ways (notice how often in this book reference was made to chapters that preceded or followed): Thus, no matter what area of linguistics you might decide to pursue in depth, I hope you will continue to read widely in the other areas. The days of working with blinders on just a single area of the grammar are behind us.

Second, the various areas of the grammar have much in common. We've seen metrical trees, morphological trees, syntactic trees, and semantic trees. We've talked about various issues of locality for sounds (the Strict Cycle Condition and the Locality Constraint on metrical grids of phonology), for forms at the word level (the Adjacency Condition of morphology), for forms at the sentence level (Subjacency for syntax), and for interpretation (the ill-defined notion of locality mentioned with respect to Binding Theory). Our grammar is cohesive. So when you walk into a linguistic puzzle in a particular area of the grammar, be sure to look for similar mechanisms and principles that you know are operative in the other areas of the grammar.

Good luck in your linguistic travels.

Problem Set 5.1: Pragmatics

(NOTE: Questions 5 and 6 are more difficult than the others.)

1. In addition to the locutionary act and illocutionary act, some speech-act theorists have argued that a speech act also includes a PERLOCUTIONARY ACT, which is defined as the speaker's intended effect on the hearer. Thus the sentence:

There's a bull!

in a context of two people walking down a street in Madrid and coming upon a loose bull would constitute the locutionary act of informing of the presence of the bull, the illocutionary act of warning the hearer, and the perlocutionary act of frightening the hearer (presumably so that the hearer runs for safety).

Give the three acts that the following utterance constitutes:

Your boss is married.

The context is this: The hearer is having a romantic relationship with his boss and is unaware of her marital status. The speaker is a co-worker and friend of the hearer.

2. Consider this discourse:

Speaker A: Kim pretends she knows a lot about computers, but I've got my doubts.

Speaker B: Looks like rain, doesn't it?
Speaker A: I thought so.

Analyze this discourse with the assumption that Grice's Cooperative Principle is operative. What maxim(s) of the Cooperative Principle is being exploited as Speaker A interprets Speaker B's utterance?

3. Syntactically we can talk about three main sentence types: declaratives, imperatives, and interrogatives. Considering only simple sentences (sentences that consist of only one clause), can you say that utterances of one or more of these sentence types are always performatives? If so, which type(s)?

4. In the 1960s and early 1970s, many linguists adopted what was called the "performative analysis," whereby every sentence was derived from an underlying source that had a matrix clause that contained an explicit performative verb. With the performative analysis a sentence like 1 would be derived from a fuller sentence like 2 (fuller in that 2 contains the performative clause overtly—whereas it has been deleted in 1):

(1) John left.
(2) I am {saying to you/telling you} that John left.

Sentence 1 is a declarative. But not all sentences are declaratives. Orders, for example, will have a different source with the performative analysis. For example, 3 would come from 4:

(3) Go home!
(4) I order you to go home.

Questions also would have a distinct source, with 5 coming from 6, like so:

(5) Is she nice?
(6) I'm asking you: Is she nice?

An alternative is called the "speech act analysis" (and this is the approach we assumed in the text). With the speech act analysis 1 is derived from 1 only. But we understand 1 and 2 to be semantically very similar (if not equivalent) because in 1 the speaker of the sentence is telling something to the listener of the sentence. So there is always an "I" and a "you" participant in this speech act, even if these "I" and "you" participants are not linguistically represented in the sentence. The same remarks go for 3–4 and 5–6. The relevant difference for the pragmatic analysis (that is, the speech act analysis) between these three sets of sentences is that the first set involves the act of telling; the second set involves the act of ordering; and the third set involves the act of questioning. But all implicitly involve a speaker and a hearer in a speech act.

The performative analysis is dead as a method of syntactic analysis today. This conforms with what you learned in the section "Transformations" of Chapter 4 and what you will look at again in Problem Set 5.9—since the performative analysis calls for a taboo syntactic deletion rule (to delete the entire performative clause). In this problem set, however, I want you to take the performative analysis seriously. And, indeed, its explanatory value for some of the data that follow is remarkable.

Part 1

Consider the following sentences, all of which are orders, with and without explicit performative clauses.

(7) For the last time, turn down that radio.
     For the last time, I order you to turn down that radio.
(8) Go home, or else!
     I order you to go home, or else!
     (but not: *She's intelligent, or else.
               *Where's the book, or else?)
(9) I know it's insane, but be blond! I hate redheads!
     I know it's insane, but I order you to be blond! I hate redheads!
(10) Go home! That's an order!
     *I order you to go home. That's an order!
(11) Please go home.
     *I order you to please go home.
     *I order you please to go home.
(12) I order you to have finished it by six.
     *Have finished it by six.
     (compare to: Have it finished by six.—which is a different sentence, so
     don't get it confused here.)

Each of these six pairs of sentences can be used to build a distinct argument either for or against the performative analysis. Give each argument and tell whether it is supportive of the performative analysis or destructive of it. (If you don't see the point of the data in 8, consider the distribution of the tag *or else*. What kind of utterances can this tag appear after?)

Part 2

Now discuss 7 through 12, each pair separately, from the perspective of the speech act analysis.

Part 3

How would the-performative-analysis proponents explain the fact that we can say both 13 and 14?

(13) Because I'm curious, why are flamingos pink?
(14) If you're not in too much of a rush, why do koalas smell sweet?

What would a speech act analysis of 13–14 be?

Part 4

Comment on the following interchange from both the performative analysis and the speech-act-analysis perspectives.

(15) Are hippos in the pig family?

(16) Who—me?

(Here the speaker of 16 is asking whether or not the speaker of 15 is addressing the speaker of 16.)

5. I'd like you to explore the notion of factivity a bit here. Begin by giving a definition of "factive predicate" based on what you read in the text of this chapter. Then do the following tasks.

(a) Classify the following predicates as factive or nonfactive and give at least one argument to support your classification:

(1) expect   regret   be annoyed   wonder

(b) Consider this pattern:

(2) ??Mary said the fact that Jeff failed the exam.
    Mary was sad about the fact that Jeff failed the exam.

The double question marks before the first sentence of 2 indicates that this sentence is highly marginal, if not entirely unacceptable.

Make a generalization about the data in 2 that can be used as a diagnostic for factive predicates. Use that diagnostic to support or refute your classifications of the predicates in 1.

(c) Is the verb *know* factive or nonfactive? Give two arguments for your answer. (Be careful, you may be surprised here.)

(d) Consider this sentence:

(3) I'm afraid that you failed the exam.

Give a context for this sentence in which the predicate *be afraid* has the force of a factive. Give another context for this sentence in which the predicate is nonfactive.

(e) Discuss briefly what (d) tells us about the classification of factive predicates.

(f) Finally, consider:

(4) She regrets that he broke his leg, but she's an idiot.
    She can't see that he's just faking.

How does 4 affect your original definition of a factive predicate? Try to revise your definition to account for all the data presented in this problem. If you can't, explain why not. If you think the whole endeavor is doomed, explain why. Please limit yourself to one side of one page at most.

Problem Set 5.2: Conceptual Semantics

1. Consider these two sentences:

(1) Abe wiped the dishes dry with a towel.
(2) Abe dried the dishes with a towel.

Give a conceptual structure for the verb of 2.

Given this conceptual structure, should 1 and 2 be conceptually equivalent?

Now consider these sentences:

(3) →←Abe wiped the dishes dry with a towel but they didn't come dry.

(4)   Abe dried the dishes with a towel but they didn't come dry.

In my speech 3 is a contradiction but 4 is not. If this is true of your speech, what does that suggest about the conceptual structure of 1 with respect to that of 2? If appropriate, now revise your conceptual structure for the verb of 2.

If you do not agree with my judgments on 3 and 4, give your own judgments and discuss their relevance to the issue of whether or not 1 and 2 are conceptually equivalent and to the issue of what the proper conceptual structure of the verb in 2 is.

2. Consider this sentence:

(1) John climbed the mountain.

It has been claimed that the conceptual structure for 1 must include the concept **TOP**, since the top of the mountain is reached if John has climbed it. (Recall that we boldface and capitalize all concepts in this theory, just to indicate we are talking about a concept, not a word or an object.) Is this true? Why can we say:

(2) John climbed the mountain all day long, but he never did reach the top.

What is it that leads us to understand that John achieved the top in 1 when no further information is given? Consider three possible answers:

A. We use the Cooperative Principle and assume that all the relevant information was given to us (Quantity), so the desired goal was achieved.
B. The concept of **UPWARD** is included in the conceptual structure of the verb *climb*, and this concept leads us to interpret 1 as involving achievement of the top of the mountain.
C. Both A and B.

Give at least one argument for favoring one of these accounts over the others.
In doing this, consider data such as:

(3)   John scaled the mountain.
(4) →←John scaled the mountain all day long but he never did reach the top.
(5)   Mary climbed up and down mountains all day long.
(6) ??Mary climbed the mountain all day long and she finally reached the bottom.

(Not all speakers use *scale* only for reaching the summit of the object climbed, so not all speakers mark 4 as contradictory. I'm sorry that I couldn't find a verb that made a nice contrast for all speakers.)

3. Consider these sentences:

    (1) The box has books in it.
    (2) There are books in the box.

The box in 2 is a **THING** that is mapped into a **PLACE** via the preposition *in*. So *the box* has a locative theta-role.

    Now it's been claimed that 1 and 2 are conceptually equivalent. Assuming that a given NP can play only one theta-role in a single proposition, we would conclude that *the box* in 1 has a locative theta-role and no other theta-role. Do you think that's true? Give at least one argument why you do or don't support that claim, based on the following sentences and how they contrast with 1:

    (3)   New York has the Empire State Building.
    (4) *New York has the Empire State Building in it.

(A context for 3 might be in response to the remark: "There are no interesting buildings in the northeast.") What's different about New York and a box that allows 1 but disallows 4? Use that difference in discussing the theta-role of *the box* in 1.
[NOTE: Allow yourself latitude in discussing theta-roles here. In Problem Set 4.8 of Chapter 4, for example, we glossed over delicate distinctions in order to try to see the larger picture. But subtle differences should be taken into account in your discussion here.]

4. Compare these sentences:

    (1) John's love of Mary was harmful.
    (2) John's can of beans was edible

In 1 we do not understand Mary to be harmful, but in 2 we understand the beans to be edible. Give me an account of this fact by answering the following questions.
    First, consider:

    (3) John's can of beans was corroded.
    (4) John's can of beans was tender.

Discuss the referential difference between *John's can of beans* in 3 and 4 that allows both of these sentences to be understood appropriately.
    Give two other noun phrases which are open to two interpretations with regard to their referent, similarly to *John's can of beans*.
    Give two other noun phrases which have only one interpretation with regard to their referent, similarly to *John's love of Mary*.
    Why does an NP like *John's love of Mary* not have the option of being understood in two ways—in contrast to *John's can of beans*? (Give a brief discussion—not more than half of one side of a page, please.)
    Now briefly discuss whether or not pairs of sentences like 3–4 suggest that a word like *can* must have more than one conceptual structure. (You might want to make some explicit

assumptions about the semantic value of *of*. Recall that sometimes *of* is semantically vacuous, as when it introduces a nominal argument following a head N or A. (We discussed the Case-marking value of *of* in the section "Nouns: Objects and Case" of Chapter 4 and the syntactic-glue use of *of* in the section "Inventory of Morphological Types" of Chapter 3.) Perhaps *of* is always semantically vacuous. Can you think of any usage in which we need to assign *of* a semantic value?)

5. Consider the sentence:

(1) John ate the ice cream with a spoon.

It's been argued that the conceptual structure of this sentence contains the concept of transfer, symbolized with **TRANS**, in the movement of the ice cream to John's mouth. This seems pretty reasonable to me.

But there are many instances of movement here that one generally does not find represented in the conceptual structure of a sentence like 1: John's hand moves to pick up the spoon, John moves his hand muscles to grasp the spoon, John opens his mouth wide enough to receive the spoon, John's tongue gets involved in there, and so on. And sometimes our speech reflects the knowledge that at least some of these movements are involved, as in a sentence like:

(2) John ate the ice cream with a spoon really fast.

The linguistic evidence for knowledge of these movements is in the modifier *really fast*. Think about what it modifies—certainly the various movements involved, not the event of eating the ice cream.

Furthermore, there are many instances of actions other than movement that are likewise omitted from most conceptual representations of a sentence such as 1—for example, John's thinking about moving his hand muscles, and on and on.

The issue I'd like you to consider is exactly how far we should go in giving a conceptual structure. What kinds of standards should we use to determine which information must appear in the conceptual structure and which is not needed? Do not write down your thoughts—but please take any opportunity you can find to discuss them with members of your class or unwitting victims you accost on the street.

After thinking about this, I'd like you to give one sentence of English and discuss a concept that must be included in its conceptual structure with one reason why it must be included and a second concept that we know is relevant to the sentence but which need not be included in the conceptual structure with one reason why it need not be included.

6. Consider this sentence:

(1) Jeff ate.

One could argue that the predicate here is the concept **INGEST**. Now **INGEST** has been argued to take two PPs, **TO** and **IN**. But these concepts have no morphosyntactic counterpart: The syntactic structure of 1 involves no PPs.

I'd like you to focus on the claim that we can have semantic entities that have no morphological or syntactic counterpart. In that light, consider these passive sentences:

(2) That absurd lecture was delivered with a straight face.
(3) The boat was destroyed in order to collect the insurance.

Use the modifier *with a straight face* in 2 to make an argument that the meaning of 2 includes a semantic entity that has no morphological or syntactic counterpart. Now use the controlled infinitival *in order to collect the insurance* in 3 to make the same argument for 3. (If you have trouble getting started on the argument for 3, look back at the section "Control Theory" in Chapter 4.)

Now consider these sentences, in which the second contains a passive NP:

(4) [Jack's destruction of the boat] was outrageous.
(5) [The boat's destruction by Jack] was outrageous.

Notice that we can say 6 but not 7:

(6) Jack's destruction of the boat to collect the insurance was outrageous.
(7) *The boat's destruction to collect the insurance was outrageous.

Contrast 7 to 3.

We can make a similar contrast between 8 and 2:

(8) *The lecture's delivery with a straight face really put me off.

In light of 7 and 8, do you really believe that 2 and 3 offer no morphological or syntactic entity that corresponds to the semantic entity you were led to posit? What is, in fact, the relevant morphological or syntactic entity in 2 and 3 (that is missing in 7 and 8)?

7. Consider this sentence (and I apologize for its brutality—it comes from the literature cited in the bibliography):

(1) John killed his teacher by shooting him in the head.

Let's take three different contexts that this sentence describes:

A. John shot a bullet through the teacher's head.
B. The gun had only blanks, but it was so close to the teacher's head that the force blew his brains out.
C. The gun has only blanks and it was far enough away from the teacher's head to do no direct damage, but the teacher had a heart attack and died.

Discuss whether or not we will need to posit a different conceptual structure for 1 for each of these contexts. If you say we do, is this a mark against a conceptual approach to meaning or not?

8. Consider this sentence:

(1) When Fred gave Mary a peach, she ate it.

It's been argued that in this sentence, *when*'s conceptual structure involves the notion of causation. Now consider:

(2) When Fred saw Mary, she was eating a peach.

There is clearly no sense of causation connected to *when* in 2. What should we do about this? Should we say there are (at least) two *when*'s in English, one that indicates causality and one that indicates only temporal relationships? Or should we say there is only one *when* and that the causality we find in the reading of 1 is due to other factors in language use?

9. Consider:

(1) I comforted John by feeding him.

Does this sentence have to mean that John's comfort came from his ingestion of the food? Do you think that's what it means?

What kinds of issues does this sentence raise for how explicit a conceptual structure should be?

Problem Set 5.3: Lexical Semantics

(NOTE: Questions 4, 6, and 9 are more difficult than the others.)

1. In Navajo nouns fall into eight different classes according to an animacy hierarchy. They are:

1. Humans capable of intent and purpose (not infants) and lightning
2. Human infants, larger animals (like horses, donkeys, mules, bulls, cows, lions, bears, elephants), and animals endowed with superior intelligence (wolves, wild-cats, dogs)
3. Medium-sized animals (sheep, goats, turkeys, cats, deer antelope, foxes, coyotes, hawks, eagles)
4. Small animals (songbirds, squirrels, gophers, snakes, frogs, turtles, mice)
5. Spiders, worms, insects, centipedes, scorpions
6. Natural forces (heat, fire, wind, flood)
7. Plants and inanimate objects
8. Abstractions (old age, thirst, hunger)

The driving forces behind these eight classes have been claimed to be capacity for intent, as well as intelligence and usefulness to people (as in the case of distinctions among animals), and the ability to move.

Part 1

Now consider the following active/passive pairs of Navajo sentences. I have marked with an asterisk the less preferred of the pair (if a preference exists). (You don't have to understand the diacritics here in order to do the problem. If you have read Chapters 1 and 2, let me tell you that Navajo is a tone language and it makes use of nasalized vowels.)

(1) a. 'Ashkii 'at'ééd yiníł'į.
　　　 boy　　 girl　　 look
　　　 'The boy is looking at the girl.'
　 b. 'At'ééd 'ashkii biníł'į.
　　　 'The girl is being looked at by the boy.'

(2) a. *Tsídii 'ashkii yishtạsh.
　　　 bird　 boy　 pecked
　　　 'The bird pecked the boy.'
　 b. 'Ashkii tsídii bishtạsh
　　　 'The boy was pecked by the bird.'

(3) a. *Kọ 'ashkii yidííłid
　　　 fire boy　　 burned
　　　 'The fire burned the boy.'
　 b. 'Ashkii kọ bidííłid.
　　　 'The boy was burned by the fire.'

(4) a. *Sạ́　　 Hastiin Nééz yiisxį́.
　　　 old age Mr. Long　　 killed
　　　 'Old age killed Mr. Long.'
　 b. Hastiin Nééz sạ́ biisxį́.
　　　 'Mr. Long died (was killed) of old age.'

Give a statement about the word order of nominals in a Navajo sentence that makes use of the animacy hierarchy.

Part 2

Translate these English sentences into Navajo with the closest grammatical counterpart that you can give, based on the knowledge you gained in doing Part 1.

(5) The cat is looking at the bird.
(6) The bird is looking at the cat.

The word for cat is *mósí*.

Part 3

Now consider this pair:

(7) a. *'Ii'ni'　　 Hastiin Nééz yiisxį́.
　　　 lightning Mr. Long　　 killed
　　　 'Lightning killed Mr. Long.'
　 b. Hastiin Nééz 'ii'ni' biisxį́.
　　　 'Mr. Long was killed by lightning.'

Are you surprised by this preference or did you expect it? If you were surprised, why? How might you alter the animacy hierarchy to account for this preference?

Part 4

Discuss briefly why dealing with these Navajo phenomena with an animacy hierarchy is more perspicacious than with a list of eight lexical features.

2. Consider these NPs:

   a loop of rope   a herd of cattle   a grain of sugar

Take one of the three words *loop*, *herd*, or *grain*, and discuss what semantic requirement it puts on the referent it can quantify.

3. Give a predicate-argument structure for *lurk*. In doing this consider the following sentences:

   (1)   John lurked in the bushes.
   (2)   *John lurked all day.

4. Some linguists make use of the idea of PREDICATORS, which can be of any syntactic category and which are theta-assigners. In the sentences that follow, tell which items are the predicators and which items they assign a theta-role to. Do not discuss which theta-roles are assigned—just note whether an item gets a theta-role (or roles) and note which item(s) gives the theta-role(s). (NOTE: there can be more than one predicator in a given sentence.)

   (1) Ralph lied to Mary about the war.
   (2) Ralph told a lie about the war to Mary.
   (3) The Huns' destruction of the city disgusted even Ralph.
   (4) The blow knocked Sally senseless.
   (5) He's out of his gourd.
   (6) Max carries such behavior to extremes.
   (7) Max took Felix to task over his behavior at the party.

   Give an example to show that a V can be a predicator. Now give examples to show that N, A, and P can be predicators.
   Can a predicator consist of a string of words rather than just a single word? Can that string be linearly discontinuous?

5. Consider these verbs:

   (1) shave   dress   bathe   shower

Describe the semantic properties that these verbs have in common.
   Now consider pairs of sentences like:

   (2) I dress at dawn.
   (3) I dress my daughter at dawn.

How many and what type of arguments (in terms of theta-roles) do these verbs take? Describe the linking of theta-roles to GFs for these verbs.
   Consider once again the semantics of a sentence like 2. Compare it to:

   (4) I dress myself at dawn.

Are 2 and 4 synonymous? If so, discuss possible ways to account for the lack of the reflexive pronoun in 2. If not, give a context which makes clear the difference in meaning between 2 and 4.

Now consider the verb *clothe*. In what significant ways does it differ from the class of verbs exemplified in 1? What does that tell us about membership in this class?

Finally, consider the verb *improve*, as in:

(5) I'll improve if you give me a chance.
(6) I'll improve this chapter if you'll give me a chance.
(7) I'll improve myself if you give me a chance.

Does *improve* appear to fall into the same semantic class as the verbs in 1? Why or why not?

Does *improve* display the same range of arguments and the same linking of arguments to GFs as the verbs in 1? If not, demonstrate with relevant example sentences.

Are 5 and 7 synonymous? If not, give a context which makes clear the difference in meaning between them.

6. It's been claimed that verbs fall into four main classes with respect to aspect:

a. Activity terms: run, walk, swim, push (a cart) . . .
b. Accomplishment terms: paint (a picture), make (a chair), build (a house), run (a mile) . . .
c. Achievement terms: reach (the summit), win (the race), die . . .
d. State terms: love, hate, want, believe, have, desire, understand, rule . . .

Actually, various refinements can be and have been made, recognizing more classes of verbs regarding aspectual distinctions. But in this problem set we will consider only these four classes.

Various tests have been offered for determining which of the four classes a given verb belongs to.

I. The progressive is compatible with activities and accomplishments, but not with achievements and states. For example, in response to, "What are you doing?", we find:

a. I'm running.
b. I'm painting a picture.
c. *I'm reaching the summit.
d. *I'm loving algebra.

II. Durational adverbials with *for* are compatible with activities and states, but not with accomplishments and achievements. For example, we find:

a. I ran for a half hour.
b. *I painted a picture for a half hour.
c. *I reached the summit for a half hour.
d. I loved algebra for a half hour.

III. Time adverbials with *in* are compatible with accomplishments, but not with activities. The same is true of the *take . . . to . . .* construction. For example, we find:

> a. *I ran in a half hour.
>   *It took a half hour to run.
> b. I painted a picture in a half hour.
>   It took a half hour to paint a picture.

There is controversy over whether this test is applicable to the other two classes. If it is, we find achievements are compatible with these constructions, but states are not.

> c. I reached the summit in a half hour.
>   It took a half hour to reach the summit.
> d. *I loved algebra in a half hour.
>   *It took a half hour to love algebra.

IV. Punctual adverbials are compatible with achievements, incompatible with states:

> c. She reached the summit at 5 o'clock on the dot.
> d. *She loved algebra at 5 o'clock on the dot.

This test is said not to be applicable to activities and accomplishments.

All of these tests are open to criticism. Please do this problem set accepting these four tests as valid. Also, please accept the given grammaticality judgments for the sentences in this problem. Then, once you have done the problem, if you want to go back and offer criticisms for the various tests, you are welcome to do so. And if you want to offer your own grammaticality judgments and discuss how the arguments are affected by them, please do.

Part 1

Use the four tests to classify these verbs:

> deliver (a sermon)
> know
> drive (a car)
> find (a book)

Part 2

Discuss whether it is verbs or, rather, verb phrases that these four tests distinguish between by comparing these sentence pairs:

> (1) John ate an apple yesterday.
>   John ate apples yesterday.
> (2) John painted on a canvas.
>   John painted a portrait.
> (3) Mary knew French.
>   Mary knew the answer.

Part 3

Are adjectival *(be tall, be noisy, become annoyed . . .)* and nominal predicates *(be a doctor, be a friend, be the leader . . .)* subject to the same aspectual classifications? Give example sentences (with all four tests) to support your answer.

7. Consider the sentences:

    (1) Dan and Eddie traded places.
    (2) Dan traded places with Eddie.

    Discuss the predicate-argument structure of the verb *trade*. What are the theta-roles of *Dan* and *Eddie* in 1? In 2? In Problem Set 4.8 of Chapter 4 we learned that Theta Theory requires each argument of a predicate to have a unique theta-role. Does *trade* present problems for this part of Theta Theory or not? Explain your answer. What problems come up in analyzing *trade*'s conceptual structure (in a conceptual semantics)?

8. It's been claimed that all predicates can be broken into two groups according to the distinction between AFFECTUM and EFFECTUM, where an affectum predicate operates on an object understood to have existed antecedently to the event the predicate describes, but an effectum predicate actually brings about the existence of the object it operates on. An example of an affectum predicate is *ruin*, and of an effectum predicate is *build*. This distinction is correlated with the ability of a wh-cleft sentence to be a paraphrase. Thus 3 is a good paraphrase of 1, but 4 is not a good paraphrase of 2.

    (1) John ruined the table.
    (2) John built the table.
    (3) What John did to the table was ruin it.
    (4) What John did to the table was build it.

    Classify the predicates *discover*, *look at*, and *overestimate* as affectum or effectum, based solely on their meaning.
    Why are the wh-clefts below problematic?

    (5) What I did to the island was discover it.
    (6) What I did to the island was look at it.
    (7) What I did to Charles's abilities was overestimate them.

(Some of you may even star 5–7 (I do). But if you do get 5–7, the question is whether they are paraphrases of their nonclefted counterparts.)
    Is this problem destructive of the distinction between affectum and effectum predicates, or is it simply destructive of the syntactic test for this distinction? Are you surprised to have discovered this problem? (That is, was there any reason to expect this syntactic test to work as a diagnostic for the semantic distinction between affectum and effectum?)
    Consider now:

    (8) Chris wrote a book.
    (9) Chris wrote a check.

What issue for classifying predicates as affectum or effectum do such sentences raise? Look back at question 6 of this problem set. Are you surprised by this new issue or did you expect it? Why?

9. Many people claim that in copular sentences (that is, sentences that make use of a copular verb, such as *be* or *become*) a nominal following the copular verb can be understood either as a predicate or as a simple alternative identification (also called equivalence) of the Subject (as we briefly mentioned in the section "Identification vs. Predication" of Chapter 4). If that characterization were correct, out of 1 and 2, which one would you say involves predication and which one involves equivalence only?

(1) Mary is a fool.
(2) R. J. Smith is Ralph Jared Smith.

Some have suggested that among NPs, only evaluative ones can be predicates. Is this so? Consider:

(3) Bill is a doctor.
(4) Bill is the doctor.
(5) Bill is the best doctor.
(6) Bill is the only doctor.

Are any of these sentences always going to be used predicatively? Which one(s)? Are any of them always going to be used as equivalencies? Which ones? Under what conditions might 4 be used predicatively? Under what conditions might 4 be used as an equivalence? To answer these last two questions, you need only give a context for each interpretation. (If you are having trouble seeing predicative uses for 4–6, play around with intonation and be sure to consider exclamative uses.)

Sometimes we can have a singular noun with no article on it alternating with that same noun plus *the* in postcopular position:

(7) John's the boss around here.
(8) John's boss around here.

But this doesn't happen freely:

(9) John's the tall child up front.
(10) *John's tall child up front.

Try a lot of them. What crucial factor determines whether or not we can drop *the* with a singular noun following the copular verb? Is this factor related at all to those circumstances under which we can interpret 4 predicatively? If so, how?

10. The position after a copular verb is not the only place we can find predicative nominals. The italicized nominals in 1–2 are predicative:

(1) I consider Milton *a child*.
(2) This picture of Milton as *a child* makes me laugh.

Which NP is *a child* predicated of in 1? In 2? Give three other sentences in which we have a predicative nominal in some position other than following a copular verb. Underline the predicative nominal and tell me which NP it is predicated of.

11. Consider:

(1) That idiot of a linguist is at it again!

Is *idiot* here used predicatively? If so, what is it predicated of? In either case, discuss the interpretation of this sentence, paying particular attention to the semantic contribution of *idiot*.

12. In Italian, a clitic that is the argument of an infinitival verb normally appears encliticized to that infinitive. In these examples I use the same infinitive and clitic repeatedly: *vedermi* 'to see me.' We see this in:

(1) Maria gode di vedermi.
'Maria enjoys seeing me.'
(2) Maria prega di vedermi.
'Maria begs to see me.'
(3) Maria odia di vedermi.
'Maria hates seeing me.'
(4) Basta vedermi.
'(It)'s enough to see me.'
(5) Ti piace vedermi?
'Does it please you to see me?' (='Do you like to see me?')

However, sometimes the clitic has the additional possibility of appearing procliticized to the verb of the next higher clause up. (In that case, the lower infinitive appears as *vedere* 'to see' and the procliticized *mi* is written as a separate word preceding the finite verb of the higher clause, even though it is a clitic.) We see this in:

(6) Maria deve vedermi.
Maria mi deve vedere.
'Maria must see me.'
(7) Maria può vedermi.
Maria mi può vedere.
'Maria can see me.'

Some speakers also allow this pattern in:

(8) Maria ha da vedermi.
Maria mi ha da vedere.
'Maria has to see me.'
(9) Maria sa vedermi.
Maria mi sa vedere.
'Maria knows how to see me.' (= she has the ability)

The pattern in the second sentence of each of the sentence pairs in 6–9 is known as CLITIC CLIMBING or CC (because it looks like the clitic has "climbed" from the infinitival clause up into the matrix clause).

It's been argued that the crucial factor determining whether or not CC can take place is the meaning of the matrix verb. Most matrix verbs pattern as in 1–5. Only a handful of verbs pattern as in 6–9.

Assume that the matrix verbs (with the senses given in the translations) in 6–9 are the only verbs of Italian that allow CC. Give a semantic characterization of the class of verbs that allow CC.

Actually, for many speakers a few more verbs allow CC than just the four seen in 6–9. Thus we find for those speakers:

(10) Maria continua a vedermi.
Maria mi continua a vedere.
'Maria continues to see me.'
(11) Maria (in)comincia a vedermi.
Maria mi (in)comincia a vedere.
'Maria begins to see me.'
(12) Maria finisce di vedermi.
Maria mi finisce di vedere.
'Maria finishes seeing me.'
(13) Maria sta per vedermi.
Maria mi sta per vedere.
'Maria is about to see me.'

Give a semantic characterization of this second class of verbs that allows CC. (If you don't know where to begin, you might want to reread the section "Verbal Inflections and Affixes" of Chapter 3.)

Finally, there is yet at least one more verb that all speakers agree allows CC:

(14) Maria voleva vedermi.
Maria mi voleva vedere.
'Maria wanted to see me.'

Does *volere* 'want' fit into the semantic class you identified in 6–9? Does it fit into the semantic class you identified in 10–13? If it doesn't fit into either group, is there any sense in which you can see it as a kind of pragmatic extension of either group? (You might not be able to make any sense out of that question, but if you can, fly with it.)

Try to give a semantic characterization that holds of all the verbs in 6–14 but does not hold of the verbs in 1–5.

Various syntactic accounts of CC have been offered. One of the most promising is that when we have CC, the two clauses have actually been reduced (syntactically) to a single clause via a process of clause union or reanalysis (a process we won't go into here). The result of this process is that the two verbs now form one verb string. My question for you is: Why should Italian allow clause union/reanalysis with only this semantic class of verbs? (If you have trouble getting started, go back to Problem Set 4.3 of Chapter 4 and look at the semantics of the verbal string in English. I hope it helps.)

Problem Set 5.4: Logical Connectives and Natural Language

Part 1

In the text we noticed that *therefore* reflects the relationship of entailment in the sentence:

> She killed him therefore he died.

While *therefore* does not always reflect entailment, it certainly can. Is *therefore* the only connective of natural language that can reflect entailment? If you say no, give at least one example complex sentence in which a different connective reflects entailment. If you say yes, give at least ten example complex sentences, each using a different connective that you claim can never reflect entailment.

Part 2

Is *and* a logical connective in natural language? That is the overall question I want you to consider here.

Support your answer by discussions of the examples given. Be complete—discuss every single example given. The examples are grouped. Please treat each group separately first, and discuss how it is relevant to the issue. When you have finished discussing all the groups separately, then you can discuss comparisons between the groups if you think further points come out from such a comparison. (But this is not necessary to do—do it only if you truly think new insights emerge.)

When you talk about the meaning of an utterance, be sure to distinguish between the readings that occur in all contexts (the readings which cannot be denied without contradiction) and the readings that occur only in some contexts. For example, in both these sentences without a context we probably will understand John to be a teacher:

> John's sure a nice teacher.
> John sure seems to be a nice teacher.

But with the second sentence we can deny that John is a teacher without contradiction, whereas we cannot do that with the first:

> →←John's sure a nice teacher, but he isn't actually a teacher (he's a principal).
> John sure seems to be a nice teacher, but he isn't actually a teacher (he's a principal).

When you look at the examples in the following data sets, consider them in many different contexts, so you'll be sure to see what meaning comes from the sentence itself and what meaning comes from the context (via principles of conversation). Play with the sentences. Move the phrases around. Add a word here or there to see how this affects the interpretation. All of these things will help you understand the meaning of the original sentence in isolation. And, remember, this is a semantics problem set, so don't get all caught up in a syntax observation. You can notice the syntax and remark briefly on it—but concentrate your efforts on the interpretation.

DATA SET A
Contrast 1–2 to 3–4.

(1a) Paris is the capital of France and Rome is the capital of Italy.
(1b) Rome is the capital of Italy and Paris is the capital of France.
(2a) Betsy and Ted are certainly nice folk.
(2b) Ted and Betsy are certainly nice folk.
(3a) She got married and she had a child.
(3b) She had a child and she got married.
(4a) The discovery of such a case would be a blow to me and the entire linguistics profession.
(4b) ?*The discovery of such a case would be a blow to the entire linguistics profession and me.

DATA SET B

(5) Laugh one more time and I'll kick you out.
(6) Come by tomorrow and we'll talk.

DATA SET C
Contrast 7–9 to 10–11.

(7a) Sue bought a keg of beer and Jeff prepared a vegetable platter.
(7b) *What did Sue buy and Jeff prepared a vegetable platter.
(7c) *What did Sue buy a keg of beer and Jeff prepared?
(8a) Bill writes novels and criticizes poetry.
(8b) *What does Bill write and criticize poetry?
(8c) *What does Bill write novels and criticize poetry?
(9a) Bart cries too much and writes sappy poetry.
(9b) *What does Bart cry too much and write?
(10a) Sharon was being a jerk and talking about her huge salary all night.
(10b) What was Sharon being a jerk and talking about all night?
(10c) *What was Sharon being and talking about her huge salary all night?
(11a) John went and bought a keg of beer.
(11b) What did John go and buy?

DATA SET D

(12) Steak and eggs cost five dollars.
(13) Milk, juice, and coffee cost seventy-five cents.

I have one final question for you. Look at the sentences in Data Set B again. They can be paraphrased like so:

(14) If you laugh one more time, I'll kick you out.
(15) If you come by tomorrow, we'll talk.

If *and* were equivalent to the logical connective $\wedge$, would you expect 14–15 to be paraphrases of 5–6? Explain your answer.

Part 3

Is *or* a logical connective in natural language? That is the overall question I want you to consider here. As you answer this, please test for both ordinary disjunction and exclusive disjunction. And use the directions given above for Part 2 (that is, be very aware of the affects of context on interpretation and be sure to discuss each group of sentences separately and every sentence within each group).

DATA SET A
Compare 1 to 2.

> (1a) Sue got married or quit school.
> (1b) Sue quit school or got married.
> (2a) Sue got married or something.
> (2b) *Something or Sue got married.
> (2c) *Sue something or got married.
> (2d) *Sue got something or married.

DATA SET B

> (3) Shut the door or I'll freeze.
> (4) Another pork chop or I'll go to bed hungry.

DATA SET C

> (5) Do you think the baby's a boy or a girl?
> (6) Inmates may smoke or drink in the lounge area only.

DATA SET D
Consider the truth conditions of 7 and 8. Are they the same in natural language? Should they be if *or* is equivalent to the logical connective $\vee$ or to the logical connective $\oslash$?

> (7) If the raccoon is either in the garden or in the attic, and in fact is in the attic, the gardener will be glad.
> (8) If the raccoon is in the attic, the gardener will be glad.

I have one final question for you. Look at the sentences in Data Set B again. They can be paraphrased like so:

> (9) If you don't shut the door, I'll freeze.
> (10) If I don't have another pork chop, I'll go to bed hungry.

If *or* were equivalent to the logical connective $\vee$ or to the logical connective $\oslash$, would you expect 9–10 to be paraphrases of 3–4? Explain your answer.

Part 4

People have claimed that *unless* and *without* are logical connectives. For example, they say that a sentence like:

I won't come unless she does.

if represented as "p unless q," is equivalent to the logical expression:

$$\sim q \rightarrow p$$

that is:

If she doesn't come, I won't come.

And they say that a sentence like:

She'll do it without telling a soul.

if represented as "p without q," is equivalent to the logical expression:

$$p \wedge \sim q$$

that is:

She'll do it and she won't tell a soul.

Evaluate these claims by looking at other example sentences that you can think of. Give one argument (supported by one or more of your example sentences) against the claim that *unless* is the logical connective shown. Give one argument (again supported with examples) against the claim that *without* is the logical connective shown.

Part 5

Express the following argument in symbolic form and determine if it is logically valid.

The butler or the cook or the chauffeur killed the baron.

If the cook killed the baron, then the stew was poisoned and if the chauffeur killed the baron, then there was a bomb in the car.

The stew wasn't poisoned and the butler didn't kill the baron.

Therefore, the chauffeur killed the baron.

Use the following symbols: b = butler killed baron; k = cook killed baron; c = chauffeur killed baron; p = stew was poisoned; m = bomb was in car.

Part 6

Does disjunction distribute over implication? That is, is the following equivalence true?

$$(p \vee q) \rightarrow (p \vee r) \equiv p \vee (q \rightarrow r)$$

If you say yes, give truth tables in support. If you say no, give one set of truth conditions for p, q, and r for which the equivalency doesn't hold.

Part 7

Symbolize each of the statements in 1–3 that follow using truth functional connectives. For example:

I'd marry Fred if he could think better.

Let p = I'd marry Fred, and let q = he could think better. Now this could be formulated as:

q → p

In that case, if Fred could think better, I'd definitely marry him, but if he can't think better, I might or might not marry him. Or it could be formulated as:

p ⇔ q

In that case, only if he can think better will I marry him and if he can think better, I'll definitely marry him.

After each formulation you give for 1–3, give the reading of your sentence in regular English (just as I have done for the proposition about marrying Fred). Please use the symbols I give below for the propositions.

(1) Martha will major in linguistics whether or not she's good at it.

m = Martha will major in linguistics; g = Martha is good at linguistics.

(2) I'll leave unless Bill shuts up and sits down.

l = I'll leave; b = Bill shuts up; s = Bill sits down.

(3) (You) say one more word and I'll never speak to you again.

y = (you) say one more word; s = I will speak to you again.

Part 8

Construct a truth table (Table 5.9) for each of the expressions in 1–3. For example, for p ∨ ~q, we have·

Table 5.9. Example Disjunction

p	q	~q	p ∨ ~q
1	1	0	1
1	0	1	1
0	1	0	0
0	0	1	1

Please order the rows of your tables with the method described in the section "Truth Tables."

(1) p → (~q ∨ p)
(2) (q ∧ p) ⇔ (p ∨ q)
(3) ((p → q) → p) → q

Part 9

Give a proposition in regular English words that is a tautology and another that is a contradiction. Then write them as formal expressions.

Problem Set 5.5: Practical Issues in Scope in English

Many linguists and philosophers have tried to account for the interpretation of certain lexical items in natural language by talking about their scope in a logical sense. Three such types of lexical items include negatives, quantifiers, and adverbs, the first two of which we discussed in this chapter. Here we'll look at all three types of lexical items and address problematic issues.

Part 1

One might claim that (1) and (2) are unambiguous and not synonymous.

(1) Many men read few books.
(2) Few books are read by many men.

From 1 and 2 one could conclude that in each case the quantifier with the widest scope corresponds to the one that is leftmost. That is, in 1 the few books can be different for the different men—so *few* does not have scope over *many*. But in 2 the few books must be the same for all the various men—so *few* does have scope over *many*.

It is not relevant whether or not you agree with the given interpretation of these sentences. All I want is for you to understand the claim.

Now consider the proposal that in English linear order (that is, order in a line from left to right) in the S-Structure (the surface structure) of a sentence strictly determines the scope relations of lexical items, such as quantifiers. That is, in 1 *many* occurs to the left of *few*, so *many* has wide scope and *few* has narrow scope. In 2 we have the reverse.

The question for you is: Is this proposal correct?

Use only the examples following in forming your answer. (Indeed, you can easily find an example in the text of this chapter to help you answer the question definitively. But right now you are to stick to the examples here, please.)

Be sure to give your interpretation of the sentences, since these interpretations vary among speakers and since the interpretation you get will determine the relevance you see in each example.

If you decide that linear order is not the only factor relevant to scope interpretations, state other possible factors that 3–7 might illustrate. (There are at least three other such factors that you might notice, depending on how you interpret these sentences.)

Warning: The more you read these sentences, the more likely you are to feel uncertain about your own interpretation of them. Please sit in a room alone the first time you read them. Read each one aloud and immediately make a decision about what interpretation(s) you give that sentence. Write down your interpretation(s) so you can have your own first reaction when you go back to them later. Then go on to the second sentence and do the same. And so on through the list. If you are doing this problem set with a group in a class, when you get together with your group, be sure to bring your own notes on your first reaction interpretation(s) of these sentences.

(3) a. Every girl took a chemistry course.
   b. A chemistry course was taken by every girl.
(4) a. A girl took every chemistry course.
   b. Every chemistry couse was taken by a girl.
(5) a. I told every child a story.
   b. I told a story to every child.
(6) a. I told every story to a child.
   b. I told a child every story.
(7) a. Joan gave a few handouts to some pedestrians.
   b. Joan gave a few handouts to several pedestrians.
   c. Joan gave a few handouts to many pedestrians.
   d. Joan gave a few handouts to all pedestrians.
   e. Joan gave a few handouts to every pedestrian.

Part 2

A. Give sentences with *all* and *not* in the same clause. (If you haven't read Chapter 4 and you don't know what a clause is, just use simple sentences with only one verb and you'll have only a single clause in the sentences. For example, *I told every story to a child* is a single clause sentence. But *I told Bill that all the stories were lousy* is a two-clause sentence.)

Does their relative linear order always determine their scope relations? If not, give examples (with your interpretations of them) to show it does not.

Consider these two sentences in the context of announcements coming over the loudspeaker as you're riding on a subway:

(8) Not all doors will open at the next stop.
(9) All doors will not open at the next stop.

Do you see a difference in interpretation? Does the context lead you to a particular interpretation of either sentence?

B. Now give sentences with *all* in one clause and *not* in another clause. You will need two-verb sentences. And the clauses can have a variety of relationships to each other. They might be conjoined:

Jack left town and Jill bought mousetraps.

One might be embedded in the other as a Subject or Object or some other type of complement:

That Jack left town confused Jill.
Jill didn't realize that Jack had left town.
Jill was upset that Jack left town.

One might modify the other:

> Jack left town because Jill bought mousetraps.
> Jack, the boy who left town, bought mousetraps for Jill.

The question is: Does the relative linear order of *all* and *not* in these complex sentences always determine their scope relations? If your answer is no, give examples (with your interpretations of the examples) to show not.

You may use the contracted form of *not* in doing this (as in *didn't, don't, can't, won't, mayn't*—that last one's a joke, sorry).

Be sure to consider sentences with as many different relationships between the two clauses as you can think of. And be sure to have *all* in clause A and *not* in clause B with a given relationship between clauses A and B and then *not* in clause A and *all* in clause B with the same given relationship between clauses A and B.

Be careful: Even when *all* and *not* are in different clauses, we can sometimes find scope interactions between them.

Part 3

Why might one talk about scope when discussing the interpretation of adverbs? What kind of things (semantic entities, syntactic entities) can adverbs have scope over? What kind of factors (linear order, hierarchical structure, lexical choice, Grammatical Function, etc.) determine this scope? In answering this, be sure to consider the following sentences. First consider 10–12.

(10) a. John filled the buckets completely.
    b. John filled the buckets, apparently.
    c. John filled the buckets slowly.
(11) a. *Completely John filled the buckets.
    b. Apparently, John filled the buckets.
    c. Slowly John filled the buckets.
(12) a. John completely filled the buckets.
    b. John apparently filled the buckets.
    c. John, apparently, filled the buckets.
    d. John slowly filled the buckets.

Commas around an adverb indicate pauses.

Now consider 13–15, paying particular attention to the contrasts between the (a) and (b) examples.

(13) a. Sam carefully sliced all the bagels.
    b. Sam sliced all the bagels carefully.
(14) a. Milton carelessly forgot his mother's birthday.
    b. *Milton forgot his mother's birthday carelessly.
(15) a. Minnie has furnished the house lavishly.
    b. *Minnie lavishly has furnished the house.

(Be sure not to read in a pause unless I've written in a comma. In particular, there is no pause in 15b. Also, the presence of an auxiliary in 15 introduces a new position for an adverb—between the auxiliary and the main verb: *Minnie has lavishly furnished the house*. For now please ignore this additional sentence and you can return to it later if you think that it helps shed light on the overall question.)

After you have discussed 10–15, consider:

(16) John deliberately didn't kiss his wife.
(17) John didn't kiss his wife deliberately.
(18) John didn't kiss his wife, deliberately.

(Again, pay close attention to the lack of a comma intonation in 17 and to its presence in 18). Discuss the scope interaction of the negative and the adverb here. Did your discussion of 13–15 lead you to expect what you found in 16–18? Why or why not?

Part 4

Now discuss in general the usefulness (or lack of it) to the linguist of talking about the notion of scope with respect to the types of lexical items you just looked at in Parts 1–3. Please limit this final discussion to one side of one page at an absolute maximum. Use examples whenever you make a claim. Refer to your answers to the questions in Parts 1–3 whenever relevant, without repeating material from those parts.

Don't drive yourself crazy here. I am not looking for any polished overview. Instead, I just want to see what kinds of problems you see arising as you try to apply logic to natural language phenomena.

Problem Set 5.6: Three Scope Problems: ASL, Hopi, and Japanese

(NOTE: the Japanese problem requires a good knowledge of syntax and is more on syntax than on semantics.)

1. American Sign Language Eye Gaze

ASL has been argued to have three types of determiners on nominals:

a) IX—the index finger (hence the symbol "IX") points to a locus in space. This can be used immediately before a noun sign. It gives the sense of a definite:

IX MAN 'the man'

b) [SOMETHING/ONE]—the index finger is oriented upward with a slight tremor. This can be used before a noun sign. It gives the sense of a specific indefinite:

SOMETHING/ONE MAN 'a specific man'

c) Ø—a bare noun sign is understood as a nonspecific indefinite:

MAN 'a nonspecific man'

In this problem set we will not be looking at the specific indefinite (in b) at all. I mention it just to let you know it exists.

This simple arrangement of three determiners is complicated a bit by the fact that IX, the definite determiner, also has other values. It can be used alone (that is, without an adjacent noun sign)—in which case it has either the sense of a pronoun ('he,' 'she,' 'they,' and so on) or the sense of an adverbial ('there'). It can also be used immediately after a noun sign to locate the referent. For example, we find:

IX_i MAN IX_i 'the man there'

(Co-indexing here indicates that both pointings are to the same locus.) Similar constructions occur in other languages:

French: cet homme-là 'that man there'
Norwegian: den mannen der 'the man there'

(By the way, SOMETHING/ONE in b contrasts here: It occurs only before a noun sign.)

Now, all four instances of IX (the prenominal use, the postnominal use, the pronominal use, and the adverbial use) may optionally occur with a nonmanual orientation of eye gaze (eg) to the locus in space to which the index finger points. Eg in ASL is a grammatical device (similar to a feature), not an extralinguistic device, as in spoken languages. And eg, as a feature of IX, can spread.

Consider these data. First, eg with a prenominal IX (the determiner use of IX) can optionally spread over the whole noun phrase, like so:

(1) $\underline{\text{eg}}$
[IX   MAN]   'the man'

(2) $\underline{\hspace{3em}\text{eg}}$
[IX   MAN]   'the man'

This is true even when a postnominal IX is also present.

(3) $\underline{\text{eg}}$
[IX_i MAN IX_i]   'the man there'

(4) $\underline{\hspace{4em}\text{eg}}$
[IX_i MAN IX_i]   'the man there'

However, if a postnominal IX is present, eg cannot spread over only the nominal sign and not the postnominal IX:

(5) *$\underline{\hspace{3em}\text{eg}}$
[IX_i MAN IX_i]

Give a tree analysis of this nominal phrase in ASL that will account for these facts:

[IX_i MAN IX_i]

Make use of the notion of scope here by assuming that eg spreads only over those nodes that determiner IX has scope over. Be sure to consider the importance of the data in 5.

Given the structure you've offered and the semantics of this NP, what do you think the function of postnominal IX with respect to the head N is most like: a determiner, an argument, or a modifier?

Based on what we've done thus far in this problem set, would you say the structure of ASL noun phrases is similar to English noun phrases or not? Offer a general X-Bar schema for ASL noun phrases.

All right, now we have more data to consider. The postnominal IX can co-occur with a bare noun sign:

MAN IX 'a nonspecific man there'

As I said, this postnominal IX can optionally have eg:

(6)   eg
   [MAN   IX]

But eg now cannot spread onto the noun sign:

(7) *_____ eg
   [MAN   IX]

Did you expect the data in 7, given the structure you offered for ASL noun phrases? Why or why not? If not, adjust the structure you offered so that you can account for the ungrammaticality of 7 with ordinary assumptions about scope.

(If you know ASL, you might have noted that 7 is grammatical with the sense 'the man there'; that is, with the same sense as 4. It is asterisked in 7 with the reading of 6, 'a nonspecific man there.' Please don't worry about the other reading of 7 for this problem set.)

2. Hopi negatives and indefinites

Part 1

In Hopi the presence of the particle *qa* makes a sentence negative:

(1) Um   ngahut   wéhekna.
    you (Nom) medicine (Acc) spilled
    'You spilled the medicine.'
(2) Um ngahut   qa wéhekna.
    you medicine not spilled
    'You didn't spill the medicine.'

Consider the sentences that follow and their translations. Then make a statement about the syntactic position of *qa* in terms of its semantic import.

(3) I'ngahu   qa wehe.
    this medicine (Nom) not spilled
    'This medicine didn't spill.'
(4) Nu'   pu' Hopilavayit qa tutuqayi.

       I (Nom) now Hopi (Acc) not study
       'I am not studying Hopi now.'

(5) David   qa tiyo.
      David (Nom) not boy
      'David is not a boy.'

(6) Itam   tuupevut   qa nöönösa.
      we (Nom) corn (Acc) not ate
      'We didn't eat corn.'

Part 2

Now consider these additional sentences and modify your statement in Part 1 about the syntactic position of *qa* with respect to its semantic import so that your new statement will cover all the data thus far.

(7) Tiyo   qa kuuyit   wéhekna.
      boy (Nom) not water (Acc) spilled
      'It's not the water that the boy spilled (but something else).'

(8) Ina   qa nuy   ngahut   maqa.
      my father (Nom) not me (Dat) medicine (Acc) gave
      'It wasn't to me that my father gave medicine (but to someone else).'

(9) Qa kawayo   pookot   kuukl.
      not horse (Nom) dog (Acc) bit
      'It wasn't the horse that bit the dog (but something else).'

(10) Pumu kawayom   qa taavok   yuutu.
      those horses (NOM) not yesterday ran
      'It wasn't yesterday that those horses ran (but some other time).'

Part 3

In Problem Set 4.5 of Chapter 4 you looked at questions in Hopi. There you learned that *hak* is the nominative singular form for 'who.' Actually, *hak* can also be interpreted as an indefinite pronoun, meaning someone. So the sentence in 11 (on which I've left off a final punctuation mark) is ambiguous—normally the context makes it clear whether we have a question or a statement.

(11) Hak wárikiwta
      'Who is running?' or 'Someone is running.'

However, when a negative is present in a sentence with *hak*, the ambiguity disappears. Thus 12 is interpreted only as a question and 13 is interpreted only as a statement:

(12) Hak qa wárikiwta?
      'Who isn't running?'

(13) Qa hak wárikiwta.
      'Nobody is running.'

The lack of ambiguity in 12 surprises me. If you see a reason for it, please discuss it with your instructor. But the lack of ambiguity in 13 is consistent with what we saw in Part 2. Explain how.

Hint: In doing this, you should consider the English sentence:

(14) Somebody isn't running.

in contrast to:

(15) Nobody is running.

3. Japanese *sika*

Here you are to figure out (1) the syntactic category, (2) the syntactic distribution, and (3) the semantic contribution of the word *sika* in Japanese. You need to have read Chapter 4 in order to be able to do this problem.

Syntactic Category

With respect to syntactic category, ask yourself whether *sika* behaves like some projection of N, V, P (here, postposition), A, or I, or like a particle.

With regard to postpositions, assume that Japanese postpositions are comparable to English prepositions for this problem set.

With regard to particles, there are at least three types in Japanese. One is the sentence particle. (You looked at some of these in Problem Set 4.6 of Chapter 4.) These particles attach to the verb or adjective that is the predicate of the clause.

Another is the GF particle. Recall from Problem Set 4.4 of Chapter 4 that Japanese assigns particles to Subject (ga), DO (o), IO (ni), and Genitive NP (no). We will not look at the Genitive particle *no* in this problem set and I ask you now to set it aside completely and not consider it as you do this problem set. GF particles can attach to both nominal phrases and clauses.

The third type of particle is often called the adverbial particle. If you have studied Japanese at all, you may well be familiar with *wa*, the particle which marks a topic. It can attach not only to phrases that play GFs, but also to phrases that have other roles, such as PPs. Another adverbial particle is *mo* 'also.'

In general, at most one particle can be attached to a given NP. No combination of GF particles would make sense, of course. Thus we never expect (and never find) combinations like *ga-o* (Subject-DO). And while a combination of a GF particle and adverbial particle would make sense some of the time, we never find them for *ga* or *o*. Thus where we might expect to find a combination like *ga-wa* (Subject-Topic), for example, we find simply *wa*.

Postpositions, likewise, cannot co-occur with GF particles. This is because the GF particles attach only to N″ and C″, so we never find the combination of postposition followed by GF particle. And it is also because the Object of a P does not have any particle of its own in addition to the P, so we never get a postposition following a GF particle. However, nothing stops us from having a postposition plus an adverbial particle. Thus we can find combinations such as *de-wa* 'from-Topic.'

One tricky problem is the behavior of *ni*, the morpheme that attaches to the IO. Earlier I called it a GF particle. However, it has some unusual properties:

a. Like the GF particles and like postpositions, it cannot co-occur with other GF particles.

b. Unlike the GF particles *ga* and *o* but like postpositions, it can co-occur with the adverbial particles *wa* and *mo* (as in *ni-wa* and *ni-mo*).

c. Unlike postpositions, it may optionally be omitted before an adverbial particle for some speakers (but not all, by any means). Thus some people would use simply NP-*wa* sometimes where others would have to use NP-*ni-wa*. (Note that this behavior is not precisely that of *ga* and *o*, since these two GF particles must be omitted before an adverbial particle.)

The analysis of *ni* could serve as the topic for a research paper or even a dissertation. For now, just note its behavior with postpostions and with GF particles and adverbial particles, because this behavior can help you figure out the correct syntactic category of *sika*.

Syntactic Distribution

Figuring out the syntactic distribution of *sika* is perhaps less difficult. Ask yourself where *sika* can appear and whether or not anything else must co-occur with it. If something else must co-occur with *sika*, what is that something else? Let us call that something else X for now. What sort of structural relationship must X stand in with respect to *sika*? Be sure to consider the structural relationships that we talked about in Chapter 4, including government, c-command, and linear precedence. (That is, must *sika* linearly precede or follow X? Must *sika* c-command or be c-commanded by X? Must *sika* govern or be governed by X?)

Semantic Contribution

With respect to semantic contribution, *sika* is relatively straightforward, so a concise statement will suffice.

Please make the following crucial assumptions as you work:

A. The Japanese clause consists of a projection of V with all arguments and modifiers of the V as sisters to the V. Japanese also has sentential particles, negatives, and tense markers which occur cliticized or affixed to the verb. Let us represent these three types of items as being part of a single word with the V root.

B. GF and adverbial particles attach as sisters to the phrasal level, and are taken to c-command all that material that the phrase they are attached to c-commands.

With these assumptions, the structure of a Japanese sentence is something like:

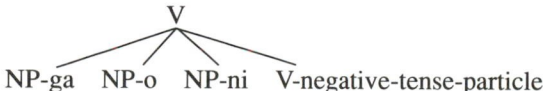

(This is an oversimplification of the phrase structure. I ask you to use this assumption because it will allow you to see the point of the problem and for our purposes no more complex structure is necessary. In fact, however, there is much evidence that at SS the Subject argument is external to the VP in Japanese. So please keep this caveat in mind for your own future research.)

Okay. Here, finally, are the data. Be sure to ask yourself what each set of examples shows you and include that restriction in your final statement.

(1) a. Taroo-sika Noriko-ni tegami-o kakanakatta.
Taroo-only Noriko-IO letter-DO write-neg-past
'Only Taroo wrote a letter to Noriko.'
b. Taroo-ga Noriko-ni tegami-o kakanakatta.

Taroo-SUBJ Noriko-IO letter-DO write-neg-past
'Taroo didn't write a letter to Noriko.'

  c. Taroo-ga Noriko-ni tegami-o kaita.
                                  write-past
     'Taroo wrote a letter to Noriko.'

(2) a. Taroo-sika Noriko-ni tegami-o kakanakatta. (=1a)
        Taroo-only Noriko-IO letter-DO write-neg-past
        'Only Taroo wrote a letter to Noriko.'

    b. *Taroo-sika Noriko-ni tegami-o kaita.
                                write-past

(3) a. Taroo-ga Noriko-(ni) sika tegami-o kakanakatta.
        'Taroo wrote a letter only to Noriko.'

    b. Taroo-ga Noriko-ni tegami-sika kakanakatta.
        'Taroo wrote to Noriko only a letter.'(not a book, for example)

(Note that in 3a many speakers insist that *ni* be present, but some optionally allow it to be omitted.)

(4) a. *Taroo-ga-sika Noriko-ni   tegami-o   kakanakatta.

    b. *Taroo-sika-ga Noriko-ni   tegami-o   kakanakatta.

    c. Taroo-ga   Noriko-ni-sika tegami-o   kakanakatta.

    d. *Taroo-ga   Noriko-sika-ni tegami-o   kakanakatta.

    e. *Taroo-ga   Noriko-ni   tegami-o-sika kakanakatta.

    f. *Taroo-ga   Noriko-ni   tegami-sika-o kakanakatta.

(5) a. Uma-ga   biiru-o   nomu koto-sika omosirokunai.
        horse-SUBJ beer-DO drink that-only uninteresting
        'Only (the fact) that horses drink beer is interesting.'

    b. Uma-ga biiru-o nomu koto-ga   omosiroi.
                                   interesting
        '(The fact) that horses drink beer is interesting.'

In 5 and the examples that follow *koto* introduces an embedded clause, similarly to *that* in English. As expected in a head-final language like Japanese, it follows the embedded clause that it introduces. *Koto* is typically followed by the GF particle that indicates whether the embedded clause is Subject *(ga)* or DO *(o)*. (Not all speakers find 5a perfectly grammatical. I have taken it from Oishi 1986, who marks it grammatical. Many of my informants agree. Please assume it is grammatical for the purposes of this problem set.)

(6) a. *Uma-sika biiru-o   nomu koto-ga omosirokunai.

    b. *Uma-ga   biiru-sika nomu koto-ga omosirokunai.

(7) a. Uma-sika   biiru-o   nomanai koto-ga   omosiroi.
        horses-only beer-DO drink-neg that-SUBJ interesting
        'It's interesting that only horses drink beer.'

    b. Uma-sika biiru-o nomanai koto-ga omosiokunai.
        'It's uninteresting that only horses drink beer.'

Okay, I think you can do it now. Let me repeat: The job is to figure out the syntactic category, the syntactic distribution, and the semantic contribution of the word *sika*.

Now translate 8 and 10. (You will learn nothing new from doing this. The idea is just to make you see how much you know about Japanese at this point.)

(8) Uma-ga biiru-sika nomanai koto-ga omosiroi.

(9) Gakusei-ga kodomo-ga kono uti-ni sundeinai koto-o tasikameta.
students-SUBJ children-SUBJ this house-in live-neg that-DO made sure
'The students made sure that children weren't living in this house.'

(10) Gakusei-ga kodomo-sika kono uti-ni sundeinai koto-o tasikameta.

Finally, there is one more complication with *sika*'s distribution that I would like to raise. Make a stab at it based on these sentences:

(11) a. Tokyo-made ikanakatta.
Tokyo-till go-neg-past.
'I didn't go up to (as far as) Tokyo.'
b. Tokyo-made-sika ikanakatta.
'I went only till Tokyo.'
c. *Tokyo-sika-made ikanakatta.

Made is a postposition. In considering why 11c is ungrammatical, be sure to consider the structural relationship between *sika* and whatever other element it must co-occur with. You probably decided that that other element must stand in a particular structural relationship with respect to *sika*. I am now asking you to propose what structural relationship *sika* must stand in with respect to that other element. Do not get frustrated. These are very few examples to go on, but your first stab at an answer will probably be correct.

*Problem Set 5.7: Reference and Formal Semantics

Part 1

Discuss the following two arguments. What interpretation would we have to assign to the premises in order for the arguments to be valid? Then discuss the use of the premises in natural language in order to explain why these would not be considered valid inferences in ordinary (non-formal-logic) settings.

1. At least one of every two people is a female.

If someone is not female, then everybody else is.

2. Exactly one of every two people is a female.

There are fewer than three people.

Part 2

Give two readings for this sentence in ordinary language (not in formal logic expressions):

(1) I'd like you to meet someone.

What is the source of the ambiguity? (Use terms that you learned in this chapter.)
Now consider the sentence:

(2) Someone is angry.

Do you see two readings here? Consider this sentence in the light of following contexts, such as:

(3) Someone is angry, and his name is Bob Dole.
(4) Someone is angry. Take a look at this anonymous note.

If you see two readings for 2, are they parallel to the two readings you found in 1, or not? (I don't think they are.) If you say they are not, what could be the source of the two readings in 2?

Part 3

The sentence:

(5) I expect all linguistics professors to know better.

is ambiguous. Paraphrase the readings in regular, nontechnical language.
  Now consider:

(6) I expect any linguistics professor to know better.
(7) I expect every linguistics professor to know better.
(8) I expect a linguistics professor to know better.
(9) I expect linguistics professors to know better.

Are all these sentences equally ambiguous? Comment on each separately, saying whether it is ambiguous and giving all its readings.

Part 4

Consider:

(10) Smith's murderer is insane.

There is an ambiguity here (at least, some people would call this sentence ambiguous). If you don't see it, consider the sentence with following contexts, such as:

(11) Smith's murderer is insane. I met him and he's a certifiable psychotic.
(12) Smith's murderer is insane. I've never met him, but just look at the crime scene and you can tell.

Discuss the ambiguity in ordinary, nontechnical language. Is the ambiguity here similar to any of the other problems raised in this problem set? If so, how? If not, try to offer a general description of the kind of ambiguity we are dealing with in this example.

Problem Set 5.8: Ambiguity

Each of the sentences that follow can be said to be ambiguous, with a different source of ambiguity in each.

(1) He's got a lot of dough.
(2) I understand what he means.
(3) The cat's got his tongue.
(4) The beaver has sharp teeth.
(5) The philosophical Greeks wrote dramas.
(6) I hate visiting relatives.
(7) I'd love a Norwegian bicycle.
(8) Nothing is better than cabbage soup.

Give the two (or more) readings for each sentence. Label each type of ambiguity, using one of the following labels:

tense
scope
syntactic
lexical
restrictive/nonrestrictive
nonspecific/specific
generic/specific
idiom/literal

(Hint: If you don't know what I mean by "restrictive/nonrestrictive," look back at Problem Set 4.1 of Chapter 4 where I introduce the contrast between restrictive and nonrestrictive relative clauses. Also, if you can't see any difference between the kind of ambiguity in 4 and that in 7, compare in your head *A Norwegian bicycle is always well-built* to 7, and then go back to 4 vs. 7. If you still don't see any difference, maybe I'm wrong and there isn't one. So discuss this with your class.)

Problem Set 5.9: Metaphor

1. Some have argued that metaphors fall into three classes:

  I. Orientational, which rely on spatial information to carry the metaphor
 II. Ontological, which treat abstract entities, states, and events as though they were concrete substances
III. Structural, which are built on other metaphors

Examples of class I would be:

  (a) Mary is getting ahead in school.
      Mary is falling behind with her work.

where the direction forward is used for positive values and the direction backward is used for negative values.
  Examples of class II would be:

  (b) My algebra is rusty.
      My nerves frayed.

where one's algebra knowledge is compared to a machine and one's nerves are compared to a material.

Examples of class III would be:

(c) All the world's a stage.
   Love is war.

In the well-known Shakespeare sentence, the world is compared to a stage, which in turn evokes the concept of a play. (The world is a play.) In the second sentence love is compared to war, but war itself is a concept which can be a metaphor for all kinds of hostile behavior.

Part 1

The sentences that follow contain expressions of English that can be considered metaphorical. Place each sentence into one of the three classes I've given and explain your answer.

   (1) That broke my heart.
   (2) Mary's in the peak of health.
   (3) His career came to a dead end.
   (4) Work is salvation.
   (5) Mary came down with the flu.
   (6) Her words pierced my heart.

Part 2

Give examples of your own of metaphors of each of the three types. Please give at least two sentences for each group, drawn from any language you know well. (If you use a language other than English, please give a word-for-word gloss or morpheme-for-morpheme gloss, as well as a colloquial translation into English.)

Part 3

Orientational metaphors are particularly problematic, because sometimes a given direction can be used primarily with a positive connotation, but secondarily with a negative connotation. For example, "up" in English is found with both positive and negative connotations:

   positive: Her remarks were upbeat. (= Her remarks were optimistic.)
   negative: Things are messed up. (= Things are problematic.)

Pick two other orientations and exemplify their problematic nature.

Part 4

Classify these Japanese metaphors:

   (7) Onaka-o kowasu. 'My stomach is upset/I have diarrhea.'
       stomach break

(8) Kondo-no   siken-ga   saigo-no   yama-da.
    this time-Gen exam-Nom last time-Gen mountain-be
    'This exam is the last mountain.'
    (= 'This exam is the last difficult thing.')
(9) Keiki-ga   uwa-muki   da.
    economy-Nom up-direction be
    'The economy is improving.'

Part 5

In Figure 5.2 you see six signs of ASL. Please discuss each one with respect to the three classifications of metaphors.

Do you think one or more classifications are going unrepresented here? If so, if you know ASL well, make a stab at why. (Don't be thrown off by this question. Some linguists believe that all three groups are represented in ASL, and examples in Figure 5.2 are brought up to demonstrate that point. Other linguists argue that this isn't so. I am not looking for any fixed answer here. Some of these signs may seem to clearly fall into classes for you; others may baffle you. Don't worry about it. Just discuss them intelligently.)

Part 6

Many linguists have criticized the grouping of metaphors into these three classes. One criticism is based on the claim that all sentences containing a metaphor can easily and naturally be followed by the phrase "so to speak." This diagnostic has been used to

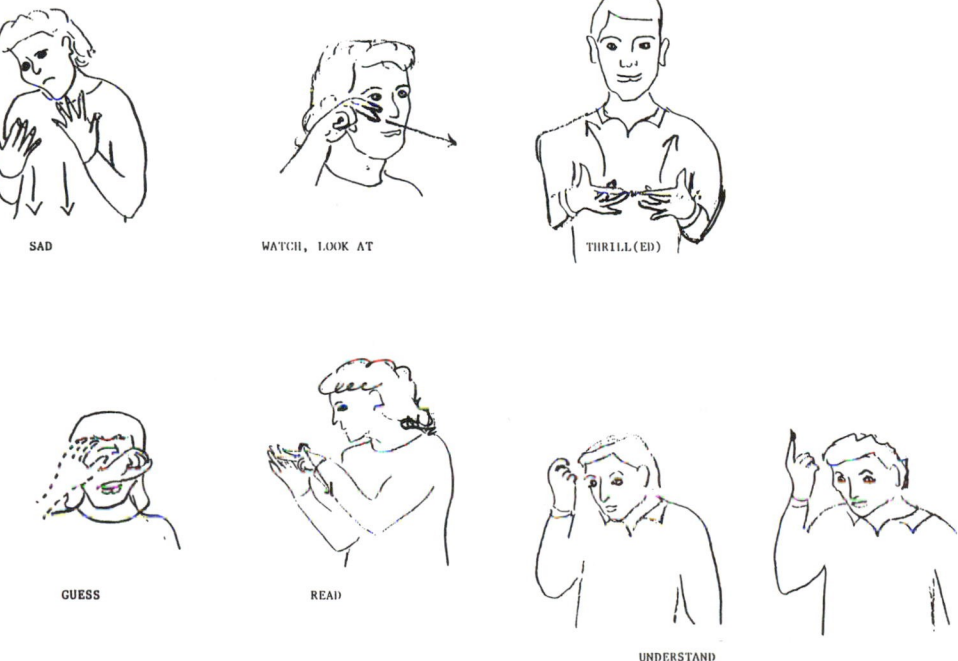

Figure 5.2. Six signs of ASL with attention to classification of metaphors.

eliminate one of the three classes given from the set of metaphors. Which class does this diagnostic eliminate?

2. We talk commonly about herds of animals and flocks of birds. But for some animals, there are special names for the groups, particularly for birds in flight. I list here some of those.

    bouquet of pheasants
    leap of leopards
    skulk of foxes
    clash of rhinos
    peep of chickens
    siege of heron
    gaggle of geese
    ostentation of peacocks
    knot of toads
    pride of lions
    troop of kangaroos
    parliament of owls
    route of wolves
    murder of crows
    unkindness of ravens
    exaltation of larks

Do you think metaphor plays a role in any of these group names? How?

Arrange these examples into classes by whatever factors you see as relevant here. Explain what the factors are. If an example belongs to more than one class, discuss that fact.

Find at least one more example of your own of an uncommon group name. Does it fit nicely into one of the classes you've already set up? Discuss your answer.

*Problem Set 5.10: Semantics and Syntax

Part 1

There was a time in modern linguistics when syntacticians proposed transformational rules to account for a wide range of semantic phenomena. Many linguists suggested and/or argued for the existence of a syntactic rule of Negative Transportation (which was also called Negative Raising and Negative Climbing) which would derive 2 from 1 by moving the negative (here the *not*) of 1 up into the matrix clause, as in 2.

    (1) I think Sue's not a fool.
    (2) I don't think Sue's a fool.

Such an analysis was reputed to have the advantage of accounting for the fact that 2 can have the same interpretation as 1. Notice further that 3 and 4 are both contradictions, as predicted by this analysis.

    (3) →←I think Sue's not a fool and I think Sue's a fool.
    (4) →←I don't think Sue's a fool and I think Sue's a fool.

I'd like you to evaluate this approach to 1–2.

First, is 2 truly synonymous with 1? If you say no, show it. (There are many ways you can test for synonymy. One way is to give a context for one sentence that excludes the other sentence. Another way is to show that one is not redundant of the other when both are used together. And I'm sure you can think of others.)

Second, give a pragmatic account of why 2 might be interpreted as equivalent to 1 without appealing to a transformation of Negative Transportation. Discuss how your account will handle 3 and 4.

Part 2

Some linguists (mainly in the 1960s) argued that a sentence like:

(1) Floyd melted the glass.

was derived syntactically from a sentence like:

(2) [Floyd CAUSED [the glass MELT]].

Here the capitalized words *CAUSED* and *MELT* stand for the abstractions of the notions of causation and melting. This is very similar to (and perhaps it is equivalent to—but I'm not sure) saying that the words *CAUSED* and *MELT* stand for the concepts **CAUSED** and **MELT** in conceptual semantics terms. The speaker would have the possibility of inserting some real lexical item for the abstract *CAUSED* and *MELT*, perhaps yielding sentences like:

(3) Floyd caused the glass to melt.
(4) Floyd made the glass melt.

(Of course, as you might have noted right away, 3 has a *to* in it that 2 does not have. There was a degree of morphological "magic" allowed in the theory of syntax in the 1960s. And some syntactic magic, too. Today such morphological and syntactic magic is eschewed. Try not to let the syntactic and morphological problems get in the way. If you were working on this problem out in the world, so to speak, and not just in this problem set, then of course you should bring all your knowledge of linguistics to bear on the issue (and on any linguistic issue). But this is a semantics problem set designed specifically to help you use the concepts introduced in the chapter. So, for the sake of this problem set, concentrate only on the semantics and assume that the syntactic and morphological problems are somebody else's kettle of fish.)

The speaker might, instead, not insert any lexical item for *CAUSED* alone, but simply take the abstract *CAUSED* and the abstract *MELT* (here intransitive) in 2 and substitute for them the lexical item *melt* (transitive), to yield 1. This derivation of 1 will automatically account for its causative sense (for, surely, 1 means that Floyd did something which brought about—that is, caused—the melting of the glass).

Many verbs have both a transitive and an intransitive use, like *melt*:

(5) John sank the boat.
    The boat sank.
(6) John opened the door.
    The door opened.

And other verbs have only a transitive or only an intransitive use—but they have a corresponding verb that is of the opposite transitivity. For example:

(7) John persuaded Bill.
   Bill agreed.

The important difference between 5–6, on the one hand, and 7, on the other, is that in examples like 5–6 the verbs are morphologically identical (*sink*, for example, sounds the same whether it's used transitively or intransitively), but in examples like 7 the verbs are morphologically distinct. (*Persuade* and *agree* do not share any morphemes.)

The proposal to derive a sentence like 1 from a source like 2 does not in any way depend on the morphological identity of the transitive and intransitive forms of *melt*. A parallel proposed derivation would be offered for examples like 7. That is, a theory that allows us to derive 2 from 1, might also derive the first sentence of 7 from:

(8) [John CAUSED [Bill AGREE]].

A lexical insertion rule would take *CAUSED* and *AGREE* and insert for them the lexical item *persuaded*, yielding the first sentence of 7. And, of course, we also have the option of just inserting the lexical item *caused* for the abstract notion *CAUSED* and the lexical item *agree* for the abstract notion *AGREE*, having 8 yield:

(9) John caused Bill to agree.

Does it make semantic sense to lexically insert the verb *kill* in place of *CAUSE (to) DIE*? I'd like you to answer this by testing whether sentences with *kill* and corresponding sentences with the string *cause to die* are semantically equivalent.

In answering this discuss the following data. (Each of the pairs of examples here brings up a distinct point—so be sure to handle each pair separately.)

(10)   John caused Mary to die and it surprised me that she did so.
       *John killed Mary and it surprised me that she did so.
(11)   John caused Bill to die on Sunday by stabbing him on Saturday.
       #John killed Bill on Sunday by stabbing him on Saturday.
(12)   John caused Bill to die by swallowing his tongue.
       John killed Bill by swallowing his tongue.

(Note that both sentences in 12 are good. But the first sentence is ambiguous, whereas the second is not. This is the point for you to discuss.)

What kind of conditions would we have to put on the rule turning *CAUSE (to) DIE* into *kill* in order to account for its failure in 11 and for its applying to only one reading of 12? Would these conditions also account for its failure in 10? If not, can you think of any conditions you might impose on this rule that would allow you to account for its failure in 10?

Part 3

In Part 2 you saw some of the reverberations of lexically inserting a verb in place of a combination of an abstract element (above it was CAUSE) and some other lexical items (such as *(to) die*). But verbs were not the only types of lexical items that this sort of lexical substitution was proposed for. For example, *orphans* could be inserted in place of *people who lost their parents*, etc. Consider the data here:

(1) The person who lost his parents misses them.
(2) *The orphan misses them.
(3) The person who played the guitar thought that it was a beautiful instrument.
(4) ?*The guitarist thought that it was a beautiful instrument.
(5) John is a person who plays the guitar and he thinks that it's a beautiful instrument.
(6) ?John is a guitarist and he thinks that it's a beautiful instrument.

In 2, 4, and 6, the * or ?* or ? indicate oddness with the reading that corresponds to 1, 3, and 5, respectively.

What problem for lexical substitution do these pairs bring up?

Why is 6 better than 4, and why is 2 the worst of the group? (If you don't agree with the grammaticality judgments here, just accept them and answer the question as though this were a foreign language for you. Once you've done that, then you can give your judgments and comment on why they might be as they are. By the way, the judgments given reflect the speech of a group of about 200 students at Georgetown University in 1978.)

Part 4

In the section "Transformations" of Chapter 4 you learned that earlier theories of syntax allowed a lot of possible transformations. In fact, there were four types of transformations considered viable in the 1960s and early 1970s:

(a) substitutions
(b) deletions
(c) insertions
(d) permutations

One assumption of this period in the theory of linguistics was that transformations would preserve meaning. So any two sentences related by a transformation had to have the same sets of readings. Accordingly, anything deleted could unambiguously be recovered. Also, anything inserted had to be semantically inert (the dummy elements we talked about in the section "Subjects and pro" of Chapter 4). Inserted elements could fill syntactic slots, but could not contribute to the meaning of a sentence and could not participate in semantic rules of interpretation.

An example of a putative substitution rule is seen in 1–2, where 2 is derived from 1 (the rule was called Reflexive):

(1) John$_i$ loves John$_i$.
(2) John loves himself.

(With the theory we developed in Chapter 4 (see the section "Reflexives"), of course, we generate 2 at DS and the grammar's job is to interpret the anaphor at SS, which it can do only if the anaphor is properly bound at SS.)

An example of a putative deletion rule is seen in 3–4, where 4 is derived from 3 (the rule was called Equi):

(3) John$_i$ hoped that he$_i$ would win.
(4) John hoped to win.

(With the theory we developed in Chapter 4, 3 and 4 would not be syntactically related. Instead, 4 is analyzed as a control structure, in which PRO is the Subject of the infinitival clause. The grammar's job is to interpret PRO at SS, which it will do in this sentence via locating the proper NP that controls the PRO.)

An example of a putative insertion rule is seen in 5–6, where 6 is derived from 5 via insertion of *it* (the rule was called Dummy It Insertion):

(5) ———— rains in Oregon.
(6) It rains in Oregon.

Here *it* is inserted into Subject position in expressions of weather and time only. (In the theory we developed in Chapter 4 we assumed a rule of dummy *it* insertion, although nothing we did hinged on this assumption, and I, for one, do not share this assumption. I have argued elsewhere that *it* is present in DS and the job of the grammar is to interpret it at SS in an appropriately ambient way.)

An example of a putative permutation rule is seen in 7–8, where 8 is derived from 7 (the rule was called Passive):

(7) The dog scared Mary.
(8) Mary was scared by the dog.

Here two movement rules were assumed, one moving the Direct Object of the active sentence into Subject position in the passive sentence, and one moving the Subject of the active sentence into Object position of a *by*-phrase in the passive sentence. (In the section "Theta Theory" of Chapter 4 we analyzed passives as involving movement of the Object into Subject position only. We generated the Object of the *by*-phrase in OP position at DS.)

Today current theories of syntax do not include substitution or deletion rules (although there are certainly deletion rules in some theories of phonology). Many theories also do not include insertion rules. And many theories don't even include permutation rules.

The reasons for the gradual winnowing away of the types of syntactic rules considered necessary and desirable are many, involving syntactic, semantic, morphological, and phonological considerations. Here we're going to concentrate on some of the semantic ones.

In the following I will not give you any formal characterization of the rules you are to consider. Just use my example sentences to give yourself an idea of what type of input the rule takes and what type of output it produces. No formal understanding is necessary for the purposes of this homework.

As you answer these questions keep in mind the rule of the day (the rule of the 1960s and 1970s): Transformations must preserve meaning.

What problem for the putative substitution rule of Reflexive (exemplified in 1–2) do these data present?

(9) Only the devil loves the devil.

(10) Only the devil loves himself.

Be sure that your discussion handles why deriving 10 from 9 is problematic in a way that deriving 2 from 1 is not. Now please extract away from the precise example here and discuss the nature of the issue. That is, what kind of semantic problem arises if we allow syntactic substitution rules?

What problem for the putative deletion rule of Equi (exemplified in 3–4) do the sentences in 11 present?

(11) John didn't know whether to act nice.
    I don't know how to do it.

Again, be sure that your discussion of 11 and of the source sentences for 11 with an Equi analysis handles why 11 is problematic but 4 is not. Now, again, extract away from this precise example and discuss what kind of semantic problem arises if we allow syntactic deletion rules.

Another putative deletion rule is exemplified in 12–13 (the rule was called Comparative Ellipsis):

(12) Mary talks louder than John does.

(13) Mary talks louder than John.

What problem for Comparative Ellipsis does 14 present?

(14) Mary likes Bill more than Sue.

What problem for Comparative Ellipsis does 15 present?

(15) Mary eats faster than a tornado.

Why do 14–15 present these problems, in contrast to 13?

What problem for the putative rule of Dummy *It* Insertion (exemplified in 5–6 above) does 16 present?

(16) It rained and ruined our party.

Again, extract away from the precise example and discuss what kind of problem can arise for semantic theory if we allow syntactic insertion rules.

What problem for the putative rule of Passive (exemplified in 7–8 above) do 17–18 present?

(17) Every person in this room speaks at least two languages.

(18) At least two languages are spoken by every person in this room.

(Hint: Pay attention to your first readings for the scope interactions of the quantifiers in these examples.) Again, extract away from the precise example and discuss what kind of semantic problem can arise if we allow syntactic movement rules.

Bibliography

Below is a list of works that I consulted as I wrote this text. Much of the information in this text, however, stems from readings I have done over the past twenty-three years. Thus the list is far from complete. I have aimed, instead, to make it somewhat representative.

With respect to the problem sets, in particular, the sources cited here are not to be taken as agreeing with the analyses that I lead you to. Rather, I have drawn materials from those sources and used them for my own purposes, sometimes in direct conflict with the conclusions of the original sources. I hereby absolve all these sources from any responsibility for errors in this text.

Chapter 1

Catford, J. C. 1988. *A Practical Introduction to Phonetics*. Oxford: Clarendon Press. (particularly helpful for ejectives, implosives, and clicks and for breathy voice, whispery voice, and creaky voice)

Cowan, William and Jaromira Rakušan. 1987. *Source Book for Linguistics*. Philadelphia: John Benjamins. (particularly for data on many languages)

Dell, François and Mohamed Elmedlaoui. 1985. "Syllabic Consonants and Syllabification in Imdlawn Tashlhiyt Berber," *Journal of African Languages and Linguistics* 7:105–130. (for the claim that any consonant can serve as a syllable nucleus)

Goldsmith, John. 1990. *Autosegmental and Metrical Phonology*. Oxford: Blackwell. (especially for syllable structure)

Hockett, Charles. 1955. *Manual of Phonology*, Baltimore, MD: Waverly Press. (particularly for data on many languages)

Keating, Patricia. 1988. "A Survey of Phonological Features," Bloomington: Indiana University Linguistics Club. (for many things, particularly a discussion of highness with regard to palato-alveolar affricates)

Kenstowicz, Michael. 1994. *Phonology in Generative Grammar*. Oxford: Blackwell. (for everything)

——— and Charles Kisseberth. 1979. *Generative Phonology*. San Diego: Academic Press. (for linear phonology)

Ladefoged, Peter. 1975. *A Course in Phonetics*. San Diego: Harcourt Brace Jovanovich. (for everything, but particularly acoustics and breathy voice, whispery voice, and creaky voice)

Smalley, William A. 1963. *Manual of Articulatory Phonetics*. Landham, MD: University Press of America. (for articulatory phonetics in general and for data on many languages)

Wolfram, Walt. 1991. *Dialects and American English*. Englewood Cliffs, NJ: Prentice Hall. (for variation in American vowels)

Problem Set 1.2

Zingarelli, Nicola. 1970. *Vocabolario della lingua italiana*. Bologna: Zanichelli.

Problem Set 1.7

Klima, Edward and Ursula Bellugi. 1979. *The Signs of Language*. Cambridge, MA: Harvard University Press.

Chapter 2

Clements, George N. 1985. "The Geometry of Phonological Features," *Phonology Yearbook* 2:225–252. (for geometric phonology)

Cowan, William, and Jaromira Rakušan. 1987. *Source Book for Linguistics*. Philadelphia: John Benjamins. (particularly for data on many languages)

Goldsmith, John. 1990. *Autosegmental and Metrical Phonology*. Oxford: Blackwell. (mainly for geometric phonology)

Echeverría, Max and Heles Contreras. 1965. "Araucanian Phonemics," *International Journal of American Linguistics* 31:132–135. (for information about and analysis of Araucanian)

Halle, Morris and Jean-Roger Vergnaud. 1987. *An Essay on Stress*. Cambridge, MA: MIT Press. (for metrical phonology and much of the data)

Hammond, Michael. 1984. *Constraining Metrical Theory: A Modular Theory of Rhythm and Destressing*. Doctoral Dissertation, UCLA. (for metrical trees)

Hayes, Bruce. 1995. *Metrical Stress Theory: Principles and Case Studies*. Chicago: University of Chicago Press. (for metrical phonology and much of the data)

Kaye, Jonathan, Jean Lowenstamm, and Jean-Roger Vergnaud. 1990. "Constituent Structure and Government in Phonology," *Phonology* 2:193–231. (for the syllabification of s-clusters in Italian)

Kennedy, George. 1953. "Two Tone Patterns in Tangsic," *Language*. 29:367–373. (for information about and analysis of Tangsic)

Kenstowicz, Michael. 1994. *Phonology in Generative Grammar*. Oxford: Blackwell. (for everything)

———— and Charles Kisseberth. 1979. *Generative Phonology*. San Diego: Academic Press. (for linear phonology)

Kiparksy, Paul. 1982. "Lexical Phonology and Morphology," in I.S. Yang (ed.), *Linguistics in the Morning Calm*. Seoul: Hanshin. 3–91. (for lexical phonology)

Krauss, Michael. 1985. *Yup'ik Eskimo Prosodic Systems: Descriptive and Comparative Studies*. Alaska Native Language Center Research Papers, No. 7. (for information about and analysis of Yup'ik)

Liberman, Mark and Alan Prince. 1977. "On Stress and Linguistic Rhythm," *LI* 8:249–336. (for metrical trees and grids)

Mester, R. Armin. 1994. "The Quantitative Trochee in Latin," *Natural Language and Linguistic Theory* 12(1):1–62. (for discussion of an instance of medial trapping)

Piggott, Glyne. 1980. *Aspects of Odawa Morphophonemics*. New York: Garland. (for Ojibwa stress clash at the end of words)

Prince, Alan. 1983. "Relating to the Grid," *Linguistic Inquiry* 14:19–100. (for metrical grids)

———. 1989. "Metrical Forms," in Paul Kiparsky and Gilbert Youmans (eds.), *Phonetics and Phonology, Vol. 1: Rhythm and Meter*. San Diego: Academic Press. 45–80. (for discussion of ternary feet)

——— and Paul Smolensky. 1993. *Optimality Theory*. Unpublished ms. Rutgers University and University of Colorado at Boulder. (for Optimality Theory and for the analysis of the Tagalog affix *-um-*)

Pulleyblank, Doug. 1986. *Tone in Lexical Phonology*. Dordrecht: Reidel. (for data and analysis of tone languages)

Pulleyblank, Edwin. 1990. "Articulator-Based Place Features of Vowels," unpublished paper. (for an argument that vowels should be described in terms of a feature of [±front] not [±back] in languages like Turkish)

Selkirk, Elisabeth. 1984. *Phonology and Syntax: The Relation Between Sound and Structure*. Cambridge, MA: MIT Press. (for metrical grids)

Steriade, Donca. 1987. "Locality Conditions and Feature Geometry," *NELS* 17(2):595–618. (for geometric phonology)

Tryon, D. T. 1970. An Introduction to Maranungku. (Pacific Linguistics Monographs, Series B, No. 14) Canberra: Australian National University. (for information about and analysis of Maranungku)

Problem Set 2.1

Clements, George N. 1987. "Phonological Feature Representation and the Description of Intrusive Stops," *CLS* 23:29–50.

Haraguchi, Shosuke. 1982. "An Autosegmental Theory: Its Expansion and Extension," *Journal of Linguistic Research* 5(2):59–80.

Problem Set 2.2

Davis, Stuart and Michael Hammond. 1995. "On the Status of Onglides in American English," *Phonology* 12(1):159–182.

Denham, Kristin. 1992. "'Y' defends cyclicity," in Chip Gerfen and Pilar Piñar (eds.), *Coyote Papers*, Vol. 8. Tucson: University of Arizona. 25–35.

Steriade, Donca. 1988. "Review of *CV Phonology: A Generative Theory of the Syllable*, by George N. Clements and Samuel Jay Keyser," *Language* 64:118–129.

Problem Set 2.3

Andrews, Henrietta. 1993. *The Function of Verb Prefixes in Southwestern Otomi*. University of Texas at Arlington: Summer Institute of Linguistics.

Klima, Edward and Ursula Bellugi. 1979. *The Signs of Language*. Cambridge, MA: Harvard University Press.

Langacker, Ronald. 1979. *Studies in Uto-Aztecan Grammar*, vol. 2, *Modern Aztec grammatical sketches*. University of Texas at Arlington: Summer Institute of Linguistics.

Perlmutter, David. 1992. "Sonority and Syllable Structure in American Sign Language," *Linguistic Inquiry* 23:407–442.

Wilbur, Ronnie. 1990. "Why Syllables? What the Notion means for ASL research," Susan Fischer and P. Siple (eds.), *Theoretical Issues in Sign Language Research: Linguistics*. Chicago: University of Chicago Press. 81–108.

———. 1993. "Syllables and Segments: Hold the Movement and Move the Holds!," *Phonetics and Phonology* 3:135–168.

——— and George Allen. 1991. "Perceptual Evidence Against Internal Structure in American Sign Language Syllables," *Language and Speech* 34:27–46.

Problem Set 2.6

Anderson, Stephen. 1972. "On Nasalization in Sudanese," *LI* 3:253–268.

Problem Set 2.7

Cohn, Abigail. 1992. "The Consequences of Dissimilation in Sudanese," *Phonology* 2:199–220.

Hayes, Bruce. 1995. *Metrical Stress Theory: Principles and Case Studies*. Chicago: University of Chicago Press.

Kenstowicz, Michael. 1994. *Phonology in Generative Grammar*. Oxford: Blackwell.

Kiparsky, Paul. 1973. "Elsewhere in Phonology," in Stephen Anderson and Paul Kiparsky (eds.), *A Festschrift for Morris Halle*. New York: Holt, Rinehart and Winston. 93–106.

Osborn, H. 1966. "Warao I: Phonology and Morphophonemics," *International Journal of American linguistics* 32:108–123.

Piggott, G.L. 1992. "Variability in Feature Dependency: The Case of Nasality," *Natural Language and Linguistic Theory* 10:33–78.

Yallop, Colin. 1971. *Alyawarra: An Aboriginal Language of Central Australia*, Canberra: Australian Institute of Aboriginal Studies.

Problem Set 2.8

Selkirk, Elisabeth. 1982. *The Syntax of Words*. Cambridge, MA: MIT Press.

Problem Set 2.9

Selkirk, Elisabeth. 1984. "French Liaison and the $\bar{X}$ Notation," *Linguistic Inquiry* 5:573–590.

Problem Set 2.10

Lamontagne, Greg and Tim Sherer. 1993. "Rutgers Optimality Workshop #1, handout," unpublished, University of Toronto and SUNY at Stony Brook.

Prince, Alan. 1990. "Quantitative Consequences of Rhythmic Organization," *CLS* 26(2): 355–398.

Chapter 3

Afcan, Paschal. 1976. "How a Unified Writing System Will Affect the Yuk Eskimos," in Eric Hamp (ed.), *Papers on Eskimo and Aleut Linguistics*. Chicago: Chicago Linguistic Society. 1–10. (primarily for data on Inuit)

Aissen, Judith. 1974. "Verb Raising," *Linguistic Inquiry* 5:325–366. (for Turkish causative sentences)

Allen, Margaret. 1978. *Morphological Investigations*. Doctoral dissertation. University of Connecticut at Storrs. (especially for compounds)

Anderson, Stephen. 1982. "Where's Morphology?" *Linguistic Inquiry* 13:571–612. (especially for a discussion of where inflectional morphology fits)

———. 1988."Inflection," in Michael Hammon and Michael Noonen (eds.), *Theoretical Morphology: Approaches in Modern Linguistics*. San Diego: Academic Press. 23–44. (for a discussion of inflectional processes)

Andrews, Henrietta. 1993. *The Function of Verb Prefixes in Southwestern Otomi*. University of Texas at Arlington: Summer Institute of Linguistics. (for data on Otomí)

Arnold, Jennier. 1994. "Inverse Voice Marking in Mapudungun," manuscript. Stanford University. (for data on and analysis of Mapudungun, particularly on the aspectual system)

Aronoff, Mark. 1976. *Word Formation in Generative Grammar*. Linguistic Inquiry monograph 1. Cambridge, MA: MIT Press. (for everything)

———. 1994. *Morphology by Itself*. Cambridge, MA: MIT Press. (for the idea that lexical morphemes like *tain* in *entertain* lack sense)

Aske, Jon. 1987. "The Accusativity/Ergativity Balance in a Non-split Ergative Language: The Case of Euskara (aka Basque)," *BLS* 13:1–14. (for data on Basque)

Baker, Mark C. 1988. *Incorporation: A Theory of Grammatical Function Changing*. Chicago: University of Chicago Press. (primarily for data on incorporating languages)

Bresnan, Joan. 1982. "Polyadicity," in Joan Bresnan (ed.), *The Mental Representation of Grammatical Relations*. Cambridge, MA: MIT Press. 149–172. (for a discussion of transitivity and of passive)

Broselow, Ellen and John McCarthy. 1983. "A Theory of Internal Reduplication," *The Linguistic Review* 3:25–88. (for reduplication)

Buckley, Eugene. 1994. "Morphosyntactic and Prosodic Dependencies in Alsea Clitics," unpublished ms., University of Pennsylvania. (for data on and discussion of Alsea)

Budiņa Lazdiņa, T. 1966. *Teach Yourself Latvian*. London: English Universities Press. (for data on Latvian)

Bybee, Joan L. 1985. *Morphology: A Study of the Relation Between Meaning and Form*. Philadelphia: John Benjamins. (for evidence and arguments that the derivation vs. inflection distinction is really a continuum)

Calabrese, Andrea. 1984. "Metaphony in Salentino," *Rivista di grammatica generativa* 9–10:1–140. (for data on metaphony)

Comrie, Bernard. 1977. "In Defense of Spontaneous Demotion: The Impersonal Passive," in Peter Cole and Jerrold Saddock (eds.), *Syntax and Semantics 8: Grammatical Relations*. New York: Academic Press. 47–58. (for data on impersonal passives)

DiSciullo, Anna Maria and Edwin Williams. 1987. *On the Definition of Word*. Linguistic Inquiry monograph 14. Cambridge, MA: MIT Press. (especially for the notion "head")

Dixon, R. M. W. 1979. "Ergativity," *Language* 55:59–138. (primarily for data on ergative languages)

Elbert, Samuel and Mary Kawena Pukui. 1979. *Hawaiian Grammar*. Honolulu: The University Press of Hawaii. (for data on Hawaiian)

Escalante, Fernando. 1984. "Moods and Modes in Yaqui," in Stuart Davis (ed.), *Coyote*

Papers: Studies on Native American Languages, Japanese and Spanish, Vol. 5. Tucson: University of Arizona. 19–31. (for data and analysis of Yaqui)

Gleason, Henry. 1955. *Workbook in Descriptive Linguistics*. New York: Holt. (primarily for data on various languages)

Goodwin, William Watson. 1894. *Greek Grammar*. London: Macmillan. (for information on the interfix in Greek)

Halpern, Aaron. 1992. *Topics in the Placement and Morphology of Clitics*. Doctoral dissertation. Stanford University. (for the theory of clitics)

Hetzron, Robert. 1990. "Hebrew," in Bernard Comrie (ed.), *The World's Major Languages*. Oxford: Oxford University Press. 686–704. (for data on Hebrew)

Janda, Richard. 1983. "Morphemes Aren't Something that Grows on Trees: Morphology as More the Phonology than the Syntax of Words,"*Papers from the Parasession on the Interplay of Phonology, Morphology, and Syntax*. Chicago: Chicago Linguistic Society. 79–95. (for general information on the relationship of morphology to phonology and to syntax)

Kaisse, Ellen. 1981. "Luiseño Particles and the Universal Behavior of Clitics," *Linguistic Inquiry* 12:424–434. (for data on and analysis of Luiseño)

Kalectaca, Milo. 1978. *Lessons in Hopi*. Tucson: University of Arizona Press. (for data on and analysis of Hopi)

Kamio, Akio. 1979. "On the Notion *Speaker's Territory of Information*: A Functional Analysis of Certain Sentence-Final Forms in Japanese," in George Bedell, Eichi Kobayashi, and Masatake Muraki (eds.), *Explorations in Linguistics: Papers in Honor of Kazuko Inoue*. Tokyo: Kenkyushu. 213–231. (for a discussion of Japanese deictics)

Kenstowicz, Michael. 1994. *Phonology in Generative Grammar*. Oxford: Blackwell. (for everything)

Klavans, Judith. 1979. "On Clitics as Words," *CLS* 15. 68–80. (for a theory of clitic types)

Klima, Edward and Ursula Bellugi. 1979. *The Signs of Language*. Cambridge, MA: Harvard University Press. (for data on and analysis of American Sign Language)

Kornfilt, Jaklin. 1987. "Turkish and the Turkik languages," in Bernard Comrie (ed.), *The World's Major Languages*. Oxford: Oxford University Press. 619–644. (primarily for data on Turkish)

Kratzer, Angelika. 1989. "Stage-Level and Individual-Level Predicates," in Emmon Bach, Angelika Kratzer, and Barbara Hall Partee (eds.), *Papers on Quantification*, NSF Report. Amherst: University of Massachusetts. (for types of predicates)

Li, Charles N. and Sandra A. Thompson. 1987. "Chinese," in Bernard Comrie (ed.), *The World's Major Languages*. Oxford: Oxford University Press. 811–833. (for data on and analysis of Chinese)

Li, Fang-Kuei. 1946. "Chipewyan," in Harry Hoijer (ed.), *Linguistic Structure of Native America*. New York: Viking Fund. 398–423. (for data on and analysis of Chipewyan)

MacKenzie, D.N. 1987. "Pashto," in Bernard Comrie (ed.) *The World's Major Languages*. Oxford: Oxford University Press. 547–565. (for data on and analysis of Pashto)

Maiden, Martin. 1991. *Interactive Morphonology: Metaphony in Italy*, London: Routledge. (for data on and analysis of metaphony in Italian dialects)

Marantz, Alec. 1982. "Re reduplication," *Linguistic Inquiry* 13:435–482. (for reduplication)

———. 1988. "Clitics, Morphological Merger, and the mapping to Syntactic Structure," in H. Hammond and Michael Noonan (eds.), *Theoretical Morphology: Approaches in Modern Linguistics*. San Diego: Academic Press. 253–270. (for clitics)

McCarthy, John. 1981. "A Prosodic Theory of Nonconcatenative Morphology," *Linguistic Inquiry* 12(3):373–418. (for templatic morphology)

———. 1983. "Phonological Features and Morphological Structure," *Papers from the Parasession on the Interplay of Phonology, Morphology, and Syntax*. Chicago: Chicago Linguistic Society. 135–161. (for data on and discussion of Bini)

———. and Alan Prince. 1986. *Prosodic Morphology*. Unpublished ms. Waltham, MA: Brandeis University. (for prosodic morphology)

Napoli, Donna Jo and Bill Reynolds. 1995. "Evaluative Affixes in Italian," *Yearbook of Morphology*. 151–178. (for a survey of evaluative affixes in Italian)

Nespor, Marina and Irene Vogel. 1986. *Prosodic Phonology*. Dordrecht: Foris. (especially for the development of prosodic phrases)

Raymond, Eric. 1993. *New Hackers Dictionary: 2nd Edition*. Cambridge, MA: MIT Press. (for information on *byte*)

Rohlfs, Gerhard. 1949. *Historische Grammatik der Italienischen Sprache und ihrer Mundarten: II. Formenlehre und Syntax*. Bern: A. Francke. (for data on Italian dialects)

Saltarelli, Mario, Mirin Azkarate, D. Farwell, J. Ortiz de Ubrina, and L. Oxederra. 1988. *Basque*. London: Croom Helm. (for data on and analysis of Basque)

Scalise, Sergio. 1984. *Generative Morphology*. Dordrecht: Foris. (for everything, but particularly evaluative affixes)

Selkirk, Elisabeth. 1982. *The Syntax of Words*. Cambridge, MA: MIT Press. (particularly for compounds)

Siegel, Dorothy. 1977. "The Adjacency Condition and the Theory of Morphology," *NELS* 8:189–97. (for the Adjacency Condition)

Smalley, William A. 1963. *Manual of Articulatory Phonetics*. Landham, MD: University Press of America. (primarily for data on various languages)

Spencer, Andrew. 1991. *Morphological Theory*. Oxford: Blackwell. (for everything)

Stemberger, Joseph Paul and Brian MacWhinney. 1988. "Are Inflected Forms Stored in the Lexicon?" in Michael Hammon and Michael Noonen (eds.), *Theoretical Morphology: Approaches in Modern Linguistics*. San Diego: Academic Press. 101–118. (for a discussion of the place of inflection in the grammar)

Wackernagle, Jacob 1892. "Über ein Gesetz der indogermanischen Wortstellung," *Indogermanishce Forschungen* 1:333–436. (for a discussion of P-2 of restrictions)

Wescott, Roger. 1973. "Tonal Icons in Bini," *Studies in African Linguistics*, 4:197–205. (for data on and analysis of Bini)

Williams, Marianne Mithun. 1976. *A Grammar of Tuscarora*. New York: Garland Press. (for data on and analysis of Tuscarora)

Woodbury, Hanni. 1975. *Noun Incorporation in Onandaga*. Doctoral dissertation. Yale University. (for data on and analysis of Onandaga)

Zec, Draga and Sharon Inkelas (eds.). 1990. *The Phonology-Syntax Connection*. Chicago: University of Chicago Press. (for the interface of phonology and syntax)

Zwicky, Arnold. 1977. *On Clitics*. Bloomington: Indiana University Linguistics Club. (for clitic types and especially for a discussion of clitics vs. affixes)

———. and Geoffrey Pullum. 1983. "Cliticization vs. inflection: English *n't*," *Language* 59:502–513. (for clitics vs. inflections)

Problem Set 3.1

McCarthy, John. 1983. "Phonological Features and Morphological Structure," *Papers from the Parasession on the Interplay of Phonology, Morphology, and Syntax.* Chicago: Chicago Linguistic Society. 135–161.

Tomoda, Shizuko. 1984. "Onomatopoeia and Metaphor", in Stuart Davis (ed.), *Coyote Papers: Studies on Native American Languages, Japanese and Spanish*, Vol. 5. Tucson: University of Arizona. 191–213.

Wilbur, Ronnie, Edward Klima, and Ursula Bellugi. 1983. "Roots: The Search for the Origins of Signs in ASL," *Papers from the Parasession on the Interplay of Phonology, Morphology, and Syntax.* Chicago: Chicago Linguistic Society. 314–336.

Problem Set 3.3

Goldsmith, John. 1990. *Autosegmental and Metrical Phonology.* Oxford: Blackwell.

Parkhurst, Naomi. 1993. "Towards an Explanation of Affix Formation," senior thesis, Swarthmore College, Swarthmore, PA.

Problem Set 3.4

Cowan, William and Jaromira Rakušan. 1987. *Source Book for Linguistics.* Philadelphia: John Benjamins.

Pena, Jesús. 1993. "La formación de verbos en español: la sufijación verbal," in Soledad Varela (ed.), *La formación de palabras.* Madrid: Taurus Universitaria. 217–281.

Shibatani, Masayoshi. 1990. "Japanese," in Bernard Comrie (ed.), *The World's Major Languages.* Oxford: Oxford University Press. 855–880.

Steever, Sanford. 1990. "Tamil and the Dravidian languages," in Bernard Comrie (ed.), *The World's Major Languages.* Oxford: Oxford University Press. 725–746.

Problem Set 3.5

Bresnan, Joan. 1982. "Polyadicity," in Joan Bresnan (ed.), *The Mental Representation of Grammatical Relations.* Cambridge, MA: MIT Press. 149–172.

Pesetsky, David. 1985. "Morphology and Logical Form," *Linguistic Inquiry* 16:193–246.

Selkirk, Elisabeth. 1982. *The Syntax of Words.* Cambridge, MA: MIT Press.

Problem Set 3.6

Kari, James. 1992. "Some Concepts in Ahtna Athabaskan Word Formation," in Mark Aronoff (ed.), *Morphology Now.* Albany, NY: SUNY Press. 107–132.

Kenstowicz, Michael. 1994. *Phonology in Generative Grammar.* Oxford: Blackwell.

Woodbury, Hanni. 1975. *Noun Incorporation in Onandaga.* Doctoral dissertation. Yale University, New Haven, CT.

Problem Set 3.7

Aske, Jon. 1987. "The Accusativity/Ergativity Balance in a Non-split Ergative Language: The Case of Euskara (aka Basque)," *BLS* 13:1–14.

Broselow, Ellen. 1984. "Default Consonants in Amharic Morphology," in Margaret Speas and Richard Sproat (eds.), *MIT Working Papers in Linguistics* 7:15–32.

Conway, Laura. 1992. "Prosodic Templates in Tigre Verb Morphology: A Phonologically Informed Analysis of Causative," in Chip Gerfen and Pilar Piñar (eds.), *Coyote Papers*, Vol. 8. Tucson: University of Arizona. 12–24.

Marantz, Alec. 1982. "Re Reduplication," *Linguistic Inquiry* 13:435–482.

Problem Set 3.8

Lieber, Rochelle. 1988. "Phrasal Compounds in English and the Morphology-Syntax Interface," *CLS* 24:202–222.

Scalise, Sergio. 1984. *Generative Morphology*. Dordrecht: Foris.

Stump, Gregory. 1991. "A Paradigm-Based Theory of Morphosemantic Mismatches," *Language* 67:675–725.

Thompson, Laurence. 1965. *A Vietnamese Grammar*, Seattle: University of Washington Press.

Problem Set 3.9

Kayne, Richard. 1975. *French Syntax*. Cambridge, MA: MIT Press.

Napoli, Donna Jo. 1982. "Initial Material Deletion in English," *Glossa* 16:85–111.

Chapter 4

Arnold, Jennier. 1994. "Inverse Voice Marking in Mapudungun." Stanford University. (for data on and analysis of Mapudungun)

Baker, C. L. 1991. "The Syntax of English *Not*: The Limits of Core Grammar," *Linguistic Inquiry* 22:387–429. (for criticisms of breaking down inflection into its component parts in the syntactic tree)

Barber, E. J. 1975. "Voice—Beyond the Passive," *Papers from the Berkeley Linguistics Society* 1:16–24. (for voice in general)

Bonvillain, Nancy. 1994. "Reflexives in Mohawk," *Kansas Working Papers in Linguistics*. 19(2):87–114. (for data on and analysis of Mohawk)

Branch, Michael. 1990. "Finnish," in Bernard Comrie (ed.), *The World's Major Languages*. Oxford: Oxford University Press. 593–617. (for data on and analysis of Finnish)

Bresnan, Joan. 1973. "Syntax of the Comparative Clause Construction in English," *Linguistic Inquiry* 4:275–343 (for the analysis of quantifiers as lexical categories)

——— and Lioba Moshi. 1990. "Object Asymmetries in Comparative Bantu Syntax," *Linguistic Inquiry* 21:147–186. (for data on and analysis of Kichaga)

Carrier, Jill and Janet Randall. 1992. "The Argument Structure and Syntactic Structure of Resultives," *Linguistic Inquiry* 23:173–234. (for arguments for ternary branching in syntax)

Chomsky, Noam. 1981. *Lectures on Government and Binding*. Cambridge, MA: MIT Press. (for the whole approach to GB here)

———. 1986. *Barriers*. Cambridge, MA: MIT Press. (for additional reading on GB)

———. 1992. "A Minimalist Program for Linguistic Theory," *MIT Occasional Papers in Linguistics*, 1. Cambridge, MA: MIT Dept. of Linguistics and Philosophy. (for the MP)

———. 1993. "A Minimalist Approach to Linguistic Theory," in Ken Hale and Samuel J. Keyser (eds.), *The View from Building 20: Essays in Linguistics in Honor of Sylvain Bromberger*. Cambridge, MA: MIT Press. 1–52. (for the MP)

———. 1994. "Bare Phrase Structure," *MIT Occasional Papers in Linguistics*, 5. Cambridge, MA: MIT Dept. of Linguistics and Philosophy. (for the MP)

Hudak, Thomas John. 1987. "Thai," in Bernard Comrie (ed.), *The World's Major Languages*. New York: Oxford University Press. 757–775. (for data on and analysis of Thai)

Iatridou, Sabine. 1990. "About Agr(P)," *Linguistic Inquiry* 21:551–576. (for criticisms of breaking down inflection into its component parts in the syntactic tree)

Jackendoff, Ray. 1973. "The Base Rules for Prepositional Phrases," in Stephen Anderson and Paul Kiparsky (eds.), *A Festschrift for Morris Halle*. New York: Holt, Rinehart and Winston. 345–356. (for the analysis of PPs and for the *right*-test)

Jaeggli, Osvaldo and Kenneth Safir. 1989. *The Null Subject Parameter*. Dordrecht: Kluwer Academic Publishers. (for the null subject parameter)

Jeanne, Laverne. 1978. *Aspects of Hopi Grammar*. Doctoral dissertation, Cambridge, MA: MIT. (for Case-marking on clauses in Hopi)

Kalectaca, Milo. 1978. *Lessons in Hopi*. Tucson: University of Arizona Press. (for data on and analysis of Hopi word order)

Kayne, Richard. 1984. *Connectedness and Binary Branching*. Dordrecht: Foris. (for evidence and arguments that syntax should allow at most binary branching)

———. 1994. *The Antisymmetry of Syntax*. Cambridge, MA: MIT Press. (for arguments that the basic branchingness direction of the syntactic tree is universally to the right, so complements follow heads in all languages at DS)

Koopman, Hilda. 1984. *The Syntax of Verbs: From Verb Movement Rules in the Kru Languages to Universal Grammar*. Dordrecht: Foris. (for arguments that there is one universal word order at DS and rules of movement account for varying orders at SS)

Kornfilt, Jaklin. 1990. "Turkish and the Turkik languages," in Bernard Comrie (ed.), *The World's Major Languages*. Oxford: Oxford University Press. 619–644. (for data on and analysis of Turkish)

Lasnik, Howard. 1993. "Lectures on Minimalist Syntax," *University of Connecticut Working Papers in Linguistics, Occasional Papers*, 1. Distributed by Cambridge, MA: MIT Dept. of Linguistics and Philosophy. (for the MP)

Lefebvre, Claire and Pieter Muysken. 1988. *Mixed Categories: Nominalizations in Quechua*. Dordrecht: Kluwer Publications. (for Case-marking on clauses in Quechua)

Lieber, Rochelle. 1988. "Phrasal Compounds in English and the Morphology-Syntax Interface," *CLS* 24:202–222. (for the analysis of compounds and for parameters on word order across languages)

Marantz, Alec. 1994. "A Reader's Guide to 'A Minimalist Program for Linguistic Theory'," unpublished ms., MIT. (for the MP)

Pollock, J.-Y. 1989. "Verb Movement, Universal Grammar, and the Structure of IP," *Linguistic Inquiry* 20:365–424. (for the claim that inflection is broken down into its component parts in the syntactic tree)

Shibatani, Masayoshi. 1985. "Passives and Related Constructions," *Language* 61:821–848. (for general discussion of passives)

Problem Set 4.2

Chung, Daeho. 1994. "A Negation Typology and NPI Licensing," unpublished ms., University of Southern California.
Talaat, Hana. 1987. *The Verb Phrase in Egyptian Arabic*, Doctoral dissertation, University of Michigan.

Problem Set 4.4

Thompson, Sandra. 1973. "Resultative Verb Compounds in Mandarin Choinese: A Case for Lexical Rules," *Language* 49:361–379.

Problem Set 4.5

Kalectaca, Milo. 1978. *Lessons in Hopi*. Tucson: University of Arizona Press.

Problem Set 4.6

Franks, Steven. 1994. "Feature Coincidence and LD Scrambling in Colloquial Russian," unpublished ms., Bloomington: Indiana University.

Problem Set 4.11

Emonds, Joseph. 1972. "Evidence that Indirect Object Movement is a Structure-Preserving Rule," *Foundations of Language* 8:546–561.
Higgins, F. Roger. 1973. *The Pseudo-cleft Construction in English*. New York: Garland.

Problem Set 4.12

Cokely, Dennis and Charlotte Baker-Shenk. 1980. *American Sign Language: A Student Text, Units 1–9*. Washington, DC: Gallaudet University Press Clerc Books.
Valli, Clayton and Ceil Lucas. 1992. *Linguistics of American Sign Language: A Resource Text for ASL Users*. Washington, DC: Galludet University Press.
Wilbur, Ronnie. 1987. *American Sign Language: Linguistic and Applied Dimensions*. Second edition. Boston: Little, Brown.
———. 1994. "Foregrounding Structures in American Sign Language", *Journal of Pragmatics* 22:647–672.
———. 1994. "Evidence for the Function and Structure of Wh-clefts in ASL," unpublished ms., West Lafayette, IN: Purdue University.

Problem Set 4.13

Burzio, Luigi. 1986. *Italian Syntax: a Government-Binding Approach*. Dordrecht: Reidel. (for the unaccusative analysis)
Napoli, Donna Jo. 1988. "Review Article of *Italian Syntax* by Luigi Burzio," *Language* 64:130–142.
Sells, Peter. 1987. "Aspects of Logophoricity," *Linguistic Inquiry* 18:445–479. (for Japanese *zibun*)
Tsujimura, Natsuko. 1994. "Unaccusative Mismatches and Resultatives in Japanese," unpublished ms., Indiana University.

Ue, Noriko. 1982. *A Crossing Constraint in Japanese Syntax*, Doctoral dissertation. University of Michigan.

Villalba, Xavier. 1994. "Clitics, Case Checking, and Causative Constructions," *Kansas Working Papers in Linguistics*. 19:125–147.

Yàlwa, Lawàn Danlàdì. 1994. "Complementation of Hausa Aspectual Verbs," *Kansas Working Papers in Linguistics*. 19:185–215.

Chapter 5

Allan, Keith. 1977. "Classifiers," *Language* 53:285–311. (for classifiers across languages)

Allwood, Jens, Lars-Gunnar Andersson, and Östen Dahl. 1977. *Logic in Linguistics*. Cambridge: Cambridge University Press. (for model theoretic semantics)

Austin, J. L. 1962. *How to Do Things with Words*. Cambridge, MA: Harvard University Press. (for performatives and the analysis of speech acts into locutionary, illocutionary, and perlocutionary acts)

Carlson, Greg and Michael Tanenhaus. 1984. "Lexical Meanings, Structural Meanings, and Concepts," *CLS Papers from the Parasession on Lexical Semantics*. Chicago: Chicago Linguistics Society. 39–52. (for a discussion of concepts and their relationship to structure)

Carlson, Lauri. 1981. "Aspect and Quantification," in Paul Tedeschi and Annie Zaenen (eds.), *Syntax and Semantics 14: Tense and Aspect*. New York: Academic Press. 31–64. (for the generic quantifier)

Chierchia, Gennaro and Sally McConnell-Ginet. 1992. *Meaning and Grammar: An Introduction to Semantics*. Cambridge, MA: MIT Press (for everything)

Geis, Michael and Arnold Zwicky. 1971. "On Invited Inferences," *Linguistic Inquiry* 2:561–566. (for invited inferences)

Grice, H. Paul. 1975. "Logic and Conversation," in Peter Cole and Jerry Morgan (eds.), *Syntax and Semantics 3*. New York: Academic Press. 41–58. (for the Cooperative Principle and implicatures)

Haas, Mary. 1942. "The Use of Numeral Classifiers in Thai," *Language* 18:201–206. (for Thai classifiers)

Heim, Irene. 1982. *The Semantics of Definite and Indefinite Noun Phrases*. Doctoral dissertation. University of Massachusetts at Amherst. (for generics and existentials)

Jackendoff, Ray. 1983. *Semantics and Cognition*. Cambridge, MA: MIT Press. (for conceptual semantics)

———. 1990. *Semantic Structures*. Cambridge, MA: MIT Press (for conceptual semantics)

———. 1991. "Parts and Boundaries," *Cognition* 41:9–45. (for conceptual semantics)

———. 1993. "On the Role of Conceptual Structure in Argument Selection: A Reply to Emonds," *Natural Language and Linguistic Theory* 11:279–312. (for conceptual semantics)

Kempson, Ruth. 1975. *Semantic Theory*. Cambridge: Cambridge University Press. (for everything)

Levin, Beth. 1985. "Lexical Semantics in Review: An Introduction," in B. Levin (ed.), *Lexical Semantics in Review*. Cambridge, MA: MIT Center for Cognitive Science. 1–62. (for an overview of lexical semantics, particularly predicate-argument structure and verb classes)

Pinker, Stephen. 1994. *The Language Instinct*. New York: William Morrow. (for a discussion of how many words are in an individual speaker's language)

Searle, John. 1969. *Speech Acts*. Cambridge: Cambridge University Press. (for speech acts)

Wilbur, Ronnie. 1987. *American Sign Language: Linguistic and Applied Dimensions*. Second edition. Boston: Little, Brown. (for classifiers in ASL)

Wilkinson, Karina. 1986. "Genericity and Indefinite NPs," unpublished ms. University of Massachusetts at Amherst. (for generics)

Problem Set 5.1

Austin, J. L. 1962. *How to Do Things with Words*. Cambridge, MA: Harvard University Press.

Problem Set 5.2

Jackendoff, Ray. 1987. "The Status of Thematic Relations in Linguistic Theory," *Linguistic Inquiry* 18:369–411

Shank, Roger C. 1973. "Identification of Conceptualizations Underlying Natural Language," in Roger Shank and Kenneth Colby (eds.), *Computer Models of Thought and Language*. San Francisco: W.H. Freeman. 187–247.

Problem Set 5.3

Carlson, Lauri. 1981. "Aspect and Quantification," in Philip Tedeschi and Annie Zaenen (eds.), *Syntax and Semantics 14: Tense and Aspect*. New York: Academic Press.

Creamer, Mary H. 1974. "Ranking in Navajo nouns," *Diné Bizaad Nánil'iih/Navajo Language Review* 1:29–38.

Fillmore, Charles. 1968. "The Case for Case," in Emmon Bach and Robert Harms (eds.), *Universals in Linguistic Theory*. New York: Holt, Rinehart and Winston. 1–88.

Frishberg, Nancy. 1972. "Navajo Object Markers and the Great Chain of Being," in John Kimball (ed.) *Syntax and Semantics 1*. New York: Academic Press. 259–266.

Mourelatos, Alexander. 1978. "Events, Processes, and States," *Linguistics and Philosophy* 2:415–434.

Napoli, Donna Jo. 1981. "Semantic Interpretation vs. Lexical Governance: Clitic Climbing in Italian," *Language* 57:841–887.

Shank, Roger C. 1973. "Identification of Conceptualizations Underlying Natural Language," in Roger Shank and Kenneth Colby (eds.), *Computer Models of Thought and Language*. San Francisco: W. H. Freeman. 187–247.

Vendler, Zeno. 1957. "Verbs and Times," *The Philosophical Review* 56:143–160.

Young, Robert and William Morgan, Sr. 1987. *The Navajo Language: A Grammar and Colloquial Dictionary*, revised edition. Albuquerque: University of New Mexico Press.

Problem Set 5.4

Allwood, Jens, Lars-Gunnar Andersson, and Östen Dahl. 1977. *Logic in Linguistics*. Cambridge: Cambridge University Press.

Gazdar, Gerald and Geoffrey Pullum. 1976. "Truth-Functional Connectives in Natural Language," *CLS* 12:220–234.

Geis, Michael. 1973. "*If* and *Unless*, in Braj Kachru et al. (eds.), *Issues in Linguistics*. Urbana: University of Illinois. 231–253.

McCawley, James. 1974. "If and Only If," *Linguistic Inquiry* 5:632–635.

Problem Set 5.5

Ioup, Georgette. 1975. "Some Universals for Quantifier Scope," in John Kimball (ed.) *Syntax and Semantics 4*. New York: Academic Press. 37–58.

Thomason, Richmond and Robert Stalnaker. 1973. "A Semantic Theory of Adverbs," *Linguistic Inquiry* 4:195–220.

Problem Set 5.6

Bahan, Benjamin, Judy Kegl, Dawn MacLaughlin, and Carol Neidle. (forthcoming). "Convergent Evidence for the Structure of Determiner Phrases in American Sign Language," FLSMVI, Proceedings from the Sixth Annual Meeting of the Formal Linguistics Society of Mid-America. Bloomington: Indiana University Linguistics Club Publications.

Kalectaca, Milo. 1978. *Lessons in Hopi*. Tucson: University of Arizona Press.

Oishi, Hitomi. 1986. *Scope Interpretation of Negation in Japanese*. Doctoral dissertation. University of Michigan.

Problem Set 5.7

Allwood, Jens, Lars-Gunnar Andersson, and Östen Dahl. 1977. *Logic in Linguistics*. Cambridge: Cambridge University Press.

Donnellan, Keith. 1966. "Reference and Definite Descriptions," *Philosophical Review* 60:281–304.

Kempson, Ruth. 1975. *Semantic Theory*. Cambridge: Cambridge University Press.

Problem Set 5.9

Jackendoff, Ray and David Aaron. 1991. "Review article on *More than Cool Reason: A Field Guide to Poetic Metaphor*," *Language* 67:320–338.

Lakoff, George and Mark Johnson. 1980. *Metaphors We Live By*. Chicago: University of Chicago Press.

Wilbur, Ronnie. 1990. "Metaphors in American Sign Language and English," in W. H. Edmondson and F. Karlsson (eds.), *SLR'87 Papers from the Fourth International Symposium on Sign Language Research*. Hamburg: Signum-Press. 163–170.

Problem Set 5.10

Fodor, Jerry. 1970. "Three Reasons for not Deriving 'Kill' from 'Cause to Die'," *Linguistic Inquiry* 1:429–438.

Napoli, Donna Jo. 1983. "Comparative Ellipsis: A Phrase Structure Analysis," *Linguistic Inquiry* 14:675–694.

———. 1988. "Subjects and External Arguments/Clauses and Non-clauses," *Linguistics and Philosophy* 11:323–354.

Indexes

Language Index

Agta, 222–23
Ahtna, 278–79
Algonquian family, 106
Alsea, 249
Alyawarra, 157
American English, 3, 29, 37, 40–41, 50, 55, 117, 151, 162, 182, 294
American Sign Language, 64–66, 147–49, 197, 222–23, 251–54, 264–65, 365, 435–36, 462–63, 536–38, 547
Amerind languages, 29–30, 207, 243, 387
Amharic, 281–82
Arabic, 29, 105–6, 110, 112–14, 116–17, 156, 217–21, 224–26, 362–63, 399–403
Araucanian. *See* Mapudungan
Athapascan family, 30, 191
Auca, 111
Australian languages, 207, 243
Aztec. *See* Nahuatl

Bantu family, 198, 207
Basque, 199, 201, 243, 277
Bini, 201–2
Breton, 283
British English, 29, 117, 162, 182
Bulgarian, 248, 266–68
Burmese, 365
Burushaski, 228
Bushman, 31

Cahuilla, 108, 110
Calabrese, 249, 288
Cambodian, 110
Catalan, 437
Caucasus languages, 29–30
Cayuvava, 157
Chinese, 182, 249, 327, 349, 409–10, 442, 461
Chukchee, 196, 199–200, 221
Comanche, 32
Creek, 106, 110
Czech, 21, 111

Dutch, 180, 193, 238–39, 434
Dyirbal, 243

Farsi, 111
Fijian, 197
Finnish, 21, 91–92, 95, 99, 101, 158, 176, 327, 355, 366
French, 9, 12, 25, 29, 32, 41, 50, 59, 79, 82, 111, 144, 150–51, 162, 180, 186, 189, 195, 197, 210, 286–87, 348, 358, 387, 395–96, 446, 464, 537

Georgian, 30
German, 12, 28, 41, 130, 168, 193, 195, 214, 228, 238–39, 297, 348, 434
Greek, 28, 81, 105, 180, 189, 197, 200, 209, 223

Hanunóo, 229
Hausa, 30, 362, 439–40
Hawaiian, 109
Hebrew, 29, 87–88, 202, 224, 362
Hindi-Urdu, 28, 111, 198, 365, 411, 538–40
Hopi, 197, 333, 365
Hottentot, 31
Hungarian, 28, 83–84, 86, 111, 130

Icelandic, 299, 442
Ilokano, 221–22
Imdlawn Tashlbiyt, 34
Indo-European, 81, 168
Inuit family, 29, 82, 106, 207
Irish, 362, 448
Iroquoian family, 106, 110, 207
Italian, 4, 12, 16, 21, 28, 58–59, 61, 63, 68, 82–83, 101, 125–27, 145–46, 149–50, 168–69, 183–84, 192–94, 202, 209, 211, 228–29, 246–51, 257–60, 264, 283–85, 287, 297, 302–4, 335–36, 347–50, 369, 395, 411–15, 434, 442, 446, 460, 464, 526–27
Itel'men, 223

Japanese, 12, 28, 32, 59, 60, 141–42, 150, 169, 171, 197, 209, 212–13, 249, 256–57, 260–61, 269–70, 349–50, 365, 410–11, 413–15, 434, 436–37, 440–42, 446, 448, 540–43, 546

Karok, 223
Kele, 28
Kichaga, 382, 419

Index of New Terminology

Subject Index